Food Security and Nutrition

A publication of Spektrum – Berlin Series on Society,
Economy and Politics in Developing Countries
edited by Georg Elwert, Volker Lühr, Ute Luig and Manfred Schulz
(Freie Universität Berlin)

Food Security and Nutrition

The Global Challenge

edited by

Uwe Kracht and Manfred Schulz

LIT VERLAG

St. Martin's Press, New York

Cover picture: A closeup of a woman with a basket of yams on her head; FAO photo, object name: 18463.

First published in Germany by

LIT VERLAG

Grevener Str. 179 D-48159 Münster

Die Deutsche Bibliothek – CIP-Einheitsaufnahme

Food Security and Nutrition : The Global Challenge / Uwe Kracht;
Manfred Schulz (Eds.). – Münster : LIT, 1999
(Spektrum ; 50.)
ISBN 3-8258-3166-3
NE: GT

First published in the United States of America 1999 by

ST. MARTIN'S PRESS, INC.
Scholary and Reference Division,
175 Fifth Avenue,
New York, N.Y. 10010

ISBN: 0-312-22249-1

Library of Congress Cataloging-in-Publication Data

Food security and nutrition : the global challenge / edited by Uwe Kracht and Manfred Schulz.
p. cm.
Includes bilbliographical references and index.
ISBN: 0-312-22249-1 (cloth)
1. Food supply. 2. Nutrition policy. 3. Malnutrition.
I. Kracht, Uwe. II. Schulz, Manfred.
TX353.F6655 1999
363.8–dc21 98-53553
CIP

Printed in Germany

Contents

Acknowledgements

Writing a book on food security was an old plan of the editors. To be exact, the idea was born in 1988 when Manfred Schulz was spending a sabbatical semester with the World Bank and Uwe Kracht visited there. Due to multiple obligations, however, the latter was only able to develop a first concept of the book after he had terminated his contract with the World Food Council.

We wish to express our gratitude to the International Food Policy Research Institute (IFPRI), Washington, especially to the Division Director of the Food Consumption and Nutrition Division (FCND), Lawrence Haddad, who hosted Manfred Schulz during another sabbatical term in 1997. This gave him the prime opportunity to work on the introduction and the sociological part of the book. At IFPRI he profited mostly from the writings of Joachim von Braun, the former FCND Division Director and now the Director of the Centre for Development Research (ZEF) at the Rheinische Friedrich-Wilhelms-University in Bonn, Germany. Section 5 of the introduction on policy design especially has drawn on Joachim von Braun's Technical Background Document "Food Security and Nutrition" which was submitted to the World Food Summit in 1996.

At IFPRI several collaborators offered their comments on earlier versions of the introduction, above all Mark Rosegrant, Claudia Ringler, Manfred Zeller, Agnes Quisumbing and John Hoddinott. In Germany improvements to the draft were suggested by Wolfgang Hein in Hamburg, as well as Peter Ay and Richard Flower from Berlin.

Our thanks also go numerous colleagues at FAO, who provided useful comments at the stage of conceptualization, proposed authors and contributed chapters themselves. We are grateful to FAO for making the book's cover photo available to us. A special thanks is due to John Shaw, the untirable writer, for his repeated encouragement as well his own contribution. And we thank all authors for sharing with us some of their most valuable time for providing contributions free of charge—many of them waiting for a considerable time to see their manuscripts finally published.

Special thanks go to Manfred Schulz's secretary, Daniela Stozno-Weymann, who did much of the hard work of editing the 692 pages of the book. This is particularly noteworthy since, owing to the financial crisis at the Free University of Berlin, there is only one part-time secretary for the section Political Sociology and Development Sociology within the Institute of Sociology.

Uwe Kracht
Manfred Schulz

Berlin and Rome
June 1998

Introduction

Manfred Schulz

1 Starting point of the analysis: our concerns

The persistence of an unacceptably high level of hunger and malnutrition worldwide presents a serious challenge to the world at the threshold of the third millenium. Though enough food is produced to feed mankind, about 840 million people go hungry; among them are 185 million pre-school children that are severely underweight for their age. Since an additional 80 million people have to be fed each year, achieving food security is a central global challenge, if not the most important development issue.

Even where the nutritional situation has gradually improved, as for example in parts of Asia, the absolute numbers of malnourished people remain staggeringly high. Moreover, man-made emergencies, natural disasters and sudden economic crises also threaten what has been achieved, notably where the positive results of development have been taken for granted. For instance, Indonesia, Papua New Guinea, the Philippines and Thailand experienced a severe drought in 1997; agricultural slash-and-burn economy and forestry activities exacerbated the usual level of forest fires and the smoky haze covered vast parts of South Asia.

The long-term prospects of food security may also depend more on weather fluctuations and climate change than was formerly thought. In 1997 we experienced the appearance of El Niño, a periodic abnormal warming of the sea surface off the South-American coast. Major weather fluctuations in many parts of the world are attributed to this phenomenon and the consequent floods and droughts have influenced food production. It is still an open question as to whether El Niño may become more frequent and whether it is related to the trend of global warming (Pinstrup-Andersen et al. 1997: 22/23).

Let us return to South-East Asia. The deep financial crisis that hit the formerly booming economies in this region in 1997 was a major and unforeseen event; it showed that the transition of the newly industrialized countries did not follow a smooth and steady upward path but was prone to interruptions, cyclical changes and even impasses. As a consequence of the chaotic developments in the various currencies, prices for staple food commodities like rice soared in a number of countries; in Indonesia, in 1997/98 for instance, food riots occurred in several urban areas. It remains an open question whether food production and markets there will meet the long-term demand for affordable food.

The food situation of Asia cannot, however, be generalized; it may be even more bleak in other parts of the world. It appears that the food and nutrition situation is deteriorating, notably in Africa. Medium-term prospects for the countries of the former USSR and Eastern Europe are uncertain, and there is a disquieting emergence of food deprivation in the rich industrialized countries. In all, the nutritional problems caused by man-made crises have reached a historical record. And in the long-term perspective beyond the year 2010, our planet's capacity to feed an ever growing population remains an issue of ardent debate.

There are, however, new opportunities to address these problems more forcefully than in the past. The 1990s have seen a sharp rise in political attention to these and related social problems, with a spate of summit-level meetings of the World Summit for Children (1990), the UN Conference on the Environment and Development (1992), the World Population Conference (1994) and the 1996 World Food Summit. These events, together with an improved understanding of the nature and causes of, and solutions to, food and hunger problems, new technological prospects—notably in biotechnology, and with growing emphasis on the ethical and human rights dimension of development—give rise to hope for accelerated progress in overcoming hunger. But seizing these opportunities and translating them into substantial action requires not only human, but also financial resources. These have been hitherto inadequate and on the decline over the last years.

2 Nutrition and food security in the light of development theories

In order to better understand the various and controversial theoretical points of view regarding food production, nutrition and food security, we consider it useful to link these problems to general development theory. This is not an easy task, since food and nutrition are usually discussed as part of agricultural development and basic needs and are somewhat removed from general development theory.

For the period from the 1950s till today we can distinguish six major theoretical approaches towards development; they have come about more or less in the following chronological order, being related to each other within a complex network of criticism and counter-criticism. They contain different implications and messages regarding the assessment of nutrition and food security. The approaches are:

- Modernization theory;
- Dependency theory;
- Basic needs;
- Neo-liberalism and structural adjustment;
- Sustainable development;
- Globalization and post-modernism.

2.1 Intellectual fashions

The particular theoretical positions aside, it can be observed that the discourse on development and food security has known certain intellectual fashions which resulted in cyclical changes of view over the last forty-five years.

In the late 1950s and early 1960s a gloomy perspective prevailed. A growing scarcity of protein-rich food was predicted and prospects for producing unconventional food like algae were put forward. Later on FAO changed its standards for measurement; instead of emphasizing protein, stress was now placed on calorific requirements. In retrospect it appears that world hunger was at that time at least partly conceived as an error of the measurement concept. Perspectives changed in the late 1960s when an era of optimism began with the Green Revolution, with research institutions offering high-yielding crop varieties in combination with other technologies for intensified production. Since then, an optimistic assessment has prevailed in the leading international development institutions even though this view has been cautiously challenged in the light of environmental concerns during the 1980s and 1990s.

2.2 Modernization theory

Modernization theory of the late 1950s and early 1960s tried to show the path from under-development to development by applying the concepts of capitalism and technology development to the Third World. By favouring capital accumulation, technical progress and mass consumption, industrial development received a priority over agricultural development.

With respect to agriculture and food the most important line of thought of the modernization theory was the rise of the "diffusion of innovations" concept. Adopter-typologies were developed to explain which type of farmer—ranging from the daring entrepreneur to those with little initiative—would accept what kind of innovation at what time in the diffusion cycle. In this model, development occurred as a trickle-down process. Agricultural innovations were, for instance, developed in international research centers, were passed on to national research stations and from there to agricultural extension services. This model assumed that progressive high-status farmers would be the first adopters until finally small-holders also accepted it.

The influence of the modernization theory on agriculture, nutrition and food security can be summarized as follows:

— This theory underestimated the potentials of local agriculture and food systems in the early stages of development.

— Within agriculture, modernization theory favours export-oriented cash crops for markets to the detriment of subsistence-economy. In the food sector attention is mostly given to cereals and not to tubers and roots which play a significant nutritional role in Sub-Saharan Africa, for instance.

— Modernization theory correctly stresses the transition from extensive to intensive modes of agricultural production, a trend also analyzed in numerous field studies, though change in remote low potential areas was found to be slow.

— Even if the trickle-down model now appears outmoded, the essential impact of the Green Revolution is assured a place. As an indicator, we can say, for example, that all segments of the Indian peasantry producing on ecologically suitable land are nowadays using intensive production techniques. The World Bank estimates that 70% of the global cereal production, today is based on the use of improved seed. To produce the same quantity with the old low-yielding varieties would have required an additional 300 million hectares of land.[1]

— Regarding access to food, modernization theory favours the monetarization of exchange modes, but pays little attention to poverty alleviation and income generation for the poor.

— Taking the industrialized countries as a model, it is no surprise that the modernization theory foresees the imitation of western consumption patterns in the Third World. This particularly holds true for high-prestige food like meat or white bread increasingly consumed by people rising in social status.

2.3 Dependency theory

The dependency theory evolved in the later part of the 1960s as a refutation of the modernization paradigm and as an answer to the development crisis in Latin America. This view understands under-development no longer as resulting from endogenous causes (culture, low level of physical development, "feudal" structures), but as caused by external factors, including colonialism and the world market, with particular emphasis on the destructive role of transnational corporations. When analyzing a particular country, exogenous and endogenous factors of under-development are molded into a specific form of peripheral capitalist development that is characterized by structural heterogeneity. Development is seen as restricted to a capital-intensive export-oriented sector, whereas the traditional, backward, marginalized and mostly agricultural sector serves as a reservoir for cheap labor. A radical consequence of dependency theory is the proposal for some sort of dissociation from the world market or at least protection from its supposed detrimental influences. The attempted goal is to attain self-reliant and self-controlled development.

What conclusions can be drawn from the theoretical position of dependency theory as regards agriculture and food?

— The agricultural sector is here seen as an important base for development in contrast to strategies which promote industrialization first. According to this theory agriculture is able to provide food for attaining self-sufficiency and also supplies a growing internal consumer market, stressing the importance of local and regional distribution.

— Dependency theory suggests the use of simple home-produced and adapted technologies that should replace sophisticated socially inadequate, repair-prone imported technologies, while at the same time providing more employment.

— Low potential areas are also viewed as deserving promotion, by providing them with a material and social infrastructure and decentralized units of decision-

1 Figures provided by Ismail Serageldin, Vice-President of the World Bank, in an IFPRI-Seminar on July 22, 1997.

making; small-scale industries are foreseen as processing agricultural raw materials. In the export sector a specific crop monoculture should be replaced by a diversified production structure.

— Backward and forward linkages between the agrarian and the industrial sector are sustained in order to develop a mode of production leading to rising incomes, thus allowing for mass consumption.

— For decreasing dependency on the world market, regional markets of neighbouring states should be fostered.

The ideas of dependency theory came under criticism with the rise of the new industrializing countries of the Far East and elsewhere which largely produced modern industrial products for the world market—an event that, according to this theory, could never have happened. Even though development without integration into the world market appears inconceivable in the present day discussion of globalization, certain aspects of dependency theory still deserve attention, notably the focus on the local and regional levels in a development strategy , the search for food security by including subsistence economy, the attempts to arrive at more self-reliance and, above all, the necessary linkages growing between various productive sectors during the development process.

2.4 Basic needs

The basic needs concept was the leading development strategy during the second development decade from 1970-1980. It started with the idea that economic growth alone does not automatically alleviate the poverty of the urban and rural masses. "Redistribution with growth" was now required. Consensus was reached that the highest priority in development politics should be to meet the basic needs; the so-called "first floor" needs were defined as: nutrition, shelter, clothes, health. In some branches of thinking these needs were broadened by "second floor" needs such as education, employment, a safe environment, social participation and political liberty. Other authors even pointed out that all needs have a cultural and social dimension which also has to be addressed.

Regarding agriculture and food we can note the following implications of the basic needs strategy:

— Access to food is the main imperative of any development policy.

— Priority is given to rural development, which implies an increase in production as well as an improvement in the standard of living.

— Increase in food production is given high priority.

— Investments should also be undertaken in the subsistence sector.

— Cheap credits should be granted to small-holders; local crafts and trade should be promoted.

— Investment in human capital should be made by supplying educational and training facilities adapted to the abilities and educational level that most people possess.

— The main strategy should be to combat unemployment with a variety of measures, including the development of agro-industries.

— Women should be integrated in agricultural production for the market, as well as in social and political life at the community level.

— The rural youth should become integrated in modernized agriculture.

— Participation in decision-making in development projects and programmes should be realized by promoting rural self-help organizations.

The strategy of stimulating food production has been successful in quite a number of cases; however farmers have also experienced falling prices for their products when the demand has not increased with the production. A counter-productive factor for local production in several cases was the prolonged distribution of food aid, creating the danger of an "expectation" mentality among the recipients. Another concern was that several donors gave food aid solely in order to ship surplus grain and meat to developing countries.

In sum, the basic needs approach has a strong orientation towards agricultural development and food security, though it is a welfare-oriented strategy with much intervention by the state and the donor community. It should be noted that land reform is not on the agenda of the basic needs strategy. Moreover, the basic needs concept does not advocate structural reforms of the world market, for instance by creating a new world trade order. A number of developing countries consequently have viewed the basic needs approach negatively since they fear it will perpetuate their inferiority for ever.

Finally: One should realize that the present debate on entitlements and a human right to food carries many elements of the basic needs concept, which has thus seen a partial ressurection (see Eide, chap. 16, this volume).

2.5 Neo-liberalism and structural adjustment

In order to counter the welfare-oriented basic needs concept and to find an answer to the growing debt crisis, a strictly economic policy based on world market orientation and foreign trade came into being in the 1980s. Relying on the theorem of comparative cost advantage, neo-liberal thinking suggested that each country produced those goods which by its specific factor allocation could be produced competitively. State-regulated prices on goods and wages, tariffs and import-export taxes should be abolished or at least reduced. State interference in the economy was, and is, regarded as ineffective if not counterproductive.

The main elements of this concept as they are pursued by the IMF and the World Bank are:

— Devaluation of overvalued currencies;

— Removal of tariffs and customs on imported and exported goods to strenghen exports;

— Better prices for the farmer (getting prices "right");

— Removal of subsidies, also on food;

— Combatting deficit spending and tightening government budgets;

— Achieving a lean civil service by firing excessive staff;

— Recovering at least part of the costs of the educational and health systems.

The overall effects of this strategy have been debated at length, since there are success cases like the Republic of Côte d'Ivoire, but also examples of countries that have made little progress when following this strategy.

What are the implications of this strategy on agriculture and food now?

— It can be confirmed that this strategy is popular with market-integrated farmers; product prices are not set, but result from market dynamics, that is, they are dependent on world market prices. The positive effects on agricultural production are believed to be greater than the negative ones, that is, the removal of subsidies on fertilizer and other imputs is compensated by higher product prices.

— In agriculture the stress is on export cash crops, so that foreign currency earnings can be used to pay back debts. There is much less regard for food crops and the subsistence sector.

— Urban lower and middle classes are negatively affected by the partial or total removal of subsidies on bread and other staple commodities. Structural adjustment policies do not advocate policies of cheap food; only specific targeted social interventions are foreseen in order to give adjustment a human face.

— Within this debate a lively discussion of world food problems has started all over again, in which the importance of market-oriented development instruments, like the fostering of micro-entrepreneurs or allowing rural financing of food security for the poor, have gained prominence (see Zeller and Sharma, chap. 26, this volume).

In sum and substance, food security within the concept of structural adjustment is arrived at by market-oriented production and "right prices"; the modernization of agricultural technology and infrastructural development form part of this approach. Obviously a conflict of interests exists between the farmers, who aim for better product prices, and urban consumers who demand cheap staple food commodities.

2.6 Sustainable development

Sustainable development is a concept introduced by German forestry in the 19th century; the meaning of the term was that only that much timber should be cut as is naturally replaced. In development politics the term only became widely known by the Report of the World Commission on Environment and Development (Brundtland Report) in 1987. Here sustainable development is defined as "development which meets the needs of the present without compromising the ability of future generations to meet their own needs" (Kirkly et al. 1995: 1). Though various definitions of sustainability exist, the most important elements are the following:

— Emphasis on the compatibility of economic activities with requirements of the environment;

— Directing economic activities to the micro-level in order to reach indigenous and poor social groups;

— Shifting to a greater local control over resources and their use; providing for greater decentralisation and more local decision-making;

— Reducing the exploitation of non-renewable resources and expanding the use of renewable ones;

— Attaining a more equitable distribution of wealth and resources;

— Changing to a more multi-sectoral approach in economic development that leads to more diversification (Abdelgabar 1997).

In essence, the concept has ecological/bio-physical as well as economic and socio-cultural dimensions. Reviewing the various development theories, sustainable development incorporates much of the previous basic needs concept, blended with ecology-oriented reasoning.

What are the implications of this concept for agriculture and food?

— Sustainability is much concerned with an ecologically compatible production of agricultural goods; it lays emphasis on diversification and not on monocropping.

— The ultimate goal of sustainable agriculture is not the short-term maximization of yields but long-term stable production quantities.

— Yields should be increased by using renewable resources as inputs and refering to local knowledge systems.

— Sustainable development is compatible with existing local food distribution systems and provides safety-nets for redistribution.

In substance, sustainability implies a resource-saving production system with stable yields, mainly achieved by relying on labour-intensive production techniques, taking fragile land and over-stretched resource bases into consideration. The provision of sufficient food is a goal compatible with sustainability. The concept also implies a changeover to more modest consumption patterns in the industrialized countries, for instance, a reduced level of meat consumption.

2.7 Globalization and post-modernism

In the current discussions on development politics it appears certain that all strategies for food security must be embedded in the framework of global accumulation and regulation, since globalization is the determining characteristic of the present worldwide development. Post World War II developments were moulded by the Fordist global accumulation structures. As regards agriculture the main traits of the Fordist model may be characterized as follows:

— Seeds are becoming standardized (high yielding varieties);

— Standardized agricultural and food products—mostly produced by transnational corporations—gained world-wide acceptance;

— Mechanization and intensive chemical treatments through the use of fossile energy are prevalent;

— Rising incomes in a number of developing countries have caused people to move up the food chain, making the consumption of high-quality foodstuffs, in particular meat, rise;

— Farms with industrial livestock breeding and raising have expanded;

— State intervention and subsidies in developed countries have caused over-production and environmental problems (Hein 1996: 25).

It must be noted, however, that the Fordist transformation process only partly spread to developing countries. In most cases the level of productivity remained so low there that higher wages could not be paid in order to induce mass consumption, a pre-requisite for a Fordist type transformation. A prominent feature of the Fordist accumulation process in developing countries is the broadening gap between larger regions, for instance the rise of economies in East Asia and the faltering structures in many parts of Africa, but also the growing differences between the regions of one country, in India for instance, where some areas have profited from the Green Revolution and others have not.

The main development trend of the current decade is the shift from the so far dominant industrial sector to the more and more important role of the tertiary sector of highly qualified services. Micro-electronics has developed to a new system of technical knowledge which has decreased transport and transaction costs and contributes to the growing internationalization of markets for goods, finance and services. This process is frequently labelled as globalization, the major developmental trend of the post-Fordist era. In the countries of the North more efficient and flexible forms of organization only allow for the employment of a restricted number of well-paid workers, above all in research, development and management. Unemployment, therefore, is a major phenomenon in the era of globalization in the industrialized countries and in the Third World. In the context of developing countries it must be emphasized that the globalization process is not all-embracing and unilinear, but is characterized by changing boundaries, inherent limitations and even contradictions. So far, only a minority of developing countries have been in any way integrated into post-Fordist accumulation patterns. In the Third World probably only one to two percent of the population have access to profits from globalization, which indicates a further widening gap between rich and poor. Altvater points out that the richest fifth of the world population enjoys 83% of the world income whereas the poorest fifth participate only with 1.4% (Altvater 1992: 156 ff.).

Among the aspects that deserve particular attention in developing countries is that the transnational corporations have gained influence over the production of export-crops and their marketing, introducing and controlling new potentials of bio-technology, screening relevant strains for plant and animal breeding and becoming able to develop new products by making use of genetic engineering. Simultaneously, the more affluent middle classes and elites in the better-off developing countries, for example in Africa, are changing to more conspicuous food consumption patterns, eating white bread and rice instead of tubers and roots;

also meat consumption has dramatically increased here. Evers explains this characteristic as a "symbolic share" in modernity (Evers 1997: 219).

The contemporary developmental pattern of this world has been fundamentally criticized by post-modern thinkers. Post-modernism is basically a philosophical school of interpretation of social change that has spread to the social sciences as well as to architecture and other disciplines. The key issue in this theory is the deconstruction of the enlightenment discourse, that is an attack on the idealistic position taken up from the eighteenth century onwards to struggle for freedom, equality and modernity. Schuurman sums up the meaning of the word deconstruction:

— Delegitimizing the enlightenment discourse by stating that there is no such thing as general emancipation of mankind and only one desirable path of development;

— Dismantling structures to find actors; for instance class is seen as an abstract concept not relevant to action; individuals or households should be chosen as units of analysis;

— The search for hidden metaphors behind and in the concepts of the enlightenment discourse, for instance the assumption of man as rational or of the state as a benefactor (Schuurman 1993: 26).

In consonance with the more flexible intellectual organization which prevails in computer-aided manufacturing, for example, a plurality of perspectives exist. At this moment we cannot fully describe post-modern development patterns in the Third World but must concentrate on post-modern research perspectives. One basic trait of post-modern research in the developing countries is the concentration on gender studies (the inequality of the sexes) and social movements in their quest for radical democracy; moreover, the observation of civic societies emerging in the Third World is also a topic of post-modern research. Schuurman, however, points out that the post-modern discourse views social movements of the Third World as an "expression of resistance to modernity" (Schuurman 1993: 27); he points out that many of these movements, on the contrary, demand access to the modern world, but they face an aborted project of modernity. In this sense developing countries in their majority are not post-modern societies.

In a recent article Simon Maxwell has attempted to condense the post-modern tendencies in the analysis of food security by highlighting three areas of change in the discourse:

— From the global and national to the household and the individual;

— From a food first to a "livelihood" perspective;

— From objective indicators to subjective perceptions (Maxwell 1996: 157).

Following this author, the following conclusions can be drawn:

— The post-modern concept of food research demands more decentralization; social structures are regarded as open systems with multiple choices and developmental trajectories; because of the importance of individual commitment, a micro-perspective in research is required.

— The "livelihood" perspective, for instance, means that individuals and households also pursue objectives other than nutritional and that food must be seen in a diverse and flexible balance with other goals also striven for.

— It can be seen that contemporary food security research already widely follows this concept, recognizes the diversity of reasons for food insecurity and analyzes the "livelihood" perspective through collective models of the household.

— Finally, attention must be paid to the fact that food requirements do not follow only objective criteria like age, sex or size but also local food habits. It is therefore a must to investigate local perceptions, local knowledge systems and local strategies in order to cope with food problems. Maxwell underlines that the currently spreading application of participatory research methods is already characteristically post-modern; this also holds true for the bottom-up approach and decentralized planning.

— In this sense research and policy implementation in the food sector already correspond to a great extent to a post-modern view of things, though it must be admitted that these changes in outlook and orientation are in the discipline of agriculture mostly realized without awareness of their roots in post-modern philosophy.

2.8 The impact of development theories on agriculture and food policies—Summary

Development theories focus with differing emphasis on agriculture and food aspects, and also carry different messages. Whilst for instance dependency theory and basic needs explicitly stress more food production even in a subsistence economy and advocate self-sufficiency, structural adjustment and modernization theory are more concerned about export crops. In recent discussions on globalization and post-modernism food issues hardly appear as an essential problem in the general development debate. The reason for this negligence appears to be a basic lack of communication between the social and the natural sciences. Post-modernism was first developed as a concept of ideology-critical philosophy; the spread of this concept to the discipline of agriculture still remains to be seen.

When reviewing development theories with regard to their influence on food security, one particular tendency becomes apparent; in former days much work was devoted to global food security and regional, national and sector analysis. Recent thinking relates the macro-level to a micro-perspective: families, households, communities and associations, as well as NGOs and entrepreneurs are seen as actors to be actively involved in the analysis, planning and implementation of development strategies. Policy issues are now, more than ever before, embracing the households and their resource allocation processes. The resulting development tendency towards more decentralization and participation appears to be beneficial, since such thinking needs to be incorporated in the development projects and activities of the NGOs and the organizations of the international development network.

3 World food projections—the macro-perspective

In the macro-view, the main questions of food security can be located by information regarding development trends in food demand and supply, for which world food projections try to provide data. The introduction gives an overview of this debate, whereas more details may be found in the contributions contained in part I of this volume, notably in the article by Peter von Blanckenburg (chapter 4).

One of the oldest questions of mankind as to whether it will have enough food tomorrow has in recent years once again provoked an ardent debate between the pessimists and the optimists. World food supply and demand projections by the World Bank are among the most important publications in this field (Mitchell and Ingco 1993); others to be mentioned are FAO (Alexandratos 1995), IFPRI (Rosegrant et al. 1995, updated version 1997) and L. Brown/World Watch Institute (Brown 1996).

The first three of these projections can be classed as professional economic studies in so far as they use simulation modelling techniques which allow interaction between variables, while the Brown study may be seen as an environmentally concerned critical study that relies on the projection of single factors. The modelling studies are, though, not superior *per se*; they depend on assumptions about future trends. The single most debated factor during the last three years has been world cereal prices and their impact on food security. These prices have been subject to sharp increases; for instance wheat and maize prices in mid 1996 were 50% higher than a year before (Rosegrant et al. 1997: 1). Brown even reports that in April 1996 wheat prices at the Chicago Board of Trade had doubled compared with one year before (Brown 1996: 19). Price rises and the depletion of cereal stocks are seen by Brown as a new reality that will persist in the future, whereas economists tend to assess this development as a momentary distortion, since North American and European governments have reduced cereal stocks and scaled down farm price support programmes (Rosegrant et al. 1997: 3). Moreover, the policy-induced slowdown in production was not only aggravated by the economic collapse in the former Soviet Union and Eastern Europe, but also by bad weather in other key grain growing areas in 1994. As a result, average wheat prices increased to \$216 in 1995/96, compared with \$143 in 1993/94 and \$157 in 1994/95 and decreased again to \$183 in 1996/97 (FAO 1997: 2). While dramatic price increases for cereals are a very important factor throughout Lester Brown's book, the experience of 1997 shows that conventional economic theory prevails in the long term. The recent price increases for wheat and maize have been rather short-term blips than a complete new trend (Pinstrup-Andersen and Pandya-Lorch 1997: 8).

Summa summarum, the economic studies show institutional optimism, whereas Lester Brown draws a more gloomy picture. The World Bank study underlines considerable improvements in the world food situation, comparing the early 1960s with the 1990s with regard to per capita food production and food supply; the increase was 18% over these 30 years (Mitchell and Ingco 1993: 31). The extension of life expectancy in all regions, even in Africa, cannot be explained without citing improvements in nutrition. However, 20% of the population in developing countries still remain chronically undernourished; though this does compare favorably with the 36% in the 1960s.

What is the outcome if you take projections as a logical extension of past trends and not as a result of abrupt changes? The FAO study presents the following picture: there has been progress in the world as a whole; but this progress has been slow and regionally uneven. Currently, about 840 million people suffer from malnutrition. Future developments will see a still slower and more uneven growth caused by the major constraint factors: population growth and degradation of agricultural and other environmental resources. In these projections, hardly any improvement is forecast for Sub-Saharan Africa. With respect to the global scenario in the year 2010, 650 million people are expected to suffer from under-nutrition as compared to 840 million today. Taking into account the increased world population in the year 2010, the absolute number of undernourished people, as well as their proportion within the total world population, will be reduced. This projection can, therefore, be regarded as moderately optimistic. Some things may have been accomplished by 2010, but the world will still be a long way from overcoming hunger completely.

What, then, is Lester Brown's message? Contrary to official forecasts, we will experience no surpluses, but an ever growing food scarcity and increasing imbalance between food demand and supply. Environmental problems will become more and more acute. Regarding supply, Brown cites a long list of constraining factors, such as overfished oceans, a growing scarcity of water for irrigation, the depletion of aquifers, increasing fertilizer requirements and decreasing yields, soil erosion and climate change. But regarding demand, he estimates that about 80 million people will be added to the global population annually and forecasts a growing demand for food and seed. Another major factor he emphasizes is changes in consumer preferences. As an example, Brown presents China with its huge population, limited possibilities for area expansion and rising aspirations for higher quality food products. He foresees China, which had a grain consumption in 1995 of 95 million tons for feeding animals, considerably increasing its grain imports from 6 million tons in 1990 to 215 million tons in 2030 (Brown 1996: 56, 107).

Whatever the final results of food projections may be, the basic reasoning in the simulation studies is, according to Brown, a single direct extrapolation of the past into the future. He believes this approach is misleading. Nothing can grow indefinitely, and facing the new realities, an S-shaped growth curve of food supply should be assumed. In contrast to this, a model builder like Mark Rosegrant of IFPRI takes the view that Brown's argument is a false representation of the modelling concept, since he also explicitly shows a declining yield of cereals. Brown's recent publication "Tough Choices—Facing the Challenge of Food Scarcity" (1996) has found a wide audience not only in the US but also in Europe. Nevertheless, in the agricultural economics community, Brown's projections are seriously questioned. In the 1997 update of IFPRI's food projections (Rosegrant et al. 1997) adjustments have been made concerning population growth and prices.

According to this study, increases in cereal yields will slow down, but will hardly reach the stagnation predicted by Brown. In the meantime, Brown's position on China also has undergone harsh criticism as being exaggerated (Alexandratos 1996, Fan and Agcaoily-Sombilla 1997).

It should be noted here that Brown has a peculiar understanding of technological change. Whereas many authors, who deal not only with the technical but also the ethical dimension of genetic engineering, finally view the future role of bio-technology and genetic engineering either in a positive or negative perspective, Brown does not give a point of view on this issue. He points out that almost all inventions so far have been made to gain profit in the markets of the industrialized countries; he assumes that in the years up to 2010, genetically engineered products will not be relevant in developing countries. Although there are good reasons for this prediction, the future role of biotechnology in developing countries does deserve careful consideration (for a detailed discussion see Wenzel and Leisinger, chap. 22 and 23, this volume).

World food projections involve a number of risks and uncertainties of supply and demand. One example is population growth: the United Nations have, till now, overestimated population growth. The medium fertility model now forecasts 9.4 billion people by 2050, which is half a billion less than expected before (UN 1996). It must be noted that health problems, for instance AIDS, may heavily influence future population growth rates.

Quite a number of other factors of risk and uncertainty should also be mentioned here, such as future income growth and distribution, changing consumer preferences and, above all, the consequences of the alarming cuts in investment in agricultural research and development aid to agriculture which we have seen during the last years. In simulation models, such risks and uncertainties are predicted by sensitivity analysis and alternative scenarios. However, models can not predict the outcome of fundamental political changes. For example, hardly anybody foresaw the transformation of the former communist states which has since had a considerable impact on the world food balance.

4 Intra-household resource allocation and food security—the micro-perspective

4.1 The household—a black box?

If one wishes to understand resource allocation processes and behavioural patterns of the actors the macro-level analysis of food security must be supplemented by a micro-perspective. Nowadays it is commonly acknowledged in food policy planning that food insecurity and malnutrition cannot be mitigated merely through increases in global, national or regional food availability, but policies must also be household-oriented (IFAD 1996: 1).

Before we discuss some important findings on intra-household resource allocation relating to food security, we should be aware that ambiguity exists concerning the definition of the household: is it a unit of people living together, a kin-related group, a unit where members share a common cooking pot, or what? We do not wish to summarize the broad methodological discussion here, but suggest reading J.A. Strauss and D. Thomas (1995). Due to limited space we shall also steer clear of attempting a summary of the recent debate on the adequate econometric model of the household; information on this is provided by L. Haddad, J. Hoddinott and H. Alderman (1997).

In the following we shall present our views on household analysis. In order that the term household make sense, though, some degree of homogeneity regarding a description of its functions is needed. For planning purposes and action programmes it would be ideal if the household were to be taken as:

— A production unit where its members work together and produce goods (farms, crafts) and an internal division of labour is possible;

— A decision-making unit which could adopt (agricultural) innovations;

— A consumption unit where its members themselves consume goods (shared cooking and feeding arrangements);

— A residential unit where members use a common infrastructure (house, energy, water);

— A social unit (family, dowry, inheritance).

However, households where all, or most, of the above conditions apply can hardly be found nowadays. Urbanization, migration, disintegration of the extended families and other circumstances have induced change towards a variation of household types. For example:

— The number of household members varies between one and twenty or more members;

— In areas severely affected by outward migration households often consist of grand-parents with their grand-children only;

— In urban centers there are many young couples without children;

— Households differ in the age structure of their members because of a trend to smaller units replacing several generations living together;

— For the composition of households it is important to know that up to 20% of the household are female-headed;

— Household members may live together but do not eat together; in other cases they may eat together but work outside the household; moreover, one may discover numerous temporary members in a household (migrant labourers, servants, apprentices, etc.) who do not participate in decision-making;

— Finally, there are also traditional social structures, for instance in West Africa, where the basic social unit has never been the nuclear family but the lineage composed by extended families; the different economic and social functions are related in a complex exchange network with the various kinship units. These traditional modes of social organization may still play an important normative role for the perception of households, even if the socio-economic conditions do not provide any base for such organization any more.

From this we conclude that there is no model of a household which has general application as a research and planning tool. Consequently, we suggest analyzing the specific conditions and using carefully designed definitions which apply to the problem areas studied and which can help in decision-making for development planning. For example:

— Households consisting of several generations (also laterally extended);
— Households with nuclear families (father, mother, children);
— Widows/widowers;
— Young one-person households (seasonal migrants, students);
— Aged one-person households.

We must stress that for the targeting of food security programmes the variation of household categories must be identified through adequate action research, since a simple definition of what the household is will not suffice. A combination of research methods, in which action research and various participatory methods are available for efficient information and data collection, would appear adequate.

4.2 Intrahousehold resource allocation: issues and findings

Research on food security at the micro-level has become broader with time; one no longer deals with food problems in a narrow sense, but relates the household perspective to changing lifestyles and social structure development. Consequently, it is no surprise to learn that intrahousehold resource allocation analysis deals with food problems in many areas, such as labour and land allocation, the use of modern inputs in agriculture, income distribution and expenditure patterns, education and health, boy-girl differences in food intake and, above all, gender differentials in farm productivity. Finally, strategies of coping with poverty are treated under resource allocation aspects. Due to limited space we only can discuss the more important points of this debate.

To begin with, it is widely assumed that the income level has an impact on the nutritional status of household members; and conversely, that the nutritional status of a family influences labour productivity and, in consequence, the income level (Behrman and Srinivasan 1995: 1886). When testing these assumptions, however, the results from cross-country research are often not so strikingly uniform as was formerly supposed.

A recent study comes to the conclusion that there are more differences in the nutritional status of household members with low incomes, whilst with rising incomes, the differences are more likely to vanish (Kanbur and Haddad 1994). In another study it is reported that in poor households there is a definite association between income and calorie intake, but when a threshold level of intake has been reached, the correlation is close to zero (Behrman and Srinivasan 1995: 1986). In sum, it is clear that calorie intake relative to requirements varies greatly between households.

The most hotly debated subject in household resource allocation anlysis is gender differentials. The main reason for this interest is that over the last fifteen years or so developmental policy has become somewhat gender-sensitive, and efforts are undertaken to give women an equitable share in development projects in order to upgrade their social position. Empirical evidence, however, once again shows that cross-cultural differences must be taken into account. It is understood that women in South Asia and possibly in South East Asia are disadvantaged in comparison to males, but that in other regions, like Sub-Saharan Africa, the situation tends to be more equal. One major finding in this context is that men and women have different expenditure patterns. Mothers care more about spending for health, education and the well-being of their children (Behrman and Srinivasan 1995: 1996), whereas men spend more money on alcohol, cigarettes, highly prestigeous consumer goods and female companionship (Alderman et al. 1995: 11). Since women purchase more goods for children and general household consumption, and not luxury goods, their ethically superior behaviour—this value judgement appears justified—should be honoured by development policies that foresee more support for women-targeted development schemes.

A second point in this debate is whether there are differences in investment and feeding with respect to boys and girls. The reasoning is as follows: many traditional societies, for instance in South Asia, do not know formal institutionalized social safety nets for old people. Sons may have to take care of aged parents whereas girls will marry away to the family of their husband. Under these conditions, it will make sense to invest more in boys than in girls. Some studies prove that girls are discriminated against in the household (Haddad and Kanbur 1992: 373), but for Africa, once again, there is less evidence of this (Haddad and Reardon 1993). Also in a study on the Côte d'Ivoire it is maintained that there is no compelling evidence of a pro-male or pro-female bias in the allocation of household resources (Haddad and Hoddinott 1994).

A third issue in the debate is the role of women in agricultural production and their productivity, since their productivity is a vital element of their income chances and, consequently, for their possibilities for spending money on food. In this context it is interesting to note that generally 20% and in special cases up to 40% of all rural households in developing countries are female-headed. When you simply compare productivity, it has been found in several studies that yields are generally higher on male-managed plots than those on female-managed plots. However, when differences in human and physical capital are controlled for, women and men are equally efficient as farm managers (Quisumbing 1996). There is broad evidence of gender biases with respect to the control of production factors, as shown by Quisumbing and others (Quisumbing et al. 1997). Women in rural areas tend to have less education. A higher educational level boosts productivity; moreover, fertility is decreasing with higher levels of education. Women have often only limited access to land, since the land tenure system does not foresee property rights for women. Moreover, women have in many cases lesser chance to mobilize extra family labour, i.e., either hired labour, because they lack the capital, or to activate labour groups, since cooperative labour associations mostly can only be convened by men. Women may also have smaller plots and frequently farm in low potential areas. If husbands migrate, either temporarily or for good, women—because of their tight time schedule—tend to farm near by the village, where the land is exhausted, since fallow periods are no longer respected. Finally, women have no close contact to agricultural extension services which generally employ few female extension workers anyway. In addition, women have only limited access to rural credit. The exception, where credit is provided without collateral to women—as in the schemes of the Grameen Bank in Bangladesh—has been replicated elsewhere but has not become standard so far (see Zeller and Sharma, chap. 26, this volume).

It must be borne in mind that the gender biases described above are findings from a so far limited number of empirical studies. Still more case studies are needed to permit cross-cultural generalizations and to explore whether these associations found so far are robust (Quisumbing et al. 1997). In essence the actual behaviour and the norms orientating the functioning of family units have not yet been fully explored. Haddad et al. rightly point out that the costs of neglecting household resource allocation analysis are often high (Haddad et al. 1997: 276 ff.). But meanwhile it has already become apparent that the complexity of cultural characteristics does not allow for one single optimal approach applicable to all situations.

To return to nutrition analysis, it is to be understood that the intrahousehold perspective must be expanded to incorporate interhousehold relations, since considerable input supply, as well the distribution of output, are governed by norms of interhousehold relations, a point that the mainstream of research is actually not yet fully aware of. The results of these studies must, then, be incorporated into policy strategies. We have to answer such questions as to whether lump-sum transfers to poor households are more efficient than price subsidies for staple food. What are the reactions of those household members that are non-recipients of transfers, e.g., does a school child that participates in a school feeding programme get less calories at home? In public work schemes it is often asked whether—if participants are male—the remuneration should be in kind instead of in cash, in view of the expenditure preferences of men. From the development policy aspect, the intrahousehold resource allocation pattern is of particular interest for avoiding as much as possible the unintended consequences of orchestrated social change. Often projects and programmes interfere with the established patterns of division of labour and income between men and women. When, for instance in West Africa, cash crops like cocoa (a male crop) are expanded women are frequently required to work as well without, though, sharing the returns. On top of this, they may have to neglect their food crop products intended for the market; i.e., one of the unwanted results of developmental efforts is that frequently additional burdens are shifted on to women. Intrahousehold resource allocation analysis possibly may help to prevent such outcomes in the future.

5 The design of food security policies and the framework for action

5.1 Basic considerations

With policy considerations it makes a difference whether one conceives food security as a human right, food insecurity as a consequence of poverty or as causing underdevelopment problems (FAO 1996b: iii). Various strategies might follow from the specific understanding of the food policy adopted.

— When designing food policies one has to rely either on market-derived approaches or transfer-based interventions. In practice a mix of both approaches is chosen, though it appears nowadays that in the long run more market orientation and some measures of liberalized economy should supersede welfare-oriented interventions.

— Another basic option in this domain is whether one starts with the removal of one critical constraint or designs a complex set of actions (FAO 1996a: i). One also has to look into the nature of food insecurity and whether one wants to combat transitory or chronic hunger.

— Finally there is a normative dimension. We are now inclined to look at food security policies in a more holistic and integrated way (IFAD 1996: 21, 31). This means that the enabling environment should be strenghtened. Policy-makers do not merely strive for increased food supply but for sustainable paths to economic development and poverty alleviation (FAO 1996a: ii), a strategy that—when successful—implies, more or less, an improvement in the food situation.

— However, a lesson learnt over the last decades is that in food policy design there is no "turnkey" or "magic bullet" solution. You cannot simply draw up a blueprint from which you can derive a strategy that always works. This has already been identified as a short-coming when applying one and the same concept of structural adjustment policy to all countries of the Third World regardless of their different stages of socio-economic development. It is now generally agreed that the specific measures in food policy programmes have to be different from country to country (FAO 1996b).

— The instruments of food policy must be related to the different global, regional, national, provincial, community and household levels and they have to take account of the different dimensions of food security such as food availability, food access and food use.

5.2 Experiences in different countries

Although caution is required, it nevertheless makes sense to consider "areas of likely success and failure" in order to arrive at some starting point for action planning. In the following we report on results from a food security assessment paper done for the 1996 World Food Summit. Here the history from 1970 to 1990 was recorded for 86 low food supply countries. It turned out that 52 countries had

fared well and improved their situation whereas 34 cases had experienced retrogression. The basic factors for improvement in the 52 success cases were:
- Countries have an above average economic growth rate;
- Countries have stemmed the growth of food imports;
- Global agriculture provided the food imports readily and without difficulty;
- Countries have seen domestic agricultural growth ;
- Improvements in some cases were made in a relatively short period of time, that is, in about 10 years (FAO 1996a: i).

It must be noted, however, that agricultural growth does not automatically improve the food security of households. The paper states further that in a number of cases improvements and retrogression in the same country follow the commodity boom-and-bust cycles. There were even cases (5 countries) where per capita food supplies were improved, although generally negative economic growth was experienced. On the other hand there are examples of countries where positive economic growth was associated with a deteriorating food supply situation. In general, however, experience shows that countries that had already had short food supplies and where many people were undernourished had made little progress in achieving food security. In 20 out of 34 negative cases there have been detrimental political factors like severe disruptions by war and civil strife and it has become evident that those countries mostly suffer from economic as well as agricultural stagnation.

From this situation one may draw the conclusion that when planning food security policies one should follow a double strategy consisting of the implementation of general economic measures supporting development, including poverty alleviating policies and programmes that on the one hand raise the purchasing power of the poor, and on the other pursue specific food policies, either targeted or non-targeted.

5.3 The framework of food policy designs

The design of successful food policies has to be done within the framework of four dimensions:
- The political framework;
- General economic policies;
- Agricultural development policies and human resource development approaches;
- Specific food security policies.

5.3.1 The political framework

In the political sphere a Third World government should respect basic human rights; the political system should be democratic or should at least be open for a democratic solution in the longer term. In most dictatorships, for instance in Africa, little progress, if any, has been made in improving the food security of the poor. Secondly, the necessary security for investments requires political stability, a factor all too evident if you again look at quite a number of African states. Thirdly, graft and corruption must be combatted; above all the money grubbing behaviour of the bureaucracy in many states is counter-productive. Finally, good governance must be striven for; that is, the ruling elite must have an interest in poverty alleviation for the poor (FAO 1996a). However, it must be admitted that progress in this domain is only likely to be possible when coalitions and alliances of the poor with segments of the middle class become able to articulate low class political interests.

5.3.2 Economic macro-policies

The second dimension in the framework is supportive general economic policies. These are appropriate macro-economic policies and development strategies (FAO 1996b: iv). They may be trade and stock-policies, adjustments to overvalued currencies, structural adjustment programmes, employment and income policies, population policies, and the like. These broad policies should face the requirements of the globalizing world market; strategies of autonomous efforts against world market influcences have failed, as the debacle of self-reliance in the dependency theory has shown.

5.3.3. Agricultural policies and human resource development

The third dimension includes the development of agriculture and complementary action in human resource development. Quite a number of strategies and instruments can be noted here; in particular we should mention:

- All strategies for yield increases and area expansion where the latter is still possible;
- Shifts from export crops to food crops for national consumption;
- Technological change by innovation diffusion;
- Expansion of irrigation;
- Sustainable production on fragile land and in an overstretched natural resource base;
- Investment in research, including concern for local knowledge systems;
- Rural infrastructure, transport and communication systems;
- Agricultural extension, adult literacy and basic education and training;
- Rural health and sanitation;
- Rural job creation outside of agriculture;
- Improving access to land, credit and other resources that allow for self-employment (FAO 1996a: 13)

In this context a rather progressive policy rationale is followed by IFAD (IFAD 1996: ii). This UN organization suggests that the agricultural policies should above all be followed in low potential areas (which is against conventional wisdom) and in areas of high concentration of malnutrition, with special emphasis on Africa; moreover, IFAD stresses that a gender perspective in development policies and programmes should be pursued, since women are the key to improved food security. The time burdens of women in agriculture and the household should be relieved, but the ability to earn an independent income should be preserved. Besides women, other vulnerable groups must be protected (IFAD 1996: 9). A third aspect in this position is the promotion of self-help and self-employment at the community level where participation, not only in planning, but also in the implementation and evaluation of projects should be realized. It is evident that many development programmes and projects so far do not follow this holistic and integrated developmental approach.

5.3.4 Specific food security and nutritional policies

Fourthly come the specific food and nutritional policies. Here we rely on an attempt at categorization by de Janvry and Subramanian (1993: 4), who suggest the following typology:

- Cheap-food policy at no direct cost to government;
- Untargeted food subsidy schemes;
- Targeted interventions, including emergency prevention and relief.

First, cheap food is represented by government policies of a suppressed rise in food prices, overvalued exchange rate, massive concessual aid or state monopolies in procurement and sale. Secondly, in untargeted food subsidy schemes one mostly has consumer food subsidies from which all strata of the society derive profit whether they are needy or not. The subsidies may accumulate to such a degree that producer costs may be at the same level as, or above consumer prices. Quite a number of countries have this kind of subsidy; among the most well known cases is Egypt, obviously showing that such a policy may be very cost-intensive, at the same time raising doubts as to whether such uniform approaches can be cost-effective.

However, expenses cannot be considered alone, but must be balanced against the benefits accrued. De Janvry and Subramanian also point out that such food policy "is politically a more legitimate instrument of income transfer than these (redistributive) other measures like asset transfer and wage policies" (de Janvry and Subramanian 1993: 12). But with a heavy food subsidy policy it is likely that domestic food production will grow only slowly. Since many people in developing countries think that food subsidies are the only profit they derive from government, even partial removal of foodstuff subsidies in order to adjust to rising world market prices, giving incentives to domestic agriculture, is a very sensitive matter. In several countries threats to remove subsidies have led to outbreaks of protests, demonstrations and rioting.

Finally, we have the targeted interventions lilke feeding programmes, micronutrient programmes, food stamps, cash transfer programmes, rationing programmes, food-for-work programmes as well as famine and catastrophe prevention and relief programmes. Targeting means that specific nutritional policies are applied in selected regions or to needy segments of a society identified by various measurement devices. It is well known for protecting vulnerable groups such as school children, pregnant mothers and babies. An instrument of particular interest is the self-targeted work scheme where the wage or the food ration are somewhat below the minimum wage. This feature is meant to assure that only the needy, that is who cannot find employment on the job market, engage for participation.

The policies of targeting transfer are often difficult to achieve (see Schubert, chap. 25, this volume). Recently, a large-scale cash-transfer scheme, GAPVU in Mozambique, where urban beneficiaries received 3$ per month, had to be reorganized, since too many ineligible people had succeeded in finding a way on to the pay roll. It is evident that the poorest countries in the Third World can only implement large-scale targeted food subsidy schemes if they have considerable access to concessional food aid.

5.4 Conclusion

To conclude, we advocate, as do other authors in the field of food policy design, that a combination of general economic promotional policies and specific food policies be developed and applied. We are aware of the fact that the success rate of such multi-sectoral nutritional planning has not been very impressive so far. Over the last twenty years we have seen a shift in policies from more basic needs approaches, with welfare-oriented measures, to more market-oriented, liberal economy approaches. Economists are frequently concerned that subsidies and transfer policies may stifle the spirit of entrepreneurship (FAO 1996a: ii), have detrimental effects on economic growth and, in the long run, reduce the welfare of the rural poor, who cannot be integrated in an otherwise growing agriculture.

We agree with de Janvry and Subramanian's point that "promotion of equitable growth thus requires a combination of targeted subsidies to protect the poor until the income effects of increased investment materialize" (de Janvry and Subramanian 1993: 21).

Last, it must be said that effective food policies demand precise operationalization of nutrition objectives as well as reliable descriptions of household food security in an international reporting and monitoring system; furthermore, an efficient organizational set-up is required, which must achieve a coordination of effort at the community level with farmers, male and female, associations, co-operatives and NGOs as well as with local, regional and national government agencies, e.g., research stations and extension agencies. Finally one has to integrate the different bilateral and multilateral donors. The experiences of this dimension of food policy are presented in part IV of this reader.

6 The concept of the reader

Food security is a complex subject, representing a special field of developmental problems. In order to sort the vast amount of publications with their different approaches, we suggest distinguishing four dimensions of food security:
- Theoretical-analytical;
- Empirical-descriptive;
- Normative-political;
- Institutional.

6.1 Part I: The theoretical-analytical dimension

This includes problem and issue oriented concepts as well as theoretical approaches to help explain the reasons and consequences of undernutrition and malnutrition. Moreover, the concept of food security must be located in the framework of general development theory. Following von Braun (chapter 1, this volume), we suggest taking three aspects, or avenues, of analysis:
a) The physical availability of food (production, storage, marketing);
b) Access to food or economic availability (mostly determined by household income, including the resource base of subsistence economy and food prices);
c) Food use (preferences for particular food items, preparation of particular dishes, distribution of meals among household members, including particular food requirements, e.g., of small children).

In former times the theoretical discussion of food security was largely concentrated on global, regional and national aspects, with particular reference to supply-oriented elements, such as production, commerce, marketing, stocks, and reserves. Over the last ten years a change in orientation has taken place. Nowadays we are more interested in the household and its members. We ask about patterns of food distribution according to gender (in adults), among children (boy/girl differences) and the old, as well as about social solidarity and reciprocal exchange relations between households. In addition, non-food aspects which are relevant for social well-being, above all, health aspects, nowadays also undergo scrutiny and are related to food considerations.

6.2 Part II: The empirical-descriptive analysis

This dimension can present structured data that are necessary to prove theoretical reasoning. Mostly, new areas of research are opened up by descriptive and empirical reports. The case studies and multi-country experience we have collected here, demonstrate the relevance of the food aspect in different areas of development. So far, the empirical discussion on food security was mainly a domain of agricultural economics. In the empirical part of the reader we have chosen, with one exception, contributions from development sociology. We hope to gain fresh insights by this choice. Sociologists, like social anthropologists, do not only present data, but strive particularly for explaining the rationality of behaviour of the people under analysis, as these people perceive it themselves. The contributions cover the major development regions of the world. This is important, since considerable regional differences in the food sector exist, for instance, between Africa and Asia; developmental trends between the continents also show considerable differences. When selecting empirical contributions we have tried to place the accent on relevant topical research themes like ecological requirements of sustainable food production or gender relations in achieving food security. In part I and II experiences from Africa are overrepresented since, of all continents, Africa has the bleakest future with regard to nutrition. The case of Germany which has also been included serves as an example of an industrialized country.

6.3 Part III: The normative-political analysis

This part of our study deals with approaches, policies and programmes to overcome hunger and malnutrition. In recent programmes and in the on-going political debate more and more emphasis has been put on the ethical dimension of development; here we discuss whether a specific human right to nutrition can be incorporated into the human rights catalogue.

Nation-based programmes to achieve food security have to seek an adequate combination of macro-policies and specific food security policies, like subsidies, food aid rationing, food-for-work programmes, etc. Therefore, the policy dimension is at first described as a framework for effective nutrition and health programmes. Because of the present ardent debate on the consequences of genetic engineering and new bio-technologies we analyse the passing from the Green to the Gene Revolution from a natural and a social scientist point of view.

Since the end of the cold war the number of armed conflicts has increased dramatically, and more and more food aid goes into famine prevention subsequent to armed conflicts. We view this problem as a growing humanitarian challenge. The spread of civil society within the previously authoritarian regimes of an increasing number of developing countries has given increased importance to non-governmental organizations, and their role in the struggle against hunger is critically assessed. Our policy discussion shows what actually has been done and what could still be done.

6.4 Part IV: The institutional analysis

Besides the national institutions through which nutritional policies are executed in developing countries, there is ample international cooperation in this field. We concentrate our efforts on the international dimension and present an overview of the international institutions active in the field of food aid and food security. Some institutions of particular relevance like the World Bank and the European Community are analysed in a special chapter. As an example of an important bilateral donor, the German Agency for Technical Cooperation GTZ is examined. The role of non-governmental organizations in international cooperation is also treated in another chapter. Finally the global commitments to eradicate hunger as they were agreed at the 1996 World Food Summit in Rome are delineated and the general significance and specific results of this conference with regard to policy implementation are discussed. This contribution ends with a policy outlook on the required action. In the appendix abstracts of all articles are provided.

References

Abdelgabar, Omar (1997): Mechanized Farming and Nuba Peasants: An Example for Non-Sustainable Development in the Sudan, Münster.

Alderman, Harold et al. (1995): Unitary Versus CollectiveModels of the Household: Is it Time to Shift the Burden of Proof, in: The World Bank Research Observer, Vol. 10, No. 1, Feb., pp. 1-19.

Alexandratos, Nikos (1996): China's Projected Cereal Deficits in a World Context, in: Agricultural Economics, 15, pp. 1-16.

Alexandratos, Nikos (ed.) (1995): World Agriculture: Towards 2010—An FAO Study, FAO, Rome, Chichester.

Altvater, Elmar (1992): Der Preis des Wohlstands, Münster.

Altvater, Elmar and Birgit Mahnkopf (1996): Grenzen der Globalisierung—Ökonomie, Ökologie und Politik in der Weltgesellschaft, Münster.

Behrman, Jere and T.N. Srinivasan (eds.) (1995): Handbook of Development Economics, Vol. III A, Elsevier, Amsterdam 1995.

Brown, Lester (1996): Tough Choices—Facing the Challenge of Food Scarcity, World Watch Institute, Washington.

Evers, Hans-Dieter (1997): Marktexpansion und Globalisierung, in: Manfred Schulz (ed.): Entwicklung—Die Perspektive der Entwicklungssoziologie, Opladen.

Fan, Shenggen and Sombilla Agcaoili (1997): Why do Projections on China's Future Food Supply and Demand Differ? IFPRI, Environment and Production Technology Division, Discussion Paper No. 22, March.

FAO (1997): Food Outlook, May/June.

FAO (1996a): Food Security and Assistance, Technical Background Document No. 14, World Food Summit Technical Background Documents, Vol. 3, Rome.

FAO (1996b): Food Security and Nutrition, Technical Background Document No. 5, World Food Summit Technical Background Documents, Vol. 1, Rome.

Haddad, Lawrence, John Hoddinott and Harold Alderman (1997): Intrahousehold Resource Allocation in Developing Countries—Models, Methods, and Policy, IFPRI, Baltimore, London.

Haddad, Lawrence and John Hoddinott (1994): Women's Income and Boy-Girl Anthrometric Status in the Côte d'Ivoire, in: World Development, Vol. 22, No 4, pp. 543-553.

Haddad, Lawrence and Thomas Reardon (1993): Gender Bias in the Allocation of Resources within Households in Burkina Faso: A Disaggregated Outlay Equivalent Study, in: The Journal of Development Studies, Vol. 29, No. 2, Jan., pp. 260-276.

Haddad, Lawrence and Ravi Kanbur (1992): Intrahousehold Inequality and Theory of Targeting, European Economic Review, Vol. 36, 1992, pp. 372-378.

Hein, Wolfgang (1996): Welternährung: Mehr produzieren, besser verteilen, anders konsumieren?, in: Peripherie, No. 63, Vol. 16, pp. 7-32.

International Food Policy Research Institute (1995): A 2020 Vision for Food, Agriculture, and the Environment—The Vision, Challenge and Recommended Action, Washington.

International Fund for Agricultural Development IFAD (1996): Household Food Security—Implications for Policy and Action for Rural Poverty Alleviation and Nutrition, IFAD Paper for the World Food Summit, Rome.

De Janvry, Alain and Shankar Subramanian (1993): The Politics and Economics of Food and Nutrition Policies and Programs, in: Per Pinstrup-Andersen (ed.): The Political Economy of Food and Nutrition, Baltimore, London.

Kanbur, Ravi and Lawrence Haddad (1994): Are Better-Off Households More Unequal or Less Unequal?, in: Oxford Economic Papers, Vol. 46, No. 3, July.

Kirkly, John, Phil Okeefe and Lloyd Timberlake (eds.) (1995): The Earthscan Reader in Sustainable Development, London.

Maxwell, Simon (1996): Food Security: A Post-Modern Perspective, in: Food Policy, Vol. 21, No. 2, pp. 155-170.

Mitchell, Donald and Merlinda Ingco (1993): The World Food Outlook, Washington.

Pinstrup-Andersen, Per, Rajul Pandya-Lorch and Mark Rosegrant (1997): The World Food Situation: Recent Developments, Emerging Issues, and Long-Term Prospects; 2020 Vision, Food Policy Report, The International Food Policy Research Institute, Washington.

Pinstrup-Andersen, Per and Rajul Pandya-Lorch (1997): Major Uncertainties and Risks Affecting Long-Term Food Supply and Demand, Paper prepared for the OECD Forum for the Future Conference on "The Agro-Food Sector on the Threshold of the 21st Century", Paris, France, June 24-25, 1997 (Revised August 1997).

Quisumbing, Agnes et al. (1997): Strengthening Food Policy Through Intrahousehold Analysis, Research Paper, The International Food Policy Research Institute, Washington.

Quisumbing, Agnes (1996): Male-Female Differences in Agricultural Productivity: Methodological Issues and Empirical Evidence, in: World Development, Vol. 24, No. 10, 1996.

Quisumbing, Agnes et al. (1995): Women: The Key to Food Security, Food Policy Report, The International Food Policy Research Institute, Washington.

Rosegrant, Mark W. et al. (1997): Global Food Markets and US Exports in the Twenty-First Century, The International Food Policy Research Institute, Washington, May 28.

Rosegrant, Mark W., Sambilla Agcaoili, Perez Merdedita and D. Nicostrato (1995): Global Food Projections to 2020: Implications for Investment, Food, Agriculture and the Environment Discussion Paper No. 5, The International Food Policy Research Institute, Washington.

Schuurman, Frans J. (1993): Beyond the Impasse—New Directions in Development Theory, London, New Jersey.

Strauss, J.A. and D. Thomas (1995): Human Resources: Empirical Modeling of Household and Family Decisions, in: T.N. Srinivasan and Behrman (eds.): Handbook of Development Economics, Amsterdam, North Holland.

UN (United Nations) (1996): World Population Prospects: The 1996 Revisions, New York: UN.

PART I

FOOD SECURITY AND NUTRITIONAL WELL-BEING: CONCEPTS, TRENDS AND ISSUES

1

Food Security—A Conceptual Basis

Joachim von Braun

1 Basic views

Food security in its most basic form is defined as the access of all people to the food needed for a healthy life at all times (FAO and WHO 1992). Food insecurity is a prime cause of undernutrition. This paper shall conceptualise food security.[1] It focuses mainly on the food security problems of the poor in low-income countries, but to some extent, the issues addressed also relate to transforming economies and the small food insecure-population groups in high-income countries.

In order to achieve food security for all, it is important that planners and policy-makers in every sector be aware of the impact that their decisions and actions are likely to have on food security. Also, however, clarity of basic perspectives of the food security problems shall be called for, as these may be viewed from three different perspectives:

- first, as a basic human right,
- second, as a symptom of broader poverty and development problems and,
- third, as a cause of these poverty and development problems.

Human-rights view

Considering food security and nutritional well-being to be a basic human right of every individual means that, in principle, no compromise is acceptable concerning the right to food. The International Covenant on Economic, Social and Cultural Rights adopted by the United Nations General Assembly in 1966 defined and formalised the right to food as a basic human right, which had already been mentioned in the Universal Declaration of Human Rights of the United Nations in 1948. Eighty-five states had signed the covenant in 1989. Although states continue to endorse the right to food, they have not translated this right into specific legal obligations, and there are no national or international mechanisms to supervise the implementation of this right.[2]

---

1 The chapter draws partly on the background paper "Food Security and Nutrition" of the World Food Summit (FAO 1996b), which had been prepared by the author in collaboration with colleagues from FAO, UNICEF, WHO, The World Bank.

2 The Universal Declaration on the Eradication of Hunger and Malnutrition adopted at the 1974 World Food Conference states: "Every man, woman, and child has the inalienable right to be free from hunger and malnutrition ... " (UN 1975).

This does not imply that the stated human right is meaningless. The consensus and its codification provide a foundation for advocacy and political pressure in the countries which signed the covenant or related declarations. The World Food Summit of 1996 provided an opportunity to revive the matter. Certainly, current monitoring of the right to food is not satisfactory.

Symptom-of-poverty view

Considering malnutrition to be a symptom of poverty and development problems (i.e. as an outcome) suggests that the availability of and access to food (being mainly functions of structural conditions and changes in income, agriculture, and trade) interact with the health and sanitation environment and human behaviour and knowledge in giving rise to nutritional outcomes. Policy is then called upon to rectify constraints in any of these domains.

While food availability may be a problem for many people when availability declines and prices rise, the problem assumes crisis proportions mostly for the poor. This is why food availability needs to be evaluated within the context of poverty when availability problems turn into access problems (e.g. when prices rise), be it at the national or household level.

Increasing the incomes of households that have malnourished members can improve their access to food. Increases in income are strongly related to nonstaple food consumption, particularly of meats.

Pre-condition-for-development view

Taking the view that nutritional well-being is a pre-condition for development argues that lack of productivity (in a broad sense) is partly a result of malnutrition. The nutritional well-being of the poor is thus not merely an outcome of development, but a pre-condition for it. The linkages between the two are of both a direct, short-term nature and an indirect, long-term one, whereby the latter also relate closely to population growth.

Improved adult nutrition leads to higher physical productivity and higher productivity in the labour market.[3] Undernutrition results in substantial productivity losses, e.g. through high levels of morbidity and impaired cognitive development (Mason, Jonsson, and Csete 1995; Scrimshaw 1994).

In addition to their current income flow, poor households build their asset bases out of incremental income. This is one of the key links between short- and long-term food security and nutrition. Expanded asset bases reduce the vulnerability of households to short-term downturns in income flows; part of the asset base

---

3 Empirical studies find nutritional status and labor productivity, as measured by wages or own-farm output or both, to be positively related (Strauss 1986; Sahn and Alderman 1988). In environments where physical productivity matters, therefore, substantial lifetime losses may be expected among adults who are stunted as a result of poor health and nutrition during childhood.

can be liquidated in times of adversity, an action that helps to maintain household-level food security.

The position adopted in this chapter is to accept each of the three views (human right, symptom of poverty, precondition of development) as having a certain degree of validity, rather than playing them off one against the other. This approach may facilitate the formation of larger and more influential coalitions internationally and domestically—coalitions which can improve food security rapidly.

2 Causes of food insecurity: the framework

Poverty, including the associated vulnerability to natural or man-made shocks, is one of the root causes of food insecurity and malnutrition. Yet, poverty and its dynamics may be seen as an endogenous outcome of limited human and natural resources and flawed policies—as discussed in above. If the root causes of malnutrition such as policy failures, poverty, and population growth remain unaddressed, both public program actions and private actions (e.g. household strategies) will have limited effectiveness in sustainably improving nutrition. A broad framework of the causes of food insecurity and malnutrition examining the linkages between food security and nutrition is presented below.

Basic causal factors

In Figure 1, the top row represents basic causal factors:

1. economic strategies and policy interacting with social discrimination and conflict,
2. resource endowments and their relationship to climate and disaster events influencing,
3. levels of poverty and food availability; and
4. population growth.

These factors directly affect the success of any policy and program interventions (such as subsidies and asset distribution). The figure is intended to highlight the primary importance of addressing the basic causes of food and nutritional problems, due to the predominance of the "downstream" links. Otherwise, for instance, public actions in the areas listed in the second row of the figure (services, transfers, etc.) can be only partial remedies.

Food security—population linkages

Food security, nutrition and population growth stand in a particularly complex, long-term relationship. Only over the medium term is the relationship in part one of food availability racing with population growth. Over the long term, improved nutrition, being an element of human welfare, may contribute to slowing down population growth. Clearly, there are strong positive relationships, on the one hand, between improved nutrition and economic development (Fogel 1994), and on the other, between economic development and the population's transition from a high birth rate and low life expectancy to longer life expectancy and, thereafter, lower birth rates. Thus, to the extent that improved nutrition fosters economic development, it is also a fundamental force for alleviating the mounting problem of population growth.

Figure 1: Food (in)security and (mal)nutrition in a broad context

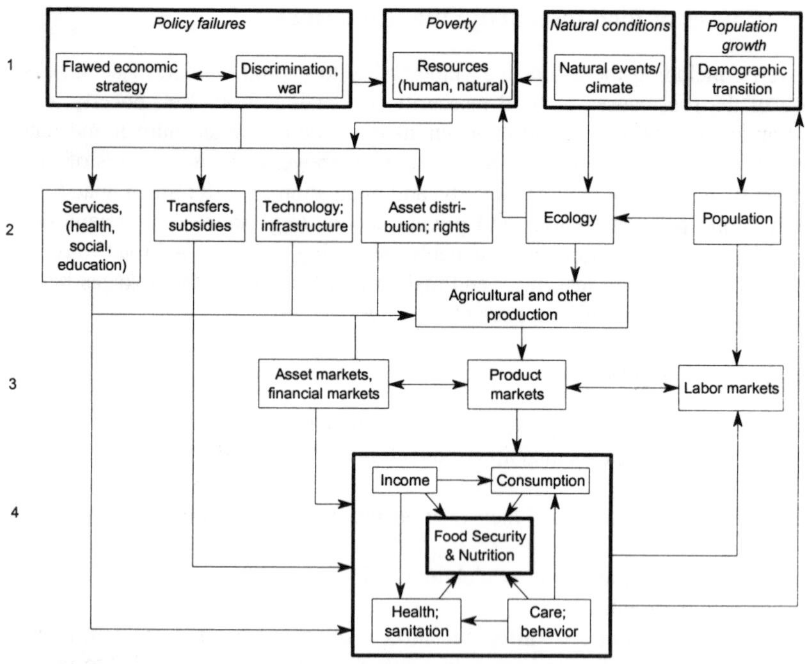

(1) Basic causes
(2) Structural/institutional conditions, areas of public action
(3) Market conditions
(4) Micro-level conditions, household, intrahousehold, gender
Source: adapted from von Braun, Teklu and Webb (1993).

The search for nutritional well-being may also have important implications for a region's demographic situation, especially if it leads to short- or long-term migration to other areas in search of employment and income or, in the extreme, in search of relief food. Such out-migration may result in an increased number of female-headed households, a higher dependency ratio in the sending area, and changes in the dynamics of the labour market. The receiving areas, mostly urban slums, experience considerable food-security strain from the influx of migrants.

The efforts of food-insecure households to acquire food may also have important implications for the environment and the use of natural resources. Many poor and food-insecure households live in ecologically vulnerable areas (Leonard and contributors 1989), and inappropriate or desperate land-use practices can cause environmental degradation that can further undermine their livelihood and that of future generations.

Food security—market linkages

Policies (such as wage policy) and project interventions (such as employment programs for poverty reduction) interact at the level of capital, labour, and product markets. These relationships determine the prices and terms of trade faced by the poor, and hence their real purchasing power.

Food Security and nutritional well-being is linked with labour markets and production (via productivity effects) and to population (via mortality, fertility, and migration), and can be influenced by direct intervention (services, incl. health, social, educational; transfers, subsidies). These linkages and their development policy implications are discussed briefly further below.

Household, gender and intra-household issues

Actual nutritional well-being is then determined by a number of interrelated factors, as depicted at the bottom of Figure 1:

- Availability of food through market and other channels, which is a function of production, stock holding and trade opportunities;
- Access to food, that is the ability of households to acquire whatever food is available, which is a function of household income (including the resource base for subsistence farming);
- Behaviour and knowledge, which under certain conditions of availability and access predispose people to buy specific foods or to grow them for home consumption, which influence the preparation and distribution of food among household members, including the meeting of special feeding needs, for example of young children, and which affect breast feeding and general aspects of care;
- Health status of individuals, which is governed by factors such as health and sanitary environment at the household and community levels, and behaviour and care-taking, as well as—in a circular link—by nutritional status itself (e.g. mother-child links/low birth weights).

Of the more directly food-linked factors of nutritional well-being, emphasis should be placed on dietary composition (incl. animal products) and energy density, the mode of processing and preparing food, and, for infants, the extent of breast feeding. The less directly food-linked factors include, for example, the allocation of women's time and knowledge, which may have significant nutritional effects through changes in breast feeding, child care and health and sanitation factors.

While improving access to food, increases in household income do not always directly contribute to improving the nutritional well-being of all household members. Intrahousehold decision-making plays a role (Alderman et al. 1995), as do knowledge and care. Even if they seem rational to the head of the household, patterns of household spending and consumption may not necessarily be optimal from a nutritional perspective. Nutrition is only one of a series of considerations that are taken into account in decisions regarding household spending and consumption. A lack of knowledge regarding the nutritional needs of household members may lead to the withholding of needed food, even when it is available. This problem may be aggravated by incorrect information from outside the household and the promotion of non-foods or non-nutritious foods. Moreover, the health and nutritional status of children are substantially affected by care behaviours. Although they play key roles as guardians of household food security and children's nutrition and fulfil many food-related, economic and reproductive responsibilities in the household, women frequently do not have commensurate control over resources or decision-making authority. This is one of the causes of poor women's increased vulnerability to nutritional risks.

3 Conceptual aspects of the dimensions of the food security problem

Measurement issues

The food security and nutrition problem has a number of dimensions, and some of the problems overlap or are parts of larger nutrition and food-related problem areas (Figure 2).

It is difficult to know how many people suffer from hunger and malnutrition, given definition and measurement problems and inadequate data. Related measurement difficulties result from regional, community-level, household, and intra-household inequalities, and from dynamics which are difficult to quantify. Many regions of the world have never been in the position to make the sizeable investment needed to put in place data systems capable of comprehensively assessing chronic malnutrition. Also, the nutritional well-being of a population may change rapidly, yet the monitoring of food insecurity and malnutrition in disaster zones and areas of armed conflict is limited, for obvious reasons.

Given the multiple dimensions (chronic, transitory, short-term, and long-term) of food insecurity, there can be no single indicator for measuring it (Maxwell and Frankenberger 1993). Proposed indicators actually relate to household food security in different ways. The relation may be temporal (leading, concurrent, or trailing indicators), conceptual (consumption, nutrition, coping strategies, resource-related, and non-household measures), and/or definition (access, adequacy, vulnerability, and sustainability) (Csete and Maxwell 1995).

- Food security at the national level (the ability to obtain sufficient food to meet the needs of all citizens) can, to some extent, be monitored in terms of needs and supply indicators; that is, the quantities of available food versus needs.
- Food security at the household level may be measured by direct surveys of dietary intake (in comparison with appropriate adequacy norms). Such data is costly due to the considerable time required for its collection and processing.
- If properly analysed, the level of, and changes in, socio-economic and demographic variables such as real wage rates, employment, price ratios and migration can serve as proxies to indicate the status of, and changes in, food security.[4]

Figure 2: Food security and nutrition problems

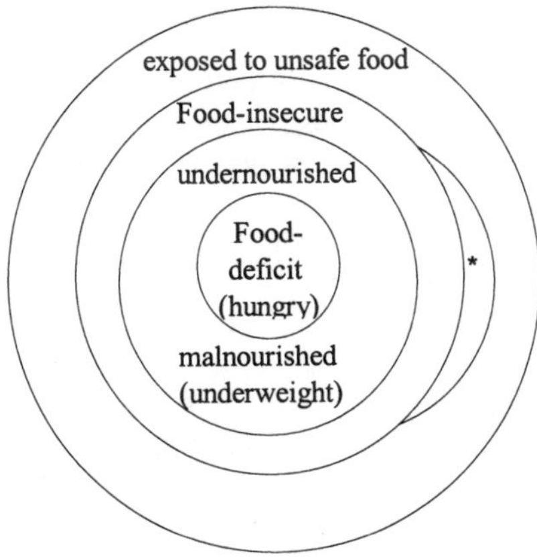

* = overnourished

Where and who are the food-insecure and malnourished?

In certain regions and in rural settings

Essentially, all estimates concur that South Asia, and particularly India and Bangladesh, holds the largest proportion of the developing world's underweight children, followed by sub-Saharan Africa (de Onis et al. 1993). The incidence of food

4 An IFPRI study identified a set of relatively simple indicators of food and nutrition security. The indicators analyzed included the number of unique foods consumed, region, dependency ratio, household size, rooms per capita, incidence of illness, vaccination status, drinking water facilities, health facilities, etc. These indicators were used as single proxies or in combinations. The study found that these simple indicators "perform well in locating the food- and nutrition-insecure." The ideal combination of indicators was observed to be dependent on local characteristics (Haddad, Kennedy, and Sullivan 1994).

deficiency as expressed in estimated energy deficiency is highest in Africa and South Asia, and considerably lower in East Asia and Latin America and the Caribbean. While the percentage of the energy-deficient persons in the populations of South Asia has decreased, their absolute number in South Asia and Sub-Saharan Africa has increased (FAO 1996a).

Regarding location of the food-energy-deficient population by agro-ecological zone it is found that deficiency tends to be least prevalent in wet zones and most prevalent in arid zones (Broca and Oram 1991). By region, most of the poor in Sub-Saharan Africa were located in the arid zone. In most instances, the distribution of the poor mirrors the population distribution in the agro-ecological zones (Garcia et al. 1995).

In different areas, food-insecure households may belong to different socio-economic and demographic groups, depending on factors such as agro-ecological characteristics, access to land, diversity of income sources, and the state of development of the economy. Food-deficient households tend to be larger and to have a higher number of dependants and a younger age-composition (von Braun and Pandya-Lorch 1991). The prevalence of food insecurity tends to be higher among landless or quasi-landless households, which are much more dependent on less reliable sources of income than farm income and on the diversification of the rural economy.

In urban areas

In urban areas, household food security is primarily a function of the real wage rate (i.e. the rate relative to food prices) and of the level of employment. The prevalence of food deficiency and malnutrition tends to be lower in urban areas than in rural areas. But the miserable sanitation environment in poor urban locations and certain aspects of urban lifestyles sometimes make the urban nutritional situation qualitatively different from the rural situation. Urban food insecurity and malnutrition will become an increasingly important problem in the future, as rates of urbanisation increase while problems with urban sanitation, diet quality and food safety grow (UNICEF 1994). For instance, by the year 2025, 57 percent of Africa's population may be urban, as opposed to only 34 percent in 1990. In South Asia, the figure may be 52 percent. In Latin America, this figure had already reached 72 percent in 1990.

Among refugees and the displaced

Unable to secure a living or adequate food, often as a consequence of armed conflicts and discrimination, vast numbers of the poor migrate to more peaceful areas in their own country or into neighbouring countries. There are now an estimated 20 million refugees, plus some 30 million internally displaced people, making a total of 50 million (WFP 1995). Another 35 million people live outside their own country in search of employment (Chen 1992; Russell, Jacobsen, and Stanley 1990). Such movements are accompanied by problems of increased food insecurity among the refugees and displaced poor, and specific nutritional problems (UN ACC/SCN 1994).

In transforming economies

Due to malfunctioning markets, lack of safety nets, and under-employment the early 1990s have seen a substantial increase in the food-insecure population groups of some economies in transition. Absolute poverty has increased, and the symptoms of nutritional deficiencies are particularly widespread in central Asian countries and parts of Russia. In Russia, preliminary estimates report that 3.6 percent of children under 2 years of age were underweight in 1993, and 21 percent stunted. During the same period, a considerable prevalence of obesity was found among Russian adults (e.g. 20 percent of those between the ages of 30 and 59) (Mroz and Popkin 1995). The significance of access to land for household food security increased. In Russia, for instance, 25 million households derive much of their staple foods from garden plots. The income earned in cash and kind from the household plots is for instance about 26% in western Russia and the contribution to household calories is large. Contrary to what one might expect, the poorest 25% of households are getting not only absolutely but also relatively less food and income from their household plots (8% of income) than the top 25% of the income distribution (32%) (von Braun et al. 1996).

In industrialised countries

In high-income countries and among the high-income groups of low- and mid-income countries, the prime causes of unhealthy diets include issues of lifestyle, social stratification and knowledge (FAO and WHO 1992). Particularly in the industrialised countries, there has been increasing recognition over the past 40 years that certain chronic, non-communicable diseases are closely related to diet and aspects of lifestyle. In the course of the 1980s and 1990s, as the distribution of income in the industrialised countries of North America and Europe has become more skewed and as social-welfare spending has been cut back in the face of rising unemployment, the need for food assistance among the low-income groups has grown (Feichtinger 1995). Homeless people are especially vulnerable to food insecurity.

Different groups of households and their members

Different types of nutritional risks affect different groups of households and their members in different ways, as is pointed out in Figure 3. The most severe nutritional problems arise when vulnerable household members are hit by negative outcomes of two or more risks simultaneously. The possible combinations are numerous. In order to improve food security and nutrition, it is necessary to identify the specific risks involved and to develop effective means of reducing them. A focus on the household and intra-household aspects of food insecurity is called for (Senauer and Roe 1997).

Figure 3: Sources of problems for food security and nutrition and examples of affected populations

Risks	Households and people at risk of food insecurity and malnutrition
Political and policy failure risks	Households in war zones and areas of civil unrest Households in low-potential areas that are not connected to growth centres via infrastructure
Lack of employment	Wage-earning households and informal-sector employees (i.e. in urban areas and, when there is a sudden crop-production failure, in rural areas)
Agricultural trade risks (disruption of exports or imports)	Smallholders who are highly specialised in an export crop Small-scale pastoralists Poor households that are highly dependent on imported food Urban poor
Food-price fluctuations (substantial, sudden price rises)	Poor, net food-purchasing households
Crop-production risks (pests, drought, and others)	Smallholders with little income diversification and limited access to improved technology such as improved seeds, fertiliser, irrigation, pest control Landless farm labourers
Health and sanitation problems (infectious diseases, incl. AIDS, for example)	Entire communities, but especially households that cannot afford preventive or curative care and vulnerable members of these households, especially women, children, elderly
Problems of care and social insecurity	Women, especially when they have no access to education Female-headed households Children at weaning age The aged

Source: Adapted from von Braun et al. 1992.

4 Aspects of priority setting

The typical problem of combined chronic and transitory food-security and nutrition problems which exists in poor households requires a well-designed portfolio of food-security and nutrition-policy actions. Such a portfolio should be based on problem assessments (i.e. assessments of the nature of nutrition problems and future risks), and on the instruments available, which are influenced by institutional capacities. In designing new programs, it is advisable to build on the past experiences of the concerned country and other countries. In order to achieve optimal impact, it is usually necessary to pay attention to complementary actions in conjunction with nutrition policies and programs. Such complementary actions include the development of an adequate market infrastructure and policies that do not impede trade. Often, however, the policy reforms needed involve changes in organisation and privatisation and new legal procedures, all of which take time. The time dimensions of optional actions vary, however.

It would be misleading to suggest that even the most serious food security problem could be overcome without substantial national fiscal costs. Not to overcome these problems, however, represents economic costs of much greater magnitude. In crude economic terms, the malnutrition problem is clearly one of the largest, world-wide waste of potential "economic resources"—the lives of billions of potentially productive people now and over the coming decades—and is probably the biggest failure of market functioning yet to be resolved. Any consideration of the costs must therefore also take into account the benefits which would be forfeited through non-action. Focusing on (fiscal) spending and ignoring the resultant benefits yields a misleading picture. Prevention of conflict and instability which may result from a more food-insecure world are part of the benefits (Pinstrup-Andersen et al. 1997).

A guiding principle when considering cost aspects of improving food security and nutrition is to achieve set goals fast, yet in a sustained way, with a portfolio of policy instruments whose costs are lowest. Following such cost-effectiveness principles should lead to the use of optimal combinations of measures, rather than to the perfection of a single policy instrument and over-reliance on short-term interventions. Integrated approaches have proven particularly cost-effective in the context of conducive growth-oriented macro-economic framework. The success of such an approach depends much on public investment in capacity for research and organisation relating to food and nutrition policy and programs.

As described earlier, food-security and nutritional risks can originate from different sources, and the effectiveness of actions in dealing with these risks over the short and long term may vary. From the outset, efforts to improve nutrition must take into account the re-enforcing, detrimental linkages between food insecurity, disease, poor sanitation, inadequate education, and undernutrition. Otherwise, progress made with specific agricultural or health measures alone will have only a limited effect on food security and nutritional improvement.

References

Alderman, Harold, Pierre-André Chiappori, Lawrence Haddad, John Hoddinott, and Ravi Kanbur (1995): Unitary Versus Collective Models of the Household: Is it Time to Shift the Burden of Proof? in: The World Bank Research Observer, 10 (1): pp. 1-19.

von Braun, Joachim, and Rajul Pandya-Lorch (eds.) (1991): Income Sources of Malnourished People in Rural Areas: Microlevel Information and Policy Implications, Working Papers on Commercialization of Agriculture and Nutrition, No. 5, Washington, D.C.: International Food Policy Research Institute.

von Braun, Joachim, Tesfaye Teklu, and Patrick Webb (1993): Famine as the Outcome of Political, Production, and Market Failure, in: IDS Bulletin, 24 (4), pp. 73-79.

von Braun, Joachim, Howarth Bouis, Shubh Kumar, and Rajul Pandya-Lorch (1992): Improving Food Security of the Poor: Concept, Policy, and Programs, Washington, D.C.: International Food Policy Research Institute.

von Braun, Joachim, Eugenia Serova, Harm tho Seeth, and Olga Melyukhina (1996): Russia's Food Economy in Transition: Current Policy Issues and Long-term Consumption and Production Perspectives, Food, Agriculture and Environment Discussion Paper No. 18, Washington, D.C.: International Food Policy Research Institute.

Broca, Sumiter, and Peter Oram (1991): Study on the Location of the Poor, Washington, D.C.: International Food Policy Research Institute (Mimeo).

Chen, R.S. (1992): Hunger Among Refugees and Other People Displaced Across Borders, in: Hunger 1993: Uprooted People., ed. Bread for the World Institute on Hunger and Development. Washington, D.C.: Bread for the World Institute.

Csete, Joanne, and Daniel Maxwell (1995): Household Food Security: The Challenge to UNICEF Programmes (Mimeo).

FAO (Food and Agriculture Organization of the United Nations) (1996a): The Sixth World Food Survey, Rome.

FAO (Food and Agricultural Organisation of the United Nations) (1996b): Food Security and Nutrition, Technical background document No. 5, World Food Summit, Rome.

FAO (Food and Agriculture Organization of the United Nations) and WHO (World Health Organization) (1992): International Conference on Nutrition. World Declaration and Plan of Action for Nutrition, Rome.

Feichtinger, Elfriede (1995): Armut, Gesundheit, Ernährung: eine Bestandsaufnahme, in: Ernährungs-Umschau, 42 (5), pp. 162-169.

Fogel, Robert W. (1994): Economic Growth, Population Theory, and Physiology: The Bearing of Long-term Processes on the Making of Economic Policy, in: The American Economic Review, 84 (3), pp. 369-395.

Garcia, Marito, Manohar Sharma, Aamir Qureshi, and Lynn Brown (1995): Overcoming Malnutrition: Is There an Ecoregional Dimension? Draft Discussion Paper, Washington, D.C.: International Food Policy Research Institute (Mimeo).

Haddad, Lawrence J., Eileen Kennedy, and Joan Sullivan (1994): Choice of Indicators for Food Security and Nutrition Monitoring in Africa, in: Food Policy, 19 (3), pp. 329-343.

Leonard, H. Jeffrey, and contributors (1989): Environment and the Poor: Development Strategies for a Common Agenda, U.S.-Third World Policy Perspectives, 11, New Brunswick, N.J., U.S.A.: Transaction Books.

Mason, John, Urban Jonsson, and Joanne Csete (1995): Is Malnutrition Being Overcome? Paper prepared for the World Bank Hunger Programme meeting on "Overcoming Hunger in the 1990s", November 7-11, 1994, Thailand.

Maxwell, Simon and T.R. Frankenberger (1993): Household Food Security: Concepts, Indicators, Measurement—a Technical Review, UNICEF and IFAD, New York and Rome.

Mroz, T.A., and B.M. Popkin (1995): Poverty and the Economic Transition in the Russian Federation, in: Economic Development and Cultural Change, 44(1), pp. 1-31.

de Onís, Mercedes, C. Monteiro, J. Akré, and G. Clugston (1993): The Worldwide Magnitude of Protein-energy Malnutrition: an Overview from the WHO Global Database on Child Growth, in: Bulletin of the World Health Organization, 71 (6), pp. 703-712.

Pinstrup-Andersen, Per, R. Pandya-Lorch and M. Rosegrant (1997): World Food Situation: Recent Developments, Emerging Issues, and Long-Term Prospects, Food Policy Report, Washington, D.C.: International Food Policy Research Institute.

Russel, S.S., K. Jacobsen, and W.D. Stanley (1990): International Migration and Development in Sub-Saharan Africa, Vol.2, Country Analyses, World Bank Discussion Paper, 102, Washington D.C.: World Bank.

Sahn, David E., and Harold Alderman (1988): The Effects of Human Capital on Wages and the Determinants of Labor Supply in a Developing Country, in: Journal of Development Economics, 29 (2), pp. 157-184.

Scrimshaw, Nevin S. (1994): Effects of Iron Deficiency and Protein-calorie Malnutrition on Cognitive Behavior and Neurological Function, in: The Damaged Brain of Iodine Deficiency, ed. John B. Stanbury, New York, Sidney, Tokio: Cognizant Communication Corporation, pp. 59-65.

Senauer, Ben and Terry Roe (1997): Food Security and the Household, Paper prepared for the XXIII International Conference of Agricultural Economists, Sacramento Cal. Aug.

Strauss, J. (1986): Does Better Nutrition Raise Farm Productivity? in: Journal of Political Economy, 94 (2), pp. 297-320.

UN (1975): Report of the World Food Conference, Conference held in Rome, November 5-16, 1974, New York.

UN ACC/SCN (United Nations Administrative Committee on Coordination—Subcommittee on Nutrition) (1994): Update on the Nutrition Situation, 1994, Geneva.

UNICEF (United Nations Children's Fund) (1994): The Urban Poor and Household Food Security. Urban Examples, Vol. 19, New York.

WFP (World Food Programme) (1995): Investing in the Poor to Prevent Emergencies, Background Paper No. 4 prepared for the European Conference on Hunger and Poverty, Nov. 21-22, Brussels.

2

Hunger, Malnutrition and Poverty: Trends and Prospects Towards the 21st Century

Uwe Kracht

1 Introduction

For the last two decades, the concept of food security has been central to efforts aimed at dealing with food and nutrition problems. However, having undergone significant changes over that period, the food security term may have become less useful as a unifying concept than originally intended. Conceived in the 1970s, the term originally referred to adequate supplies to meet food requirements at global, regional and national levels, focusing on production, trade, marketing, stocks and reserves. Gradually, emphasis has shifted towards food security at the level of households and individuals, giving greater attention to physical and economic access to adequate food and moving the focus from a largely commodity orientation towards an orientation concerned with the human condition. As such, the term of food insecurity has become to be used frequently as a synonym for hunger (the latter being more of an advocacy than scientific term), meaning an individual's inability to consume a sufficient amount of adequate food to lead a healthy and active life. But while food insecurity may lead to, and is often characterized by, hunger, its principal meaning refers to the risk of people being hungry. In this sense, food security is not just the absence of hunger, but it is about the absence of risk relating to adequate food consumption (Webb and von Braun 1993).

Moreover, the "mutation" of the food security concept has gone beyond the food dimension, highlighting important linkages to non-food, social components, such as access to health services and a healthy environment, adequate care of children and women, as well as education, to achieve nutritional well-being (Jonsson 1993: 10). As such, food security is a means, not an end in itself; it is a means to achieve nutritional well-being. While food availability and access to it are the cornerstone of nutritional well-being, they are not sufficient by themselves. In particular, the synergistic relationship between inadequate food intake and infectious diseases is often so strong that the separate role of each is difficult to assess (FAO/WHO 1992: 32).

Thus, contrary to frequent terminological usage today, food security is not identical with nutritional well-being; and food insecurity is not necessarily synonymous with hunger, under- or malnutrition. To reflect the complexity of nutrition problems beyond food supply and access, the terms "nutrition security" or "food and nutrition security" are increasingly used in recent literature, both covering all components of food security (i.e. access to adequate food by all people at all times) plus health factors and care for women and children (Oshaug et al. 1992). Despite the potential merits of having a single umbrella term—such as food insecurity or hunger—for all food and nutrition problems, policy and operational considerations call for a breakdown of these problems into actionable components. Such a breakdown comprises four—or even five—distinct problems:

- famines and starvation now increasingly caused by civil strife;
- chronic and transitory undernutrition largely due to inadequate access to food by large population groups;
- protein-energy malnutrition especially among mothers and young children, caused by a combination of educational, sanitary, health and food-quality and -quantity factors; and
- specific micronutrient deficiency disorders with substantial health and development implications (e.g. Vitamin A deficiency, iodine deficiency disorders, nutritional anaemia related to iron deficiency).

A fifth category of quite a different nature is that of overnutrition, which affects both rich and poor population segments alike.

Globally, it is difficult to know how many people are affected by the different types of food and nutrition problems, because of definition and measurement problems and the inadequacy of data (FAO 1996b). Many regions of the world have never been in the position to make the sizable investments needed to put in place data systems capable of comprehensively assessing and monitoring the nutritional well-being of their populations.

In disaster zones and areas of armed conflict, the scope for monitoring food and nutrition conditions is limited, for obvious reasons. Estimates of the number of chronically undernourished people depend on the reliability of statistics on per caput daily energy supplies (DES), as derived from national food balance sheets, and their distribution within countries, as well as on assumptions concerning human energy requirements. As is well known, the reliability of food supply and distribution data is a matter of great concern in many countries, especially in low income developing countries where food and hunger problems are likely to be particularly pronounced. Assumptions concerning energy requirements are based on estimates of the basal metabolism rate (BMR)—i.e. the energy expenditure of an individual in a state of fasting and complete rest; those assumptions have been changed several times over the years, resulting in different estimates of undernourished people for the same time period. At the core of these changes has been the question of an appropriate additional energy allowance over and above the BMR. The corresponding energy requirement, below which an individual would be considered undernourished (the so-called "cut-off point"), has been increased from the original 1.2 BMR in FAO's earlier World Food Surveys to 1.4 BMR in the Fifth Survey in 1987 and to 1.5 BMR in the latest Survey of 1996 (FAO 1996a: 37), taking into consideration that nutritional well-being of an individual means his or her ability to live an active, healthy life.

Malnutrition among young children is generally assessed through anthropometry, using various ratios of weight, height and age (height/age for stunting, an indicator of chronic malnutrition; weight/height indicating wasting or acute malnutrition; weight/age as a general indicator of malnutrition). Anthropometric data have become more widely available thanks to expanding nutrition surveillance activities in the health sector, but the data base on child malnutrition is still limited in most countries. Greater attention has recently also been given to the use of anthropometry in measuring the nutritional status of adults, notably through the body mass index (BMI). The BMI is expressed as the ratio of weight/height squared and serves to indicate under- or overnutrition (WHO 1995). Specific micronutrient deficiency disorders are generally identified through clinical assessments or simple medical examination. As is the case with other nutrition statistics, existing micronutrient data are very much of an *ad hoc* nature, but they do permit inferences, at the global level, concerning the geographical spread of the major deficiency disorders.

Given the measurement and statistical data constraints, absolute numbers of under- and malnourished people must, therefore, be interpreted with great caution. Probably more important is the analysis of trends, where data permit, with a view to assessing future prospects for reducing specific food and nutrition problems. The following sections will look at trends and prospects particularly with regard to assessing the degree of realism of the often ambitious food and nutrition goals adopted at the various global development conferences of the 1990s[1] and the feasibility of their realization in the early 21st century.

2 Famines and starvation

Famines and the starvation caused by them have traditionally been associated with crop failures. In one of the following chapters, P. von Blanckenburg cites 22 major famines, starting with India's Bengal famine in 1770 which is believed to have starved some 10 million people to death, to China's 1876/79 famine with a similar number of victims, to a series of famines of various proportions in this century. The staggering absolute numbers of starvation victims of some of the Asian famines seem to dwarf the importance of one of Europe's fiercest famines, the notorious Irish potato famine of 1846/47. Most recently, in 1997, North Korea was at the brink of a major famine potentially affecting millions of people, following three consecutive years of flood- and drought-induced crop failures (FAO/WFP 1997). However, timely international assistance was able to avert a major disaster.

It is generally assumed that war and civil strife are replacing natural disaster as the main source of famines in our times—a point taken up by Marc Cohen elsewhere in this book.[2] Recent violent conflicts have put an estimated 80 million

1 See Chapter 32.

2 See Chapter 19.

people at risk of severe food deprivation, if not outright famine and starvation. While it is true that civil strife emergencies have surged, it should not be forgotten that past famines were often not the exclusive result of natural causes. Two considerations, in particular, need to be kept in mind.

First, some of the seemingly "natural disaster" famines were at their roots man-made, as A.K. Sen pointed out almost two decades ago (Sen 1981). While the Irish famine in 1846/47 was triggered by the failure of the potato crop, Ireland had adequate cereal supplies to avert famine—but much of these were instead exported. A similar situation occurred in Bangladesh in 1974, when at the height of famine the country actually exported cereals. Sen explains these situations as entitlement failures, i.e. the inability of hungry people to establish command (or "effective demand" in economic terminology) over available food supplies—a phenomenon which is clearly man-, not nature-made.

Second, it must not be forgotten that for millennia wars have dramatically reduced food supplies to the point of generating famines by preventing farmers from tending their fields or by destroying or diverting crops. And it has long been common practice to use food as a political weapon through sieges or embargoes, when political pressure and military force failed to be effective. The last 1,000 years of Europe's history provide a host of prominent examples. Today, at a time of globalization of national and regional affairs, an evolving new humanitarian aid regime seeks to avert or alleviate conflict-driven famines—or "complex humanitarian emergencies", as they are now frequently called—by pursuing international assistance even involving military support, if necessary. The development of a kind of "military humanitarianism" (Weiss and Campbell 1991) would have been unthinkable some 15 years ago. A stark contradiction to these new humanitarian efforts is the continuing application of food embargoes in various forms within and between countries—and sometimes with international sanction at the highest level, the UN Security Council, as in the case of Iraq, for example. While such embargoes may not lead to famines, they can have severe nutritional consequences among helpless populations which cannot be blamed for the politics leading to such action.

It is famines which get most public attention, because of their dramatic immediate impact on the human condition. But the numbers of people affected by famines at any time account for only a small fraction of the large population groups suffering from chronic undernutrition which saps their physical energies and diminishes their development potential.

Table 1: Estimated and projected incidence of chronic undernutrition in developing countries

Region/ Economic group	Year (three-year averages)*	Total population (millions)	Percent under-nourished	Number of people undernourished (millions)
Region				
Sub-Saharan Africa	1969-71	268	38	103
	1979-81	357	41	148
	1990-92	500	43	215
	2010	874	30	264
Near East & North Africa	1969-71	178	27	48
	1979-81	233	12	27
	1990-92	317	12	37
	2010	513	10	53
East Asia	1969-71	1 147	41	476
	1979-81	1 393	27	379
	1990-92	1 665	16	269
	2010	2 070	6	123
South Asia	1969-71	711	33	238
	1979-81	892	34	303
	1990-92	1 138	22	255
	2010	1 617	12	200
Latin America & the Caribbean	1969-71	279	19	53
	1979-81	354	14	48
	1990-92	443	15	64
	2010	593	7	40
TOTAL DEVELOPING COUNTRIES	1969-71	2 538	35	918
	1979-81	3 228	28	906
	1990-92	4 064	21	841
	2010	5 668	12	680
Economic group				
Low-income countries	1969-71	1 928	39	752
	1979-81	2 372	33	783
	1990-92	3 026	23	696
Middle- to high-income countries	1969-71	664	25	166
	1979-81	878	14	123
	1990-92	1 107	13	144

* Projections for 2010 cover the 93 developing countries of FAO's study "World agriculture: towards 2010" (FAO 1995) accounting for 98.5 percent of the total developing country population.

Source: FAO 1996a; FAO 1996b: 9; FAO 1996c: 6.

3 Chronic and transitory undernutrition

According to FAO's latest World Food Survey (FAO 1996a), these large population groups suffering from chronic undernutrition numbered some 840 million people—or about 20 percent of the developing countries' population—in the early 1990s (Table 1).[3] Close to two-thirds of them lived in Asia and one-quarter in Sub-Saharan Africa (Table 2). Latin America and the Near East/North Africa held the smallest shares, with 8 and 4 percent respectively. Of the total, 83 percent lived in low-income countries.[4]

Table 2: Geographical distribution of the undernourished population in developing countries, 1990-92 and 2010 (projected), in percent

Region/Economic group	Percent of total undernourished population			
	1969-71	1979-81	1990-92	2010
Region				
East & South Asia	78	76	62	47
(East Asia)	(52)	(42)	(32)	(18)
(South Asia)	(26)	(34)	(30)	(29)
Sub-Saharan Africa	11	16	26	39
Latin America & the Caribbean	6	5	8	6
Near East & North Africa	5	3	4	8
Total developing countries	100	100	100	100
Economic group				
Low-income countries	82	86	83	
Middle- to high-income countries	18	14	17	
Total developing countries	100	100	100	

Source: FAO 1996a: 45; FAO 1996c: 6.

Chart 1 provides a graphic overview of the trends since 1970 in the prevalence of undernutrition and that projected to 2010. The total number of undernourished

3 FAO's Sixth World Food Survey cautions that its estimates of people with "food inadequacy" as shown in Table 1, strictly speaking, can not be equated with "undernourished people", one major reason being that the methodology of estimation does not take into account the incidence of infectious diseases and thus potentially higher requirements. For this reason, "the assessment of food inadequacy presented may well underestimate the true prevalence of undernutrition" (FAO 1996a: 4). It also points out that "as it is presented here, the prevalence of food inadequacy refers to the situation prevailing on the average over a relatively long period", i.e. three year averages, and does not show transitory, short-term food inadequacy variations (p. 44). It finally emphasizes the uncertainties of its estimates arising from the problems of statistical and measurement errors noted in the introduction of this chapter.

4 Countries with a per caput GNP of US$ 695 or less in 1993.

people has decreased since 1970, with an accelerated decline between 1980 and 1990, and is projected to continue its decline towards 2010 at a faster pace than over the past two decades. However, the decrease over the past 20 years was a bare 8 percent. At surface level, this may appear shamefully low, given the world's food, economic and scientific resources. Yet viewed against the background of a total population increase in developing countries of over 1.5 billion people or 60 percent during that period (Table 1), the result is not unimpressive. Between 1990-92 and 2010, the number of undernourished people is projected to fall by almost 20 percent, while population increases will amount to some 40 percent, or another 1.5 to 1.6 billion people. Globally, there has therefore been a significant decline of the share of undernourished people in the developing regions' total population: from 35 percent in 1970, to 28 percent in 1980, to 21 percent in the early 1990s, with a projected fall to 12 percent in 2010.

The fall in the total number of undernourished people conceals major regional differences. The sharpest decline occurred in East Asia, where the number of the undernourished dropped by 43 percent over the last two decades and is projected to fall by another 54 percent by 2010. South Asia experienced a major increase (27 percent) in undernutrition between 1970 and 1980, followed by a decline, leaving it with 7 percent more undernourished people in the early 1990s than in 1970. Between 1990-92 and 2010, South Asia should see a decline of over 20 percent in the number of its undernourished people.

The greatest concern rests with Sub-Saharan Africa, which has experienced a continuous increase in undernutrition since 1970 that is expected to continue towards 2010. By the early 1990s, the Continent's number of the undernourished had more than doubled and is projected to increase by another 23 percent by 2010. As Chart 1 illustrates, before the year 2000 Sub-Saharan Africa will have scored the deplorable record of overtaking—in terms of absolute numbers of undernourished people—the much more populous sub-regions of East Asia and South Asia.

In contrast, the share of the developing world's undernourished people in Latin America/Caribbean and the Near East/North Africa is almost negligible in relative terms, though not in absolute numbers. Both regions experienced a slight decline in undernutrition between 1970 and 1980, followed by an increase in the 1980s, which is projected to continue in the Near East/North African region, while Latin America should experience a significant decline by 2010.

The differences in regional trends have naturally changed the geographical distribution of the undernourished, shifting the importance of undernutrition as a largely Asian problem towards a major African problem, as shown in Table 2. While in 1970 almost 80 percent of the undernourished lived in Asia and only some 10 percent in Africa, Asia's share had decreased to just over 60 percent by the early 1990s, while Africa's had increased to more than one-quarter. According to current projections, Asia's share of the developing world's undernourished people would further decline to less than one-half by 2010, while Africa would approach 40 percent.

The conclusions to be drawn from this summary review suggest a considerably mixed past record and medium-term prospects for different developing regions. The overall reduction in undernutrition has not been insignificant when compared to total population growth, but must be considered well below our globe's potential. The outlook is brightest for East Asia, and certainly much more could be achieved in South Asia than is currently projected for 2010. A special effort is needed in Sub-Saharan Africa, where the traditional challenges in the fields of science and technology and their application, economic management and overall governance are exacerbated by increasing problems of violent civil strife.

How do current projections compare to the vision and commitments of the leaders at the World Food Summit held in Rome in November 1996? The Rome Declaration on World Food Security states prominently: "We pledge our political will and our common and national commitment to achieving food security for all and to an ongoing effort to eradicate hunger in all countries, with an immediate view to reducing the number of undernourished people to half their present level no later than 2015" (World Food Summit 1996: 1). This commitment goes way beyond the 20 percent reduction in the number of undernourished people currently projected towards 2010. There is no question that if by 2015 a 50 percent reduction is to be achieved, a major concerted effort beyond current policies and programmes will be required. Such an effort will have to focus on Sub-Saharan Africa and South Asia.

As noted before, the estimates of chronic undernutrition refer to "habitual" food inadequacy calculated on multi-year averages. They do not capture what is generally termed transitory—or temporary—undernutrition. The most common manifestation of this kind of undernutrition is its seasonal variant: for millions of rural people, the months preceding the harvest are a time of extreme food shortage with debilitating effects on farmers just as they prepare to face the heavy physical demands of the forthcoming harvest. Seasonal undernutrition may also be linked to the cyclical increases of infectious diseases, which increase food requirements. On the other hand, short-term non-seasonal undernutrition may result from external shocks such as natural disasters or economic hardship such as sudden unemployment or a sharp rise in food prices—events often associated with structural adjustment programmes. It is evident that various forms of transitory as well as chronic undernutrition require different kinds of responses, which is the subject of Part III of this book.

4 Protein-energy malnutrition among young children and pregnant and nursing women

Food and nutrition problems among young children and pregnant and nursing mothers as well as the elderly are more complex than undernutrition affecting poor populations at large. These so-called vulnerable groups have special food and health requirements involving higher quality foods, special dietary and feeding practices, particular measures in the fields of health and sanitation, and generally special care. Meeting these special needs also requires certain basic health and nutrition knowledge, notably among women. It is therefore not surprising that reducing malnutrition among vulnerable groups tends in practice to be more difficult than dealing with undernutrition where the main emphasis is more on adequate food quantity. These greater difficulties are reflected in the trends of protein-energy malnutrition among children under five years of age—the age group in which malnutrition matters most since even in its milder forms it increases the risk of death and inhibits cognitive development in children, leading to less fit and productive adults. Moreover, it perpetuates the problem from one generation to the other, through malnourished women having low birth-weight babies. The proportion of children being underweight provides the most common indicator of malnutrition.

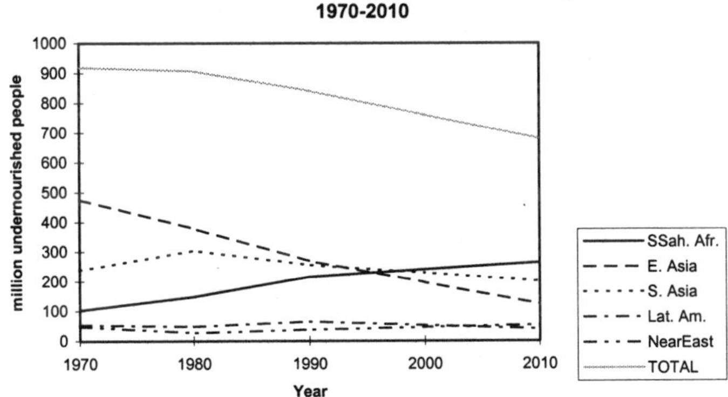

Source: FAO 1996b: 9.

If the number of undernourished people declined at least modestly—by less than 10 percent—over the past two decades, the number of young children affected by protein-energy malnutrition (as measured by underweight according to age) is estimated to have increased by about 10 percent over 15 years: from 168 million "under fives" in 1975 to 184 million in 1990 (Table 3). Some 100 million of them, or 55 percent, lived in South Asia alone; with a total of 145 million malnourished children, the Asia region as a whole accounted for 79 percent of the developing countries' child protein-energy malnutrition. The increase in the number of malnourished children is largely explained by population growth; in relative terms, their share in the total "under fives" population decreased from some 42 percent in 1975 to 34 percent in 1990. Thus, there has certainly been progress over the past 15 years—but how much progress? Protein-energy malnutrition among one-third of the developing countries' preschool children does not appear a record to be particularly proud of, given global knowledge and resources.

Table 3: Prevalence and numbers of underweight preschool children (0-60 months) in developing countries, 1975-1990

Region	Year*	Percent underweight	Numbers underweight (millions)	WSC goals for 2000**	
				Percent	millions
Sub-Saharan Africa	1975	31.4	18.5		
	1980	28.9	19.9		
	1985	29.9	24.1		
	1990	29.9	28.2		
	2000A	32.0	38.0		
	2000B	27.0	30.0	15	18
Near East & North Africa	1975	19.8	5.2		
	1980	17.2	5.0		
	1985	15.1	5.0		
	1990	13.4	4.8		
	2000A	11.0	5.0		
	2000B	8.0	3.0	6	2
South Asia	1975	67.7	90.6		
	1980	63.7	89.9		
	1985	61.1	100.1		
	1990	58.5	101.2		
	2000A	54.0	110.0		
	2000B	49.0	100.0	29	59
South East Asia	1975	43.6	24.3		
	1980	39.1	22.8		
	1985	34.7	21.7		
	1990	31.3	19.9		
	2000A	24.0	17.0		
	2000B	22.0	15.0	16	11
China	1975	26.1	20.8		
	1980	23.8	20.5		
	1985	21.3	21.1		
	1990	21.8	23.6		
	2000A	22.0	30.0		
	2000B	16.0	24.0	11	15
Middle America & the Caribbean	1975	19.3	3.4		
	1980	17.7	3.1		
	1985	15.2	2.8		
	1990	15.4	3.0		
	2000A	16.0	4.0		
	2000B	10.0	2.0	8	2
South America	1975	15.7	4.8		
	1980	9.3	3.1		
	1985	8.2	2.9		
	1990	7.7	2.8		
	2000A	6.0	2.0		
	2000B	2.5	1.0	4	1
TOTAL DEVELOPING COUNTRIES	1975	41.6	168		
	1980	37.8	164		
	1985	36.1	178		
	1990	34.3	184		
	2000A	32.0	206		
	2000B	27.5	175	17	108

* Year 2000 projections—A: pessimistic, B: optimistic scenario.

** Goals adopted at the 1990 World Summit for Children.

Source: United Nations 1992: 10 and 67.

A regional analysis of child malnutrition prevalences and trends follows roughly the patterns of undernutrition. In 1990, the prevalence of malnourished children was—with almost 60 percent—highest in South Asia, followed by South East Asia and Sub-Saharan Africa with some 30 percent. The lowest shares were observed in Latin America and the Near East/North Africa, ranging from 8 to 15 percent. Percentage-wise, trends were declining in all regions between 1975 and 1990.

In terms of trends in absolute numbers, Sub-Saharan Africa again held the deplorable record of a 50 percent increase, while South Asia and China saw increases of some 12-13 percent. In contrast, South America, with already low levels of child malnutrition, achieved a 42 percent reduction, followed by Middle America/Caribbean and South East Asia with a decline of 18 percent each; the numbers of underweight children also decreased in the Near East/North Africa.

Alternative projections to the years 2000 and 2020, prepared by the ACC Subcommittee on Nutrition for 2000 (United Nations 1992) and by the International Food Policy Research Institute (IFPRI) for 2020 (García 1994), provide a mixed, but generally disappointing outlook. They are based on historical trends, but account for future trends in fertility. The optimistic scenario (B) is based on the best five-year historical trend between 1975 and 1990; the pessimistic scenario (A) uses the worst five-year trend during the same period. Under the latter, the number of underweight children in the developing world would still increase, between 1990 and 2000, by some 12 percent to 206 million. According to the optimistic scenario, there would be a modest five-percent decline to 175 million (Table 3). The outlook for the year 2020 under scenario A suggests that there would still be some 200 million malnourished children in over 20 years from now. But even the "best-case" scenario B would leave some 100 million under-five children underweight in 2020.

Among the goals of the 1990 World Summit for Children, the first of a series of global development conferences in the 1990s, was the reduction—between 1990 and 2000—of severe and moderate malnutrition among under-five children by half (UNICEF 1990). In Table 3, this global goal has been translated into regional targets in terms of both percentage and numbers of underweight children. A comparison between the optimistic scenario projections for 2000 and these regional targets suggests that only one region, i.e. South America, could meet the Summit goal, although the Middle America/Caribbean and Near East/North Africa regions would not fall much behind. In contrast, South Asia and Sub-Saharan Africa, in particular, would be way behind. Globally, the 175 million underweight children projected under scenario B would exceed the Summit goal of 108 million by 67 million children. According to IFPRI's "best-case" scenario, the Summit goal for 2000 would be achieved around 2020.

However, recent estimates for the period 1990-95 and a review of the data for 1985-90 in the light of newly available information (United Nations 1996) give rise to some optimism. While the most recent data broadly follow the trends shown in Table 3, one major change stands out: a revision of South Asian data has led to a significant downward adjustment in child malnutrition estimates, with a prevalence of some 50 percent for 1990, corresponding to some 85 million underweight children or about 16 million less than previously estimated. Between 1990 and 1995, little change is estimated to have occurred. Given South Asia's overwhelming share in the total number of underweight children, any change in that region obviously has a significant impact on the total number of malnourished children.

Table 4 shows prevalence and numbers of underweight children in 1995, together with the changes in prevalence rates for the two periods of 1985-90 and 1990-95. Globally, 29 percent of all under-fives were estimated to be underweight in 1995. This corresponds to 158 million children or some 10 percent less than projected under the optimistic scenario for 2000—although still a long way apart from the Summit's goal of 108 million at the turn of the century. Overall trends in prevalence rates, i.e. the share of malnourished children in the under-five population, have been declining in the two periods, although the rate of decline has significantly slowed down in the 1990s, to -0.28 percentage points per year, compared to -0.72 percentage points in the preceding five-year period. It should be noted that prevalence rates in Sub-Saharan Africa, which according to recently revised data were increasing between 1985 and 1990 (at a rate of 0.44 percentage points per year), have declined in the first half of the 1990s (-0.16 per year). Overall, these rates of decline in the prevalence of child malnutrition are well below of what would be needed to reach the global goal of the Summit. At the 1990/95 rates, the number of malnourished children in the year 2000 would probably still be in the area of 40 percent above the level stipulated by the Summit.

Table 4: Prevalence and number of underweight preschool children in 1995, and trends in prevalence rates in 1985-90 and 1990-95

Region	Percent underweight 1995	Numbers underweight 1995 (millions)	Prevalence trends (changes in percent underweight, in average percentage points per year)	
			1985-90	1990-95
Sub-Saharan Africa	27.2	27.8	0.44	-0.16
Near East & North Africa	9.6	3.4	-0.62	-0.06
South Asia	48.8	85.2	-1.04	-0.26
South East Asia	32.4	19.1	-1.12	-0.36
China	15.0	16.6	-0.98	-0.56
Middle America & Caribbean	15.2	3.0	-0.56	-0.02
South America	8.4	2.7	-0.18	-0.01
TOTAL DEVELOPING COUNTRIES	29.3	157.6	-0.72	-0.28

Source: United Nations 1996: 3.

The conclusion from the above analysis is that even the optimistic outlook, including the most recent data, is just not good enough if the Summit goal for under-five malnutrition is to be realized. The slow-down in the reduction of prevalence rates in the first half of the 1990s gives rise to additional concern. This does not mean that the Summit goal is unrealistic or unreasonable. A number of programmes and policies aimed at dealing with child malnutrition in countries as diverse as Thailand, Zimbabwe, Indonesia, Costa Rica, Chile, and in India's Tamil Nadu State have proven extremely effective. In Thailand, for example, the prevalence of underweight children was reduced from 36 percent to 13 percent in only eight years, through a combination of anti-poverty programmes and direct nutrition interventions (García 1994). What is clear, however, is that a much more concerted and focused effort will be needed in the future, especially in South Asia and Sub-Saharan Africa. Such an effort will, of course, also require greater resource allocations to fight poverty and malnutrition.

5 Micronutrient malnutrition

Malnutrition resulting from deficiencies in micronutrients, i.e. vitamins and minerals, have long tended to receive less attention than other forms of under- and malnutrition as they appeared of lesser importance for nutritional well-being or less damaging to human development and performance—conditions which also gave these deficiencies the popular name of "hidden hunger" (WHO et al. 1991). However, three micronutrient deficiencies—vitamin A, iodine and iron—have become recognized as major nutrition and public health problems. All three have serious consequences in terms of increased mortality, morbidity and disability rates, affect large numbers of people and can be controlled relatively easily and at low cost. They are most devastating for preschool children and pregnant women, but are debilitating for all ages. And they are debilitating for the national economy as well (World Bank 1994).

Table 5: Population at risk of and affected by micronutrient malnutrition (millions)

Region	Iodine deficiency disorders		Vitamin A deficiency		Iron-
	At risk	Affected (goitre)	At risk*	Affected* (xerophthal mia)	deficient or anemic
Africa	181	86	52	1.3	206
Americas	168	63	16	0.1	94
South/South East Asia	486	176	125	10.0	616
Western Pacific & China	423	141	42	1.4	1 058
Europe	141	97	--	--	27
Eastern Mediterranean	173	93	16	1.0	149
TOTAL	1 572	655	251	13.8	2 150

* Preschool children only.

Source: WHO 1994 for vitamin A, WHO 1993 for iodine, WHO 1992 for iron.

Virtually every developing country has a deficiency in vitamin A, iodine or iron that is large enough to constitute a public health problem; many developing countries have multiple deficiencies. More than 2 billion people worldwide are at risk from deficiencies of these nutrients, and more than 1 billion are actually ill or disabled by them.

5.1 Vitamin A deficiency

Vitamin A deficiency (VAD) is most known for the progressive damage it inflicts on the eye, eventually leading to blindness. The general term for this is "xerophthalmia", which ranges from the mildest form, night blindness, through reversible signs in the eye to the destruction of the cornea and thus blindness. Less known is its contribution to reduced physical growth, ill health and mortality, since it impairs resistance to infection.

There are at least some 250 million preschool children, half of them in South and South East Asia, with subclinical levels of vitamin A malnutrition, putting them at risk of the clinical manifestations of VAD (Table 5). Considering that a large number of countries has no data available, the actual number of preschool children is likely to be considerably higher. Moreover, the size of the at-risk population increases greatly if other age groups are included, such as school age children and women of child-bearing age. Actual clinical cases of VAD in the form of xerophthalmia are, at less than three million, considerably fewer than estimated until recently.[5] VAD is known to currently constitute a public health problem in over 65 countries, and another 28 countries are likely to have such a problem.

The most desirable, sustainable way of controlling vitamin A deficiency is through dietary diversification, increasing the consumption of specific vegetables and fruits, of red palm oil and animal foods; breast milk is an outstanding source of vitamin A. Other approaches include food fortification (e.g. sugar, dried skim milk) and administration of vitamin A capsules.

5.2 Iodine deficiency disorders

According to most recent estimates,[6] close to 1.6 billion people live in iodine-deficient areas around the world (Table 5). These are generally regions where iodine, normally supplied from soil and water, has been leached from the topsoil by rain, flooding, glaciation and snow. These regions therefore tend to be mountainous as well as flood plains. Out of the total population living in such regions, some 655 million are estimated to have goitre, a prominently visible enlargement of the thyroid gland and the most common manifestation of iodine deficiency. About half

5 Until recently, the number of preschool children affected by xerophthalmia was estimated at some 14 million, the at-risk cases at 190 million (WHO 1992).

6 The figures used here are updates by WHO, UNICEF and the International Council for the Control of Iodine Deficiency Disorders (ICCIDD); they are substanially higher than WHO's earlier, widely published estimates.

of the global goitre problem is found in Asia. But beyond goitre, the consequences of iodine deficiency are reduced mental function, increased rates of still births and abortions, and infant deaths. Severe mental and neurological impairment known as cretinism occurs in babies with severely iodine-deficient mothers. Such cases of overt cretinism are estimated at at least 6 million. Iodine deficiency in later infancy and childhood cause mental retardation, growth failure, neuromuscular disorders and speech and hearing defects (WHO 1992).

Control of iodine deficiency disorders (IDD) is mainly through fortification of salt with iodine or periodic distribution of iodized oil, either administered orally or by injection. Increased sea foods consumption would help in IDD control, but is frequently not feasible because of the geographical location of IDD or for economic reasons. Both the World Summit for Children and the 1992 International Nutrition Conference had called for the elimination of iodine deficiency by 2000. A recent progress report suggests that "tangible progress in universal salt iodization ... is being made in the 118 countries currently known to be affected by these [iodine deficiency] disorders," and that "despite the magnitude of the problem, it seems realistic to anticipate that IDD will indeed be eliminated as a major public health problem by the year 2000" (FAO/WHO 1996).

5.3 Iron deficiency

Iron deficiency is the most common nutritional disorder in the world, affecting over 2 billion people (Table 5), half of them with clinical iron deficiency anemia. Particularly affected are women of reproductive age and preschool children in tropical and sub-tropical zones. It also has a serious impact on school children and working males. If uncorrected, it leads to anaemia of increasing severity, reduced work capacity, diminished learning ability, increased susceptibility to infection and greater risk of death associated with pregnancy and child birth (United Nations 1992: 40-43). It results from diets with insufficient iron contents or reduced iron availability, increased iron requirements to meet reproductive demands, and losses due to parasitic infection. These factors often operate concurrently.

Analogous to vitamin A control measures, there are three possible approaches to controlling iron deficiency: dietary diversification, with emphasis on certain fruits and vegetables, pulses, and liver and red meat; fortification (e.g. salt, cereals or cereal flour); and the administration of iron/folate tablets.

6 "Overnutrition" and diet-related non-communicable diseases

"Overnutrition" can be the result of an excessive intake of any macro- or micronutrient, but most frequently refers to the excessive consumption of energy, especially in the form of fat. Its most visible manifestation is obesity, but there is a host of health-damaging, life-threatening diseases associated with it, such as cardiovascular disease, hypertension and stroke, some form of diabetes, various forms of cancer and other gastro-intestinal and liver diseases. Collectively, these illnesses are responsible for more than 70 percent of deaths in developed countries (FAO/WHO 1992: 17).

"Overnutrition" is often thought of as a typical form of "industrialized-country malnutrition", where obesity affects 7 to 15 percent of adults approximately 40 years of age. However, it is already prevalent in the developing world, particularly (and ironically) among poor people in middle-income countries as well as the elite in low-income nations. For example, among urban women in several Caribbean countries, prevalence of obesity exceeds 30 percent (FAO/WHO 1992: 22, 23). High rates of obesity are also evident in preschool children, reaching or exceeding, for example, 10 percent in Chile and Jamaica. Similar rates of overweight preschoolers have been observed in countries as divers as Canada, Mauritius and Iran.

7 Trends in poverty as the root cause of hunger and malnutrition

That poverty is at the root of hunger and malnutrition needs no special emphasis. One-third of the developing countries' population—or 1.3 billion people—has to make ends meet with one US dollar per person per day (1985 PPP$[7]).[8] Three-quarters of them live in Asia, close to 20 percent in Sub-Saharan Africa (Table 6). Between 1987 and 1993, there have been modest improvements, at best, in the prevalence of poverty, i.e. the percentage of poor people in the total population. While many aspects of food insecurity and malnutrition can be resolved ahead of poverty elimination, as illustrated by policy and programme examples in Parts II and III of this book, greater progress in poverty reduction will be necessary to achieve some of the ambitious food- and nutrition-related development goals adopted at this decade's global summit conferences.

There has also been growing concern in recent years over poverty and hunger in the industrialized countries—a concern conspicuously absent from the documentation and debate at the World Food Summit. While it may appear inappropriate to talk about poverty in the developed world against the background of well over one billion people living on a dollar a day, one cannot ignore the fact that amidst the affluence of the economically most advanced countries there is a growing number of people in great distress. They do not live on one or two US$ a day, but on less than some $14 (1985 PPP$).[9] While this is 14 times the subsistence amount of their "poor cousins" in the developing world, it is too little to meet basic needs in the environment in which they live—with the result of growing queues at soup kitchens and food banks and growing numbers of shelterless people, among other things. Using the US$ 14 poverty line, 80 million people in the western

7 In 1985 purchasing power parity.

8 The 1.3 billion people living in poverty include 110 million Latin Americans and Caribbeans for whom the poverty line has been set at two, instead of one PPP$.

9 The US poverty line stands at 14.40 PPP$ (1985).

industrialized (OECD) countries are classified as poor. They constitute 12-14 percent of the total population in countries like Germany, Belgium, France, United Kingdom, USA and the Netherlands (UNDP 1997: 36).

Table 6: Recent poverty trends in developing countries, 1987-1993

Region	Percentage of people below the poverty line*		Share of all poor people (in percent)		Number of poor people (millions)
	1987	1993	1987	1993	1993
East/South East Asia	30	26	38	34	446
South Asia	45	43	39	39	515
Sub-Saharan Africa	38	39	15	17	219
Latin America & Caribbean**	22	24	7	9	110
Arab States	5	4	1	1	11
TOTAL	34	32	100	100	1 301

* At 1 US$ per person per day (1985 PPP$).
** At 2 US$ per person per day (1985 PPP$).
Source: UNDP 1997: 27.

To a large extent, poor people in the industrialized countries can count on some support from state social safety nets as well as private charitable assistance to meet their food and other basic needs. In the USA, for example, 26 million people receive food assistance through the Government's Food Stamp Program. A similar number benefits from food assistance provided by a network of some 150,000 private charitable agencies (Cohen and D'Costa 1996). Cash assistance through various forms of safety nets is widespread throughout the industrialized countries. But the globalization of the world economy and its effects on the industrialized countries' economies puts governments under heavy pressure to cut the costs of these social programmes. Such cuts are bound to have serious repercussions for food security and nutrition of economically vulnerable populations, even though they may be less dramatic than those experienced in many of the countries in transition in Central and Eastern Europe and the former Soviet Union.

With the rapid dismantling of costly social programmes during the transition from planned to market economies in Central and Eastern Europe and the newly independent states (NIS) of the former Soviet Union, the number of poor people in the region is estimated to have soared eightfold between 1988 and 1994. Drawing the poverty line at US$ 4 per person per day (1990 PPP$), the poor numbered 14 million (or 4 percent of the total population) in 1988; by 1994, their numbers had risen to 119 million (or 32 percent). With almost 60 million poor people in 1993-94, Russia alone accounted for half of the region's poor (UNDP 1997: 34, 35). Sharply rising food prices and reduced health and related services during this period exacerbated food insecurity and malnutrition among the rapidly growing number of poor people. On the other hand, soaring poverty has, to varying degrees, been accompanied by soaring riches: Russia holds the record in income inequality among 25 western and eastern industrialized countries (followed by the USA and Australia, while income inequality is lowest in the Slovak and Czech Republics) (Cohen and D'Costa 1996).

There are certain parallels between the poverty and food insecurity situations in the economic transition countries of the former "Second World", the western industrialized countries facing the need for economic realignment in response to the challenges of economic globalization, and the developing countries under pressure to undertake structural adjustments of their economies. All three groups of countries are undergoing profound economic and social changes with potential short-term negative effects in terms of increased poverty and food insecurity and all need to put in place special measures to protect economically and nutritionally vulnerable groups during a transitory period. But in each case, the challenges and the existing capacities to deal with them are significantly different.

The western industrialized countries have both the economic resources and the political and administrative management capacity to address a problem of a limited magnitude within their borders. The eastern industrialized countries are more heterogeneous in terms of their economic resources, their management capacities and the magnitude of their problems: for some, notably in Central and Eastern Europe, the situation is not unlike that in the western countries, but for many of them the challenges are much greater, considering lower economic resource levels, reduced management capacity due to political volatility, and a greater magnitude of poverty and food insecurity problems. But the problems of these countries are dwarfed by those in the group of the developing countries where the vast majority of the poor and under- and malnourished live: in the Asian and Sub-Saharan regions. The concerned Asian countries generally have the management capacity and a discrete economic resource base, but the sheer magnitude of poverty and food insecurity within their borders slows progress. In turn, many—certainly not all—Sub-Saharan African countries lack the economic resources, the political stability and the administrative management capacity to face the poverty and hunger challenges without substantial assistance.

8 Conclusions

Three broad conclusions emerge from the foregoing assessment of trends in hunger, malnutrition and poverty.

First, the record of addressing global hunger and malnutrition in its various manifestations over the past two decades is not one for the international community to be particularly proud of—nor is it one of total failure and despair. All in all, the world is today feeding 1.5 billion people more than some 20 years ago; the absolute number of undernourished people has decreased, albeit slightly; the share of undernourished people in the total population has come down considerably; and some regions and countries have achieved impressive success. Progress in reducing child malnutrition has proven more difficult to realize, given the greater complexity of its causes and remedies, relative to the problem of hunger or undernutrition. Achievements notwithstanding, the absolute numbers of people affected by various forms of under- and malnutrition are morally unacceptable, since what has been achieved is much below mankind's capacity in terms of advanced knowledge and economic and human resources, and is in stark contrast to rhetorical expressions of political determination. Projections into the early 21st century suggest progress well below the objectives and goals adopted at the many global development conferences of the 1990s, unless current efforts are considerably stepped up and improved.

Second, while undernutrition and child malnutrition very much remain an Asian problem (above all in South Asia) in terms of the numbers of people affected, their relative importance is rapidly shifting from Asia to Sub-Saharan Africa. Reducing global under- and malnutrition will, above all, require special efforts at national, regional and international levels in support of Sub-Saharan Africa and South Asia.

Third, without distracting attention from the overwhelming problems in Asia, Africa and the developing regions on the whole, greater attention is needed in the eastern and western industrialized countries to the fact that problems of food insecurity and poverty are growing within their own boundaries and need to receive greater policy attention while they move from planned to market economies or realign their economies to meet the challenges of economic globalization.

The political determination to eradicate hunger, malnutrition and poverty has been strongly reaffirmed by governments in this decade. Operational goals have been agreed upon. The means to realize them exist. Civil society has pledged and demonstrated its own contribution. The challenge to each and every institutional and individual member of society is to work together to realize the achievable.

References

Cohen, Marc J., and Jashinta D'Costa (1996): Overview of World Hunger, in: Bread for the World Institute (BFWI): Hunger 1977, Silver Spring, MD, pp. 9-25.

Food and Agricultural Organization of the United Nations (FAO)/World Food Programme (WFP) (1997): Special Alert No. 277 - FAO/WFP Crop and Food Supply Assessment Mission to the Democratic People's Republic of Korea, Rome.

FAO (1996a): The Sixth World Food Survey 1996, Rome.

FAO (1996b): Food Security and Nutrition, World Food Summit Technical Background Documents, Document 5, Rome.

FAO (1996c): Food, Agriculture and Food Security: Developments Since the World Food Conference and Prospects, World Food Summit Technical Background Documents, Document 1, Rome.

FAO (1995): World Agriculture: Towards 2010, Rome.

FAO/World Health Organization of the United Nations (WHO) (1996): Joint FAO/WHO Progress Report on the Implementation of the ICN World Declaration and Plan of Action for Nutrition, Rome.

FAO/WHO (1992): Nutrition and Development—a Global Assessment; International Conference on Nutrition, Rome and Geneva.

García, Marito (1994): Malnutrition and Food Insecurity Projections, 2020, IFPRI, Washington D.C.

Jonsson, Urban (1993): Nutrition and the United Nations Convention on the Rights of the Child, Florence.

Oshaug, Arne, Asbjorn Eide and Wenche Barth Eide (1992): Food, Nutrition and Human Rights, paper prepared at the request of the Royal Norwegian Ministry of Foreign Affairs for the First Preparatory Committee for the International Conference on Nutrition, Oslo.

Sen, Amartya (1981): Poverty and Famines, An Essay on Entitlement and Deprivation, Oxford.

UNICEF (1990): The World Summit for Children, New York.

United Nations (1996): Update on the Nutrition Situation 1996—Summary of Results for the Third Report on the World Nutrition Situation; Administrative Committee on Coordination—Subcommittee on Nutrition (ACC/SCN), Geneva.

United Nations (1992): Second Report on the World Nutrition Situation, Vol.1, ACC/SCN, Geneva.

United Nations Development Programme (UNDP) (1997): Human Development Report 1997, New York/Oxford.

Webb, Patrick, and Joachim von Braun (1993): Ending Hunger Soon: Concepts and Priorities; Technical Paper for the World Bank "Overcoming Global Hunger" Conference, International Food Policy Research Institute, Washington.

Weiss, Thomas, and Kurt Campbell (1991): Military Humanitarianism, in: Larry Minear, Thomas G. Weiss and Kurt M. Campbell: Humanitarianism and War: Learning the Lessons from Recent Armed Conflicts, Providence, RI , pp. 50-71.

World Bank (1994): Enriching Lives—Overcoming Vitamin and Mineral Malnutrition in Developing Countries, Washington D.C.

World Food Summit (1996): Rome Declaration on World Food Security and World Food Summit Plan of Action, Rome.

WHO (1995): Physical Status: the Use and Interpretation of Anthropometry, Report of a WHO Expert Committee, WHO Technical Report Series No. 854, Geneva.

WHO (1994): Global Prevalence of Vitamin A Deficiency, MDIS Working Paper No. 2, Geneva.

WHO (1993): Global Prevalence of Iodine Deficiency Disorders, MDIS Working Paper No. 1, Geneva.

WHO (1992): National Strategies for Overcoming Micronutrient Malnutrition (doc. A45/3), Geneva.

WHO et al. (1991): Proceedings of Ending Hidden Hunger (A Policy Conference on Micronutrient Malnutrition), Montreal.

3

Population Growth: Its Implications for Feeding the World

John C. Caldwell

To a very large extent, population numbers determine the needed food supply. It is true that the very poor will increase their food intake as they become better-off, but beyond a certain point food consumption does not rise as people or countries become richer. Certainly, there may be a demand for a greater variety of food, giving rise to more specialized agriculture.

This relationship between the number of people and the food required was the theme of Thomas Malthus's *First Essay*, which may be regarded as the origin of modern demography. He pictured human well-being as dependent on the outcome of a race between the growth of human population and the increase in the food supply. He did not believe that food supplies were likely to grow rapidly, and hence there was a constraint on human numbers operating largely through malnutrition maintaining a high death rate. One of the constraints on increasing food production was that the best land was already being employed, and new lands brought into production were likely to be inferior and to yield less. The classical economists broadened this hypothesis into the theory of marginal productivity.

The Malthusian cap on population growth has been termed the Malthusian limit. When food production is growing only very slowly or not at all there is a Malthusian equilibrium where population growth is nearly stationary because death rates are as high as birth rates. In most years death rates are probably lower but the undernourished condition of the population makes them susceptible to death from periodic famines which return the population to its near-stationary level. Indeed, for most of the world's history something like a Malthusian equilibrium must have prevailed, for, until the last two centuries, population growth has been very slow indeed. It is difficult to explain this slow growth in any other than Malthusian terms. Certainly, societies exhibited different fertility levels, usually as a result of social institutions not meant primarily to affect births, and occasionally in pre-modern times by voluntary birth control. Infanticide was also practised in some societies to keep down family size. But the equilibrating force that kept long-term mortality almost exactly at the level of long-term fertility must have been Malthusian.

One modification of this thesis must be noted. Ester Boserup (1965) has plausibly argued that even the long slow growth of population, whereby the human race took hundreds of thousands of years to reach 250 million people around the beginning of our era and 500 million by the seventeenth century, had not been a continuous process, but occurred in steps. When population growth pushed against a ceiling, it was the desperation induced by the population growth itself and resultant famine and other crises which forced people to adopt technical innovations which allowed them to grow more food. Examples are the replacement of the digging stick by the hoe, the replacement of the hoe by the plough, the move from shifting to settled cultivation, irrigation, terracing, crop rotation, and the use of fertilizers. Nevertheless, although Boserup does not seem to accept the point, the attainment by the population of the Malthusian limit was probably succeeded by population decline caused by disaster far more often than it resulted in innovational breakthroughs to higher population carrying capacities. The long periods between such breakthroughs were probably characterized by Malthusian equilibria.

Ironically, Malthus wrote at a time when the Malthusian equilibrium was disappearing from significant parts of the world. The explanation was the commercial, industrial and scientific revolutions. In Europe they increased the availability of food both by dramatic rises in production and food and by allowing the import of grains from European-settled areas overseas. In these settlement colonies, in the Americas and later in Australasia, both food production and population grew even more rapidly, as Malthus himself recorded. The colonial changes were brought about by vast innovational changes in agriculture, arising not from population pushing against a Malthusian ceiling but by the import of innovations with an invading and settling population. This spread of agricultural innovation globally has continued ever since, although less frequently accompanied by invasion and settlement. It is the theme of this book.

1 Demographic transition

The modernizing technological revolutions brought with them a decline in the death rate. Population was certainly growing consistently in England from the seventeenth century (Wrigley and Schofield 1981 end paper) and in Sweden from the eighteenth century, and probably more widely in Europe. There were material reasons, such as more food or better-distributed food, better housing and better clothes, but social and behavioural change probably played its part (P. Caldwell 1996). In the nineteenth century public health measures helped to accelerate the decline, as in the twentieth century did biomedical advances. The changes were only gradual and Europe has not known sustained periods of population growth much above one per cent,[1] implying population doubling only every 70 years.

In contrast, populations in the settlement colonies of the New World were, as Malthus pointed out, growing at three per cent per annum or multiplying eightfold each 70 years. This was a harbinger of what was to come in parts of the developing

1 Thompson (1953); Mitchell (1962); Bogue (1969). In the nineteenth century England and Wales attained a rate of natural increase between 1800 and 1870 of 1.5 per cent (Wrigley and Schofield 1981: 183) but this was eroded by massive emigration. Germany, Norway and the Netherlands rose as high as 1.3 per cent at the end of the nineteenth and early twentieth centuries. In the first three decades of the present century Russia and Poland reached 1.5 per cent.

world in the second half of the twentieth century, although in the settlement colonies immigration, as well as unprecedented levels of natural increase, also played a role. The latter owed a great deal to plentiful food supplies and something to the dispersion of population which reduced the incidence of epidemics.

Curiously, China's population also grew at an unprecedented pace after 1600, although not above 0.5 per cent per annum, mainly, it seems, because of the extension of irrigation and internal migration to the South China settlement frontier.

It would seem a plausible hypothesis that continuing mortality decline would lead to ever-faster rates of population growth in the West and ever-greater population numbers. This did not happen because birth rates also began to decline. This occurred first in small elite populations, such as the bourgeoisie of Geneva, and then nationally in France from the late eighteenth century. Human fertility began to decline more generally over much of Northwestern and Central Europe and in English-speaking colonies of overseas European settlement during the last three decades of the nineteenth century. Whether this was primarily a matter of the new social and economic conditions or whether it was a recognition at the family level that more children were surviving remains a matter of dispute. What is certain is that fertility is inevitably high in largely subsistence, poor, uneducated, high-mortality populations, and low in rich, urbanized, educated, low-mortality populations where most men and women work outside agriculture in a full market economy.

In the early twentieth century fertility also began to fall in Eastern and Southern Europe but fertility transition was to remain almost entirely a Western phenomenon for another half-century. Nevertheless, in the first half of the twentieth century mortality began to fall in the Third World, especially in colonial areas. In 1921, in spite of the recent experience of the influenza epidemic, the chief census officer of India could report that persistent mortality decline had begun in that country. Studies in the early 1940s showed decisive mortality decline in such British colonies as Egypt, India and Ceylon (Sri Lanka), in Dutch-colonized Java, in the American colony the Philippines, and in the Japanese colonies of Formosa (Taiwan), Korea and Manchukuo (Manchuria) (cf. Caldwell and Caldwell 1986: 13-15).

The realization that the world was faced with a new demographic experience of a kind of which it had no previous knowledge outside frontier settlement colonies came with the compilation of demographic figures by the new United Nations Population Division in 1948 and especially with the release of figures from the 1950-51 census round. In the early 1950s levels of natural increase were already above three per cent in Africa in Northern Rhodesia (Zimbabwe) and Uganda, in spite of the latter having a life expectancy of only 40 years, in the Americas in several Caribbean and Central American countries, and in the Pacific in Fiji (United Nations 1995).[2] Natural increase was 2.5 - 3.0 per cent in Asia in Malaysia, Philippines and Sri Lanka, in the Middle East in Iraq and Turkey, and in

2 Where the source is not otherwise specified, post-1950 demographic data are from this source.

South America in Colombia, Nicaragua, Panama, Ecuador, Paraguay and Peru. The explanation was a startling fall in mortality, largely connected with the globalization of world society and its health provision and also specific mechanisms that are still debated. Japan and Sri Lanka both recorded in the half-dozen years after the Second World War rises in life expectancy of 12 years from 46 to 58 years in the latter, an increase that had taken Sweden 45 years.

This was an unexpected challenge to food scientists. The demographic forecast to the meeting that planned the establishment of FAO at Hot Springs, USA, in 1943 was for a world population of three billions by the year 2000, and, at the time, this was regarded as a challenge—the addition of more than a billion people in a little over half a century. By 1951 the United Nations Population Division was forecasting (in its medium projection) that the three billion mark would be reached by 1980: in actuality it was attained 20 years earlier at the beginning of 1960. Every successive United Nations projection until 1968 raised the estimates of future populations, largely because of increasing evidence that mortality was falling faster than had been anticipated among the poor populations of South Asia and sub-Saharan Africa (Caldwell and Caldwell 1986: 21-25). In recent decades there has been agreement that the six billion figure will probably be reached before 2000, a trebling of global human numbers in little more than half a century.[3]

2 The demographic challenge of the second half of the twentieth century

The reaction to population growth rates of one per cent and life expectancies of 40-50 years had led to Europe reducing its fertility rate, but birth rates had not begun to fall outside France for up to 200 years after child survival began to improve. No one knew how the Third World would react to growth rates which by 1950-54 were already 2.4 per cent in Africa and West Asia and 2.1 per cent in the whole developing world, driven by life expectancies which were nearing 60 years in Sri Lanka, Lebanon, Trinidad, Jamaica and Costa Rica, and 55 years in Panama and Venezuela.

These growth rates were an obvious challenge to food producers. However, it was increasingly believed that the difficulties were broader still and that high rates of population growth might impede or prevent further economic development (Coale and Hoover 1958). This was a particular problem if fertility decline could not be triggered until certain minimum levels of economic development were attained (Leibenstein 1957). The result was a broadening consensus that voluntary and national agencies had to work together to induce a fertility decline in countries where fertility was unlikely to fall spontaneously. Starting with India in 1952, most Asian countries and some African countries organized national family planning programmes. But, apart from the West, temperate South America and Japan, fertil-

3 The most recent estimate for reaching six billion is March 1999, cf. Haub 1996: 1.

ity declined nowhere for two decades after the Second World War. It began to look as if Western family structure might be unique. Theorists began to suggest that the family structures found elsewhere were such that fertility was unlikely to fall.

Nevertheless, from about 1965 substantial fertility declines began to occur in some countries in every region except sub-Saharan Africa. This is brought out clearly in Table 1. The onset of fertility decline in Latin America occurred at similar socioeconomic levels with regard to occupation, urbanization and education as had been the case in Europe. These declines were little assisted by national family planning programmes, largely because of the opposition of the Catholic Church, but were certainly helped by an increasingly strong global belief in the virtue of family limitation and by new methods of contraception. It was in Asia that national family planning programmes appear to have brought on earlier and steeper falls than had been the Western experience at the same socioeconomic levels (Caldwell 1993). From the 1980s there has been a steep fertility decline even in one of Asia's and the world's poorest countries, Bangladesh, while India's total fertility rate is now little more than three children per woman.

Table 1: Population growth rates, major world regions, from 1950

Region	1950-54 % p.a.	Highest growth rate		1990-95 Annual % rate of population growth	Year when growth projected to fall to 0.5% p.a.
		Level (%)	Years		
World	1.8	2.0	1965-70	1.6	2050-55
Developed countries	1.2			0.4	1985-90
Developing countries	2.1	2.5	1965-70	1.9	2060-65
East Asia (exc. Japan)	1.8	2.4	1965-70	1.6	2020-25
Southeast Asia	1.9	2.5	1965-70	1.8	2045-50
South Central Asia	2.0	2.4	1965-70	2.1	2050-55
West Asia and North Africa	2.4	2.7	1960-65	2.4	Late 21st century
Sub-Saharan Africa	2.4	3.0	1990-95	2.8	22nd century
Latin America and Caribbean	1.8	2.1	1960-65	1.8	2045-2050
Oceania (exc. Australia and New Zealand)	2.0	2.5	1960-65	2.1	Late 21st century

Source: United Nations 1995.

Table 1 charts these changes. It shows that the population growth rate in the world as a whole, and in developing countries, reached its peak at 2.0 and 2.5 per cent per annum respectively in the late 1960s. Since then there has been a significant, but not huge decline in levels. There are two exceptions. The first is East Asia where especially steep fertility declines in China and other areas in its cultural sphere have led to a drop of almost one per cent in growth rates. The other exception is sub-Saharan Africa, where fertility decline has only recently begun in a small number of countries and where there is no convincing evidence as yet that the regional growth rate is falling. The problem in Africa is not merely poverty but also culture, for fertility has declined in Asian countries which were as poor as, or poorer than, many African countries (Caldwell and Caldwell 1988).

Two points should be emphasized with regard to Table 1. The first is that population growth rates, although falling, are still positive and high, so that the size of the population base continues to grow. As we will see later, the absolute size of population increments has continued to rise over the last 30 years and is only now reaching its maximum. The second point is that there is a momentum to population growth so that declining fertility will not result in low population growth rates, identified here as being 0.5 per cent per annum, until a quarter of the way through the next century in East Asia, half way through the century in the rest of Asia and in Latin America, late in the century in the Arab world, and not until the 22nd century in Africa. For much of the world, the family planning crusade has only now brought population growth rates back to the rather high levels of the early 1950s.

Table 2: Population growth, 1950-1990

	1950		1995		1950-95	
	Population (millions)	**% of world population**	**Population (millions)**	**% of world population**	**Increase (millions)**	**Multiplication since 1950**
World	2520	100	5717	100	3197	2.27
Developed countries	809	32	1167	20	358	1.44
Developing countries	1711	68	4550	80	2839	2.66
East Asia (without Japan)	587	23	1298	23	711	2.21
Southeast Asia	182	7	484	8	302	2.66
South Central Asia	499	20	1381	24	882	2.77
West Asia and North Africa	104	4	329	6	225	3.16
Sub-Saharan Africa	171	7	567	10	396	3.32
Latin America and Caribbean	166	7	482	8	316	2.90
Oceania (without Australia and New Zealand)	2	0.1	7	0.1	5	2.78

Source: United Nations 1995; United Nations 1996.

3 Differential challenges

It should be repeated that the challenge both to population control programmes and to food producers shows significant and increasing differentials, which would be unimportant only in the unlikely event of population flowing freely over national borders and of food flows not being restricted by price levels or import policies. Since 1950 the population of developed countries has increased by only 44 per cent, while that of developing countries has grown by 166 per cent, with growth ranging from 121 per cent in East Asia to 232 per cent in sub-Saharan Africa.

These differentials are going to increase, but even in the period 1950-1995 they caused changes of great significance in terms of food and other consumption. The population of developed countries fell from almost one-third to one-fifth of the world's numbers, while South Central Asia increased from around one-fifth to almost one-quarter and sub-Saharan Africa increased its number of people more than three-fold and raised its proportion of the world's population to almost half as much again.

4 Demographic and non-demographic factors in increasing food supply

Most agricultural analyses seem to suggest that global food production can be doubled and possibly trebled. This, however, appears to depend greatly on the advance of scientific farming. This depends in turn on food selling for a high enough price to make agricultural investments worthwhile. The determinants of this in turn are real per capita income which provides purchasing power, and national levels of urbanization which provide markets beyond the farming sector. Table 3 accordingly examines per capita income in US dollars, change in real per capita income over a decade just completed, and level of urbanization.

Table 3: Other influences on farming and food production

	pci (US$)	pci growth p.a 1985-1994 (%)	% urbanized
World	4740	0.9	43
Developed countries	18130	1.9	75
Developing countries	1320	0.7	35
East Asia (without Japan)	804	6.9	35
South East Asia	1240		30
South Central Asia	340	2.7	27
West Asia and North Africa	2518	-0.4	54
Sub-Saharan Africa	550	-1.2	27
Latin America and Caribbean	3290	0.6	71
Oceania (without Australia and New Zealand)	1302	3.0	23

Source: World Bank 1996.

Table 3 emphasizes the problems ahead. South Central Asia and sub-Saharan Africa with over one-third of the world's population are the poorest regions in the world, with per capita incomes one-fiftieth and one-thirtieth respectively of the developed world. Furthermore, the disparities between richer and poorer developing regions are growing. Sub-Saharan Africa's real per capita income actually declined over the decade, while that of South Central Asia grew at less than half the rate of East and Southeast Asia. The main anomaly in the table is Latin America, the richest of the developing continents, but comparatively poor in economic growth.

The urban markets vary greatly. In sub-Saharan Africa there are almost three times as many farmers as urban consumers, while in Latin America the proportions are almost reversed. There are countries in Africa like Niger, Malawi, Rwanda and Burundi where over five-sixths of the population are farmers and where the proportion is likely to be two-thirds or more in 30 years' time. Farmers cannot sell food to other farmers, and, unless they can get reasonable prices for their produce, they cannot invest enough in inputs to the soil to maintain its quality, let alone increase production.

5 The real challenge

Although population growth rates have been declining for 30 years, the absolute number of people added to the world's population has not. This is because the base population to which the rates are applied, namely the population of the world, is still growing. If Malthus was right that agriculture expands only in arithmetical progression then the major challenge is only just beginning.

There are really two main challenges ahead. As can be seen from Table 4, the first is that we have only just entered the period when the greatest additions to the world's population are being made. The second is that a dramatic change has occurred, and will intensify, in the regional distribution of that growth.

This quinquennium will see a net addition to the world's population of almost 450 million people, probably the largest addition that the world will ever experience. The real problem, however, is that there is no pronounced peak and hence quick falling-off in these numbers. The increments are almost identical, around 440 million per quinquennium or 88 million per year, for the 30-year period from 1985 until 2015. Even subsequently the decline in the quinquennial population additions will be slow and will still be around a quarter of a billion in the middle of the next century. The annual population increment has now been declining for a decade in East Asia, and is now reaching stability in Southeast Asia, but this has not yet occurred in South Central Asia. Increments will grow in size until around 2025 in Western Asia and North Africa, and a later date still in sub-Saharan Africa.

There have been dramatic changes in the regional distribution of these population increments. In the early 1950s, 21 per cent of the world's population

Table 4: Quinquennial additions to population, major world regions from 1950

	World	Developed countries	Developing countries	East Asia	Southeast Asia	South Central Asia	Western Asia and North Africa	Sub-Saharan Africa	Latin America and Caribbean	Oceania
(a) Numbers (millions)										
1950-1954	234	50**	184	55	18	53	13	20	24	0.3
1985-1990	439	31	404	90*	41	130	36	67	41	0.6
1990-1995	431	23	408	70	42	138	37	79	42*	0.6
1995-2000	442*	19	423	67	43*	145	39	87	42*	0.7
2000-2005	436	14	422	56	42	146*	40	95	40	0.8
2005-2010	439	13	426	53	38	145	41	107	39	0.9*
2010-2015	437	9	428*	54	36	137	41	117	38	0.9*
2015-2020	419	8	411	47	35	122	42*	125	35	0.8
2020-2025	406	6	400	39	34	120	42*	129†	33	0.7
2045-2050	246	-7	253	2	21	74	28	107	20	0.5
(b) Percentage of total addition										
1950-1954	100	21	79	24	8	23	6	9	10	0.1
1985-1990	100	7	92	21	9	30	8	15	9	0.1
1990-1995	100	5	95	16	10	32	9	18	10	0.1
1995-2000	100	4	96	15	10	33	9	20	10	0.2
2000-2005	100	3	97	13	9	33	9	22	9	0.2
2005-2010	100	3	97	12	9	33	9	24	9	0.2
2010-2015	100	2	98	12	8	31	9	27	9	0.2
2015-2020	100	2	98	11	8	29	10	30	8	0.2
2020-2025	100	1	99	10	8	30	10	32	8	0.2
2045-2050	100	-3	103	1	9	30	11	44	8	0.2

Notes: * quinquennium
** of greatest numerical addition
† quinquennium of greatest numerical addition beyond 2025 (actually 2030-2035)
Source: United Nations 1995.

growth was found in developed countries. Now it is four per cent and in the coming century it will reach zero followed by population decline. East Asia has also experienced a decline in the proportion it contributes to world population increase from one-quarter in the 1950s to one-sixth now and soon to less than one-eighth. The massive challenges in terms of food production will be in South Central Asia and sub-Saharan Africa. The two areas together account for one-third of global population growth in the 1950s, around half now, and three-quarters by the middle of next century. For most of this period South Central Asia's contribution to world growth will be fairly stable at around one-third, but sub-Saharan Africa will continue to grow, from one-tenth in the 1950s to one-fifth now, and to over half shortly after the middle of the coming century. For the next 60 or more years additional food will have to be found in sub-Saharan Africa for an increment of 20-25 million people each year. This may have to occur in circumstances where incomes are too low and income growth is so meagre that there are very great obstacles to proceeding to more scientifically based agriculture.

6 The global future

The situation now is that growth rates are declining rapidly in East Asia and Latin America, moderately in South Central Asia, slowly in West Asia and North Africa, and barely at all in sub-Saharan Africa.

In Asia national family planning programmes have played a role in producing fertility declines over much of the continent. Indeed, the national family planning programme was an Asian invention, and the most successful examples are found in that continent. They have been instrumental in reducing India's total fertility rate to 3.4 per cent per year and more recently Bangladesh's rate to the same level. China, with a programme with coercive elements, has gone further and has attained long-term replacement level. The anomaly in Asia is Pakistan with 140 million people, a birth rate which has barely begun to decline and a rate of natural increase of three per cent per annum. Over four million additional inhabitants are currently being added to its population each year. It has not had good family planning programmes, partly probably because of its feudal rural social structure and partly because its political history has been so turbulent that national priorities lie elsewhere.

Globally, the great anomaly is sub-Saharan Africa (Caldwell and Caldwell 1987). Its population is growing at almost three per cent per year in spite of the world's highest death rates with life expectancy averaging barely 50 years. The growth rate is achieved by a total fertility ratio[4] still over six, a level that Europe or much of Asia may not have experienced for a millennium. A decline from this high level may be largely offset in terms of population growth by mortality decline, for which there is still very great potential. The birth rate is kept high by universal

4 The average number of births to each woman over her reproductive span if fertility rates remain constant.

female marriage and remarriage after widowhood or divorce made possible by the institution of polygyny. Contraception is slowly increasing but this is partly offset by a shortening of traditional postpartum periods of sexual abstinence.

Family planning programmes have been hindered in sub-Saharan Africa by the fact that nation states are new and not deeply rooted and by the absence of national elites accustomed to providing political and moral leadership. Nevertheless, fertility is now definitely falling in more economically developed Southern Africa, certainly South Africa, Zimbabwe and Botswana, and probably in Namibia, Swaziland and Lesotho. It is also declining in Kenya and probably Ghana. These declines have been among too small a fraction of the total regional population to have as yet any significant fertility impact in reducing regional or growth levels. Furthermore, they have occurred in the countries with the lowest child mortality and the highest levels of female education. Much of the region is decades behind in this respect.

An unknown factor in the African situation is the AIDS epidemic which is particularly intense in an area stretching from the Central African Republic through Southern Sudan, Uganda, Rwanda, Burundi, Kenya, Tanzania, Malawi, Zambia, Zimbabwe, Botswana, Namibia and South Africa, especially KwaZulu-Natal. This is the main AIDS belt where 175 million people, or less than three per cent of the world's population, are infected with over half the HIV/AIDS in the world. Rural HIV levels are typically 10-16 per cent, and some capitals reach levels of over 30 per cent. Within a few years AIDS will be the cause of half of all deaths and will reduce life expectancy by up to 20 years. This alone will not be Malthusian because of the previously high population growth rates. However, recent evidence suggests that the retrovirus also has a biological impact on fertility, perhaps reducing it by at least one-third (Boerma et al. 1997). New population projections, which incorporate both these factors, show the likelihood of population decline at least in Zimbabwe and Botswana (Stanecki and Way 1997). The present evidence is that the intensive epidemic will be confined to sub-Saharan Africa, and AIDS is unlikely to reach anything like the same intensity in most of the rest of the region. Where it is intense, it may reduce the number of people who need to be fed but it is also likely to reduce food production because it kills disproportionate numbers of younger adults.

Ironically, while much of the world's population is growing rapidly, four-ninths of the world's people now live in countries which have achieved not merely long-term stationary population but below-replacement-level fertility. Not all are yet declining in numbers but, within a few years, as their age structures conform to the new situation, they will do so. Countries now at or below long-term replacement level include the whole of Europe with the exception of Albania, the whole of East Asia except Mongolia, elsewhere in Asia Singapore, Thailand and Georgia (with Sri Lanka marginally above the level), the whole of North America, in Latin America and the Caribbean the Bahamas, Barbados, Cuba, Guadeloupe and Martinique, and in Oceania Australia and New Zealand. It would seem that

Table 5: United Nations medium population projections, 1995, 2025, 2050

	Numbers of persons (millions)				Annual population growth rate in 2045-2050 (%)	Distribution %			
	1950	1995	2025	2050	2050	1950	1995	2025	2050
World	2520	5716	8294	9833	0.5	100	100	100	100
Developed countries	809	1167	1238	1208	-0.1	32	20	15	12
Developing countries	1711	4550	7056	8626	0.6	68	80	85	88
East Asia (without Japan	588	1298	1616	1687	0.1	23	23	19	17
Southeast Asia	182	484	713	851	0.5	7	8	9	9
South Central Asia	499	1381	2196	2673	0.6	20	24	26	27
West Asia and North Africa	104	329	573	738	0.8	4	6	7	8
Sub-Saharan Africa	171	567	1227	1800	1.1	7	10	15	18
Latin America and Caribbean	166	482	710	839	0.5	7	8	9	9
Oceania (without Australia and New Zealand)	2	6	12	15	0.7	0.1	0.1	0.1	0.2

Source: United Nations 1995.

replacement fertility is incompatible with being a developed market economy with well educated and usually employed women.

Thus the world is now divided into two almost equal camps, on the one hand slowly growing or declining populations and on the other populations with the potential for substantial further growth. The latter are found mostly in South Asia and sub-Saharan Africa. Table 5 presents the most recent full publication of United Nations population projections (United Nations 1995). It shows world population increasing in the 30 years, 1995-2025, by 45 per cent and in the 55 years, 1995-2050, by 72 per cent. Nevertheless, by the mid-21st century global growth will be dwindling and the world's most dramatic period of human increase will be over. Only sub-Saharan Africa is likely to have a growth rate still over one per cent.

The redistribution of world population numbers will also be almost finished. Today's developed countries, which constituted one-third of the world's population in 1950, will have declined to one-eighth and will probably stabilize around one-tenth at the end of the 21st century. In contrast, sub-Saharan Africa, containing one-fourteenth of mankind in 1950 and one-tenth now, will probably stabilize at one-fifth. Changes elsewhere are on a smaller scale although over the whole period the Arab world will double its proportion.

Very recent faster declines than had been expected have occurred in parts of the Third World, particularly Africa, where the impact of the AIDS epidemic had been underestimated; and Asia, where the continuing success of national family planning programmes had been underestimated, and fertility has declined even further below the long-term replacement level in developed countries, especially in Eastern Europe, where the extent of post-Communist declines had not been foreseen. As a result, the United Nations has reduced the levels of its population projections below those forecast as recently as 1994. The 1994 and 1996 revisions are compared in Table 6.

Over the course of two years it has been necessary to reduce the medium projection for the year 2050 by almost five per cent. This has clearly unnerved the United Nations demographers and the result has been three sets of projections with the high projection almost 50 per cent above the low projection. This margin is sufficient to weaken our confidence in all population projections. This is one reason why the present study has concentrated on the shorter term, namely up to about 2025 when the margins between the projections are much smaller.

The challenge to agriculturalists is to prepare for a possible doubling of human numbers over the next 55-75 years. The harder struggle, assuming that most food will still be produced within each region, will be to multiply production in West Asia and North Africa by 2.25 to 2.5 and in sub-Saharan Africa by over three by 2050 and eventually by four.

Looking further ahead still, in a world where 44 per cent of the population lives in countries where population is set to decline, it is now hard to escape the conclusion that global population will ultimately begin to decline, probably early in the 22nd century. That decline may, centuries hence, bring us down to our present

Table 6: New United Nations projections of world population in the year 2050 (millions)

	Medium projection				1996 projections		
	1994	1996	change	%change	low	medium	high
World	9833	9367	-466	-4.7	7662	9367	11156
Developed countries	1208	1162	-46	-3.8	959	1162	1352
Developing countries	8626	8205	-421	-4.9	6703	8205	9805
Africa	2141	2046	-95	-4.4	1731	2046	2408
Sub-Saharan Africa	1885	1789	-96	-5.1	1523	1789	2096
Asia	5741	5443	-298	-5.2	4405	5443	6501
Latin America and the Caribbean	839	810	-29	-3.5	650	810	1001
North America	389	384	-5	-1.3	301	384	452
Europe	678	638	-40	-5.9	538	638	742
Oceania	46	46	0	0	37	46	53

Source: Haub 1997.

numbers again. Farmers will probably make up much less than the five per cent of the work force that they now do in the developed world, in contrast to the 60-70 per cent they still constitute in East and South Asia and in sub-Saharan Africa.

A still unanswered question is what will happen to the age composition of the rural work force. All over the world farmers are becoming older. This is just as much the case in developing as developed countries. Southern Nigeria is probably a typical example. Young people nearly all go to school and assume that this implies seeking a non-farming job. Most farmers are now over 50 years of age. Clearly this is an unsustainable situation and bodes ill for Nigeria's and Africa's chances of increasing food production by at least three per cent per year and eventually quadrupling it.

References

Boerma, Ties, Kofi, Awusabo-Asare and Basia Zaba, eds. (1997): The Socio-Demographic Impact of AIDS in Africa, Supplement to Health Transition Review, Vol. 7, Canberra.

Bogue, Donald J. (1969): Principles of Demography, New York.

Boserup, Ester (1965): The Conditions of Agricultural Growth and the Economics of Agrarian Change under Population Pressure, Chicago.

Caldwell, John C. (1993): The Asian Fertility Revolution: Its Implication for Transition Theories, in: The Revolution in Asian Fertility: Dimensions, Causes and Implications, ed. Richard Leete and Iqbal Alam, Oxford.

Caldwell, John C. and Pat Caldwell (1986): Limiting Population Growth and the Ford Foundation's Contribution, London.

Caldwell, John C. and Pat Caldwell (1987): The Cultural Context of High Fertility in Sub-Saharan Africa, in: Population and Development Review, Vol. 13, No. 3, pp. 409-437.

Caldwell, John C. and Pat Caldwell (1988): Is the Asian Family Planning Program Model Suited to Africa? A Comparison of Asia and Sub-Saharan Africa, in: Studies in Family Planning, Vol. 19, No. 1, pp. 19-28.

Caldwell, Pat (1996): Child Survival: Physical Vulnerability and Resilience in Adversity in the European Past and the Contemporary Third World, in: Social Science and Medicine, Vol. 43, No. 5, pp. 609-619.

Coale, Ansley J. and Edgar Hoover (1958): Population Growth and Development in Low-Income Countries, Princeton.

Haub, Carl (1996): World Population Expected to Reach 6 Billion in Early 1999, in: Population Today, Vol. 24, No. 6/7, pp. 1-2.

Haub, Carl (1997): New UN Projections Depict a Variety of Demographic Futures, in: Population Today, Vol. 25, No. 4, pp. 1-3.

Leibenstein, Harvey (1957): Economic Backwardness and Economic Growth: Studies in the Theory of Economic Development, New York.

Mitchell, B.R. (1962): Abstract of British Historical Statistics, Cambridge.

Stanecki, Karen A. and Peter O. Way (1997): The Demographic Impact of HIV/AIDS: Perspectives from the World Population Profile, IPC Staff Paper No. 86, Washington DC.

Thompson, Warren S. (1953): Population Problems, New York.

United Nations (1995): World Population Prospects: The 1994 Revision, New York.

United Nations (1996): World Population 1996 (Chart), New York.

World Bank (1996): From Plan to Market: World Development Report 1996, New York: Oxford University Press.

Wrigley, E.A. and R.S. Schofield (1981): The Population History of England, 1541-1871: A Reconstruction, London.

4

The Feeding Capacity of the Planet Earth. Developments, Potentials and Restrictions

Peter von Blanckenburg

1 Introduction

Rarely in the history of mankind has food been available in plentiful supply for consumers. The normal case was that it was scarce and that a major or minor part of the people had to struggle to find enough food for their families. Differences in the overall availability have always occurred, varying from period to period, e.g. due to drastic short-term weather fluctuations or wars. Regional and social inequalities in supply have never been overcome. The land-man ratio had a substantial influence: where the population grew fast, it was difficult to mobilize use of land and other resources for additional agricultural production in time. Many scarcities and hunger catastrophes are man-made, e.g. caused by wars, political upheavals or inadequate political measures. Epidemics among populations played a major role too, particularly evident in the medieval "black death" in Europe, which carried off millions of people, leading to losses in the productive capacity, to impoverishment and diminution of purchasing power.

The factor which has found prominent attention with respect to the long-term availability of food is the increase in population, as opposed to the development of food production. The thoughts of the British author T.R. Malthus have strongly influenced the debate from the beginning of the 19th century onwards. Since the appearance of his "Essay on the Principle of Population" in 1798 scientists, politicians and "futurologists", as they are called today, have commented on his basic thesis, that mankind is, biologically speaking, in a position to increase geometrically, i.e. to double the population in each generation, whereas food production can increase in arithmetical sequence only. Malthus saw that such an unequal development is impossible in long-term view, and he introduced the term of the so-called "checks" as variables which limit the population growth. He distinguished between "preventive" checks, e.g. sexual restraint, and "positive" checks such as wars and other events diminishing population growth from outside.

Malthus recognized that, over longer periods of time, the development of the size of population cannot differ much from that of food supply. However, the weak point in his thoughts was that he underrated the potential for raising food production. The agricultural revolution which gained momentum in the 19th century with its changes in the land tenure systems, strong increase of agricultural productivity by availability of new technologies, of chemical fertilizer and pesticides and, moreover, the stimulation of agriculture by the process of industrialization, was still ahead.

Until today "Malthusianism" has played an important role in public debate. The former polarity of opinions on the basic correctness or incorrectness of Malthus' theses has, however, ceased. Modern research has provided better insight into the dynamics of population processes on the one hand and of agricultural productivity developments on the other. Today, the population dynamics can be appraised well, but the future development of agricultural production and the relevant socio-political conditions only with more difficulties. Malthusian fears regularly become virulent during periods of temporary scarcity, as they occur from time to time, and they fade out of discussion again when the crisis is over.

Nevertheless, there remains the nagging question how long the almost incessant growth of demand for food can be matched by productivity increases. Additional land resources are limited, in many areas of the world essential natural resources even get lost instead of being built up. Research and development can contribute substantially to the opening up of additional resources, but it is not clear whether the productivity increase will come fast enough and where it will reach definite technological and institutional limits. Another decisive question refers to the political environment. Wars and unrests have far too often wrecked the technological and economic development reached earlier, and the chances are low that this will happen less frequently in future. Recent experiences with international crisis management in developing countries are sobering. Thus, many unforeseeable factors exist in these fields, and this makes projections difficult.

2 The historical perspective

Food scarcities and hunger have accompanied mankind in history from time immemorial. There are very few quantitative data on extent and consequences of early hunger catastrophes. Information is sketchy even for the most recent decades. Sometimes governments have hidden, for political reasons, the extent of major catastrophes. For the period from 1770 to 1996, Oltersdorf and Weingärtner (1996: 13) have listed 22 very severe hunger catastrophes in the world, in which often millions of people died. The most dramatic ones among them happened in:

— India, Bengal (1770, 10 million dead)
— Ireland (1846/47, 2-3 million)
— India (1866, 1 million; 1869, 1.5 million; 1876/78, 5 million)
— China (1876/79, 9-13 million)
— Ethiopia (1888/92, 1/3 of the population)
— Russia (1920/21, several millions)
— China (1929, 2 million)
— Russia (1930, 3 million)
— India, Bengal (1943, 1.5-3 million)
— China (1946/48, 30 million affected)

— Nigeria, Biafra (1966/70, 2 million)
— African Sahel Zone (1973/74 and 1983/84, millions affected by drought)
— Africa, East and South (1992/93 and 1995/96, millions affected).

It is obvious that hunger catastrophes have occurred in all parts of the world, but they were particularly severe in Asia. For Europe the notorious Irish famine in the middle of the last century (caused by potato blight) and famines in the Soviet Union in the twenties and early thirties of this century (largely politically caused) are to be noted. During and after the two last world wars many millions of Europeans have suffered from hunger. Undernutrition and diseases brought about a high death rate.

However, by the thirties of this century, Malthus and his sombre predictions were almost forgotten in the Western world, as Poleman (1985: 516) pointed out. The world food security problem became obsolete in the Western world, it shifted to Asia, Africa and Latin America, to the "developing countries", as they were called henceforth. The character of the problem changed, too. Extensive undernutrition, not necessarily leading to widespread death, but seriously impairing their quality of life, became the prominent feature now. The global political and economic systems, the improved international transport systems, new approaches to health care and to food aid prevented the worst, although it was not possible to eradicate hunger.

3 The world food and nutrition situation and population growth

Several international institutions and many research institutes all over the world are doing research work on international food security problems. Most of them took up work after the end of the second world war. First and foremost are to be mentioned
— the Food and Agriculture Organization (FAO) of the UN, Rome,
— the World Health Organization (WHO), Geneva,
— the International Food Policy Research Institute (IFPRI), Washington,
— the World Bank, Washington,
— the World Watch Institute, Washington.

FAO, IFPRI and World Bank, which have remarkable expertise and also funds for research, dominate the international discussion. They have presented significant studies in the past decades. Statements on the world population development are mainly based on the work of the Population Council of the UN in New York. University and other research institutes have dealt less with global aspects, they have usually concentrated on specific problems and they carry on a critical dialogue with the big organizations.

The following presentation is mainly based on results of FAO and IFPRI studies. The most relevant new FAO publications, dealing with the present and future situation of world agriculture and nutrition, are the 1995 study "World Agriculture Towards 2010" (Alexandratos 1995) and various papers prepared for the World Food Summit of 1996 (FAO 1996). IFPRI has published, within its programme "2020 Vision", a number of studies with projections, which have another time horizon than FAO (cf. e.g. Islam 1995).

3.1 The population problem

At first a short look is to be cast at the population development. This is, in the long run, the most influential demand factor. Within the last four decades the number of people in the world has more than doubled: from 2.52 billion in 1950 to 5.3 billion in 1990. In 1995 there were 5.8 billion people on earth. As Table 1 shows, the population growth was and will be in future far higher in developing countries than in developed countries. The population of the developing countries grew from 1.68 to 4.08 billion (= + 143 per cent) during the 40 years from 1950 to 1990. The increase in the developed countries was 44 per cent in the same period.

Table 1: Population development in the world 1950-2025

	Population (billions)			Increase in per cent	
	1950	1990	2025*	1950-1990	1990-2025*
Developed countries	0.84	1.21	1.40	44	15
Developing countries	1.68	4.08	7.07	143	73
World	2.52	5.30	8.47	110	60

* Projected.
Source: Bongaarts 1995: 7 f.

The growth is highly disquieting. "More people have been added to the world since 1950 than in all of human history before the middle of this century" (Bongaarts 1995: 7). The world growth rate has reached its peak in the late sixties and is now—very slowly—declining. From the present 1.6 per cent p.a. it will presumably go down to 1.3 by 2010 and 1 per cent by 2025 (FAO 1996, Vol. 1: 1/16). The growth in the developing countries will add another 6.1 billion between 1990 and 2100. The total world population may then be 11.7 billion, provided, it is possible in fact to double the carrying capacity of the earth. Extremely strong efforts will be necessary to provide food and other means of living for the people in developing countries. The task will be to sustain 2.5 times more people who would live in this group of countries in 2100 (increase from 4.1 to 10.2 billion between 1990 and 2100).

Table 2: Regional differences in population growth between 1990 and 2025

	Pop. 1990 billions	Pop. 2025 billions	Increase 1990-2025 per cent
Western countries (OECD)	0.80	0.91	14
CIS / Eastern Europe	0.40	0.48	20
Asia	2.87	4.49	56
Latin America	0.44	0.70	59
West Asia/North Africa	0.27	0.56	107
Sub-Saharan Africa	0.50	1.30	160

Source: Bongaarts 1995: 12.

The growth of population will predominantly take place in developing countries. The worldwide rate of increase will amount to 60 per cent between 1990 and 2025, but it will be much lower in the West and the East European countries (Table 2). Around 2025 more than half of the world population (53 per cent) will live in Asia, but the rate of increase will be the strongest in Africa. It is to be seen whether a corresponding growth rate of production of food and other needed goods can be achieved. At least for Africa it can be doubted.

3.2 The present and future food and nutrition situation

The most recent data available about the state of food and agriculture in the world refer to the first half of the nineties. The supply of food energy in developed countries is plentiful, as Table 3 shows. But it has also improved in developing regions, this mainly in Asia, the least in Africa.

Table 3: Per caput food supplies for direct human consumption

	Calories/day		
	1979/81	1990/92	2010*
Developed countries	3 280	3 350	3 390
East Asia	2 360	2 670	3 030
South Asia	2 070	2 290	2 520
Latin America	2 720	2 740	3 090
Near East and North Africa	2 840	2 960	3 010
Sub-Saharan Africa	2 080	2 040	2 280
World	2 580	2 720	2 900

* Projection.

Source: FAO 1996, Vol. 1: 1/7.

Considering that the population of developing countries grew from 2.1 to nearly 4 billion people between the early sixties and the early nineties, it is clear that this improvement of per caput food supply is a great achievement.

Data on the incidence of undernutrition allow an insight into the distribution of food within the populations. As Table 4 reveals, 21 per cent of all people in developing countries (839 million) were regarded as chronically undernourished around 1990. Again, Africa comes off most badly with 43 per cent. FAO expects a reduction of undernutrition to 12 per cent of the total population of developing countries until 2010. This means a number of 680 million chronically undernourished people.

Table 4: Estimates of incidence of undernutrition in developing countries

	Undernourished					
	1979/81		1990/92		2010*	
	million persons	% of total	million persons	% of total	million persons	% of total
East Asia	378	27	268	16	123	6
South Asia	303	34	255	22	200	12
Latin America	48	14	64	15	40	7
Near East and North Africa	27	12	37	12	53	10
Sub-Saharan Africa	148	41	215	43	264	30
Total	905	28	839	21	680	12

* Projection.

Source : FAO 1996, Vol. 1: 1/9.

3.3 The food supply side

In spite of the enormous increase in the number of consumers, the agricultural production systems have, as shown, maintained and even slightly improved the per caput supply of food. Between 1970 and 1990, the world agricultural production increased by 2.3 per cent per annum. In the developed countries the growth was much smaller due to inbuilt retarding mechanisms: it amounted to 1.4 per cent only. In 93 developing countries it reached 3.3 per cent p. a. or, on a per caput basis, 1.1 per cent in the period 1970/90 (Alexandratos 1995: 80). This is a noteworthy improvement.

On the other hand, it cannot be overlooked that the growth of production in world agriculture has slowed down recently. The growth rate fell from 3.0 per cent p.a. in the sixties to 2.3 per cent in the seventies and to 2 per cent between 1980 and 1992. “These developments have given rise to expressions of concern that production constraints are becoming more stringent and may ultimately threaten world food security" (Alexandratos 1995: 39 f.). Fears have been increasingly pronounced since the middle of the nineties that the food and nutrition situation is "at a turning point to the worse" (Alexandratos 1995: 41). An influential advocate of such thoughts is Lester Brown (1996). He thinks that the FAO projections are too optimistic and have also methodological shortcomings. He points firmly at the ongoing processes of resource degradation and the increasing scarcities, especially in densely populated parts of the world.

At the moment we will leave this question behind and point once more to the regional disparities in agricultural production development. Between 1970 and 1990, East and South East Asia had a p.a. growth rate of 4.1 and 3.1 per cent respectively. In Near East/North Africa the growth reached 3.1 per cent and in Latin America 2.9 per cent. Sub-Saharan Africa fell back with 1.9 per cent p.a. FAO expects for the period of 1990 to 2010 a slow growth in all developing regions except for Africa (Alexandratos 1995: 80). The annual growth rate until 2010 for all 93 developing countries studied is projected at 0.8 per cent; it will be highest in East Asia with 1.5 per cent, and only Africa will have a decrease rate of -0.2 per cent p.a.

It should not be overlooked that the nutritional situation of countries and regions does not depend solely on their own food production. There are countries whose agriculture contributes less to the national food supply than food imports. They have a high non-agricultural export capacity, for instance as oil exporters. Their problem is, however, that such a food economy is subject to the fluctuations on the world market, this mainly for cereals, the major import commodity.

One of the main problem regions with respect to food security will be South Asia with its large and dense population. In future, several countries may be forced to fill a gap by more imports from developed countries. The chances for Sub-Saharan Africa to reach adequate food security are still more unfavourable, although substantial untapped resources exist in this region. International technical and financial assistance plus a continuing readiness of donor countries to provide food aid will be indispensable in order to avoid substantial food scarcities (cf. Alexandratos 1995: 134).

4 The resource potential

In the following the natural and human resource potential of developing countries will be observed. Will it be possible to comply with the challenge of feeding 7.1 billion people who will be living in developing countries around 2025—3 billion or 73 per cent more than in the mid-nineties? It has to be kept in mind that the demand for additional food will still be higher than these 73 per cent, as the growth of demand results not only from population increase, but also from that of incomes. The following account will be confined to some particularly important resources and point to requirements and starting points. The discussion of strategies will be left to other contributions in this book. The quantitative data presented here are again mainly based on studies of FAO and IFPRI.

4.1 Land use

"Land currently used in crop production in the developing countries (excl. China) amounts to some 760 million ha, of which 120 million are irrigated ... These 760 million ha represent only 30 per cent of the total land with rainfed crop production potential, which is estimated to be 2 570 million ha ... The remaining 1.8 billion ha would therefore seem to provide significant scope for further expansion of agriculture" (Alexandratos 1995: 151 f.). FAO hints at the fact that the real potential of reserve land is far lower. The regional distribution of unused land is rather uneven. Moreover, a substantial part of this land is under forest (probably more than 45 per cent) and there are other hindrances, e.g. in land use in the mountains. Finally there is competition for land: for human settlement, infrastructure, forest etc. FAO concludes (Alexandratos 1995: 158) that out of all reserve land only 90 million ha will be additionally available for food production until 2010.

Obviously, a land growth rate of 0.1 per cent p.a., as projected by FAO, cannot contribute much to meeting the overall additional food demand, although some regions have a higher potential for expansion. Most of the needed additional produce must come from other approaches. The cropping intensity (more harvests per year from a piece of land) can often be increased. More land can be irrigated, resulting in higher and safer yields. Finally, improved practices of crop and animal husbandry, use of high yielding varieties and, not the least, more economic use of fertilizer and of means of crop and animal protection have to be employed.

However, there is no reason for assuming that a major additional potential can be released here. These approaches have been applied over decades and have resulted in steady, but only slow improvements. What is needed is a second "green revolution" which will bring about another increase of productivity, comparable in effect to the green revolution in Asian agriculture in the seventies. However, one should perhaps better not expect a very dynamic expansion of food production. There are also major forces which impede positive developments. The much discussed land degradation, leading to lower yields and losses of productive soils, is not the only danger in developing regions, and we will come back to that.

4.2 Water and irrigation

Most farming in the world is rain-fed. Great efforts have been made to extend irrigation, which brings about a higher productivity than rainfed farming and makes agriculture less dependent on the vagaries of changes in rainfall. Irrigated land is, on average, 2 1/2 times more productive than rain-fed land. The expansion is, however, restricted by high costs of establishment, by shortage of physically suitable places and very often also by scarcity of water. It has also to be considered that cultivation under irrigation has a high water demand, and agriculture is already the greatest consumer, using 70 per cent of all water worldwide. Water has indeed become a scarce good. Since 1950 water consumption of the world has more than tripled, and agriculture competes here more and more with other consumers.

However, globally almost 40 per cent of all agricultural goods are produced on irrigated land (FAO 1996, Vol. 2: 7/6). By the mid-nineties 120 of the 760 million ha (16 per cent) of crop land in developing countries were irrigated. 2/3 of all this irrigated land lies in Asia. FAO assumes that in future the majority of the additional food demand will be satisfied from irrigated farming. Irrigation is expected to expand in developing countries by 23 million ha (19 per cent). There will be, on the other hand, losses of irrigated land, caused by water shortages and degradation of land due to salination. It was estimated that in each year 2.5 per cent of the irrigated land must be rehabilitated or substituted by new installations (Alexandratos 1995: 159). Frequent mistakes observed are an excessive, non-economic use of water and too little attention given to field drainage. Estimates have shown that on a global scale about 20 to 30 million ha of irrigated land are severely affected by salination, and additional 60 to 80 million ha by waterlogging (FAO 1996, Vol. 2: 7/54). Such observations are discouraging, but on the other hand they show that there is still a substantial potential for improving the productivity of irrigation agriculture by better management.

4.3 Agriculture's contribution to environmental decline—the sustainability issue

Agriculture has recently been exposed much more than earlier to environmental criticism. It is reproached for contributing substantially to the damaging of natural resources, especially to soil degration. It is, moreover, accused to influence changes of the climate, e.g. due to emission of greenhouse-effect gases by ruminant livestock or by rice cultivation. Other reproaches are the ill-considered conversion of forests into farm land, and finally pollution of underground water by overdoses of fertilizers and pesticides. The fear of a loss of irreplaceable natural resources is growing. Sustainability in production has now become a matter of public concern.

Public reactions to these developments have become virulent from the seventies onwards. Many aspects of sustainable agriculture have been examined since the Brundtland Commission report came out in 1987. It is obviously a particularly difficult task to translate the concept into a framework for poor rural people and for farming on a low technological level. Food insecurity, poverty and endangerment of the natural environment form a self-reinforcing vicious circle in many countries. Particularly the poverty which induces people to clutch at each straw, irrespective of environmental consequences, is a barrier to sustainable agriculture. Poor people with little formal education do not care much about protecting resources when fighting for survival. It cannot be expected that farm families below the poverty line and with little knowledge of the modern world take environmental consequences much into consideration, even if they obviously endanger their own future.

4.3.1 Land degradation

In the following, some other relevant problems will be discussed. The degree of land degradation in many developing countries gives particular cause for concern. "It occurs mainly in the form of soil nutrient mining as a result of low fertilizer availability, use of marginal land because of land shortages or tenure constraints, soil erosion resulting from poor knowledge and lack of income to carry out protective measures and pollution by agrochemicals because of insufficient understanding of application methods" (FAO 1996, Vol. 2: 11/14). The most frequently used scientific source for the quantification of soil degradation is the so-called GLASOD assessment of 1991 (ISRIC/UNEP 1991). It shows that damage has occurred on nearly 2 billion ha or 15 per cent of the world's soils. "Nearly 1 billion ha of arable land in developing countries are estimated to be so degraded that productivity is being moderately or severely affected. Some 9 million ha worldwide, of which 5 million ha are in Africa, have had their original biotic function fully destroyed and reached the point where rehabilitation is probably uneconomic" (Alexandratos 1995: 355).

The main factors responsible were water erosion (55 per cent), wind erosion (28 per cent), decline of nutrients in the soils (7 per cent), salination (4 per cent), and physical compaction by pressure of heavy vehicles (3 per cent) (FAO 1996, Vol. 2: 11/15). There are a number of other factors which impair the ecological balance and the increase of food production. For instance, pollution of groundwater by excessive use of chemicals (fertilizers and pesticides) for agriculture frequently takes place, but this more in developed than in developing countries.

4.3.2 Overexploitation of fish and forest resources

Aquatic resources play an important role in the world food economy. They contribute 19 per cent to the total animal protein consumption and 4 per cent to the total protein for human consumption. In many societies, fish is an absolutely indispensable foodstuff. The continuing overuse of the world fish resources, taking place at present, is likely to bring about a substantial decline of supply. Until 1989, the world production of fish had increased, but afterwards it started to drop. By the mid-nineties the total annual production of fish amounted to 100 million tonnes, of which about 50 million tonnes were available for direct human consumption.

FAO (Alexandratos 1995: 241 f.) maintains that fish production from all sources could still increase, provided that better resource-saving techniques and better management are applied. However, an intensification of production, as it is practiced in crop and animal husbandry, is hardly possible in fisheries, apart from aquaculture. Some experts have even pointed out that fish production has passed a turning point. The capital-intensive industrial fishery with ist superior technology is repressing the local coast fishing and often endangering the fish stocks. Further overuse of resources will have an increasingly negative effect, this mainly in marine fisheries, but not much less in inland fisheries. Aquaculture's fish production is growing, but it can fill only part of the gap. The total per caput supply of fish is likely to fall anyway. This is serious for many poor countries. The people in these countries can also hardly cope with the higher prices to be expected.

"Measures likely to bring about environmentally sound fisheries resource management include restrictions on the present free and open access to resources, but this requires ensuring equitable allocation of resources and establishment of use rights. In artisanal fisheries, use rights are particularly important in protecting fishermen from unequal competition with industrial vessels" (FAO 1996, Vol. 2: 11/27). The chances to arrive soon at international agreements on effective control of fish catch, with the intention to realize the concept of "responsible fishing", are not promising. It would require, among others, to restrict the target of catch to a maximum of 80 million tonnes p.a., i.e. 20 per cent less than is caught now.

Another important subject which here can only be treated briefly, is the function and the future of forestry. The majority of the land in many regions of the world had been covered with forests in earlier times. Throughout history, forests have served as land reserve, and the clearing for purposes of agriculture, pasture land, human settlement, construction, and infrastructure has been a slow process. Over centuries, forest reserves were abundant. Recently, they have decreased rapidly, particularly in the tropics, and have become definitely scarce in many countries.

Around 1990 the forest areas in the world amounted to 3.4 billion ha plus 1.6 billion ha woodland. This is more than 50 per cent of the total land area. In the tropical countries—they are mainly developing countries—1.76 billion ha were under forest cover in 1990. Deforestation has progressed steadily. Between 1980 and 1990, it amounted to more than 15 million ha p.a. in the developing countries (Alexandratos 1995: 207 ff.) or 0.7 per cent of total forest land, in Asia even to almost 1 per cent.

The disappearance of forests is partly due to the transformation of forest land to crop and pasture land. Other causes are the overcutting of fuel wood and the commercial demand for timber. This last-mentioned cause is being much discussed, especially with a view to the growing timber exports. But the other cause, the cutting of trees and bushes for household purposes (cooking and heating) does much more harm to the forests, as it takes place usually without any control. Almost 2 billion people in the world depend on bio-fuels (not only wood) as their main source of household energy. The most intensive forest clearing in developing countries takes place around the centres of population, followed by established farming areas. High population density stimulates deforestation, too.

The widespread disappearance of forests has far-reaching ecological consequences. Forests play a decisive role for the maintenance of the environmental balance. Among others, they contribute to conservation of soils and water, they help to prevent desertification, they have an influence on the climate, this, for instance, by sequestering CO_2 and diminishing in this way the greenhouse gases. The economic, social and cultural function of forestry for people can only be mentioned here.

There are many approaches to diminishing deforestation: control of tree cutting, assistance in replacing fuel wood by other energy sources, and education of rural people, who often do not understand the consequences of destructive action or are lacking knowledge of other instruments for cooking and heating. These issues cannot be discussed here. Reforestation is practiced increasingly, but its expansion is hindered by financial or land tenure problems. Changes in the attitudes of people to care more for conservation of forest resources, are taking place, but they are slow, they require education and realization of participation by local groups.

5 Improvement of the agricultural knowledge system

5.1 Education and agricultural extension

"There is increasing evidence and recognition that what matters for development, more than natural resources and man-made physical capital, is the capability of people to be effective and productive economic agents, in short, human capital" (Alexandratos 1995: 338). Activation of rural people for coping with the future challenges has been recognized as a development target since long. Education and agricultural extension, two major components of the agricultural knowledge system, are very important instruments for enhancing the rural human capital (von Blanckenburg 1982: 348 ff.).

The interest to make these instruments more operational, seems, however, to have diminished recently. The subject is treated unenthusiasically by international and national development agencies. Whether this phenomenon is due to lack of recent positive experiences or of innovativeness among the organizations in charge, is disputable. Anyhow, not many new conceptual ideas have been developed in this field recently.

It must be admitted, however, that substantial financial inputs have been made during the recent decades to improve the formal educational system in developing countries, of which primary and professional schools are the main components. In this group of countries public expenditure on education has climbed from 2.9 per cent of GNP in 1970 to 4.1 per cent in 1988, this, however, with major regional differences. The rural illiteracy rates are rather high in Africa with more than 70 per cent and are the lowest in Latin America and South Asia with 20 to 40 per cent of the people (Alexandratos 1995: 343). Illiteracy occurs much more among females than among males. This discrimination of women in education is particularly unfortunate for food security, as regularly more women than men are working in food production.

Beside the formal educational systems, of which primary and secondary schools are the most important components, non-formal educational institutions have been established in all countries. Agricultural extension services, in which agricultural advisers help farmers to improve technically and economically, are the prominent instrument. They are mainly governmental services, but non-governmental agencies play an increasing role, often in connection with development aid. The equipment with personnel and other means varies considerably, but on the whole it is inadequate. Whereas in Western countries typically 1 extension agent is available for about 400 farmers, the ratio is much more unfavourable in developing countries—often around 1:2500 farmers.

This extension density is much less determined by the need of upgrading the knowledge of farmers than by budgetary restrictions. It would be indicated to make more funds available for extension and to improve its efficiency, but this has rarely happened recently. The structural adjustment programmes of the World Bank, with their strict call for cutting down public expenses, have, unfortunately, led many governments to reduce costs of extension, too. It is another point that not all farmers accept the extension advice. Often no really new technical messages are available which could attract the interest of the farmers. This hints at insufficient cooperation between research and extension. Moreover, extension agents often lack important equipment, such as vehicles to reach the farmers. Budgetary restrictions are thus not the only, but a major reason for an unsatisfactory extension efficiency.

Agricultural extension is usually in the responsibility of the agricultural Ministry, but a second service, namely that for training in nutrition matters, is under another authority. Nutrition education and advice are important in all developing countries, as most families know little about physiological needs of the body, the nutrient content of foods and preparation of suitable new dishes. However, the nutritional extension work often leads a shadowy existence. The work is more difficult than that in agriculture, as, beside lack of modern knowledge, also deep-rooted traditions and cultural patterns influence the behaviour of the clients.

5.2 The role of agricultural research

Hopes for future increase of agricultural production are based on two avenues: 1) to use more land for crop and animal production and 2) to intensify production on the cultivated land and obtain higher yields per ha. The first approach has primarily contributed to the previous growth of production in developing countries. But land suitable for production has become scarce and therefore the second, intensification of production, has moved into the foreground. Beside various organizational and technical steps, attention focuses primarily on agricultural research. It is hoped to attain, via research, major improvements in development of technologies, to reach higher productivity and food security and to decrease poverty. These expectations are nourished, among others, by the positive experiences with the "green revolution" in Asia in the seventies, which started from a breakthrough in plant breeding.

The growth of agricultural production in developing countries has slowed down recently, as mentioned, and this raises the question in how far agricultural research will be a motor in safeguarding an adequate food supply in future. It is alarming that the so far generous international financing of agricultural research has decreased recently. During the sixties and seventies increasing sums had been invested worldwide into agricultural research. The growth rate was lower in the eighties and became stagnant in the nineties (FAO 1996, Vol 2: 9/9). It is indispensable to reverse this trend and to search for new financial and organizational means, which help to make full use of the potential which agricultural research holds.

First the national agricultural research systems (NARS) of the developing countries must be strengthened. More money is needed for state-run research institutes, for research at universities and the private sector research (chemical and machine industries, plant breeding, etc.). Moreover, the link between these institutions needs improvement. There exists a proven international cooperation between developed and developing countries in the form of the Consultative Group for International Agricultural Research (CGIAR). It procures and channels funds of donor countries and international organizations into research activities in developing countries, maintains a number of research institutes of its own and coordinates projects. The CGIAR activities deserve further strong support.

To conclude it may be said that agricultural research offers undoubtedly a major potential for the future. Whether and how far it will fulfill the hopes and play a decisive role in future safeguarding of food security, is difficult to judge. The issue will be approached further in some of the following papers.

6 Final remarks: confident versus sceptical expectations

As shown, the world-wide food and nutrition situation has slightly improved lately. The rate of progress has, however, slowed down in the most recent period. Various critical observers are afraid that, due to the increasing economic and environmental restrictions, a turning point has been reached.

History teaches us to be cautious in predicting complex future developments, and this is certainly advisable with respect to the world food situation. The majority of the observers of the scene have given an all-clear signal, whereas others, as indicated, are afraid that deteriorations are inevitable. The "confident experts" are confirmed in the fact that extreme worries have not come true and that new solutions for upcoming food security problems have everywhere been found so far. They base their view on the assumption that the development will go on in future more or less as in the past, and they hint to the undisputable fact that there is still a major resource potential for maintaining worldwide food security. The last resort would be a massive transfer of foodstuffs from surplus to deficit regions.

The "sceptical experts", offspring of the neo-malthusianists, have doubts about the capability of the systems to generate technological and economic progress and to extend the carrying capacity of the world substantially. They hint at the fact that the resource potential is not inexhaustible. They put question marks at least to the long-term future and to the chances to develop the potentials in time. In view of the increasing resource constraints, they doubt that more than the double of the present world population can be fed in 2100. Continuous large food aid transactions from rich to poor countries are considered to meet insuperable budgetary problems.

At any rate some very serious questions are open:

— Family planning and other efforts to control population growth have shown success which, however, is rather limited. Economic development and basic education are still regarded as the most effective instruments, but even where these have been continuously positive, the population growth rate declines only slowly. Will it be possible to find additional approaches accelerating the reduction of human fertility?

— For how many more years to come can additional resources—not only land, but also water, energy and mineral resources—be mobilized in developing countries? Will this mobilization counterbalance demand and growing restrictions?

— Which instruments—political, economic, technical—are available to cope with the increasing regional and social imbalances in food supply? The recent development policy has not achieved much in this field.

The precept to be cautious has induced the forecasters not to look too far ahead, as the parameters, relevant in far-off future, can hardly be assessed. Therefore, most of the recent projections of the food and nutrition situation do not go beyond the years 2010 or 2025. International institutions and many experts assume that until then the world-wide food security can be kept up at least at the present level. However, most statements are cautious. They are usually based on certain assumptions, they are highly conditional with respect to actions to be taken by all means. The most frequently named requirements are:

- Efforts in family planning must be increased.
- More agricultural research is necessary.
- Much more attention is to be paid to sustainability, i.e. to maintaining land and water resources and bio-diversity.
- Education and agricultural extension work must significantly be upgraded.
- International trade agreements have to pay more attention to the needs and constraints of developing countries.
- Efforts in rural industrialization and service development as contributions to more rural employment and improvement of purchasing power are indicated.
- The states need political stability to facilitate undisturbed economic development.

From the point of view of development strategists the proposed actions are required immediately in order to avert imminent catastrophes. Here, mainly the governments are challenged. The last international conference, the World Food Summit of 1996, had the aim to make this clear to politicians and governments and to initiate soon the steps needed. One may not expect very much, but it is to be hoped that the warning has been understood within some of the mainly affected nations.

References

Alexandratos, N. (ed.) (1995): World Agriculture Towards 2010. An FAO Study, Rome, Chichester: FAO, Wiley and Sons.

von Blanckenburg, P. (1982): Aktivierung der bäuerlichen Landwirtschaft durch Bildung und Beratung, in: Handbuch der Landwirtschaft und Ernährung in den Entwicklungsländern, 2nd Edition, Vol. 1, Stuttgart: Ulmer.

von Blanckenburg, P. (1986): Welternährung. Gegenwartsprobleme und Strategien für die Zukunft, München: Beck.

Bongaarts, J. (1995): Global and Regional Population Projections to 2025, in: Islam, N. (ed.): Population and Food in the Early Twenty-First Century, Washington: IFPRI.

Brown, L.R. (1996): Tough Choices. Facing the Challenge of Food Scarcity, New York, London: Norton.

FAO (1996): Documents on theWorld Food Summit, Vol. 1, Vol. 2, Rome: FAO.

Islam, N. (ed.) (1995): Population and Food in the Early Twenty-First Century, Washington: IFPRI.

ISRIC/UNEP (1991): World Map of the Status of Human-Induced Soil Degradation. Global Assessment of Soil Degradation, Nairobi: UNEP.

Oltersdorf, U. and L. Weingärtner (1996): Handbuch der Welternährung, Bonn: Dietz.

Poleman, T.T. (1985): World Food. A Perspective, in: Science, 188.

5

Food Security in the Context of Global Markets, Agricultural Policy and Survival Strategies of Rural People in Sub-Saharan Africa

Theo Rauch

1 The present situation concerning nutrition: a great deal of data but non the wiser

No one is really sure if the situation concerning nutrition in the countries of the so-called "Third World" has improved or deteriorated over the last three decades. The number of people affected by malnutrition has variously been estimated as being between 400 and 800 million, depending on the method and definition used in the assessment (cf. FAO 1994a, Meyns 1992, Bohle 1992). According to conservative estimates, though, even with a sharp increase in global food production "the problems of starvation and nutrition continue unabated" (Meyns 1992: 197).

According to the FAO figures which are based on estimates of national production, the percentage of people worldwide suffering from a lack of adequate nutrition is on the decline, while at the same time in absolute terms, there is an increase in the numbers affected. Promising developments are being reported mainly from South, South East and East Asia. There, the statistics would even seem to indicate an absolute drop in the number of undernourished people. However, what remains indisputable is simply the fact that in many countries of the region (e.g. India and China) the average per capita consumption of food has greatly increased. Equally indisputable is the fact that the increase in food production proceeded hand in hand with a retrenching of farmers and farm workers, thus limiting the access of an unknown number of people to securing their food needs. Statistics emanating from sub-Saharan Africa paint a picture of continuous deterioration. Here again it is possible that an unrealistic picture may result from the statistics. The impression that there are situations of scarcity in many African countries is often incorrectly heightened by only focusing one-sidedly on cereals when collecting data, whereas the root crops such as manioc and yams which constitute the main staples of significant sections of the rural population are not taken sufficiently into consideration. The same point can be made for the contributions made by hunters and gatherers within nutrition.

The deficiencies of the data base would require some further consideration in order to avoid giving credence to dubious facts and questionable conclusions. Thus, the sometimes large discrepancies noted in the data presented by FAO, World Bank, UNICEF and those from the National Statistical Bureaux, would seem to indicate that there are some basic problems connected with data gathering. For example, production data is often based on the harvest forecasts (!) of agricultural extensionists who, if they do not simply arrive at the figures by multiplicator factors and projections, then are more likely than not to concentrate on too narrow a product range and too few farmers. Data relating to the supply of nutrients such as carbo-hydrates and proteins are in turn arrived at by estimating the figures for production, imports and exports and thus contain all the error sources inherent in the production figures. The physiological data relating to nutrition (as for example available from UNICEF) is based on the nutritional status of small children who are of course affected to the same degree by illness as by their food intake. Since it was only in the eighties that a unified system for collecting data was established in the majority of countries, a prediction of trends is not all that easy. Given this lack of solid data it is not surprising that there is sufficient leeway allowing for both an optimistic as well as a pessimistic spin on the situation; this fits the bill of various support organisations who can then claim: We have made progress, but many are the problems that still lie before us.

Furthermore, the information that can be gleaned from micro-analytical case studies is also not of much use when attempting to predict middle-term trends in the nutrition situation. If the macro data are prone to over-standardisation, insufficient consideration of the real correlations between the nutritional systems and are purely quantitative in analysis, then it can equally be said that many micro-studies leave much to be desired as far as dimensioning, proportionality and quantitative trends are concerned. As a result of the differences in approach and methodology they are by nature clearly not comparable. The difficulties faced when trying to determine the extent of the nutrition problem are rooted in some basic methodological problems. If food security is not primarily a problem of production but a problem of the possibility of gaining access to food, then it becomes clear that one should examine how many people have sufficient and secure access to food, be it through own production, purchase or transfer. There is at once no simple answer to the question as to what is "sufficient", given the range of nutritional requirements from a physiological point of view. What makes establishing the extent of the problem especially difficult is in addition the fact that the problem situations vary to a very large degree:

- Seasonal food shortages in the weeks and months before the harvest ("hungry seasons") is a widespread regular occurrence in many peasant societies, affecting the majority of the people.
- Chronic malnutrition, meaning in this case a deficiency in certain nutrients, is often encountered in places where acute starvation is relatively rare.
- In many peasant societies certain groups of people within households (particularly women and children) are systematically put on a lower rung when it comes to foodstuffs which are rare and of higher nutritional value (e.g. fish, meat and eggs). In many countries more than 30% of the children are malnourished even where there is no general shortage of food.

- In many communities there are individuals who are social cases and are permanently undernourished. These tend to be old or chronically ill people without any family members looking after them who for one reason or another cannot avail themselves of the traditional extra-familial support systems.
- Occasional or periodic events of food insecurity or crises tend to affect people who are normally able to feed themselves.

All these chronic or temporary shortages appear from year to year, place to place or family to family in differing degrees of severity as well as in different combinations. There are those, for example, who subsist at a level which is chronically but only slightly deficient, yet relatively free from times of severe crisis, and then again others who in normal years are relatively well supplied with food, but in times of crisis experience really severe cutbacks. People in regions of rural Africa, South Asia and Latin America who have continuous and secure access to nutritious food are still very much the exception. In view of this broad spectrum of deficient or risk-prone situations it is clear why the search for data relating to the scope and extent of the problem is fraught with many difficulties.

The point on which all observers would appear to agree is: not only on a global scale but also locally within many countries of the South more food per person is being produced today than was the case in the sixties. The number of countries with an insufficient total output has dropped significantly. In countries such as India, China and Indonesia it would be possible to feed the population adequately with the food being produced at present. It is also indisputable that since 1960 famines have been milder. The crisis management systems at national as well as international levels have become more efficient, not least because they could fall back on global and regional buffer stocks. Pernicious famines are mainly encountered in areas where they consciously form part of a means for waging war.

The questions which need to be answered within the scope of this paper are: how has the "normal" food supply and food security situation for the populations in these countries developed? Has the number of precariously and poorly nourished people increased or diminished? Is a polarisation of the situation taking place in such a manner that for a decreasing number of people scarcity and risks are intensifying whereas others are now in a position to escape the zones of shortage and insecurity? The answers will, in view of the above-mentioned information deficit, perforce have to be in the form of circumstantial evidence and trends rather than in the form of corroborative representative data. They will be restricted to sub-Saharan Africa and will, at the same time, concentrate on the situation of rural people. With the aid of a nutrition system model the most important factors which need analysing will be described (section 2). We will then proceed with the help of macro-level observations in section 3 to obtain an overview of the availability of food in separate countries, while section 4 will deal with influencing factors and the way they are likely to develop. Section 5 will attempt to convey an impression, using selected examples from micro-level analyses, of the nature and the degree of vulnerability faced by rural households and of the strategies they employ to cope with food crisis situations. Finally, some conclusions regarding food security policy will be drawn.

2 The present state of the scientific discourse: a nutrition system model

The present discourse on the subject of starvation, food scarcity and crises is centred on two essential paradigms, represented by the terms "entitlement" (Sen 1981) and "vulnerability" (Chambers 1989). By adopting the "entitlement" approach (the right to access to food) the notion that global nutrition issues cannot simply be reduced to a question of food production has gained currency in the debate on nutrition. It has come to be realised that distribution (of land, purchasing power, food and so on, within local communities and families) plays an eminently important role. By employing the "vulnerability" concept, an awareness is spreading that starvation is not a static phenomenon but that the problem can be characterised by the lack of protection against risks and threats to one's livelihood. Situations of vulnerability are caused on the one hand by external factors (e.g. droughts), on the other hand by people's own capacity to deal successfully with such crisis events (for example by turning to other sources of food—"the coping capacity") or, in cases where shortages have appeared, to affect a complete recovery without a deterioration in their (re)productive potential (cf. Bohle 1993a). To summarise: today in the field of famine and food security research, the emphasis has come to be placed on the risks affecting people's access to food. The focus is on vulnerable groups whose physical or economic existence is endangered in the event of an acute deficiency situation. The range of factors influencing levels of nutrition and food security can best be illustrated by using a nutrition system model (see Figure 1).

Nutritional status and nutritional security thus depend on whether someone is able to produce enough food for him- or herself, if he or she is able to buy food—or where both these options are not possible—he or she has the possibility and/or the right, that is the entitlement, to be provided for by others. The nutritional status is, however, also influenced by eating habits and by the way food is prepared. The nutrition system model indicates in which way these household related factors are dependent on the global market, the political system (especially agricultural policies, but also whether economic policies can create mass purchasing power and conflicting group interests can be settled amicably), furthermore on the nature and viability of socio-cultural norms and of course on the respective natural environments.

Before looking at the question in which way these conditions have influenced food security in the rural areas of tropical Africa, it is necessary to obtain an overview of the way in which food supply has developed in these countries over the last decades.

Figure 1: Nutrition System Model

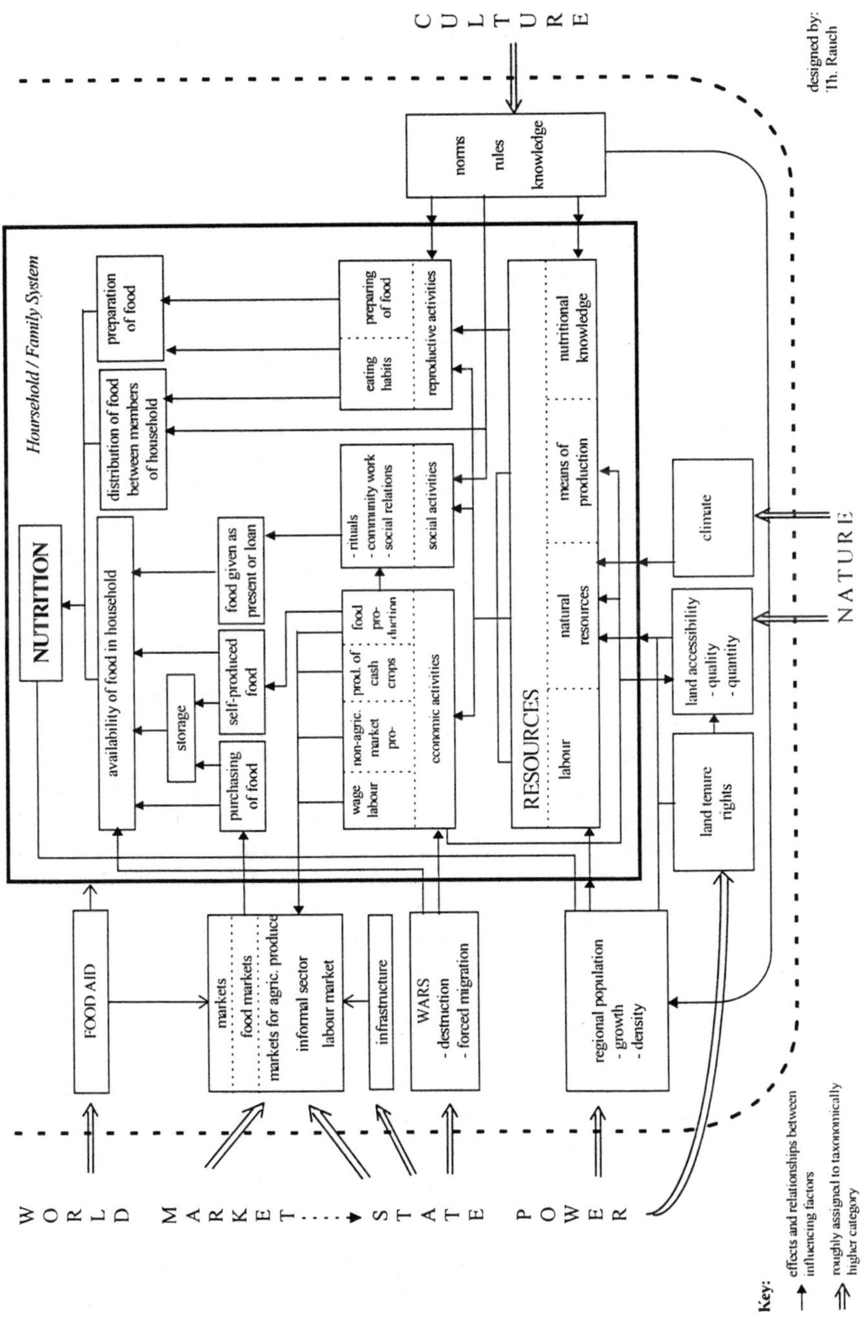

3 The availability of food in the countries of tropical Africa—a macro-level overview

In view of the inadequate data situation outlined above, the question arises whether it is at all possible to arrive at any conclusions concerning food security on the continent. One has to be somewhat daring in making the following estimates which are essentially based on an attempt to compare various indicators with each other, to check for consistency as well as to establish whether it is simply the case that they all originate from one and the same source. The indicators used come from various sources such as the FAO, the Worldbank and UNICEF and consist for example of production figures for various agricultural products, cultivated area, yield levels, import and export volumes for food, calorie/protein intake and the nutritional status of children. Their reliability was also looked at by taking into consideration country-specific analyses, local case studies and the author's own experience. The result of all this is most certainly a more thorough-going collection and use of data than is usually the case encountered in the majority of "guestimate" analyses, it nevertheless still represents a "best guess" attempt, relying as it does on a shaky information base. Accordingly, the reader should maintain a certain amount of caution when drawing conclusions, deriving results and interpreting them.

Tropical Africa is, on average—and this is confirmed by all the estimates—a food deficit region. The average value for the nutritional intake as established by the FAO (2100 kilo calories per day) lies below the minimum daily requirement, as also defined by the FAO. The percentage of people normally not in a position to satisfy this minimum need is estimated to be roughly between 30% and 35%, which means 150 to 200 million people. The percentage of children who are underweight is estimated by UNICEF to be equally high. These figures include in the equation imported food, which in fact goes to make up 10% of the total supply. It would, however, be incorrect to assume as a result of these figures that agriculture in Africa is not capable of meeting the needs of the populations in the respective countries. Often cereals are imported solely to satisfy the luxurious needs of the urban elites and their desire for wheat bread, and subsidised imports displace locally grown foodstuffs from the market (cf. section 4).

The long term trend for the continent would appear, all in all, to neither indicate a marked improvement nor a general deterioration in the situation; growth in food production is just keeping up with the growth in population. The same applies to the per capita calorie intake. The figures for the segment of people who fall under the category of the insufficiently nourished have also remained fairly constant since 1970. Any increase in food production is largely due to an increase in the area under cultivation and only to a very limited degree to intensification of farming production, i.e. an increase in productivity per unit land.

An analysis in which different groups of countries are differentiated clearly shows that during the period from 1990 to 1994 in the majority of countries affected by significant, continuous and worsening food shortages, wars or civil wars were prevalent. More than 25% of the population of sub-Saharan Africa lived in countries in which destruction caused by war and forced migration led to the creation of emergency situations. In comparison to this, the majority of African countries are, during good years, in a position to meet their needs; in bad years shortages appear so that in good years the supply of food grows faster, in bad years slower than the general growth in population.

The annual fluctuations in food production in individual countries can vary quite considerably, on occasion exceeding 20%. Extreme fluctuations (of well over 50%) can be observed in the case of cereals. Root crop yields (manioc, yams, etc.) are, as a rule, far less affected by climatic changes than is the case with cereals. This is incidentally also true for many types of export produce (which are usually the tree crops, such as coffee, tea and cocoa). In spite of the limitations of the available data, the following provisional conclusions can be drawn:

- The catastrophic scenario that is frequently depicted is not characteristic for the countries of tropical Africa as a whole, but is only found in those countries affected by war.
- For the remaining majority of African countries one can safely say that very little has changed over the last three decades as far as the food situation is concerned; production has more or less been able to keep pace with the growth in population. Neither has the prophecy of a catastrophe been fulfilled nor the expected breakthrough in production expansion achieved. The region is as prone to crises as ever before.

From all this we must therefore assume that the majority of the population which lives on or near the poverty line continues to be vulnerable to food crises (cf. section 5).

4 The factors which influence food production and supply in sub-Saharan Africa

4.1 Natural conditions

The issue of famine in Africa simultaneously triggers two types of association in the majority of people: drought and population growth. In fact, the irregularity and poor distribution of precipitation represents the biggest risk to food security for those 15-20% of the African people living on the southern edge of the Sahara (in the area referred to as the Sahel), south of the 16th parallel below the equator. This is nothing new, as has been confirmed by reports from previous centuries (cf. Cissoko 1968 for Mali). However, whether there has been an increase in the frequency of these climatically mitigated catastrophes or not remains undecided. Many observers feel that population growth rates of more than 3% "in view of the ecological disadvantages of the Tropics," represent a real threat to food security for the growing numbers of inhabitants. These fears need to be placed in context and seen against the relatively low population densities still the case in the majority of sub-Saharan countries. In the permanently settled regions south of the Sahara the population density is approximately 35 people per square kilometer (India: 260; China: 120). At present, about 10% of the surface area of Africa south of the Sahara is used for cultivation. As opposed to this, it is estimated that 13% to 16% of the total surface area comprises land suitable for fairly unlimited agricultural utilisation, i.e. also for rain-fed agriculture (Brandt et al. 1986: 67). Also these figures are likely to be misinterpreted: Africa's population is distributed extremely unevenly. In well-endowed agricultural regions one can already find concentrations of population above the 500 per square kilometer mark. However, it is indisputable that in many regions the supporting capacity has not been exhausted by a long shot by the prevailing extensive types of farming. "For the humid inner tropics ... a four-fold increase in supporting capacity is imaginable, given the right kind of agricultural and technical innovations. In the dry outer tropics ... it would only be possible, with the transition to appropriate intensive forms of farming, to achieve a doubling of supporting capacity" (Brandt et al. 1986: 65).

According to a supporting capacity study conducted by the FAO et al. (1982), approximately 35% of the tropical African population live in the 14 countries which without any form of agricultural intensification, that is to say only by an expansion of acreage, would be in a position to produce surpluses (measured against the number of inhabitants expected by the year 2000). A further 50% live in 13 countries where self-sufficiency, through an intensification on the basis of local intermediate production technologies (with modest external inputs), would appear feasible. In six countries, comprising 11% of the population, food self-sufficiency would only be possible through the use of high yielding crop varieties and through a high level of external inputs. Rwanda is, according to this study, the only country in Africa south of the Sahara where it would not be realistic to expect to achieve food self-sufficiency even if all the agricultural and technical possibilities available are used.

Notwithstanding the problems involved in setting up such large-scaled and highly aggregated supporting capacity prognoses, there are nevertheless clear signs that the phase in which food security was achieved by expanding cultivation areas or by opening up and developing new arable areas, is in most but not all the regions of Africa coming to an end. However, almost everywhere there is still plenty of leeway for intensification of production based on labour intensive and environmentally suitable techniques. It is striking that the majority of countries which experience significant shortages at present belong to the group of countries with a surplus producing potential, while those countries producing surpluses are predominantly countries where the possibilities for extensifying production has to a large extent already been exhausted. This demonstrates clearly that it is not the given natural resource limitations that are crucial for food security but that other factors come into play. It is only in Rwanda, Burundi, Mauritania, Kenya and Somalia that, amongst other things, the natural conditions constitute a limiting factor (even though there is of course still some degree of flexibility).

4.2 The global market

The integration of the African countries during the pre- and post-colonial eras within the global market influenced the production of food in two ways: On the one hand, arable land was used for the production of export crops and thus was no more available for food production. On the other hand, the USA and the countries of the EU swamped the global cereal markets with their subsidy-created surpluses, in the process forcing down the world prices and the profit margins for staple foods in the developing countries. The bottom line of global integration undoubtedly represented a negative balance-sheet for food self-sufficiency in the developing countries. On the other hand, the surpluses of many South and South East Asian countries have demonstrated that this does not automatically have to be the case. Whether or not such linkages to the world market will eventually lead to diminishing food security (in contrast to food self-sufficiency), has still to be decided.

The stepped up production of agricultural produce for export, during the colonial period and its subsequent reappearance in the last decade within the framework of the IMF's Structural Adjustment Programme, has been repeatedly criticized especially by the Left, who see in the slogan "Coffee instead of food" a declaration explaining the main causes of starvation. To be sure, there are many examples of how the production of food has been forced to shift to less fertile land to make way for cash crops or how the latter led to peasants becoming involved in the cash economy to the detriment of their own food production. However, in view of the possibilities for increasing acreage or intensifying production and in view of the fact that many rural inhabitants do not have access to markets and thus to a source of monetary income in their villages, one should not overemphasise the negative impacts of export crop production, in as far as it is done by small-scale farmers. In Ghana and Nigeria we see an expansion in food production running concurrently with the production of food. Cases have also been reported where, when the maize harvest was lost, income from the cultivation of coffee secured the family's nutritional requirements. All in all, the amount of land set aside for the production of export crops is small compared to the total area of arable land (e.g. Tanzania: 15%). The area under cultivation and the amount produced have remained fairly constant since 1980 and their significance has consequently been reduced. The real problem with agricultural produce destined for export is that the markets in the industrialised countries have stagnated and that prices, in view of the worldwide oversupply triggered by Structural Adjustment, have fallen. The price index for sub-Saharan Africa's agricultural exports has continuously dropped in the period from 1979-81 and 1992 to an index of 84 (FAO 1994b: 90).

There is absolutely no doubt that the agricultural subsidies in the industrialised countries (together with the de facto imposition of taxes levied against the producers of food in the developing countries) have held back the production of food in these countries. Whereas the production of food in the EU enjoyed a subsidy of 49% and in the USA of 30%, by 1991 the Low Income Countries faced an average levy of 25% and were thus often enough not in a position to compete against imported grains on their own local markets. The amount of grain exported from Europe reached 42 million tonnes in 1991/92, the equivalent of approximately half of Africa's total grain production for 1992 (UN 1993: 161). Calculations based on models carried out by the U.N. (ibid.: 162) have come to the conclusion that the total abolishment of protectionism on the part of the industrialised countries would turn those same countries into importers of food whereas the developing countries would in turn become food exporters.

The liberalisation of the world trade in food, as decided upon by the Uruguay Round of the GATT negotiations in 1994, tends to contribute to a higher degree of self-sufficiency in food in those regions where there is still room for an increase in production. This is to be expected since the prices for grain on the world market will not only increase in absolute terms but also relative to the classical tropical export crops. An increase in the degree of self-sufficiency would of course imply a decrease in dependency of the food deficit countries, however not necessarily greater food security for all sections of the population. What pleases the farmer may irk the city dweller. There will not only be an increase in producer prices but correspondingly also in consumer prices.

In the same way in which subsidy-created surpluses of the industrialised countries proved to be a double edged sword for food security in the "Third World", the food aid given to regions threatened by crises also falls into this category. The global system of stockpiling for emergencies can certainly reduce the risk of famine in crisis situations (always assuming that war activities have not rendered it unworkable), but of course can also increase the likelihood of crisis situations by undermining the capacity for autonomous food security at an individual, local, regional and national level. It lowers the risks of those who are dependent on buying food, while it increases the vulnerability of those who produce their own food by leading to the abandonment of the search for own coping strategies to deal with the crisis. An effective food aid policy would require careful fine tuning in order to achieve the desired short-term emergency relief effects, without exacerbating the long-term food risk. Since food aid is invariably accompanied by vested political interests—both on the part of the farmers in the surplus producing countries and on the part of the politicians in the recipient countries who would much like to boost their popularity by distributing cheap grain—in reality fine tuning is mostly not ensured, even with the help of improved instruments and techniques.

Thus, the agricultural grain policies of the industrialised countries go a long way to explaining why the majority of countries in sub-Saharan Africa have to date not been able to produce sufficient food to securely cover the needs of the population, despite being well-endowed on the whole with resources. The example of many Asian states which have gone from scarcity to surplus would seem to indicate, however, that negative influences emanating from the global market need not necessarily lead to food shortages. Country-specific factors would also appear to play an important role.

4.3 National agricultural policies

Since the middle of the 1990s, the majority of African countries have seen far reaching changes in agricultural market policies, away from the state controlled system which favoured low and stable consumer prices, towards a free market system with private enterprise. The effects of these two systems on the production of food and food security are very different and in certain cases even of a contradictory nature. The old, state controlled system can be seen as offering an explanation for why production potential was inadequately utilised and why there was a high degree of dependence on the importation of food. The price and market conditions were not attractive incentives which would induce farmers to produce surpluses. There was indeed a far greater incentive for enterprising and dynamic people to try their luck in the towns where they were able to take care of their food needs by availing themselves of the cheap price-controlled staple foods sold on the regulated markets. The governments did not only gladly accept the grain sold at dumping prices—a result of surplus creating policies—by the industrialised countries. What is more, they made the price of imported grain even lower by devaluing their own currencies. According to certain estimates, deregulation and the scrapping of intervention mechanisms by the governments in the developing countries would increase the rate of food self-sufficiency by 16%, compared to the 1991 bench mark (U.N. 1993: 162).

Agricultural research policies and their attendant agricultural extension systems are also not in a position to make a positive contribution towards the utilisation of the potential for intensifying production. The attempt to latch on to the success of the "Green Revolution" in certain Asian countries was bound to fail under African conditions. Whereas the promotion of monoculture high input production systems was ecologically compatibile and at the same time not too risky in the traditional irrigated rice cultivation areas of Asia, in the African highlands the one-sided promotion of monocultural dry land maize farming gradually led to ecological degradation as well as to extreme fluctuations in yield. Important food crops such as manioc, yams, millet and sweet potatoes have for a long time been neglected by agricultural researchers. The intensive capital investment that accompanied hybrid maize programmes was often not well-suited to the location, in addition to which it represented too big a jump in intensification for the majority of the production units of the small-scale farmers. In short, what was lacking were not only incentives for the mass of small holders to embark upon intensification but suitable options for intensification as well.

Given the amount of negative effects stemming from the old agricultural policies, it is only natural to expect improvements to be in the offing in the event of radical change. However, since experience with liberalisation and privatisation of the agricultural markets is so new, and since the scene is still far too influenced by transitional states, it is not possible as yet to make any general statement about the effects on agricultural policy. Observations made here and there would seem to indicate that privatisation and liberalisation create new problems, which make it difficult for small-scale farmers to benefit from production incentives and which prevent the food security situation from improving. An example of this would be the fact that price increases for food are not passed on down to benefit the producers, but that the main profiteers are the middlemen. In Tanzania, liberalisation brought about extreme seasonal and geographical price differentials. Small-scale farmers who do not have sufficient storage and transport facilities, apart from being burdened by limited cash reserves, find themselves forced to sell their goods locally immediately after the harvest at extremely low prices, only to be frequently forced to then buy at higher prices, before the harvest, when their own stocks become depleted. What they lack are insights into the workings of the market as well as the material and financial means to make use of the market mechanisms to their own advantage. In these cases the incentives and possibilities for intensification or expansion of food production are no greater than before. This is especially true for producers in remote regions, where the increase in transport costs have shrunken their profit margins. What has increased, is their vulnerability: fixed prices guarantee a certain element of food security. In contrast, prices that fluctuate and monopolistic dealers only to eager to exploit situations of short supply, increase the danger of artificially induced scarcity which in turn drives prices up to a level beyond the limit of what those dependent on buying are able to afford.

Hence, while the old agricultural policies—reflecting the need to satisfy urban consumers—caused food insecurity by discouraging food production, the total absence, on the other hand, of any pro-active agricultural market policies endangers food security by limiting the ability of poor people to afford food from the market during periods of short supply and high prices.

4.4 Wars

The worst famines in Africa are caused at present by wars, civil wars and the attendant expulsions and movements of refugees. The rate of food self-sufficiency in those countries which were affected by war at the beginning of the 1990s (Angola, Mozambique, Somalia, Liberia, Sierra Leone, Sudan, Rwanda and Burundi) was 60%, compared to an average of 100% for those countries at peace. War and forced migrations do not only mean huge drops in production but also that the little food being produced is often destroyed as part of starvation strategies directed against the enemy or that food aid from outside is blocked. "Starvation was in certain instances not only the consequence but indeed the aim of warfare" (U.N. 1993: 170). The nutritional systems of the refugees and the exiles are, as a rule, completely destroyed. By the end of 1991 the UNHCR had registered about 5 million refugees outside their countries of origin, and about 14 million internal residents who were forced to be resettled as a result of war.

4.5 The role of socio-cultural norms in the distribution of food

In societies where food is scarce and where the principles of the market economy have not caught on in every section of society, access to food is, as a rule, regulated by social norms. This applies to the distribution of prepared food between members of the same household, especially between men and women as well as between different generations. It applies too, to groups of people in need of special care who live in social formations such as village communities or extended families. And it usually also applies to special cases of individual emergencies (e.g. sickness), which can lead to members of the community being unable to collect the harvest. Issues relating to the manner in which these traditional social systems of food security have developed in recent decades will be looked at within the framework of the insights arrived at from the micro-analyses in section 5.

4.6 A summary of the above mentioned tendencies

How the determining and influencing factors which we have described are likely to develop in their effects on the food security situation of the rural population—if we ignore wars—can best be described as being contradictory. On the one hand, production possibilities have been curtailed and the utilisation of the remaining expansion possibilities has been adversely affected by the implementation of international as well as national agricultural policies, so that self-sufficiency has come to stagnate and is on an insecure footing. On the other hand, the options available for food security have grown; the dependence on one main food crop has decreased in recent decades as a result of more mobility, import possibilities and other potential sources of income. No less contradictory—but just the other way round—are the effects of Structural Adjustment and liberalisation. They tend to strengthen the potential for increasing self-sufficiency but they also increase the vulnerability of those who have to depend on purchasing food using cash derived from income.

5 Nutritional deficits, risks and food security strategies of rural households—insights obtained from micro-analysis

Stemming from the fact that macro-analysis has left many questions concerning food security unanswered, nutritional researchers have begun, over the last few years, to concentrate more on micro-analytical case studies.[1] These analyses usually pose two central questions: which groups of people in which regions are constrained or endangered by which kinds of threats when attempting to secure their nutritional needs (vulnerability analysis)? Which strategies do people employ to avoid these dangers, to limit their negative effects, or when they do appear, to deal with them (coping strategy analysis)? Both questions are closely interrelated; the

[1] Cf. especially the anthologies published by H.G. Bohle et al. (1991, 1993a and 1993b) concerning geographical research on hunger crises, as well as the work of A. Haas (1995) and B. Lohnert (1995).

fewer the avoidance and coping strategies individuals and groups have at their disposal, the greater the danger and vice versa. These two aspects should therefore be looked at in context. The presentation is based on selected examples, which appear to the author to be typical for the range of situations encountered in rural regions south of the Sahara. The examples have been subdivided—in accordance with the nutrition system model described above—into the following categories: food production, the use and storage of food, the selling of food and food distribution.

5.1 Production

The type of production system has an all-important influence on the food security situation of small-scale farming households in Africa. Generally speaking the rule is: the greater the specialisation, the higher the risk. This is especially true with the specialisation of cereals using rain-fed systems, and where the variety grown is not suited to local conditions. There are abundant examples in the literature which illustrate how African farmers attempt to avoid the risks associated with specialisation. The Kaonde, for instance, of north western Zambia, who primarily grow sorghum as their main food crop would also plant manioc, considered a less valuable foodstuff, in order to bridge the gap in the hunger season before the sorghum harvest, and in the event of a bad sorghum harvest they have something to fall back on in times of crisis. For the neighbouring Luvale and Lunda who favour manioc as their staple, the fact that they also cultivate maize, primarily for selling, proved to be their salvation when, in the middle of the 1980s their manioc fields were almost totally destroyed by a certain pest. Krings (1991: 73) reports on how the Senoufo of Mali grow maize in addition to rice and millet because the latter two can be harvested earlier, thus serving also to bridge the gap in the proverbial season of hunger. In northern Cameroon amongst the Massa it is common to grow different varieties of sorghum which can be consumed, should the need arise, even before it is properly ripe (de Garine 1991: 85). A survey of regions affected by drought in Kenya showed that those households who were led into swapping their relatively drought resistant crops, millet and sorghum, for the higher yielding maize, were hit much harder by the 1984 drought than the farmers who continued to grow at least some millet and sorghum (Downing 1991: 48). The same study shows that the majority of farming households managed to survive the food crisis of 1984 because they were able to buy food. Cash crops such as coffee and tea, which were not exposed to the same climatic risks as the staple foods, proved to be a real boon by lessening the risk (ibid.: 52). Mortimore (1991: 15) illustrates with examples from the drought affected regions of northern Nigeria, how it was possible not only through the diversification of crops but also by using a clever system of different methods of adaptation for timing and spacing (e.g. the planting date, plant spacing and the type and time of fertilisation) to respond to the periods of drought in such a way so as to limit the amount of damage.

Farmers living in the drought threatened regions of Africa are familiar—and a generalisation is permissible here—with the risks of drought and have developed techniques for keeping the risk down to a minimum. Effective and successful strategies can be subsumed under the heading: Diversification. But not, however, under the heading: "Preservation of the traditional subsistence farming system". Making use if necessary of the possibility to buy food with the proceeds from cash crops, can be just as effective at lessening the risks as continuing to plant appropriate local drought resistant food crops. It all depends on getting the location-specific combination between traditional and modern varieties and methods right. A combination of subsistence- and market-oriented approaches have proved in many instances to be less risky than a one-sided concentration on either the own production of food or alternatively market products. Besides diversification, many small-scale farming production units are attempting to achieve a certain amount of accumulation of the means of production (land, seeds and livestock, etc.). This is in order to avoid having to sell those essential assets vital for reproduction, but instead to make use of productive reserves that can be mobilised to compensate for the losses that may be incurred. The ability, or not, to avail oneself of this option represents an all-important criterion for social differentiation in African villages. Thus, the borderline between poor and not poor, in the respective local context, can be drawn between the social class faced with insecurity and the class faced with security.

5.2 Use and storage

The use and storage of food are closely interconnected in a situation of partial integration within the market. In the cases where there are well-established and secure systems for storing food reserves, it is but a logical step, to build up stocks of food to cover ones own needs rather than being open to the risks emanating from the market. Conversely, it is the case that where market conditions are stable and advantageous to the producers (for example where one is able to buy subsidised flour the whole year round, at fixed, stable and cheap prices set by the state), systems for building up foodstocks are not frequently embarked upon.

Even in farming households, where sufficient food is produced to take care of the needs of all the family members for the whole year, it is not that usual any more to store the total amount which would be required to meet the family's own consumption. There are many reasons for this. Manioc farmers, for instance, use the ground for storage, only digging out the roots when they need them to prepare food. Storing food as a reserve never came to be developed in this system of production. When the farming households in the north western province of Zambia proceeded to supplement their food with maize meal, they did not have the technical know-how necessary for the storage of cereals and thus tended to sell their maize first and then if the need arose, to subsequently by maize meal. This situation continued to be advantageous for food security, so long as maize remained a government subsidised commodity available more cheaply on the market than could have been produced given the costs of storage and processing. Today, after the advent of liberalisation, the absence of a viable system for food reserve stores has revealed itself to be a factor that adds to food insecurity. The maize price, before the harvest, can be twice as high in certain regions than after the harvest. An additional reason for the inadequate maintenance of reserve stores is that the losses incurred during storage are high, estimated to be about 20% in most regions. The private enterprise trading system—where it functions, that is to say where there is sufficient competition—is sometimes in a position to undertake food storage more economically than the producers themselves can. In addition, there are various social and economic pressures forcing the farmers to sell immediately after the harvest. Consequently, since farmers have started producing for the market, it has become customary to view the period after marketing as the time for increased spending, for settling outstanding debts, for celebrating, for honouring one's social commitments and for investing (for example buying cattle). The social pressures urging one on to such expenditure tend to be quite strong. De Garine (1991: 86) gives a vivid description of an example of this in his analysis of a starvation crisis in northern Cameroon. The Massa and the Mussey who place a high premium on food self-sufficiency in order not to be dependent on the exploitative middlemen, usually, however, do not succeed in this, because of the social pressure to bestow presents, organise celebrations, purchase cattle for bridal price downpayments and last but not least to spend for purposes of prestige to secure their social status. The pressure is at times so strong that they have no option but to sell their stores of reserve food at dumping prices. All these investments are necessary to secure one's status within the community. This is especially relevant when it comes to starting a family and thus to securing biological reproduction. As the example shows, it is, however, of very little help as a means of avoiding a food crisis. If, as a result of drought, all the people have had a bad harvest and the social net does not work, then everyone is forced to fend for him- or herself.

The examples show: reserve food stores, as one of the most important means of avoiding a food crisis, are not always that easy to realise, given the social and economic conditions under which small-scale farmers have to survive and work. The results of a survey from Ghana would seem to reflect the reality in many rural regions of sub-Saharan Africa, when it states that two thirds of the food needs of poorer small-scale farming households are covered directly by own production and one third is sold and subsequently re-bought on the market.

5.3 Securing food needs via the market

As the previous examples from the areas of farm production and reserve food storage have already implied, becoming involved in production for the market economy can reduce risks in that dependence on the success of one main crop is lessened. But, there can also be an increase in risks, in that market involvement can entice or even force people to relegate the storing of food reserves to second place behind the demands stemming from other needs and necessities. A few examples may serve to make clear that not only the opportunities but also the dangers that lie in obtaining one's food via the market are not simply hypothetical, but are very much part of the reality in rural Africa.

All the studies concerning crises of starvation prove one thing: mobility is the most important strategy when it comes to dealing with a crisis situation. It could always be seen wherever a crisis threatened to develop or actually did occur. Mobility can mean taking advantage of trans-regional networks in order to send family members (e.g. children) to relatives living in less affected areas. Mobility also means, however, searching for alternative sources of income so as to be in a position to buy food in other places which have not been hit by exorbitant price rises caused by scarcity. The migration south out of the Sahel which can be observed during periods of drought have a long tradition (Haas/Lohnert 1994). In Kenya during the drought of 1984/85, non-agricultural sources of income proved to be invaluable. De Garine (1991: 89) in his case study of the famine in Cameroon in 1984/85, quotes an old man at the height of the crisis as saying: "You call this a famine? Nowadays all you have is a bunch of weaklings! Today you can simply go off to some other place or go to the city. In the olden days we had to starve in this place, or were killed or taken as slaves if we dared to leave our own area" (translated by the author).

The same study highlights the risks of integration into the market economy: The market for cereals was controlled as a monopoly by a few local traders. They worsened the famine by buying and hoarding food at a time when shortages were already predictable, only to sell it again at the height of the crisis at unbearably high prices. Whereas in normal times a goat was bartered for 150 kg of sorghum, in 1985 the going rate for the same goat was only 4 kg (ibid.: 87). Similar changes in the scale of prices were noted in other regions affected by drought. In remote rural areas, if markets are allowed to determine prices without any regulation this can easily, in times of short supply, result in a hunger catastrophe, triggered by speculation on the part of local monopolistic traders. The example of Kenya points to a possible solution: the partial integration of rural households into the market economy led to a reduction in the vulnerability to crisis, simply because the Kenyan government imported food which was put on the market in time, thus counteracting any speculative hoarding by the traders—food continued to remain available at normal prices on the local markets.

Even though the studies on the food crises cited above clearly illustrate how the search for sources of cash outside the region as well as outside agriculture has come to represent an important option in coping with crisis, one is hardly able to find representative data on how often such searches were crowned with success or met with failure. Based on studies conducted in the 1970s, Hugo (1991: 138) was able to claim: "many case studies have shown that mobility has helped to prevent many deaths through starvation in recent famines in Africa and South Asia." In times of crisis in the modern urban sectors of the economy and the general loss of jobs occurring within the framework of Structural Adjustment Programmes, in times when the city dwellers of certain countries are trying their luck again in the countryside, in such times, the employment opportunities of people forced by starvation to migrate are, however, also very limited. The one "advantage" that they have over the older more established workers on the casual labour job market is that they are willing to work for less. Hugo (ibid.: 136) comes to the conclusion that people who have become hunger migrants have a harder time finding their feet on arrival at their destination than do other migrants, because they are less-well prepared for the situation that awaits them and less willing to integrate.

The survey results outlined above would seem to indicate that the partial integration of small-scale farming population groups into the market economy—to the extent that this is successful—will increase the range of opportunities to gain access to food. However, the ability to make use of these opportunities are tied up with certain pre-conditions which cannot, at present, be fulfilled by many African countries. Sources of income outside the sphere of agriculture or outside the region have to be available, and policies relating to the agricultural market have to find ways and means of keeping prices below a certain level, even in times of scarcity. Thus for the large majority of African small-scale farmers as well as for the many households whose source of income stems from involvement in non-farming activities, subsistence farming will continue to represent the main prop in their food security strategy.

5.4 The distribution of food within communities

There are and were in all farming societies in Africa systems of social security aimed at reducing the food risks of the individual and at providing a net for those age groups which are not able to take care of themselves. Local communities had devised different ways of looking after the old and frail. In some societies care for the aged was provided for by an intra-familial arrangement across the various generations, in others, communal farming land would be cultivated by young unmarried men, thus providing for those who were no longer able to participate actively in production, or alternatively there would be a form of community service involving the young men cultivating the fields of those no more in a position to do so themselves. These systems were good at reducing the food risks of "social cases" within communities; where they did not work so well was against risks which affected the community as a whole.

The literature contains numerous examples of how and why the viability of these systems of redistribution is on the decline: a high degree of mobility tends to cause the dissolution of village communities. In many African villages people do not live any longer in units of the extended family, presided over by a recognised normative authority. Vacillating between village subsistence production, on the one hand, and the world of commodity production on the other, has produced a kind of value pluralism in which there is no clear and unambiguous social orientation any more. The literature of course also contains plenty of examples of how, even over enormous distances and even in the urban world of commodity production, relationships based on solidarity are kept alive in order to reduce the risks in the daily struggle for survival. From experience we can say: Both of these tendencies can exist, both can exist at the same time, in the same place and even within the same family. While the maintenance of social networks and orientation towards a cash economy may contradict each other on certain occasions, they can as well supplement or reinforce each other over a wide range of situations.

Migration as a hunger crisis avoidance strategy is only likely to be viable when one has relatives living in other locations who can be of assistance with board and lodging until such time as they have helped one to secure a job. Civil servants can be seen transporting a sack or two of maize meal to their villages in order to help out when there has been a bad harvest, gladly taking advantage of their social connections in the village to garner a free chicken or two while they are about it. De Garine's accounts of the situation in northern Cameroon draw attention to the parallels between the maintenance, on one hand and concurrently the destruction on the other, of social norms. While ritual ceremonies, which serve to bond and maintain the community (such as extensive burial celebrations) are still practised, at the same time negative manifestations during a food crisis, like the pilfering of food (even amongst family members) can readily be observed.

By no means can all the traditional norms of distribution in African societies be seen as being positive for all the members of a community when it comes to the question of food security. An institutionalised discrimination of women and children as far as the access to foodstuffs of higher value are concerned, is a commonplace occurrence in rural Africa (but of course not only there). Certain food tabus against women and children would often merely seem to serve the purpose of reserving scarce but desirable foodstuffs (for example eggs) for the men. That is why it is not uncommon to come across high rates of malnourished children (approximately 30%) in areas where there is normally no problem with staple food shortages.

Given the cautious approach necessitated by a lack of representative and comparative analyses on the subject, it would however still be possible to tentatively draw the following conclusion: The maintenance and fostering of social networks continues to be an important strategy of nearly all the people in rural Africa for the prevention of starvation. The commitment to the social rules that govern the duties of helping each other on a mutual basis is however on the decline almost everywhere. The high percentage of undernourished children can not only be put down to the general situation of scarcity or to bad eating habits, but is a direct result of neglect when it comes to the children (UNICEF 1991: 12). Less well documented is the number of old and frail people in the villages who die of starvation, because they now fall through the social net. All the signs seem to point to an increase in the numbers of those whose food security needs can no more be adequately covered by the rules that govern the redistribution of food (cf. Elwert 1985: 79).

6 Conclusion

There is hardly any reliable information available regarding the nutritional situation in the rural regions of sub-Saharan Africa. All the indications and estimates point to the fact that over the last three decades there has been no general improvement in the situation. There has, however, been no dramatic deterioration or catastrophic intensification of the problem either, except in cases where wars or civil wars were being waged. Everywhere else food production was able to keep up, on the whole, with growing needs. It is not easy to say with any degree of certainty whether food security has actually increased or decreased (measured in terms of the numbers affected by food insecurity and the magnitude of the risks), as risk increasing tendencies and their converse, risk decreasing tendencies, run together. It is also necessary to distinguish between the previous situation in the largely state-controlled societies and current tendencies resulting from economic crises and the policies of liberalisation.

The following picture summarises the situation:

- High population growth rates, increasing settlement in the proximity of sites blessed with infrastructure and the growing expansion of arable land set aside for cash crop cultivation have led since the 1950s to an increase in population densities in relation to the land available for growing food. These population concentrations already exceed the capacity of traditional farming systems in many regions.
- The grain surplus of the industrialised countries in combination with the urban bias encoutered in agricultural pricing policy in Africa, in addition to an inappropriate focus in the sphere of agricultural research, have contributed to the fact that the necessary innovations and intensification measures, because of a lack of incentives, did not take place on the whole. As a further consequence, the "superfluous" inhabitants of the countryside prefered to look for a source of livelihood in the cities. As a result of a partial and one-sided promotion of high yielding cereal varieties, which are relatively susceptible to risks and which were cultivated in the form of a monoculture, the nutritional risk situation was exacerbated in many cases.
- Cash crop farming, migration and growing wage labour impede the ability, on the one hand, to achieve self-sufficiency in food at the level of the household, on the other, it leads to a diversification of the sources of income and to extending the social and physical radius of action. For the people living in rural areas the dependence on the purchase of additional food increased at the same time as did their opportunities to buy food. The dependence on one main crop has decreased. In addition, the availability of imported food in emergencies means a reduction in risks or catastrophes. There is now a greater range of coping strategies, one of which is still the traditional strategy of diversified production systems.
- The crises and the policies of liberalisation of the 1980s and 1990s tended to reduce the old nutritional risks and at the same time to create new ones. In the

field of food production the conditions for intensification and thus for an increase in the degree of self-sufficiency were partially improved. This effect can only be observed where peasant farmers or the agricultural market policies of the government succeed in ensuring that the price incentives actually reach the masses themselves who are involved in production. Usually it is only those commercial farmers who have the capacity to build up strategic reserves and gain access to means of transport, who are able to use the market mechanisms to their own advantage (cf. Tekülve 1997, Taube 1992); elsewhere it is only the middlemen who stand to make any profit. For those with a structural dependence on opportunities to buy additional food and who have come to rely on non-agricultural sources of income, the food security situation has taken a turn for the worse in two ways: The number of options and the real income level in the non-agricultural sectors have gone down while food prices have experienced an increase and are frequently unpredictable. The conditions influencing accessibility to food via the market have worsened.
- Social norms which worked in favour of food security no longer attract the same level of commitment. The number of individuals finding themselves outside a social network is on the increase.

This scenario (which of course generalises the diversity of the real conditions somewhat) suggests two conclusions:
— the number of people faced with insecurity will tend to increase,
— the risk of dying of starvation by the people faced with insecurity will tend to decrease.

What can be expected is a growing dependence of more and more people on the ability, when emergencies arise, of statal and international relief organisations to redistribute the food surpluses they obtained from the victors in the fight to secure access to good land as well as the means of production, to the losers in that same fight.

What are the approaches (cf. Rauch 1996) that can be used in policies for food security, approaches that are not limited to simply making emergency food redistribution more efficient?

- Agricultural research and extension should concentrate on supporting the search for possibilities for intensification which are appropriate and which also take into consideration the strategies for diversification devised by the farmers.
- Agricultural policies relating to the market economy should not attempt to merely substitute interventionary market policies by liberalisation, at the expense of the farming population. They should be directed at ensuring that the production of food remains worthwhile to all concerned, and that food remains affordable even in times of scarcity. This can be achieved with the aid of market information systems, price stabilising intervention mechanisms and measures to strengthen the market position of poorer farmers (e.g. enabling them to build up reserve stocks, to organise shared means of transport and to build up savings to bridge the periods when selling prices are low).

Agricultural policies, however, cannot by themselves bring about food security. To accomplish this you need to create mass purchasing power outside the sphere of agriculture by specifically promoting the establishment of labour intensive enterprises based on local resources, in such sectors which stand a chance of competing on a long-term basis on the local market with world market production.

References

Bohle, Hans-G. (1992): Hungerkrisen und Ernährungssicherung, in: Geographische Rundschau, 44, pp. 78-87.

Bohle, Hans-G. (1993a): The Geography of Vulnerable Food Systems, in: Bohle et al. 1993, S. 15-30.

Bohle, Hans-G. (Ed.) (1993b): Worlds of Pain and Hunger. Geographical Perspectives on Disaster Vulnerability and Food Security, Saarbrücken.

Bohle, Hans-G., Terry Cannon, Graeme Hugo and Fouad N. Ibrahim (eds.) (1991): Famine and Food Security in Africa and Asia. Indigenous Response and External Intervention to Avoid Hunger, Bayreuth.

Bohle, Hans-G., Thomas E. Downing, John O. Field and Fouad N. Ibrahim (eds.) (1993): Coping with Vulnerability and Criticality. Case Studies on Food-Insecure People and Places, Saarbrücken.

Brandt, Hartmut et al. (1986): Afrika in Bedrängnis. Entwicklungskrise und Neugestaltung der Entwicklungspolitik (Deutsche Welthungerhilfe), Bonn.

Chambers, Robert (1989): Vulnerability, Coping and Policy, in: IDS Bulletin, (20) 2, pp. 1-7.

Cissoko, S.-M. (1968): Famines et épidémies à Tombouctou et dans la boucle du Niger du XVIe au XVIIIe siècle, in: Bulletin de l'IFAN, série B, 30.3, pp. 806-821.

De Garine, Igor (1991): Seasonal Food Shortage, Famine, and Socio-Economic Change Among the Massa and Mussey of Northern Cameroon, in: Bohle et al. (1991), pp. 83-100.

Downing, Thomas E. (1991): African Household Food Security: What are the Limits of Available Coping Mechanisms in Response to Climatic and Economic Variations? in: Bohle et al. (1991), pp. 39-68.

Elwert, Georg (1985): Überlebensökonomien und Verflechtungsanalyse, in: Zeitschrift für Wirtschaftsgeographie, 29, pp. 83-97.

FAO (1994a): Production Yearbook 1994, Rome.

FAO (1994b): The State of Food and Agriculture 1994, Rome.

FAO/UNFPA/IIASA (1982): Potential Population Supporting Capacities of Lands in the Developing World, Rome.

Haas, Armin (1995): Hunger und Logistik. Der Beitrag des Transportwesens zur Ernährungssicherung im Niger-Binnendelta der Republik Mali, Saarbrücken.

Haas, Armin and Beate Lohnert (1994): Ernährungssicherung in Mali. Zehn Jahre nach der letzten großen Sahel-Dürre, in: Geographische Rundschau, 46, pp. 554-560.

Hugo, Graeme (1991): Changing Famine Coping Strategies under the Impact of Population Pressure and Urbanization: the Case of Population Mobility, in: Bohle et al. (1991), pp. 127-148.

Krings, Thomas (1991): Indigenous Agricultural Development and Strategies for Coping with Famine—the Case of Senoufo (Pomporo) in Souther Mali, in: Bohle et al. (1991), pp. 69-82.

Lohnert, Beate (1995): Überleben am Rande der Stadt. Ernährungspolitik, Getreidehandel und verwundbare Gruppen in Mali. Das Beispiel Mopti, Saarbrücken.

Meyns, Peter (1992): Hunger und Ernährung, in: D. Nohlen and F. Nuscheler (eds.): Handbuch der Dritten Welt 1, (1992), pp. 197-212.

Mortimore, Michael (1991): Five Faces of Famine. The Autonomous Sector in the Famine Process, in: Bohle et al. (1991), pp. 11-36.

Rauch, Theo (1996): Ländliche Regionalentwicklung im Spannungsfeld zwischen Weltmarkt, Staatsmacht und kleinbäuerlichen Strategien, Saarbrücken.

Sen, Amartya (1981): Poverty and Famines. An Essay on Entitlement and Deprivation, Oxford.

Taube, Günther (1992): Wirtschaftliche Stabilisierung und Strukturanpassung in Tansania. Die Auswirkungen des Economic Recovery Programme 1986-1989 im ländlichen Bereich. Fallstudie West-Usambara Berge, District Lushoto, Hamburg.

Tekülve, Maria (1997): Krise, Strukturanpassung und bäuerliche Strategien in Kabompo, Zambia, Berlin.

UNICEF (1991): Zur Situation der Kinder in der Welt 1991, Oxford.

United Nations (1993): World Economic Survey 1993. Current Trends and Policies in the World Economy, New York.

6

Economic Liberalization and Food Security in Sub-Saharan Africa

David E. Sahn

1 Introduction

For the past decade much of the policy debate in sub-Saharan Africa has been focused on the need for, and effectiveness of measures to promote, economic liberalization. Much of the contentiousness over that debate has been over the impact of economic reforms in agriculture and food markets on the food security and welfare of the poor. In this paper, I explore these issues, with particular attention accorded to the impact of reforms aimed at promoting agricultural exports, and those designed to liberalize domestic food markets. I attempt to generalize from the experiences of a large number of countries. Doing so, however, has its perils, as not only are the numbers of countries in Africa large, but their differences great. In fact, one could easily argue that the most obvious generalization about sub-Saharan Africa is its vastness, in geography, diversity in human and natural resources, as well as policy environment. Thus, the challenge of this paper is to synthesize generalizable findings from amongst this diversity, and draw some lessons that are applicable to a broad spectrum of countries.

2 Context

Africa remains largely agrarian. Consequently, agriculture is the most important sector. As a share of GDP, agriculture often accounts for over 40 percent of the total. It is usual that over two-thirds of Africa's labor force is engaged in the agricultural sector, with figures over 90 percent not being uncommon. And agricultural exports presently account for on average 18 percent of total exports, although these numbers vary widely. In many countries, particularly those without large mineral or oil exports, agricultural exports comprise more than half of the total (Table 1). It is also worth noting that household survey data reveal that the poor are integrally involved in the production and sale of tradable products, both export crops and food crops (see Table 2). These figures imply that the poor will benefit from the expansion of commercial agriculture. It is therefore clear that a healthy agriculture is critical to Africa's economic vitality in general, and the need to increase exports and improve the balance of trade in specific.

Table 1: Structural features of African countries

	Share of Agriculture in GDP (1994)	Share of Labor Employed in Agriculture (1980-1992)	Share of Food in Total Expenditures	Share of Exports in GDP (1993)	Share of Agriculture in Total Exports (1993)	Major Agriculture Export Crops
Angola	14	...	...	48	00	Coffee
Benin	41	...	...	22	18	Cotton
Botswana	05	52	...	61	04	Groundnuts
Burkina Faso	34	...	57 (1995)	11	28	Cotton
Burundi	44	97	...	09	72	Coffee
Cameroon	35	87	...	19	17	Coffee/Cocoa
Cape Verde	12 (1993)	29	...	15	02	
Central African Republic	42	95	60 (1993)	15	19	Coffee
Chad	45 (1993)	...	...	13	52	Cotton
Comoros	40	52	...	19	38	Vanilla
Congo	11	...	...	44	01	Coffee
Côte d'Ivoire	33	...	30 (1995)	34	43	Coffee/Cocoa
Djibouti	...	...	...	...	...	
Equatorial Guinea	44	73	...	39	08	Cocoa
Eritrea	...	...	...	34	01	
Ethiopia	43	...	...	09	30 (1992)	Coffee
Gabon	10	...	...	46	00	Cocoa
Gambia (The)	25	85	...	56	04	Groundnuts
Ghana	43	...	39 (1992)	20	28	Cocoa
Guinea	26	...	73 (1991)	22	06	Coffee
Guinea-Bissau	54	35	...	11	54	Cashew nuts
Kenya	24	...	54(1992/3)	39	33	Coffee
Lesotho	12	28	...	16	12	Wheat
Liberia	...	...	...	41 (1986)	05	Rubber
Madagascar	34	...	...	15	28	Coffee/Vanilla

Table 1 — Structural features of African countries continued …

	27	87	…	16	86	Tobacco
Mali	46	73	…	16	64	Cotton
Mauritania	28	…	…	46	09	
Mauritius	07	18	…	61	19	Sugarcane
Mozambique	33	…	…	21	10	Cashew nuts/Cotton
Namibia	14	…	…	58	09	
Niger	38 (1993)	…	32 (1993)	13	19	Groundnuts/Cotton
Nigeria	34	…	67 (1992)	36	03	Cocoa
Rwanda	44	97	…	07	42	Coffee
Sao Tome and Principe	…	52	…	31	25	Cocoa
Senegal	17	…	…	23	08	Groundnuts
Seychelles	04	12	…	61	01	
Sierra Leone	39	…	64 (1989/90)	22	05	Cocoa
Somalia	64 (1990)	…	…	10 (1990)	82 (1990)	Bananas
South Africa	06	…	48 (1993)	24	06	Maize
Sudan	28 (1991)	74	…	07 (1991)	96 (1991)	Cotton
Swaziland	11	…	…	88	32	Sugarcane
Tanzania	52	…	70 (1993)	18	39	Coffee/Cocoa
Togo	42	64	…	23	27	Coffee
Uganda	48	…	63 (1993)	07	76	Coffee
Zaire	31 (1989)	…	…	26 (1990)	06	Coffee/Palm kernel
Zambia	11	41	75 (1993)	35	02	Cotton
Zimbabwe	14 (1993)	67	…	34	32	Tobacco
Median	33	66	60	22	18	

Source: World Bank 1996.

Table 2: Agriculture income shares of poor rural households disaggregated into tradables and nontradables in selected countries

Country/Region	Share of Agricultural Income			
	Nontraded Food	Traded Food	Export Crops	Total
		(Percent)		
Ghana				
Forest	70	18	12	100
Savannah	73	26	1	100
Tanzania				
All	61	35	4	100
Côte d'Ivoire				
Forest	41	14	45	100
Savannah	46	32	45	100
Malawi				
South	24	53	23	100
Madagascar				
Coast	46	23	31	100
Plateau	69	30	1	100
South	58	36	6	100

Source: Dorosh and Sahn (1993).

Beyond the critical role that agriculture plays in terms of the performance of African economies, the typical household allocates most of its resources, both time and money, to achieving household food security. As shown in Table 1, among a sample of countries for which household survey data are available, a media value of 60 percent of the budget is allocated to the purchase of food and achieve food security. A large share of the food budget, however, is in the form of subsistence production. In fact, in countries such as Madagascar, Tanzania, Cote d'Ivoire and Ghana, over half of the food consumed is home-produced. This implies that poor consumers are to some extent insulated from the fluctuations and increases in market prices.

Despite these figures which underscore the importance of agriculture and the related food sector in African economies, both at the macro and household levels, food insecurity and poverty remain serious problems. In fact, living standards in Africa are generally worse than in other regions of the world, and likewise have been slower to improve than elsewhere. Estimates indicate that around half of

Table 3: Average daily calories per caput in Africa

	1965	1970	1975	1980	1985	1987	1988	1989	1990	1991
Angola	1897	2030	1905	2177	1956	1818	1740	1725	1710	1694
Benin	2009	2160	1999	2041	2193	2176	2167	2145	2123	2100
Botswana	2019	2115	2115	2152	2244	2251	2276	2269	2262	2255
Burkina Faso	2009	1998	1993	2029	2085	2225	2311	2061	1812	1562
Burundi	2048	2348	2398	2304	2340	2389	2436	2253	2070	1887
Cameroon	2079	2180	2323	2130	2040	2018	2007	2161	2315	2469
Cape Verde	1767	1879	2179	2567	2744	2690	2663	2635	2607	2580
Central African Republic	2135	2177	2254	2136	1927	1970	1992	1980	1968	1956
Chad	2399	2200	1817	1799	1740	1772	1832	1852	1872	1892
Comoros	2296	2217	2096	2074	2107	2110	2111	2113	2115	2116
Congo	2259	2153	2326	2472	2609	2637	2655	2512	2369	2225
Côte d'Ivoire	2360	2393	2310	2546	2563	2584	2603	2365	2128	1890
Djibouti	....	....	....	....	....	....	....	....	....	....
Equatorial Guinea	....	....	....	....	....	....	....	....	....	....
Eritrea	....	....	....	....	....	....	....	....	....	....
Ethiopia	1824	1714	1553	1806	1604	1728	1749	1658	1567	1476
Gabon	1881	1917	2050	2274	2508	2555	2587	2396	2207	2019
Gambia (The)	2194	2313	2108	2154	2353	2495	2599	2703	2807	2913
Ghana	1950	2218	2162	1795	1707	1811	1864	2209	2552	2895
Guinea	1923	1986	1885	1906	2128	2244	2302	2042	2336	2630
Guinea-Bissau	1910	2003	1972	1806	1763	1759	1745	2360	2418	2477
Kenya	2289	2249	2230	2225	2268	2071	2027	1973	1919	1865
Lesotho	2065	2013	2044	2400	2312	2299	2295	2307	2319	2331
Liberia	2154	2209	2242	2375	2376	2385	2390	2270	2152	2033
Madagascar	2462	2460	2523	2491	2379	2410	2400	2101	1805	1509

Table 3: Average daily calories per caput in Africa continued ...

	1965	1970	1975	1980	1985	1987	1988	1989	1990	1991
Malawi	2244	2360	2473	2406	2397	2258	2195	2009	1823	1637
Mali	1859	1860	1785	1720	233	2135	2196	2181	2168	2154
Mauritania	2064	2002	1815	2065	2278	2359	2398	2528	2658	2788
Mauritius	2272	2316	2618	2715	2721	2755	2767	2679	2592	2506
Mozambique	1979	2064	1901	1810	1573	1575	1558	1632	1705	1778
Namibia	....	....	....	....	....	....	....	....	....	....
Niger	1994	2102	1974	2363	2363	2457	2507	2340	2175	2011
Nigeria	2185	2140	2075	2254	2143	2169	2192	2039	1888	1737
Rwanda	1665	2029	1992	2007	1874	1786	1741	1786	1891	1875
Soa Tome and Principe	2186	2160	1900	2297	2365	2299	2261	2223	2184	2146
Senegal	2479	2360	2267	2401	2321	2373	2396	1989	1582	1176
Seychelles	1735	1901	2162	2306	2261	2210	2180	2150	2120	2089
Sierra Leone	1837	1960	1937	2034	1894	1820	1785	1806	1827	1848
Somalia	2167	2224	1973	2099	2008	2120	2136	1736	1336	1100
South Africa	....	....	....	....	....	....	....	....	....	....
Sudan	1938	2213	2090	2417	2178	2125	2102	1996	1890	1785
Swaziland	2100	2266	2482	2482	2511	2588	2610	2631	2652	2674
Tanzania	1832	1882	2134	2310	2246	2186	2172	2151	2144	2130
Togo	2378	2361	2083	2178	2225	2189	2172	2133	2094	2055
Uganda	2360	2240	2207	2151	2296	2444	2548	2013	1800	1750
Zaire	2187	2282	2288	2123	2163	2168	2173	2034	1896	1757
Zambia	2094	2129	2334	2227	2126	2108	2098	2026	1954	1881
Zimbabwe	2105	2194	2049	2137	2168	2139	2146	2232	2318	2404

Sources: African Development Bank 1992: Appendix A42, Table 40; FAO 1992: 21-25, Table 3; FAO 1991: 237-238, Table 106; World Bank 1989b: 276, Table 33; Salih 1995: 16-17, Table.

Africans live in poverty, living on less than one dollar per day (Chen, Datt and Ravallion 1993). Approximately 3 out of 4 of these poor people live in rural areas. Over half the adults in Africa are illiterate, and life expectancy is barely over 50 years. Malnutrition afflicts approximately 30 percent of pre-school age children (ACC/SCN 1992). And estimates are that 38 percent of the African population are food insecure (Braun et al. 1992).

While the severity of Africa's economic and social crisis is clear, so too is the realization that Africa's economic failures are an important cause, and manifestation, of the food security problems that are so pervasive. Stagnating production and consumption have characterized the African continent over the past 20 years, despite that agriculture remains the mainstay of African economies. This, coupled with a deteriorating balance of payments situation which limits opportunities for imports, is manifested in calorie figures that show little sign of growth over the years (Table 3). Labor productivity, particularly in agriculture has remained stagnant, falling behind other regions of the world (Singh and Tabatabai 1993). Technological innovation has also been slow, leaving Africa lagging behind other regions of the world. At the same time, land and resource constraints are increasingly important problems. Desertification, deforestation, land degradation, and polluted water are a direct consequence of growing population pressures and distorted incentive structures.

While these problems are generally recognized, the causes and solutions are far more contestable. Of particular interest is the question of whether the economic transition from state-dominated to free market economies is consistent with the objectives of improving food security, or instead, simply represents another in a long chain of events that imperils the poor and threatens the vulnerable. In order to address this issue more fully, I next turn to a discussion of the underpinning of Africa's food security problem.

3 Causes of Africa's food security crisis

Food insecurity in Africa has a long and complex history, with plenty of blame to apportion to various circumstances and events since the period dating back to colonialization. In the process of opening up external trade opportunities, particularly in agriculture, colonialism often destroyed the indigenous institutions and practices that helped promote food security as part of the larger effort to exploit human and natural resources. For example, colonial authorities in Malawi introduced the concept of individualized holdings parallel to traditional tenure. The appropriation of customary land led to land scarcity and the emergence of tenancy relationships which facilitated the colonialist's need for cheap labor. Likewise, in countries as diverse as Guinea, Tanzania and Mozambique, the exploitation of land resources by colonial powers forced peasants to become estate laborers. The labor markets thus developed not as expected according to the neo-classical theory of institutional change, where external trade and population growth induced the development of a labor market, but instead through coercion (Sahn and Sarris 1994).

Thus, colonialism weakened indigenous institutions that defined land tenure rules and mutual assistance relationships that helped protect the food security of the population. Crop choice was often taken away from the peasants, and the rules of exchange were redefined in a way that the state assumed control over economic relations. While such intervention was efficient from the point of view of the colonialist powers, it was often contrary to traditional systems. This contributed to increased food insecurity and increased inequality as the centralized authority needed to manage estates, administer marketing boards, and build transport infrastructure that not only neglected the underlying food security needs of the population, but contributed to the demise of traditional institutions that were instrumental in protecting the poor and vulnerable.

Beyond the historical role of the colonialist powers, the post-independence leaders in Africa have adopted policies that have also proved counterproductive to promoting a healthy agriculture and achieving both household and national food security. The socialist paradigm that was in good currency among Africa's new leaders at independence, first and foremost led to rejecting a growth strategy based on external trade. The state apparatus was conceived as a means of allocating resources and centralizing decision-making. Resources were in turn required for such an expansive role. This led to the distortionary policies that have contributed to extremely high rates of taxation on export crops in most of sub-Saharan Africa.

Governments have found taxation of agricultural exports an easy target. Not only are producers generally rural, and without a strong political voice, but trade taxes are generally easy to levy, as compared with general taxes on sales or income which demand a tax administration that is more capable and honest. A further explanation for the tendency to heavily tax cash crop production was the export pessimism that led to the erroneous belief that improved price incentives would not translate into substantially higher exports. Thus, in practice, the agricultural sector in general, and the export sector in particular were heavily taxed in the years after independence. In some countries, such as Ghana, taxes on cocoa accounted for nearly one quarter of all revenues in the 1975-1977 period, an amount similar to that levied on export crops in Madagascar. To achieve these high shares, the overall rates of taxation in much of SSA have been startling. This point is illustrated in Figure 1 which graphically presents the official producer price for major export crops, the world market price denominated at the official exchange rate, and the world price at the parallel exchange rate. The difference between the official and world price (the bottom two lines in the figures) is an approximation of explicit taxation, while the difference between the middle and top line is the implicit taxation, which operates primarily through the overvalued exchange rate. It is obvious that in the mid-1980s, prior to the initiation of economic reform programs, the farmers were receiving an extraordinarily low share of the world market price for their output. For example, in Guinea, prior to liberalization in 1985, the nominal

Figure 1: Trends in producer prices for major export crops in selected African countries

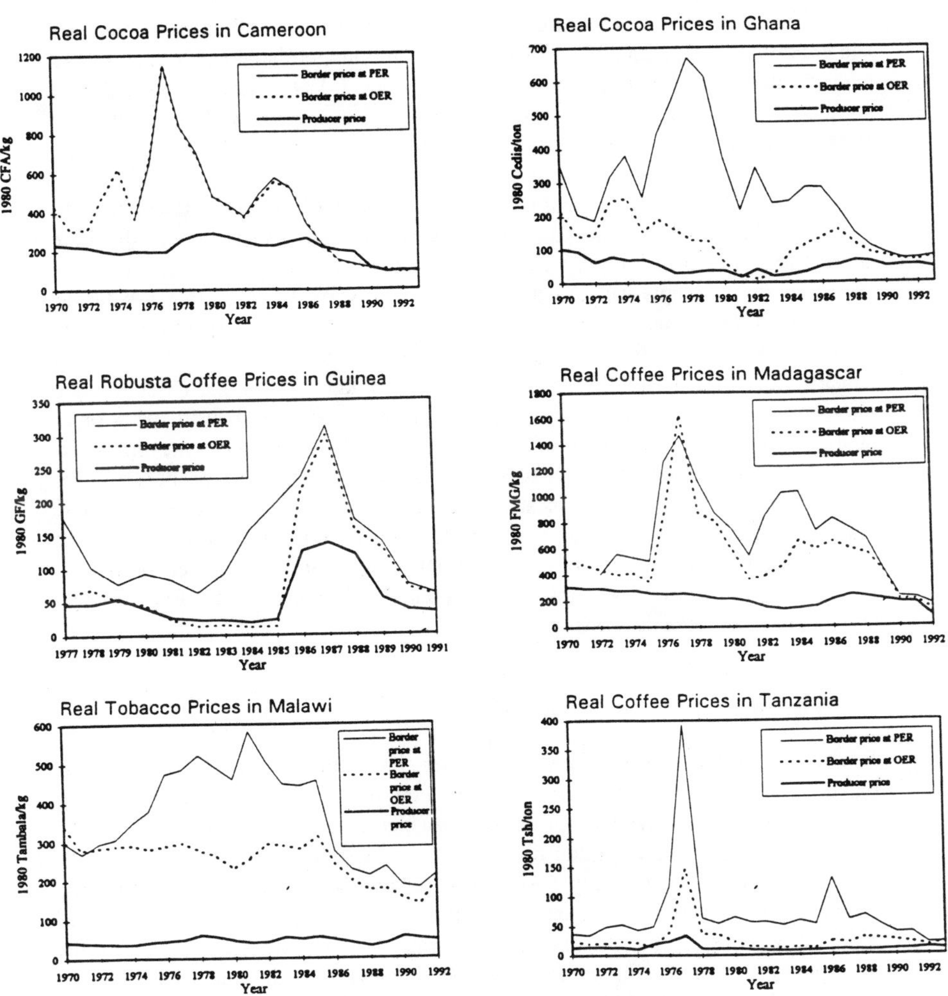

Sources: Cameroon: IMF 1994. Ghana: Alderman 1991; Sahn, Dorosh and Younger 1997. Guinea: Arulpragasam and Sahn 1996. Madagascar: Dorosh, Bernier and Sarris 1990; Dorosh and Bernier 1991. Malawi: Donovan 1993; Jaeger 1992; Sahn, Arulpragasam and Merid 1990. Tanzania: Sarris and van den Brink 1993

protection coefficients, evaluated at the parallel exchange rate, was 0.12 for coffee and 0.33 for palm kernels and groundnuts. And in Tanzania, domestic producer prices were 79 percent below border prices, based on the parallel exchange rate, between 1977 and 1988.

These distortionary measures certainly had an adverse effect on production and exports. For example, by 1979 cashew nut production in Mozambique was 42 percent lower than the pre-independence (1973) level. Even more dramatic are the numbers from Guinea: coffee exports in 1980-1985 averaged 580 MT, down from 10,000 MT, between 1960-65; palm kernel exports fell by two-thirds, and banana exports declined even more precipitously.

Pervasive state involvement in agriculture was not limited to the export crop sector. In the more extreme cases such as Guinea and Mozambique, the state endeavored to control virtually all food production. Land rights were re-defined, and strenuous attempts were made to collectivize agriculture in state run farms. Similarly in Tanzania, the government attacked virtually all aspects of private sector involvement in food marketing. Socialist villages were formed. The latter consisted of peasants forcibly removed form their land. While the cases of state intervention in Guinea and Mozambique were more extreme than in many other countries, the fact is that much of Africa was committed to direct intervention by the state in order to extract the surplus from food and export crops producers alike. Mechanisms for doing so, such as state marketing boards and overvalued exchange rates, were pervasive. As a result of these policy distortions, the food security of the poor suffered. In fact, it was not until a virtual collapse of the formal economy that the demand for reform was heard and precipitated action on the part of government and international organizations.

4 The impact of liberalization

Economic liberalization, as indicated earlier, has been the hallmark of policy-making in Africa over the previous decade. Few would disagree with the contention that the changes have been profound. Key elements of these reforms have been exchange rate devaluation, trade liberalization, including the reductions in tariffs, and fiscal reforms, particularly designed to reduce the excesses and improve the efficiency, of government expenditures. Reforms in agriculture, and the related food sector, have been at the heart of this strategy. Most important have been the attempts to (1) increase international competitiveness through reducing taxation of agricultural exports, and (2) reduce the interference of the state in the marketing of food products, including the widespread practice of subsidizing consumer prices. I next turn to a discussion of each of these areas of reform.

4.1 Export crops

Raising exports of agricultural products seems like a logical objective of economies where agriculture plays such a prominent role. However, policies aimed at reducing taxation, and thereby promoting export crops through increasing incentives for farmers to produce cash crops, have proved contentious. Such an outward-looking strategy has been the source of considerable criticism from those concerned with food security and related nutrition issues. Specifically, critics have charged that reducing both explicit taxation, as well as implicit taxation operating through the overvaluation of the domestic currency, implies food security risks for the poor in Africa. This viewpoint arises from a number of testable assumptions.

First, as articulated by Singh and Tabatabai (1993), there is a concern that expanding production for export will take place at the expense of production for domestic consumption. Second is the assertion that the types of policies that will increase export crop incentives, particularly exchange rate devaluation that reduces implicit taxation of export crops and raises the price of tradables relative to non-tradables, will increase income inequality. Third, there is the concern that even if increases in export crop production raises farm incomes, the implied change in the source of the income and to whom it accrues will have adverse effects on women and children. This would result from women's loss of control over income, and consequently, women having less of a voice in the choice of the consumption bundle. Of course, such an outcome is based on a number of assumptions, such as male preferences being less for purchasing nutritious food, as well as male preferences regarding the intra-household allocation of goods and services not favoring children and women to the extent that female preferences would (Elson 1991; Due and Gladwin 1991; Saito and Spurling 1992). Another related, and potentially adverse outcome of shifting cultivation to exports, from food crops, is that the burden of maintaining food production at the household level will continue to fall on women (Haddad 1990; Meena 1991), who have less access to land and productive inputs. As such, women face even greater demands on their scarcest resource, time.

Each of these propositions, if true, would represent a detraction from whatever benefits would otherwise accrue from increased export orientation in agriculture. However, while there is legitimate concern over these issues, and there are instances where the types of perils listed above are undoubtedly real, the preponderance of the evidence indicates that on balance, increasing export crop production does not represent a serious threat to the food security of the household, or individual members therein.

To amplify on the points above, first, with regard to the tradeoffs between food and export crop production, empirical evidence indicates that countries with trends of increasing food production are also those that have witnessed increases in export crops. While farmers do substitute between crops, and there are certainly short-term tradeoffs between food and export crops in response to relative price

Table 4: General equilibrium impacts of elimination of export taxes: model simulations

	Cameroon	Gambia	Madagascar	Niger	Tanzania
			Percentage Change[a]		
Agricultural export commodities	coffee, cocoa	groundnuts	tree crops	cowpeas, cattle	tree crops
Change in export tax / producer price	-38.03	-20.00	-72.00	-20.00	-26.46
Real GDP	1.09	0.18	0.79	0.06	0.48
Consumption / GDP	0.48	-0.05	0.78	0.31	0.14
Total investment / GDP	0.62	0.23	0.02	-0.25	0.33
Government recurrent expenditures / GDP	0.00	0.00	0.00	0.00	0.00
Government revenue / GDP	0.00	0.00	0.00	0.00	0.00
Exports / GDPb	1.36	0.22	0.85	0.51	0.60
Imports / GDPb	1.36	0.22	0.85	0.51	0.60
Change in foreign savings / GDPb	0.00	0.00	0.00	0.00	0.00
Real exchange rate	-12.73	-1.96	-10.30	-3.07	-8.17
Real wage rates					
Skilled labor	2.02	-0.36	2.64	1.23	-1.67
Semi-skilled labor	1.12	-1.28	2.30	—	—
Unskilled labor	10.01	5.46	4.65	2.19	5.96
Real incomes					
Direct tax	4.12	1.00	1.57	0.92	2.10
Urban non-poor	-8.20	-1.96	1.72	0.63	0.36
Urban poor	-1.27	-1.97	2.67	0.79	-0.06
Rural non-poor	2.87	2.15	0.98	0.33	0.63
Rural poor	2.24	2.25	2.16	0.81	-0.35
Small farm — export-oriented	—	—	4.93	0.64	—
Total	0.30	-0.07	1.78	0.60	0.14

Notes: [a] Percentage change relative to base simulation. [b] Exports and imports valued at the base simulation real exchange rate.
Sources: Model simulations; Dorosh and Sahn (1993); Sahn, Dorosh, and Younger (1996).

movements, it is also the case that factor use is generally not fixed. As such, when the economic incentive structure and non-price environment is favorable to one aspect of agriculture, it is usually the case for all of agriculture. Thus, one generally observes an overall increase in input use and resources devoted to agriculture in a favorable policy environment. This results in increases in both food and export crop production (Braun and Kennedy 1986; Weber et al. 1988).[1]

Second, with regard to the issue of the impact of increased export orientation on earnings of the food insecure, as well as on income distribution, the evidence is quite persuasive that policy measures that reduce taxation of export crops increase incomes. Thus the ability to buy food among the poor is enhanced. Likewise, lower taxes contribute to reduced income inequality. The results from one comparative study on the impact of reducing export crop taxes on incomes and income inequality is summarized in Table 4. The simulations are based on the use of computable general equilibrium models, and involve the elimination of agricultural export taxes while holding foreign savings fixed. Also of note in these simulations is that revenues are held constant; there are offsetting tax increases on households and firms to compensate for the loss of export crop revenues. Even in the short-term, not accounting for any dynamic growth effects, the elimination of export taxes raises exports. Real GDP also increases slightly in each country. Rural households, poor and non-poor, also generally benefit. The exception is the rural poor in Tanzania, in which case, owing to the fact that returns to capital and land from tree crops is quite trivial for these households, they do not benefit from the reduction in export crop taxes (Sahn, Dorosh and Younger 1997).

Beyond this study, others have reported similar findings. For example, Donovan (1996) points out that smallholders in Malawi were discriminated against consistently in the tobacco sector. They were penalized through policies that prevented them from producing and marketing tobacco (and other export crops) at remunerative world prices. In fact, smallholders were paid for their tobacco approximately one third of the price the commodity realized at auction. They were also not permitted to grow either flue-cured or the profitable burley tobacco, which accounted for most of the increase in tobacco production in Malawi in the 1980s. This was reserved for the estates. Donovan argues that this was the single most important area where the policy climate held back development of the smallholder sector, particularly since there was no other cash crop that could provide the capital for them to support crop diversification and use of modern inputs.

Beginning in the 1990/91 agricultural year, Malawi smallholders have been permitted to grow burley tobacco with consequent positive effects on the incomes of rural producers. Similarly in the case of agriculture, the response to the effects of devaluation and external competition has been an increase in both export and import-substituting commodities. The major beneficiaries of such changes have

1 This point is also made by Donovan (1996) in the case of Nigeria where he shows that the shift in relative prices in favor of the rural sector contributed to both an increase in the production of cash and food crops.

been those growing export commodities with relatively few imported inputs, many of whom are low income households (Muir-Leresche 1994).

Indeed, at first glance these findings of the beneficial income and equity effects of eliminating export crop taxes, both explicit, and implicit through exchange rate and related trade reforms, seem counterintuitive. However, recall the figures presented earlier that indicate that the poor are heavily engaged in the production of tradables, including export crops. Likewise, the poor in Africa remain heavily reliant on subsistence for their food. So even if real prices of some commodities rise concurrent with devaluation, the poor are largely insulated from these price increases. But another major reason that increased export orientation and devaluation improves food security and reduces inequality is that it eliminates the economic rents that are associated with the parallel market premium that accompanies heavy implicit taxation through overvalued exchange rates. The evidence from Africa, prior to the reform of exchange rate regimes, is that such rents were a significant share of GDP, and that they accrued primarily to the urban elite. The elimination of the parallel market premium and associated rents was thus a redistribution of the value of those rents to exporters, among which are the poor.

Finally, the concern that food insecurity will be compromised as a consequence of the loss of income control among women, and shifts in the source of income away from food production, is most difficult to validate, and clearly most challenging for economists (as well as other social scientists) to model. There are some examples, reported in the literature, of agriculture projects that encouraged cash crop production and eroded the overall earnings of women relative to men (Gladwin and McMillan 1989; Carney 1988). However, most of the research designed to examine the food security and nutritional implications of shifting incentives to export crop production have concluded that on balance, the benefits of higher incomes outweigh the potential deleterious consequences of shifts in income sources and control. This point is well illustrated in the case of Malawi where eliminating taxation of tobacco would have raised the income and food security of the household, and nutrition of the pre-school age children (Sahn, Van Frausum and Shively 1994). A similar finding was observed in the case of the elimination of taxes of coffee and cocoa in Cote d'Ivoire (Sahn 1992). In large measure this was attributable to the fact that households in the bottom 40 percent of the income distribution were extensively engaged in the production of these crops, and to the extent that shifts in income control occurred, there were not any adverse impacts observed.

Besides these two cases, a broader examination of the impact of cash crop production on nutrition and food security found no general pattern of adverse impact on food security and nutrition, although the positive effects from moving toward an export orientation were limited, as measured in terms of nutritional improvement (Braun and Kennedy 1986). This was explained by factors other than food consumption, such as the quality and availability of health care, being limiting factors in terms of nutritional improvement, along with the possibility of changes in how resources are allocated within the household dampening what would otherwise have been larger positive impacts.

4.2 Food crop liberalization

Even more than adopting outward looking agriculture policies, the prospect of liberalizing domestic food markets is often portrayed as a formidable threat to food security. This is particularly so for the urban population, as well as low income, rural households who are net food consumers. The primary concern is that state disengagement from food markets will first and foremost result in higher food prices as explicit subsidies are eliminated. The related contention is not only that food prices will rise concurrent with subsidy removal to levels more closely approximating world markets, but that predatory traders and inefficient markets will conspire to result in shortages and high prices to urban consumers, as well as unstable and low farm-gate prices.

The legitimacy of these concerns is a function of three factors. First is the extent to which governments in fact successfully intervened to maintain low and stable food prices for low income households prior to liberalization. Second is who paid the costs associated with such policies, e.g., the treasury or the farmers. Third is the response of markets and marketing agents to liberalization, and the nature of price movement subsequent to state disengagement from procurement, distribution and price administration. On all of these scores, most of the evidence would suggest that liberalization of food markets did not result in the feared adverse consequences for food security.

To amplify, it is initially important to emphasize that there was (and remains) a great degree of variability in terms of: (1) the level of state involvement in food markets, and (2) the extent to which the dual objectives of access to low and stable food prices among the vulnerable were achieved. In most countries in West Africa, including both CFA and non-CFA countries, interference in food markets has been relatively limited. This in part reflects the practical reality that a wide variety of roots, tubers and coarse grains dominate the food bundle, particularly for low-income households. These products, numerous in variety, are not amenable to state control owing to their production, marketing and processing characteristics. Thus, to a large extent, where food market intervention occurred in much of West Africa, it involved a vain attempt to raise the domestic production, as well as stabilize and influence the price, of increasingly important products such as rice.

This is well illustrated by Cameroon's efforts to influence the production and marketing of rice, despite its very small share of the national food basket, and the evidence that the country did not have a comparative advantage in rice production. Nevertheless the government made extensive capital intensive investments in irrigation projects in the hope of increasing rice production with the help of the World Bank and bilateral donors (World Bank 1989a). While the promotion of food security and foreign exchange savings were the purported objective, the inappropriate policies were, according to Van de Walle (1989), primarily motivated by rent-seeking behavior of bureaucrats, and misguided ideologies in terms of the striving for self-sufficiency in the name of improving food security.

While the generalization about limited involvement of the state in West Africa's food markets has some exceptions, such as in Guinea where rice is increasingly a staple food over which the state had attempted to exert significant influence, the region nevertheless contrasts markedly with East and much of Southern Africa. In these regions, extensive interference in food markets in the name of ensuring food security was the rule, not the exception.

The countries in East and Southern Africa are generally single staple economies where maize is the major agricultural product and represents a very large share of the consumption bundle, especially among the poor. The island nation of Madagascar, off the east coast of Africa, is also a single staple commodity, but in this case it is rice. It too interfered extensively in food markets. Maize and rice are best characterized as tradable products, although the combination of exchange rate and trade distortions often led to domestic prices diverging dramatically from those on world markets.

It is possible to distinguish between two categories of countries that were actively involved in the marketing of staple foodgrains (maize in most of east and southern Africa, and in the cases of Guinea and Madagascar, rice): those with and without explicit consumer subsidy programs. In the case of the former, the paramount issue from a food security perspective is who received the subsidized food. In other words, was the subsidy targeted to the poor? The answer to that question is a resounding no in all cases for which reliable data are available. This in part is a reflection of the fact that food subsidies in countries like Guinea, Madagascar and Mozambique served primarily (or only) persons living in urban areas. Given that the vast majority of poor are rural, coupled with the fact that the incidence of poverty is much higher in rural areas, regardless of how well targeted the urban subsidies were, they excluded the vast majority of the poor. This reality is coupled with the fact that in many instances the cost of urban based subsidies was borne not by the treasury (and as such by progressive taxation of income, consumption and so forth), but by the farmers themselves who received low prices from state marketing boards. Thus, not only did the rural poor not benefit from these subsidies, they often were actual losers as a result of state intervention.

Making matters worse are indications that urban food subsidies were not effective in terms of food security objectives. In the best case scenario, that of the food subsidy program in Antananarivo (Madagascar), the poor received a greater share of the subsidy as measured by shares of their income, but not so in terms of the total value or quantity of rice. In Guinea, where we only have information on the value of the subsidy received by functional groups of households, we also see that those presumably at the lower end of the income distribution, such as workers in the informal sector and the unemployed, received a smaller amount of rice than upper income households, such as civil servants (see Table 5). A similar story applies to the experiences in Ethiopia and Mozambique (Sahn and Desai 1995).

Table 5: Structural features of CFNPP study countries, early 1980s

Countries	Share of Agriculture in GDP	Share of Labor Employed in Agriculture	Share of Food in Private Consumption	Share of Exports in GDP	Share of Agriculture in Total Exports	Major Agricultural Export Crop(s)
	(1980-82 average)		(Percent)			
Cameroon	28	70	55	20	42	Coffee/Cocoa
The Gambia	41	84	58	30	24	Groundnuts
Ghana	57	65	64	25	64	Cocoa
Guinea	31[a]	81	51	31	3	Coffee
Madagascar	32	81	60	12	77	Coffee/Vanilla
Malawi	37	83	61	25	86	Tobacco
Mozambique	59	85	73	23	51	Cashew/Cotton
Niger	31	91	56	23	31	Groundnut/Cotton
Tanzania	53	80	68	20	63	Coffee/Cotton
Zaire	31	72	71	39	8	Coffee/Palm Kernel

Note: [a] 1985-86 average.

Source: World Bank 1993.

By implication, market liberalization which results in the elimination of poorly targeted subsidies will have limited adverse consequences for food security. In addition, however, there is evidence that in many cases, liberalization and related trade reforms contributed to moderating food prices without any deleterious consequences for the poor. This point is well illustrated in the case of Guinea. Results from a multi-market analysis reveals that reducing tariffs on low quality imported rice would have benefited the urban poor in relative and real terms far more than the state-run ration system. At the same time, there would have been little disincentive effects on producers. In fact, on balance, the rural poor, who also consumed a substantial amount of low quality imported rice, would have benefited from the increased availability of products that would result from the reduction in trade barriers (Arulpragasm and del Ninno 1996). A similar story applies to Mozambique, where the elimination of the ration system would have first saved the government large sums of money; the foregone revenues that were in fact accruing to parastatals and state-sanctioned traders. Those savings could have been used to import larger quantities of yellow maize, which if sold on the open market would have improved the food security of the poor. Since yellow maize is self-targeting to the low-income household (given its inferior qualities), the net effect of higher yellow maize imports would have been to substantially reduce poverty and increase calorie consumption (Dorosh, del Ninno, and Sahn 1995).

The story from other countries that did not have rationed food distribution programs, but nevertheless intervened extensively in food markets, likewise suggests that such efforts, on balance, did more harm than good in terms of the economy in general, and food security in specific. This is particularly well illustrated in the cases of Malawi, Tanzania and Zimbabwe. In the case of the former, there was a substantial subsidy to maize, which at times reached a value close to one percent of GDP, and over three percent of total government spending during the 1980s. However, the evidence indicates that the rural poor had only limited access to official prices. Instead they paid open market prices, not having access to the distribution outlets, or the cash requirements to purchase maize grain in the large quantities in which the product was packaged at government-run distribution sites (Arulpragasm and Sahn 1991).

The history of state involvement in Tanzania's food markets is one of far more extensive involvement, and far greater failure. Policies, such as nationalizing production, marketing and even retailing functions in the mid-1970s were the most extreme. Shortages and rationing ensued, not just of food, but consumer goods as the incentive for producers to work declined commensurate with the low prices offered by the state for their output (Bevan et al. 1989). The avoidance of the official marketing channels eventually led to the perverse situation where, in urban areas, official producer prices climbed above those in the parallel market. Government, determined to rectify this situation, turned to imports, an extremely expensive response. Ultimately the failure of the system to achieve food security objectives, despite unsustainable resource costs, contributed to the liberalizing of maize markets, albeit at a somewhat lethargic pace (Sarris and van den Brink 1993).

Indeed, Tanzania's experience with liberalization has not proved a panacea, as impediments to efficient and competitive markets remain, such as inadequate market infrastructure, and uncertainty in the private sector regarding the future actions of the state (Amani, van den Brink and Maro 1992). However, the bottom line seems to be well summarized by Donovan (1996), explaining that subsequent to the beginning of market reforms in 1983, maize marketing costs were reduced and the real price of food fell, with a consequential positive impact on food security. Likewise, other benefits to the economy, such as the near elimination of food imports, are noted.

Zimbabwe's efforts at state disengagement from maize markets was also relatively recent. Beginning in 1992, the government began lifting controls on marketed maize. This included abolishing the controls on the movement of maize that were designed to ensure regional food security, and eliminating restrictions that had prevented private traders and small-scale millers from being actively engaged, particularly in urban areas. After these measures were instituted, the government moved to eliminate costly subsidies on refined maize meal. Given the importance of the maize meal in their consumption bundle, this gave rise to concerns over food security of the poor. The overall effect of such changes, however, was that the potential welfare loss of the food subsidy removal was mitigated by complementary market reforms that made new lower cost products available, and which lowered marketing and processing costs (Jayne et al. 1995). Within a span of two years of the liberalization of markets, the proportion of staple maize meal procured through informal distribution channels soared from 8% to 50%. The market reforms also allowed urban households to acquire maize meal at 60% to 70% of the cost of maize meal manufactured by large-scale millers prior to reform; this presumably was achieved by relying on the small scale hammer mills in Harare, which increased from 57 to 85 in the 18 months between 1992 and 1994 (Jayne and Jones 1996).[2] The cost saving to consumers equaled 7% to 13% of average household income among the lowest income quintile in the capital city (Rubey 1995). Furthermore, it is claimed that the reforms have led to between 10% and 25% higher cash incomes for at least 200,000 low-income rural consumers and a reduction in government treasury losses equal to 2% of the country's GDP.[3] On the macroeconomic front, Muir-Leresche (1994) also observed that the liberalization of the trade regime has increased imports in general. Of note is that the food security of low-income workers has benefited from the increased availability of motor transport, fish, and cheap consumer goods.

---

2 A similar story of market liberalization spurring the growth of the small scale milling industry, based on hammer mill technology and production of a whole meal at much lower production cost than large mills is reported for Mozambique and Zambia. Also noted is that market liberalization in Mozambique stimulated the growth of informal food marketing activities (Jayne et al. 1995).

3 See Food Access Synthesis Studies Fact Sheet (1997).

5 Discussion

From the experiences recounted above we can conclude that there is little evidence that market liberalization of both the export crop sector and domestic food markets has had deleterious consequences for household or national food security. Rent seeking, weak institutions, lack of analytical capability, and so forth, were characteristic of the over-extended and predatory state. Its disengagement has thus had positive effects. This in large measure is a consequence of the fact that liberalization has eliminated the ineffectual intervention of the state in the food and agricultural sector, and thus lowered transaction costs, eliminated parallel markets and reduced exploitation of peasants.

While there is little historical evidence in support of the state exerting a positive role in agriculture and food markets, this does not mean that unfettered free markets are the answer to Africa's food security ills. More caution is especially warranted since the supply side response to liberalization has, for the most part, been modest. Thus, we should not confuse the fact that the actions of African states during the pre-reform period may have been misguided, and at times predatory, with the notion that government action is irrelevant to, or will necessarily adversely affect food security, and related growth objectives in agriculture. In other words, the arguments in favor of state disengagement are not to say that a different, and more appropriate role for government is not required to promote household food security.

Examples of appropriate roles for the state in improving food security, beyond the process of liberalization, are first and foremost, ensuring macroeconomic stability and a macro policy set, such as an outward looking trade regime and a market-determined exchange rate, which will foster a healthy agriculture and promote equity. Furthermore, there remains a potential role for the state in the area of targeted food security interventions. Cooperation with non-governmental institutions is particularly commended in this arena, especially in light of the past failures of the state. The evidence is also compelling that a prerequisite for success of such interventions is active community participation in their design and implementation, something in which non-governmental organizations have a comparative advantage.

Likewise, enhancing other public inputs into agriculture, such as investing in agricultural research, improving information systems and fostering more relevant and widespread agricultural extension are required. It is also the case that greater efforts need to be made to address problems such as decreasing soil fertility and related environment degradation. Here too, government plays a potentially powerful role, even if it is limited to helping develop appropriate regulatory mechanisms and incentive structures that ensure the protection of natural resources. Of course, such measures require institutional capacity that has been absent in much of Africa. So too, financial resources are required. Some of the latter may be culled from otherwise inappropriate support for inefficient agricultural parastatals. However, it is also noteworthy that despite agriculture's prominence in terms of generating incomes, providing employment, and earning foreign exchange, government spending in agriculture has, at best, stagnated over the previous decade. And in certain categories, such as agricultural research, the level of domestic support is on the decline (Pardey, Roseboom, and Beintema 1995). Thus, at a time when debilitated market infrastructure and related constraints limit growth and responsiveness of African agriculture to improve price signals, there is a need to consider how to mobilize public resources. In turn, these resources must be focused on increasing factor productivity, lowering transaction costs, and in general, raising forward and backward linkages, including outside agriculture.

Regarding this last point, while the emphasis of this paper has been on the food security implications of market liberalization in the agricultural sector, it is also important to recognize the important linkages between sectors and markets that will not only affect the performance of agriculture, but the achievement of food security objectives as well. For instance, the imperfections in capital markets prevent many small farmers from gaining access to capital that is required to benefit in a meaningful well from improved incentive structures, technology and agricultural projects. Likewise, complex problems with land markets often limit both the responsiveness to economic signals, but more seriously, result in an unequal distribution of benefits associated with economic reforms. Thus, tackling Africa's food security problems demands a multi-faceted approach, starting from understanding the micro-foundations of household and intra-household decision-making, to an appreciation of the role of macroeconomic policies in economic performance and income distribution. The need to further strengthen analytical capacity in Africa, including improving the availability of data, is therefore a high priority. Most important, however, is a renewed commitment to promoting food security in countries that have gone through the economic transition to a market economy, which while a first step, needs to be complemented by a strategy that focuses on ensuring food security and protects Africa's human resources.

References

Administrative Committee on Coordination/Subcommittee on Nutrition (ACC/SCN of the United Nations) (1992): Second Report on the World Nutrition Situation. V.I Global and Regional Results, Geneva, Switzerland.

African Development Bank (1992): African Development Report, Abidjan.

Amani, H.K.R., Rogier van der Brink, and W.E. Maro (1992): Tolerating the private sector: grain trade in Tanzania after adjustment, Working Paper No. 32, Ithaca, NY: Cornell Food and Nutrition Policy Program.

Arulpragasam, Jehan, and Carlo del Ninno (1996): Do cheap imports harm the poor? Rural-urban tradeoffs in Guinea, in: David E. Sahn (ed.): Economic reform and the poor in Africa, Ithaca, NY: Cornell University Press, pp. 53-95.

Arulpragasam, Jehan, and David E. Sahn (1991): The Stagnation of Smallholder Agriculture in Malawi: A Decade of Structural Adjustment, in: Food Policy, 16(3), pp. 219-234.

Bevan, David, Paul Collier, Jan Willen Gunning, Peter Horsnell, and A. Bigsten (1989): Peasants and governments: An economic analysis, Oxford: Clarendon Press.

Braun, Joachim von, Howarth Bouis, Shubh Kumar, Rajul Pandya-Lorch (1992): Improving Food Security of the Poor: Concept, Policy, and Programs, Washington, DC: International Food Policy Research Institute.

Braun, Joachim von, and E. Kennedy (1986): Commercialization of subsistence agriculture: Income and nutritional effects in developing countries, Washington, DC: International Food Policy Research Institute.

Carney, Judith A. (1988): Struggles over land and crops in an irrigated rice scheme: The Gambia, in: Jean Davison (ed.): Agriculture, women and land: The African experience, Boulder: Westview Press.

Chen, Shaohua, Gaurav Datt, and Martin Ravallion (1993): Is poverty increasing in the developing world? Poverty and Human Resources Division, Policy Research Department, Washington, DC: World Bank.

Donovan, W. Graeme (1996): Agricultural and Economic Reform in Sub-Saharan Africa, Africa Technical Department Working Paper No. 18, Washington, DC: World Bank.

Dorosh, Paul and David E. Sahn (1993): A General Equilibrium Analysis of the Effect of Macroeconomic Adjustment on Poverty in Africa, Cornell Food and Nutrition Policy Program Working Paper 39, Ithaca, N.Y.: Cornell University.

Dorosh, Paul, Carlo del Ninno, and David E. Sahn (1995): Poverty alleviation in Mozambique: a multi-market analysis of the role of food aid, in: Agricultural Economics, p. 1156.

Due, Jean M., and Christina Gladwin (1991): Impacts of structural adjustment programs on African women farmers and female-headed households, in: American Journal of Agricultural Economics. 73(5), pp. 1431–1439.

Elson, Diane (1991): Gender and adjustment in the 1990's: An update on evidence and strategies, Presented at the Inter-Regional Meeting on Economic Distress: Structural Adjustment and Women, Lancaster House, London, June 13–14 1991.

Food Access Synthesis Studies Fact Sheet (1997), East Lansing, MI: Department of Agricultural Economics, Michigan State University.

Food and Agricultural Organization of the United Nations (FAO) (1992): Production Yearbook, Vol. 46, Rome.

Food and Agricultural Organization of the United Nations (FAO) (1991): Production Yearbook, Vol. 45, Rome.

Gladwin, C., and D. McMillan (1989): Is a turnaround in Africa possible without helping African women to farm? in: Economic Development and Cultural Change, 37(2), pp. 345–364.

Haddad, Lawrence (1990): Gender and economic adjustment in Ghana and Côte d'Ivoire: Executive summary, Washington, DC: International Food Policy Research Institute.

Jayne, T.S. and Stephen Jones (1996): Food Marketing and Pricing Policy in Eastern and Southern Africa: Lesson from Increasing Agricultural Productivity and Access to Food, MSU International Development Paper No. 56.

Jayne, T.S., L. Rubey, D. Tschirley, M. Mukumbu, M. Chisvo, A. Santos, M. Weber, and P. Diskin (1995): Effects of Market Reform on Access to Food on Low Income Households: Evidence from Four Countries in Eastern and Southern Africa, MSU International

Development Working Paper No. 19. Department of Agricultural Economics, Michigan State University.

Meena, Ruth (1991): The Impact of Structural Adjustment Programs on Rural Women in Tanzania, in: C. Gladwin (ed.): Structural Adjustment and African Women Farmers, Gainesville: University of Florida Press.

Muir-Leresche, K. (1994): Market liberalization, equity, and efficiency in Zimbabwe's agricultural sector, in: Agricultural competitiveness, market forces, and policy choice, Proceedings of the 22nd International Conference of Agricultural Economists, August 22-29, Harare, Zimbabwe.

Pardey, Philip G., Johannes Roseboom, and Nienke M. Beintema (1995): Investments in African agricultural research, Environment and Production Technology Division Discussion Paper No. 14, The Hague, The Netherlands, and Washington, DC: International Service for National Agricultural Research and International Food Policy Research Institute (Photocopy).

Rubey, Lawrence (1995): Maize Market Reforms in Zimbabwe: Linkages between Consumer Preferences, Small Scale Enterprise Development and Alternative Marketing Channels, Ph.D. Dissertation, East Lansing, MI: Department of Agricultural Economics, Michigan State University.

Sahn, David E. (1992): Public expenditure in sub-Saharan Africa during a period of economic reforms, in: World Development, 20(5), pp. 673–693.

Sahn, David E., and Jaikishan Desai (1995): The emergence of parallel markets in a transition economy: The case of Mozambique, in: Food Policy, 20(2), pp. 83–98.

Sahn, David E., Paul A. Dorosh, and Stephen D. Younger (1996): Exchange Rate, Fiscal and Agricultural Policies in Africa: Does Adjustment Hurt the Poor? in: World Development, 26(4), pp. 719-747.

Sahn, David E., Paul A. Dorosh, and Stephen D. Younger (1997): Structural Adjustment Reconsidered: Economic Policy and Poverty in Africa, Cambridge: Cambridge University Press.

Sahn, David E., Yves van Frausum, and Gerald Shively (1994): Modeling the nutritional and distributional effects of taxing export crops, in: Economic Development and Cultural Change, 42(4), pp. 773–793.

Sahn, David E. and Alexander Sarris (1994): The Evolution of States, Markets, and Civil Institutions in Rural Africa, in: The Journal of Modern African Studies, 32(2), pp. 279-303.

Saito, Katrine A., and Daphne Spurling (1992): Developing agricultural extension for women farmers, World Bank Discussion Paper No. 156, Washington, DC: The World Bank.

Salih, Siddig A. (1995): Food Security in Africa, World Development Studies 3, The United Nations University, World Institute for Development Economics Research.

Sarris, Alexander H. and Rogier van den Brink (1993): Economic Policy and Welfare during Crisis and Adjustment in Tanzania, New York: New York University Press.

Singh, Ajit, and Hamid Tabatabai (1993): Economic crisis and Third World agriculture, New York: Cambridge University Press.

Van de Walle, Nicolas (1989): Rice politics in Cameroon: State commitment, capability, and urban bias, in: The Journal of Modern African Studies, 27(4), pp. 579–599.

Weber, et al. (1988): Informing food security decisions in Africa: Empirical analysis and policy dialogue, Staff Paper 88-50, East Lansing: Michigan State University.

World Bank (1989): Cameroon agricultural sector report, Vols. 1–2, Washington, DC: World Bank.

World Bank (1989b): Sub-Saharan Africa: From Crisis to Sustainable Growth, Washington D.C.: World Bank

World Bank (1993): African Development Indicators, Washington, DC: World Bank.

World Bank (1996): Africa Development Indicators, Washington, DC: World Bank.

Part II

Empirical Studies: Cases and Multi-country Experience

7

Stress, Crisis and Catastrophe. Communication and Survival Strategies of Tuareg Nomads During a Famine

Gerd Spittler

1 Introduction

How do the people affected behave during a famine? Several theories, both complementary and contradictory, attempt to explain their behaviour. We can distinguish three such theories: 1. the disaster or victim theory; 2. the survival theory; 3. the crisis theory.

1.1 The disaster or victim theory

Pictures of victims—skeletons of camels on dried-out land, people with no possessions fleeing the drought, drought-driven beggars in the cities, starving children, refugee camps where food is distributed—are most widely available through the media. According to popular opinion, those depicted are victims of a natural disaster. Experts however, are reluctant to accept this explanation without modifications. In their opinion, a drought needs not necessarily lead to water shortages, loss of crops, loss of cattle, and finally to hunger and death. Drought does not automatically result in famine, unless political, social and economic conditions favor one. From this point of view, it would be better to speak in terms of a social rather than a natural disaster. The reasons for famine have not been sought in natural events like drought or locusts, but in export-oriented colonial and postcolonial economies which destroy the subsistence basis of local markets.

The theory of socially and politically induced disasters, developed as a critique of the natural disaster theory, argues that it is not nature that is to blame but corrupt governments or neocolonial dependencies. Despite these conflicting views, both theories share a basic assumption: they portray the people affected as victims. In one case people are victims of natural events, in the other, of political maneuverings. Each represents victims as helpless, innocent and incompetent. The solution for both must be aid which comes from outside and from above: from international donors and national administrations, from foreign and local experts.

1.2 The survival theory

During the 1980's this victim and disaster paradigm came under more and more criticism and was eventually replaced by the theory of survival strategies. Here, people are no longer seen as victims waiting for aid but as actors whose survival depends foremost on their own activities. The titles of many publications already indicate this new perspective: "Strategies for Coping with Severe Food Deficits in Rural Africa" (Campbell 1990); "Survival Strategies of a Sahelian Society" (Chastanet 1992); "Coping with Uncertainty in Food Supply" (de Garine and Harrison 1988); "Combating Famine by Grain Storage in Western Sudan" (Ibrahim 1987a); "Survival Strategies of Sahelian Peasants" (Ibrahim 1987b); "Adapting to Drought" (Mortimore 1989); "Local Strategies for Coping with Hunger" (Richards 1990).

Key terms here are "coping", "survival strategies", "combat" and "adaptation". Nearly all publications since the eighties stress the variety of strategies applied by peasants and nomads in the Sahel in order to survive during a famine (for summaries see Campbell 1990; Shipton 1990):

- Peasants diversify their crops in order to reduce the risk of bad harvests caused by drought.
- Nomads lower their risk by diversifying livestock; keeping not only cattle and sheep, but drought-resistant camels and goats as well. They also add agriculture or trade to their pastoral activities.
- Peasants store grain for several years to have enough food in the event of a bad harvest.
- Nomads keep large herds, part of which can serve as a buffer in an emergency.
- Kinship as well as patron-client structures can be mobilized during a famine.
- The collection of wild seeds, fruit and leaves, compensates for grain shortages.
- Migration to less affected areas constitutes an essential survival strategy as well.

It is important to distinguish between short term and long term survival strategies. Survival in the former sense means finding food and food substitutes, in which a long term perspective is sacrificed for immediate needs. In the latter, heavy sacrifices are made in the present in order to safeguard the future. It is commonly believed amongst outsiders that in a famine immediate survival interests prevail over long term ones. Contrary to this opinion, we can often observe in the Sahel that even during severe famines, people will not sacrifice the future for the present. For example, de Waal (1989) describes how, in the 1984 famine in Darfur (Sudan), people did not spend all their money on food. Instead of selling their seed and cattle, they preferred to suffer hunger.

Although at first glance the survival theory appears to be in direct opposition to those based on victim and disaster paradigms, the two are actually combined by many writers who argue that in precolonial times, peasant and nomadic economies were well adapted to the climatic conditions of the Sahel. Due to the implementation of a variety of survival strategies, people were able to reduce the effects of famines, and in some cases to prevent them altogether. In colonial and postcolonial times, the structures on which these survival strategies were based were destroyed. Instead of active participants coping successfully with drought and famine, the peasants and nomads became victims of colonial and postcolonial economies.

This combination of the survival and victim theories is widespread and supported by most authors in the two volume collection, "Sécheresses et famines du Sahel" (edited by Jean Copans in 1975). In "Silent Violence" (1983), Michael Watts presents this argument forcefully and in great detail, making him the best-known exponent of the position in the anglophone world. He claims that there was a "moral economy" in Northern Nigeria during precolonial times which prevented famines, or at least reduced their disastrous effects. During the colonial era this moral economy was displaced by a market economy, resulting in more frequent and acute subsistence crises. Only then did droughts begin to lead to severe famine and disaster.

The position taken by Watts and supported by other authors seems doubtful to me for the following reasons. First, there is a great deal of evidence that even today peasants and herders are successfully applying locally-developed survival strategies which, although they may have changed since precolonial days, certainly have not been lost. The second objection seems to me even more striking, for, although it may be the case that a moral economy and other survival strategies did exist in Hausaland in precolonial times, it is quite doubtful whether they could be applied in practice. During the 19th century, the entire Sahel region was convulsed by war and slave raiding. It is therefore quite probable that under these conditions, food procurement was much more insecure then than in the 20th century.

To conclude, I would like to stress that survival theories have greatly improved our understanding of how people behave in droughts and famines, explaining the actions of peasants and nomads far better than victim theories do. However, there is one serious weakness to be found in survival theories: they postulate a rather mechanical connection between a "stress" situation and its corresponding strategies. Whereas the weakness of victim theories lies in their assumption that the people concerned are helpless, passive victims of a disaster, the flaw in survival theories lies in the opposite assumption: that people always react actively and rationally. In this approach, people have no doubts or fears; they always know how to behave in a crisis.

1.3 The crisis theory

The crisis theory, which I favour, starts from the assumption that a crisis is an open situation. In my opinion we should take the term "crisis" more seriously than is usually done. Compared to a situation of "stress," a crisis is more severe. Unfavorable and irregular climatic conditions in the Sahel produce constant stress. Nomads have adapted to these stress conditions by developing survival strategies which they routinely apply. However, a crisis constitutes a more severe threat which routine alone cannot resolve, as people have doubts and fears, and are not sure how to behave. A crisis constitutes an open situation in which the result is not known in advance, either by the social scientist or the people affected. During a crisis, the action taken depends on how people communicate with each other, and this communication is at least as important as the above-mentioned survival strategies.

If a crisis is managed successfully, it may be interpreted as having become a "stress" situation in which the usual survival strategies could be applied. If coping with the crisis fails, then it becomes a catastrophe, resulting in a breakdown of the social order.

After this short introduction to my theoretical frame of reference, I would like to proceed with a more detailed illustration by describing and analyzing the handling of a crisis by the Kel Ewey Tuareg in Niger, where I conducted research during the famine of 1984-85 (Spittler 1989; 1993).

2 The Kel Ewey Tuareg and the Drought of 1984-85

The Kel Ewey Tuareg have lived in the Aïr, a mountain range in south central Sahara in Niger, for hundreds of years. Annual rainfall is between 50 and 150 mm. Here, both a pastoral economy and irrigation-dependent gardening are possible. My investigation concentrates on the Kel Timia, whose lives represent the traditions and economic system of the Kel Ewey with singular clarity. This group (approximately 4000 people) lives in the centre of the Aïr in the vicinity of the Timia Oasis. Its economy consists of the following four mutually complementary elements:

- A triangular caravan trade between the Aïr, Bilma and Kano.
- Camel husbandry based on a transhumance of camels between the Aïr and Hausaland, which covers southern Niger and northern Nigeria.
- Goat husbandry in the Aïr, for which women are responsible.
- Horticulture based on irrigation in the Aïr valleys.

The supply of millet, their dietary staple, is circulated by the caravan trade based on a complicated triangular transaction. In October the Kel Timia travel 500 km eastwards through the desert to obtain salt and dates, either for cash or in exchange for millet or garden products. After their return to the Aïr they rest for several weeks before travelling south in December to Kano in Nigeria, 900 km away. In Hausaland they sell salt and dates, and from these earnings buy not only the quintessential millet but also clothing and other products. A large camel load of millet (180 kg) is usually enough to satisfy the yearly alimentary requirements of one person.

The caravan trade is connected to a transhumance of camels which covers two completely different pasturelands. During the rainy season from July to September, as well as during the short rest period after the return from Bilma in November, the camels graze in the Aïr. After this they are moved to Hausaland where they are kept during the cold, dry season (December to February), and sometimes during the hot, dry season (April to June). The latter was usually the case when the previous rainy

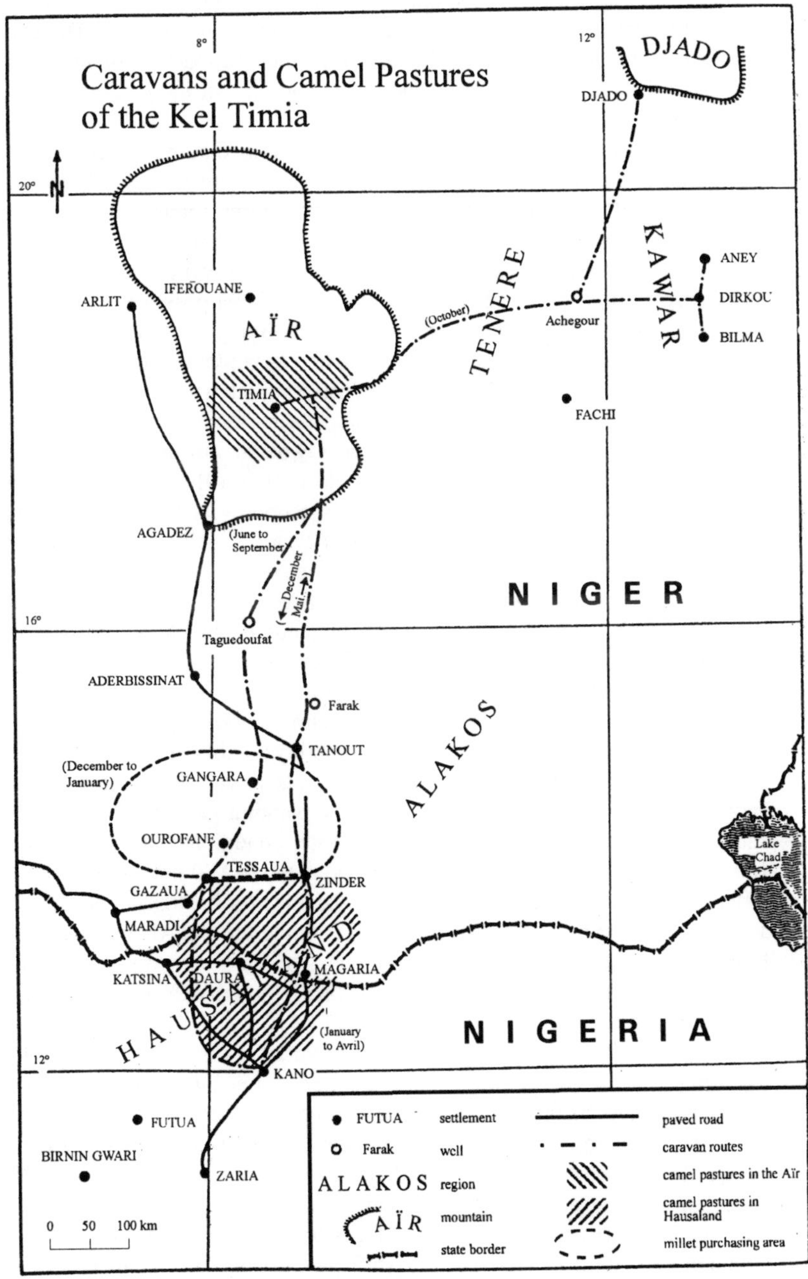
Caravans and Camel Pastures
of the Kel Timia
8°
12°
20°
16°
12°
N
DJADO
DJADO
AÏR
ARLIT
IFEROUANE
TIMIA
AGADEZ
(June to September)
(October)
TENERE
Achegour
KAWAR
ANEY
DIRKOU
BILMA
FACHI
NIGER
(December Mai)
Taguedoufat
ADERBISSINAT
Farak
TANOUT
ALAKOS
(December to January)
GANGARA
OUROFANE
TESSAUA
ZINDER
GAZAUA
MARADI
KATSINA
DAURA
MAGARIA
HAUSALAND
(January to Avril)
NIGERIA
Lake Chad
KANO
FUTUA
BIRNIN GWARI
ZARIA
0 50 100 km
FUTUA settlement
Farak well
ALAKOS region
AÏR mountain
state border
paved road
caravan routes
camel pastures in the Aïr
camel pastures in Hausaland
millet purchasing area

season in the Aïr had been poor, and had thus led to inadequate grazing conditions. Goats are kept in the Aïr year-round and are tended by women. The economic significance of goats is principally based on their production of milk, which is consumed daily by the goatherds and their children, but the production of cheese also plays a fundamental role.

In contrast to the centuries-old activities described above, gardening was only introduced in the twentieth century. Although date-palm groves had been worked for hundreds of years, artificially irrigated horticulture, founded on the cultivation of wheat and maize, was only introduced after 1914 in Timia.

The Kel Ewey's economic system consists of several characteristics which make adaptation to the extreme conditions in the Sahel possible. A relatively high income secures for them a modest standard of living in "normal" years. When drought and millet shortage occur, people can reduce their consumption of "luxury" goods, and buy the more expensive millet with the money they have saved from this personal sacrifice. This compensates them at least partially for price increases resulting from the millet shortage. Ownership of livestock can also serve as a financial buffer, as animals can be sold during a drought. With camels and goats as primary livestock, the Kel Ewey's economy is tailored to dry periods. Cattle and sheep are less common, since they are usually the first victims in a drought. As a result of irrigation, gardens in the Aïr are better able to survive a dry season than agriculture which is solely dependent on rain. Diversification of the economy offers additional protection. Participants in the caravan trade, who also own goats and cultivate gardens have a better chance of surviving a crisis than those who are only gardeners or camel owners.

In the Sahel, we not only find extreme climatic fluctuations from year to year but also from place to place. Physical mobility is therefore a vital strategy in reducing risk. The herding of camels and goats is mobile in the Aïr, and even gardeners carry out horticulture like nomads, planting gardens in different valleys and cultivating those which have the best water conditions. Although a rainfall of 100 mm is considered good in the Aïr, Kano receives 870 mm. This great climatic difference between the Aïr and Hausaland accounts for the transhumance of camels and the supply of millet. A drought which is limited to the Aïr and does not affect Hausaland in the south is easy to overcome. The gardens and goats still suffer in this case, but if the caravans can bring back enough reasonably-priced millet, survival is assured.

Returning to a subsistence economy provides a further protection. Normally the Kel Ewey do not have a self-sufficient economy but obtain their goods and foodstuffs predominantly from outside. However, in emergencies they return to their own resources. The goatherds and their children live increasingly from milk, the gardeners from wheat. These products are usually earmarked for sale. Now the collection of wild plants, frowned upon in normal years, contributes to survival. This is particularly true for leaves and fruits from trees, but not for grasses, which, although they could also serve as foodstuffs, are usually lost first in a drought.

In 1984-85 the Kel Ewey Tuareg experienced one of the severest droughts of this century. Agadez, for example, had only 3% of its 150 mm average yearly rainfall. Tanout at the northern edge of the millet-growth area had only 17%. The situation was aggravated by the fact that 1984 was the climax of a series of bad years which began in 1981. Between 1981 and 1985 half of the goats were lost. More critically, however, during this period the remaining goats did not produce milk. This lack of milk seriously undermined the Kel Ewey's diet, in particular the nutritional needs of women and children. Even more dramatic was the situation of camels. Half of the camels died between 1981 and 1985. The percentage of losses was the same as for goats, but in the case of camels the effects were more disastrous as the recovery of a camel herd is a great deal slower than that of a goat herd. The yearly salt caravan to Bilma is one of the pillars of the Kel Ewey economy. Only twice within this century had it ever been cancelled—both times during the Kawsan War (1917-19)—and even during the century's heaviest drought (1913-14) a large caravan did march to Bilma. It was not until 1984 that the Bilma caravan was cancelled due to drought.

Millet constitutes the staple food of the Kel Ewey. At the beginning of 1985 the price of millet was four times higher than in a normal year. The price of goats and camels, however, fell sharply to about half or a third of their normal price. Thus by selling a goat a Tuareg could only get 1/8 of the quantity of millet obtained in a typical year; by selling a camel, the ratio was even worse: 1/12. Obtaining food was much more difficult during this famine than in normal years. What were the strategies employed by the Kel Ewey?

— To buy millet, they not only sold salt and dates but also animals, jewelry, weapons (i.e. swords), and cloth.

— Since there was a shortage in Niger in 1984-85, the millet normally exported from Niger to Nigeria was not available. Thus, because northern Nigeria was less affected by the drought than Niger, the Kel Ewey travelled all the way to Kano, 1000 km from their home, to buy it. In spite of a Nigerian government ban on the export of millet, the Tuareg succeeded in smuggling it across the border. This was quite dangerous as Nigerian soldiers either shot at smugglers or confiscated their goods. However, in buying millet the Tuareg sometimes had the support of Hausa peasants in Nigeria whom they had known from caravan trading and transhumance in the past.

— Many men fled to Algeria and Libya not only to find work and food for their own survival but also with the hopes of bringing back enough food for their families.

— The collection of wild roots, leaves and fruits became essential for survival. However, at that time there was even a shortage of wild plants. The seed of wild grass which could serve as a substitute for millet was even rarer than millet, since due to the severity of the drought there was no grass. The only wild plants which could be collected were leaves and fruits from trees (such as *maerua crassifolica* and *acacia raddiana*, respectively). These leaves and fruits were mixed with a little millet so that meals had at least some resemblance to ordinary porridge (*ashin*).

Because the strategies described above are individual ones, they have received less attention from most anthropologists who have primarily focused on another type of strategy. Networks of relatives, friends, neighbours and clientship are part of the social structure in these societies, and each has ist function in everyday life. Since a moral economy exists among the Tuareg, a lot of food, animals and other goods circulate within this network and can be of great help to individuals, especially in an emergency. On a public level, an alms tax (*asadakat*) is collected by Islamic scholars and distributed among the poor.

However, under the stress of a severe drought and famine when more aid than usual is needed, this rule of reciprocity, generosity and help does not function as well as at other times. Even the total amount of alms tax available for distribution tends be to much smaller than otherwise. No one contests the rules of hospitality and generosity, but most people try to hide their food supplies. Within households, the pooling and distribution continues to function but outside the household people become more reluctant to help others. The reason for this behaviour is clear: the network functions as long as the emergency affects only a few individuals. However, when the emergency becomes a collective phenomenon, these networks fail.

3 Communication During the Famine

The search for food is a short term strategy which aims at survival during the immediately following days or weeks. From this we can distinguish long term strategies which attempt to safeguard the future over the coming years. In the case of nomads this primarily means the maintenance of animals, which during a drought are threatened in two ways. First, the animals have to be saved from the effects of the drought. Second, they should not have to be sold for foodstuffs.

The prevailing behaviour among the Kel Ewey during the famine reflected a stronger influence of the long term rather than the short term perspective. They did their utmost to protect their camels and goats, generally selling very few animals. Here, however, long term and short term strategies were in conflict. The preservation of animals meant strenuous work and in many cases hunger, which might have been prevented had the animals been sold. I will illustrate this conflict by the example of the behaviour of female goatherds. During the cold season the millet stock of most goatherds was totally depleted. Relatively few goatherds sold their goats in order to buy millet, with the majority selling few or no animals. Instead of satisfying their immediate needs they chose to suffer hunger and survived on wild leaves (especially *maerua crassifolia*). Their behaviour was not at all self-evident and thus requires an explanation, since at the time it would have been quite rational to sell the goats for the following reasons:

— Grain stocks had been exhausted, and by selling their goats the women would have received enough money to buy the necessary food.

— The goats were of no immediate use, since as a result of the drought they were not producing milk.

— It was doubtful whether the goats would survive the following hot season (April to June), and even if they did survive, they certainly would not make it through another drought-year.

— Herding goats was particularly strenuous during the drought. No grass or leaves remained in the valleys. Herding goats meant feeding them. Some goatherds shook leaves from trees with long sticks, while others went to considerable trouble to drive the goats up steep mountains in search of leftover grass. Watering the goats was equally strenuous because the water level in area wells was much lower than usual.

— Paradoxically, while goatherding was only possible far away from the settlements, it was only in these same settlements that the goatherd could obtain food.

— Since the goatherd was in no way sure she could survive the next months, why should she continue to herd her goats instead of selling or killing them?

Despite these many reasons for selling the goats, there was one overwhelming reason not to do so: in order to secure people's future existence. But why should the goatherds have had faith in the future? They had had some experience with the alternation of good and bad years, but how could they have known whether the rain would come back the following year or whether the drought would continue? The future could have been even worse. Instead of a cycle of good and bad years they could have been faced with a continuous degradation of the climate or even the end of the world. Such interpretations could very well justify short term survival strategies or fatalism and apathy.

In 1984-85 such explanations were often heard among the Kel Ewey but they never convinced the majority. One reason for this was the communication of Islamic scholars. At the beginning of the famine, these scholars could not agree on how to interpret drought and famine although none of them doubted that ultimately the disasters had been sent by Allah. But what could have been his reason? Did he want to punish the Tuaregs for their sins? If this were the case, some of them argued, then repentance and penance might change the will of Allah. Other scholars insisted, however, that the will of Allah was unfathomable and that men could in no way influence him. It was this last view which gained the upper hand. Even though it left no room for influencing the will of Allah, it did provide at least some hope for the future—more hope than did another interpretation which exerted some influence among a minority. According to them, this heavy drought heralded the end of the world, and the most appropriate behavior under the circumstances would have been to give alms and repent in order to ensure Allah's favourable judgement.

It was not only the explanations and counsels of Islamic scholars which influenced the people. Storytelling by old men and women who had experienced the great famine of 1913-14 was equally important. Several years before it had only been me, as an anthropologist, who had expressed interest in these stories. Now, everybody was sitting around when stories about former famines were being told.

Children were learning the names of past famines. Elders described past famines as having been much worse than those being experienced in the present. But even back then, the famine ended and most people survived. Hearing that in the past others had suffered even more than they were now, was a source of consolation. Thus these famine-tales gave the younger audience hope that the present condition would also come to an end and that they would also survive.

Interpreting the crisis historically became imperative. How could the famine fit into their understanding of the course of history? Although this was not a question which held much academic interest at the time, ordinary people were consumed by it and thus discussed it incessantly. Another central issue in a crisis of this nature is how to cope with death. The goatherds, for example, were preoccupied by a fear of death. It was a topic of many conversations amongst them, and as a participant in these discussions I could feel their fear. In my opinion, it was one of the most admirable achievements that the women, rather than being overcome by panic, maintained their composure.

As believers in the Moslem faith they could imagine paradise, but it is doubtful that they derived any hope from this, since an afterlife of punishment in hell was just as likely. Everyone could describe for me in detail the pleasures of his or her paradise: plenty of water, milk, millet and dates. However, I think there remained some uncertainty about what this paradise really was. One day a young woman, describing the pleasures of paradise for me, suddenly stated: "We are terrified of death. We don't want to die. It's only under compulsion that we die. Life on earth is better than all the pleasures of paradise." More important than any speculation about paradise was the concept of a dignified death, of a death surrounded by one's relatives, of an honorable burial. When I was talking about death with another young woman, she said: "If I die my relatives and neighbours will organize a burial. If the others die, I will organize it for them."

Although the Tuareg were afraid of death they knew how to cope with it. They were willing to accept that death might be possible during a famine, and this attitude, far from being one of fatalism, was fundamental to their behaviour during the crisis. Rather than give in to despair, the Kel Ewey remained very active. However, as I have shown, their activities were more oriented to long terms solutions than to immediate survival strategies. Acceptance of their own eventual death was a prerequisite to the success of this approach. A great famine constitutes a threat to men, and, paradoxically, many survival strategies themselves contribute to this threat. Contrary to a common assumption reinforced by the survival theory, peasants and nomads of the Sahel are not exclusively preoccupied with survival. For them, living and dying with dignity counts more than survival at any price.

In times of stability, men share their meals with others instead of eating alone. They cook cultivated plants, but not wild roots, leaves or fruits. They do not eat raw food, but prepare it in complicated ways. They not only acquire the food they need for survival, but buy clothing and jewelry as well. They not only work to provide for their immediate needs, but also enjoy elaborate feasts with relatives and neighbours. During a famine, this intensely social way of life is threatened by many of their own survival strategies. Humans become closer to some animals in that they now eat wild roots and leaves and also tend to eat alone instead of sharing their food. Because they are preoccupied with obtaining food, they may neglect buying clothes, jewelry and other luxuries. Under normal conditions, a Tuareg shows how civilized he is by never talking about food, and by always leaving scraps, whereas in a crisis he thinks and talks incessantly about food and leaves nothing in his bowl.

During the famine there was a tendency towards this animal-like behaviour. Had it completely displaced traditional, civilized conduct, the society would have collapsed. However, most Tuareg made great efforts to maintain the human foundations of their society. Although it would have been reasonable to spend all of their money on food during the famine, many continued to purchase cloth. They preferred starvation to presenting a ragged appearance at public gatherings. For example, the great feast of the prophet's birthday was celebrated in the traditional manner on December 6, 1984, despite the famine. Men and women presented themselves in their most beautiful clothing; the singing competition and camel race took place as usual.

To conclude, we can assert that a dignified life could be maintained during the famine with great effort. The crisis could be managed and did not lead to a breakdown of the social order. There was at least one catastrophe which remained engraved in the memory of old people, during which the social order broke down. These elders were very concerned that such a disaster could recur. During the Kawsan War of 1916-17, neighbours robbed each other, and some people had their clothes ripped off their backs so that they stood naked. A number of people also wore skins instead of cotton. Many died during the war, but it was not the fact of dying itself which terrified the elderly who today tell stories of the Kawsan War. What was engraved in their memory was the fact that those who died did not do so honourably. Men did not die in open combat but were slaughtered like goats. Dead bodies were not buried, but were instead left lying around like animals. For them, the Kawsan war was distinguished from a severe drought not by the number of human lives lost but by the denial of human dignity. This fact remained much more deeply embedded in the memories of elders than hunger, illness and death. Although the Kawsan catastrophe was an isolated incident, the knowledge that it could happen again made people afraid. The great efforts undertaken to maintain the moral order during the famine of 1984-85 can at least in part be explained by the fear of this possibility.

To cope with a famine requires not only survival strategies but most importantly, communication between men. The Tuareg put their fears into words and asked their Islamic scholars and elders for advice. They talked about death, not only because they were afraid of it, but because they wanted to calm their fears by talking. Up until now communication during a famine has been neglected by research. It is impossible to understand behaviour in a famine without taking this crucial element into consideration, since it is through communication that people make sense of famine and lend conviction to their actions. Without communication, survival strategies would result in a Hobbesian war where all fight against each other rather than cope with the crisis. People would either act fatalistically or wait passively for help, like victims. Most of the time we observe neither a struggle for survival nor fatalism during a famine. The reason for this must be sought in the communication between those affected. Hence research focusing on communication under these conditions should receive top priority.

References

Campbell, David. J. (1990): Strategies for Coping with Severe Food Deficits in Rural Africa: A Review of the Literature.

Chastanet, Monique (1992): Survival Strategies of a Sahelian Society: The Case of the Soninke in Senegal from the Middle of the Nineteenth Century to the Present, in: Food and Foodways 5, 2, pp. 127-149.

Copans, Jean (ed.) (1975): Sécheresses et famines du Sahel, 2 Vols., Paris.

Garine, Igor de, and G.A. Harrison (eds.) (1988): Coping with Uncertainty in Food Supply, Oxford.

Ibrahim, Fouad N. (1987a): Combating Famine by Grain Storage in Western Sudan, in: Geojournal 14, 1, pp. 29-35.

Ibrahim, Fouad N. (1987b): Überlebensstrategien der Sahelbauern, in: H. Schrettenbrunner (ed.): Hunger in Nordafrika, Software für den Geographieunterricht, Lüneburg, pp. 55-66.

Mortimore, Michael (1989): Adapting to Drought: Farmers, Famine and Desertification in West Africa, Cambridge.

Richards, Paul (1990): Local strategies for Coping with Hunger: Central Sierra Leone and Northern Nigeria Compared, in: African Affairs 89, pp. 265-275.

Shipton, Parker (1990): African Famines and Food Security: Anthropological Perspectives, in: Annual Review of Anthropology 19, pp. 353-451.

Spittler, Gerd (1989a): Dürren, Krieg und Hungerkrisen bei den Kel Ewey, 1900-1985, Stuttgart.

Spittler, Gerd (1989b): Handeln in einer Hungerkrise. Tuaregnomaden und die große Dürre von 1984, Wiesbaden.

Spittler, Gerd (1993): Les Touaregs face aux sécheresses et aux famines. Les Kel Ewey de l'Aïr (Niger) (1900-1985), Paris.

Waal, Alexander de (1989): Famine that kills. Darfur Sudan, 1984-1985, Oxford.

Watts, Michael John (1983): Silent Violence. Food, Famine and Peasantry in Northern Nigeria, Berkely.

8

Urban Agriculture in Africa with Special Reference to the Former Zaire
Social, Ecological and Land Use Aspects

Friedhelm Streiffeler

1 Introduction

Although urban agriculture has existed for a long time, it has only very recently become a topic in scientific research. The reasons for this scientific neglect are manifold. First, there is the common view that "urban space" applies solely to "habitation" and that economic activities are limited to the secondary and tertiary sectors, agriculture being reserved to rural areas. Second, since urban agriculture forms part of the informal economy, it has, so far, been overlooked, as were the other sectors of this informal economy. Finally, in the perspective of development research, urban agriculture did not attract much interest because its development in a non-agricultural environment is not easily conceivable. Urban agriculture is in fact situated in an environment which is "non-agricultural" as regards the availability of sufficient land, but also regarding the economic environment, the administrative organisation, social relations of people living in the urban space, and some other aspects.

However, as explained in the next paragraph, in view of the growing importance it has recently experienced urban agriculture could no longer be overlooked. It has become a major research topic with different aspects, the ecological one being the most recent. Its advocates stress that urban agriculture can contribute to the "greening" of cities as a strategy to combat the current urban environmental crisis. Without denying the significance of the ecological aspect, it is nevertheless important to understand the different economic and social functions of urban agriculture; in order to avoid, among other things, a style of urban planning with affinities to the old colonial model of garden cities.

2 Recent trends in African urbanization

The countries of Sub-Saharan Africa which were long characterized by the lowest degree of urbanization in all world regions, now show the highest rate of urbanization growth. According to the statistics of the United Nations Population Fund (1996: 74 ff.), the urban growth rates in Africa between 1995 and 2000 are, on the average, 4.3% whereas the numbers for Asia are 3.2%, for Latin America 2.3%, for

Europe 0.5% and for North America 1.2% respectively. Most of this growth is due to migration. Contrary to a widely held view, the migrants are not attracted by the "city lights", the majority of villagers migrating to the towns are realistic enough to see that they cannot all find employment in the formal economy, namely, private enterprises and in the civil service. First, with the exception of the group of migrants which come to the towns in order to complete their school education (Streiffeler and Mbaya 1987), the majority of migrants have a lower level of school education than the already established urban residents and thus, lesser chance of employment. Secondly, the migrants are well aware of the fact that in the present situation the number of people still living in towns largely exceeds the number of occupations available in formal economies, and that they will join those surviving by other means. The migrants hope that, by coming to the towns, they can increase the number of different activities which, in various combinations, can guarantee their survival. Basically, the logic behind this is not so very different from that of the subsistence farmer who combats the natural risks of agriculture by spreading production over different crops (mixed culture), different sites and different growth periods. In towns, however, (the limitation of) risk spreading (in agriculture) is no longer necessary, and the inclusion of other activities from the secondary and tertiary sectors is possible.

The situation in Zaire (DRC) shows some specific aspects. As in other central African states, the country had low urbanization levels during the colonial period, but later the highest growth rates. The population of Kinshasa in 1990 was estimated at 4 403 000 (Marysse et al. 1995: 87), which meant that Kinshasa was the second largest city in Sub-Saharan Africa after Lagos.

However, it is not clear that the subsequent catastrophic economic and political situation has parallelled a rural-urban migration. There certainly is a decrease of migration components, such as the migration of young people coming to towns in order to complete their school education because they cannot afford it at home or simply because rural schools are closed; but on the other hand, there are also new motives for migration, such as the movement of people dispersed in the country, who leave the regions formerly inhabited by them because they do not belong to the ethnic majority groups of those regions. Typically, such people go to the metropolitan area of Kinshasa.

Instead of "de-urbanization", it is perhaps more correct to speak of "less permanence" of life in the city. Thus many young men from the cities are now working in gold and diamond mines, but from time to time they return to the city, and their perspective is "urban" life. So the breakdown of the "formal" economy more often results in the land and the equipment being used informally rather than by people who were formerly employed returning to the country-side. However, this "informal" use remains debatable.

3 Growth of urban agriculture as a response to the present economic crisis

Even if the formal economy in post-colonial African cities never offered sufficient employment to the urban population, the discrepancies increased dramatically in the eighties with the implementation of structural adjustment programmes in many African states. One main reason for this is the fact that the public sector provided a high proportion of the employment in the formal economy. In Zaire, the breakdown of the formal economy, which, however, was not only due to structural adjustment programmes but also to the breakdown of the official state, was particularly dramatic. Thus, at the beginning of the nineties only 5% of the population of Kinshasa was employed in the formal economy.

In essence, dramatically in Zaire, but often also in other African states, the formal economy has mostly been replaced by the informal economy as the material basis of livelihood. When this informal economy is realized in the form of a petty commodity economy, e.g., in the form of production of goods for everyday life, small trade and so on, it has the essential feature of high competitiveness and cheapness, and can only be afforded if the prices do not necessarily secure the reproduction of the labour force. One of the most common solutions to this problem is urban agriculture. A survey of the frequency of this practice in the cities of some African countries is presented in the following list quoted from UNDP (1996: 55).

Burkina Faso	36% of families in Ouagadougou are engaged in horticultural cultivation or livestock breeding (activities).
Cameroon	In Yaounde 35% of urban residents are farmers.
Gabun	80% of families in Libreville engage in horticulture.
Kenya	67% of urban families farm (80% of which are low-income units) on urban and peri-urban sites; 29% of these families farm in the urban areas where they live. 20% of urban dwellers in Nairobi grow food in the urban areas.
Mozambique	37% of urban households surveyed in Maputo produce food; 29% raise livestock.
Tanzania	68% of families in six Tanzanian cities engage in farming; 39% raise animals.
Uganda	33% of all households within a five-kilometre radius of the centre of Kampala engage in some form of agricultural activity in 1989.
Zambia	A survey of 250 low-income households in Lusaka showed that 45% grow horticultural crops or raise livestock in their backyards or gardens on the periphery of the city.

This strategy of securing survival in the city signifies that urban agriculture is obviously carried out more with the objective of production for self-consumption than as production for sale. Thus, a survey the author did in 1987 in the Zairian town of Kisangani on 426 people engaged in urban agriculture showed that only 0.3% of those questioned declared that they produced for sale and 32.6% that they produced for their own consumption; the majority of 63.4% produced for both purposes, but the proportion of those who use the larger part for their own consumption is nearly double that of people who produce the larger part for sale (59.4% versus 30.1%). In Kampala, Maxwell and Zziwa (1992) found 69.3% subsistence production, 7.3% commercial production, and 23.3% production primarily for the household but also for the sale of significant amounts. In a study of urban agriculture in Nairobi executed in 1987, Freeman (1991) found that 70.7% of cultivators sold nothing from their harvest; 13.4% sold half and more, the rest between 1 and 39%. These numbers show clearly that urban agriculture has the primary function of securing food to the urban poor. Since food needs increase with family size, it is clear that the probability and the amount of urban agriculture increase with the number of children in the family. From a theoretical view point, intra-urban agriculture at least could be considered as an interesting field of application for the theory of the Russian agro-economist Chayanov, who considered the area cultivated as being not so much dependent on class differences as on differences in the stages of the family development cycle.

Urban agriculture is though not only practised by families who are not employed in the formal economy. It may persist in the traditional role of the women who have to assure the subsistence of the household; but rapid inflation with a slower growth of wages can also create a situation where even formal employment does not guarantee survival of the household and reproduction of the labour force. In such cases, even households who are in part employed in the formal economy may be forced to engage in urban agriculture. This phenomenon, which may be termed "subsidiarisation of wage labour by subsistence production" has been observed in Kisangani, where Alaruka and Choma (1985) in their survey executed between 1981 and 1983 found that 26.9% of the women farming had husbands who were civil servants. In the survey conducted by the author in 1987 a similar number of 28.2% of such households were found, but here the private sector also was represented with 15.6%. It should not be forgotten either that those with formal employment have often larger households (their own family or kinship) than those without. Even where the public sector has not simply dismissed many former civil servants, the situation of a decrease in real income has spread over a fair number of African states.

It should be remembered that this phenomenon of subsidiarization of wage labour by subsistence production goes back to deep-rooted practices from colonial times. We find it still reflected today in the name of one of the most important vegetables of Nairobi, collard (Brassica Carinata) as "sukuma wiki"; this Swahili expression signifies "push the week" and means that the weekly wage was not sufficient to survive during the week thanks only to wages but also to necessitated vegetable production.

Typically, urban agriculture is also practised by households with members in the formal economy who also complement their incomes with activities in petty commodity production and trade, because the high competitiveness of the informal economy alone is not sufficient to fill the income deficit of the formal income. In other words, the informal economy, which in many aspects is subsidiary to the formal economy in surviving the crisis, could not itself survive if it were not supported by urban agriculture. Or using the image of a house: the "bel-étage" of activity in the formal economy is fostered by the "rez-de-chaussée" of the informal economy which, in turn, is sustained by the "souterrain" of staple crops.

The astonishing direct relationship between the increase in urban agriculture on the one hand and inflation or the increase of food prices on the other hand, which often followed liberalisation policies under the influence of the IMF can only be explained by the high proportion of expenditure for nutrition in the total household budget. So the Mazingira study (1987) in Nairobi found that the urban poor spend 30% of their household budgets for nutrition, a percentage which amounts to 45-50% if we add the costs for fuel. These numbers are confirmed for Brazzaville with 48% and 56% for Dakar in 1979 (O'Deye 1985, 64).

In Zaire, these percentages reach a higher level with the economic crisis. So Pain (1984) found in Kinshasa an average of 60% of household expenditure for nutrition; this percentage increased for the year 1994 to 65.3% in the Zone of Matete at Kinshasa (D'Souza et al. 1995), and it can be assumed that in the poorer quarters this percentage is even higher. This high percentage is certainly related to the fact that, in economic crises, households allocate the small amounts of money they still possess to the most primary needs of survival; on the other hand, it is also important to consider that as a result of the collapse of the road infrastructure in Zaire and deterioration of vehicles, the availability of agricultural products from the countryside no longer meets the urban demand, and this increasing gap between availability and demand results in food becoming ever more expensive.

It appears to be the "norm" that two thirds of those who practise urban agriculture for subsistence are women. In his survey of 618 cultivators, conducted in 1987, Freeman (1991) found a male-female proportion of 35.8% to 64.2%, respectively. Similar proportions were found in Kisangani, Lusaka and elsewhere. There are two main explanations for this sex distribution: first, women have a lower educational status and consequently less chance of being employed in the formal economy; secondly, they tend to continue their tradition of securing the subsistence of the family by producing crops for consumption.

However, with the aggravation of the economic crisis this sex distribution may also change as a result of changes in the domestic units. One of the most alarming effects of the present catastrophic economic situation in Zaire is the fact that many people can no longer afford their rents or have to sell their houses, and that newly married couples cannot start their own households. As a result, the latter remain in their parents' homes and the former are lodged with the extended family or with people of the same ethnic origin or religion (see Ngondo and Pitshandenge 1996). However, housing them is a moral obligation, which is also profitable because one of the most important contributions of these poor people is urban agriculture.

In essence, the important role of informal activities in petty commodity production, trade and urban agriculture indicates that the household is not only a consumption unit, but a productive one, a "productive house" (see Neupert 1992). Therefore, questions relating to other production factors than the labour force for urban agriculture, mainly land, are significant.

4 The land question in urban agriculture

4.1 Main types of urban agriculture

Before presenting a typology of urban agriculture based on location of the plots, some words must be said with regard to the special structure of the fast growing African cities.

Some towns exist with one centre, generally the historically oldest part of the town with the highest population and housing densities, and declining densities the greater the distance is from this centre; but many more cities are less centralized and more "pluralistic", in the sense that they consist of several more or less centralized quarters or districts. In such cases, we have declining population and building densities with increasing distance from these sub-centres, with vacant land, green belts and zones of lower building density between them. One implication of this multi-centered structure is that the spatial distribution of urban agriculture does not correspond to the von-Thünen-model, which asserts declining intensity in land use in proportion to the distance from one presumed central point (Obara 1988). There is also a tendency toward the development of spontaneous "satellite-settlements" of poor migrants around the very big cities (e.g. Kulinda west of Nairobi). We thus have metropolitan areas of spaces with low density between the new settlements and the older metropolis as well as spaces with low density between the new settlements.

It seems reasonable to distinguish three types of urban agriculture where the location is the distinguishing criterion: intra-urban agriculture, household gardens and peri-urban agriculture.

The category of intra-urban agriculture covers spaces between, and at the peripheries of the different quarters or agglomerations constituting the whole city, spaces on "no man's land" (though not from a legal point of view), along roads and rivers, the railway, etc., also seasonally flooded land (such as in Nairobi), land on slopes not suitable for buildings and parks and often a heritage of colonial times. Whereas these spaces can form coherent areas, there is still the other category of squatter areas which may be public property (e.g. land around public buildings) or privately owned vacant land.

Generally, people who practise urban agriculture on these spaces are the poorest. The fact that they have no land rights also has implications for the type of plants which are cultivated. When there is no land security, no perennial or even annual crops are cultivated, but only fast-growing short-cycle crops, such as leaf vegetables. However, designation of the legal situation as a total absence of land rights would be only partly true; often, a local legitimation develops with respect to user's rights, when a person of this quarter grows plants with a certain continuity and visibly invests labour in order to maintain the plot in a good state. Another category of this informal land right which is of great importance in Zaire is the use of land by state employees, arguing that Zairian legislation stipulates that all land is the property of the state.

The importance of household gardens in many African countries cannot be over-estimated. Unlike the situation in rich-income countries, where they are often cultivated only for pleasure, in developing countries, cultivating urban household gardens may constitute an essential component of the spectrum of activities assuring nutritionally sufficient alimentation. Production is generally for consumption. Typical for household gardens are vegetables and fruits as dietary supplements. The advantages of household gardens in comparison to intra- and peri-urban agriculture are fourfold (Sanyal 1986: 24):

— Usually, the land is more secure in that there are less problems with property rights. At least, the household garden is not less secure than the house or the hut. Because in many traditional legal systems of Africa the right to plant trees is closely connected to rights over the land, it is logical that many plots are not only used for vegetables but also for trees and bushes.

— Work in household gardens is less time-consuming because distances from the house to the field are short. In most cases the cultivation of household gardens is done by women, who use household waste as compost.

— As opposed for instance to roadside fields household gardens can be irrigated.

— There are less problems with theft, which is one of the major problems of intra-urban agriculture in general and of roadside fields in particular.

Naturally, the frequency and areas of household gardens depend on the type of town and the centrality of the location. In Lusaka, even in the high density areas, half of the residents maintain a vegetable garden with an average size of 30 m^2 (Schlyter quoted by Jaeger 1985: 4). In Kisangani, an extended town without much industry, household gardens are also more or less the rule. In other towns with less land available, the poorest households have the least chances of using a household garden, at least those who are living in areas with very high population density. Thus, the Mazingira study found that 55% of the households in Nairobi had no household garden, and that these were generally the poorest, living not in the periphery and thus being forced to cultivate the insecure "open spaces" of the town (and/or the periphery).

The category of peri-urban agriculture is the most heterogeneous. First, there is the sub-type of village agriculture which is generally transformed by the inclusion of the villages into the urban periphery. If there is no demand for land in the peri-urban areas, land can be leased, often by the traditional custodians of the land, to urban-based people for one or two years. This is, for instance, the case in the peri-urban region around the Zairian town of Kikwit in the sparsely settled Region of Bandundu (Mpuru 1993).

Since colonial times, the state has organized agricultural projects in the peri-urban areas in order to feed the cities and to create jobs. These projects were generally organized as cooperatives and used land which, due to the land legislation of the colonial and post-colonial periods, was declared to be state-owned; an example is the great agricultural project in the Ndjili-valley near Kinshasa. On the other hand, such projects in the urban periphery, which are often technically highly developed and often supported by external assistance exist also in the form of private ownership. In this case, it is often a close relationship with the state which facilitates access to the land. An example of these types of capitalist farms near Kinshasa is the former presidential domain at Nsele (DAIPN) with the highly mechanized breeding of poultry, cows and pigs. It often happens that the people working on these capitalist farms are paid by an allowance to cultivate plots on the land of the capitalist farm.

However, because of the disappearance of clear traditional land rights in the peri-urban areas, such as in the supplanting of "traditional" ownership by modern ownership, land is also used by poor urban residents, especially recent migrants, who have not found intra-urban spaces for agriculture because they have not yet acquired informal land rights. This is the most under-privileged group because they have no land security as well as long distances to cover between their homes and their fields.

4.2 Changing attitudes of urban authorities towards urban agriculture

In the past, urban administration in almost all African states had a clearly negative attitude towards urban agriculture which was sometimes even expressed in the destruction of intra-urban fields (as Hake (1977) has described for Kenya). This negative attitude is explained by the widespread development model which placed responsibility for development of the secondary and tertiary sectors of the formal economy with the administration. Public administration was and still is more interested in the reservation of land for future industry or of new quarters with modern buildings for administrative, commercial or habitational purposes and considered non-certified agricultural use as a hindrance to this aim and as "anarchic" and illegal. The fact should also be mentioned that the administration received no taxes from this unlicensed use which also explains its negative attitude. This negative attitude mostly concerned only intra-urban agriculture and not house gardens, if the land holding title was in order.

However, the reported negative attitude of administrations towards urban agriculture knows historic changes. One of the first examples of this change in attitude was Lusaka, where formerly maize plants were slashed, street vendors were jailed and squatter houses demolished (Sanyal 1986). Since these actions had no discouraging effect on the ever growing population of Lusaka and the financial crisis of the local and national administration could not offer any income alternatives, a policy change was brought about, and the Zambian President Kaunda declared in 1977, "The 450 000 people of Lusaka must grow their own vegetables and cereals" (Sanyal 1986: 9). This declaration was followed by the organized sale of seeds, tools, and other agricultural input.

Zambia was not the only country which changed its attitude. It is mainly the profound economic crisis of the eighties throughout Africa which explains the spread of this change in attitude to other African countries, Tanzania being one of the first. Even in Nairobi where, because of firm hopes placed on rapid industrial development, a complete lack of indulgence towards the informal economy had become institutionalized, a change in attitude took place: the informal activities, renamed "small-scale enterprises", were respected, among other things, for their positive contributions, and intra-urban agriculture on public spaces was authorized, if no trees were planted.

In view of the survival efforts of an ever growing urban population living under seriously deteriorating economic conditions, the contradiction between formal laws concerning land rights and illegal land use in intra-urban agriculture was resolved in different ways. First, the old legislation regarding land use is maintained, but sanctions are usually not applied. Instead of a new legislation clearly in favour of urban agriculture, we often see attitudes of "laxity" (Mosha 1991), "tacit approval" (Stren 1992) or "benign neglect" (Maxwell and Zziwa 1992). Also, a difference between the various administrative levels can be observed. The higher levels of urban administration defend the existing formal regulations prohibiting "illicit" use of vacant public land, whereas the lowest local members of the administration in the popular quarter openly support it (Maxwell and Zziwa 1992).

Another attempt to resolve this conflict over illegal land use both for housing and urban agriculture consisted in drafting subsequent legislation on informal and illegal land occupation. This policy played an important role at the Habitat Conference in Istanbul in 1996 and at its pre-conferences, such as the Abidjan Conference (21 - 24 March 1995), under the heading "Urban land management regularization policies and local development in Africa and the Arab States" and in the New Delhi Declaration (17 - 19 January 1996). This pre-conference, held under the heading "Global platform on access to land and security of tenure as a condition for sustainable shelter and urban development", recommended general legalization policies for urban housing, which were summed up under the following headings: "C. Sustainable human settlements development in an urbanizing world: 8. Improving urban economies and the promotion of urban agriculture": "113. To provide opportunities for productive employment and private investment, governments at all appropriate levels, including local authorities, in consultation with labour unions, chambers of commerce, industry, trade, consumer organizations, and the financial sector, including the cooperative sector, should: ... d) facilitate opportunity for urban agriculture." This tendency towards legalization of urban agriculture as commercialized agriculture can also be found in the "Sustainable Dar es Salaam Project" under the Global Sustainable Cities Program of the UN Center for Human Settlements.

However, urban agriculture is not per se sustainable. In Harare, it was the Department of Natural Resources which focused the attention of urban authorities on de-forestation and tree-felling as a result of illegal urban agriculture. It invited the mayor and some councellors to fly over the city in order to give them an aerial view of the damage to natural resources within and around the city as a result of cultivation and tree felling. The mayor of Harare commented that the suburbs looked like deserts and that here should be positive encouragement for tree planting at all levels. He also called for structured enforcement of laws against uncontrolled cultivation especially along riverbanks (Mbiba 1995: 89, 90).

From this it follows that an effective policy of really sustainable development would imply a combination of controlling illegal housing and permitting urban agriculture, the latter in the form of household gardens with fruit trees and peri-urban area schemes of agro-forestry. In the short run, however, intra-urban agriculture as a survival strategy of the urban poor should also be accepted. In Harare, laws against illegal (intra-)urban agriculture were not observed by the urban poor, and technical officers were attacked by the cultivators. The most positive result of the legislation against illegal (intra-)urban agriculture was that urban cultivators founded formal cooperative organizations in order to get access to urban land. In 1991 and 1992, illegal intra-urban agriculture was no longer legally prosecuted in the light of the drought and hunger in rural Zimbabwe (Mbiba 1995).

Between long-term perspectives and survival strategy, there is still the medium-term alternative of "temporary use licences." This can refer to public land which is not yet reserved for any purpose (e.g. between quarters, riverside land) or to land which is scheduled for further public buildings but where construction has not yet begun. As Smits (quoted by Sanyal 1986) has found, the realization of these plans normally takes many years, and during this time land could be used for agricultural purposes. Land around public buildings could also be designated for agricultural purposes.

In Zaire, the situation is somewhat special. In 1975, the master plan for Kinshasa first included areas zoned for horticulture in the eastern, central and southwestern sections of the city (Pain 1985). The urban zones also had agricultural advisors. In the late eighties, urban agriculture was theoretically promoted as an aspect of the "Programme Alimentaire Minimum" which attempted to increase agricultural production. Later on, with the breakdown of the formal Zairian State, it was in the personal interest of the non-paid state officials to maintain urban agriculture as one of the main sources of survival.

5 Urban ecology and urban agriculture

Apart from the administrative and commercial centres and some high-class residential quarters, many cities in Sub-Saharan Africa are very dirty. This negative environmental quality reaches its highest degree in the spontaneous settlements, where the absence of urban services embraces also the lack of any official refuse collection. Garbage remains on streets and empty spaces, is dumped anywhere at hand, thrown into rivers and streams, and so on. The environmental quality has an influence on the hygienic situation in these quarters, with frequent diseases through infection and parasites.

From this point of view, it is a tempting idea to try to resolve the nutrition problem in the poor parts of African cities by integrating it into the hygiene problem and using suitable waste as compost for the plots in urban agriculture. This integrative solution of two problems would also seem to be applicable to waste water. This is also important because water is becoming more and more scarce in many cities, especially in the poor areas. Certainly, this integration of waste "recycling" and plant nutrition has always existed, on a small scale and without external promotion, in the form of plant nutrition in kitchen-gardens by using kitchen refuse and by means of "unorganized" garbage collectors who collect the organic material to bring it to places where it can be composted. The idea of promoting this integration in an organized manner and also directing external development cooperation projects was pioneered in the eighties with the "Food-Energy Nexus Programme of the United Nations University" (see Sachs and Silk 1990).

This integration is particularly interesting in poor parts of Third World cities, because the percentage of compostable organic material is generally high, often over 50%, and the percentage of plastic, metal and glass very low; ash has also a high percentage. This material could well be used in urban agriculture where the decline in soil fertility is a problem of high priority. Due to the limitations of available fallow fertile land is rarer than in rural areas. Certainly, some plant rotation exists in different African cities, but there is also a tendency to replace older nutrient-demanding plants by less demanding plants, such as cassava. This tendency is to be found in Zaire but also, for instance, at Bangui (Adrien-Rongier 1980). Some form of plant rotation generally exists, but at a lower degree than in the villages because of more limitation in space and the greater need for staple food.

In principle, the use of composted organic material, in combination with chemical fertilizers, could contribute to reducing one of the major problems of urban agriculture, namely the high rate of plant diseases (see for instance Percival et al. 1993). If the organic fertilizers were applied in the correct combination and at the right times, they could strengthen the resistance potential of the plants. In the Kisangani survey plant pests and diseases were mentioned as representing 30.5% of the main problems of urban agriculture. The reasons for the importance of plant diseases are manifold:

— Apart from a minority of urban cultivators who work (typically) in peri-urban agriculture, chemical products for plant protection are not used.

— Except for the technique of mixed cultivation, traditional techniques of plant protection (for example, the use of the excrement of elephants in the rural surroundings of Kisangani) are not applicable in the urban context.

— The urban environment: primarily as a consequence of the replacement of natural vegetation or of agriculturally used land by construction and industrial sites, the temperature in the urban environment is much higher than in the rural surroundings, and this heat stress constitutes an attack on plant health. The same danger stems from pollution of the air, water and soil. However, we have here big differences at city level: in many African cities lacking important industry and without much motor traffic, the real problem is in the high concentration of smoke in the air originating from poor quality stoves or open fires needed for the preparation of meals without electricity and also from the burning of organic waste due to the absence of a waste collection system (see Noe Gui-Diby 1991).

— Plant infections play a major role: contrary to rural areas, systematic plant rotation is not the rule; as coordination between urban producers regarding crop diversity is also largely absent, plant infections spread more readily than in rural areas, where we often find coordination between the peasants; and finally, because of the higher degree of integraton of urban areas into inter-regional and international areas, new diseases spread here more rapidly than in remote rural areas. The problem with the idea of integrating waste removal and plant nutrition in urban agriculture consists in its realization in urban settlements of high density in African cities, which are often very poor—not only with regard to the residents of the poor quarters but also on the administrative level.

In principle, the integration of waste removal and plant nutrition could be mastered either in a more decentralized or in a more centralized manner. The former, where in extreme cases each household is composting its organic waste itself, is realistic only where there is sufficient land for compost material and household gardens. At the other extreme, centralized systems presuppose first of all efficient systems of garbage collection; these imply, at the primary level, the transport of garbage to local central collection points by the garbage producers or by garbage collectors working with wheel-barrows and, at the secondary level, the collection of this material by garbage trucks. One big problem with these systems is that the number of trucks is often insufficient and, because they are too much in demand, they do not function properly. Because in many African states the financial potential shrinks progressively from the level of the national state downwards to the municipal and local levels and because the scarce financial means are used up mostly for salaries, there is rarely enough money to invest in trucks and keep them in good condition. However, the situation improved in the CFA-Zone with the devaluation of the CFA, which brought with it higher prices for imported chemical fertilizers which were of more interest to the commercial peri-urban producers of organic fertilizers.

The process of centralized composting is highly land-intensive and can only be organized with low-cost techniques in the peri-urban area. To avoid sanitary problems, monitoring of the safety of the end product is an absolute necessity. Technically, it is also possible to include human excreta from urban quarters which have no access to the recycling process without dangers to human health, but these techniques, for instance waste stabilization ponds, are also highly land-intensive, and they can only be set up in the peri-urban areas.

In Kinshasa, a private collection system of usable garbage developed in the eighties, mainly as a consequence of the collapse of the official collection system "Transvoirie". This system did not receive financial means after 1985 and processed only garbage material from enterprises for cash payment; the households were serviced, also for cash, by "pousse-pousseurs" (handcar-drivers) who transported garbage material to official refuse disposal tips, to unofficial tips or to spaces where the material was composted and then sold to cultivators (see Mashindi and Mwanza 1992: 117). Later on, garbage collection in Kinshasa was transferred to the "Programme National d'Assainissement" (P.N.A.), but the system collected only 7% of the estimated waste material because it received only 5.23% of the financial means provided for its functioning and only 9.12% of the means provided for further investments (Lubuimi 1995: 133). This also concerned the task of garbage collection being largely taken over by small handcar drivers who, in 1992 removed 8.2% of the household waste. Like the P.N.A., they also offer the composted material to urban and peri-urban cultivators (0.3 US$/m^3).

Nevertheless, the city of Kinshasa and other Zairian cities are becoming more and more dirty (see Numengi 1995), mainly those quarters with high settlement density and a population which can no longer pay for refuse collection. This deteriorating hygienic situation is one important cause for the alarming spread of infectious diseases; another danger comes from the high concentration of smoke in the air because 40% of households are using fuel or charcoal as their energy sources (Mpasi 1992) despite the fact that, theoretically, enough electric energy could be available from the Inga river basin.

This situation would be even more dramatic if urban agriculture with its potential to absorb organic material had not also dramatically expanded. With the breakdown of the formal economy in the middle of the nineties, urban agriculture spread more and more in all parts of the urban areas, and spaces formerly used by industrial plants or public institutions, such as schools, universities, public traffic and so on, have now been remodelled for urban cultivation as the core survival strategy of urban residents.

6 Social aspects of urban agriculture

The expression "social aspects" is used here to describe relations among urban cultivators. Despite the fact that research on this topic up to now has been extremely rare, it is not less important than in rural agriculture, where the structures and content of cooperation, social norms in relation to efficient agriculture, and so on, have had a long research tradition. The few research projects on urban agriculture which do include social aspects bring to light great differences between rural and urban agriculture:

With few exceptions, urban agriculture in Africa is practised without labour cooperation beyond the level of the nuclear family. Thus, the Mazingira study found for Nairobi that, if the work was not done individually by women or by men, it represented, in 93% of the cases, cooperation only by members of the household. As the Kisangani survey showed, cooperation among household members is generally more important for fields not immediately adjacent to the house than for household gardens; but only 15.6% of the households cooperate with each other, and 84.6% work without mutual help. The fact that this percentage is higher than that found in Nairobi can be explained by the social structure of Kisangani, which still contains agglomerations of its original inhabitants (the Komo or Mbote) and of long-established immigrants, such as the Bangwana (Swahili).

These cooperation structures differ sharply from those observed in rural areas of Sub-Saharian Africa, where labour cooperation and labour rotation were not only of great importance in the past but still are in the present. There is also no coordination between urban cultivators with respect to production programmes, especially regarding special distribution and the plants to be grown. This lack of coordination between producers—which normally does exist in rural areas—is one of the causes for the frequency of plant diseases.

However, the most important aspect of the lack of cooperation between urban producers is the general lack of a common "defence strategy" concerning the most important factors of urban agriculture: land, water and compost material. The organized cooperatives existing in many urban peripheries are the only exceptions, and they are, typically, geared to production for sale—an exemple is the case reported by Schilter (1991), where peri-urban producers of mainly "European" vegetables with a limited sales market organized themselves, in order to avoid exploitation by middlewomen, who were themselves organized.

The great majority of urban producers are relatively widely dispersed and without much influence in their relations with the urban administration. Notably urban agriculture for consumption by the producers themselves is normally not organized and cannot profit from the advantages of being organized in one way or the other. In a way, this group is, in economic terms, in a position similar to that of the "populo minuto" in medieval Florence, who were subject to political prohibition with regard to organizing themselves in guilds like other social groups were allowed to.

It is interesting to note that this lack of organization is not accepted by urban agriculturists as an immutable fact, but, on the contrary, is seen as the main obstacle to the further development of urban agriculture. In the Kisangani survey only 15.6% of those asked gave a negative answer to the question "Would you wish for intensification of collaboration with other cultivators?" Positive answers were also given regarding traditional systems of labour collaboration on a rotation basis and the transfer of land in case of need ("logo boemo": initially, in the village, the transfer of land to members of other clans in relation to their needs). The more direct question "Would you wish to participate as a member in a production cooperative?" was also answered in the affirmative by 94.4%. In Nairobi 64% of the persons interviewed said that they would like to join formal organizations for urban agriculture, but only 1% was already effectively organized (Mazingira study). In Kampala 6.7% of the persons interviewed were members of an organized cooperative (Maxwell and Zziwa 1992). It seems that not only those who write about urban agriculture consider its organization to be the key question, but also urban agriculturists themselves.

These wishes and aspirations towards formally organized cooperatives seem to stem from the people realizing that they can exert pressure in urban agriculture only if and when they are formally organized. There are many examples to support this, not only in Africa (the afore mentioned successful agricultural cooperative at Harare, for instance) but also in Europe; where the urban gardens of German industrial workers ("Schrebergärten") received their decisive developmental push when the Social-Democratic Party of Germany (SPD) organized the worker-gardeners at the turn of this century.

This formal organization of urban agriculture is facilitated where some other sort of formal organization already exists. In Zaire there are many cases where members of a formal organization (e.g. teachers at school) organize themselves in agricultural cooperatives. The reason is that they can no longer support their families with the income from their teaching activities, because their salaries are not paid regularly and are ridiculously small when they are paid at all (see Mufuta 1994).

7 Conclusions

7.1 Research requirements

Due to the fact that scientific research has focussed its attention on urban agriculture only recently, the research deficit is considerable. Generally speaking, the task should be to improve the present level of research, which is still largely characterized either by descriptive and monographic studies of urban agriculture in particular cities, or by often very abstract generalizations describing the practical application of urban agriculture. The next objective would be to explain the forms of urban agriculture, their quantitative importance and their differing stages of development. Notwithstanding the importance of theory and explanation, the practical relevance of the research must remain the central element. The most difficult obstacle to a theoretical approach is the lack of a multi-disciplinary concept and also of a multi-level approach comprising macro-, meso- and microlevels. There are scientific disciplines applicable to the natural conditions for urban agriculture: soil and climate; the specification of criteria for urban conditions; disciplines relating to plant production, with the trend centered on plant nutrition and plant protection; most important is the question of the potential for intensification in limited urban spaces. The economic aspect concerns questions of the quantity and prices of food imports from rural areas and foreign countries; the relative importance of different economic sectors in the cities; the income and the purchasing power of different groups within the urban population.

The aspect of administrative science centres mainly on the question of land access, but other aspects, such as the organization of agricultural extension and the supply of agricultural input (seeds, organization of the collection of organic waste), should also be included. Finally, the social aspect of the social sciences is to consider the socio-economic situation of the urban producers, with particular emphasis on combined incomes, strategies for acquiring access to land, labour allocation and labour distribution within the household group; on questions of cooperation and exchange, and also agricultural knowledge in an urban context. As elsewhere, the research problem is on different levels: the micro-(individual) level, where the adaptation of agricultural knowledge of a migrant coming from rural areas to urban conditions is studied, and a meso-level, where processes of knowledge exchange and processes of specialization in an urban quarter are examined. The aspect of development in urban agriculture could thus bring into perspective an aspect which seems to be more significant in household gardens and intra-urban agriculture than in the highly industrialized cases of peri-urban agriculture which are often stereotyped copies of models imported from industrialized countries.

For intra-urban agriculture at least, a field of special importance is the field of intersection between the urban administrative situation and the informal legal conditions and activities. Land rights in the urban context of Africa often belong neither to the type of modern (European) land right titles nor to customary African land rights. Nevertheless, this land is not devoid of security rights, and the precise legal status of these rights and the methods of documenting it constitute an important research issue. The question of land access by privileged groups, especially in urban administration, and client-oriented land procurement, as well as land security in exchange for votes in urban elections, which are of importance for urban administrators at the most local level, is also addressed in the aforementioned intersections. Finally, it is a matter of concern that the recent African policy of formalization of the statut of land with illegal squatters on it and the overall tendency towards formalization of informal activities should not have the effect of alienation and thereby deprive informal activities of their innate dynamism.

7.2 Suggestions for practical action

As the previous points have shown, African urban agriculture is largely underdeveloped, in spite of its enormous social and ecological significance. In principle, the development of urban agriculture constitutes a task for African municipalities. But given their chronic financial weakness, especially in the present situation, they cannot afford these tasks alone. Since the provincial and national administration are now also undergoing a financial crisis, international support could be conceivable. Nevertheless, each level has its special attributes, and close collaboration and coordination is needed. The active participation of the population within an institutionalized framework in exercising control is still more indispensable here than elsewhere. Projects need complex organization with the municipality as its centre.

Many projects which are supported by administration and external donors concern commercial agriculture (cf. the aforementioned projects at Lomé or Kinshasa), especially in peri-urban areas. Given the urban need for vegetables and fruit, the labour force which can be employed and the often sub-optimal character of commercial agriculture, these projects are certainly of great importance. They often have the form of institutionalized cooperatives and must exist in a balance between the market, administrative cooperation and cooperation between the members (Ganapathy 1984). But informal urban agriculture which focusses mainly on subsistence production should not be overlooked either. A limitation on projects for commercial agriculture would tend to discriminate particularly against disadvantaged social groups, such as women and the poor, who often find it difficult to buy the products of commercial agriculture. In order to assist also these groups, first the crucial question of land access for the urban poor should be resolved. The recent tendency towards more "tolerance" must be developed in the direction of more security in land holding.

But the best technical solutions can fail if they are planned and executed without popular participation. As Mabogunje (1990), the well-known Nigerian specialist for urban development, has described, predatory and individualistic class attitudes prevail in many urban residential areas of Nigeria and have created a sense of anomie, and means and public institutions are misused by those in power for their own personal purposes. In order to change this tendency and re-install a sense of community, the author suggests transferring the British model of neighbourhood councils to Nigerian cities. It seems likely that such institutions would be highly recommendable to assure more equal distribution of the benefits of a developed urban agriculture. Moreover, such institutions could also help overcome the overall lack of cooperation and coordination which is one of the most fundamental problems of urban agriculture.

References

Adrien-Rongier, M.-F. (1980): Les *kodro* de Bangui: un espace urbain "oublié", Cahiers d'Etudes Africaines, Vol. 21, No. 81-82.

Alaruka, A.A. and N.K. Choma (1985): Les femmes de Kisangani et la pratique agricole, Annales de l'Institut Supérieur Pédagogique de Kisangani Etudes, Série A, No. 14, Juillet, pp. 83-95.

D'Souza, St., M.M. Makaya and Kalendi, M. (1994): Evaluation du niveau de la pauvreté à Kinshasa: cas de la zone de Matete, Zaire-Afrique XXXVe Année, No. 294, 219-236.

Freeman, D.B. (1991): A City of Farmers: Informal Urban Agriculture in the Open Spaces of Nairobi, Kenya. Montreal etc.

Ganapathy, R.S. (1984): Urban Agriculture, Urban Planning, and the Ahmedabad Experience, Ahmedabad.

Hake, A. (1977): African Metropolis: Nairobi's Self-Help City, New York: St. Martin's Press.

Jaeger, D. (1985): Subsistence Food Production Among Towndwellers—The Example of Lusaka, Zambia, Amsterdam: Royal Tropical Institute, Research Paper.

Lubuimi, M.L. (1995): Exemple de la stratégie de lutte contre la pauvreté et développement efficace: le rôle du secteur informel dans la gestion des déchets à Kinshasa, in: Stefan Marysse et al., pp. 131-141.

Marysse, Stefan et al. (1995): Le secteur informel au Zaire. Partie I.: Concept, ampleur et méthode, Antwerpen: Universitaire Faculteiten Sint Ignatius.

Mabogunye, A.L. (1990): The Organization of Urban Communities in Nigeria, Intern. Social Science Journ., No. 125, pp. 355-366.

Mashindi, D.M. and M. Mwanza (1992): Pour une éducation mésologique: l'exemple de l'utilisation des ordures ménagères dans la ville de Kinshasa, Bulletin Géographique de Kinshasa-Géokin, Vol. III, No. 1, janvier-juin, pp. 103-130.

Maxwell, D. and S. Zziwa (1992): Urban Farming in Africa. The Case of Kampala, Uganda, Nairobi: African Centre for Technology Studies.

Mazingira Institute (1988): Urban Food Production and the Cooking Fuel Situation in Urban Kenya, African Urban Quarterly, pp. 849-870.

Mbiba, B. (1995): Urban Agriculture in Zimbabwe, Aldershot etc.: Avebury.

Mosha, A.R. (1991): Urban Farming Practices in Tanzania, Review of Rural and Urban Planning in Southern and Eastern Africa, No.1, pp. 83-92.

Mpasi, Z.M. (1992): Quelques facteurs qui amplifient le déboisement dans l'auréole d'influence de Kinshasa, Bulletin Géographique de Kinshasa-Géokin, Vol. III, No. 4, janvier-juin, pp. 27-35.

Mpuru, M.B. (1993): Approvisionnement vivrier immédiat de Kikwit. Aperçu préliminaire, Bulletin Géographique de Kinshasa-Géokin, Vol. IV, No.1, janvier-juin, pp 37-47.

Mufuta, K. (1994): Les intellectuels au champ, in: F.O.N.C.A.B.U. (ed.): La sécurité alimentaire au Zaïre, Bruxelles, pp. 9-10.

Neupert, R.F. (1992): Extended Households: A Survival Strategy in Poverty, in: C. Goldschneider (ed.): Fertility Transitions, Family Structure, and Population Policy, Boulder, Colorado, pp. 197-208.

Ngondo a Pitshandenge (1996): Nucléarisation du ménage biologique et renforcement du ménage social à Kinshasa, in: ZAIRE-AFRIQUE, XXXVIe Année, No. 308, Octobre 1996, pp. 419-444.

Noe Gui-Diby (1991): Les conséquences urbaines d'une démographie incontrôlée. Développement et Coopération, No. 4, pp. 14-17.

Numengi, D. (1995): Le mal zaïrois. Le Monde Diplomatique Novembre, p. 20

Obara, D. (1988): Urban Agriculture, African Urban Quarterly. pp. 849-870.

O'Deye, M. (1985): Les associations en villes Africaines, Paris: L'Harmattan.

Pain, M. (1985): Kinshasa: La ville et la cité, Paris: O.R.S.T.O.M.

Percival, G.C., J.A.C. Harrison and G.R. Dixon (1993): Biological Control of Seed Potato Tuber Pathogens, Abstract for the 14th World Plant Pathology Conference, Montreal, Canada.

Sachs, I. and D. Silk (1990): Food and Energy. Strategies for Sustainable Development, Tokyo: United Nations University Press.

Sanyal, B. (1986): Urban Cultivation in East Africa, Paris: United Nations University/Food Energy Nexus Programme

Schilter, Ch. (1991): L'agriculture urbaine à Lomé, Paris: IUED-Karthala.

Schlyter quoted by Jaeger, D. (1985): Subsistence Food Production among Town Dwellers—The Example of Lusaka, Zambia, Amsterdam: Royal Tropical Institute, Research Paper.

Streiffeler, F. and M. Mbaya (1986): Village, ville et migrations, Paris: L'Harmattan.

Stren, R.E. (1992): African Urban Research Since the Late 1980s: Responses to Poverty and Urban Growth, Urban Studies, 29, 3/4, pp. 533-555.

United Nations Development Programme (1996): Food, Jobs and Sustainable Cities, Urban Agriculture. New York.

United Nations Population Fund (1996): Weltbevölkerungsbericht (German version), Bonn.

9

Women in Rural Production, Household and Food Security: An Iranian Perspective

Parto Teherani-Krönner

1 Introduction

Women have been ignored in the food security discussion for a long time. The analysis of gender relations will be of significance when problems in food production, processing, and household economy are dealt with. Women in Iran, for example, play a tremendous role in the economy, not only at the household level, but on the national level as well. They are the producers of the most important export good besides oil. Even if not statistically registered as such, most women and girls are the creators of the well-known and treasured Persian carpets. This handicraft production makes up 90 percent of the family income in regions where agricultural production is low. In regions with intensive farming, women's share in rice and tea production is 77 percent according to detailed case studies in villages on the Caspian Sea. Looking from the outside, it is not easy to understand the power structure behind the veil. This article will give some insights into the Iranian situation on the basis of recent field research and gender policy in Iran.

I will first present the food security discussion in Iran, influenced by the 1992 United Nations Food and Agricultural Organisation conference, with respect to findings and the status of women seen as "vulnerable" (section 2). Section 3 is devoted to the discourse on women in development with special emphasis given to rural women in agriculture and to carpet weaving as an important source of household security and national income. This combination gives us two images of women: one as vulnerable, the other as an economic resource—powerful agents of social change. Finally, I point out the missing link between the food security debate and women: It is the household that is the key to food security and gender relations (section 4). My conclusion is that food security needs to be engendered with respect to the sociocultural and normative system of nutrition (sections 5 and 6).

2 The food security discussion in Iran

2.1 In the footsteps of international conferences

Food security has become an important topic of discussion in Iran in recent years. The United Nations Food and Agricultural Organisation's (FAO) 1992 conference in Rome put the issue of worldwide food security on the international agenda. The

FAO's 1992 declaration called for the institution of national plans up to the year 2000, and Iran was one of the countries that committed itself to the implementation of the goals of this resolution. The resonance of the FAO conference and the official discourse on food security in Iran was documented in 1994 in a special issue of the *Journal of Agricultural Economic Studies* on food security.[1] Djazayer (1994: 247) summarizes the aims of the FAO conference declaration as follows:

- political responsibility to improve food security,
- development with a view to protecting the environment and guaranteeing sustainability,
- economic growth that benefits all the people,
- priority given to the most vulnerable groups—this means that women and children should be given special consideration,
- more public participation,
- giving women due respect,
- offering nutritional services and guaranteeing healthy food through technical cooperation among developing countries.

These points were intended to provide the basic framework for policy orientation in Iran and elsewhere; in particular, they underline the fact that policy must respect the role of women. Women were targeted at the 1992 FAO conference because they were regarded as a vulnerable social group that must therefore be taken into account in food security policy planning. Looking after the vulnerable—attending to the needs of the weak and the underprivileged—was not supposed to be a new objective for the Iranian regime. This basic premise has been a mainstay in the overall policy of the Islamic Republic of Iran. *Mostasaf*, meaning literally, "the weak", refers to the oppressed and most deprived segments of the population as well as women; it was included in the core concept of the revolutionary policy some 19 years ago.

Although none of the articles in the food security special issue of the *Journal of Agricultural Economic Studies* deals with gender issues exclusively or focuses specifically on women, they are at least noted in several contributions. So, aside from only brief mention, women have tended to be excluded from the food security debate in general. In the majority of subsequent publications from the Research Institute of Agricultural Planning and Economic Studies in Iran, women were either overlooked, marginalized, or dealt with separately (*JAES* 1995a) (I shall examine some of these publications in greater detail in the following section).

1 This special volume gives an overview of the food discussion at international level. The FAO conference is mentioned alongside a number of other UN conferences such as the United Nations Conference on Environment and Development (UNCED) in Rio 1992, the Social Summit in Copenhagen, the United Nations Conference on Population and Development (ICPD) in Cairo in 1994, and the 4th International Conference on Women in Beijing in 1995 (JAES 1994: 317), in which women had an essential role. JAES is the house journal of the Agricultural Planning and Economic Research Institute, Ministry of Agriculture. It is published in Persian.

2.2 Research on food security in Iran and the findings

Indicators in food security research are taken from the general discussion with reference to the international FAO and World Health Organization (WHO) standards on the availability of food, average per capita consumption in terms of calories, proteins, iron, calcium and other nutrients, or the food basket combination. Food security research in Iran can be characterized as follows.

2.2.1 Abundance of food but no food security

Even taking the rapid rate of population growth into account, statistically there is still plenty of food in Iran, yet the country has no food security. Although in recent decades agricultural production has increased, and this in turn has contributed to improvements in the country's self-sufficiency, a relatively high percentage of the Iranian population still suffers from malnutrition (Djazayer 1994: 249). Nevertheless statistics indicate that there should be enough food in the country for everyone. Ghasemi and Najafi (1994) suggest that Iran has the capacity to feed 100 million people but, in fact, it has not been able to supply its 60 million inhabitants proper nourishment. Twenty percent of the calories consumed by the population are from imported foodstuffs; agricultural productivity is low; one-fourth of all Iranian consumers are malnourished and another fourth lack an adequate intake of vitamins and minerals (Ghasemi and Najafi 1994: 257).

2.2.2 Food consumption in Iran is unbalanced

Norusi (1994) discusses the results of field studies conducted in nine provinces of Iran by the Ministry of Agriculture's Research Institute and the Research Institute for Nutrition and Food Technology. According to these studies 25 percent of the households investigated were not food secure, while 35 to 40 percent actually had more than they needed (Norusi 1994: 41 ff.; Djazayer 1994: 249). This imbalance has been generally confirmed by the Nationwide Household Food Consumption Pattern Survey Project carried out by a number of research institutions, ministries and universities between 1991 and 1993. The Iranian National Nutrition and Food Technology Research Institute (NNFTR) published some of the results of this survey in November 1995 (see NNFTR 1995b). "In 1993, out of every six individuals two were at the risk of qualitative and quantitative nutritional deficiency; one had an intake over requirement, and only three enjoyed good nutrition. Significant efforts have yet to be made to make many households food secure" (NNFTR 1995b: 9). In order to redress this imbalance, the undernourishment of some social groups and overnourishment of others, Norusi (1994: 41 ff.) suggests that changes in consumption patterns be encouraged through information and extension services.

2.2.3 The gap between the poor and the wealthy, the urban and the rural populations

The lower classes face the most severe lack of food security (Djazayer 1994: 249). Differences between the urban and rural populations are significant. Ghasemi (1994) compares the access to food in urban and rural areas among the lower and upper classes in Iran, with reference to other countries like India, Pakistan, Thailand, Indonesia, Egypt, and Brazil. He states that the discrepancy between the upper and lower classes in the urban areas is greatest in Iran, followed by India. In all other countries (using calories as the main indicator) food consumption by wealthy rural inhabitants is higher than it is for all urban dwellers—again, except in Iran (Ghasemi 1994: 23).

The Iranian National Plan of Action for Nutrition also stresses the greater discrepancy between the country's northern and the southern provinces, whereby inhabitants in the south part of the country are confronted with many more difficulties in meeting household requirements (NNFTR 1995a). Energy protein malnutrition (EPM), afflicting mainly children under five years of age, is identified as the country's primary nutrition problem. "In 1991, four percent of the Guilani children (in the north) and 47 percent of the Sistani-Baluchestani children (in the southeast) had a body weight below standard (third percentile for girls) . . ." (NNFTR 1995a: 11).[2]

2.2.4 Subsidies do not reach the vulnerable

In order to attain food security for everyone, including Iran's poorest, the government has devoted much of its resources to subsidizing nutrition, in particular, to making bread available to everyone. Iran is among the countries that continuously import the greatest amounts of wheat per annum. "Over the past ten years eight countries more or less consistently have imported more than one million metric tons of cereals a year: the former Soviet Union, Japan, China, the Korean Republic, Egypt, Mexico, Iran, and Italy" (Jiggins 1994: 67).

In 1993 about 18 percent of the state budget was spent directly on a variety of subsidies. "Seventy percent of consumer subsidies and 53 percent of the total subsidies were spent on wheat for bread production; this was the largest subsidy, followed by vegetable oil and sugar subsidies. The urban inhabitants get a larger share of subsidies as compared with the rural population" (NNFTR 1995b: 9). This is especially the case because of the significant gap between social groups, and the unbalanced situation between rural inhabitants and urban dwellers who benefit more from subsidies (Djazayer 1994: 249). The disadvantages associated with

2 For a more detailed overview, see the research project, "Nationwide Household Food Consumption Pattern Survey" (NNFTR 1995b), which presents data on the caloric, protein and other nutrient intake in accordance with FAO and WHO expert recommendations for individual households. These data show average daily intake for persons in different provinces, distinguishing between urban and rural areas, but not revealing differences among the households or household members (NNFTR 1995b).

living conditions in rural areas have induced migration which, in turn, has changed the relationship between the urban and rural populations in Iran in recent decades. Agricultural production has also been affected by this policy of subsidizing food. "Due to price differences and heavy subsidies on bread, farmers sell their wheat to the government and buy subsidized bread from the bakeries, although there are some households who still bake their own bread" (NNFTR 1995b). If subsidies are supposed to reach the most vulnerable another strategy should be reflected and the structure of food policy must be thought over.

2.2.5 Waste and loss in food production and processing

Compared with other developing countries, the recorded amounts of production waste and loss are extensive and serious. Norusi calculates the food loss at approximately 25 to 30 percent. This figure is even higher when fresh vegetables and herbs, essential to the daily diets of many Iranians, are added to the equation. Losses can then amount to an estimated 50 percent. "This means that, on the basis of FAO standards, 10% of our production is lost, and this also includes loss of resources like soil and water and other inputs in the production process" (Norusi 1994: 41).

Norusi and others argue that improvements in storage capacity, conservation, and the processing of agricultural products coupled with necessary infrastructural development are of the greatest importance to the country (Kimiagar and Pajan 1994; Ghasemi and Najafi 1994).

2.2.6 Different views on how to achieve food security

Assuming an increase in consumption based upon a higher intake of calories and protein by a growing population in Iran over the next 20 years, Norusi's prognosis differs from the political aim of achieving food self-sufficiency in the country. According to her calculations, Iran can either attempt to achieve self-sufficiency in wheat production or animal proteins, each to the exclusion of the other. If it opts, for instance, to produce more animal proteins, self-sufficiency in cereals will not be possible (Norusi 1994; compare also section 5.3 Changes in customs and food habits).

As in the general discussion on food production and food supply, food security cannot be generated in terms of figures and statistical averages. It is not the amount of food or food supply that provides us with sufficient indicators for food security; rather, it is purchasing power that has become the more significant factor at the core of this discussion. The capacity to buy food is central to dealing with the problem (Ghasemi and Najafi 1994: 258).

Amartya Sen's (1981) thesis on entitlement, focusing on the household level, is considered a novel approach which will become increasingly relevant for food security as this century draws to a close and the next millenium begins (Ghasemi 1994: 13). Ghasemi and Najafi (1994: 257-288) call for more social science oriented research and planning to resolve the problems of food security in Iran, which heretofore have been regarded mostly from a natural science perspective, focusing primarily on medical indicators. Ghasemi and Najafi concentrate on the political and economic aspects of bread production, distribution, and consumption, as well as subsidies for this key commodity. The reasons for their particular focus are political, relating in part to the recent period of war.[3]

Despite political and economic orientation in food security approaches, the perception remains too narrow. As a complex sociocultural issue, food security should not be reduced solely to political strategies based on economic data of calculated averages and differences among social groups in Iran. A solution cannot be reached, if people themselves, their nutritional habits, and their cultural attitudes towards food in the context of the social order and gender relations are not respected (see below).

2.3 Women as a target group: the vulnerable

In the National Plan of Action for Nutrition women are depicted among the weakest social elements of Iranian society that must be protected. Their image is that of a marginalized social group. "The vulnerable and deprived groups include women and children, the handicapped, the elderly, the unemployed, foreign immigrants and refugees, landless farm workers, and rural immigrants to suburban areas. The care of these groups, and investments to promote and protect their health and to increase their work efficiency are essential in national development plans. At present, about 24 percent of the population throughout the country benefit from economic, social, and health supporting services. However, the numbers and proportions of the deprived and vulnerable groups are not known precisely" (NNFTR 1995a: 31).

Khadijeh Rahmani (1992) conducted a number of research projects on food security and health in the most remote areas in Khorasan in the southeastern part of the country. The results were more or less similarly dramatic.[4] She gave special attention to vulnerable women and children and presents an overview of the misery in these regions where, for most of the villages, undernourishment is not exceptional. Rahmani's research concept is directed towards nutrition at the household level, focusing on the health conditions of mothers and children in this rural region of Iran. She collected data on the daily meals of individuals based on 24-hour cycles. In addition to this she used anthropometric methods to assess the level of

3 It is remarkable that difficulties associated with food security have not been particularly attributed to the conditions that prevailed during the war in this special volume of the JAES on food security. Two exceptions to this are an article on bread by Ghasemi and Najafi (1994: 257-288) and an article by Jamshid Payujan (1994: 147 ff.) on food security at household level, focusing on the food basket, that refers indirectly to the war issue.

4 "Research on the Situation of Nutrition and Health in the Region of Machunik, South Khorasan" was a project conducted in cooperation with the Department of Medicine at Beheshti University and the National Institute of Nutrition and Food Industry in 1992.

health among mothers and children in different villages of the Khorasan region. Rahmani found that Iranian women in this area in general suffer from malnutrition: their weights and heights are below average; their daily intake of calories, proteins, minerals and other nutrients are below the desired WHO standard. In view of the fact that there is theoretically sufficient food in Iran to nourish all of its population adequately, Rahmani's research on the single household level shows the absurdity of general statistics.

Women have become one of the main target groups in terms of guaranteed food security in Iran, and they are addressed by family planning organizations as well as mother-and-child care programs at national and local level, in rural and urban settings. One of the positive results from this kind of social counselling and engagement in terms of improved nutrition and health care has been the increase in breast feeding among new mothers from 65 percent in 1979 to 98 percent in 1994 (Djazayer 1994: 250).

Population growth in Iran, despite the tremendous efforts made to reduce it, will still be a significant factor affecting the development process up to the year 2010.[5] This means that there is a great pressure to increase and improve infrastructural services (Nejatian 1995) in a country where half of the population is under 15 years of age (NNFTR 1995b: 9).

The Ministry of Health in conjunction with the United Nations Population Fund (UNFPA) has successfully established a countrywide network of local medical houses engaging a significant number of women volunteers to assist in primary health care services. "The Iranian program is in many ways a model, since it is strongly supported from the top by national leaders; it is organized at the grassroots level, with a local volunteer being responsible for roughly 50 families; it offers a full range of contraceptive services" (Brown 1996: 125). Insofar as this program has been recommended as one of the most effective ones in terms of providing food security (Foster 1992), it represents an important part of struggle against malnutrition.

In general, strategies for attaining food security are still based upon an image of women that depicts them as vulnerable or deprived, and that wholly underestimates women's active share to food and household security. The visible and the invisible contributions of women have not yet been fully recognized and appreciated in the mainstream of food security debate—either in Iran or at international level. Women are not included in the core concept of food security debates: they are marginalized. But, if "household entitlement" is regarded as the latest approach to food security, then a new concept of "household" is needed. Engendering[6] food policy might help to overcome deficiencies and shortcomings. Women's vital role

5 "...the annual population growth rate decreased from 3.9% in the period 1976-1986 to 2.82% in the period 1986-1993" (NNFTR 1995b: 9). The Ministry of Health announced a further reduction by 1.8% in 1995 (Maroofi 1997: 125).

6 For engendering policy in general see as well Lachenmann (1997) and Teherani-Krönner and Altmann (1997).

for the household economy and livelihood of the family as well as their share in the agricultural sector in food production and food processing is part of the ongoing discussion of women in development (WID) and WID approaches in rural areas which will be the subject of the following section.

3 Discovering the power behind the veil

3.1 Women as a key to development

Since the early 1990s attempts have been made to make women's work more visible. In fact, the activities undertaken in Iran during this relatively short period of time represent some remarkable steps. Official programs began with the establishment of the Bureau of Women's Affairs (BWA) in December 1991 as a department in the Office of the former President Rafsanjani. The BWA was designed to "coordinate the development of the government policies and the programs formulated to improve the status of women" (WAD 1994). One important task of the BWA during the initial period of its operation was the preparatory work for the UN's international conference on women in Beijing in 1995. The required country report made it necessary to collect available data; thus a number of research projects were undertaken. Activities at ministerial level began to try to reach local level and to devote some attention to rural women in Iran. A total of 46 old and new women's non-governmental organizations (NGOs) were discovered, or created and institutionalized, and coordinated to form a delegation to the NGO Forum[7] in Huarou, 60 kilometers from Beijing (see the Iranian country report, BWA 1995).

Domestic activities were based on the initiatives and engagement of a number of well-educated women activists in Iran—not to forget the participation of the many women who, for example, voted for the President Khatami in May 1997, hoping for a more liberal political culture in Iran (*Zanan* 1997b). In the most recent times women have created a lively press in the country. Articles about women's issues and women's rights were published in a number of selected journals, showing women as a key to development.[8] *Zanan* ("women"), for example, is a journal that mirrors the intellectual discourse on women's empowerment in Islamic Iran, discussing even feminism and the possibility of women finding their own interpretations of issues (see the article by Motiee in *Zanan* 1997a).

In addition to these domestic efforts, there has been a very decisive push from the outside by international organizations like the various UN institutions (represented in Iran). The United Nations Development Programme (UNDP)

7 The woman who represented the NGO delegation, Massoumeh Ebtekar, became Vice-president and Head of the Organization of Environmental Protection in Iran under the new President, Khatami, in 1997. She is head of the Center for Women's Studies and Research, and editorial director of the journal, *Farzaneh* (journal of women's studies and research) which publishes articles in Persian and English.

8 *Mahjubeh*, *Farzaneh* and *Zanan*, for instance, present different views of women's space for maneuver within an Islamic society.

supported a report on the situation of women in Iran (Nassehy 1993). In the WID discussions the United Nations International Children's Emergency Fund (UNICEF) played a notable role in organizing seminars, supporting workshops on gender awareness, and training (reported by UNICEF Tehran and OESRF 1993 and UNICEF 1994).[9] Recently, the World Bank has also provided funding for agricultural research projects, making it one of their preconditions that the women's situation be taken adequately into account (Pandam 1997).

Women in rural development have at least become an issue at ministerial level: WID is on the agenda of both organizations active in rural development, the Ministry of Jihad and the Ministry of Agriculture (Maroofi 1997: 122 ff.). It looks as if these ministries are becoming aware of the importance of gender studies and projects to be addressed to the female population in different parts of the country. In a way, it appears easier to set as a requirement that special attention be given to the female population in a country where obvious gender segregation is practiced. In order to reach the female population in the rural areas, female advisors and other female personnel are needed. The Rural Women's Development and Extension Office (RWDEO), for instance, wants to station female extension service workers at the provincial branches of the Ministry of Agriculture to address local farming women or other rural women.[10] The Agricultural Bank of Iran intends to provide grants and other forms of financial support to the so-called "vulnerable" women (Agricultural Bank 1994). The Ministry of Jihad has a special Bureau of Women's Affairs that offers a set of programs and instructional activities directed towards women in the Iranian countryside (Ministry of Jihad 1993).

The Center for Agricultural Planning and Economic Research of the Ministry of Agriculture (APERI) devoted a variety of research activities to women's issues, of which I will mention only the two national conferences on Women in Rural Development: the first held in 1995, and the second and most recent in September 1997.[11] The papers from the first conference were published in 1995 in a special issue of the quarterly *Journal of Agricultural Economics* titled "Women's Role in Agriculture". The most interesting aspects to this first conference were the controversial positions on WID concerning the institutionalization of women's cooperatives in rural areas. Different standpoints were discussed concerning whether these cooperatives should be based on the traditional type of women's collective work

9 The effects of various UN programs on rural women have already been studied in some detail by Professor Jaleh Shaditalab (1997).

10 To support women's economic activities and to promote their participation on a wider scale, a special Rural Women's Cooperative Office was established within the Department of Agricultural Cooperatives (Maroofi 1995, 1997; Tohid 1996).

11 The Bureau of Women's Affairs of the Ministry of Jihad was not officially invited. This was mentioned to me and criticized, when I visited that office a few days later. Participation and cooperation among the ministries must be improved if there is a common aim to elevate the status of women and improve the living conditions in rural areas by the year 1400.

called *vareh* (Farhadi 1995) or implemented according to a new, Western-influenced type of agricultural cooperative.[12]

The second national conference on WID, held in September 1997, was set under the title, "Women, Participation and Agriculture in the Year 1400".[13] The conference presented a number of empirical reports which can be seen as preliminary research designed to lay the foundations for policy formulation (Fanni 1997; Shaditalab 1997; Ghorayshi 1997; Lahsaizadeh 1997; Warzgar and Azizi-Babai 1997; Sarhadi, Malmir and Sarichani 1997). However, the future of women's participation in agriculture was not yet clearly articulated in terms of policy programs or alternative scenarios. Although this conference was hosted by the Ministry of Agriculture and titled "Women, Participation and Agriculture in the Year 1400", there were no rural women present.[14] Even if the new trend towards empirical field research in different rural areas can be seen as one positive outcome, there is a methodological shortcoming (see section 4.2): research still follows mainstream statistical quantitative survey research without considering qualitative or participatory methods like participatory rural appraisal (PRA).[15]

3.2 Women's role in agricultural production

Women have been the objects of many different types of programs, but independent of planning and project designing for women, they have also been the subjects of and active agents in the development process—engaged in economic, social, and cultural change throughout the country. Now, even in the Islamic Republic of Iran, economic argumentation has become quite significant in women's studies as a means to promote "progressive" gender policy. Treating women as an economic factor is designed to increase their productivity and to promote income-generating activities, along the lines of the "efficiency approach" in WID (see Moser 1989). "Considering the important role played by Iranian rural women in agricultural products, livestock raising, handicraft products as well as other productive rural activities, throughout recent years a number of projects have been carried out to increase their productivity and efficiency" (Maroofi 1997: 123).

More recent studies on women in rural areas have tried to emphasize their share in production, degree of participation, and their workload—factors that have

12 It is remarkable that at this time an open controversial scientific debate was possible in Iran.

13 Which will be in about 24 years or ca. 2022 by the Gregorian calendar. In accordance with the Persian calendar, the Gregorian year 1997, for instance, corresponds to 1376.

14 The Minister of Agriculture opened the seminar with the critical and cutting remark: "I do not see the rural women taking part in this conference on women's participation. Where are they?" Prof. Jaleh Shaditalab responded to this remark by saying: "We do not have problems with rural women; we are addressing this conference to the policymakers, planners, national and local administrations, and the persons in charge at ministerial level." The comments of both persons raise an important point about top down versus bottom up approaches in project planning and policy making that is worthy of more intensive consideration.

15 The 1997 conference also failed to address adequately the issue of sustainable development and the ecological problems entailed by an intensification of agricultural production.

not been registered thus far in the general statistics of the country. Official statistical data on the economically active population in Iran have calculated women's share in the agricultural sector as less than 10 percent (Motiee 1995; SCI 1986, 1991). Azimi (1997) in an effort to correct official statistics, calculates women's share of agricultural production to be around 20 percent. Still other surveys indicate that the role of women in agriculture is clearly more significant than heretofore acknowledged: "According to the surveys with regard to the role of rural women in production, rural women have carried out 40% of the activities in the agricultural sector" (Hashemi 1996: 2; Maroofi 1997: 123).[16] A figure of 40 percent looks like a wise political compromise—not too low to be ignored, important enough to be recognized, but not so high as to imply that the contribution of women might be equal to (i.e., close to 50%) or greater than that of men—a notion that for many is still unthinkable.

Over and above these general data, the most valid information can be obtained from more in-depth case studies. For example, in the northern part of Iran where rice and tee cultivation is common, 70 percent of the work is carried out by women (Sarhadi et al. 1991). This figure must be further differentiated according to class structure (Sarhadi, Malmir, and Saruchani 1997: 289).

Other, more exploratory empirical research methods indicate an even higher share for women in agricultural production that ranges from 50 to 90% (Motiee and Sarhadi 1994, cited in Ghorayshi, Sarhadi, and Motiee 1997: 7). Thus, the national census data obviously cannot be taken for granted, nor are these data free of gender bias. There are significant regional differences. Ghorayshi, Sarhadi, and Motiee conducted their field research in the northern part of Iran, where women are known for their economic independence.[17] Regional bias cannot be entirely excluded for research conducted in this area. The diverse cultural ecological conditions in Iran influence living situations, social interaction, and the construction of gender relations throughout the country. Statistical averages alone are not of any great help in attempting to understand and elucidate the many differences and contradictions.

No matter whether women are statistically registered as "economically active" or not, they do in fact produce the country's next most important good for export after crude oil.

3.3 Carpet weaving as a source of household security

Generally we identify rural activities with agricultural production, but in Iran this must be broadened to include another important income-generating activity in the rural areas, namely, carpet weaving, the best known handicraft in Iran. Persian rugs, the products of women's handicraft, are not just part of a subsistence economy: they are present in nearly every household in Iran. Persian carpets are sold on the

16 Fatimeh Hashemi and Parvin Maroofi were both engaged in the preparatory work for the UN International Conference on Women in Beijing.

17 Elderly illiterate women who still do the paddy work call themselves "gil mard", men of Gilan.

local markets and exported nearly all over the world; thus the role of this product is by no means marginal and much more attention should be paid to the producers of this typical and important Persian good. It is astounding how undervalued such an important economic activity still remains. Insofar as the household economy and entitlement are important sources for guaranteed food security, such productive activities at household level should not be ignored. In fact, however, the producers of carpets at household level are not counted as economically active. Although the statistical data on such an important handicraft is more confusing than illuminating, there are a few facts that can be generalized.

- In addition to crude oil, carpets are Iran's most important export good.
- Eighty percent of Iran's carpets are produced in rural areas of the country.
- Nearly all Persian carpets are produced at the household level.
- More than 80 percent of Iran's carpet producers are women and young girls.
- In regions where agricultural production is low, carpet weaving can cover a high percentage of individual household budgets.

The Ministry of Jihad's 1993 report (volume 2), "Research on the Situation of Rural Women in Iran", states that: "One of the important income-generating activities of women and young girls in the rural areas is the weaving of all kinds of floor coverings—carpets and rugs as well as *kelims* and *silu*. The production and export of carpets accounts for the greatest source of income in Iran after [crude] oil" (Ministry of Jihad 1993, vol. 2: 370). According to different sources, some 400,000 to 600,000 households were engaged in carpet production in 1989. It was estimated that a total of nearly 3 million people were involved in this handicraft production, including 639,868 skilled female weavers and 92,601 males, and that 80 percent of all these workers live in rural areas (Ministry of Jihad 1993, vol. 2: 370; Maroofi 1992, 1997).

Another more recent source, the Statistical Center of Iran (SCI), calculates 1,167,077 households that have their own small production of carpets, rugs, *kelims*, and *silu* for 1994. The number of persons living in these households engaged in this type of handicraft production were calculated at 6.5 million, including children. Among the economically active persons in this group, women had a share of 84.1 percent. Carpet weaving still appears to be seasonal or occassional work. According to SCI data, in 1994 small household production units worked an average of 166 days per year at five hours per day to produce carpets, *kelims*, and other floor coverings (SCI 1995: 55). A collection of statistical data given by the Ministry of Jihad in 1996 shows an increase in carpet production in Iran. In 1981, 1.6 million carpet weavers were registered; in 1994, 13 years later, the number of carpet weavers had increased to 2.5 million, nearly 2 million of which were engaged at household production level (Ministry of Jihad 1996: 2). The Ministry of Jihad's 1996 statistics are concerned with carpets as an export good and they make no mention of women in this essential industry.

No matter how diverse or divergent the various figures are, there is nevertheless evidence that carpet weaving has increased over recent decades and that it remains an important source of income for rural households and even for some urban households. This means that female family members are the ones who contribute the most to this part of the household budget and to the national income from this export good. In regions where agricultural productivity is low, carpet weaving can account for up to 90 percent of a household's earnings (Maroofi 1992). In regions with a less intensive agricultural production, household economies depend much more on carpet weaving and *kelim* production (SCI 1995).

The fact that most carpets are created in rural areas by skilled (although not acknowledged as such) female weavers (at least of 80 percent on the household level), is a good reason to give greater attention to the well-being of the female rural population and the household. Giving more attention to women's work in order to improve handicraft production in rural areas, at the same time acknowledges that women are an important economic factor (Hashemi 1995: 179 f.).[18]

3.4 Empowerment through economic activities?

An economic interest in the income-generating activities of women does not automatically mean more empowerment for them. "Research on the Situation of Rural Women in Iran" (Ministry of Jihad 1993, vol. 2: 370 f.) reports that in the winter of 1979[19] the Iranian Carpet Corporation carried out a feasibility study in the villages of Ilam Province. The surprising fact was that the men were absent in the villages. They had emigrated to nearby cities to seek employment. In order to improve the economic situation in this region, the Iranian Carpet Corporation offered the villagers high quality raw materials. As anticipated, the carpets of this region became a valuable market commodity. The head of corporation visited this region not long ago and reported that, in the meantime, men had returned to the villages, but that now they controlled the work of the women, who were required to complete at least eight rows of knots per day, otherwise they would be chastised (Ministry of Jihad 1993, vol. 2: 371). The comment on this turn of events by the Ministry of Jihad was: "The income from carpet selling is remarkable [but] these men who do not participate in the production process collect and spend the earnings and do not permit their wives to have any say in the matter. The situation for women in this region is self-destructive" (Ministry of Jihad 1993, vol. 2: 371).

Thus even with increased production and increased productivity by women, it has not necessarily been to their benefit. In this case, the oppression of women was reinforced because they were compelled to produce more in order to generate more

18 As a traditional creative skill, carpet weaving requires the artistry and very specific local knowledge of the female population. Carpet patterns tell us stories, fairy tales, or myths from ancient times. Formerly, women in carpet weaving communities had to master a whole set of preparatory tasks and crafts, like spinning wool, silk, cotton; the extraction of colors; dying, designing, and developing artistic combinations in weaving. This has changed over the course of history because of the introduction of raw materials to the market and imported dyes. Local knowledge and skills have been ignored by dismissing these women as "illiterates". For the social and historical aspects of carpet weaving see Helfgott (1994).

19 This was the year of the revolution, at that time the Ministry of Jihad did not exist.

income, and they were now fully under the supervision and control of men (Teherani-Krönner 1995b: 228). We can only hope that programs developed by the Ministry of Jihad to improve the carpet weaving industry and conditions for women will not take this same direction.

A similar situation was described by Haleh Afshar (1981) in her article on carpet weaving in the village of Asiaback, 80 kilometers southwest of Qum. She pointed out that only men have access to the bazaar to sell carpets. "Women's work brought a new prosperity to the village. Fathers and husbands all began saving to buy a three-wheel truck to take the produce to the market. Women were placed under enormous pressure to earn more to buy and maintain the vehicle and even to replace it with a better one" (Afshar 1981: 84).

This type of work can be seen as means of oppression and source of disadvantage especially for young girls. "Probably young girls in villages shoulder much of the burden of early employment, compared to boys, because of girls' lower level of education and because girls are generally involved at a very early age in productive, income-generating activities such as carpet weaving" (Agricultural Bank 1994: 2).

Young girls are becoming the most important target group in rural development (UNICEF/*Farzaneh* 1997). Their literacy rate has steadily improved, although it is lower than that for young boys. New statistical figures show that 40 years ago there where nearly no literate individuals among rural women. Now, according to the 1996 figures given by Azimi (1997) 62.5 percent of rural Iranian women are literate. The figures vary according to age group: women under the age of 24 have an even literacy rate, 78 percent; literacy among girls aged 10 to 14 years reaches 91 percent (Azimi 1997: 20). The question remains whether literacy programs will indeed promote women's empowerment. It appears as though literate women will be less willing to remain in typical areas of rural production.

Some literate young girls and women I met in Gilan in September 1997, told me that they were no longer willing to stand in rice paddies or work in the fields like their mothers and grandmothers. Mothers today aspire to getting their daughters away from agriculture. They prefer (and encourage) them to stay at home, become housewives, or pursue other types of work (even though this aspiration may not represent a very realistic perspective because of the high rate of unemployment in Gilan and much of the rest of Iran).

4 Women in household security

4.1 The missing link in the chain

Considering the food security debate in Iran, on the one hand, and following the discussion and work done so far in WID, on the other hand, we are confronted with two main images of women: one approach (for instance, food security programs) treats women as vulnerable, whereby concerns are directed toward the issue of welfare and anti-poverty campaigns; the other approach treats women as an economic factor or resource to be developed and made more efficient and effective. The introduction of women's cooperatives to better organize income-generating activities in rural areas is one example of a typical WID approach in Iran (Tohid 1996; Maroofi 1997; *JAES* 1995a). Carpet production as shown above, although it is a flourishing economic activity, will not by itself guarantee more empowerment to Iranian women. The question, then, is whether income generation can really broaden the scope for action and decision making for and among rural women. Treating women as an economic factor or resource is part of the process of modernization. "The growing literature on rural women in Iran tends to focus on the economic role of women, speaks for rural women, but considers them as a 'problem' that has to be solved. 'Vulnerability' is one face to this approach" (Ghorayshi, Sarhadi, and Motiee 1997: 21).

There has been no direct, basic research on the important and active contribution of women to food security from the perspective of the household economy and income-generating activities in household production. Carpet weaving is just one example, quite typical for Iran, to illustrate the relevance of women in this domain of survival. Carpets or the simpler type of *kelim* or *silu* are not just export goods: they are highly valued and sometimes represent the only furnishing in an Iranian household. Living space is defined by the carpet or *silu*. Selling one's only carpet means that one has lost everything (figuratively, metaphorically, and literally, the ground under one's feet—one's foundation). Carpets also speak a language of their own in Iran. They have material as well as symbolic value. Wealth ranking, for instance, can be defined in terms of this item.

In carpet weaving, we find a most important source of household income and national wealth in the hands of Iranian women. These small household production units are not comparable or reducible to the so-called reproductive sphere of private family life and consumption typical for the occident.[20] Food security concepts in Iran must therefore include the household economy and gender relations. Insofar as the household economy is the key to food and entitlement, carpet production by women can provide, on the first order, household security.

There has been almost no research undertaken to investigate, for instance the psychological and social impacts on women doing this work—that is, studies of how their self-confidence is or can be effected. As already stated, this important contribution by women in Iran has yet to be really fully appreciated. A few articles do deal with home-based carpet production as part of the informal economy in a patriarchal structure maintaining the subordination of women (Ghavamshahidi 1995, Afshar 1981). Ghavamshahidi, for instance, recommends acknowledging the importance of this skilled work demonstratively by paying the artisans an appropriate wage. Further, it is questionable whether carpet production in Iran can be properly classified as "part of the so-called informal sector," since this commodity

20 Typical Western constructions nevertheless still continue to influence Iranian national statistics and the approach (by no means exclusive to Iran) that tends to classify work done at home as non-productive.

is of such major importance to the national economy. It is necessary, therefore, to rethink the categories or to redefine the formal versus the informal economy, as well as the typology of productive and reproductive activities. Carpet weaving has a very old historical and cultural background that makes it necessary to examine this activity and the importance of the household for the national economy more closely, from a gender perspective.

Up to now, the missing link between the food security debate and WID approaches has been the household. It is within this social space that age and gender relations are defined by different dimensions of the power structure. A new concept of household will give a different meaning to the visible but undervalued work of women as well as to the invisible work within this basic space of socioeconomic and sociocultural interaction. Persian carpets are beautiful works of art; they are pervasive, highly visible, valuable commodities; how strange it is, then, that their creation belongs to the realm of the "invisible"—women's work! Actually, however, the problem is not a matter of "the invisible women"—making women's work in the household visible—as discussed in UNESCO (1980); rather, the problem is that of the blindness of economists and economic theory. Taking household activities into consideration in the food security debate is to do no more than to insist that policymakers open their eyes.

A new concept of household must overcome traditional and modern cultural barriers and gender ideology (Razavi 1994). According to Islamic law and cultural norms in Iran, men are supposed to be the guardians/protectors, the heads of households and the breadwinners. They are responsible for the welfare and financial support of the family—especially the female family members. Men lose face—they are dishonored—if they cannot fulfill these obligations. This makes it difficult, therefore, to clarify a situation where women are *de facto* the breadwinners or household heads (Motiee 1997b). Zohreh Ghavamshahidi addressed this issue in her research on women's subordinated roles in home-based carpet production: "What are the strategies employed by low income families to resolve the contradiction between gender ideology—for example, men as breadwinners and women as housewives—and harsh economic realities like [the need] to bring in a cash income?" (Ghavamshahidi 1995: 137). Similar to conditions reported in other research done on home-based handicraft production—for instance, Mies' (1982) study of the lacemakers in Narsapur, India, or Beneria's study (1989) on domestic maquila in Mexico City, Mexico—Ghavamshahidi (1995: 137) points out that home-based carpet production is built upon low income earnings, precarious working conditions, and the vulnerability of labor.

By contrast, in her case studies on female-headed households, Nahid Motiee (1997b) confronts us with a very different situation and set of circumstances for those women labeled vulnerable. As household heads, such women face immense problems. They are vulnerable, on the one hand, in the sense that they have very little vocational/occupational opportunities, and that they face social discrimination outside and inside the family. On the other hand Motiee gives us to understand that such women are not victims: they accept their fate, but try to change their situation.

She shows the strength and power of these women who manage their everyday lives even under extremely difficult conditions. Motiee concludes that not all of these women are helpless and not all of them accept uncritically the ideology of female subordination or subjugation. "Many fight back, are powerful and have taken control over their lives. The life experience of these women shows that women are powerful agents and [that they] constantly work for change within their limitations and the external constraints imposed upon them. A study of these women's lives warns us to avoid simplistic views and generalizations" (Motiee 1997b: 8).

Thus, in considering ways to improve the situation for women, we should acknowledge their power and potential, as well as the material and immaterial constraints imposed upon them by normative systems. More attention should be given to the scope for action and to women's own gender perceptions and how they see themselves (Teherani-Krönner 1989, 1997a, b). Women have their own ways of constructing social reality and defining their own identities. They develop strategies within asymmetric structures and they do have autonomous spheres of action, especially in a segregated society. Women operate within their social networks with distinction. They encourage and strengthen social and emotional ties among family members and relatives; they organize meetings and festivities, provide services, and present gifts—not the least of which includes the preparation of meals—that link gender relations and social interaction. This will be discussed in the following section after some remarks on methodology and women's studies done in Iran thus far.

4.2 Some remarks on methodology and women's studies in Iran

Methodologically speaking, women's studies have taken a "gap" approach, confining themselves to analyses of constraints. Rural women are compared either to men or to urban women in terms of level of literacy, level of productivity, or their share in the labor force or market economy. Women's share in the labor market is the main focus of much of this research, even that carried out by female scientists (Kar 1994). The household remains the underestimated field of women's active participation, social interaction and female management capabilities. Much more attention should be given to everyday life, to women's informal networks, and their scope for action. There is a need to look beyond the veil. "A study of everyday life also makes it clear that women, as individuals and as agents, are social subjects who actively build their universe and are aware of the structural constraints within which they operate. Women are subjects/agents who make choices, have a critical perspective on their own situation, and link and organize collectively against their oppressors. Each individual, man or women, within their limits, has the power to change the conditions of daily life" (Ghorayshi, Sarhadi, Motiee 1997:12).

Research carried out in "Rostamkola",[21] represents an exceptional case with a decisively qualitative approach. Most Iranian research projects on women in rural areas use mainstream quantitative methodology—in particular, statistical data and surveys based upon pre-structured questionnaires. Ghorayshi, Sarhadi and Motiee mention some of the shortcomings in the available literature—despite its steady increase—on women's studies in Iran thus far. Among other things, they criticize in particular the low credibility of quantitative methods and the structured interviews used in order to obtain some view of rural women in Iran: "By relying on structured interviews, these studies freeze women in time and space and do not allow us to grasp the complexity of gender relations" (Ghorayshi, Sarhadi, and Motiee 1997: 21). Only very few (female) sociologists and anthropologists do field work in Iran using qualitative methods of research (see, for instance, Afshar 1981, Mir-Hosseini 1987, Wright 1981, Hegland 1991, Razavi 1994, or Ghavamshahidi 1995). Their data and articles are usually published outside the country. Articles in *Farsi*, an Iranian publication, normally do not represent research based upon qualitative methodology. Participatory approaches in research have not been used, nor were they even discussed, for example, during the conference on "Women, Participation and Agriculture in the Year 1400" hosted by Iran's Ministry of Agriculture in 1997. The Ministry of Jihad's Rural Research Center (RRC) has begun to undertake some projects designed to reach the people in the countryside. The RRC projects have adopted some of the new participatory approaches in research and planning (RRC 1997, Emadi 1997). Ghorayshi, Sarhadi, and Motiee (1997: 21) underscore the need for this type of approach in field research, based upon pluralistic and qualitative methods, in their article, "An Alternative Approach to Understanding Rural Women's Lives."

"We need concepts which reflect the reality of women and enable us to comprehend how differing social and material contexts interact to produce specific gender relations. It must be acknowledged that the experiences of women vary in many ways; that women are diverse, often in relations of domination and subordination" (Ghorayshi, Sarhadi, Motiee 1997: 22). Interactions on the household level are crucial to gender arrangements and, ultimately, food security. Thus food security needs to be "engendered".

5 Engendering food security reseach and policy

5.1 From food to nourishment

To give an idea about the possible understanding of food security in Iran, I will refer to the translation of this term into Persian. Translating a word with different connotations can prove quite complicated, but it is a challenge to clarify the meaning or even discover the connotations that are connected with a term.

21 "Rostamkola" is the fictitious name given to a village in Gilan Province where Ghorayshi stayed and researched for over a year.

Food security, I think, has found a most adequate translation in the Persian, *amniate ghazai—amniat* meaning "security" and *ghaza* which has been taken as equivalent to "food". By translating food security as *amniate ghazai* I should mention, that *ghaza* primarily means a prepared meal or dish. It is a term, however, which cannot be used semantically correctly for cereals like wheat, corn, barley, rice, or other natural products. These are raw materials or ingredients, that need to be turned into *ghaza*, a meal that can be eaten. Whereas the English term "food" can be applied to food for human consumption, including cereals, or to animal feed, this is not the case for *ghaza*. Even if there are similarities between some foods for animals and some foods for people, there is a slight difference: For example, human beings do not eat raw, unprocessed wheat nor do they generally prefer other cereals even though these might be healthy. Rice must be prepared with special sensitivity. It cannot be cooked simply. Rice, *berenj*, changes it's character depending, for instance, whether it is prepared as *polow* or as *chelow*. And, depending on its mode of preparation, it is named differently. The preparation of rice is almost treated like a sacred act, an art in the culinary culture of Iran. It is called the pride of Persian cuisine (Zubaida and Tapper 1994: 10).[22]

Agricultural products must be transformed, converted, changed—they must be turned into *ghaza* before they are served and eaten. Various activities in numerous steps must be coordinated in order to transfer food into a meal. The way we select, taste, prepare, and organize all this is a complicated procedure of social interaction and gender relations.[23] Human nutrition is deeply rooted in customs and beliefs present in everyday life. This should be reflected in the perception of food security as part of human maintenance. Semantically *amniate ghazai* corresponds better to this intention than does "food security", but I fear that the Anglo-Saxon influence has already narrowed the perspective even in a Persian-speaking country.

5.2 Who prepares the meal?

This may sound like a ridiculous, rhetorical question, but such an obvious necessity of everyday life has not really entered the food security discussion or influenced it very much. Even if living conditions are very diverse in Iran and the share of women in agricultural production and handicraft varies according to ecological conditions and crop requirements over and above considerations of ethnic identity and class cleavage, there is general agreement that food processing and the preparation of meals are female tasks. As mentioned before, 90 percent of food processing is carried out by women (Maroofi 1997: 123). No systematic research

22 Uncle Ben's parboiled rice has no chance of acceptance in Iran, even at a low, subsidized price. See as well the section in this contribution on changes in food habits.

23 "Food is essential to the subsistence and survival of individual human beings, who can prepare and consume it alone. Almost universally, however, the jobs involved in food preparation (from the production or procurement of ingredients to the cooking of meals) are allocated to specific categories of people, commonly by gender; and equally universally people prefer to eat with others. This specialization and sharing mark a wide range of social distinctions and relationships" (Zubaida and Tapper 1994: 11).

has been conducted on this issue—the question of who prepares the meal. In Iran it is hardly ever part of empirical field research: it is simply taken for granted. " It is only at the household level that economic and need-based assessments, quality considerations (including aesthetic ones), and the sociocultural factor that govern access to food (such as a person's age and gender) are incorporated into definitions of food security. This is unfortunate, as it is these aspects that are central to the determination of the level and distribution of actual hunger and malnutrition" (Jiggins 1994: 70).

The active role of women in food security in the sense of a culture bound, gender specific form of human maintenance is generally overlooked. Cooking is a female task as long as there is no financial compensation for it. Food preparation is too ordinary an activity for it to be registered as a scientific problem worthy of investigation and research. This may be one reason why it has been neglected for so long. Cooking and preparing meals are part of everyday life that belongs to the sphere of women's activities at home. Normally it is not a part of the man's world, even though men love to eat. Food preparation and the rituals that accompany the whole process of nutrition continue to be important links in the chain of social interaction and gender relations in the household, and in the system of communication. Ute Reichel (1996) mentions the vital importance of personal relationships and networks in Iran. The social status of men in Iranian society depends greatly on the traditions of generosity and hospitality at home. Here, the women have their exclusive domain and scope of action. It is within their responsibility and part of their power to prepare food and to determine the appropriate meals to be served (Reichel 1996: 17).

Eating outside the home—a consequence of modernization that can be observed among city dwellers—is still not very commonplace in Iran (Zubaida and Tapper 1994: 5; Fragner 1994: 66). Generally, cooking and eating takes place at home, where women are in charge of a whole set of processing activities. Even if men do the shopping and purchase the food—which is not seldom in Iran—they usually depend on women to maintain the kitchen. This stereotype persists in the normative system of gender relations, regardless of whether there are exceptions to it. Singles, people who live and eat alone, are seen as tragic.[24] Djamshid Payujan,[25] a (male) scientist, who acknowledged this fact, gives a good example of it in his article on the household budget. Even if someone has enough money to buy all the necessary items to prepare *ab gusht*,[26] a common meal in Iran, he cannot eat and

---

24 According to cultural norms, these individuals are considered the real poor: having no one to share with means poverty.

25 Djamshid Payujan is professor at the Alame Tabatabai University of Tehran. In his article (JAES 1994) he classified food priorities according to household budget and expenditures for major household commodities in rural and urban areas.

26 *Ab gusht* (meat broth) is a soup with legumen, different types of beans, tomatoes, potatoes as well as dried lemons and at least a little bit of meat and fat, that is called a simple meal, but became most prominent while meat becoming relatively expensive. You eat the soup with bread and squeeze the ingredients to a porridge.

enjoy it immediately. All the purchased foodstuffs need to be processed and prepared (Payujan 1994: 162). Usually this means that cleaning or washing, carving, cutting or chopping, boiling, roasting, frying or baking is necessary. Some technical equipment, like pots and pans, and some type of energy, like fire, are needed. Finally, one must have the right recipe for adding the seasonings, and the knowledge and skill to prepare a dish.[27] The combination of different ingredients must be turned into something that will fit one's taste, diet, as well as one's claim to satisfaction and expectations of health.[28] With his example of *ab gusht*, Payujan admits that all these activities give food products an added value or dimension that has not been recognized thus far (Payujan 1994: 162).

Time allocation is another important aspect to be considered. Cooking and preparing a meal takes time, but as long as this is women's time invested in the household, it is not calculated and registered as real work. This fact has been underscored by other examples of household activities performed by women that are income generating, for instance, carpet weaving. However, according to a modification of Iranian divorce law in 1992, which traces back to an Islamic principle that women are not obliged to work gratis for their husbands, a woman can claim the so-called *ojratol mesl*, or equivalent wage for the period of her marriage. Provision 6 of this law "determines the reparation to which a woman is entitled after the divorce" (WAD 1994: 5). Even if this appears very theoretical and far removed from everyday life, it is a remarkably progressive step.[29]

But, while women are doing the washing up, men are occupied with the food security debate and food security policy. The whole food security issue is a male-dominated discourse with a strong gender bias. The missing link is the one between food and nourishment, which can be traced back to the ideology of the kitchen.[30] In Iran and other places, it could be difficult for men (scientists) to enter this female-

27 Payujan gives reference to Gary Becker's article "A Theory of the Allocation of Time" (1965). Professor Günther Lorenzl was kind enough to give me the reference: Coleman and Young 1989: 113-124, with remarks on household production theory based on Becker's approach. This discussion could provide a useful frame of comparison in terms of the economic aspects to household activities in the field of food preparation.

28 It is also worth mentioning that in Iran most medical prescriptions are still combined with some recommendations concerning the proper things to ingest or avoid. The mode of preparation is essential to the diet. The traditional medical classification of foods in warm or cold dishes, and edible versus non-edible substances still plays a significant role in healing common diseases. Regardless of whether people take patented medicines (if they are available), they believe in this traditional classification which remains a vital part of everyday communication.

29 A female lawyer in Tehran told me in 1994 that she had been successful in obtaining the *ojratol mesl* for her clients in single cases.

30 In the struggle for emancipation, women were often pushed "back to the kitchen". In Western feminist debate the kitchen is a symbol of oppression and therefore it nearly amounts to a taboo where its analysis is concerned. Although more intention is directed to equality between men and women in the West, most western women nevertheless continue to take the responsibility for the daily meals, even if this activity is continuously bargained. This is a process that can be expected in Iran and other countries as well, as women enter the formal labour market and attempt to gain more equity. But not all women are willing to give up their very domain of relatively autonomous action.

dominated sphere of activity. But making the gender element an essential part of the discourse on food security could bring some light into the marginalized area of food preparation and distribution. The so-called "unproductive housewives" are busy producing many different types of marmalades, mixed pickles and sweets, and other salty or sour supplements that are usually prepared at home. Some of these goods even get into the market, but they are not registered as such because they are part of an informal household or subsistence economy (Payujan 1994: 163).

Motiee (1997a) describes the increased burden of housework among middle-class city dwellers in recent years. In the process of modernization in Iran, more and more people are living in the constellation of small, separate nuclear families. According to Motiee's observations, household activities have become more complicated than they were in former times. Formerly, women had a dense social network and they were able to build upon the help and cooperation of the extended family and the neighborhood in meal preparation, child rearing and other activities.[31] Now women must take care of everything in the household just by themselves. In sum, Motiee states that the process of modernization has not been in the favor of the female population in Iran up to now (Motiee 1997a). Women in modern times are confronted with increased expectations in their ability to prepare and serve plentiful meals as a symbol of the family's social status. Cookbooks like "Cooking Art" by Rosa Montazami have become recent best-sellers in Iran. In former times, women had their own modes of communication and knowledge transfer. Fragner (1994) stresses the fact that, originally, Persian cookbooks were not written for housewives. "Until the end of the 19th century, none of the Persian cookbooks we now know were written for housewives, who obviously had their own methods of transmitting recipes from one generation to another. . . . They were used to maintaining their very own, gender-specific methods of transmitting recipes among themselves, both horizontally within generations as well as from one generation to the next. ... Early, pre-modern cookbooks were, as far as we know, written by men, prominent masters of the art of cookery, most employed at princely courts" (Fragner 1994: 65). It is fair to assume that such men also surely received generous financial reward for their services.

5.3 Changes in customs and food habits

Looking to the historical background of food habits Fragner states: "The habit of rice eating was imported to this region from China following Mongol rule in Eurasia. In China and to a certain extent in India, rice has always been regarded as a basic means of nutrition, whereas in the area described above (Iran) rice is traditionally an extraordinary and highly prestigious kind of food" (Fragner 1994: 64).

Bromberger (1994) distinguishes the regions in northern Iran according to diet. The bread-eating and rice-eating areas have their own cultural backgrounds as

31 There are not yet very many day-care facilities for mothers with young children in Iran. The longer period of attending school for her school-aged children represents an additional burden for mothers.

well as ecological boundaries in combination with their modes of production. Different food habits are the markers of ethnic identity, distinguishing between the rice cultivating *rashdi* and the nomadic *talesh*, an ethnic group still maintaining their pastoral way of life and seasonal migration with their herds.

In addition to this cultural ecological distinction on a regional and local level in northern Iran, there are trends that we can observe on a more general level: "The most notable shift in food distribution and consumption in the region since the 1940s has been the shift to wheat and, to a lesser extent, to rice" (FAO 1965: 25-28 cited in Zubaida 1994: 93). Zubaida argues that in addition to shifts in production patterns, and the reclamation and irrigation of new lands, the most important changes have been the vast acceleration of world trade in wheat and rice and the subsidized export of large quantities of wheat from North America and Western Europe, amounting to two million tons per year by 1993 (Kalantari and Khademadam 1997: 82). In the meantime this amount has become even higher.

"Rice, too, is exported to the Middle East from America and the Far East, making it more readily and cheaply available in many markets and altering consumption patterns. Rice, however has not supplanted wheat as the staple. In most places, it is not served at every meal, and when served it constitutes the main dish, or one of the main dishes, while bread is present at every meal as an auxiliary to whatever else is eaten, including rice. To most, a meal without bread is unthinkable" (Zubaida 1994: 93 f.).

Bread has become the metonym for "food" in general. Although people have adopted bread as part of their regulary diet, the mode of consumption cannot be changed easily. Iranians prefer very different types of pita bread, most of which must be eaten fresh. This means that bread must be baked tree times a day and purchased from the bakery to eat warm at every meal; families must organize the shopping and queuing up at bakeries. On the national level this pattern of consumption is dealt as a strategic problem of bread supply. This was discussed in the *JAES* special issue on food security policy (Kimiagar and Pajan 1994; Ghasemi and Najafi 1994) For most of the people—city dwellers and rural inhabitants alike—plastic wrapped, factory bread sold in ordinary shops is still quite unacceptable. This makes bread supply labor intensive, in terms of efficiency and cost-benefit calculations. The habit of eating warm, fresh bread simply does not give way quickly to a fast-food mentality. In the meantime, many of the younger generation in urban Iran have begun to accept and eat sandwiches as a new symbol of prestige and sign of modernity.

"... Farhad Khosrokhavar (1989) analyses radical changes in *mentalité* in modern urban Iran as reflected in eating habits. He notes the increase in consumption of exotic fruits and other imported foods, even under the xenophobic Islamic Republic. Meat, despite its escalating cost, has become the expected base of most household dishes, at the expense of traditional vegetable-based soups and stews as well as local varieties of cheese and other products" (Zubaida and Tapper 1994: 5 f.).

Meat that has become part of everyday meals for the better off among the urban populations, still is not part of the daily diet in rural areas, like the remote areas in Khorasan, where Rahmani (1992) investigated household security and health conditions of family members. She mentions that the only occasions where people ate meat were religious or other types of celebrations where a lamb was sacrificed in the village, prepared, and distributed among the village households (Rahmani 1992).

Meat remains a symbol of prestige. It should be served if guests are invited to one's home, where wives are in charge of preparing and offering the meals—the most important link in the chain of social relationships. Social interaction and communication begins by offering someone something to drink or to eat. This can start with water or tea, and end up with the sacrifice of a lamb or chicken as a sign of hospitality and honour to one's guest. Social relations are structured and combined with the rituals that go along with offering and serving meals. The social hierarchy determines the exact grading of the meal served. This grading is a reflection of how highly the guest is esteemed and also a measure of the host's prestige. The status and honor of the host depends upon the number of guests served, and the quantity and quality of the meal presented. One should offer as much as possible, not as much as is sufficient. Having leftovers is important. These are distributed among those who have not joined the meal because of social stratification, including persons of lower social status, or to neighbors.

So long as waste and losses are considered a problem for food security in Iran, as mentioned in section 2 above, this important cultural aspect, lavishness with food and meals, must be taken into account. The sharing of food can be compared to potlatch ceremonies in the traditional societies of North America, where distribution of food and even destruction of one's own property are ways of distributing and showing one's wealth. This attitude towards food and food sharing is deeply rooted in customs and beliefs—it remains even if food habits change. Food is essential in the construction of social order. Social relationships are unthinkable without all the various types of meals and festivities which are mostly organized and prepared by women who spin the yarn, weave the threads, and tie the knots that make up the social network. Each meal offered can be seen as a node in the net of social order, sometimes as colorful as the carpets. In a country where state social security services do not exist for everyone, people depend upon their social networks to provide security and services. Meals are the ties that bind.

6 Conclusion

If food security is oriented towards the survival of human beings, much more attention should be given to the fact that human nutrition is culturally bound. It is a process by which humankind embodies nature through culture (Brock 1996). All living species need food for survival, but human beings are governed by cultural norms and taboos regulating this process of incorporation of natural products. Even under difficult circumstances, human beings will not accept and eat anything just to supply their need for calories, vitamins, proteins and minerals, even if they are hungry (Teherani-Krönner 1997b: 354). This process of human accommodation is tied to the normative system of a culture, no matter how wealthy or poor—economically—its people are.

Food security is not to be understood as a problem of single, isolated factors calculated in terms of, for instance, average calories (or some other indices) per person. Rather, it is a process of social interaction embedded in the cultural and ecological conditions of the local environment. Food security includes more than just production, marketing, food supply, distribution, and consumption. If household security is the aim, the process of food security cannot stop at a household's "front door". Food and nutrition are indeed the materialized symbols of social networks. Because they are so vital to the maintenance of human beings, the "behind-the-door" processes are as important as the marketing and distribution of commodities. Cooking customs as well as changes in food and nutritional habits must also be considered in terms of the reciprocal impacts between symbolic items and social interaction, stratification and gender relations. Household constellations in terms of age, gender, the distribution of goods, workload, and time allocation are important elements in the equation.

If the food security debate would focus more on food culture and not just on some particular market-oriented food or cash crop, then the whole sociocultural process of food preparation, sharing and eating can become an important part of scientific reflection on nourishment. Not raw products, but meals people eat should be at the center of food security discussion. "Food is a marker of social status—not surprisingly, since we are what we eat . . ." (Zubaida and Tapper 1994: 11; Meyer-Renschhausen and Teherani-Krönner 1997). Efforts to prepare a meal could become one of the core concepts of scientific reflection oriented towards household maintenance. This kind of approach can be seen as an enrichment for the food security debate, for food security policy and food security perspectives, and it will probably affect women's status in society, their empowerment, and gender relations significantly—not only in Iran.

References

Afshar, Haleh (1981): The Position of Women in an Iranian Village, in: Feminist Review, No. 9, pp. 74-86.

Agricultural Bank (1994): Special Scheme on Protection of Vulnerable Women in Rural Areas (Seinab Kobra Scheme), Teheran.

Azimi, Hossein (1997): Basis and Specification of Women's Participation in Agriculture—Present Situation and Perspectives. Additional information to report Nr. 4, contribution to the national seminar on Women, Participation and the Agriculture in the Year 1400, APERI, Tehran (original in Persian).

Becker, Gary (1965): A Theory of the Allocation of Time, in: Economic Journal, Vol. 75.

Beneria, Lourdes (1989): Subcontracting and Employment Dynamics in Mexico City, in: Alejandro Portes, Manuel Castells and Lauren Benton (eds.): The Informal Economy: Studies in Advanced and Less Developed Countries, Baltimore.

Brock, Bazon (1996): To Embody the World by Eating, in: Lorenzl, Günter (ed.): Urban Perception of Nature as a Chance to Agrarian Market?, Berlin, pp. 51 - 62 (original in German).

Bromberger, Christian (1994): Eating Habits and Cultural Boundaries in Northern Iran, in: Sami Zubaida and Richard Tapper (eds.) pp. 185-201.

Brown, Lester E. (1996): Tough Choices. Facing the Challenge of Food Security, The Worldwatch Environmental Alert Series, New York.

BWA (Bureau of Women's Affairs) (1995): Iranian Country Report on the Situation of Women, Tehran.

Coleman, D. and L. Young (1989): Principles of Agricultural Economics, Cambridge.

Djazayer, Abolghasem (1994): International Conference on Food Security and it's Messages to Iran, in: JAES, Special Issue on Food Security, Vol. 2., pp. 241-256 (original in Persian).

Emadi, Mohammad (1997): Women's Participation in Rural Development, Ministry of Jihad, Tehran (original in Persian).

Fanni, Sohreh (1997): Structure of Women's Cooperation in Agriculture, contribution to the national seminar on Women, Participation and the Agriculture in the Year 1400, APERI, Tehran, pp. 119-136 (original in Persian).

Farhadi, Morteza (1995): Mutual Help and Traditional Institutions of Cooperation, in: JAES, Special Issue on Women's Role in Agriculture, Vol. 3, Spring, Tehran, pp. 107-129 (original in Persian).

Farzaneh, Journal of Women's Studies and Research (1993-1997), Tehran (Persian and English).

Foster, Philips (1992): The World Food Problem. Tackling the Causes of Undernutrition in the Thirld World, London.

Fragner, Bert (1994): Social Reality and Fiction: the Perspective of Cookbooks from Iran and Central Asia, in: Sami Zubaida and Richard Tapper (eds.), pp. 63- 72.

Ghasemi, Hossein (1994): Definition and Meaning of Food Security, in: JAES, Special Issue on Food Security, Vol. 2., pp. 12-36 (original in Persian).

Ghasemi, Hossein and Bahaeddin Najafi (1994): Food Systems Management, in: JAES, Special Issue on Food Security, Vol. 2., pp. 257-288 (original in Persian).

Ghavamshahidi, Zohreh (1995): The Linkage between Iranian Patriarchy and the Informal Economy in Maintaining Women's Subordinate Roles in Home-Based Carpet Production, in: Women's Studies International Forum, Vol. 18, No. 2, pp. 135-151.

Ghorayshi, Parvin (1997): Women's Role in the Sustainability of Peasant Agriculture, contribution to the national seminar on Women, Participation and the Agriculture in the Year 1400, Ministry of Agriculture, Tehran pp. 151- 173 (original in Persian).

Ghorayshi, Parvin; Parvin Sarhadi and Nahid Motiee (1997): Plural Methodology: An Alternative Approach to Understand Rural Woman's Life (unpublished).

Hashemi, Fatemeh (1996): The Profile of Rural Women in the Islamic Republic of Iran, presented at Expert Group Meeting, Kuala Lumpur, Malaysia, April 1996 (original in Persian).

Hashemi, Marjam (1995): Socio-Economic Role of Carpet Weaving Rural Women, in: JAES, Special Issue on Women's Role in Agriculture, Vol. 3, Spring, Tehran, pp. 179-202(original in Persian).

Hegland, Mary Elaine (1991): Political Roles of Aliabad Women: The Public-Private Dichotomy Transcended, in: Keddie, Nikkie and Beth Baron (eds.): Women in Middle Eastern History: Shifting Boundaries in Sex and Gender, New York, pp. 215-230.

Helfgott, Leonard Michael (1994): Ties that Bind: a Social History of the Iranian Carpet, Washington.

JAES (Journal of Agriculture and Economic Studies) (1995a), Special Issue on Women's Role in Agriculture, Vol. 3, Spring, Tehran (original in Persian).

JAES (1995b), Special Issue on Population and Labour Force, Vol. 2, Winter, Tehran (original in Persian).

JAES (1994), Special Issue on Food Security, Vol. 2., Vol. 2, Autumn, Tehran (original in Persian).

Jiggins, Janice (1994): Changing Boundaries: Women-Centered Perspectives on Population and the Environment, Washington.

Kalantari, Issa and Nasser Khadamadam (1997): A Policy for Reforming Nutrition Patterns. Nutrition Physiology and Foodstuff Economy, APERI, Tehran (original in Persian).

Kar, Mehrangiz (1994): Women in the Labor Market of Iran, Tehran (original in Persian).

Khosrokhavar, Farhad (1989): La Pratique Alimentaire, in: Yann Richards (ed.): Entre L'Iran et L'Occident: Adaptation et Assimilation des Idées et Techniques Occidentales en Iran, Paris, Maison de Sciences de L'Homme, pp. 143-154.

Kimiagar, Massud and Rasul Pajan (1994): Report on the Special Meeting on Bread, in: JAES, Special Issue on Food Security, Vol. 2., pp. 310-316 (original in Persian).

Lachenmann, Gudrun (1997): Future Perspectives of Rural Women's Projects—Intervention, Interaction or Empowerment?, in: Teherani-Krönner, Parto and Uta Altmann (eds.), pp. 31-52.

Lahsaizadeh, Abdolali (1997): Investigation on the Class Structure of Rural Women in Iran, in: contribution to the national seminar on Women, Participation and the Agriculture in the Year 1400, Ministry of Agriculture, Tehran, pp. 99- 118 (original in Persian).

Mahjubeh (1996-1997): Monthly Journal on Women in the Islamic Republic of Iran.

Maroofi, Parvin (1997): The Development of Rural Women's Institutions in Iran, in: Tehrani-Krönner, Parto and Uta Altmann (eds.), pp. 122 - 134.

Maroofi, Parvin (1995): Country Paper: Iran. Contribution to the Seminar: Women in Farming and Improving Quality of Life in Rural Areas in Asia and the Pacific, 27th September - 7th October, 1994, Tokyo, Japan, Asian Productivity Organisation, Tokyo.

Maroofi, Parvin (1992): The Role of Rural Women in Carpet Weaving in Iran, Rural and Economic Research Centre, Ministry of Agriculture, Tehran (original in Persian).

Meyer-Renschhausen, Elisabeth and Parto Teherani-Krönner (1997): Colloquium on: Der Mensch ist, was er ißt (Human's are what they eat), Faculty of Agriculture and Horticulture of the Humboldt-University of Berlin, Berlin (original in German).

Mies, Maria (1982): The Lace Makers of Narsapur: Indian Housewife Produce for the World Market, London.

Ministry of Jihad (1996): Production and Export of Handmade Persian Carpets in the last 25 Years, Tehran (original in Persian).

Ministry of Jihad (1993): Research on the Situation of Rural Women in Iran, Vol. 1 and 2, Tehran (original in Persian).

Mir-Hosseini, Ziba (1987): Impact of Wage Labour on Household Fission in Rural Iran, in: Journal of Comparative Family Studies. 18, 3, pp. 445-461.

Montazami, Rosa (1969/1989): Cooking Art, A collection of Iranian and Foreign Meals, 17th edition 1989, Tehran (original in Persian).

Moser, Caroline O.N. (1989): Gender Planning in the Third World: Meeting Practical and Strategic Gender Needs, in: World Development,Vol 17, No. 11, pp. 1799-1825.

Motiee, Nahid (1997a): Iranian Housewives in the Process of Development, contribution to the national seminar on Women, Participation and the Agriculture in the Year 1400, Ministry of Agriculture, Tehran, pp. 137-150 (original in Persian).

Motiee, Nahid (1997b): Female Headed Households in Iran: Vulnerable or Powerful, in: UNICEF: State of Children in Iran, Autumn, Tehran.

Motiee, Nahid (1997c): Feminism in Iran. In Search of an Indeginous Interpretation, in: *Zanan*, Nr. 33, pp. 20-25 (original in Persian).

Motiee, Nahid (1995): Changes of Women's Role in Agricultural Activities in Iran, in: *Zanan*, Nr. 14, pp. 19-23 (original in Persian).

Nassehy, Guitty (1993): Women: A Situation Analysis, UNDP, Tehran.

Nejatian, Hossein (1995): The Changing Trend of the Human Population Fertility Level in Iran, in: JAES, Special Issue on Population and Labour Force, Vol 2, Winter, Tehran, pp. 38-52 (original in Persian).

NNFTR (National Nutrition and Food Technology Research Institute) et al. (1995a): National Plan of Action for Nutrition, Tehran.

NNFTR et al. (1995b): Nationwide Household Food Consumption Pattern Survey Report, Tehran.

Norusi, Farahara (1994): Food Production and Distribution in Iran, in: JAES, Special Issue on Food Security, Vol. 2., pp. 37-94 (original in Persian).

Pandam (Consultant engineers) (1997): Development of Women's Issues, Irrigation Project in Behbahan, Iran, draft report to the Ministry of Agriculture, Tehran (original in Persian).

Payujan, Djamshid (1994): Household Food Security, in: JAES, Special Issue on Food Security, Vol. 2., pp. 147-173 (original in Persian).

Rahmani, Khadijeh (1992): Research about Health and Nutrition in the Region of Mochunik in South Khorasan, NNFTR et. al., Tehran (original in Persian).

Razavi, Shahrashoub (1994): Agrarian Change and Gender Relations in South-East Iran, in: Development and Change, Vol. 25, pp. 591-634.

Reichel, Ute (1996): Women and Food Security in Iran, Contribution to the Research Paper by Tehrani-Krönner, Parto et. al. (1996b), Berlin (original in German).

RRC (Rural Research Center) (1997): Ministry of Jihad: Information on the RRC, Tehran.

Sarhadi, Farideh; Pouran Malmir and Nahid Sarichani (1997): Summary of the Research on Women's Productivity in Rice Production, contribution to the national seminar on Women, Participation and the Agriculture in the Year 1400, Ministry of Agricul-ture,Tehran, pp. 289- 313 (original in Persian).

Sarhadi, Farideh; Azar Nikzat; Zahra Saremi; Nahid Motiee and Marzieh Khojastefar (1991): Research on the Social and Economic Role of Women in the Village of Ahandan, Centre for Agricultural Planning and Economic Studies, Tehran (original in Persian).

SCI (Statistical Centre of Iran) (1995): Statistics on Households with Industrial Activities in 1994, Tehran (original in Persian).

SCI (Statistical Centre of Iran) (1991): Statistical Data of Iran, Tehran (original in Persian).

SCI (Statistical Centre of Iran) (1986): Statistical Data of Iran, Women's Participation in Work Labor, Tehran (original in Persian).

Sen, Amartyra (1981): Poverty and Famine, Oxford.

Shaditalab, Jaleh (1997): Effects of International Efforts on Rural Women in Iran, Report Nr. 2, contribution to the national seminar on Women, Participation and the Agriculture in the Year 1400, Ministry of Agriculture, Tehran (original in Persian).

Teherani-Krönner, Parto (1997a): Changes in Women's Scope of Action in Agrarian Cultures, in: Dieter Steiner (ed.): Human and Living Space. Questions of Identity and Knowledge, Opladen (original in German).

Teherani-Krönner, Parto (1997b): Strategies and Arts of Survival. Women Dealing with Scarce Resources in Agrarian Cultures, in: Kurt J. Peters (ed.), pp. 349-363 (original in German).

Teherani-Krönner, Parto (1996a): Ecofeminist Positions on Nature, in: Günter Lorenzl (ed.): Urban Perception of Nature as a Chance to Agrarian Market?, Berlin pp. 123-150 (original in German).

Teherani-Krönner, Parto et. al. (1996b): The Cultural Ecology of Nutrition: Women in Food Security, Research Paper, Faculty of Agriculture and Horticulture, Humboldt-University of Berlin, Berlin (original in German).

Teherani-Krönner, Parto (1995a): Research on Gender Relation in Rural Areas, in: Uta Altmann and Parto Teherani-Krönner (eds.): Women in Rural Development, Humboldt-University of Berlin, Berlin, pp. 10-69 (original in German).

Teherani-Krönner, Parto (1995b): Improving Local Knowledge for Appropriate Technologies in Agriculture: Women's Co-operatives as a Space for Maneuver for Rural Women, in: Women and Technology, International Seminar on Women in Agriculture and their Participation in Development of Agricultural Technologies, January 1995, Beijing, pp. 227-233.

Teherani-Krönner, Parto (1994): Women in Food Security and Family Planning, in: Josef Schmid (ed.): Population, Environment. Development. A Human Ecological Perspective, Opladen, pp. 179-193 (original in German)

Teherani-Krönner, Parto (1992): Human Ecology and Cultural Ecology - A Contribution to the Sociology of Environment, Wiesbaden (original in German).

Teherani-Krönner, Parto (1989): Human Ecology—A New Orientation in Development Projects, in: Bernhard Glaeser (ed.): Human Ecology, Opladen, pp. 194 - 208 (original in German).

Teherani-Krönner, Parto and Uta Altmann (eds.) (1997): What have Women's Projects Accomplished so far? Proceedings of the Second International Conference "Women in Rural Development, June 1996", Faculty of Agriculture and Horticulture, Humboldt-University of Berlin, Berlin.

Tohid, Leila (1996): Rural Women's Co-operatives in Iran, paper prepared for the International Seminar of Co-operatives in Bangkok, Thailand, Teheran.

UNESCO-Kurier (1980): The Invisible Women, Vol. 7 (original in German).

UNICEF (1994): Mainstreaming Gender Issues in UNICEF Tehran, Programmes for 1994-1995, Tehran.

UNICEF/*Farzaneh* (1997): Young Girls in Rural Areas, Tehran (Englisch and Persian).

UNICEF and OESRW (Office of Extension Services for Rural Women) (1993): Gender Analysis Workshop Proceedings for Female Agricultural Extension Workers, Tehran.

WAD—Women and Development (1994): A Report on Important Measures Taken for Women since the Victory of the Islamic Revolution, Tehran (original in Persian).

Warzgar, Sharareh and Mastaneh Azis-Babai (1997): Research on Women's Participation in Cotton Production in Gorgan and Gombad Region, contribution to the national seminar on Women, Participation and the Agriculture in the Year 1400, Ministry of Agriculture,Tehran, pp. 217- 257 (original in Persian).

Wright, Susan (1981): Place and Face: Of Women in Doshman Ziari, Iran, in: Shirley Ardener (ed.): Women and Space, New York, pp. 136-157 (original in English).

Zanan (1997a): Journal on Women, Tehran, Nr. 33 (original in Persian).

Zanan (1997b) Journal on Women, Tehran, Nr. 34 (original in Persian).

Zubaida, Sami and Richard Tapper (eds.) (1994): Culinary Cultures of the Middle East, New York, London.

10

Food Production, Transformation Processes and Changes of Gender-specific Division of Labour in Rural Africa

Gabriele Zdunnek and Peter Ay

> "Africa is the land of the most intensive hoe culture. ... There are, however, degrees of intensity, and these again closely connected with the division of work. Where women undertake the hoe culture, it is often very superficial; where the man takes part, it is intensified, and the intensity of cultivation increases in proportion to the man's share in the hoe culture. ... the ... tribes ..., where the men participate largely in the actual work of hoe culture, are the best agriculturalists, ... where women undertake the cultivation, the work is often deplorably bad." (Baumann 1928: 294/295)

1 Introduction

The importance of women for agricultural production and food security, especially in Africa, has been emphasized since the 1970s and particularly during the UN women's decade. According to FAO (Food and Agriculture Organization of the United Nations), women in the so-called developing countries produce more than half of the consumed food and in sub-Saharan Africa even about three quarters. Estimates assume that in Africa women are responsible for about 90% of the work connected with the processing of food and the provision of water and firewood for family consumption, for 80% of the work involved in storing of food and transporting of farm products, for 90% of fieldwork with hoes and weeding, and for 60% of the harvesting and marketing. Due to the importance of women for the production of food, the reasons for food crises in Africa are often attributed to the fact, among others, that women are neglected by agricultural policies and development projects (Quisumbing et al. 1995: 1/2).

As one of the first authors Boserup (1982, first edition 1970) examined the systematic exclusion of female producers in colonial and post-colonial agricultural policies and in extension services of African countries. She showed that in the course of an increasing modernization of the agricultural sector, this exclusion creates and reinforces differences in productivity and income between men and women. By prefering male producers when new technologies, methods of cultivation or products are being introduced, a broadening gap appears between men who cultivate cash crops mainly for export with modern methods and women who produce food for subsistence or for local markets with traditional methods. The first part of this contribution summarizes Boserup's study which is generally seen as a "watershed" (Kabeer 1994: 2) in the discussion on gender and development. Subsequently, many studies, following her example, have illustrated the extent and levels of discrimination of women by colonial and post-colonial administrations as well as their exclusion from formal modern sectors of agriculture and urban labour markets. From the point of view of the 1980s and 1990s, however, several critical comments to Boserup's study have to be made.

Whereas in the 1970s opportunities to integrate women into modern production processes had been discussed, in particular by the WID (Women in Development) lobby, the debates of the 1980s and especially the 1990s, after the "lost" decade of development of the 1980s, are far more sceptical as regards the direction as well as the possible success of previous efforts towards modernization. This involves a reassessment of women's work in agricultural production. While Boserup saw women's work and productivity as being static due to a lack of knowledge and technology, this is in part being reinterpreted, especially in the debate on ecology, as a sustainable use of natural resources based on indigenous knowledge. In this reconceptualization women in rural areas often are seen not only as the "key" to food security, but also as the safeguard for sustainable development. In our view both approaches neglect the multitude of agricultural systems, patterns of gender-specific labour division and diverse influences of modernization and transformation processes in rural areas of Africa. By taking southwestern Nigeria as an example, in the second part of the contribution it is tried to show the complexity of factors influencing food security and agricultural production in general as well as patterns and changes in the gender-specific division of labour. In the last part an attempt is made to assess recent development trends.

> "Men deal with modern things. They use modern equipment while women do degrading manual work; ... men drive bicycles and steer lorries, while women carry headloads as did already their grandmothers. In short, in the village the men represent modern agriculture and the women the old drudgery." (Boserup 1982: 51; translation by the authors)

2 From systems of female to systems of male agriculture—from "primitivity" to complexity?

Boserup was one of the first authors to use gender as a social category in the comparison of countries and to prove that women do not necessarily gain from development and modernization. On the basis of previous studies, she examines the effects of modernization in agriculture, of industrialization and of urbanization on the economic and social situation of women in African, Asian and Latin American countries. She emphasizes the important economic role of women, particularly in

African agriculture, and concludes that women in comparison to men are at a disadvantage in the process of modernization as their "traditional" production sectors lose importance while modern opportunities remain inaccessible for them.

When she describes the gender-specific division of labour in African agriculture at the beginning of the century, she largely refers to Baumann's study on the division of work in African hoe cultures which appeared in 1928. She adopts his distinction between a "female" and a "male" system of subsistence agriculture, depending on whether the field work is done mainly by women or mainly by men, and describes Africa in comparison to Latin America and Asia as a "region of female agriculture par excellence" (Boserup 1982: 13). She also partly adopts Baumann's model of an evolutionary development from systems of female to systems of male agriculture. In Baumann's view systems of female agriculture were characterized by low population densities, the predominance of root and tuber crops over grains, a minimal soil cultivation, segmentary formation of societies and simple technologies. Boserup describes systems of female agriculture as labour-extensive shifting cultivation combined with communal land property and land use rights for women. The men's work is limited mainly to land clearing. All further field work, such as planting, weeding, harvesting, etc., are entirely or largely the task of women. In systems of female agriculture women, therefore, work hard and the support of their husbands is limited, but they often enjoy considerable freedom and mobility as well as economic independence to some extent by selling the agrarian surplus.

Boserup explains the necessity of a transition from systems of female to systems of male agriculture with an almost inevitable increase in population. She forecasts that with an increasing population density land will become a scarce production factor, which will require the transition from extensive shifting cultivation with the use of the hoe to permanent plough culture with draught animals. She assumes that men will take over the ploughing even in regions of formerly female agriculture. As a consequence the workload of men will increase whereas women's workload will be reduced, owing, among others, to the fact that plough cultivation without irrigation requires less weeding. Under the pressure of further population increases the necessity arises to apply more labour-intensive techniques and to cultivate labour-intensive products. Accordingly, the share of women's as well as of men's labour increases, e.g. when the introduction of irrigation agriculture requires more weeding and leads to a higher workload of women, while men will have additional tasks such as digging irrigation feeders, fixing terraces and dams etc. (Boserup 1982: 29-32).

The models that Boserup uses to characterize systems of male agriculture are societies in Asia in which plough cultivation and an intensification of production prevail. Men use the plough with the help of draught animals, and only the manual labour, or part of it, is done by women. Due to the existence of private property of land and a comparatively large section of landless families which are forced to do wage work, it is possible to "free" a considerable proportion of women from field-work. They only fulfill tasks within the domestic sphere or, in landless families, work as paid labourers in the fields of male landowners. In these systems of male agriculture women depend on the economic support by men. Husbands largely have to provide for their wives and children (Boserup 1982: 21-23, 45/6).

In Boserup's view the exclusion of women from productive spheres in the course of transition from systems of female to systems of male agriculture in Africa is caused by the fact that women have less access to land rights, education, professional training and new technologies. In particular, she blames colonial and post-colonial administrations for their prejudiced perceptions and the preferential treatment of male producers in agricultural policies and development projects. Thus, in the course of modernization of the agricultural sector, the differences in productivity between men and women increase as mainly men produce with modern equipment and modern agricultural methods for the market while women continue to cultivate subsistence products with traditional methods. Boserup describes a multitude of processes which reinforce the gap between the income opportunities of men and women. Men can use part of their income from marketing to further improve their production while women only dispose of a modest cash income for investments. They are at a disadvantage when land is commercialized because they can raise less funds for buying land. Therefore, even in regions where women are entitled to inherit land, landownership may slowly pass over from women to men. In part, land reforms of colonial and post-colonial governments lead to women losing access to land. In the formal sector men are being employed preferentially, thus a gender-specific segregation of the labour market evolves. In addition to discriminating employment practices, socially conveyed prejudices and preferences keep women from seeking an employment in the formal sector (Boserup 1982: 48-55).

Boserup concludes that in the course of modernization, intensification and mechanization of agriculture and of a growing specialization and differentiation of non-agricultural occupations women will be increasingly excluded from production. She sees as a consequence not only a deterioration of the social status of women but also a slowing down of development and economic growth because productive resources are not used. Therefore, she demands the integration of women into the process of development and modernization, their access to education and professional training, equal conditions in school education and professional training for girls and boys, equal chances in the labour market including sectors being outside the typically female domains as well as a reduction of domestic duties of women (Boserup 1982: 204-14).

3 Boserup revisited[1]

In her study Boserup summarized the knowledge of the late 1960s concerning the "economic role of women in Africa, Asia and Latin America." Her work was paradigm and starting point for many studies to follow which largely confirmed her

1 See Beneria/Sen 1997.

findings, i.e. an increasing gender-specific differentiation and a relative discrimination of women in the course of modernization processes. Partly due to a multitude of empirical data collected since then, however, her evolutionist approach and the assumption that the transition from systems of "female" to systems of "male" agriculture would be almost inevitable due to technological innovations, appear to be deterministic and no longer tenable from today's perspective. The observation that in Asian societies where plough cultivation is prevalent and specific crops are cultivated, men perform the largest part of agricultural work does hardly allow the general conclusion that technological innovation and changes in the patterns of gender-specific division of labour are direcly interrelated in general. Beneria and Sen (1997: 45) criticize that "one is left to presume that technical variation exercises some mysterious, if powerful, impact on the division of labour by sex."

Furthermore, the characterization of systems of female and male agriculture as stages of development, associating the female system with an early "primitive stage", does not correspond to more recent research findings. According to Guyer (1995: 30/1) the system of "female agriculture" which has been described in the literature on agriculture in Africa at the beginning of the century is particularly characteristic for the production of maize and cassava, products which had been imported from the New World since the end of the 15th century and had been integrated into existing production structures. The cultivation of old African products such as yam, sorghum, millet and rice in contrast had not been characterized as female work but had been organized in complex groups with intertwining sequences of tasks of men and women. Equally untenable is the assumption that modernization and technological changes, like the transition of hoe culture to plough culture, are inevitable consequences of population growth. Charles (1993: 164) annotates that population growth might be a result of an intensified agriculture instead of its cause.

Particularly Beneria and Sen (1997: 45-48) criticize that Boserup ignores processes of social differentiation in rural areas caused by modernization since the colonial period, and that she does not discuss the problems arising with the model of (capitalist) modernization but only the fact that women do not gain from it.

> "Everywhere ... more boys than girls went to school. Thus, while formerly analphabetism, traditional behaviour and superstition had been common for all villagers, these signs of backwardness in rural communities gradually became more characteristic for women ... subsequently, this gap seemed to justify ... prejudices against female farmers." (Boserup 1982: 51-52; translation by the authors)

4 From "invisible" women to female agricultural producers—the development of gender-specific labour division in southwestern Nigeria

The example of the Yoruba in southwestern Nigeria, who are with approximately 25 million people one of the predominant ethnic groups of the country, may illustrate some basic problems of research on gender-specific labour division and the effects of modernization. Until the 1970s it was a generally accepted perception, even if it was not widely supported by empirical data, that Yoruba women "usually do not work in the fields" (Baumann 1928: 313, see also Johnson 1973, Fadipe 1970, Boserup 1982, Sudarkasa 1973). Some authors emphasize that women have an important role in the processing of agricultural products, in trade and in some handicrafts and that, owing to substantial financial obligations towards their household, children and relatives, almost all women have one or more income generating occupations, but that in agriculture, at most, they "help" during the harvest or fulfill "simple" tasks.

Since the 1970s, gradually the "role" of Yoruba women in agriculture has been reevaluated. Several studies show that even if only few women cultivate their own fields, many work in the fields of husbands and relatives, in addition to their work in trade, in food processing and in the keeping of small animals. Their "help" includes a multitude of agricultural activities, such as planting, weeding, applying of fertilizers, harvesting and transporting of agricultural products (headloads) (see e.g. Berry 1975, Grant/Anthonio 1973, WORDOC 1988).

The study of Berry (1975) already shows that it is untenable to assign a (large) ethnic group to a distinct form of gender-specific labour division without differentiations and consideration of other factors. Based on data from three villages close to Ife, she shows that the increasing integration of cocoa into local production systems and rising incomes from the cultivation of cocoa lead to a differentiation of employment structures and to an increase of non-agricultural occupations, for men als well as for women. In the village of Orotedo cocoa had only been cultivated for a relatively short period, in Abanata it had been cultivated since the 1950s. In both locations a relatively high proportion of men and women were working in cocoa plantations. In Orotedo 91% of the men were working as independent farmers or farm labourers, in Abanata 79%. 96% of the women in Orotedo and 48% of the women in Abanata were working on the farms of husbands and relatives or as paid farm labourers. New cocoa plantations were exclusively owned by men. In Orotedo only 12% of the men and 16 % of the women were working in trade, handicrafts or services, in Abanata this were 30% and 50% respectively. In Araromi-Aperin where cocoa had been cultivated since the 1920s, only 60% of the men and 22% of the women were working in agriculture. Only in Araromi-Aperin a small number of women owned inherited cocoa plantations (Berry 1975: 132, 164-5, 172-5).

In the following the results of two panel studies are being presented, indicating a much larger proportion of women being independent producers. Further studies would be necessary to see whether these are entirely new developments or special local features and also to assess the extent of "gender blind" perceptions that made the productive activities of women "invisible" in earlier studies.

Guyer carried out her panel study in 1968/69 and 1987/88 in Ibarapa, a district with about 6,000 inhabitants in southwestern Nigeria about 100 km from the city of Ibadan. Being situated on the border of the cocoa belt in the savannah area, Ibarapa has belonged to the supplying hinterland of Ibadan and Lagos for more than 100 years. Since the beginning of the century the local production systems have been changing gradually. Several products had been selectively integrated into regional systems of distribution, beginning with savannah grass (to thatch roofs) and egusi (protein-containing melon seeds), following with yam and cow peas in the 1940s, cassava and maize since the 1950s and diverse vegetables (tomatoes, chili pepper, okra) in the 1960s and 1970s when transport systems and marketing opportunities were improving.

Guyer estimates that in the 1960s only 10% of the women had been working in agriculture on their own account. Of 60 farms which she had visited in 1968 only two had been owned by women. The majority of the women had earned an income by processing and preparing food and from activities in trade. In agriculture they had been working predominantly as family labourers or as paid labourers, for example as paid harvesters, also for husbands and close relatives. Some women had been employed as daily paid labourers in tobacco cultivation and harvesting. In the 1960s only few motorable roads existed in the district, and the women had to transport almost the entire agricultural production by headload from the fields to the villages and the markets. Women had the obligation to render this service to husbands and male relatives and in general did not receive any remuneration. Men decided on the production and were in control of the incomes from product proceeds. Small-scale agriculture and a low degree of mechanization prevailed in the whole area, and only the Nigerian Tobacco Company, which employed a small number of men as contractual producers, owned some tractors (Guyer/Idowu 1991: 263, Guyer 1995: 34).

In comparison to her study of 1968/69, in 1987 Guyer observed several changes, especially regarding the size of cultivated areas, the establishment of larger farms and an increase of female producers working on their own account. The expansion period began in the middle of the 1970s with improved transport facilities, an inflow of migrant labourers and the establishment of a hire service for tractors. From the end of the 1960s until the end of the 1980s the small-scale producers had increased the cultivated areas by 40% from, on average, 2.9 acres to

4.1 acres, more than half of them (59%) were using tractors. The improvement of transport facilities reduced the unpaid transport services of women. Due to the extension of cultivated areas, the amount of their paid labour during peak periods grew, and men were increasingly dependent on their working capacities. Wages for farm labour were relatively high and partly had even risen. The extension of production furthermore led to an increase of income opportunities for women in small-scale food processing, especially cassava processing. In the late 1970s and early 1980s, local large-scale producers emerged. They used savings and income from non-agricultural sectors to finance mechanization and the employment of workers. In 1988, nine farms with more than 10 acres existed, the largest one having more than 50 acres. In the middle of the 1970s, multinational agrobusiness enterprises established large-scale farms in Ibarapa. Two of them (Obasanjo farms), had more than 1,000 acres, the third one (United African Company/Marquis) had 700 acres of land. The large-scale farms offered jobs for a large number of women as harvesters and to a smaller extent in other activities such as the application of fertilizers. At the time when men extended the cultivated areas, women started to cultivate their own fields. Two thirds (69%) of the 222 women Guyer had interviewed in 1988 had farms with an average size of almost two acres. Only 9% were having farms for 20 years or longer, which coincides with the data Guyer collected in 1968/69. In 1988 about 20% of the entire cultivated area had been cultivated by women. At the end of the 1980s land was not yet scarce in Ibarapa due to the relatively low population density (approximately 50 inhabitants per square kilometer in the district, in some areas only 14 per sqare kilometer) which does not mean that there did not exist land conflicts (Guyer/Idowu 1991: 264-9, Guyer 1995: 33-6).

The majority of women started farming on their own account in the 1970s or 1980s. Guyer and Idowu describe the socio-economic background and the characteristics of different cohorts. The findings show that women who had own fields before 1976 were rather an exception. For them farming was the main occupation. Reasons to start included that they were left alone to care for their children and could not travel as required for activities in trade, for example. After the end of the Biafra War in 1970 and also due to a rising urban demand following the oil boom, transport and marketing opportunities were improving. The women who started farming in the middle of the 1970s had up to then been doing business quite successfully in food processing and marketing for urban demand. Owing to increasing competition, however, they had been facing losses of income since the middle of the 1970s, and partly they were having problems with the supply of agricultural products necessary for a continuous production and marketing. These women used farming in addition to their other occupations to reduce risks and to obtain raw material for processing. Since the beginning of the 1980s Nigeria had been faced with an increasing economic crisis and rising costs of living. The women who had started to work on their own farms after the middle of the 1980s mainly tried to cope with the crisis. Before, they had predominantly been working on a very small scale in food processing and preparation and were then no longer able to manage financially. A large proportion of the very old as well as very young women belonged to this category. They started farming following the example of other women in order to "try it" (Guyer/Idowu 1991: 267-8, Guyer 1995: 42).

Comparing farms of men and women, Guyer and Idowu found that male producers had larger farms with more diversified cultivation patterns. Women who had started farming before 1976 were cultivating areas of an average size of 3.4 acres, which is almost as large as those of men (81% of the average cultivated areas of men). Women who had started their farms in the 1970s or 1980s disposed of an average of 1.7 and 1.3 acres of cultivated land respectively. The main product of women was cassava, requiring 59% to 69% of the area under cultivation. The longer women were engaged in agriculture, the more diversified was their production and the lower was the share of cassava (54% for the first, 61% for the second and 70% for the third cohort). On the whole, female producers employed more workers as male. While men cleared 19% of their cultivation area themselves, women rarely did this work themselves. They had 42% of their cultivation area cleared by tractor services and 57% by paid labourers. They equally employed more workers for weeding than men (Guyer/Idowu 1991: 268, Guyer 1995: 36-41).

In a panel study in 20 villages east of Ibadan in 1975 and 1990 it became evident that in the complex cultivation systems of the forest areas also problems of perception may lead to an undervaluation of women's labour (Ay 1980, 1989, 1990a, 1990b, 1992, 1996). In 1975 a representative sample of 235 farmers had been interviewed about their agricultural production. According to the literature available up to the 1970s the assumption prevailed that men were the heads of farm households and women and children contributed to the work on the family farms. Field visits and informal interviews seemed to support this assumption, thus at first giving no reason for further investigation. The men mentioned in the interviews that the tasks of women consisted in the assistance in weeding, harvesting and transporting of the products from the fields to the villages. In 1975 as well as in 1990 the men questioned about the farm production of their wives explained that they were producing cassava, maize and vegetables mainly for household consumption. The main objective of the study of 1975 was to examine the effects of an agricultural development project of the University of Ibadan which did not include women as agricultural producers, therefore the agricultural production of women was not systematically analysed (Ay 1980). Participatory observation and qualitative interviews showed already in 1975 that there were women who had their own farms, but like in the study of Guyer they were perceived as exceptions.

In the following years the sensitivity regarding the significance of women's contribution to agricultural production generally increased, one reason being the amount of empirical studies which had been carried out during the "women's decade". Studies in the framework of "Farming Systems Research" indicated for western Nigeria and the villages in the research area a much larger share of women in agricultural production as had been assumed before. The second representative survey of the panel study in 1990 therefore included a sample of 127 women. 135 farmers who were included in the 1975 sample were interviewed again. Altogether, a total of 309 men were interviewed. The research results showed that the majority of women were working on their own farms and cultivating, like the men, up to 15 of the approximately 60 different crops of the region. In the production year 1989/90, about one quarter of the entire crop output had been produced by female farmers. That this proportion basically had existed already in 1975 had been found out in several group interviews in which women participated who had already had their own fields at that time.

In the production years 1974/75 as well as 1989/90, women on average cultivated a larger share for subsistence than men. Women's share in the total market production was about one fifth. In 1989/90, women's returns from selling farm produce amounted to an average of US-$540, whereas men obtained an average of US-$1,960. There was considerably less economic differentiation among women than among men. While for the women the maximum of returns was six times higher than the average (US-$3,600), it was 18 times higher for the men (US-$35,200).

Differences in the agricultural production of men and women are partly due to differences regarding the access to land. "Traditionally" land is not perceived as personal property, and rights arise, among other factors, from work applied for the cultivation of farm products. Tree plantations secure long-lasting rights which may be inherited. Women only exceptionally inherit land rights. On the death of a husband the inheritance falls to the sons or the male relatives of the husband. Often a widow, however, is granted the right of several years of use before the land is ultimately divided between the male heirs. In 1990, 80% of the men disposed of long-term land use rights, but only 20% of the women of whom some had bought the rights with income from food processing, trade and/or agriculture. Two thirds of the men and most of the women owning tree plantations controlled only small stocks of trees, partly this were only a few and sometimes even single trees. In 1990, less than 20% of the men were in control of land use rights for larger areas, partly in different villages. Almost no women in the research area, comprising about 12,000 inhabitants, belonged to this category.

Agricultural producers without inherited land use rights mostly obtain access to land only for a limited period and are restricted to areas between oil palms, cola nut or other trees. After three or four periods of cultivation the soil loses its fertility, the cultivation of arable crops is abandoned until the area, after lying fallow for several years, is being redivided, often between other users. For short-term use men as well as women mostly obtain access to land without any problems. Most women get land through their husbands.

Especially in remote villages sufficient land is still available. Here, even today the recompensation for land use is of a more symbolic nature, such as the biggest yam tuber of the field or a basket of cassava. For the owners of the trees the advantage of granting the land use is that, because of the clearing of the land for arable crops, they have an easy access for harvesting the trees. In the more densely populated villages there is more pressure on land, and a part of the harvest or today more often money is being paid as rent. Cocoa is cultivated as sole crop on the most productive soils. As a consequence short-term users in villages with extended cocoa production, especially women, have only access to less productive land.

In the perspective of the inhabitants of the research area their farms consist of the products they cultivate. Therefore, land use rights of several people may overlap on the same fields. The following example illustrates the complexity of these land use systems. On the same field the oil palms belonged to a woman, cola nut and orange trees were owned by another farmer and arable crops between the trees had been cultivated by a migrant labourer from eastern Nigeria, whose wife furthermore cultivated several vegetables between his cassava and maize plants. In the interviews they all indicated the same field as being their "farm".

"Traditionally" all the land is being distributed by the "bale" (father of the land) whose family descends from the first settlers in the region. However, he is usually only involved personally when the negotiations between holders of long-term rights and potential users are already settled. But the bale has the important function to publicly announce the current distribution of land use rights and thus securing them for the temporary occupants. Owing to the different growth periods of the crops and also to the parallel rights on the same land, conflicts often arise so that in 1975 as well as in 1990 the most frequent appeals to the village chief and the elders were to settle conflicts over land use issues. These evolve, for example, when old trees are no longer productive and other users argue that this land is not cultivated anymore whereas the old users emphasize their inherited rights. Women rarely are involved in these conflicts as they have less tree plantations, and if they succeeded to obtain trees they secure them by special care and by regenerating unproductive trees in time.

In the vicinity of transport facilities and towns the demand for land to cultivate fresh vegetables for urban markets has increased in the last decades. For seasonal products, such as various green vegetables, young maize, tomatoes, chili pepper and okra, long-term rights are required as investments in the improvement of soils, in fences and water supply are necessary. Instead of selling permanent land use rights mostly contracts on the basis of regular payments are negotiated orally and secured by involving esteemed persons as witnesses. This system is more and more comparable to a lease system allowing for a trend towards commercialization of land use rights. Some of the women were able to "capitalize" on this trend and aquired longer duration land use rights with funds they had obtained from their trade and/or processing activities.

From 1975 until 1990 there were several changes in the cultivation patterns of men and women. In 1975 women mostly cultivated their products between those of the men on the same field, which is one of the reasons for an underestimation of women as independent producers. It was usually not realized that the crops planted by the women on the same fields were managed, harvested and partly sold by them in their own responsibility.

In the period from 1975 to 1990 a fundamental change of the production system had been the doubling of the output of cassava which had been cultivated mainly together with maize. In order to increase the production of maize and cassava, men increased the plant densities which reduced the space for the "farm" of the women on the common field. As a consequence women started to cultivate their products on seperate fields. Men and women equally conceived this change not as an alteration of the patterns of labour division but as a mere transfer of the woman's "farm" to a seperate location. The previously existing rules of gender-specific division of labour were still valid. The husband continued to be responsible for clearing and land preparation on the woman's farm, either doing the work himself or hiring paid labourers. As a recompensation the women were still supposed to do the weeding on the men's cassava-maize fields, to apply fertilizer and to help in the harvest. The exchanges of labour between men and women usually seem to be balanced quite exactly. If, for example, the woman's work on the larger fields of the husband does not correspond to his work on her fields, she stops her activities or demands a recompensation. Thus, in 1990 more women were working as paid workers in weeding, harvesting and transporting of products than in 1975. Children considerably contribute to all farm work, and girls as well as boys help their mothers in all activities. This applies also for paid labour, the work is being paid per task and not depending on the time it requires. Women with larger farms hired more paid labourers, men and women, than men with farms of comparable size. In families of the lowest income groups women often carried out tasks which "normally" were men's tasks as they had no funds to pay labourers. In 1989/90 about a quarter of all women and men respectively had an income from paid work for other farmers in addition to their own farm returns. This income was partly used by men as well as women to hire migrant labourers for land clearing.

In contrast to the results of Guyer's study in the savannah region, women in the villages of the forest zone developed a diversified farming systems comparable in complexity to those of the men. Cropping patterns and produced quantities differ more depending on socio-economic categories than on gender. In spite of the discrimination of women regarding long-term land use rights and, in comparison to men, their generally lower production, similarities exist in proportions of income sources of men and women for different crops. Men obtain 61% of their farm income from long term crops (50% from trees and 11% from other perennials) as compared to 51% (37% from trees, 14% other perennials) for women. Perennials include bananas and plantain, leaves to wrap up food, black pepper and several medicinal plants.

Whereas cocoa had been the most important export product and "cash crop" for several decades, it lost importance mainly for small-scale producers from 1975 until 1990. Other trees such as oil palms, oranges and some local tree species gained in importance during this period. In 1975, 80% of the men had been cultivating cocoa, gaining an average of one third of their farm income with it. At that time cocoa had only a marginal importance for women. In 1990, still 70% of the men were having cocoa trees. Those who had abandoned cocoa planted food crops instead, one reason being that small cocoa quantities entail relatively high costs for harvesting, processing and marketing which are not compensated for even by higher producer prices. For women investment into oil palms was more attractive than into cocoa as they could increase their income considerably with the processing of palm oil. In 1975, the largest part of oil processing had been carried out by women as a kind of commission business for men who were almost exclusively the owners of the palm trees. Men received the red palm oil while women kept palm kernels and the by-products as recompensation for their work. Until 1989/90 the women's income from their own oil palms amounted to US-$126, representing 26% of their entire farm income. Men gained with US-$303 about twice the average amount of women, which represented, however, only 15% of their farm output.

In 1990, women and men were cultivating cassava as main food crop. Other roots and tubers such as cocoyam and sweet potatoes were of minor importance. Only yam had been cultivated by several men on a larger scale but had considerably lost in general importance since 1975. Roots and tubers contributed 26% to the farm income of women and 19% to that of men. Cereals, mainly maize and sometimes also sorghum and rice, had a share of 16% for women and 12% for men. Vegetables had the same rank for men and women with an average of 7%. Although more women than men were growing vegetables, men on average were producing larger quantities for the market, as a few of them specialized on vegetable cultivation on fertile land near streams or rivers.

In the period from 1975 until 1990, the incomes from non-agricultural occupations have increased for women as well as for men. In the research area trade, handicrafts and services offer more than one hundred different occupations from which more than 80% of the men and almost all women earned additional income. As compared to 1975, there had been no additional occupations, but the income levels had considerably changed due to specialization. In 1989/90 women derived on average US-$724 or 57% of their total income (US-$1,270) from non-farm occupations while for men this were US-$1,140, representing 37% of their total income (US-$3,100).

Most women earned income from food processing such as palm oil or several cassava products. Other income generating activities were the preparation of various meals which they sold in the villages. The majority were processing food for the household, selling only small quantities. But a minority specialized in specific products and made them a main source of income. In 1975, cassava flour had been frequently sold on the markets whereas gari had been produced only in small quantities by manual work for home consumption. Cassava flour is milled from sundried cassava after fermenting whole roots which are broken up by hand. Gari is derived from grated cassava roots, the mashed cassava is fermented in bags and dewatered by pressing. The storable end product is obtained by roasting over fire. In 1990 the main cassava processing for the market was gari. An expansion of gari processing was favoured by the fact that cassava could be harvested throughout the year. The roasting over fire allows to produce gari also during the rainy season and offers a regular income source for women specializing in it. The importance of the gari production increased in the 1980s when graters and mechanical presses had been introduced in the research area and the roasting had switched from using clay pots to iron pans which need less firewood and allow a faster roasting because of higher temperatures. Several women's groups and also several business-women established production facilities with capacities for the processing of several tons of cassava per day. The utilisation of the machines increased the productivity of the gari processors who were now able to buy fresh cassava roots in larger quantities, giving incentives to cassava farmers to increase their production. To give further incentives for an expansion of cassava farms the processing women often paid for the cassava harvest several months in advance, giving the farmers the opportunity to use the money for the establishment of new cassava fields. In mechanized gari productions sites men and women are being employed as paid workers for the different processing activities. Mainly women are, for example, employed for washing and peeling cassava roots, for roasting or sieving, packaging and marketing. Men are usually employed to operate the engines, graters and presses and are also responsible for their maintenance. In 1989/90, only about 1% of the women in the research area were working in the production of gari, but they were producing almost the entire marketed quantity. In the same year about half of all women had produced palm oil, but the main part of the palm oil marketed was produced by only about one thenth of them. For the production of larger quantities of palm oil as well as for the processing of cassava to gari an increasing number of paid female workers had been hired since 1975, who transported palm fruit, carried water and firewood, or mashed the steamed oil fruits. Similar to many craftsmen's occupations (e.g. blacksmith, carpenter, tailor) apprenticeship systems have developed in food processing, enabling women to learn the complex working processes before they start their own business with machines and paid labour.

As a source of income for women trade is equally important as food processing. The numbers of women and men working in trade are almost equal and their activities partly overlap, but there are differences concerning the kind of products they buy and sell. Men deal, for example, more often in the "classical" cash crops like cocoa, coffee and black pepper. Women mainly deal in food products which they often process before marketing. Small-scale trade for household use (salt, matches, detergents, spices, spare parts for lamps, etc.) is for the most part "women's business". Women as well as men sell beer and soft drinks. Less than 10% of the men and even less women were having income from a regular employment, e.g. working for the health stations in the villages or for the authorities or industrial plants in the town.

> "The archetypal female farmer scratches the impoverished earth around her homestead with a hoe to produce 'subsistence' crops. Her husband, meanwhile, manages the complex technology of hybrid seeds, small-scale irrigation schemes, tractors, etc. to produce export agricultural crops. So powerful is this image in contemporary thought that this structural dualism is often conceptualized as lying at the heart of the link between the food crisis and the sexual division of labour." (Whitehead 1991, quoted according to Bryceson 1995: 6)

5 Development trends

The results of the two panel studies show that the farming systems of the Yoruba may not be described as a predominantly "male agriculture" as it has been done quite undifferentiatedly especially in a part of the older literature. In both research areas women are producing a relatively large share of the agricultural production on their own account, particularly food for local and regional markets and for household use. Since the middle of the 1970s, the Nigerian oil boom economy had induced improvements in infrastructure and increases in urban demand, inputs for agricultural production were subsidized either by direct investments or as a result of the overvaluation of the national currency (Naira). New opportunities for economic activities emerged for men as well as for women and developed often as parallel instead of competing options.

In the beginning of the 1980s, Nigeria had to face an increasing economic and debt crisis. In 1986, a structural adjustment program of neo-liberal orientation, including the standard measures such as devaluation of the national currency, reduction of state expenses, liberalization of imports and exports, cuts in subsidies, had been carried out to cope with the crisis. The devaluation of the currency and the liberalization of trade resulted in an increase in producer prices, in particular for export crops. Before, in Nigeria, like in other African countries, agricultural exports had been highly taxed. As an immediate reaction to the liberalization of the marketing boards cocoa exports boomed largely induced by businessmen trying to obtain hard currencies. A particularity of the Nigerian structural adjustment programs had been that, contrary to the ideology of free markets, the import of some food products, e.g. wheat and rice, had been prohibited in order to protect domestic production. Due to the import restrictions and drastically rising prices of imported goods owing to the currency devaluation, the demand for locally produced food increased. Female producers in particular gained from rising food prices (see Guyer/Idowu 1991: 262, Lele 1991: 48).

However, it has to be assumed that in the long run the structural adjustment program will have negative effects also in rural areas, affected are for example some of the agricultural production and food processing sectors. The devaluation of the Naira and cuts in subsidies caused drastically increased costs for imported production inputs such as tractors, transport vehicles, fertilizers and insecticides.

The cuts in the expenses for maintenance of roads and infrastructure have impaired public transport facilities and thus also marketing opportunities especially in remote production areas.

Significant drops in production were to be observed for the cultivation of maize, for example, which had been extended in the last decades mainly due to the propagation of new varieties developed by research institutes. These varieties, however, produce high yields only with mineral fertilizers. Even though Nigeria, due to the crude oil reserves, disposes of the necessary raw materials and energy to produce mineral fertilizers, the only fertilizer production plant never met more than 10% of the national demand. With rising import prices most producers could no longer afford mineral fertilizer. In the villages of the panel study east of Ibadan, the farmers, men as well as women, who had cultivated maize for the market in 1990, had reduced or abandoned the production in May 1997. Surveys in Kogi State in the same period have shown that maize had been reduced in favour of sesame. Without mineral fertilizer insect pests had multiplied on the weaker maize plants. In their complex mixed cropping systems women mostly cultivate a multitude of local varieties of different plants, thus also contributing to the preservation of genetic resources. Local varieties mostly are more resistant, but as seeds for the new maize varieties had been easily available for several years, women also had replaced the local varieties. The reduction of maize yields impaired the income opportunities of women who had specialized in the preparation of different meals with fermented maize which were being served mainly for breakfast and eaten especially by children and elder people. Partly, these dishes have been replaced by cassava meals which contain less proteins and vitamins.

The expansion of the agricultural production in Ibarapa during the 1970s had mainly been possible because of the low import prices of vehicles and tractors owing to the overvaluation of the Naira. Guyer and Idowu assume that when production inputs become more expensive the cultivated areas will be reduced. According to them, mainly women will reduce production when fewer tractors are available and when costs for farm labourers rise because of a growing demand for workers (Guyer/Idowu 1991: 264-73). Also in other sectors where women are working, e.g. food processing, newly established capacities could not be maintained. A visit in the research area east of Ibadan in 1997 revealed that the production sites for gari which had been established in the 1980s had for the greater part been closed down again due to problems with maintenance because of excessively rising prices of spare parts and difficulties in the regular supply of cassava on eroded roads.

Basically, the structural adjustment measures, originally meant to reduce the "urban bias", rather seem to contribute to a growing regional, social and gender-specific differentiation in rural areas. Even Lele (1991: 48) who in principle advocates structural adjustment programs criticizes the speed and simultaneousness in the implementation of different measures. It is expected that in particular large-scale farms will gain from rising producer prices as they can overcome bottlenecks in the supply of production means more easily (Guyer/Idowu 1991). In addition to rising costs for production inputs, small-scale producers, men as well as women, have to face rising costs for medical care, education of their children and basic consumer goods. In how far they are able to gain from rising prices for agricultural products also depends on their capacity to increase their output when new opportunities arise. But only a part of the men and a much smaller part of the women, who are at a structural disadvantage as regards the access to land and production inputs, dispose of the required means and prerequisites to rapidly adjust. Data from empirical studies indicate for many sectors, especially in marginalized areas, a trend to give up cultivation and processing capacities at the expense of rural and urban food supplies. In how far these deficits may be compensated for by a shift to other products or by increasing the output in other regions with better infrastructure cannot be assessed from the available data.

References

Ay, Peter (1980): Agrarpolitik in Nigeria, Produktionssysteme der Bauern und die Hilflosigkeit von Entwicklungsexperten, Hamburg: Arbeiten aus dem Institut für Afrika-Kunde, Nr. 24.

Ay, Peter (1989): Datenauswertung von Langzeitstudien in Entwicklungsländern, das Beispiel von Feldstudien in Westnigeria, paper at Institut für Sozialökonomie der Agrarentwicklung, Technische Universität Berlin.

Ay, Peter (1990a): Women in Food Processing—Traditional Palm Oil Production and Changes Through the Introduction of Appropriate Technology, Ibadan: Book Builders for UNDP, ILO, Federal Department of Rural Development Abuja.

Ay, Peter (1990b): Changes in Traditional Agricultural Production Systems in Western Nigeria from 1975 to 1990, paper at Research Seminar IITA, Ibadan, January.

Ay, Peter (1991): The Dynamics of Economic Change in Traditional Production Systems, seminar paper, Economic Development Institute of the World Bank, Washington D.C., August.

Ay, Peter (1992): Umweltprobleme in afrikanischen Bauerngesellschaften, in: Bruhns, B. and R. Kappel (Ed.): Ökologische Zerstörung in Afrika und alternative Strategien, Münster, Hamburg: Bremer Afrika Studien, Bd.1.

Ay, Peter (1996): Die Steigerung der Maniokproduktion in lokalen Systemen als Beitrag zur Ernährungssicherung, in: Peripherie, Nr. 63, pp. 73-101.

Baumann, H. (1928): The Division of Work According to Sex in African Hoe Culture, in: Africa, Vol. 1, pp. 289-319.

Beneria, Lourdes and Gita Sen (1997): Accumulation, Reproduction, and Women's Role in Economic Development: Boserup Revisited, in: Nalini Visvanathan, Lynn Duggan and Laurie Nisonoff (eds.): The Women, Gender and Development Reader, London, New Jersey, Dbaka, Bangkok, Halifax, Cape Town: Zed Books, White Lotus, Fernwood Publishing, David Philip, pp. 42-51.

Berry, Sara (1975): Cocoa, Customs and Socio-Economic Change in Rural Western Nigeria, Oxford: Clarendon Press.

Bisi, Grant and Q.B.O. Anthonio (1973): Women Cooperative in the Western State of Nigeria, in: Bulletin of Rural Economics and Sociology, 8, 1, pp. 7-36.

Boserup, Ester (1982): Die ökonomische Rolle der Frau in Afrika, Asien, Lateinamerika, Stuttgart: Edition Cordeliers, first edition 1970.

Bryceson, Deborah Fahy (1995): Wishful Thinking: Theory and Practice of Western Donor Efforts to Raise Women's Status in Rural Africa, in: Deborah Fahy Bryceson (ed.): Women Wielding the Hoe. Lessons from Rural Africa for Feminist Theory and Development Practice, Oxford, Washington D.C.: Berg Publishers, pp. 201-219.

Charles, Nickie (1993): Gender Divisions and Social Change, Harvester Wheatsheaf: Barnes & Noble Books.

Fadipe, N.A. (1970): The Sociology of the Yoruba, Ibadan: Ibadan University Press.

Guyer, Jane I. (1995): Women's Farming and Present Ethnography: Perspectives on a Nigerian Restudy, in: Deborah Fahy Bryceson (ed.): Women Wielding the Hoe. Lessons from Rural Africa for Feminist Theory and Development Practice, Oxford, Washington D.C.: Berg Publishers, pp. 25-46.

Guyer, Jane I. and Olukemi Idowu (1991): Woman's Agricultural Work in an Multimodal Rural Economy: Ibarapa District, Oyo State, Nigeria, in: Christina H. Gladwin (ed.): Structural Adjustment and African Women Farmers, Gainesville, Florida, pp. 257-80.

Johnson, Samuel (1973): The History of the Yorubas. From the Earliest Times to the Beginning of the British Protectorate, Lagos: C.S.S. Bookshops, first edition 1921.

Kabeer, Naila (1994): Reversed Realities. Gender Hierarchies in Development Thought, London, New York: Verso.

Lele, Uma (1991): Women, Structural Adjustment and Transformation: Some Lessons and Questions from the African Experience, in: Christina H. Gladwin (ed.): Structural Adjustment and African Women Farmers, Gainesville, Florida, pp. 46-80.

Quisumbing, Agnes R., Lynn R. Brown, Hilary Sims Feldstein, Lawrence Haddad and Christine Pena (1995): Women: The Key to Food Security, Washington, D.C.: Food Policy Report, The International Food Policy Research Institute.

Sudarkasa, Niara (1973): Where Women Work: A Study of Yoruba Women in the Marketplace and in the Home, Anthropological Papers, 53, University of Michigan.

Whitehead, Ann (1991): Food Production and the Food Crisis in Africa, in: Tina Wallace and Candida March (eds.): Changing Perceptions. Writings on Gender and Development, Oxford: Oxfam, pp. 68-78.

WORDOC (Women's Research and Documentation Centre) (1988): Women in Agriculture, African Notes, Special Number 3, Instiute of African Studies, University of Ibadan.

11

Local Knowledge and the Improvement of Food Production—A Case Study in Bénin

Georg Elwert and Lazare Séhouéto
with the collaboration of Albert Hoegner

1 The problem

Agricultural production in least-developed countries seems to be in a crisis. Development aid is therefore concentrated upon the rural sector. Both the perception of a crisis and the weight of aid motivate considerable research on the farmers' responses to this aid (see Grillo and Rew 1985, Boiral et al. 1985, Richards 1986, Geschiere and Schlemmer 1987, Long 1989, Lühe 1989, Cernea 1991, Croll and Parkin 1992, Long and Long 1992, Floquet et al. 1996, Bierschenk and Elwert 1997). This response to all this well-meaning aid was rather reluctant. It can, however, be doubted whether it is appropriate to speak of a crisis. In many of the countries concerned the production increased with the pace of the population increase (Bierschenk 1996). This is a considerable increase although it does not alleviate the risk of hunger. It is, however, appropriate to speak of a crisis of agricultural aid projects (Floquet et al. 1996). These projects had no measurable impact on the agricultural production. The increase came mostly from regions or sectors which did not benefit from aid. Since neither land nor capital increased, it is a good guess that this increase was due to knowledge.

Local knowledge, a concept earlier forged by Clifford Geertz (1983), made a career as a reference to the strength of peasant production in a context where, beforehand, the same peasants were rather seen as feeble and ignorant (among the first critics of this perspective was Paul Richards [1985]). Could a reference to local knowledge by donor agencies and natural bureaucracy help to alleviate hunger? That the peasants themselves rely on their knowledge more than on the authority of rural extension services is obvious (see Elwert et al. 1989, von der Lühe 1991, Floquet et al. 1996). But in how far could technologically advanced communication contribute to it? Before we can proceed to these questions we have to get a clear picture of how local knowledge appears in the rural world.

1.1 Definition

We define local knowledge as knowledge essentially transmitted by oral face-to-face communication (and therefore rather localized). Insofar we give the element "local" in this established concept a rather metaphorical meaning. Local knowledge must not necessarily be known to the majority of the population of a locality. It can be shared by farstretching networks of oral communication. There is the possibility to control the input of knowledge, i.e. the authors are known and the effects of its application can be seen. The encoding of this knowledge into an oral discourse (not in literary language) and the use of sensual (especially visual) demonstration distinguishes local knowledge from scientific or technical knowledge.

Two contradictory hypotheses cover our field. Firstly, the hypothesis of peasant ignorance, the basic premise of rural extension up to its most pedagogized latest version of the "training and visit approach". Secondly, the new romanticism (Séhouéto 1996) of applied local knowledge research which grants peasants, in contrast to development experts, in most cases superior mastership of their production knowhow. We[1] asked peasants in five regions of Bénin about their knowledge and the sources of their knowledge. We participated in work processes and observed in how far the knowledge as defined by oral discourse was really that was put into practice. In contrast to other studies we did not restrict our interview partners to those which were locally considered to be the best experts. We took samples of people in the same locality which were informed about the same subject in order to find out whether this knowledge is a shared one or whether there is an unequal distribution to be observed.

2 Spirituality and holism

It is a widespread belief among western intellectuals that knowledge systems in Africa derive from spirituality. It is assumed that priests play the role of professors and that they form an invisible academy. This knowledge is presented as holistic, that means that all its components are interconnected and that, thus, any knowledge has a spiritual element (cf. Brouwers et al. 1997). We tested this hypothesis. In the analysis of the local knowledge systems of the Lokpa and the Fon of Ayogo we (Séhouéto) looked for links with religious beliefs and institutions. Only 5-8% of the people interviewed saw linkages between elements of agricultural knowledge and the world of the gods. In the study on bee-keeping in northern Bénin we found no reference to religious wisdom in the field of productive knowledge. The transcen-

1 The senior author, Georg Elwert, started his research on this topic in 1989 in the village Ayou among Ayizo in Bénin's southern region (province de l'Atlantique) and in the northwestern region in Bassila (province de l'Atacora). For the sake of this article he is especially grateful to Klikpo Cece and Anato Raimond. Lazare Séhouéto did fieldwork 1991-1993 in Ayogo (central region, province du Zou) among Fon and in Ouaké among Lokpa in the northwestern region. He is especially grateful to Alice Massim-Ouali, Kalixte Avognon and Paul Gnagna. Fieldwork was supported by the DAAD and the Graduiertenkolleg Gesellschaftsvergleich of the Freie Universität Berlin. His Ph.D. thesis was supervised by Georg Elwert. Lazare Séhouéto supervised, himself, some students' work on the subject including Hanna Schmuck-Widmann's M.A. thesis on peasant knowledge in Bangladesh (see Hanna Schmuck-Widmann 1996), which brought us new comparative perspectives. Albert Hoegner, a semi-professional bee-keeper did fieldwork in northern Bénin among Betamaribe in 1996, financed by the GTZ, supervised by Georg Elwert. He is especially grateful to Barbara Gugel and Antoine Nda.

dental is, however, not absent. To protect beehives in the house against theft and magic actors (witches) a deity (*omonekwango*) receives an offering. Similarly, a growing minority of peasants among Ayizo and Fon protects their fields by magic charms. But it would stretch the concept too far to call this activity as being directed against—assumed—social actors' production knowledge. The study on agricultural knowledge in southern Bénin brought only one reference to a religious authority: two varieties of millet, a cereal there no longer cultivated, have to be conserved by the priest of the local *vodún*.

The problem with studies which insist upon spirituality and holism is that they take their assumptions for granted and do not test them against a negative hypothesis. The association of facts in the mind of the researcher is no proof for an association in the mind of the peasants. Thus Brouwers et al. (1997) noticed that the Aja in Bénin relate some plant diseases to rains in May, the month when the triple stars *ezàn* (*éza* in their self-made orthography) appear. That a mythological ancestor identified with these stars exists is, in our view, no proof that the observation of untimely rains and their damaging effect is spiritual knowledge.[2]

Some informants—used in the interaction with missionaries and anthropologists—develop readily theories of origin when asked for the assumed reasons of extraordinary phenomena. But these etiological theories have to be distinguished from practical knowledge. That such theories exists, or can be produced, is no proof for the assumption that peasant knowledge is produced by deduction from such spiritual theories.[3] Where knowledge is drawn from, has to remain an open question.

There are two models which govern the study of systems of knowledge. The first is that of "a determined structure which individuals are seeking to express or interpret" and the other is that of a "creation by particular individuals of systems of understanding out of a series of given building blocks ..." (Goody 1997). As conspiracy theories have often more appeal than stories of accidental events, the idea of a grand design, of a determined structure, was for a long time more popular than that of a creation with differentiated individual inputs. In all studies we tested also the hypothesis of a grand design of one holistic system covering all the knowledge at least in the field of agriculture. We found, however, no deductive or hierarchically organized explicative or semantic model. This does not mean that people had no references when talking about their knowledge. They referred to fields of experience which were clearly distinguished and they referred to competent persons.

In all cases we found inconsistencies in the information we collected. People were conscious about these inconsistencies and explained them in respect to the

2 Their elaboration on the month names of the lunar calendar does not convince us either. They count "16 to 17 lunar months" where most Africans and Europeans would come to 13 and give only 12 month in their table (p. 252).

3 Unfortunately Brouwers et al. (cf. p. 254) give no indications on the methods and context of research, thus that projective questionning could be excluded.

differentiations of fields of experience and in relation to the different competent persons from whom someone drew his wisdom.

Inconsistencies widened, once we touched religious fields. There especially the study in the centre revealed a systematic practice of double discourse. There was a pious discourse pronounced in public—one was supposed to believe all the miracles proclaimed by religious groups. And there was "off-stage" (Scott 1990) a private discourse rather sceptical and realistic close to everyday practice. It seems that the idea of a holistic belief system is rather a travesty of the western model of a unified science (and of its hierarchical character) which is combined with a longing for lost worlds of religious security and homogenity.

3 The production and the productivity of knowledge

That African agriculture is not only dynamic in respect of increased production but also in respect of adding new knowledge to the old established one can best be demonstrated by the use Africans made of the Amerindian tuber fruit *manihot* called maniok or cassava in Africa. Three hundred years ago *casawa* seedlings of less than ten varieties were brought from South America to Africa. Out of these African peasants created more than two hundred and fifty (see von Oppen 1991). This enabled revolutionary changes in some regions of Africa. This relatively drought-resistant crop turned hitherto scarcely populated areas with semi-deciduous forests into "fertile" savannah. Compared with plant breeding in modern Europe this success seems to be not less impressive than potato breeding in Europe till 19th century. We have no written records on this plant-breeding. But we can see that the variation is largest in those regions where there was a mosaic of differentiated cultures. These mosaics should be seen as a highly productive social setting—and not at all as a kind of splintering as the German concept "Volkssplitter" suggests. The differentiation of cultures allowed for a diversification of experience which was made an element of an evolutionary process through exchanges between neighbours.

How plant-breeding works can be demonstrated by our case-study in southern Bénin. The Ayizo are a rather endogenous group of lineages which always lived on the margins of the powerful Fon. Within Ayizo villages reigned a segmentary political system—an acephalic political structure. If one searches for peasant knowledge about varieties of maize and beans in the village of Ayou one is directed by the other peasants to specific persons in each of the quarters. One of those considered to be an expert by the other peasants (although he has no formal schooling, as is the case for them too) is Klikpo Cece (interviews Sept. 7 and 8, 1989). He knows nine varieties of maize and 20 varieties of beans. He classifies maize in respect of five old varieties (*alokpadeé*) and a new one. One of the old varieties is split into four sub-varieties. Fourteen of the twenty varieties of beans are old ones, they were brought during his life-time from other places. He explained to us that his classification of maize is just a rough classification because "there are many cross-breeds. The new breeds appear especially because there are some peasants who gamble. They just produce enough for the family's survival. They ate everything till the moment of seed. They ask for maize seeds from all sides. In this way the maize (different varieties from different sources, G.E.) cross-breeds in their fields."

On his own fields he "saw mostly a cross-breed I have crossed myself of the new variety *cankpó* and the old variety *asódúkwe*. I often asked for varieties I do not have. I often look at other people's fields to see if a variety yields well. One can buy new varieties, exchange them or receive—in small quantities—as a gift. People also often bring me varieties of maize and beans because they know that I keep them." This is a reference to the fact that keeping varieties, experimenting with them, detecting new ones is a special social role. "A good peasant sorts the fruits out—discovers thus changes (spontaneous cross-breeds and mutations, G.E.)—and sows each of them separately. ... God gives these things. There are, for example, red grains in the maize. This is like albinos with human beings." We notice that there is an intensive observation of nature and routine practice of cross-breeding with maize. The cross-breeding is done with the same technique as would be done on experimental fields in agronomical research stations. They are perfectly aware of the need to separate the male from the female part of the flowers as any scientific experimenter would be.

This special role of the one who receives varieties and keeps them for other peasants who, in general, cultivate just one variety is coupled with a specific economic situation: "it were only the big peasants (*glesì klógbó*), those who produced a surplus, who conserved many varieties and gave other people seeds. There were eleven of them in the whole village. ... One knows their names well because they were able to sell maize (to people from the outside and to give it free to those of the village, G.E.) in big famines." Whereas most people were only able to name three to six different varieties of maize these specialists knew by heart not only the twelve varieties they each preserved, but also all its characteristics in respect of cycle of vegetation, need of water, tolerance of pests, storing capacity, consistency of the grain in respect of grinding, milling or cooking, and, last but not least, the taste and its assumed nutritive qualities. Their ambition went further. They tried to bring in new varieties. They even ordered young men to go to the agricultural research station of Hinvi in order to steal seedlings and plants from the experimental fields. They then made experiments themselves on their own fields. In most cases they were not entirely satisfied by these experiments and so they started to cross the plants.

What motivated these treasurers of genetic variety? Their own answer was: "It allows me to make gifts to other people." From other informants we heard that this was a considerable source of prestige and, so it was added, every gift creates an obligation. The economic system of reciprocity was basic for the economy of seed reproduction and breeding. Till the seventies these peasants were the main source of old and new seeds for their neighbours, then migration and also markets contributed to it.

The result of these activities for the peasants of Ayou was that they had varieties of maize and beans which spread over a wide spectrum. Some had shorter and some longer vegetation cycles than those offered by the extension services. The varieties included also two high-yielding varieties propagated by the extension services, but included also some which could be harvested from bad soils and after scanty rainfall, something which the "scientifically selected" varieties could not offer. They were proud of varieties which were particularly pest-resistant and especially self-protecting when stored in peasant granaries.

4 Distribution of knowledge

Peasants in the village Ayogo in central Bénin which we (L.S.) interviewed had only immigrated to their site over the last hundred years. Since they came from the high plateau to a swampy area, this new environment forced them to recreate their knowledge. The dominant contribution to this new knowledge is neither imported knowledge nor undefined "tradition" but it comes from experience. Experience means experiments which force them to give up "certainties", to reformulate their initial questions by increasing the complexity of the assumed model and resulting in new experiments. The number of persons who are more or less continuously engaged in these experiments is not larger than one twentieth of the producers—a figure which is confirmed by our (Elwert's) research in southern Bénin.[4] The results of this local research are remarkable. Agriculture in Ayogo which started as a poor and marginal village is now flourishing. People take advantage of maize planting on flood plains—an innovation for them—in the counter-season and thus profit from high prices. They even developed a type of green manuring for the non-flooded fields.

In how far local knowledge is shared knowledge or not can be demonstrated with the case study we (Séhouéto) realized in Ouakité among Lokpa. We choose this example for the sake of demonstration because there the local knowledge about types of soils is highly differentiated and thus easy to quantify. Most people (58%) had quite a differentiated knowledge of the five types of soil; a third was doubting, when asked to identify differentiations of soils; 3% were in error. The top level of differentiation was only realized by 30%. We expected the oldest persons to be best informed. This was not the case. From the age of 60 on the level of differentiation showed a clear regression. This research result should make us cautious in respect of the romanticism implicit in the generalisations about "the" members of an ethnic group whose "local knowledge" is then opposed to "the western knowledge" of agricultural research. Obviously intellectual competence plays a role. Some people are more receptive and curious than others. But this cannot be the only explanation

4 The bee-keepers in northern Bénin we (Hoegner) studied have a higher percentage - about a third - of actively experimenting persons. This should be seen in the context that they, themselves, form a minority among their neighbours.

for differential distribution. The access to, and selection of knowledge mediated by other persons, play a role too, as we have seen yet with the example of Ayou.

It is conventional in studies of this type to insist upon the formal structure of networks which transport knowledge. We think that the question of trust should receive at least equal attention. In all three case studies the sharing of knowledge followed those social relations where trust was established. Market relations, friendship and membership in a group all played a role. Knowledge is purchased, received generously in the form of generalised reciprocity or, more often, exchanged in the form of balanced reciprocity. Migration is an important opportunity for the acquisition of knowledge. Sometimes knowledge is connected to theft. This is the case when seedlings are taken from agricultural research stations. These cases which were reported to us in the central and in the southern region show that there is no traditionalist "mentality" which inhibits peasants to take advantage of modern science. But there is caution. In all the cases where people admitted to us that they had stolen seedlings, they made experiments on different soils before they decided to share this knowledge with other persons. No-one of those interviewed trusted the advice of rural development officers (who should be instructed by the experts from the research stations). Knowledge acquisition requires activity. "The lazy ones know nothing," said some peasants in Ayogo.

The transmission of knowledge implies demonstration. The knowledge is not only stored in the verbal register of our brains. People may know something without being able to verbalize it. They know it by eyesight or by smell. Peasants in Aiogo and neighbouring villages we asked about soil qualities in an abstract interview situation identified soils by colour and were unable to bring in all the differentiations which we were told about when we discussed soil differentation in the context of cultivation, especially on the fields.

Development aid played, in spite of the considerable expenses for building a whole bureaucracy and providing it with scientifically tested and reproduced seedlings, almost no measurable input. This was explained by the peasants by their deep mistrust against this institution. The main justification for this mistrust was the general behaviour of the officers in this business who were not very reliable, if asked for services, and repressive and corrupt once they saw a chance to extract money from the peasants (see Elwert et al. 1989, Floquet et al. 1996). If mistrust and caution are dominant features of this peasant world, how then could trust in the information of these wealthy peasants, and later also of some of the migrants, be established? The concept of truth (*nugbó* in the Fon and Ayizo language) has a very high value. This value is not only expressed by proverbs and declarations but by special practices related to it. One has to say where one got knowledge from (at least in this field of agricultural knowledge). If one transmits information one talks in general in the presence of witnesses. It is expected that one tests the new knowledge in order to have proof of its efficiency. This, together, can produce either considerable honour or considerable shame for the author of the original information.

5 Screening knowledge

Peasant knowledge is often presented as "traditional". With this concept one associates inertia or rather slow transformations. Two explanations come implicitly or explicitly with this assumed traditionalism. Firstly, the concept of a prelogic mentality (Lévy-Bruhl 1922). This conception supposes rather associative thinking than logic to structure the human mind in primitive culture. Secondly, the dominance of the cognitive grid produced by the semantics of oral language (Whorf 1942).

A different perspective is gained through the work of Roumasset (1971) and Scott (1976) who argue that peasant conservativism makes sense. The option for traditional seeds, e.g., can be shown to be perfectly rational in the face of high risks. Peasants appear, in this perspective, not as traditionalist but just as cautious. This brings us to the question left aside by the first two perspectives: if they innovate, how do people operate selections of knowledge (a question asked as well by Robin Horton (1961)). In order to see the forms in working by which people create certainty, we selected a field of knowledge which is often portrayed as a core of spiritual and magic thinking. If a prelogic mentality might be found, it should be found there. We present here in the following the results obtained from our study among the Anii in Bassila in the north of Bénin (see Elwert 1995).

The ways certainties are created are just two: empirism and logical deduction with generalisation. Logical deduction from which people generalise, can never be based only upon personal experience, it implies always also deduction from other experience presented by persons which are considered as trustworthy, authoritative experience. The ways empirism and deduction may be combined are, however, manifold. In order to demonstrate the working of logical deduction and to see its linkage to empirism, we choose the paradox example of people believing that the common cold is caused by drinking fresh rainwater from the ponds. This belief was considered to be a typical example of magic or prelogic reasoning. If we go into detail we see, however, how logical deduction and experience interact to produce this conclusion

In the days of the first rains when the rainy season starts, the temperature drops, the huts get wet; thus, sneezes and related symptoms occur or increase. The temporal correlation between the first days of the rainy season and occurrence of the cold is valid. The observation of temporal coincidence or sequence is linked to a more general explanatory model for illnesses. Illness may be hereditary, may be due to injury—rather rare cases—or is caused by wrong nutrition. The main danger comes from what you consume. There is ample evidence for this, including the practice of poisoning. Since this etiology looks empirically valid, there is no doubt that the cold has to be caused by something taken in through the mouth. The only nutrition which is specific for this period and thus can be the reason for the illness is the clear "new water". So there are two arguments which build this etiology: one rather empirical, namely, the observation of a temporal correlation, and the other rather deductive, namely, illness comes from what you take in. What made this idea that cold is caused by fresh water look especially odd was, however, a new variation of this belief. Since development aid introduced wells there was no longer the possibility to drink this "dangerous" fresh water "floating" above the brown water of the water ponds. Therefore, the health experts (old women) concluded that the common cold became slightly more rare. This again is a deductive argument.

Other illnesses, especially diarrhoea, reduced their occurrence considerably after the wells were introduced. Thus, since the quality of water was connected to several illnesses it was a logic conclusion that the incidence of the cold might have been reduced as well. This deduction is valid in so far as the empirical evidence about the incidence of the common cold is of a type we call diffuse evidence. Diffuse evidence is the counter-concept for distinct evidence. Distinct evidence is any evidence which immediately causes one to question the validity of generalisations. An example for that is the belief of the origin of the illness called guinea worm, a parasite transmitted through drinking water. The old emic theory blamed heredity. Wherever the worm occurred, the whole hamlet was infected. (In a hamlet people are related through patrilineal kinship and they get their water from the same pool.) In 1980s wells were drilled and thus clean water was available at a short distance from the houses. The guinea worm had vanished. This constituted distinctive empirical evidence and was recognized as such. Without propaganda from the health education team people switched to another theory about the guinea worm. Now, of 36 people interviewed, only 6 believed heredity as being the cause of the illness whereas 16 argued that parasites were transmitted through water or food (Elwert and Elwert-Kretschmer 1991: 124). Evidence on the common cold, in contrast, is diffuse evidence. Neither are the number of cases counted nor the gravity of infection measured.

Logic and empirism are intertwined. To come back to the belief about the common cold, there is a clear five-step deduction implying deduction and strong empirical evidence:

1. Illnesses are in most cases the consequence of something taken in by mouth.
2. The common cold appears with the first rains.
3. The only nutrition which is specific for this period is the fresh water floating on the old water of the water ponds.
4. Now, there is a new source of water: the wells.
5. Therefore the cold has to occur less often.

If there is no statistical analysis which transforms diffuse evidence into distinct evidence people in Europe, as people in Africa, create their certainties first by logical deduction.

Distinct evidence makes people change their generalisations. They may modify them or they may opt for alternative statements. Diffuse evidence can be transformed into distinct evidence by means of statistical tests. In this respect any evidence accepted by a scientific reader is a distinct evidence. (What we call diffuse evidence is called evidence only because it can be made distinct).

One conclusion of our observations is that societies of oral communication and literate societies are not different in their ways of creating certainties. Knowledge is organised by empirism and by logical deduction. Both principles necessarily have to clash from time to time to produce contradiction. This is nothing special for African nor for European societies.

Deduction can be, as we wrote above, not only a deduction from generalisations based upon personal experience by means of formal logic, it can also be a deduction from sources of information which have shown their credibility in other contexts. This applies to scientific environments as well as to environments of oral communication. But there is one difference we see at least based upon our Bénin material. Oral societies seem to be more sceptical in respect of authoritative information they can not control. They are in this sense more empiricist than people in intellectual worlds. There are more people who make their own experiences and who draw, themselves, their logical deductions. At least of the people we have observed we can say they are more empiricist than average European peasants. Being empiricist means also less inclined to deduce from sources of authority that a new statement of this source would be valid. These African peasants have a long experience with state officers considering state authority merely as a means for personal appropriation of wealth. This peasant experience reinforces their caution against authoritative statements. (It should be no surprise that state-organised information about AIDS—a diffuse evidence—finds few believers in this environment.) There are no institutions which control the validity of knowledge. For this reason the rural extension officer (*glègaán*) is less credible than persons from the same village.

6 Structures of relevance and neglected sectors of knowledge

As we have seen, the central problem of local knowledge systems in their working is that the structures of relevance of the people active in these systems leave small space for diverging interests and specialisations to create fields for knowledge evolution. Knowledge evolution has to be based upon variation as widely as possible and simultaneously upon selection according to criteria as consistently as possible.

We have seen this problem in the study we undertook on bee-keeping (Hoegner 1997). Bee-keeping and honey-hunting (we use this term because in most cases the hive is destroyed after harvesting) is a minority occupation. Not even every village has a bee-keeper. There is some accumulation of knowledge. But there is almost no regional circulation of knowledge. As a result, there are too few cases to allow for comparison which might generate the play of variation and selection. Since there are too few cases, there are only limited possibilities to identify parameters responsible for success or failure of specific measures. The success in bee-keeping is a typical case of what we call diffuse reality. It is only with great numbers that one can transform this diffuse reality into a distinct one.

And to record these great numbers would be possible only with the help of written protocols and statistics.

Four parameters allow us to make a prognosis as to whether, in a specific field, there will be a rapid or a slow diffusion (or evolution) of information: relevance, contact, complexity, and evidence. If the relevance is high, the contact direct, the complexity of information rather low and when the new information is based upon distinct evidence, then there will be a rapid diffusion of the information through oral communication systems articulated with local knowledge. Typical cases are the mango tree (see Taylor and Soumaré 1983) and the green manuring with the plant *kétra* we studied in Ayogo. However, if the relevance is low, the contact indirect, the complexity of information rather high and the information itself is based upon a rather diffuse evidence, then the new information will travel very slowly, if at all, and there may be few, mostly not sufficient people who will experiment with this new idea. Typical examples are the information about bee-hives and mulching.

7 Rural extension as a mock version of scientific knowledge diffusion

The problem of the selection of knowledge, whenever the relevance of a field of knowledge appears to be low, affects not only local knowledge systems. The planned economy approach of administrative innovation (Bierschenk et al. 1993: 95-96) which is practiced in rural extension services suffers from the same problem. It is impossible to deal with great numbers of specific demands if one is bound to a command economy approach and oral communication (which is characteristic of the Training Visit Approach of the World Bank). If a peasant wants to decide whether he adapts a new variety or not, he will ask nine different questions: identification of the variety, length of the vegetative cycle, demand in water, demand upon soil quality, resistance against pests, harvest quantity, problems in conservation, condition in the preparation as food, and taste and consistence of the food.

These nine parameters are difficult to retain by oral communication, and the World Bank's "Training and Visit approach" is essentially oral. How would one just communicate the pros and cons of three varieties if the information should be vehicled through a chain of three persons? Each case is specific, each asks for another solution. The maximum number of peasants who might pose a structurally similar problem to an extension officer was below 50% in all villages studied. What is too complex for a centrally-planned bureaucracy can, however, be treated with a measurable increase of productivity by a local community if the product is one of high relevance. This explains the relative strength of local knowledge systems as compared to centrally-planned services, when common crops or new ones of high relevance are the object.

Local knowledge systems are often opposed to a generalised other one, to "western knowledge systems". In empirical studies rural extension services organised by state bureaucracies or by development aid are taken as representatives of this western model. This is, however, a wrong representation. Rural information in Europe is based upon a dense network. This network consists of research journals, specialized agricultural journals (often with university and technical school-trained journalists), reports in general newspapers, trade fairs (such as the Berlin Grüne Woche), radio publicity, practical demonstrations by state services and by agents representing the rural trade, meetings of farmers interested in a special problem, scientific congresses or lectures and farm visits organised by farmers' unions.

This information network is characterized by five main features which lack completely or partially in both the local knowledge systems we are studying and in the agricultural extension services organised by national bureaucracies and propagated by foreign aid, and especially the World Bank.

1. Specialization: even producers who are specializing in a product which is a minority product in the respective region are touched. It is, therefore, no problem if diverging directions or specialization cause every producer in a village to be in a minority. Specialization implies not only the selective accumulation of knowledge but also the development of special registers of language able to cover fine details of the production process.

2. Feedback structures: wrong information is corrected by letter to the editor, by scientific re-studies and by success and failure on the market. Irrelevant information reduces the audience in oral presentations or the sale of the respective publications.

3. The use of writing: writing is a powerful means to store information over time and to make it accessible also to isolated single persons who specialize in a field not covered by other people in the same locality. The modernization of European agriculture is linked to books which compared methods from different regions of Europe as Estienne (1567), Coler (1665) or Thaer (1810-12).

4. A sandwich structure of oral and written communication (Elwert 1988): the strength of both types of communication is linked by chains of written invitations to visits on the farm-site, by oral discussions there, by written reports about these discussions, by oral information about a report's contents which makes other people read it, by letters between peasant, by phone calls, etc. In this sandwich structure it is orality which provides for the quick selection, for rapid feedback and for the specification of information in dialogue. The contribution of the written communication is the stabilization of information and the capacity to make it available over long distances at a low price.

5. Motivation by commercial and prestige interests combined: that information can have a market value is evident. This is the basis for information media. It is much less known that the western idea of "publication" reflects not a pure market logic. The prevalent individual motive is the acquisition of prestige. Someone who helps other people, someone who is an explorer or inventor earns a high reputation. This reputation helps to overcome the problem that the monopolization of informa-

tion can be highly rational on the individual level. That knowledge also follows reputation motives causes the sharing of knowledge to be a general pattern also there where individual motives might lead to other solutions.

8 Conclusions

The strength of local knowledge systems is based upon the fact that parameters of production, which are too complex to deal with by centrally-planned approaches are covered by a meticulous empirical research. This peasant research, the basis of local knowledge systems, forms a decentralized network adapted to local conditions and close to the consumers of knowledge. This research follows basically the same methods as scientific endeavour: namely, logical deduction plus empirical falsification. And, as in the world of modern science, deduction implies belief into the source's authority when there was an experience of trustworthiness connected with it. Both trust and caution towards authority's propagating scientific knowledge can constitute problems. Highly relevant is, whether the differentiation of advances in knowledge from power interests and economic interests is effectively managed by this institution (Luhmann 1984). It is decisive whether these institutions, in fact, screen knowledge for its realism and whether the consumers of this knowledge are aware of the interests of the institution and its strong or weak screening capacity.

Local knowledge, peasant research and the accumulation of knowledge associated with it are, however, remarkably unevenly distributed. It is a small minority which is really engaged in this; and the commonly shed version of this knowledge (as often with computer share-ware) is only a shed version of this knowledge. But this distributional structure is of no problem for the overall performance of the agriculture in the key nutritional sectors of the peasant production system. Peasant forms of transmission and screening of knowledge do, however, not show this performance in fields which have, now, a low relevance.

If, however, a sector of production which is now of low relevance should play a larger role in the future, then local knowledge systems face a problem. The web of communication and the network-based storage of knowledge are too holeridden to allow for systematic selection. The potential evolution of knowledge which implies variation and selection is thus severely hampered.

Any future knowledge systems which should increase productivity should therefore keep the decentralized structure of research and storage of the oral local knowledge systems. They should include, as well, written communication and information storage. They should network scattered local experience in order to create larger numbers for comparison and better and wider variation to allow for selection. Written communication implies the building of institutions which are able to guarantee trustworthiness and a systematic selection of information. These institutions have to be shielded off from power and economic interests. That means that power and profits should not interfere as motives with decisions about truth.

References

Bierschenk, Thomas (1996): Le Secteur Rural dans l'Économie Rentière du Bénin, in: Thomas Bierschenk, Pierre-Yves Le Meur and Mathias von Oppen (eds.): Institutions and Technologies for Rural Development in West Africa, Weikersheim: Margraf Verlag.

Bierschenk, Thomas and Georg Elwert (eds.) (1997): Entwicklungshilfe und ihre Folgen. Ergebnisse empirischer Untersuchungen, Frankfurt: Campus.

Bierschenk, Thomas, Georg Elwert and Dirk Kohnert (1993): The Long-Term Effects of Development Aid: Empirical Studies in Rural West Africa, in: Economics (Tübingen) Vol. 47, pp. 83-111.

Boiral, Pierre, Jean-Francois Lanteri, Jean-Pierre Olivier de Sardan (eds.) (1985): Paysans, experts et chercheurs en Afrique Noire—sciences sociales et développement rural, Paris: Karthala.

Brouwers, Jan, Constant Dangbénon and Valentin Agbo (1997): La connaissance agricole des Adja, in: Jon Daane, Mark Breusers and Erik Frederiks (eds.): Dynamique paysanne sur le plateau Adja du Bénin, Paris: Karthala, pp. 240-264.

Cernea, Michael (1991): Putting People First—Sociological Variables in Rural Development, Oxford: Oxford University Press.

Coler, Johannes (1665): Economia ruralis et domestica, Mainz: Nicolaus Heyll.

Croll, Elizabeth and David Parkin (1992): Bushbase: Forest Farm—Culture, Environment and Development, London: Routledge.

Elwert, Georg (1988): The Social and Institutional Context of Literacy, in: Adult Eduction and Development, Nr. 31, pp. 355-407.

Elwert, Georg (1995): Changing Certainties and the Move to a 'Global' Religion. Medical Knowledge and Islamization Among Anii (Baseda) in the Republic of Bénin, in: Wendy James (ed.): The Pursuit of Certainty. Religious and Cultural Formulations, London: Routledge, pp. 215—233.

Elwert, Georg, Etienne Beaudoux, Augustin Durand, Karin Janz and Dieter Orlowski (1989): Ländliche Regionalentwicklung: CARDER Atlantique. Evaluation Report, Berlin: Freie Universität.

Elwert, Georg and Karola Elwert-Kretschmer (1991). Mit den Augen der Béniner. Eine andere Evaluation von 25 Jahren DED in Bénin, Berlin: Deutscher Entwicklungsdienst.

Estienne, Charles (1567): L'agriculture et maison rustique, Paris: DuPuys.

Floquet, Anne, Niko von der Lühe, and Hans-Joachim Preuss (1996): Paysans, vulgarisateurs et chercheurs au sud du Bénin: le trio déconnecté, Münster: Lit.

Geertz, Clifford (1983): Local knowledge, New York: Basic Books.

Geschiere, Peter and Bernard Schlemmer (1987): Terrains et perspectives—anthropologie face aux transformations des sociétés rurales, aux politiques et aux idéologies du développement, Paris: ORSTOM.

Goody, Jack (1997): Representations and Contradictions, Oxford: Blackwell.

Grillo, Ralph and Alan Rew (eds.) (1985): Social Anthropology and Development Policy, London: Tavistock.

Hoegner, Albert (1997): Erfassung des sozialen, ökologischen und ökonomischen Stellenwerts der Bienenhaltung bei der Bevölkerung in der Projektregion Bassila, Republik Bénin, Lehrforschungsbericht, Berlin: Institut für Ethnologie der FU.

Horton, Robin (1967): African Traditional Thought and Western Science, in: Africa 37, pp. 1-2.

Lévy-Bruhl, Lucien (1922): La mentalité primitive, Paris: Alcan.

Long, Norman (ed.) (1989): Encounters at the Interface—a Prospective on Social Discontinuities in Rural Development, Wageningen: Agricultural University.

Long, Norman and Ann Long (eds.) (1992): Battlefields of Knowledge. The Interlocking of Theory and Practice in Social Research and Development, London: Routledge.

Lühe, Niko von der (1991): Transfer of Technology or Barter Trade? The Rural Extension Service in the Atlantique Province of Bénin as a Market for Negotiating Ressources, in: Quarterly Journal of International Agriculture, 30, 3.

Luhmann, Niklas (1984): The Differentiation of Advances in Knowledge: the Genesis of Science, in: Nico Stehr and Volker Meja (eds.): Science and Knowledge, London: Transaction Books.

Oppen, Achim von (1991): Cassava, "The lazy man's food"? Indigenous Agricultural Innovation and Dietary Change in Northwestern Zambia (ca. 1650—1970), in: Food and Foodways 5, 1, pp. 15-38.

Richards, Paul (1986): Coping with Hunger: Hazard and Experiment in an African Rice Farming System, London: Allen and Unwin.

Roumasset, James (1971): Risk and Choice of Technique for Peasant Agriculture: Safety First and Rice Production in the Philippines, Economic Development and International Economics No. 7118 (University of Wisconsin).

Schmuck-Widmann, Hanna (1996) Leben mit der Flut. Überlebensstrategien von Char-Bewohnern in Bangladesh, Berlin: FDCL.

Scott, James (1976): The Moral Economy of the Peasant—Rebellion and Subsistence in Southeast Asia, New Haven: Yale University Press.

Scott, James (1990): Domination and the Art of Resistance. Hidden Transcripts, Yale University Press: New Haven and London.

Séhouéto, Lazare (1996): Savoirs locaux ou savoirs localisés? La production et la diffusion des savoirs agricoles paysans au Bénin: éléments empiriques pour une anthropologie sociale des savoirs "locaux", Phil. Diss. Berlin: Freie Universitaet.

Taylor, George F. and Moustapha Soumaré (1983): Strategies for Forestry Development in the Semi-arid Tropics. Lessons from the Sahel, Bamako:US-AID (24/25).

Thaer, Albrecht von (1812): Grundsätze der rationellen Landwirtschaft; Bd. 1-4, Berlin.

Whorf, Benjamin L. (1942): Language, Mind and Reality, New York: Wiley.

12

Ecological Requirements for Increased Food Production: Towards an Integrated Habitat-Farm System in South India

Bernhard Glaeser

This contribution begins with an assessment of kitchen gardening in the Chengai-Anna (earlier Chengai-MGR) district near Madras, India—the facts about it and some proposals. To bolster the recommended propagation of kitchen gardens in villages, some information has been compiled in a more systematic manner. A habitat model including house and kitchen garden, is designed as a concrete example of what a housing compound could look like before more general conclusions are drawn.[1]

The concern for an integrated habitat farming system is part of a wider issue which raises the following question: What are the most urgent needs felt by the rural population? How high do housing problems rank in relation to other needs? What are the most significant economic constraints, cultural traditions and social conditions affecting the provision of housing? What interior functions and what external environmental factors must be taken into account? To what extent are the house and household, as part of a human-ecological system, integrated into the village and landscape development? Is the kitchen garden a common feature and is there a real demand for it?

1 Kitchen gardens in the investigated area

The above questions were raised in specific areas of the South Indian state of Tamil Nadu, particularly in the Chengai-Anna district, located about 40 kilometers southwest of Madras. The project objectives were defined in the spring of 1985, followed by initial observations in villages and the establishment of contacts. Experts were consulted and various South Indian housing projects scrutinized. In the spring of 1986, a questionnaire survey was carried out among roughly 300 households in 20 selected villages, supplemented by observation data and expert information in 1986, 1987 and 1989. In 1987 and 1988 the data collected were computerized and evaluated. In 1991 and 1992 the remaining open questions and

1 See Glaeser, 1995 (chapter 8): 189-223: "The 'House' as a Habitat Organism: Environmental Compatibility."

some housing technology implementation measures were followed up, and the manuscript was finalized thereafter.

Among the 291 interviewed households in the investigated area, 205 have a front or back yard, yet only 27 use this space as a kitchen garden. However, 212 interviewees believe that a kitchen garden is necessary, including 152 of the 205 households who have a yard around the house. Two families even designate "having no garden" as their house problem. Only 42 respondents consider a kitchen garden to be unnecessary, among them most of the "flower farmers" from the village of Pushpagiri.

The result sounds contradictory. Whereas the majority considers a kitchen garden to be useful, comparatively few people have one. The case of the flower farmers is special: they may need all the time available to cultivate their cash crops. The returns from the flower cultivation are higher than those from food cropping. Yet cash crop growers form only a minority among the sample households.

A more general problem seems to be water supply. Thirteen of the 27 using a garden, i.e., almost half, suffer from water shortage during the dry season. Of all the interviewed households, 233 lack water for irrigation. Thus an insufficient water supply may be the major factor in explaining why most people wish to have a kitchen garden, whereas only 27 families actually have one. Clearly irrigation is an obstacle to establishing kitchen gardens.

On the other hand, the desire to cultivate a kitchen garden ought to be backed by objective socioeconomic data before a more reliable water supply is planned and undertaken. An indicator would be food expenditure in relation to income. Among the 291 interviewed households, 266 have a per capita annual income of between Rs 500 and 3,000. This represents a marginal income. At the same time, food expenditures among 216 households vary between Rs 300 and 1,000. Differentiated according to income categories, the expenditures are as follows:

Annual Income	**Food Expenditures**
up to Rs 0,500	up to Rs 0,300
Rs 0,501 - 1,000	up to Rs 0,600
Rs 1,001 - 3,000	up to Rs 1,000
more than Rs 3,000	Rs 1,500 - 2,000

The lower the income, the greater the proportion spent on food. This is a well-known economic law that was formulated on statistical grounds by Ernst Engel in 1857. The problem here is the extremely high percentage of food expenditures amounting to almost two-thirds in the largest income category (up to Rs 1,000) with 85 households. Such a relation clearly and objectively favors the promotion of kitchen gardens.

Unfortunately, there is no clear evidence that food expenditures of kitchen garden owners in the project area are significantly lower than among non-owners. One reason was mentioned above: lack of water and drought. Other possible

Table 1: Kitchen gardens in the investigated area

Household Number	Type of Garden Product	Produced for Own Consumption (o. c.) or for Sale (f. s.)	Amounts Produced in Kilograms or Rupees per Year		Number of Family Members	Food Expenditures in Rupees per Year	Income	
			Kilograms	Rupees/Year			1984	1985
1107	chilies	50% o. c., 50% f. s.		500	10	3,500	n. a.	7,000
1512	brinjals, tomatoes	o. c.			9	4,000	7,000	8,000
2101	greens, beans, bitter gourds	o. c.			3	2,200	n. a.	3,000
2103	lime tree, drumstick tree, beans	o. c.			4	7,800	n. a.	12,000
2104	greens, drumstick tree	o. c.			6	12,000	n. a.	21,000
2105	coconut, palm tree				5	2,400	3,600	4,200
2108	mango tree	o. c.			6	2,000	3,600	4,000
2111	vegetables, lime, coconut	o. c.		1,500	5	7,200	15,600	18,000
2116	mango tree				6	2,400	3,600	4,000
2201	pumpkins brinjals	o. c. f. s.	3 (per week) 47 (per week)		4	700	1,000	1,500
4104	fruit tree vegetables	o. c. f. s.	8 12		4	2,000	1,500	1,600
4117	vegetables	o. c. and f. s.		500	8	1,000	3,500	4,000

Source: Glaeser 1995: household schedule.

reasons could be the following: poor soil, plant diseases, lack of working time, small acreage and thus insufficient quantity and variety of products.

Due to the small number of gardens and because water shortage overrides other reasons, a complete and reliable answer cannot be given. Some tentative answers concerning type and purpose of gardens, however, can be inferred from the 12 households that provided further details (Table 1). Vegetables and fruits are grown. They serve mainly for home consumption: only four families sell some of their garden products, thereby improving the household budget considerably. But the expenditure on other food products in relation to income is still high.

One exception, not in relative but in absolute figures, is household No. 2201. Both income and food expenditures are low. It seems that the family (a young married couple with a six-year-old child and a 60-year-old grandmother) must profit from their garden products. Both parents work as agricultural coolies and do the kitchen garden work.

An entirely different situation was found in the village of Kattankulathur. The seven families maintaining a kitchen garden are Brahmins. They own sufficient land, have funds for irrigation (deep wells) and time or money to do the work themselves or to pay servants to do the work.

We can summarize as follows. There are relatively few kitchen gardens in the study area, most probably due to irrigation and perhaps to other problems. On the other hand, a need in favor of kitchen gardens was expressed. This need is supported by the existence of low cash incomes in the area and by the proportionally high food expenditures in relation to incomes.

A consequence for village development planning is the promotion of kitchen gardens, particularly among the poorest income strata. The major obstacle, water for irrigation, must be removed. In the following, further elements and information as to the nutritional advantages, possible cropping combinations and integration in the habitat sphere are provided.

2 Kitchen gardening: a factor in nutrition and ecology

According to the 1971 Census of India, one of the major objectives of the Five Year Plan Schemes was to make the country self-sufficient in the matter of foodstuffs by adapting more land for production through irrigation and reclamation and by stepping up productivity along scientific lines. Nationally, this goal has largely been achieved; India has become a net exporter of grains. This does not imply, however, that everybody has access to food. Production is one matter, distribution another. Kitchen gardening could be a different way to help achieve local self-sufficiency and improve distribution.

It is, however, not only this quantitative aspect that ought to be stressed. More important perhaps, is the nutritional value of a proper diet upon which physical well-being and mental health depend. A proper diet includes proteins, carbohydrates, fats, vitamins and minerals (cf. Schäfer 1980: 5-9). A well-balanced diet is particularly important for children and pregnant women; its absence is often a sad reality in underdeveloped regions.

High amounts of protein are contained in meat, milk products, pulses and green leaf vegetables. As South Indian Hindu culture is basically vegetarian, it may be worthwhile to emphasize that the daily consumption of about 200 g of fresh weight vegetables provides a person with 6-14 g of protein. Green leaf and yellow vegetables are eminent sources of high value carotene, a pre-form of vitamin A, which is basic to cell structure formation (SLE 1982: 67-69). A maximum of proteins, vitamins, and minerals are found in green leaf vegetables, beans, and other legumes. Table 2 shows the nutrients contained in a variety of vegetables that are familiar in Tamil Nadu.[2]

Table 2: Some vegetables with high nutrient content

Vegetable	Protein in g per 100 g fresh weight	Vitamin A 1 U/100 g (in mg/100 g)	Vitamin C mg/100 g	Iron mg/100 g	Calcium mg/100g
Horse tamarind leaves	12.0	17,800 (5.3)	64	2.5	1,500
Papaya leaves	8.0	18,250 (5.5)	140	0.8	353
Bird chillies	4.7	11,000	70	2.5	45
Garlic	4.5		15	1.0	42
String bean leaves	4.1	5,240 (1.5)	29	6.2	134
Pumpkin leaves	3.6	2,750	36	3.7	138
Winged bean	2.9	595	19	0.3	63
Mungo bean sprouts	2.9	10	15	0.8	29
String bean	2.7	335 (21)	21	0.7	49
Bamboo sprouts	2.6	20	4	0.5	13
French bean	2.4	630	19	1.1	65
Carrot	1.2	12,000	6	0.8	39

Source: Dafter Komposisi Bahan Makanan, Directorat Gizi, Departemen Kesechatan, Jakarta, 1979. Quoted in: Seminar für Landwirtschaftliche Entwicklung (SLE) 1982, pp. 68-74.

A kitchen garden also contributes to a "sound" environment of the house. A more or less constant plant cover prevents the soil from being dried out and eroded. The roots of plants, especially deep ones, fix the soil and enhance its water retention and filter capacities. A further result is a more comfortable micro-climate with slightly more moderate temperatures and fewer extremes in humidity (cf. Seymour and Girardet 1985).

---

2 For vegetable production in the tropics, see Tindall 1983; Agricultural Information Centre 1979; in the Indian context: Chauhan 1986; Choudhury 1967; Katyal and Chadha 1985.

These factors indicate that the kitchen garden is part of the habitat (house and household) system, comprising social and ecological features. Figure 1 illustrates these interrelations in a schematic manner. Food production and soil conservation are integrated. Vegetable production and animal husbandry complement each other. Trees provide fruits for consumption, mulch material as soil cover and, not least of all, shade. A few selected aspects of this human-ecological system are now briefly explained in their relation to mixed cropping.

Figure 1: Integrated kitchen garden system

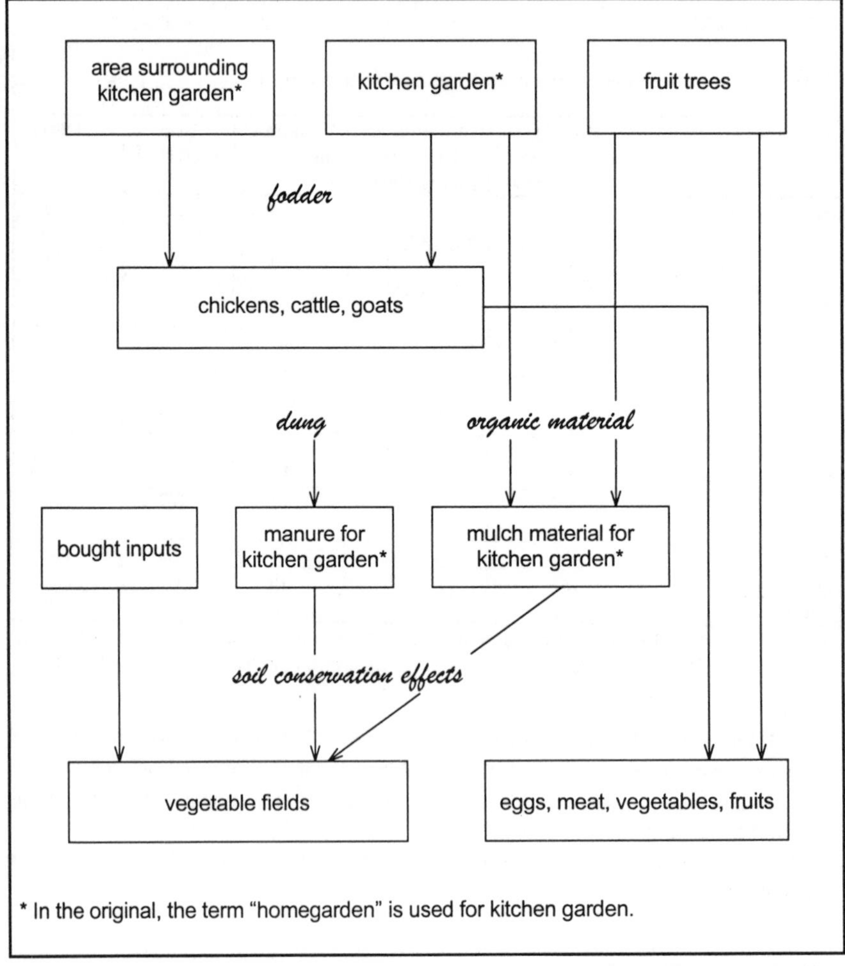

Source: Seminar für Landwirtschaftliche Entwicklung (SLE) 1982: 232.

Mixed cropping is a central feature in kitchen garden plant and soil management, as it is on a larger scale in organic farming. It includes various cropping plants that need various soil properties and that have different heights, sowing, and harvesting times. Imitating natural cycles in a managed crop system, food supply and labor management are optimized in an ecologically balanced way. Different species are combined so as to provide a variety of products (possibly all year round) that do not compete for nutrients, water, or light. In this way, sowing as well as harvesting peaks are avoided. The plant multiplicity guarantees a continuous presence of microorganisms in the soil and a permanent top cover. Plant residues are recycled and fed back into the soil. Pests and diseases are minimized.

Table 3: Tropical fruit trees

Crop	Plant Height (m)	Space Between Plants (m)	Climate Requirement*	Maximum Altitude (m)	Maturity (years)	Inter-cropped with**	Seed storage
Avocado	8	10	W	2,500	5	2, 3, 8	moist
Banana	4	3	W	1,000	4	3, 7, 9	moist
Breadfruit	15	12	D/W	1,500	5	2, 3, 5, 6, 8	moist
Cacao	2	3	W	1,000	4	1, 3, 5	moist
Cashew	3	8	D	1,500	3	2, 3, 8, 9	dry
Chico	8	10	D/W	1,500	5	5, 9	dry
Coconut	22	10	D/W	1,500	4	1, 2, 3, 4, 5, 6, 7, 8	dry
Coffee	3	3	W	1,000	4	1, 2, 4, 9	moist
Durian	30	15	W	2,500	5	3, 6, 8	moist
Guava	10	6	D	1,500	3	1, 3, 8, 9	dry
Guyabano	7	6	D	300	3	1, 3, 8, 9	dry
Jackfruit	10	8	D/W	1,500	4	1, 3, 8, 9	moist
Lanzones	15	8	W	200	10	1, 3, 8, 9	moist
Lime	5	5	D/W	1,500	4	1, 9	moist
Mango	30	15	D	500	6		moist
Orange	5	8	D/W	1,000	5	1, 9	moist
Papaya	4	2	W	900	1	1, 9	dry
Pili nut	20	14	W	1,500	14	1, 2, 6	dry
Pineapple	1.5	1	W	1,000	1.5	2, 3, 4, 8, 9	dry
Pomelo	5	8	D/W	1,500	5	1, 9	moist
Rambutan	13	10	W	1,000	10	1, 9	moist
Santol	15	12	D/W	1,500	12		moist
Star apple	10	10	D/W	1,500	5	2, 3, 5, 6, 8	dry
Sugar apple	5	5	D/W	1,000	3	1,9	dry
Tamarind	25	16	D	500	16		dry

* D = only 5 to 6 months wet, W = 9 months wet

** 1 = pineapple, 2 = banana, 3 = coffee, 4 = ipil-ipil, 5 = anona spruce, 6 = lanzones, 7 = avocado, 8 = cacao, 9 = coconut

Source: The Unicef Home Gardens Handbook. Quoted in: Sommers 1983: 7.

Table 4: Kitchen garden crops

Plants for wet areas (near water pumps)	Plants for dry areas
taro swamp cabbage sugar cane banana	legumes cassava pineapple tamarind mango sugar apple jackfruit grapes cashew guava sour-sop
Plants for trellis	**Plants that make good natural fences**
(a) climbing legumes string bean lima bean yardlong bean winged bean yam bean (b) climbing fruit vegetables squash gourd cucumber bitter melon	giant ipil-ipil madre de cacao drumstick plant casuarina bamboo (poles) hibiscus pineapple cassava cactus
Plants for under the trellis	**Plants that suppress weed growth**
taro swamp cabbage sweet potato (for leaves) ginger	sweet potato swamp cabbage squash bitter melon

Source: The UNICEF Home Gardens Handbook, quoted in Sommers 1983: 8.

Some typical mixed crop combinations are (Riotte 1977: 34-35; SLE 1986: 66):

- banana, pineapple;
- coconut, cow-peas;
- legumes, cereals;
- maize, ground-nuts;
- maize, beans;
- maize, string beans, cucumbers;
- rice, maize, mung beans;
- millet, cow-peas, pigeon-peas;
- millet, ground-nuts, maize, ladyfingers;
- egg-plants (brinjals), bird chilies, papaya;

- egg-plants (brinjals), gourds, long chilies;
- egg-plants (brinjals), cucumbers, string beans.

Perennial crops such as coconut, mango and lime trees (Table 3) have to be positioned carefully in a kitchen garden. They provide shade for humans, animals and some smaller plants, and should protect the house and animal shed. Annual crops can be planted around the trees and changed from one season to another (Table 4). Trees and hedges, if densely grown around the plot, may protect fruits and vegetables from being eaten by passing cows or goats. They also assure privacy. Leguminous trees, such as the tamarind or the neem, are included to improve soil fertility because of their nitrogen-fixing capacity. The neem tree is a multipurpose plant and can be used as an insect repellent.

Other protecting crops are castor, cotton and marigolds. Many tropical plants are famous for their wide variety of useful qualities and functions (cf. Acland 1971; Dastur 1985). Above all, the coconut (cf. Thampan 1981; Nair 1979) can be used as a food crop, for cooking oil and fuel, and as a raw material for mats, furniture and household utensils (Table 5).

Table 5: Functions of kitchen garden crops

Banana	Coconut	Bamboo
animal feed shade protection for transplanted seedlings leaves for cooking food compost pit mushroom growing	fuel building material mats scrub brushes seed storage stakes for vines weed control fencing cooking oil lamp oil water (juice) furniture baskets shade animal feel natural trellis food coconut oil as a food preservative cooking utensils drinking cups	fuel trellising crop protection animal sheds plant nursery housing furniture baskets fishing rods plant stakes fence posts seed storage water containers cooking utensils drinking cups mulching bed frames

Source: The UNICEF Home Gardens Handbook. After Sommers 1983: 10.

A major, if not the main, objective of soil management is to improve soil fertility. Avoiding ploughing and deep digging leaves the microorganisms undisturbed and living near the surface, and thus contributes to maintaining or increasing topsoil fertility. Mulch, i.e., plant material from leaves, grass, weeds, or bark, covers the soil to preserve its humidity and to improve its humus constitution by supporting the living conditions of the microorganisms in the topsoil. Finally, leguminous plants and composted animal dung, plant materials and kitchen waste, supplemented by biogas slurry, add to soil fertility by fixing nitrogen, by virtue of their decomposition in the tropical climate.

3 A habitat kitchen garden model

To round this up, a concrete example is to be provided of how family life and the kitchen garden could be integrated. The model is based on the information given

Figure 2: Static habitat-kitchen garden model

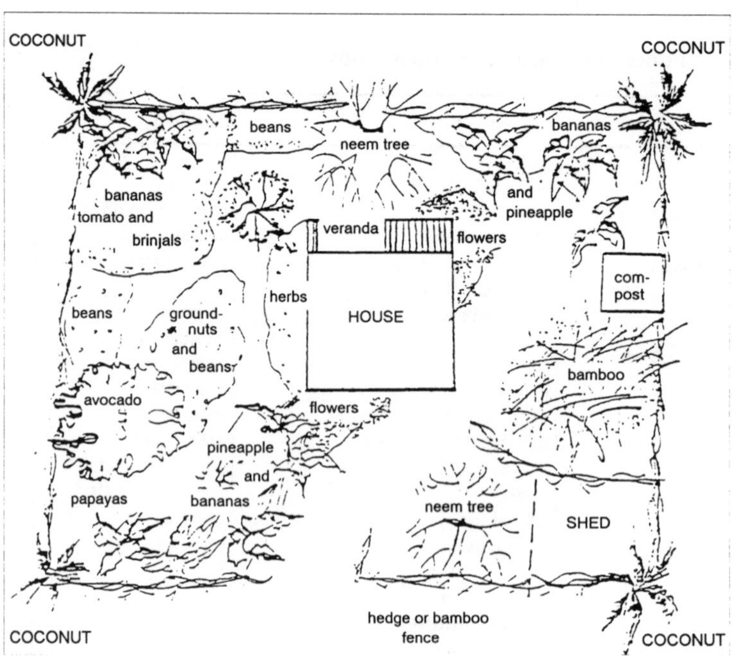

Design: E. Janz

above. It goes without saying that it allows for a multitude of variations. A kitchen garden design depends on the type and quality of soil, on the size and shape of the plot, the location of the house, the availability of certain trees, vegetables, animals and, last but not least, on the needs and preferences of those who plan and work it.

The static model (Figure 2) designs a 500 m², almost square plot with a small to medium-sized house, perhaps a local, triangular truss "khatri hut" or "Housing Board house" of 46 m² in the center. The house is protected by a large neem tree on the south side. The back entrance leads to the cattle shed which is shaded by another neem tree and bamboo. Between the bamboo and some intercropped pineapple and banana trees, compost is produced from kitchen and garden wastes. On the east side of the house, typical vegetables are grown, interspersed with a variety of fruit trees. The compound is surrounded by a natural fence. An outdoor toilet and a biogas plant could be added.

The process model (Figure 3) illustrates the compost heap (alternatively, a biogas converter could be imagined), fed by organic wastes from kitchen and garden, supplemented with cow dung. The garden provides food and firewood for the people, feed for the animals, and is fertilized with dung and compost. Trees provide shade and a comfortable microclimate so that the kitchen (cooking place) can be located outside during the dry season.

Figure 3: A habitat kitchen garden as a human-ecological process

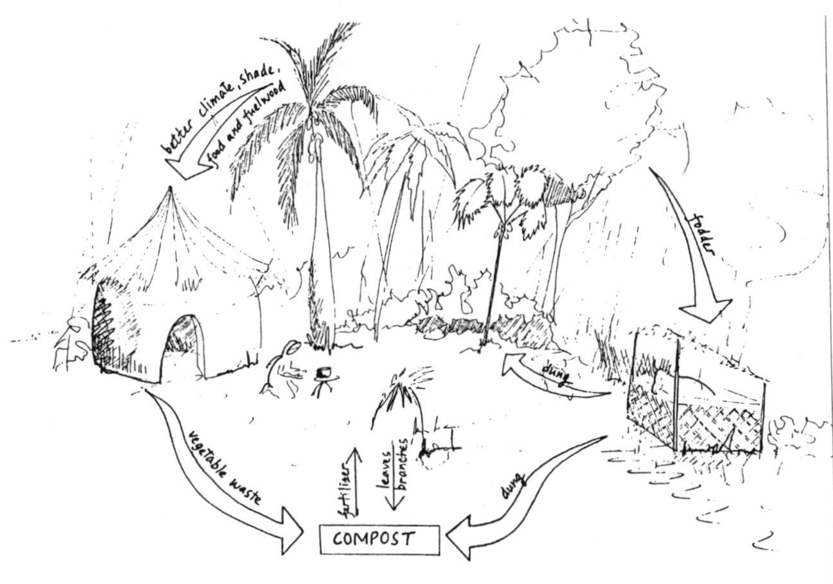

Figure 3: A habitat kitchen garden as a human-ecological process
Design: E. Janz

The two models depict a complete human-ecological system and cycle as favored by the ecodevelopment approach, covering the human habitat, the provision of the household and intake of food and energy, as well as the process of a natural recycling system by means of a complete, even if minute, anthropogenic ecosystem.

4 Results and conclusions

4.1 Ecofarming

The methods for preserving and improving soil fertility that were briefly presented have two things in common: they are economically viable in a low-cash rural economy, and they are environmentally sound. In actual fact, they are elements of an appropriate agricultural technology: ecofarming. This technology is locally available (self-reliance), at least partly related to traditional know-how (sociocultural orientation), and it integrates ecologically an anthropogenically transformed natural system of agriculture (environmental compatibility).

Pursuing the environmental aspect, it is stressed that cultivation conditions are improved without the addition of chemical fertilizers in the soil. And the latter is protected against erosion. Thus, it would seem that these methods of fertilization (farmyard and green manuring, composting, crop rotation and mixed cropping) are highly recommendable and that their utilization should be increased.

Statistics indicate a trend contrary to ecofarming recommendations. For instance, cattle dung was utilized in only one-sixth of the agricultural land as fertilizer (1973), and from 1969 to 1972 the area under green manure decreased by 15%. Two main reasons can be found for this development. First, the income situation in rural India must be taken into account. As opposed to 40% in 1962, in the late 1970s more than 70% of the rural population was no longer in a position to provide for itself with sufficient food (Eggeling et al., n.d.: 6). If farmers had utilized green manure on their fields as fallow vegetation in this situation, they would not have been able to grow crops during that period. Under such socio-economic circumstance, it is clear that present needs outweigh long-term considerations regarding soil preservation.

Secondly, due to their income situation, people need cheap burning materials. Traditionally, firewood was utilized for cooking. But since wood has become very scarce in the study area, as elsewhere, and since a substantial part of the daily or weekly schedule is needed for the collection of firewood, more and more people are forced to use cow dung for cooking.

4.2 Afforestation

In view of these growing problems, an conclusions concerning village development have to take the rural energy crisis into account. Although the "potentially natural vegetation" is humid savannah, suggesting forests as the dominant vegetation, there are no forests left in the villages visited. The first and most paradoxical finding, however, is that in the depleted environment in question, there are obviously still enough trees, bushes or shrubs to make firewood the number one burning material.

The reason for this paradox lies in the fact that the distances covered to find wood have been appreciably extended. Villagers spend on average two hours a day accomplishing this task; in extreme cases they need five hours and sometimes even more. The burden and hardship involved, as well as the share of the family time budget are delegated to the female members. Beyond housework, child-rearing and agricultural field work, they now receive an additional burden resulting from environmental degradation.

A differentiation in energy consumption habits exists on the basis of income. With rising incomes the use of firewood and dung decreases. This is understandable because cooking with firewood and dung is time consuming. It also causes ecological damage. Deforestation removes certain capacities for protection against the ravages of nature, e.g., the windbreaking function of forests. Winds and monsoons wash away the fertile topsoil, and the land is eroded. As a result, water-retaining capacities dwindle; the groundwater households vary enormously and catchment areas become unreliable. Reversing such damages entails measures aimed at reforestation and substitution of firewood and dung by other sources of energy.

4.3 Biogas: energy for an integrated habitat system

For the investigated area, biogas could be a reasonable alternative to firewood and cow dung. In biogas plants, organic matter is mineralized by anaerobic fermentation with the help of various microorganisms whose metabolic products are biogas (CH4 and CO2) and mineralized sewage sludge.[3] Nearly all organic matter can be processed in biogas reactors, but the most effective way is the processing of dung, excrements, plants and organic waste water (Werner et al. 1986: 62; Figure 4).

The advantage of these digesters is that all products can be used: gas for cooking and lighting, the mineralized manure as fertilizer. The slurry has a higher fertilizing value than decomposed dung because it contains more nitrogen and potassium. As a result of the processing, weed seeds and insects are almost completely destroyed. Less money is needed for weed killers and insecticides. Fertilization with slurry as opposed to direct fertilizing is also more hygienic. This has positive effects on vegetable cultivation and cattle breeding. Pasture grounds fertilized with slurry improve the health of animals, since parasites are by and large destroyed. As a result of odorless fertilizing, the appetites of the animals are hardly reduced. In addition to these advantages, positive physical effects on the soil texture take place, similar to the case of farmyard manure, since the volume of the slurry is hardly reduced and all solid components are still present (Werner et al. 1986: 43).

3 For an energy input-output analysis, see Auer 1978: 64 f.

Figure 4: Biogas technology

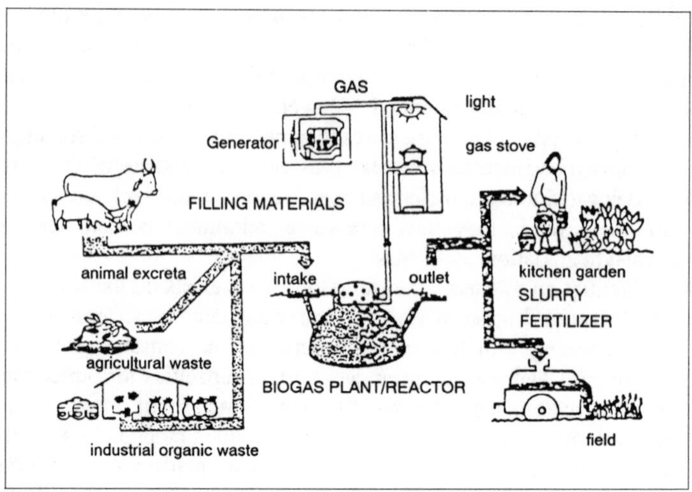

Source: Werner et al., 1986, p. 9

Figure 5: Integrated habitat farm system

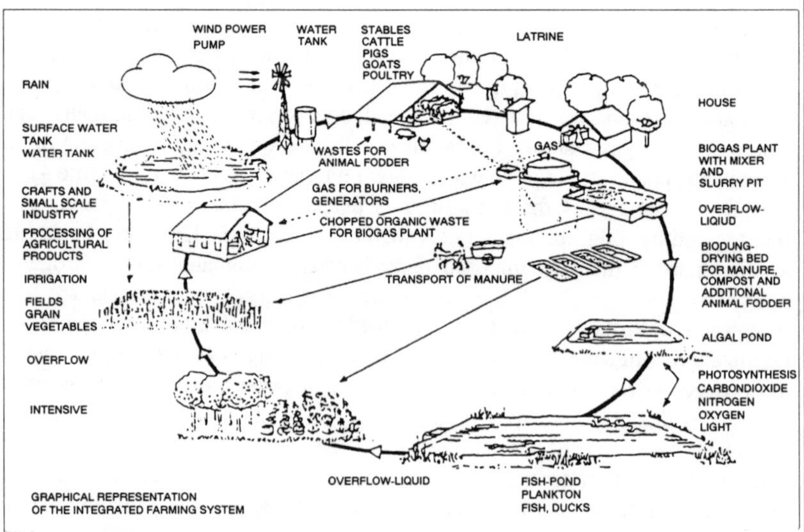

Source: Eggeling et al., 1980, p. 101

If firewood need not be collected, the time thus saved could be invested in home food production, i.e., in kitchen gardening if "land"—including rooftops—is available. Biogas residues fertilize the garden which, in turn, supplies the reactor with plant material. Just as biogas substitutes time and money for energy, kitchen gardening enhances the self-sustaining features of the household. The cycle of matter and energy forms an integrated habitat system, starting with the house as shelter and the household as consumption center, and combining energy and food production with a recycling regime for all organic wastes from humans, animals, and plants (Figure 5).

4.4 Social, environmental and developmental constraints

Kitchen gardening can be managed if a family's vocation is farming, if women are not required to be wage earners or if children are able to do gardening before and after school. The greatest limiting factor is climate, particularly rainfall. Investing time, labor, or money to improve soil, for instance, is a futile exercise if rainfall is insufficient. As responses in the questionnaire survey indicate, the availability of water in many villages, particularly an adequate supply of drinking water, is a serious problem all year round.

Relying on an economy based on biomass, however, becomes increasingly difficult with growing environmental degradation through deforestation, depletion of plant cover and variety, and soil erosion. Even if planners consider the modern cash economy to be advantageous for integrating rural areas into the national economic cycle, they cannot but acknowledge that the effects on the rural environment, the lowest income groups and women in particular, have been adverse, if not disastrous.

This difficulty can only be solved with the help of communal development activities and, in many cases, by state or national schemes. Such activities are recommended with a view to the greater self-reliance of rural areas and better nutrition for the villagers. Reforestation and substitution of firewood and dung by other sources of energy are necessary. As has been shown, there is no panacea to this problem, particularly because alternative sources of energy are often more expensive and cannot be afforded by low-income families. The environmental problem is a social one and can only be tackled by socioeconomic and village development measures.

This is not the place to discuss whether or not the measures taken are appropriate, or whether all communities are satisfied with them. All that needs to be pointed out here is that the government is aware that the traditional Indian social structure poses a problem and measures have been taken to deal with it. The findings of the present survey indicate that in the investigated area the chances that the poorest segments and lowest strata in the rural society will be able to overcome their miserable plight appear to be limited. It is recommended, in line with the governmental measures taken, that these poorest of the poor be extended assistance in their housing efforts. This includes the provision of water and energy. Moreover, true developmental efforts should be incorporated, ranging from the provision of a piece of farmland, at least for a kitchen-garden, to the creation of job opportunities in agriculture, handicrafts, small-scale industries and housing.

If a nationwide rural employment scheme, involving complete integration with the urban cash economy is considered unrealistic, the only immediate relief would be to lessen the excessive workload of women without further destroying the environmental basis of the village subsistence economy. This can be done and has been done by developing and disseminating appropriate technologies such as fuel-conserving solar cookers or smokeless *chulhas* for cooking, hand pumps for easier water collection, fuel and country wood plantations for energy and building materials, biogas plants to supplement other sources of energy, and nearby latrines to avoid long walks to the next forest grove in an otherwise deserted environment.

It is recommended, therefore, that development include women not only as a "target group" but also as counterparts—partly because their support contributes considerably to the living conditions in the village, and partly because experience has evidenced higher success rates for projects oriented towards women.

References

Acland, J.D. (1971): East African Crops, London: Longman.

Agricultural Information Centre (1979): Fruit and Vegetable Technical Handbook, Nairobi: Ministry of Agriculture.

Arakeri, H.R. (1982): Indian Agriculture, New Delhi/Bombay/Calcutta: Oxford & IBH Publishing Co.

Auer, P. (1978): Advances in Energy Systems and Technology, Volume I, New York/San Francisco/London: Academic Press.

Bansil, P.C. (1986): Economic Problems of Indian Agriculture, New Delhi/Bombay/Calcutta: Oxford & IBH Publishing Co., 5th revised edition.

Chauhan, D.V.S. (1986): Vegetable Production in India, Agra/Bhopal: Ram Prasad & Sons.

Choudhury, B. (1967): Vegetables, New Delhi: National Book Trust.

Dastur, J.F. (1985): Useful Plants of India and Pakistan, Bombay: D.P. Taraporevala Sons & Co. (originally published in 1964).

Eggeling, G., H. Guldager, R. Guldager, G. Hilliges, L. Sasse, C. Tietjen, and U. Werner (n.d.): Biogas—Manual for the Realisation of Biogas Programmes, Bremen: Bremen Overseas Research and Development Association (BORDA).

Glaeser, B. (1995): Housing, Sustainable Development and the Rural Poor. A Study of Tamil Nadu, New Delhi/Thousand Oaks/London: Sage Publications.

Katyal, S.L. and K.L. Chadha (1985): Vegetable Growing in India, New Delhi/Bombay/Calcutta: Oxford & IBH Publishing Co., 2nd edition.

Nair, P.K.R. (1979): Intensive Multiple Cropping with Coconuts in India: Principles, Programmes and Prospects, Berlin/Hamburg: Verlag P. Parey.

Riotte, L. (1977): Der kleine Gemüsegarten: Bessere Erträge mit biologischem Anbau, Fulda: pala-verlag.

Schäfer, K. (1980): Hausgarten und Ernährung in den Tropen (Reihe dü-scriptum), Stuttgart: Dienste in Übersee, 2nd edition.

Seminar für Landwirtschaftliche Entwicklung (SLE) (1982): Vegetables in East Kalimantan: Agro-Economic, Nutritional and Ecological Aspects of Promoting Vegetable Production and Marketing in Three Districts of East Kalimantan/Indonesia, Berlin: Technische Universität Berlin.

Seminar für Landwirtschaftliche Entwicklung (SLE) (1986): Demand for Major Fruit Tree Seedlings Including Coconut by Village Farms and Farmers in the Lowland Areas of Tanga Region (Tanzania), Berlin: Technische Universität Berlin.

Seymour, J. and H. Girardet (1985): Fern vom Garten Eden: Die Geschichte des Bodens: Kultivierung, Zerstörung, Rettung, Frankfurt am Main: S. Fischer Verlag.

Thampan, P.K. (1981): Handbook on coconut Palm, New Delhi/Bombay/Calcutta: Oxford & IBH Publishing Co.

Tindall, H.D. (1983): Vegetables in the Tropics, London: Macmillan.

Vasudevan, K. and M. Gosh (1985/86): Agricultural Economics and Problems in India, New Delhi: New Heights Publishers, 4th revised edition.

Werner, U., U. Stoer, and N. Hees (1986): Praktischer Leitfaden für Biogasanlagen in der Tierproduktion, Rossdorf: TZ-Verlagsgesellschaft (edited by the German Agency for Technical Cooperation—GTZ).

13

Health, Food and Nutrition in the Hands of the People—Some Lessons from the Philippines

Detlef Schwefel, Benjamin Ariel Marte, Noriko Kashiwagi

1 From dependence towards self-help

Food and nutrition comprise one of the most basic human needs. It is an issue at the level of governments, and at the level of families and communities. For many nations in the poor world, food security is not a given. This is the case when many families are not assured that there will be food—much less enough—to eat from day to day. Actually, food security is not just an issue of the poor world. At the level of the family, we face such problems increasingly in the impoverishment processes all over the world. This is due to a rapid expansion of the capitalistic system after the collapse of the Second World. Social security networks face a grim outlook in the poor countries, and for poor people everywhere (Schwefel et al. 1987; Schwefel et al. 1976).

1.1 Imbalances between need, demand, and supply of food

Need, demand, and supply of food are out of balance. What the human body needs for survival in terms of calories, proteins, amino acids, minerals, vitamins and the like is quite a given. Each and every warm body counts! Given the growing number of people in the Philippines, it is very well predictable what the nutritional needs or requirements are that have to be met in the near and more distant future. We development workers must begin with this very notion of needs when analyzing what development means, or how it should proceed. Indeed, such a notion of needs introduces the principle of solidarity: everybody shall avail of their needed nutritional intake.

Demand is driven by the purchasing power of the families. Many other factors intervene, of course: food habits, cooking styles, food price variations, diseases, other competing basic needs, et cetera. Quite a number of scholars have drawn up flowchart presentations of the many systematic linkages between food demand and the natural, social, cultural, environmental and economical determinants thereof. When measured against the yardstick of needs, however, we see realities that transcend a pure economic analysis. We see demands that are unjustifiably high or unjustifiably low relative to need. This can lead eventually to an imbalance of food intake. Undernutrition and malnutrition are the consequences. Diseases and deaths result that could otherwise have been prevented or avoided.

Negative health effects can highlight the discrepancy between needs and demands for food. In medical statistics, some indicators are quite apparent of this imbalance. Infectious diseases comprise the leading causes of death and disease among an inordinately high proportion of the very young and the very old. Due to the interaction between under- or malnutrition and infection, this suggests that the nutritional requirements are not being met on a regular basis for these higher-risk segments of the population. The unavailability of supply can not be blamed for this imbalance as such. There is enough supply of nutrients available in the Philippines for everyone to avail of a proper diet. Even if domestic rice production does not catch up with the rising national demand, there are secondary staple foods, and there are many potential substitutes for any other nutritional items that might be in short supply. It is easy to demonstrate that with proper diets, or a kind of "rational consumption", the food supply in the Philippines is appropriate to satisfy the basic human needs of nutrition for all Filipinos (Schwefel 1982).

The improper interaction between demand and supply seems to be a problem. Either there is a demand that does not match with the needs, or the demand does not match with the available supply, or the supply is not patterned after the needs and/or the demand. It does not matter whether we approach the problem from the demand side or from the supply side.

— A demand driven strategy would be to empower families to know better what their best choices are. This means that ultimately they adopt a kind of health economics attitude. Why strive for such a goal? By definition, health is the capability to lead a socially and economically productive life. Family health management is health economics at the family level. It means choosing the best way to manage the family's resources in order to provide an affordable and effective diet for all members. Moreover, since information is a by-product of good management, this approach will be able to forewarn us if the family's basic nutritional needs are being satisfied. The smartest families among the poor know best how to address these issues. Let us learn from them and their community organizations. This will be one of the messages of our article (Schwefel 1975a; Schwefel 1978a, 1979a).

— A supply driven strategy was adopted at national levels a long time ago in Norway, in the Dominican Republic, and in Peru, for example. These were the so-called national food-and-nutrition strategies, where the production and supply of food was to have been patterned after the nutritional needs of the people. At national levels this strategy simply failed because of the "microeconomics" involved. In short, businessmen expect cash; therefore, cash crops become the objective of agricultural production. This is regardless of what nutritional value they may or may not have, relative to the nutritional requirements of the population (Schwefel 1978b, 1978c, 1979b).

In terms of social economics both strategies have a common denominator—need satisfaction. Need satisfaction of each and everyone! There is, moreover, a peculiarity—indeed, an urgency—in the context of nutrition: the satisfaction of nutritional needs must be met on a regular and daily basis. This can be achieved by a diverse set of human diets. Unfortunately, no matter how flexible human nature is, nor how smart family nutrition management might be, supply shortages are a regular experience of human beings in most poor countries. Theoretically and in practice, such shortages can be alleviated by a shift to secondary or even tertiary staple foods, and through many other ways of adjusting demand. But the shortages can also be alleviated through changes in the supply structure. This would take into account a planning and management of demand and/or supply that anticipates and addresses food and nutrition security. Many papers in this book show that this is not properly done anywhere. Rather than searching for innovative options of survival, many governments and people see catastrophes in food and nutrition as the consequences of natural or man-made calamities, and declare such occurrences as therefore "inevitable".

1.2 Risk reduction and security strengthening strategies

During the past decades we got to know of many fashionable proposals and strategies on how to deal with the food security issue. We need mention but three of them.

— One strategy was to channel agricultural production nutritionally for the basic needs satisfaction of the people. This failed because, macro- and micro-economically, cash counts more than food. In this context, food is just a commodity. Income is the primary concern. Whether this income is fairly distributed, or if it is being used for addressing the basic needs of the poor, is a secondary concern (Schwefel 1987a, 1987b).

— A second strategy was a challenge provided by innovative and seemingly appropriate technologies. Knowing that food security has also to do with the security of energy supply for cooking, we hoped very much that solar cookers could be helpful. We looked carefully into the physical, social, cultural and economic context of such solar cookers. We took into consideration technical matters as well as the social situation, food habits, cooking habits, cost-effectiveness and other aspects of acceptancy. It turned out that indeed it is a promising technology, but when properly and comprehensively assessed, it is not, at least for the time being, a solution for the poor (Kuhnke et al. 1990).

— Nutritional bypass tactics are quite fashionable nowadays. The catch phrase is: micronutrient supplementation. Specific vitamin and mineral deficiencies lead to morbidity and mortality which could well be reversed and prevented. Micronutrient programs target such specific deficiencies, and are supposed to proceed in two general phases. The replacement or curative phase attempts to boost the micronutrient levels among the high-risk or even the general population. Since the biological effect tends to be transitory, this should be followed very soon after by a supplementation or preventive phase. In this latter phase, more lasting measures must be adopted to ensure that the micronutrient level does not again subside among the population. Micronutrient supplementation might be a good additional strategy for food and nutrition security. Very often, however, the curative aspect tends to be emphasized, perhaps because the impacts are more politically apparent in the short term, even if the expense is greater and the biological effects are less lasting than the preventive aspect. A more comprehensive approach to micronutrient supplementation might be more effective. But be that as it may, there is a precaution that when we deal with micronutrient supplementation, we might well be skirting the issue of generalized undernutrition while focusing instead on a more circumscribed aspect of malnutrition which is therefore more convenient to deal with.

Such strategies—and others that we have not discussed, such as protein enrichment programs, income subsidies for the indigents, rationing schemes, food vouchers, and the like—promise a lot. Nevertheless, when carefully assessed, the advantages and disadvantages are not in a balance. It is nice to talk on such options at international conferences, and to weigh their cost-effectiveness. People have seldom benefited from those options.

1.3 Self-help initiatives

Are food and nutrition catastrophes inevitable? Some people and some groups are not so stoical nor lethargic that they will accept such statements on inevitability and uncertainty at face value. These are those that would rather take food and nutrition into their hands. In the subsistence economy of the Garden of Eden, God produced for Adam and Eve what they needed. Need, demand, and supply were in a balance. "Rehabilitation of subsistence economies" is a slogan addressing the issue of food and nutrition security. There are so many other such slogans: "wartime nutrition economics", "food rationing", "food stamps", to name a few. Some people and some groups do not care that much about such slogans. They would rather take the issue into their own hands, and to act on it.

"Health in the hands of the people." This is the battle cry of a Philippine movement towards self-help and self-help-empowerment. People's empowerment is part of the development strategy of the Philippines. It started with the toppling of a martial law and its perpetrators by the people in the streets of Manila. Of course, by and large, the power of the people diminished in favor of the survival of the prevailing power structures. Nevertheless, it is still the basic strategy for health to the present time. This is not just a nostalgic reminiscence of the power of the streets. It is a counterbalance against the insecurity imposed by the vested interests and wasted resources of governments that are not for the people. It is a counter-strategy against lethargic local and national governments. It is a battle cry against policies that do not satisfactorily address the basic needs of the people.

Seen from a general point of view, people's empowerment is the incarnation of the "subsidiarity principle". What families and communities can do for themselves, let them do it! Governments should just be prepared for back-up strategies if lower levels can not do it themselves. But local and national governments must also be prepared for emergencies that hit entire populations. This is a kind of division of labor within a civilian society. It is also a kind of supportive "let alone policy" that favors individual enterprise over state control. But as industrialization proceeds, and most people are getting dependent on other sources of income and survival—away from the primary sector of agriculture, this "let alone" aspect of the subsidiarity principle can not apply when it comes to nutrition. If the market forces can not guarantee the basic survival of populations, than the government has to step in. Supply management is the focus, and becomes a primary key to survival. If that fails, the repercussions fall back on the individual. Demand management must then become the secondary key for survival.

2 Risk and security assessments

Families and communities, naturally, have an interest in the risks related to food and nutrition security insofar as this knowledge might provide them the edge in survival. Governments and committed outsiders, for whom such risks do not necessarily spell survival or doom, have also had an interest in this issue. Let us start this section by first examining some risk assessment methodologies in the hands of committed outsiders.

2.1 Risk and security assessments by outsiders

The world has seen a large compilation of literature on risk and security assessments. National indicator systems on nutrition surveillance were prominent for a certain time. Many years ago, it was discovered that rising prices for secondary staple foods, as well as the pawning of kitchen utensils, proved to be good proxy indicators for predicting impending food crises in Indonesia. Such proxy indicators can be detected when applying a comprehensive systems analysis of the interactions between nature, the economy, and death, as depicted in Figure 1. This is a fascinating subject, converting interconnected indicator systems into a tool for addressing the issue of food and nutrition security. Nevertheless, this knowledge often remains just in the hands of universities or governments. It's up to them, if ever, to convert this knowledge into action by convincing governments (Schwefel 1980).

Such a systems analysis as described above can be converted into a socio-economic path analysis (Schwefel 1975b, 1984, 1987c, 1987d, 1989; Schwefel et al. 1976). This traces the fate of economic products, commodities, or services down to the basic consumption patterns of those in need. The "product path analysis" (PPA) was invented to study, for example, the nutritional implications of large-scale investment projects, such as an irrigation dam or a railways network. The PPA tries to identify the demand for the final end product from different groups, strata, or classes of the society, and to analyze this demand according to its potential for satisfying basic human needs. With regard to this demand—the first focus of the PPA—one has to raise the following questions:

Figure 1: A simplified model on links between nature, economy and death

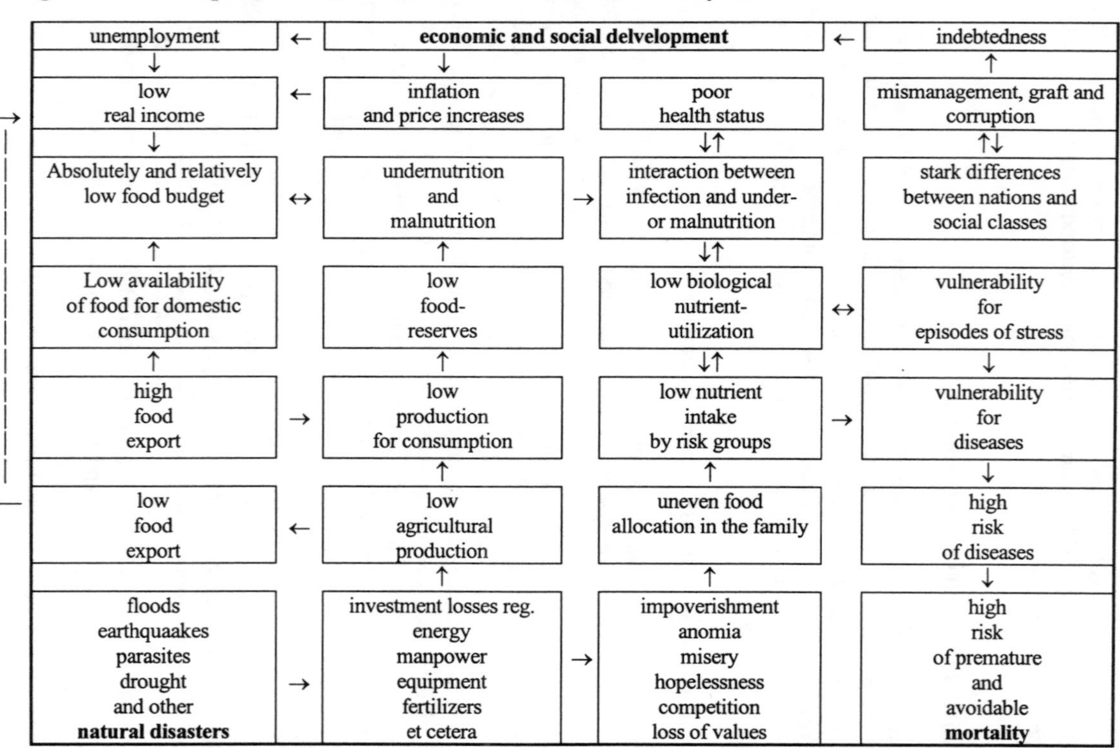

a) What is it that is produced or made available by means of the project, in terms of use values?

b) What are the intermediate uses of this product (or service) until it is transformed into a final human consumption?

c) Which groups, strata, or classes of the society demand these products of final consumption?

Having identified the social demand, the PPA continues to ask and to analyze, if such a demand satisfies basic human needs. The PPA analyzes the paths of the production between the project, the intermediate use, the final human consumption, and the basic needs of different social groups. The PPA tries to identify what benefits derive from the production side of the project, and who benefits from production. These are precisely some of the most important questions of social evaluation. Another important question that derives is this: Who benefits from employment? This was extensively applied when looking into the nutritional implications of large-scale development projects for the poor. The grim result most often was: "Sorry, it's just for the rich!"

2.2 Risk and security assessments by the people

Some people and some groups are not content with these information systems being in the hands of outsiders, even if they might be compassionate and with empathy. They would rather "take matters into their own hands." On the island of Mindanao, in the Philippines, we discovered quite some volunteer health workers that maintained an information system that they call "Databoards" (Remotigue et al. 1994). It is an information system that is not imposed on them from above. It was introduced a long time ago by certain academicians and health managers sympathetic to the poor. Even after they were assigned somewhere else, the Databoards continued to be maintained by the volunteer health workers. This Databoard is a spot map of the households in the villages where the volunteer health workers live, and these are those whom they work for. Each household is assessed quarterly according to basic indicators of health, which the volunteer health workers look into, i.e.

- environment: waste disposal, water supply and toilets;
- nutrition: undernourished children;
- family health: immunization, family planning, prenatal care.

These three issues—environment, nutrition, and family health—are considered as the basic needs in a community. The volunteers collect the data and present them in color-coded manner on the spot maps. This color-coding is in the form of traffic lights: red means danger, green means things are doing well, while yellow indicates borderline danger or a change in status either toward green or red. A fourth color, blue, was added when the indicator does not apply to the particular household; for instance, immunization status does not apply where there are no children.

This display of information in the Databoard, we have observed, stimulates community discussion and dialogue. It converts data into information, and thence into action. It reinforces community support of the knowledge of the volunteer health workers. It also empowers these health workers to bargain with the presidents of the blocks of families, or with the captains of the villages, or with the mayors of the municipalities or cities. A color-coding of the indicators according to the traffic lights opens the eyes of everybody regarding past, actual and impending crises. This is why the volunteer health workers maintained the Databoard as a kind of subsistence information system: the producers of the data consume the data and get stronger with it. After we discovered and promoted this system it was adopted as a national program of the Department of Health. Indeed, the national anti-poverty strategy of the government has also adopted the Databoard, and tries to add more indicators on basic needs. In the hands of volunteer health workers, the Databoard can be a powerful tool to address the problem of nutrition security at the family and community level.

As a back-up information system at the level of provinces we developed a socioeconomic information system that contains data on the health-and-wealth features of a village (Schwefel et al. 1995). This we call the Barangay Socioeconomic Information System, "barangay" being the term for villages in the Philippines. The information system answers the need to define and identify socioeconomic, environmental, and ecological variables at the barangay level that may be affecting the health and nutrition status of communities. This is the backdrop against which health occurs—or does not occur—in a community. The Barangay Socioeconomic Information System is a compilation of basic socioeconomic data that may be affecting the health status of communities. These include such factors as the terrain, language, agricultural profile, wealth and poverty indicators, and others. In addition to socioeconomic data, the Barangay Socioeconomic Information System contains data on environment, culture, as well as the provision of, and access to, health care at the local levels. Such an information system is being updated whenever needed. Its inclusion of information on agriculture and community organizations can make it useful for nutrition surveillance.

3 Health, food and nutrition in the hands of the people

Under the auspices of a people's empowerment, we were commissioned by the German Development Cooperation[1] to strengthen the **h**ealth **a**nd **m**anagement **i**nformation **s**ystem in the Philippines at the start of this decade (Schwefel et al. 1995). This we called HAMIS, a Philippine-German technical cooperation project. It is very fitting that "hamis" is a Filipino word that can mean "smooth" as well as

1 We acknowledge the generous support of our projects by the German Ministery for Economic Cooperation and Development (BMZ) and the German Agency of Technical Cooperation (GTZ) as well as by the Philippine Department of Health – an exemplary partnership of two people for the benefit of the poor.

"sweet". And so we say that "the HAMIS way" is "smooth and sweet." Of course, we used medical informatics and indicator systems that contained information on food and nutrition, too. We had some radically different points of view, however:

— Let us not concentrate on data and information only, but let us especially consider understanding and wisdom when developing health and management information systems.

— Let us not be contained with computers as the holders of information, but especially with human beings as the real expert information systems.

— Let us learn from the best managers in the Philippines what good management is, before we presume to tell them what the state of the art is, according to books and papers.

This is easy to say, but how do we get to know the best managers? Our source of information was to discover and analyze examples of outstanding health care management. Sponsored by Germany, three national contests were conducted in the Philippines by the Department of Health to recognize exemplary health care activities (Schwefel and Pons 1993, 1994; Schwefel and Palazo 1995a).

— More than 400 applications for the three HAMIS Contests were received from all regions of the Philippines. The applications were submitted to intensive screenings. Representatives from Department of Health, academe and non-governmental organizations were asked to give a standardized peer review. Many projects were visited by three evaluators who were guided by a checklist of 73 criteria to check quality, innovativeness, effectiveness, equity, efficiency and sustainability. Distinguished members of the selection committees for the three HAMIS Contests chose 160 projects that were given diamond, gold, silver and bronze awards. The plaques of recognition were presented to the winners by the President of the Republic of the Philippines in 1991, 1994 and 1997.

— The HAMIS Contests show that there are many innovative ways of improving effectiveness and efficiency of health care for those in need. The HAMIS Winners demonstrate that good management makes improvement in health care possible under any given circumstances. The experiences of the Winners show that good health care management does the right things despite scarcity of resources and immobility of institutions and people. Good health care management discovers untapped resources, mobilizes human and intellectual resources, combines existing resource patterns resulting in multiplicative effects, and reconfirms productivity gains through self-organization and banding together. Good health care management in this sense is the more productive use of otherwise overlooked resources for the benefit of those in need.

— After the first Contest, the 52 Winners formed a southern and a northern association, and a national Federation to strengthen and to be lobbyists for good management. HAMIS Winner Clubs were built upon issues of mutual interest, e.g., community health workers, herbal medicine, drug cooperatives, community health financing and social health insurance. The first Winners were co-equal partners for preparing, implementing and using the second Contest to bring into the fold 68 new excellent health care managers, and to establish and renew self-sustainable reassurance networks to benefit the poor. The Federation of the 160 HAMIS Winners in the Philippines nowadays is an important consultative body to influence policy-making and law-making to strengthen good health care management.

This strategy of discovering good health care management provided us with a lot of insights on health management. Good health management is not focused on medicine and hospitals alone. It is, first of all, preventive and promotive in character. Prevention of disease incorporates a balanced satisfaction of basic needs. Food, nutrition, employment, housing, water, income and all the other key ingredients of basic needs are at stake when a cost-effective health care is under discussion. Not all the projects that we discovered are that comprehensive. But all of them show us ways and means how people and good managers take health and health management into their hands.

3.1 Health in the hands of the people via community-managed projects

Let us just mention a very few projects that were declared to be outstanding examples of health care management in the hands of the people.

— Stimulated by an enlightened group of medical students, urban poor in a community of garbage collectors in Manila realized cost sharing through donation of some seed money. This enabled voluntary community health workers to provide some preventive and medical care that was complemented by services of volunteer doctors. Additionally, they collect contributions from families so that they can avail of a 50% discount of the factory prices of drugs when buying prescribed drugs in the cooperative store. Others in the catchment get drugs at prices below retailers price. The contributions are according to family income but not according to family size, thus providing a progressive risk sharing component. The lesson of this project is that self-organization and cooperation can save money for all in the catchment, not just for the members of the cooperative. Under the name "community drug insurances" this project is now being replicated as a national program in 1.000 local areas all over the Philippines.

— A voluntary association of diabetic patients in Quezon Province reduces public costs by early discovery (and prevention) of complications through monthly blood sugar testing and health training. It reduces private costs by having reduced drug and consultation fees due to economies of scale and managed care. At the same time, social and mental suffering is alleviated through banding together and consoling each other. Membership fees and donations are collected. The lesson of this project is that cooperation brings about private and public savings.

— A network of Mothers' Clubs on the islands of Surigao City initiated a comprehensive blend of activities to develop skills among mothers, their families, and other individuals in the community. This allows them to achieve an acceptable level of health and well-being in a self-reliant way. These activities include health care, health education and training in nutrition and food production, environmental sanitation, building of infrastructure, livelihood projects, day care centers, weekly radio program, bargain incentives for Mothers' Club members in city stores including drug stores, emergency credit arrangements, scholarships, regular self-evaluation and awarding of good performance, and last but not least, diversified fund raising. The lesson of this project is that good health care management should be comprehensive, and that comprehensiveness, sustainability and expansion are achieved if people understand and share it. One of the components of this project—a databoard in the hands of volunteer health workers—was proclaimed a national program and is being replicated now all over the Philippines by the Department of Health.

In all these cases, people got sick and tired when waiting for a support from local or even national governments. They took health and health management into their own hands.

3.2 Herbal medicine as a crucial option and a strategic tool

Herbal medicine in the Philippines is an old tradition but a new science. Indeed, when the Winners of the first HAMIS Contest were awarded in 1991, only a very few of the 52 community organizations were involved in herbal medicine. Specifically, only 9 of them had any involvement either in promoting the use of herbal medicine, or actually going into producing herbal preparations, either for their own consumption or for more widespread distribution. Remarkably, though, one of these HAMIS Winners is headed by a university professor who is in fact a pioneer in pursuing herbal medicine as a science in the Philippines.

Shortly after the HAMIS Winners established their Federation, one of the first things they did was to organize a Herbal Medicine Conference. Many had come to realize that herbal medicine was an activity that was very much needed by their communities. The Conference brought together the expertise of a few of the Winners with the consuming interest of many others who were eager to learn the technology for themselves, and to pass on the benefits to the communities they represented. A subsequent follow-up Conference brought in many more experts, and came up with a training manual that was disseminated to any and all interested HAMIS Winners.

In 1994, there were 68 new HAMIS Winners awarded in the second HAMIS Contest. Many very soon learned from the experiences of the first HAMIS Winners, and quickly adopted the practice of herbal medicine in their activities. Many, many more have since demanded this sharing of knowledge. The informal gatherings and workshops soon became quite inadequate to meet the growing demand. The herbal medicine training therefore had to be formalized as a course offering in our HAMIS Academy. The HAMIS Academy is in itself an innovation. It is a sort of open people's university and self-help referral center. Anybody is welcome to learn the new technologies developed by the HAMIS Winners from their own experiences in health management. It is the venue for sharing with many others the lessons learned by the HAMIS Winners.

The offshoot of this historical evolution is that, now, more than half of all the HAMIS Winners include a herbal medicine component among the services they offer. Moreover, the standards of quality in the preparation and practice of herbal medicine have been refined and standardized among the HAMIS Winners. Why did herbal medicine become so popular so quickly among the HAMIS Winners? Herbal medicine is a crucial option by which people can effectively manage their own health.

— Herbal medicine makes use of resources that are readily available, often in one's own backyard or garden. These are the medicinal plants, many of the most useful of which grow like weeds. Sadly they are often treated as weeds, precisely because people are ignorant of their true value. And one doesn't need to internalize an encyclopedia of herbal knowledge in order to effectively practice herbal medicine. A dozen or so of the most common of these "weeds" could be effective for most of the illnesses that poor communities in the Philippines suffer from (Marte 1996). As in the practice of Western medicine, it is important, firstly, to know which plants are good for which conditions. Secondly, one must know what is the proper mode of preparation, and how to go about it. Thirdly, one must know how to administer the drug, and in what amounts. In the experience of the HAMIS Academy, it does not take very much to transfer this knowledge even to community health workers who have hardly any formal education at all.

— Herbal medicine makes use of technology that is commonly used in daily activities of the household, particularly the kitchen. Herbal medicine has a scientific basis that is not just a hit-or-miss thing. The scientific aspect of herbal medicine does not mean, however, that herbal preparations can only be done in the laboratory. It is possible to produce quality herbal preparations in the home, using kitchen measurements and kitchen implements. The "kitchen technology" or "kitchen laboratory" approach to herbal medicine is necessary because very few people have access to laboratory instruments, but every household has a kitchen and kitchen implements. Not everybody may have clocks, even, and so preparation time may have to be approximated by other means. For example, "boil until only one-half is left" might be more appropriate than "boil for 15 minutes" if there are no clocks in the community (de Padua 1996). And so, preparing herbal medicines is essentially very much like cooking vegetables, except that these vegetable preparations have medicinal value; meaning, they can prevent, attenuate or cure illness episodes.

— Herbal medicine is a very much less expensive alternative to synthetic pharmaceuticals, but not necessarily less effective. In many instances they could even be more effective. The conventional wisdom is that, if herbal medicine fails, shift to synthetic pharmaceuticals. Our experience with the HAMIS Winners, however, is that the other way around may also be true. If synthetic pharmaceuticals fail, it may be beneficial and proper to shift to herbal medicine. In fact, herbal medicine may also be used together with synthetic pharmaceuticals. Some principles of herbal medicine, moreover, promote the rational use of drugs. For instance, herbal medicine advocates that it is best to use ingredients individually, in order to monitor the desired and adverse effects of a given herbal plant. If several herbs are in combination, we may not know which is producing a desired or adverse effect.

Herbal medicine has certain strategic implications that "extend beyond the kitchen," so to speak.

— Herbal medicines in general, but particularly the ones advocated by the HAMIS Academy, have a wide margin of safety. This means that the preparations can be used liberally or ad libitum as it were, without much fear of adverse effects. The implication is that, for most of the common ailments that people suffer from, a well-informed family need not seek consultation with a doctor without first trying out the herbal remedies on their own. This does not necessarily do away with doctors, but it does minimize the use of, and dependence on, medical services. The practice of herbal medicine must of course be according to accepted standards. These standards cover a wide gamut of the process of herbal medicine:

-- from planting, harvesting, and storing the plants,
-- to compounding the infusions, decoctions, syrups, and ointments, and finally
-- administering the drugs and monitoring the effects.

These standards, developed and compiled with the HAMIS Academy, try to assure the quality of herbal products and services rendered to patients. The effect has been to refine a traditional practice into a popular science.

— Herbal medicine has a great potential for community enterprise. The income generating potential for producing herbal preparations is quite recognized, but the concerted effort of a community—even and especially of the poor—could take this to further heights.

Even a relatively small scale industry for herbal medicine production would have to involve an agricultural aspect, which is basically the growing and harvesting of the plants. Initially this could even be done on a backyard gardening basis. Eventually it could grow into contract farming. The other aspect is of course the preparation of the herbal products. This involves the preparation and packaging of the dried herbal products, as in tea bags, or the preparation of the end-product itself such as tablets, capsules, syrups, ointments, soaps, and many others. Interestingly, government rules and regulations may actually favor such a community enterprise. The law is quite stringent on licensing the herbal medicines as pharmaceuticals if they are produced in commercial quantity. In the form of tea bags or soaps, however, they are considered food supplements or toiletries, and the pertinent laws are not as stringent. There are also tax incentives if such an enterprise is entered into as a community cooperative.

Herbal medicine is in fact a way beyond an informed self-medication. It is an informed production of drugs for some of the most common illnesses. "Health in the hands of the people" acquires a very active and productive meaning by this very issue.

3.3 Nutrition security as a strategic issue

Herbal medicine is a way of preparing and consuming plants—just a step away from preparing and consuming food. Some people say, the best herbal medicine is a good and balanced diet. Some of the HAMIS Winners are actively dealing with this issue.

For many years, the efforts of nutrition intervention programs have been directed mainly toward increasing the food available at the household level. The strategy to improve such "food security" was either to increase agricultural production, or to increase the income of these households. This is based on the premise that as long as food is available at the household level, the nutritional status of every member of the household would be assured. Unfortunately we have seen through the years that food security does not by itself lead to "nutrition security". The model developed by the UNICEF (1990) shows quite clearly that there are many variables and determinants of nutritional status, and that food security is but one of them (Figure 2; see Maxwell and Frankenberger).

— The model shows that a combination and interaction of inadequate dietary intake and disease lead directly to malnutrition and death. Moreover it bears reemphasizing that disease, in particular infectious disease considering its relative importance in developing countries, adversely affects dietary intake and nutrient utilization. These immediate causes of malnutrition and death in turn arise out of a combination of three inter-related factors: insufficient household food security, inadequate maternal and childcare, and insufficient health services and unhealthy environment. These latter are termed the underlying causes.

— The model can also be stated positively. In this case, when household food security is available, when maternal and child care are adequate, and when health services are sufficient and the environment is healthy, then dietary intake will be adequate and disease episodes would be controlled. This is when we might say that nutrition security has been achieved, and the eventual manifestation would be that proper nutrition is assured and avoidable deaths are prevented.

— Food security by itself is a necessary but not a sufficient condition for adequate nutrition. Technically, food security is defined as "access by all people at all times to the food needed for a healthy life" (Kaufmann 1994, quoting from World Bank 1986). This does not include the fact that, for example, inadequate caring capacity within the household (due to traditional beliefs, lack of knowledge, etc.) can lead to inadequate distribution of food among the members, even though food is generally available to the household. Health care is another important condition that is closely related. When the environment is conducive to disease (e.g., diarrhea) and sufficient health services are not available, the interplay between disease and dietary intake is likely to make sure that adequate nutrition is not going to be achieved.

— Nutrition security goes beyond food security to include certain other dimensions. Indeed, it is defined "access to food by all people at all times including the adequate utilization in order to live a healthy life". Nutrition security comprises aspects as fair distribution of food between and within communities, conducive living conditions, proper and adequate health care, education, physical work, frequency of childbearing, health conditions, etc.

Figure 2: Causes of malnutrition and death

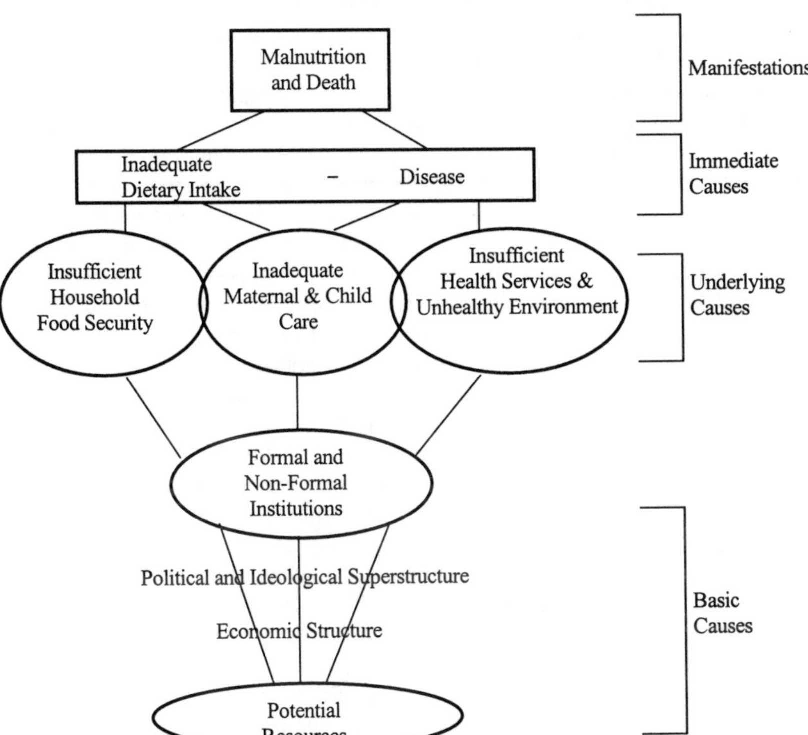

A major difficulty with many nutrition programs is that, in most cases, the interventions were decided and implemented without the participation of communities. Experience has shown and proven that nutrition programs of this sort have generally not been successful. The determinants of nutrition security are very complex indeed. These determinants encompass several interrelationships between the cultural, the economic, the behavioral, as well as the biological and physiological. And only if the community is fully involved in the design, implementation, monitoring and evaluation of nutrition programs—with several approaches considered—can the likelihood be improved that they would be more effective and sustainable (FAO 1993).

About 50% of our HAMIS Winners in the Philippines are focusing their activities on the improvement of the nutritional situation in their communities, especially the poor and malnourished children. A lot of them are directing their activities toward more than one intervention. Their approach has been to improve the household food security, the maternal and childcare, and the health services and environment in order to improve the dietary intake at the family level. This also considers the health situation of the individual. The overall goal in effect contributes toward improving the nutritional situation in the Philippines.

— One of the outstanding HAMIS Winners is the "Federated Primary Health Care (PHC) Mothers' Clubs", a self-help, non-governmental organization in Surigao City, in the northeastern part of Mindanao. It is supporting their people in the communities to develop skills in order to improve their health situation in a self-reliant way. The activities try to include the active participation of everybody—in the household and in the community. Mothers are organized in "Mothers' Clubs", "Barangay Environmental Sanitation Implementation Group (BESIG)" is involving the husbands, and "Youth Clubs" involve their children. Besides the approach to involve everybody—an embodiment of "health in the hands of the people"—the approach of the project is quite comprehensive. The mothers have the opportunities to be trained in health, nutrition, and family planning, so that they are being trained as Barangay Health Workers (BHW) who have direct contact to the people in the village. The participation of fathers/husbands in health-related activities minimizes the dropouts among the mothers/wives. The activities range from primary health care supporting activities, skills training and financial support for income generating projects, and environmental sanitation, to include even community infrastructure.

— Another outstanding HAMIS Winner is the "Implementation of Integrated Nutrition Program" in the Municipality of Hilongos, Leyte. The local government of Hilongos, aware of the magnitude of malnutrition problem in their locality, implemented an integrated approach to nutrition. The beneficiaries of this project are all the households in the 50 barangays in Hilongos, with special emphasis on pre-school children, elementary school children, pregnant and lactating mothers. The range of their activities comprises food assistance and supplementary feeding in schools, nutrition education, day care centers, cooking demonstrations, teacher-child-parent (TCP) approach, mother's classes, backyard gardening (bio-intensive gardening, poultry raising etc.), and assistance in food production (school garden, livelihood). This project is supported by different government ministries including the Department of Agriculture (DA), the Department of Social Welfare and Development (DSWD), the Department of Education, Culture and Sports (DECS), and the Department of Health (DOH).

— A project that is engaged in the rehabilitation of severely malnourished children is supported by the Theosophical Order of Service. This "Intensive Rehabilitation of Severely Malnourished Children and Self-Reliance Program" is addressing the families in depressed barangays of Metro Manila and has started with two approaches. On the one hand, severely malnourished children are immediately supported with medical check-ups, medicines and food for a short period. The parents act as direct implementors of the program. They are responsible for meal planning, marketing, cooking, cleaning the feeding center, etc. Non-formal mother's classes on basic nutrition and primary health care are also conducted. On the other hand, parents of the malnourished children are at the same time involved in the Self-Reliance Program, where they are being offered income-generating opportunities with interest-free loan assistance. The purpose is to secure the food availability at household level, and thereby the nutritional well-being of the whole family. Lately, they have started to give trainings on producing herbal medicine and encouraging the community for backyard vegetable and herbal gardening.

— "Good nutrition through good income generation" is the objective of the project "Urban Family Development Program (UFDP)" which is implemented by the Nutrition Foundation of the Philippines, Inc. (NFP) since 1991. It is a holistic and muti-sectoral program that focuses on the development of the whole family. The beneficiaries are the economically and nutritionally depressed families in different barangays of Metro Manila. The components of the UFDP range from community organization (Mother's Clubs and Youth Groups), training (leadership training, skills training), and livelihood activities (cash loan assistance, product development, rice/salt vending), to nutrition and health classes, as well as medical, nutrition and health services. One of the causes of malnutrition, according to the NFP, is ignorance or lack of knowledge on food and nutrition. Therefore nutrition education is one major pillar of the project. There are nutrition and health classes for mothers and preschool children, involving the community organizations in the planning, implementation and monitoring of the activities.

These above-described four projects are examples of many more existing innovative and community-based approaches to eradicate hunger in the Philippines. They are very likely to achieve nutrition security because of their participatory and multi-sectoral approach. The problem of malnutrition is tackled by different interventions. Food production, income generation, education on meal frequency, etc., will lead to food security at the household level. Knowledge on childcare, nutrition and health, awareness of time constraints, and reduction of workload for women will improve the maternal and childcare capabilities. Awareness about, access to, and improvement of water supply, waste disposal, latrines and health services are crucial conditions to improve the health status of the people. Food security, maternal and childcare, and health services are working together to increase the household dietary intake and to reduce the prevalence of diseases. These conditions are important to achieve nutrition security for the people.

The HAMIS Winners are already powerful because of their networking system as the national Federation of HAMIS Winners in the Philippines and their regional formations into the northern and southern associations. Additionally, with the HAMIS Winners' Clubs, projects with similar activities and interests are sharing and exchanging their experiences, with mutual benefits for all. The experience of the HAMIS Winners' Clubs has shown that this kind of networking will not only support themselves but strengthen them to influence local and national health policies.

The plan of the Federation of the HAMIS Winners for the year 1997 is to set up a "Nutrition Club". This is a great opportunity to spread the wisdom and skills about nutrition security. The Nutrition Club will facilitate conferences where experiences, knowledge and wisdom of each member can be shared and exchanged. Like the other Clubs of the Federation—health insurance, herbal medicine, women's health, information systems etc.—the Nutrition Club might most probably develop policy papers especially on community nutrition. They could also produce a training module to be included in the HAMIS Academy. The Nutrition Club will certainly serve as a networking strategy to strengthen the different projects in their efforts to improve the nutritional situation in the Philippines. Our HAMIS Academy will serve as a kind of self help empowerment center.

3.4 From income generating projects to food generating projects, from health to wealth, from food and nutrition towards a productive life style

Quite a number of the best grassroots managers in the Philippines include income generating projects on their agenda. Piggeries, buying-and-selling, and backyard farming of cash crops are quite prominent examples. Income is the aim. This is quite understandable, since money is a universal tool to satisfy basic human needs. But are we sure that this income is turned, indeed, into basic needs satisfaction including food security?[2]

In situations of widespread poverty, the relationship between spending and saving money is of crucial importance. Money management at the household level has an enormous impact on health and social life. This has to be seen in the wider context of saving, and what is being called "negative saving."

Saving has many faces. Webster defines "to save" as:

- to rescue or preserve from harm or danger,
- to preserve for future use,
- to prevent or lessen,
- to prevent loss or waste,
- to avoid expense, waste, etc.,
- to store up money or goods.

To pick but one of these definitions and to declare it the only valid one would be inappropriate and insufficient, especially when considering what saving really means, its determinants, and its effects. Much more, saving is a social concept, a social reality, and a social problem—this is what we will elaborate in this chapter (see Figure 3). Rational household behaviour—this is what we can learn from the smartest HAMIS Winners.

2 The following chapters are taken from: Schwefel and Leidl 1987 and Schwefel and Palazo 1995b.

Figure 3: Concepts and examples of negative, nominal, real and rational savings

<table>
<tr><th rowspan="4">Purposes / outcomes of savings
Inputs / sources of savings</th><th>Past</th><th>Present</th><th colspan="4">Future</th></tr>
<tr><th colspan="3">consumption</th><th colspan="3"></th></tr>
<tr><th colspan="2"></th><th colspan="4">accumulation</th></tr>
<tr><th>Past consumption</th><th>Short-term consumption delay</th><th>Long-term consumption goods</th><th>Investment in human capital</th><th>Insurance against unknown risks</th><th>Investment in production technology or other profitable assets</th></tr>
<tr><td>Income from a reduction of assets</td><td rowspan="3">Indebtedness, negative saving</td><td rowspan="4">Smoothening consumption patterns over shorter time periods (storing food between harvests, etc.)</td><td rowspan="3">Buying durable consumer goods, which at the same time could serve as insurance capital or profitable assets</td><td rowspan="3">Health and education expenses</td><td></td><td>Commercial dealing with, e.g., valuable household goods</td></tr>
<tr><td>Money income</td><td colspan="2">SAVING IN THE TRADITIONAL ECONOMIC SENSE</td></tr>
<tr><td>Resources income (goods and services)</td><td colspan="2" rowspan="2">PROMOTION OF REAL AND RATIONAL SAVINGS

Expenditure for consumption goods which could be sold in view of a consumption crisis
Expenditure of resources or money for foodstalls, street vendor equipment, rickshas, tools for sandal production
Social security oriented activities, e.g., child rearing behaviour or stabilizing social networks
(opposed to non-productive consumption)</td></tr>
<tr><td>Behaviour / lifestyle / way of life</td><td></td><td></td><td>Performing rational consumption patterns, avoiding costly risks</td></tr>
</table>

In situations of poverty, as among the poor in the Philippines, the usual economic concept of "positive saving" is not the general option. The poor frequently do not have a choice between consuming or saving. Often, they are forced to go into "negative saving" (indebtedness to money-lenders) in the present, in order to avert an existing crisis, such as a catastrophic illness or catastrophically rising food prices. Not to loan and spend in such a situation would worsen the crisis. Thus, we have to look at credits and loans for health, food and nutrition from a different perspective. On the one hand, real saving, as we know it, if practiced by the poor may worsen their health and nutrition, and may not even be possible to achieve. On the other hand, negative saving, or loans from money lenders, though a depressing fact of the lives of the poor, can indeed be life-saving.

3.4.1 First Concern: Widespread indebtedness as the starting point

In a situation of poverty, "negative saving", i.e., the widespread indebtedness of poor people, is the point of departure for any realistic analysis of savings. The poor produce deficits every month, as can be seen from income and expenditure surveys and, more validly, from qualitative case studies. Borrowing is often used to satisfy consumption instead of investment needs, especially in the case of emergencies (necessary as opposed to excess). Everywhere, a tight hierarchical system of more or less informal mini-loans exists, which is based on trust and memory and which can exceed the loan conditions usually imposed in the formal sectors. This system penetrates families, friendships, businesses, and villages, and is not restricted to the exchange of today's and tomorrow's money, but includes goods, services, and social relationships as well. Implicit and explicit negative savings forced by high prices, e.g., of food, could be added to this picture. Sophisticated research on this topic is still very scarce. It would need promotion.

3.4.2 Second Concern: "Healthy" savings in cash and kind

Income statistics are especially poor for an economic analysis when applied to informal sectors linked with shadow, exchange, and subsistence economies. To regard only the monthly or yearly money left-overs as potential savings has a pragmatic appeal, but some inconveniences as well. To mention only two points: reserves in kind have to be added and debts have to be subtracted. The first bias could not even be corrected by using family expenditure surveys; instead, non-standard research would have to be undertaken. These could show, for example, a stock of mini-production factors such as a bicycle, or of durable consumer goods as radios or TV sets, which could be sold when needed. Such sales are a first sign of a coming consumption crisis. Non-cash savings in kind are an important aspect of the problem under consideration.

Let us go further and be provocative: child-rearing may sometimes be considered a specific form of sacrifice of present family consumption, made in view of a future security for parental consumption. This, too, is a social facet of real savings.

It implies that not only stored money or goods may be seen as savings, but also behavior or activities aimed at securing future consumption. Another example could be the construction of toilets in the present to avoid the expense of treating diarrheal diseases in the future.

Another aspect of saving may be stored fitness through good nutrition and health in order to be prepared for health crises, such as infections, which are easier to overcome when well nourished. The rationale behind this aspect of real savings is that activities to prevent possible crises in the future may be labeled as saving, because the expenditure that would have been required to cure and care later has been saved by preceding activities to prevent disease and to promote health.

Thus, in order to study the social meaning of saving in the informal sector in Third World countries, we have to look for real savings. This we do by applying a blend of social research designs, case studies, behavioral studies, as well as health and nutrition surveys, and not only income and expenditure studies in order to operationalize nominal savings in terms of income minus expenditure.

3.4.3 Third Concern: Rational household economics and a healthy lifestyle

The latter two aspects of real savings introduce a normative concept of "rational" behavior: refraining from "bad" or "conspicuous" consumption in favor of "good" consumption is interpreted as saving as opposed to squandering. This is the case when future benefits can be expected from actual behavior. More generally, savings in the sense of avoiding future consumption crises can be achieved by present consumption patterns, in the extreme case, even without any further reductions in the level of consumption. Hence, substantially "rational" consumptive behavior can be looked upon as an activity of saving, since it might help to enlarge human and environmental capital stocks for future consumption. Healthy diets and life-styles or better education (as a precondition for a self-initiated improvement of the standard of living) are common examples for this type of saving. In short, saving can mean not only a reduction of consumption, but also a change of consumptive behavior towards healthier lifestyles.

One purpose of saving is to have a risk remedy at hand when needed. Not to spend all of one's money and to save some of it may be one instrument of fulfilling this purpose. It may be bad advice in times of inflation or in cases where social networks, friendship, good health, power, or love are the backbone of a minimal social security. To spend money for fiestas, where the gains may be intangible but desirable, may then be good advice to achieve the purpose of savings. This contradictory argument refers to the level of the individual.

Similar problems may arise when individual activities are linked with societal consequences. Individual saving, with the side effects of increased undernutrition or a diminished safety at work, may not only lead to later losses in production, but also to an increased use of public goods and services such as hospitals. This is the situation of saving in the wrong places. Thus, individual saving may have social costs.

To overcome such dilemmas one has to avoid the naive definition of saving, i.e., to consider saving only as the difference between current income and current expenditure and forget about all the rest.

3.4.4 Fourth Concern: Health promotion as a rational saving behavior

Saving means generating reserves to overcome future crises. To try and minimize the impact of crises could be one aspect of "preventive saving." There are more examples: spending money for good nutrition of the children, not spending money for excessive tobacco and alcohol consumption, and spending time for one's physical condition are examples of individual endeavors to strengthen health, and to be fitter during ill health and consumption crises. At the social level, prior investment in such projects as clean drinking water, environmental hygiene, and road safety may later save expenditures for cure and care. In short, the rational spending of individual time, energy, and money, and of public funds, is an effective and efficient kind of saving.

Let us imagine a family hit by a catastrophic illness following unemployment of the father. The resulting income reduction may lead, via the distributive patterns of intra-family consumption, to undernutrition and disease of the socially weakest parts of the family, i.e., mostly younger girls and dependent older people. Let us then assume that some members of the family indulge in gambling in an attempt to recoup the family's fortunes. Not unemployment, then, but gambling reduces food consumption for the family. In this case we could not speak of bad luck or misfortune, but of irresponsible behavior that further drives the family into distress.

The above reasoning implies that nominal (irrational) saving in a situation of poverty may have unacceptable side-effects; an unthinking mobilization of the savings of the poor may have, for example, unhealthy consequences for the weakest parts of society. The lack of rational saving, in the form of lack of health-promoting behavior (smoking or gambling), spells doom for the family in crisis.

3.4.5 Fifth Concern: The social meaning of mobilization of savings

Poverty is a widespread reality for our people. What is the social meaning of mobilization of savings in such a context? Let us take a rural electrification program as an example. Sixty-four percent of the electricity produced is spent for private lighting, 24% for television, 11% for public lighting, and 1% for radio. Current monthly expenditures are P10 for TV, P4 for light and P2 for radio. About 30% of the households with electricity bought a secondhand TV for about P1,000 that includes 45% import taxes and 10% other taxes; additionally, an average business profit of 30% can be assumed. These data imply that, in the wake of a rural electrification program, enormous savings were mobilized for the benefit of state and commerce and not for immediate productive use by the local population or for building up a reassurance fund for coping with future crises.

This example points to what the social meaning of mobilization of savings should be: to spend money, resources, and energy rationally to satisfy basic human needs now or in the near future. In other words, the mobilization of the savings of the poor should be channeled into meeting basic needs, such as health, food, nutrition, and shelter. Not to do so would be to continue the present wasteful consumption in non-productive uses.

This is exactly the message that we can learn from many HAMIS Winners. A good family health and household management is a very important step towards basic needs satisfaction, including security of health, food and nutrition. Smart people and smart people´s organizations can show us the way.

4 Summary and conclusions

Food and nutrition security has to be seen in the broader perspective of a development strategy that is aimed at satisfying the basic needs of the population with a perspective of self reliance and sustainability (Satzinger and Schwefel 1982; Schwefel 1985; 1997). Health, food and nutrition in the hands of the people is a tool and an aim, at the same time.

References

FAO (1993): Guidelines for participatory nutrition projects, Rome.

Kaufmann, Silvia (1994): Nutritional Baseline Survey for Integrated Food Security Programme, German Agency for Technical Cooperation (GTZ), Germany, May.

Kuhnke, Klaus, Marianne Reuber, and Detlef Schwefel (1990): Solar Cookers in the Third World. Evaluation of the Prerequisites, Prospects and Impacts of an Innovative Technology, Braunschweig: Vieweg Verlag, 228 pages.

Marte, Benjamin Ariel (1996): Wisdom of the Weeds: A Learning Manual for Herbal Medicine, prepared for the HAMIS Academy, Manila.

Maxwell, Simon and Timothy R. Frankenberger: Household food security: Concepts, indicators, measurements—A technical review.

de Padua, Ludivina S. (1996): Kitchen Technologies for the Preparation of Herbal Medicines, prepared for the HAMIS Academy. Laguna, Philippines.

Remotigue, Teofila E., M. David, R. Yapchiongco, O. Banias, T. Bonoan, and Detlef Schwefel (1994): Health Databoards for Communities. An Orientation Guidebook on the National Implementation of Community Health Databoards, Manila: HAMIS at the Department of Health, Popular Papers No. 2, 198 pages.

Satzinger, Walter, and Detlef Schwefel (1982): Entwicklung als soziale Entwicklung. Über Irrwege und Umwege entwicklungstheoretischer Strategiesuche (Development as social development. About wrong ways and detours in search of a theoretically based development strategy), in: Dieter Nohlen and Franz Nuscheler (Eds.): Handbuch der Dritten Welt, Hamburg: Hoffmann und Campe Verlag, pp. 312-331.

Schwefel, Detlef (1975a): Planificación, administración y organización de los servicios de salud (Planning, administration and organization of health services), in: Revista Centroamericana de Ciencias de la Salud, Vol. 1 (1), pp. 92-115.

Schwefel, Detlef (1975b): Who Benefits from Production and Employment? Six Criteria to Measure the Impact of Development Projects on Poverty and Need Satisfaction, Berlin: German Development Institute, Occasional Paper No. 29, 91 pages; 3rd edition 1976.

Schwefel, Detlef (1978a): Papel y funciones de los departamentos de nutrición de los ministerios de salud en los servicios descentralizados de salud pública (Role and functions of nutrition departments in ministries of health within the context of decentralized public health services), in: José Aranda-Pastor and Bernd Breuer (Eds.): Programas de nutrición en los servicios descentralizados de salud en América Central, Guatemala: INCAP, pp. 69-84.

Schwefel, Detlef (1978b): Grundbedürfnisse und Entwicklungspolitik (Basic needs and development policy), Baden-Baden: Nomos Verlag, 298 pages.

Schwefel, Detlef (1978c): Basic Needs. Planning and Evaluation, Berlin: German Development Institute, Occasional Paper No. 50, 358 pages.

Schwefel, Detlef (1979a): Nahrungsmittelpreispolitiken und Ernährung. Bericht über einen Workshop der Universität der Vereinten Nationen in Mexiko 1978 (Food price policies and nutrition. Report on a workshop of the United Nations University in Mexico 1978), in: Vierteljahresberichte, Probleme der Entwicklungsländer (Forschungsinstitut der Friedrich-Ebert-Stiftung), No. 77, September, pp. 237-253.

Schwefel, Detlef (1979b): Basic Needs, Planning and Policies, in: intereconomics, Vol. 14 (3), pp. 132-138.

Schwefel, Detlef (1980): Nutrition Monitoring, Evaluation, Planning, and Surveillance in Indonesia. Assignment report to WHO-SEARO. Jakarta, 27.12.79-24.2.1980, New Delhi: WHO-SEARO, 38 pages.

Schwefel, Detlef (1982): Product Path Analysis and Rational Consumption Budgets ....., in: M. Buchmann et al. (Eds.): Basic Needs Strategy as a Planning Parameter, Berlin: German Foundation for International Development, pp. 541-564.

Schwefel, Detlef (1984): Evaluación de efectos sociales de grandes represas (Evaluation of social effects of large dams), in: Centro Interamericano de Desarrollo Social (CIDES) de la Organización de los Estados Americanos (OEA) & Instituto Latinoamericano de Planificación Económica y Social (ILPES) de la Comisión Económica para América Latina (CEPAL) (Eds.): Efectos sociales de las grandes represas en América Latina, Montevideo: Fundación de Cultura Universitaria, pp. 231-273.

Schwefel, Detlef (1985): From Cost Containment to Effect-Assessment, in: World Health Forum, Vol. 6 (1), pp. 17-19 (also in Arabic, Chinese, French, Russian, Spanish).

Schwefel, Detlef (1987a): Inestabilidad económica, nutrición y salud (Economic instability, nutrition and health), in: Antonio Correia de Campos et al. (Eds.): Sociedade, Saúde e Economia. Lisboa: Escola Nacional de Saúde Pública, pp. 99-109.

Schwefel, Detlef (1987b): Crisis económica y salud (Economic crisis and health), in: Boletín Económico de Información Comercial Española, No. 2078, pp. 1159-1164.

Schwefel, Detlef (1987c): Evaluation sozialer Auswirkungen und Nebenwirkungen von Projekten. Ein Überblick über Themen, Tendenzen und Trugschlüsse (Evaluation of social effects and side-effects of projects. A synopsis of topics, tendencies and traps), in: Detlef Schwefel (Ed.): Soziale Wirkungen von Projekten in der Dritten Welt, Baden-Baden: Nomos-Verlag, pp. 15-50.

Schwefel, Detlef (1987d): Soziale Auswirkungen von Infrastrukturen und Industrien (Social impacts of infrastructures and industries), in: Detlef Schwefel (Ed.), Soziale Wirkungen von Projekten in der Dritten Welt, Baden-Baden: Nomos-Verlag, pp. 191-249.

Schwefel, Detlef (1989): The Product-Path-Analysis. A Method of Socioeconomic Project Appraisal, in: Canadian Journal of Development Studies, Vol. 10 (2), pp. 211-223.

Schwefel, Detlef (1997): Grundbedürfnisbefriedigung durch Entwicklungspolitik? Sisyphos und der Großinquisitor als entwicklungspolitische Leitbilder, in: Manfred Schulz (Ed.): Entwicklung: Die Perspektive der Entwicklungssoziologie, Opladen: Westdeutscher Verlag.

Schwefel, Detlef, Luis Gurmendi, Thomas Müller-Debus, Karin Röhrbein, Rainer Rosenbaum (1976): Producción, empleo y consumo racional. Hacia una cuantificación de implicaciones nutricionales de proyectos de inversión (Production, employment and rational consumption. Approaches to quantify the impacts of investment projects on the nutritional status), Berlin: Instituto Alemán de Desarrollo, Occasional Paper No. 41, 131 pages.

Schwefel, Detlef, Per-Gunnar Svensson, Herbert Zöllner (Eds.) (1987): Unemployment, Social Vulnerability, and Health in Europe, Berlin: Springer-Verlag, 325 pages.

Schwefel, Detlef, B.A. Marte, Teofila E. Remotigue, M.R. David, B.C. Magtaas, V. Pantilano, F. Quijano, R. Delino, M. Ringor, and M. Pons (1995): HAMIS. A Health and Management Information System for the Philippines, Manila: HAMIS at the Department of Health, Occasional Papers No. 11, 703 pages.

Detlef Schwefel, and Reiner Leidl (1987): Remarks on the social meaning of savings of the poor, in: Development, No. 2/3, pp. 142-144.

Schwefel, Detlef, and Melahi C. Pons (1993): Discovering Good Management. An Information System on Innovations in Health Care Management in the Philippines, Manila: HAMIS at the Department of Health, Occasional Papers No. 5, 190 pages.

Schwefel, Detlef, and Melahi Pons (1994): Winners Show the Way to Good Management in Health Care, in: World Health Forum, Vol. 15, Number 4, pp. 348-352.

Schwefel, Detlef, and Emma Palazo (Eds.) (1995a): The Federation of the HAMIS Winners in the Philippines, Manila: HAMIS at the Department of Health, Popular Paper No. 3, 635 pages.

Detlef Schwefel, Emma Palazo (Eds.) (1995b): Policy Papers on Community Health Care Financing of the Federation of the HAMIS Winners, Manila: HAMIS at the Department of Health, Occasional Paper No. 14, 104 pages.

UNICEF (1990): Strategy for improved nutrition of children and women in developing countries, New York.

World Bank (1986): Poverty and Hunger: Issues and Options for Food Security in Developing Countries, Washington D.C.

14

Food Security and Nutritional Well-Being in the Context of Structural Poverty Alleviation

An example from an extremely deprived Andean region in Bolivia

Hans Schoeneberger

1 Introduction and conceptual framework

Part one of this book describes in detail current global trends and the scale of food and nutrition security and malnutrition. Also at a global level, the conceptual framework for analyzing nutrition insecurity—drafted by UNICEF (1992) and modified by the author (Figure 1)—identifies insufficient access to food, education, primary health care and basic sanitation as well as local resources and decision making as the underlying causes of widespread nutrition insecurity and malnutrition.

Figure 1

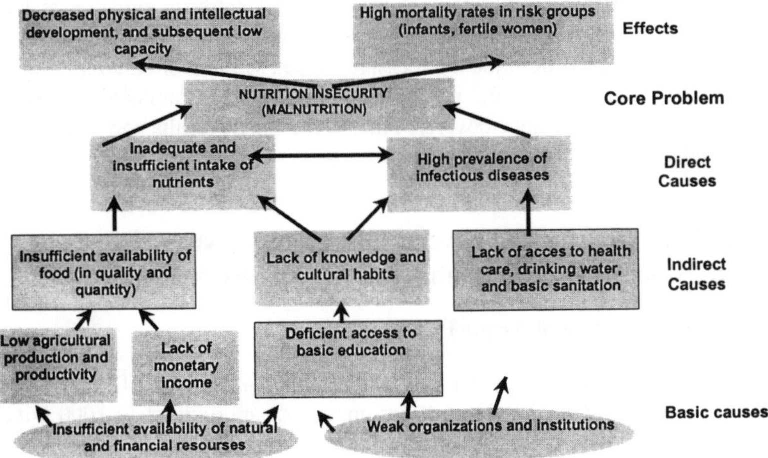

Recent concepts and definitions of poverty, though aware of the shortcomings of viewing this phenomenon in strictly economic terms by taking into account only per capita income or low purchasing power, define poverty as the inability to reach a minimum living standard, as the lack of access to basic human needs (UNDP 1997). As may be seen, this definition links poverty directly to food security and nutritional well-being as defined by the UNICEF model (see Figure 2).

Figure 2

It is important to emphasize that this concept of poverty is referred to as absolute poverty. The terms “basic needs” and “adequate way” do not imply comparison with other individuals or households. The needs are “basic” when they must be satisfied for the individual to achieve a physical development adequate to her/his genetic potential. In this sense, attempting to achieve nutritional well-being means reducing or alleviating poverty.

This article describes and analyzes the food and nutrition situation at local level in an extremely poor Andean region of Bolivia, employing the UNICEF model. It then goes on to describe the measures taken within a bi-national program to improve this situation and the parallel structural reforms implemented by the Bolivian government to reduce poverty. Finally, the initial results and conclusions of these joint efforts are presented.

2 Nutrition security and poverty alleviation in Arque Province, Department of Cochabamba, Bolivia—a case study

2.1 A brief description of Arque Province

Arque Province is located in the Andean region of the Department of Cochabamba (see Map 1), in the heart of Bolivia. It has an area of approximately 1000 km^2, a very rough terrain, and a variety of agricultural zones ranging in altitude from 2,400 to 4,500 meters above sea level.

Map 1: Arque Province's Location

Although the Arque region was in the past covered by forests, it is nowadays almost completely deforested, with the ensuing problems of high erosion levels and loss of fertile soils. Arque's nearly 20,000 inhabitants are Qeshwa speaking Indians of Aymara origin; about a third of the men and a sixth of the women also speak Spanish. Illiteracy prevails in 66% of the population older than 15, the women being those most affected with 83% illiteracy.

People in Arque live in some 180 small dispersed communities, which mostly do not have roads for vehicle access. Their economy is based on subsistence agriculture which, due to the small size of plots, low soil fertility and ancient, non-technical farming methods, allows peasants only in exceptional agricultural years to obtain marketable surpluses. The estimated present annual income from this agricultural activity is US $150 to $200 per person, an amount that generally does not fulfill the households' basic needs and forces household heads to migrate temporarily—mostly to the areas where coca leaf is produced—for supplementing their incomes.

The low productivity of Arque's fragile agro-ecosystems is also a direct consequence of the province's advanced ecologic deterioration, characterized by severe soil erosion, lack of vegetal coverage and degradation of pastures caused by overgrazing. Although the indigenous peasants have over centuries developed complex strategies for survival, they do not manage to maintain a sufficient, sustainable food production. The *Mapa de Pobreza* (Poverty Map) (MDH 1994) situates Arque Province as the second poorest province in Bolivia, itself considered to be the poorest country in Latin America.

This situation of extreme poverty mostly affects Arque women, since they are in charge not only of raising and caring for children, but also perform many tasks of agricultural and cattle-raising production, particularly during the long periods when men migrate.

2.2 Food and nutrition situation

In 1992, when program activities began in the region, the food and nutrition situation was dramatic. The following data are based on studies and assessments carried out by the Food and Nutrition Security Program for the Arque Province (PROSANA).

Anthropometric measurements of 1,048 pre-school children of the province revealed 56% prevalence of stunting and 2.5% of wasting (NCHS-Standard, cut-off point-2SD), indicating a situation of chronic malnutrition.

As Figure 3 shows, the height/age indicator z-score of children separates from the mean between the 6th and 24th month of their lives, settling on average below the second standard deviance, while the weight/age indicator remains close or even above the mean. Everything leads one to conclude that low height is a biological accommodation to a long term insufficient intake of nutrients.

Figure 3

Nutritional Situation of Pre-school Children
According to Different Indicators

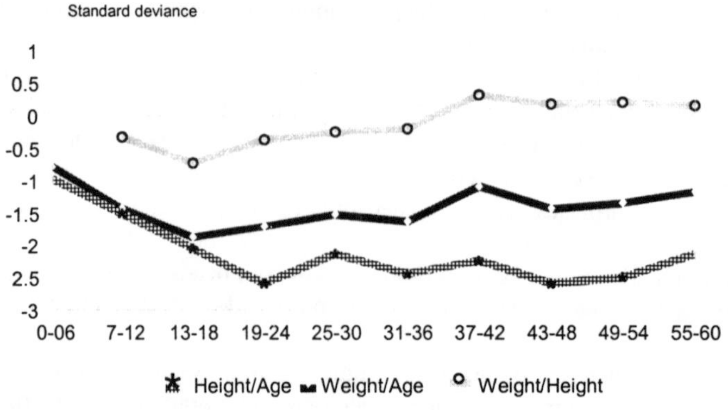

Sample: 1,048 children (< 5 years)

Another sign of the deficient nutritional situation is the high prevalence of anemia, which affects 45% of the women between the age of 15 and 45, as well as 74% of children under five years old.

In direct relationship to the region's malnutrition problems is child mortality. Unfortunately, it was not possible to calculate either the infantile or the child mortality rates, due to the lack of accurate data about the birth and death dates of every child born, and to the small number of children who are born in the province in one year. The project obtained from interviews with 500 women the Dead Children Ratio (DCR), this measurement being taken as an indirect indicator of infantile mortality.

From the total number of Children Born Alive (2,343) to the women interviewed who belonged to the age group 15 to 49 years up to the time of the study, 738 had died, which is 32%, showing a loss of one third of the children brought forth by these women during their reproductive age. From the total 738 dead children, 83% (612) died in their first year of life. Taking these 612 dead children as a new total (100%), we see that 64% of them (385) died in the first month of life. These ratios are well above national averages, according to INE 1990 (average: DCR = 0.17; DCR of women older than 45 years: 0.23), and clearly show the high mortality of children in Arque Province which, nutritional problems aside, is obviously related to an absence of pre- and post-natal care, deficient care as regards child delivery and low tetanus vaccination coverage.

Following the conceptual framework already illustrated in Figure 1, the direct causes of infantile malnutrition are the inadequate food intake and the high prevalence of diseases. Case studies in Arque of 14 pre-school children to determine the nutrient intake using 24-hours direct observation and measurement, showed an energy intake of only 50% of the recommended requirement for the respective age group, whereas protein intake covered 73% of the recommended amount. Even taking into account the low height and weight of the children, the energy intake covered only 60% of the recommendation per kilogram of bodyweight (Ibisch 1992).

While some nutritional habits of Arque people are highly positive, such as the prolonged breast-feeding (83% of women continue for more than 12 months) and the introduction of weaning foods at 5-6 months of age, other feeding habits have a bad effect on child health and nutrition: colostrum is frequently discarded and the nutrient density of the mostly liquid weaning food is extremely low (20 to 60 kilocalories per 100 grams). (For pre-school children the optimum energetic density of foods is 100 kcal per kg, considering the tiny stomach capacity they have.) This is aggravated by the quite low feeding frequency of these small children: more than half of them do not in fact ingest the four daily meals they need, considering the low density of nutrients (Gütschow 1996).

The typical diet of the Arque inhabitants is basically vegetarian, characterized by:

- High consumption of tubers (mainly potatoes), which along with cereals (wheat and corn) compose the basic diet;

- Low consumption of legumes (dried beans, lupins, etc.) in terms of quantity;
- Low consumption of fruits, as well as foods of animal origin;
- Low consumption of high energetic density foods (fat), in terms of quantity.

As to the prevalence of diseases directly affecting the increased utilization of nutrients, epidemiological data of 500 families showed a point prevalence of 30% of Acute Respiratory Infections (ARI) and 10% of Acute Diarrhea Diseases (ADD) among children. Considering that a temperature rise of one degree centigrade—a symptom that accompanies many respiratory infections—means a 10% increase in calorie consumption, one can assess the dramatic damage caused by these diseases in children who already have an extremely low intake of nutrients. Also, diarrheal diseases decrease the absorption of the few ingested nutrients.

Coming to the underlying causes of malnutrition, the low ingestion of nutrients is mainly related, apart from the feeding habits discussed above, to a scarcity of foods. According to case studies, food availability frequently does not fulfill household requirements, due to the limited areas of arable land owned by the peasants and to reduced production through lack of irrigation, agricultural inputs and the persistence of inadequate farming technologies.

As for the underlying causes of the health situation, one cannot but note the barely incipient medical service, where there is only one doctor and three assistant nurses for almost 20,000 people, and the insufficient access to drinking water and sanitation. In 1992, only 2.5% of the population received water through a drinking water system; there was no service for disposing of excrement.

The access of the Arque population to economic resources and to decision-making instances that could influence their province's development was also extremely limited. Municipal governments lacked democratic legitimacy, because they had not been elected by all the population that had the right to vote; the peasants' incomes barely reached US $1,200 per year, an amount that clearly does not allow for any development-oriented measure. Decisions concerning the few projects for the region, such as opening up a road or building a school, were taken far away at the departmental or national capital.

2.3 Measures for improving nutritional security and alleviating poverty

Facing the situation described above, the Bolivian government, with the technical and financial support of the German government through the German Agency of Technical Cooperation (GTZ), in 1991 introduced firm measures to uphold this region's development through a Food and Nutrition Security Project referred to as PROSANA.

Together with the local authorities and peasant representatives, the following objectives were defined:

- to enable peasant households to sustainably increase their food production;
- to improve the population's nutritional and health knowledge and attitudes;
- to create access for the population to primary health care and basic education;

- to strengthen peasant organizations and local state and non-governmental service institutions.

The project's time period of 10 years was subdivided into three phases:

In the first 3-year phase, called the Orientation Phase, the project staff, together with the peasant population, designed and tested in selected communities concepts, strategies and measures for food security in a process of action-research. This process allowed serving those specific needs felt and expressed by the people while, at the same time, with their participation, researching problems and potentials in peasant communities.

After the 3-year Orientation Phase the project already had a documented, validated multi-sectorial strategy which, based on extensive situation analysis, put forward a package of measures resting on four axes:

1. Increase in food production through small-scale irrigation, soil conservation, agroforestry, and integrated plant protection;
2. Implementation of a local primary health care system, combining traditional and modern medicine, and building up small drinking water systems;
3. Education and training in topics such as health, nutrition, agriculture and others, including a literacy campaign;
4. Strengthening of local governmental and non-governmental institutions to improve service delivery, and of peasant organizations to increase their self-help potential.

The second phase for Replication, also lasting three years, considered the massive implementation of the measures tested on the previous phase as its priority. For this replication the project supported the creation of an Interinstitutional Committee for Provincial Development, whose objective is to elaborate and coordinate a Development Plan and follow it up during its later implementation. Implementation proper is left in the charge of a network of governmental, non-governmental and peasant institutions and organizations.

This development process receives active support through the structural reforms implemented by the Bolivian government, aimed at actively increasing the people's participation and empowerment, particularly of marginalized groups, through:

- Decentralization of authority and jurisdiction for planning and implementing development processes at a municipal level;
- Transfer of financial resources to the municipalities for them to fulfill their newly assigned functions;
- Improvement of the quality of education and training.

In a third phase for Consolidation, the project aims to reinforce its achievements through strengthening the institutional network for development implementation, which is gradually taking complete responsibility for implementing the strategy.

2.4 Achievements

Probably the most important achievement of the project was the fact that the strategy for Nutritional Security and Poverty Alleviation became—through the participatory planning processes established by the democratic reforms in Bolivia—the official development strategy for all of the municipalities of Arque Province. This strategy was thereby institutionalized, embracing all social actors in its implementation.

The strategy is currently in full operation via an institutional network. First results show that it has been possible to date (1997) to improve the intermediate indicators of nutritional security in the various areas.

The recently built small-scale irrigation systems have allowed increased outputs of some crops—40% in average (see Figure 4). This crop increase results in an increased quantitative availability of foods: the 14 irrigation systems have improved the production of 287 ha for the benefit of some 700 households, which have on average increased by 25% their energetic availability (410 kcal daily per person).

Figure 4

Output Increase of Some Crops
trhough Irrigation in Arque Province

(ton/hectare)

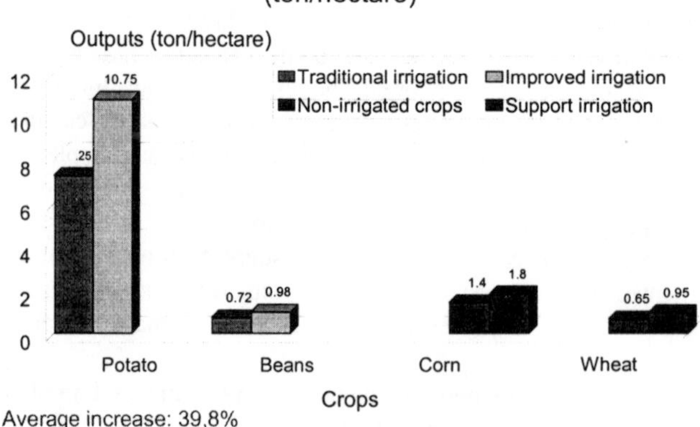

Note: These data area means for several years and diverse agroecological zones, based on technical estimates.

Regarding access to health services, a set of seven health centers was built and equipped and staffed by local indigenous personnel, that had previously been trained and qualified. The work of these semi-professionals was complemented by volunteer village health workers in each small community. Both the wider coverage and the improvement of the services' quality lead to an increase in service demand, from nearly 600 contacts with patients in 1991 to more than 5,000 in 1996. At the same time, the percentage of the population with access to drinking water rose from 2.5% to 10% after the small drinking water systems were built.

In the educational field, 16 teaching modules were elaborated for health, nutrition, agroecology, and other subjects. More than 500 local teachers and 550 peasants were trained accordingly, and now fulfill a disseminating role within their communities. School facilities were also supplemented with the construction and equipping of 22 schools in the rural area.

In the organizational field, a strengthening of peasant organizations was attained at micro-regional and provincial levels. Now, these organizations are actively engaged in planning and implementing projects and works in the municipalities, they also exercise a social control through Vigilance Committees established by a recent law.

No less important is the process of strengthening the recently created municipal governments which gained democratic legitimacy in the last general elections, thereby becoming responsible actors of local development. The continuous qualification courses for mayors, councillors, and technical personnel, along with on-going coaching, allow these authorities to gradually fulfill their new, complex roles within the framework of the decentralization process, with particular emphasis on implementing the food and nutrition security strategy.

The structural reforms also led to an epochal redistribution of financial resources in favor of poor municipalities. For the first time in Bolivia's history, 20% of the taxes collected are distributed to all municipalities at a national level on an equitable basis according to their population figures. This mechanism allows municipalities to rely on their own resources for implementing their development strategies. Figure 5 shows the increased financial support for the Arque Province's development.

Figure 5

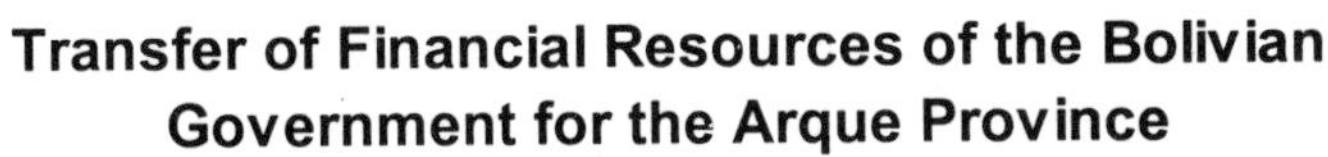

Transfer of Financial Resources of the Bolivian
Government for the Arque Province

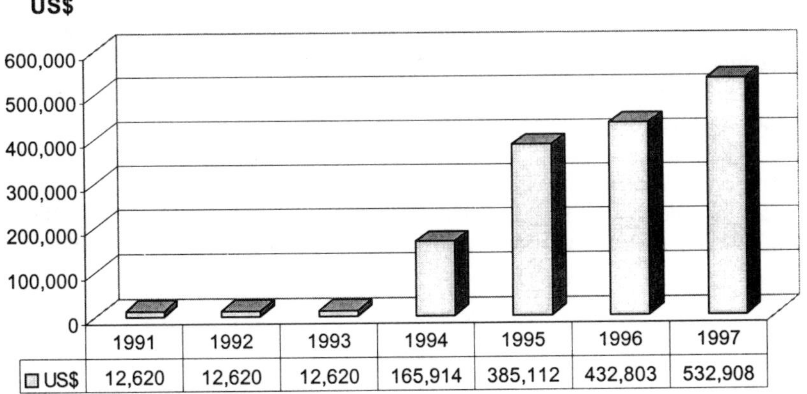

Despite the dramatic increase of the municipal budget, it is clear that these resources are still insufficient for multiplying and replicating the indispensable measures for achieving a sustainable development in a region marginalized and relegated to obscurity for centuries. This problem was also faced by the Bolivian government's policy which, jointly with the International Cooperation, made poverty alleviation its priority. Thus, the governmental Social and Productive Investment Funds assigned significant financial resources for projects that focused on the strategies mentioned above. Other bilateral and multilateral agencies also contribute directly to the strategy; Figure 6 illustrates the amazing increase of the resources which have become available.

Figure 6

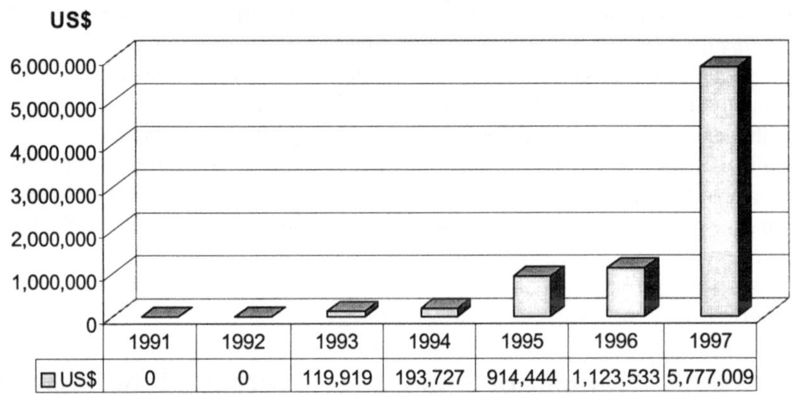

	1991	1992	1993	1994	1995	1996	1997
US$	0	0	119,919	193,727	914,444	1,123,533	5,777,009

It must be underscored that the achievements attained to date and the indicators mentioned represent only intermediate steps towards ultimately attaining nutritional well-being and reducing the Arque population's extreme poverty. Nevertheless, they show that the road chosen by the province is leading it closer to its main objectives.

It is also encouraging to observe that the interesting, positive experiences of Arque Province are being repeated in the neighboring provinces of Bolívar and Tapacarí and that the strategy's components and instruments for poverty alleviation have been incorporated into national and departmental norms, procedures, and plans.

3 Final Remarks

In regions of extreme poverty, the concept of food and nutrition security coincides with poverty alleviation strategies.

Every intervention focused on improving the nutritional situation requires previous participatory analysis and diagnosis of the related problems and causes. Only after this diagnosis, and with the involvement of the population affected, should specific activities be implemented.

Usually, a sustainable, sizable improvement of food and nutrition security is obtained only through the simultaneous combination of direct nutritional interventions and structural economic and socio-political reforms. Although nutritional interventions usually have direct and immediate effects, they frequently lack sustainability when they are not paralleled by structural processes focused on alleviating the underlying causes of poverty. On the other hand, there is no doubt that far-reaching economic and socio-political measures that promote a sustainable, equitable development take a long time to have any noticeable effects on the nutritional situation of a population, unless they are accompanied by directly nutrition-oriented activities.

References

Gütschow, Kathrin (1996): Die Einflußfaktoren des Ernährungszustandes von Kleinkindern als Indikatoren für Ernährungssicherheit. Giessen: Focus Verlag.

Ibisch, Claudia (1992): Ernährung in der Provinz Arque, Department Cochabamba, Bolivien, und die sie bedingenden Faktoren, Thesis, University of Bonn, Germany.

Ministerio de Desarrollo Humano (1994): Mapa de Pobreza, Una Guía para la Acción Social, La Paz, Bolivia.

UNDP (1997): Human Development Report, Oxford University Press, New York.

UNICEF (1990): Strategy for Improved Nutrition of Children and Women in Developing Countries. A UNICEF Policy Review, New York.

15

Conspicuous—and Thoughtless—Food Consumption. A Critical German View on Modern Eating Habits

Elisabeth Meyer-Renschhausen

1 Introduction

Since 1989 McDonald's and other fast food restaurants have been springing up in Berlin and eastern Germany at an increasingly rapid rate. The American sociologist George Ritzer has spoken of a "McDonaldisation" of the world. What he means is a radical process in which people voluntarily give up their kitchens and communal meals without any personal advantage, and are prepared to stand in line for bad food and consume it surrounded by mountains of trash. Snacks, an endless chain of quick bites, are increasingly replacing the meal, that social event at an appointed time around which the rhythms of work were organized in peasant and other traditional societies. The kitchen and the communal meal are disappearing.

Since the triumph of monocausal thinking with Descartes and particularly the narrow market orientation ushered in by Adam Smith, the modern world-view has lost sight of those realms of human everyday life and physical needs that have, since the eighteenth century, been connoted once and for all as female. In the mid-nineteenth century, with the emergence of the new science of economics, women's unpaid work in the household was dislodged from public consciousness (Duden and Hausen 1978). From that time forward, the work devoted to maintaining everyday life has been undervalued and forgotten, particularly those tasks which were regarded as female in traditional societies.

This process went hand in hand with a structurally similar disrespect for agricultural work, which is expressed in the unjustly low prices paid for agricultural goods, in relation to the amount of labor required to produce them.

Historically, both phenomena taken together promoted the development of quite novel ecological problems, which are beginning to whittle away at our very substance. The corporeality suppressed along with the female and peasant subsistance economies is taking its revenge in the form of new illnesses: diabetes, obesity, permanent fatigue, addictions, cancer, allergies and ever-new immune deficiency diseases, along with new phenomena of physical and mental backwardness, melancholy and rage. It would be no exaggeration to say that the ecological problems are, in a sense, imperiling the very foundations of democracy in our societies.

Recent nutritional research has shown that the older dietary systems of both "primitive" and "civilized" peoples were astonishingly well adapted, in their traditions and eating habits, to their respective environments (Maurizio 1927, Spittler 1987, 1993). For centuries, coarsely ground cereal porridges, coarse-grain bread, sour milk products and fermented cabbage, legumes, bacon and small beer provided Europeans with a physiologically rather balanced diet (Gamerith 1956). With the introduction of industrially produced luxury, with sugar, coffee, white flour, cheap spirits and more highly alcoholic lager beer, a systematic knowledge of nutrition should have replaced the lost dietary customs, but it is still not taught in the schools even today (Mintz 1986).

It is precisely because of this ignorance about nutrition, war-related and culture-specific dietary deficiencies and misapprehensions in the third, fourth or even sixth generation, along with a lack of satisfaction owing to the disappearance of relaxed meals and of foods with characteristic flavors, and the prevalence of full-time employment outside of the home, that all of us now have to struggle with various addiction problems. We fluctuate between childish "needs" to snack and be fed and manic phases of hunger (Kleinspehn 1987). As for the ritual of a communal meal with friends and family members, we, above all in northern Germany, claim to have no time for it. The long commutes in a society which obliges all of its members to perform a "normal workday" does its part as well. Nowadays we find ourselves in an almost permanent state of panic, in the hectic pursuit of so-called "careers" and the restless consumerism that this produces (Sloterdijk 1990).

This situation is today exacerbated by the permanent stress caused by the constant assault of "modernizing" industry on a humane way of life. The question is: how are we to deal with these problem foods? After all, researchers believe that 80-90% of cancer cases, which have risen sharply here since 1945, are environmentally related (Koch et al. 1986: 137). The current international anti-smoking campaign serves particularly to distract us from the carcinogenic potentials of conventionally grown foods, along with our constant poisoning by automobile exhaust.

So what can we still eat? In the face of these endless problems, what is a proper way of life? Fixed habits, as "institutions" (Arnold Gehlen) that make life simpler, were already steadily disappearing among previous generations, along with traditions and customs and religious guidelines for a wholesome good life.

Around the end of the nineteenth century, the resulting lack of orientation, lost "meaning of life", fear of pauperization and anger of the victims of capitalist dominance led to a virtually enlightened enthusiasm for hygiene. Our mothers began to scrub their kitchens in such a cleaning frenzy that we hate to cook. In today's kitchens—rendered blindingly white in the effort to achieve absolute antisepsis—we do nothing but read calorie tables and vitamin recommendations from experts, to whom we have entrusted our physical weal and woe.

By the end of the last century, the first international women's movement already saw the complete dominance of the masculine view of society as unbearable and proclaimed "feminine culture" and "organized motherhood", which would be just to the poor and downtrodden, to women, children and the private individual more generally, as the alternative (Meyer-Renschhausen 1989, Taylor 1990). The social reforms that resulted are being dismantled today.

In the face of general unemployment, the continued dominance of a "masculine" ideology of paid work represents an obviously outdated eight-hour-day model. A kind of blind trust in the so-called "self-regulating powers of the market" on the part of politicians supports land speculation and a kind of "economic growth" to which our self-determination is increasingly being sacrificed. We are constantly given advice by scientists in white coats, experts with an astoundingly unreflective faith in the truth of the results of their research.

These ways of thinking and this kind of perpetual having one's mind made up for one has so robbed us of any desire to act on our own that, resigned, impatient and against our better judgment, we buy prepared foods at the supermarket. Children and adolescents troop daily to McDonald's because it is "cool", although they know that the hamburgers there are unhealthy and full of fat. Instead of eating with one another, of celebrating meals, eating has become a joyless solitary process akin to the feeding in animal "production".

2 Too many cooks spoil the broth

Thus, we nowadays let the many cooks employed in the laboratories of the worldwide "food industry" do the cooking for us. There, the natural foods of all countries are lovelessly manipulated and artificially reconstituted in the farthest-flung corners of the globe. The brutal competition among the gigantic multinational corperation of the "life-industry", bestows upon us foods which, indeed, have been made to keep during endless transport and storage periods, but which contain so many different preservatives, pesticide residues and illegal additives that ever-increasing numbers of people suffer from cancer, allergies, and chronic fatigue. Not only pregnant women, even healthy people should be urgently warned against consuming them. It should hardly surprise us if the minister of health were one day to require that the warning: "Eating this food is hazardous to your health" be added to certain advertisements.

We ingest two kilos of leavening agents per year if we eat only normal store-bought bread. A Frenchman or woman unwittingly consumes one and a half kilos of pesticides when he or she eats conventionally grown food. Ninety-four percent of normal commercial foods contain usually minute amounts of pesticide residues. Ninety percent of all the heavy metals and poisons that are found in the human body stem from foods, including about three-quarters of the brain-damaging lead that we ingest. Forty percent of the meat sold in supermarket chains has passed the expiration date and is already in the process of decomposition. Cheap orange juice tastes of the mouldy oranges that were not sorted out during the pressing and thickening processes. After consuming a harmless-looking fish sandwich we may experience the kind of massive dizziness that accompanies medium-grade lead or mercury poisoning (Tietze 1978).

Today, humans, animals and the environment are being subjected to chemical bombardment, mainly via the food industry and agriculture, of over 50,000 applied chemicals, 1,500 pesticides, 4,000 drugs, 2,500 approved food additives and 3,000 approved preservatives. In Germany alone 30,000 tons of pesticides are sold every year, including herbicides, fungicides and insecticides. In at least 10% of cases, the concentration of pesticides in the groundwater exceeds values considered to be harmless (Umweltbundesamt 1997: 124), to which the fertilizers that are introduced into the soil in not insignificant amounts must be added. An excess of nitrates in greenhouse lettuce makes it a doubtful pleasure which can promote stomach cancer (Koch et al. 1986: 125 f.).

In the face of this drug cocktail, the significance of the laws on "threshold value" with which legislators have attempted to minimize the amount of undesirable residues in food, appears dubious. Any amount of poison, however small, affects the body, changes it, even if there is no immediately visible reaction. Suddenly and unpredictably, a critical point is reached: the synergetic result is that the body, which has hitherto tolerated certain pesticide residues "administered" previously, ceases to do so when these occur in combination with other pesticides, fertilizers or preservatives and other food "additives". When repeatedly ingested in combination, various pesticides, nitrates, preservatives, additives and artificial flavors can cause the body to become polluted like an overfertilized lake. People no longer feel well, and suffer from acne, rashes, neurodermatitis and other allergies, they become weak and nervous, cannot sleep and have a compromised immune system, rendering them susceptible to infection. Phosphates enter the human body as fertilizer residues from plant and animal "production". In conventionally produced milk, phosphates are usually present in high amounts, taken up by the cow through its well-fertilized feed. In addition, orthophosphates are added to the milk in order to stabilize it during heating, a process which facilitates cheese production (Lücke 1985: 70). In excessive doses, phosphates increase psychomotor functions, making for fidgety children and nervous adults.

In addition, phosphates cause the body to lose calcium. Thus, the desired effect of calcium in milk, to help build children's bones, is no longer guaranteed. And women who drink milk during menopause in order to prevent osteoporosis (i.e., also a loss of calcium in the bones) are in danger of developing osteoporosis precisely by drinking conventional commercial milk. Only unprocessed milk from cows allowed to graze freely in unfertilized fields can combat this problem.

Ten percent of Americans are considered to be permanently ill and unfit to work. Many illnesses which today are considered to be psychosomatic in origin might possibly be traced back to poisons in our food. It is not inconceivable that a good proportion of today's alcoholics and drug addicts are also victims of hidden food "additives" (Randolph and Moss 1980). We might begin to ask ourselves whether one of the factors that makes today's urban youth so aggressive is a constant low-level poisoning via their normal "food consumption" (see Cremer 1980). In experiments with rats, those who had been poisoned with insecticides and other pesticides not only developed all sorts of illnesses, visual impairments and exhaustion but also responded with a heightened degree of irritability and excitability (Ernst et al. 1986: 159 ff.). Children who have ingested greater than usual amounts of lead through leafy vegetables and canned foods have been shown in experiments to be either hyperactive or less capable than normal, as well as being impulsive and aggressive. After medicines to rid their bodies of lead were administered they became somewhat calmer, but continued to have problems in school.[1]

In 1988, annual per capita meat consumption in Germany reached an all-time high of 70 kilos, and it has not decreased significantly since then (Ernährungsbericht 1988). In the meantime it has become known that the not unproblematic additives used in market-oriented "animal and plant production" are present in particularly massive amounts in meat thanks to the cumulative effects of the food chain. Human beings thus become the "permanent waste disposal site" for the residues of fertilizers, herbicides and pollution which can no longer be catabolized by the body. And on top of that comes the illegal use of additives by farmers: artificial sex hormones, such as the estrogen drug DES, which is intended to fatten cows more quickly, can have carcinogenic effects in pregnant women. It frequently causes miscarriages and stillbirths as well as reproductive tract cancer and later infertility in children. The commercial aspect takes precedence over everything else; hardly any consideration is spared for the consumer. Eleven micrograms of DES, the equivalent of 11 birth-control pills, have occasionally been found in a single jar of baby food. Artificial hormones, such as DES, cannot be catabolized by the body and can cause cancer (Kapfesberger and Pollmer 1992: 35).

3 "Cannibals, don't eat Germans!"

"Cannibals, don't eat Germans!", a Berlin newspapers headlined some years ago, and indeed, the DDT we consumed in our youth until it was banned will never leave us, the body is unable to discharge it (Tietze 1978: 87, 90 ff.). Legal and also illegal drugs are administered to cattle, pigs and poultry as part of meat production. Cattle are legally given antibiotics usually used to guard against infectious disease in order to make them metabolize feed more efficiently. Animals being prepared for slaughter also receive anabolic steroids, i.e., sex hormones produced naturally or by genetic technology, so that they grow 20% faster than normal. The animals are provided with thyreostatics that reduce the activity of the thyroid gland, thus increasing the fluid in the muscle tissue and making steaks look "nice and juicy." Animals are also given lung medications to make them produce more protein and less fat.

Thirty percent of global grain production currently goes to animal husbandry in the countries of the North, and is thus unavailable to the starving people of the South. The unchecked use of pesticides, particularly insecticides, has produced

1 According to studies by the American Academy of Sciences, quoted by Kapfelsberger and Pollmer 1992: 158.

varying degrees of poisoning among the rural laborers and populations of the South (Pestizid-Aktions-Netzwerk 1991).

But the large-scale meat producers of the North are dependent upon the import of feed from the Third World. This now normal mass production of meat represents a general attack on the health of consumers, since feed from the Third World brings pesticides such as DDT, which have long been banned in the West, back to our dining tables. The imported concentrated feedstuffs, which have long ship journeys and storage periods behind them, are usually full of molds, and such aflatoxins are known to be carcinogenic for human beings. All of these practices are perfectly legal and amount to the maintenance of animals under inhumane conditions; in tiny cages and sheds they suffer from inadequate exercise and the immense stress of living crowded together with too many others. The animals taken to slaughter from such "mass production centers" are sad, overfat, nervous and hypersensitive. They are given psychiatric drugs to prevent premature death from stress on the way to the slaughterhouse. After eating such meat human beings become tranquilized, tired and often slightly depressed, like the animals themselves. The tranquilizers given to the animals, often veritable cocktails of different substances, such as chlorpromazine, which is used in psychiatry, can cause liver damage, changes in the red blood cells, bone marrow damage and Parkinson's Disease (Schäfer 1993: 109). Thus the sad state of the animals we eat can make us, too, feel melancholy and resigned.

Meat normally becomes grey and green quite quickly after slaughter. In earlier times the meat of pigs slaughtered in the autumn was salted or cold smoked, thereby retaining some of its red color. Nowadays meat is preserved and kept red or pink by the addition of nitrates and nitrites. In the human body harmless nitrate can, when other proteins such as cheese enter the stomach at the same time, produce nitrite and then nitrosamine, compounds that do not occur in nature and which, as we have known since 1956, can lead to liver cancer (Kapfelsberger and Pollmer 1992: 104).

When the groundwater was found to contain so much nitrate from fertilizers that animal "production" was affected, research finally began on this subject. The now common practice of the quick hot-smoking of meat releases polycyclical aromatic hydrocarbons, which are referred to on cigarette packages as "tar." These substances include benzypyrene, which is also suspected of causing cancer. In traditional society meat, consumed in moderate amounts, represented little danger to the eater, thanks to careful preservation methods. In contrast, the large amounts of meat, with its chemical additives, which consumers eat today may, thanks to modern production methods, certainly be considered a health hazard. To be sure, some substances are now banned or restricted in use, but this has little effect. Just as European firms unscrupulously continue to export long-banned poisons such as E 605 or DDT to the Third World, and allow them to be applied there without education about the dangers, European "meat producers" continue to use many prohibited antibiotics, artificial hormones and drug cocktails under the extreme pressure of artificially low prices and international competition. Understaffed and underfunded government food inspection departments intervene too late and much too seldom.

And people who try to bring light into this area do so at their own peril. The Belgian veterinarian Karel van Noppen, who worked for the Veterinary Inspection Institute of the Belgian Ministry of Health and sought to prevent the use of illegal drugs, was shot in broad daylight, apparently at the behest of the illegal drug rings.

Black marketeers are well-informed about the limitations of food inspectors' drug testing methods and are thus always coming up with new tricks for circumventing surveillance. It has also been reported that the pharmaceutical companies include these illegally sold products in their calculations (Winkler 1996: 23). This life-threatening black market in carcinogenic hormones reminds us of the problems of a market economy. Even if the market is a "regulator" without which our complicated social system could not exist, the history of food markets in particular shows that they were always and everywhere subject to strict controls. The market overseers in medieval towns were unrelenting in their insistence on the strict observence of weights and measures. Throughout European history millers and bakers were constantly being suspected of stretching flour with illegal additives (such as sawdust) or cheating their customers in regard to weight, and were thus everywhere subject to official surveillance. The French Revolution of 1789 was also a result of frequent bread riots, in which the poor protested against the hoarding of and speculation with grain because they could not pay the inflated bread prices. Fine white flour without the germ, which is not very nutritious, became so popular in France and England around the time of the Revolution in part because it was more difficult to introduce unwanted additives into it without being detected.

4 The mad marketing of animal bone meal

On 30 March 1996, the weekend before Easter, the German minister of agriculture had to cut short a visit to South America in order to take measures to confront the British beef scandal. The British government had announced that human beings could contract bovine spongiform encephalopathy, popularly known as BSE or "mad cow disease." At the end of March, no one in the world wanted to buy or eat British beef (Sentker 1996). German butcher shops complained of a 50% drop in beef sales (Die Tageszeitung: 29 March 1996). The British meat industry, fighting to win customer confidence, called for the destruction of the entire stock of 12 million British cattle, much to the dismay of British farmers, since they could not hope for appropriate compensation from their own government or the European Union (The Times: 28th of March 1996).

Scientists in Edinburgh had announced that young people were dying after a period of illness twice as long as that considered typical (13 months) for the similar Creutzfeld-Jakob disease (CJD). After depression and fits of rage, the patients became paralyzed and finally fell into madness and coma. Autopsies revealed not only a spongy brain structure, but also protein deposits (plaques) that are rare in classic cases of Creutzfeld-Jakob disease, but typical of the sheep disease scrapie and of BSE. Protein structures that were smaller than the viruses found previously appear to have lodged in proteins occurring naturally in the body and, like viruses, to have reprogrammed them to develop in adverse ways. The system began to "run amok", in a manner vaguely similar to cancer, without any clear explanation (Der Stern: 28th of March 1996).

Events as they unfolded revealed that all sorts of dissidents within the scientific establishment had already developed theories on mad cow disease, but that they had been systematically silenced. For many years, the organic farmer Mark Purdey had been saying that BSE among British cattle was not solely the result of feeding them sheep's meal. More importantly, Great Britain had engaged in a more radical program than other European countries for eradicating the sheep nostril fly, which, in his view, had meant an increasing poisoning of cattle with organophosphates. These toxic pesticides, he claimed, triggered the transformation of a latent cattle disease into an acute one (Kröning 1996).

This might explain why BSE cases also appeared in Switzerland, where phosphoric acid esters, e.g., in the form of E 605, are still deployed against microorganisms. Although degradable, they are highly toxic, attacking the central nervous system in particular (Walletscheck and Graw 1995). Deployed in agriculture as an allegedly decomposible means of internal pest control, phosphoric acid esters have produced extremely poisonous effects particularly in persons who eat mainly fruits and vegetables (Ernst et al. 1986).

It is more likely that a number of different factors come together here. Cattle whose bodies have been weakened by the intake of poisonous substances in agriculture are probably more susceptible to BSE than other animals. The pathogene has not yet been discovered. All we know is that very similar brain diseases have been detected in different species of animals, and that different species can infect each other. Since 1967, in North American sheep-growing regions, even wild deer have been found to have died from a disease very similar to scrapie. A scientist found through experiments on apes that spongiform diseases among human beings as well as scrapie could be infectious to other species (Köster-Lösche 1995: 24, 28).

American scientists who injected hamsters with white blood cells from healthy human beings found that this caused spongiform brain disease. Anthroposophists would probably say that this result shows that the diseased individuals had come into contact with too many alien protein molecules, which they could not catabolize because they had entered their bloodstreams.

5 Uncritical science and the politics of appeasement

The majority of scientists today believe that the pathogene may simply be infectious proteins: prions. "According to the prion hypothesis, the prion succeeds, as soon as it has penetrated a healthy nerve cell in the brain, in [starting] the construction of wrongly folded" proteins. This thesis represents a serious challenge to received medical wisdom, which has previously recognized bacteria and viruses as practically the only agents of infection. As the veterinarian Kari Köster-Lösche warns, the fact that the prion theory is now preferred to the virus theory may simply be the result of funding considerations. Additions to the existing research on viruses are less likely to win Nobel Prizes and thus more research funding tends to flow into new fields. In addition, the prevailing legal situation means that, unlike with the prion hypothesis, the mere suspicion of a viral infection inspires a rapid response from government (Köster-Lösche 1995: 53).

What is particularly terrifying is the extent to which, even at the government level, the decisions being made still favor a market-oriented food industry, rather than paying serious attention to the many warnings about dangers to consumers. An anonymous super-regional and global market, which is permitted, through advertising, to disseminate misleading or actively false information or at least to manipulate the public, is apparently in danger of sacrificing the health of all consumers to short-term sales. This cannot be in anyone's long-term interest. A social system that sacrifices the physical well-being of its citizens to commercial interests will, in the long run, destroy itself.

The most common vehicle of misinformation nowadays is advertising, which likes to operate with phrases such as "medical research shows ..." Whatever "research shows" is considered sacrosanct. The necessary monocausality of such results, which is what characterizes science as a process dependent upon reductions, is forgotten. That "scientific facts" can always be "invented," as the physician Ludwik Fleck showed in the 1930s, is ignored, as is the circumstance that today's food science derives from the narrowly market-oriented realm of "animal and plant production."

Today, if genetically manipulated foodstuffs are to be pushed through against the opposition of 80-90% of consumers, government and the scientific community will be acting as the willing servants of the large corporations—at best. If what is really at stake here is not in fact genetic technology at all, but rather the ability to patent natural resources—i.e., plants (the neem tree) and animals (genetically engineered mice)—this is both irresponsible and unscrupulous towards the poor of this world. The transformation of natural resources such as trees and their fruits into private property of giant corporations by means of genetic research and subsequent patenting is a life-threatening dispropriation of such groups as the rural population of India, who are dependent on the fruit of the neem tree as a source of food in times of crisis. As the poor can often not afford to buy enough food, they are forced to go hungry if they are excluded from food by new patents. When an industry seeks, with the aid of science, to seize power for itself in order to dictate what people eat against their will, it is high time that we warned of a new totalitarianism, a dictatorship of multinational industrial corporations.

It is indeed science that has led to an evergrowing alienation of people from the food we eat. The protein theory was proposed by Justus von Liebig in 1830, and the first agricultural research station was set up in 1851. With the advent of mineral fertilizers, the new discipline of nutritional physiology arose in medicine, based on developments in veterinary medicine. Beginning with Liebig's meat extract, it intensified the industrialization of food culture (Teuteberg 1990). The rationalization of military provisions facilitated the invention of prepared foods and also the mass cattle production which now prevails, for example in Argentina and Brazil, to the detriment of local landless peasants.

The food sciences, which developed later, were only renamed ecotrophology a few years ago. Only very recently, and by no means everywhere, has this field of research begun—in the name of cutting healthcare costs—to study the ecological and health consequences of current dietary and food production habits. This research goes beyond questions of the problematic overuse of fertilizers and food additives.

6 The burden of the modern luxuries market

The problems of modern dietary habits began with the modern era, with the emergence of the purely market-oriented large-scale production of sugar, coffee and tea on plantations using slave labor. Later, they were exacerbated by the industrial production of bleached white flour, spirits and meat. Sixty percent of Germans today weigh more than the "ideal weight" that was suggested by American life insurance companies in the 1930s. If we take into account that people with a few extra pounds tend to live longer than others, then probably about 50% are truly overweight. The tastelessness of industrially produced foodstuffs may well be leading people to seek satisfaction in eating more. The result, however, is the opposite—too much of a good thing is making us sick. Many of us have become accustomed to considering what used to be a holiday meal—several courses and meat everyday—as a necessity. Even in the Middle Ages, though, the prosperous knew that roast meat and too much wine every day could be deleterious to their health. One probably needs a good deal of cold-pressed olive oil and salad in order to eat "the king's white bread" (baguettes) everyday without the permanent constipation that afflicts up to 60% of Germans, according to the authoritative nutrition report. White bread, or bleached white flour, lacks the aleuron, the vitamin-B and mineral-rich protein layer necessary for digestion which, because it is highly perishable, is generally removed along with the bran.

Nowadays we are increasingly purchasing packaged foods in the supermarket with fancy names and think we have to hide our secret attachment to plain old-fashioned dishes. When we invite someone to dinner, we believe we have to put together some elaborate meal involving expensive cuts of meat and heavy wines. We feel an obligation to luxury and want to make sure everyone knows that we live well. We are caught up in a culture of prestige where appearance, simulation and advertising have put our senses and their capacity to distinguish between different flavors out of commission. It is no wonder that so much pretense has become indigestible, and that many young girls increasingly find vomiting to be the best response.

This development is the result of the increasingly profane nature of our eating habits. In the course of the nineteenth century, "sacred" bread and porridge were permanently replaced by the elaborate Victorian meal. The middle classes, having become involved in the exercise of power, sought symbolic ways of expressing this. Restaurant culture, which developed during and after the French Revolution, was a demonstrative culture derived from courtly custom, in which men got together to display their power and wealth (Meyer-Renschhausen 1990: 127-140). For this reason the heavy roasted meats and rich wines, along with exotic vegetables and fruits from distant lands, that recalled baroque royal feasting were an important part of this culinary culture. What these men forgot was that constant feasts and gorging were unhealthy even for the most powerful ruler, unless he intended to go in for daily "purging" (enemas) like the unfortunate Louis XIV.

The problems began with sugar, which, thanks to colonialism in Central America, and with the help of slave labor, was the first foodstuff to be produced in large quantities for the expanding European market on the eve of industrialization. (Previously honey and dried fruits had been used as sweeteners.) The manner of production with the help of slaves already contained the seeds of punishment for its consumers. First the ladies and gentlemen of the court ruined their teeth by eating sugar. At the English court in the eighteenth century, decaying brown teeth were the norm, even for the queen. In early modern Europe, sugar was thus the first attribute of a new more splendid way of life. Sweet puddings and cakes grew in popularity and helped, together with the enjoyment of meat, to make kings stout, gouty and short of breath (Mintz 1986).

Refined industrial sugar, which has been produced on a larger scale since 1800, together with large quantities of meat and fat, makes people obese because it speeds up the digestive process to such an extent that not everything can be utilized but is instead stored as fat. Sugar, particularly a simple sugar like glucose, enters the bloodstream almost immediately. A balanced blood sugar level is the necessary precondition for stamina. An elevated blood sugar level has an invigorating effect. It causes more rapid digestion. This, however, leads to higher vitamin B requirements, since thiamine is necessary for digestion. Once it is used up, the blood sugar level drops with the metabolism. One becomes tired and feels the need for more quickly digestible food, and develops a need for sweets. This is particularly the case with children, all of whose metabolic processes are more rapid.Theoretically, this need for sweets could be fulfilled by carbohydrates from porridge, bread, legumes, roots and vegetables. But refined sugar acts more quickly than the old sweet porridges made of grains; sugar enters the bloodstream more rapidly. As soon as people became accustomed to refined sugar they tended to prefer it. Thus, people nowadays are more or less dependent on sugar.

Vitamin B does not act on its own. In order to digest carbohydrates, we need the insulin produced by the pancreas. If the pancreas is constantly required to produce higher levels of insulin, it may become overtaxed and slow down. People so affected always feel thirsty, since fluids stimulate circulation and thus metabolic processes and also insulin production. Later the pancreas gives up altogether, and one develops diabetes, a typical disease of the modern age (Liehr 1996: 112 ff.).

The first coffeehoue was founded in England in 1620. Coffee, and later tea, became the drinks of the new middle-class public sphere. Only with the addition of sugar was the bitter coffee drinkable in large quantities. In northern Europe, coffee had become popular even in the countryside by the eighteenth century, since farmers too had learned to appreciate coffee and cake as something to serve visitors. Frederick II of Prussia tried to ban it for reasons of taxation policy, but to no avail: coffee had become a symbol of the new age. In the opinion of the historian Jules Michelet, coffee, which had a rather more enlivening effect than the old popular drink, small beer, represented a new era, in which people expected to think for themselves and to participate in politics (Schivelbusch 1983).

Coffee also had its disadvantages, for its triumph meant that in the course of the nineteenth century, morning gruel or porridge was displaced among both urban workers and, ultimately, also peasants by—to put it bluntly—drugs. Coffee and sugar were the first stimulants and people became addicted to them. Coffee acts on the heart, speeds up the pulse and stimulates the circulatory system. It sparks the production of adrenaline, which enables human beings to perform astounding physical feats in dangerous situations. However, an elevated adrenaline level which (for example, when driving) is not worked off by physical activity, hinders complete digestion and is probably the most important cause of the high cholesterol levels common today among middle-aged men (Borges 1993).

With the disappearance of the morning bowl of porridge, people began to consume more cakes and, later, bread and jam at breakfast, a trend that prevailed from Scandinavia to Italy. When young rural women were pushed into factory work, which occurred in the Zurich uplands as early as the late eighteenth century, gruel, soups, polenta and cooked cereals made of oats, buckwheat or millet disappeared from the breakfast table. The old naturally sweet porridge, which we now know mainly from fairy tales, disappeared (Meyer-Renschhausen 1991: 95-120).

Around 1800 bakers began producing larger quantities of white breads and cakes, which was made possible by the availability of cheap refined sugar and new milling processes. But along with the aleuron layer, white bread also lost protein and a number of minerals that the old wholemeal breads contained and which made them aromatic. White flour without the germ is also lacking in roughage. Thus some 60% of the population is now told to eat a little cup of wheat bran everyday as a nutritional supplement. In the old days, the bran was fed only to cattle.

A new method of milling grain, which was invented in 1770 and became widespread around 1820, made it possible to remove the entire germ layer, the aleuron stratum, from the grain. This made the flour finer, whiter, and above all easier to store for long periods. Without the highly perishable protein layer, flour can be kept "indefinitely". More coarsely ground flour, which still contains the vitamin-rich aleuron stratum, cannot be kept for long because of the protein content of this germ layer. Protein is highly perishable. In contrast to coarse groats, which, for example in combination with bacon or sour milk, represents a complete food, white bread is not nutritionally complete. It must be supplemented by food containing protein and minerals. Bleached white flour is also not as sweet as the old porridges. If they were made of whole grain groats, a gentle saccharification process began after drying in the oven or long cooking in oven or pan, giving the porridge a natural sweetness (Gamerith 1956).

In the old society of peasant Europe, bacon was the main source of fat. As late as the 1950s, for the farmers of the village of Atany near Budapest, "good food", as the most important element of the good life, meant bacon, bread and wine (Fèl and Hofer 1972). This changed with urbanization, however. In the nineteenth century it became common throughout society to eat larger amounts of meat, which in the twentieth century came to be a symbolic replacement for workers for the independent farm life they had given up. Meat makes the man, meat consumption was a symbol of dominance and recalled "Adam the hunter." England, the first capitalist nation, had already produced a veritable cult of meat in the seventeenth and eighteenth centuries and used the lands of the colonized Scots and Irish in particular in order to satisfy its growing need for meat before moving on to the North American prairies as cattle grazing land (Fiddes 1993).

Nineteenth century middle-class men, in particular, and many of the well-to-do in the twentieth century, developed something like an addiction to meat, and insisted on their right to a daily steak, regardless of the destructive effects of such customs on the global ecosystem and on their own health (gout, cancer, etc.).

7 New life styles: "alternative" eating habits

With its ruthless exploitation of distant lands, unscrupulous use of slave labor, expulsion of rural folk from the land, and the death of the small farm, modern society has set in motion a luxuries industry whose deleterious effects endanger our health today. Glycol-tainted wines, noodle scandals, salmonella outbreaks and genetically manipulated tomatoes: suspect foods have brought about a process of reflection about the "female sides" of life, and returned the significance of everyday life and the housework and subsistence activities that make it possible to public consciousness. An alternative movement arose in the 1970s as a culture opposing the politics of "everything is for sale".

This "silent revolution" (Inglehart 1977) even engendered a political party—the Greens—in West Germany around 1980; it has received over 30% of the vote in some inner-city areas of Berlin (Kreuzberg, Schöneberg). Many younger people are organized in ecological associations as Friends of the Earth (BUND in Germany) and local environmental initiatives. Increasing numbers of young people are taking an interest in their own daily diet, which they regard as a central component of the environmental question. The strict and principled vegetarianism of some 15-20-year olds appears intensely aggressive to some of us older people, and is the exact opposite of the devil-may-care attitude which even verbally "green" "1968er" teachers and mothers have towards their daily food. Despite the ritualized anti-ritualism of their "wild" but still festive communal dinners, the generation of protesting students leant a new significance to the celebration of their own way of life in a group of like-minded people.

Instead of the acceptance of "excess" which is our normal state nowadays, the new "alternative" people are trying to return to a way of living with a different sense of time, one that acknowledges the interdependence of people and "things" and moves through everyday life with peasant composure, as it were (Sloterdijk 1990). Instead of orienting themselves towards careers and profit, the protagonists of "alternative culture" seek to rediscover the moment and to heal themselves through a new dedication to enjoyment. But it is not only the restoration of pleasure that is at stake here; it is also a question of the "meaning of life" (Van Otterloo 1993). Even if our "daily bread" has irrevocably lost its sacredness, the consumption of organic bread is connected with the "global resistance" to the pull of the worldwide market. Buying wholemeal bread has thus become a symbol of the "new internationalism" of the Kreuzberg "autonomous" Left, and, not unjustifiably, recalls Immanuel Kant's idea of cosmopolitanism. Thus, daily consumption has once again become "charged" and significant: "politically correct shopping" restores a little bit of the lost "meaning of life" with every alternative cheese sandwich—a meaning completely absent from the sandwich as pure commodity. As in the world of mothers and children, each everyday act in the "alternative scenes" regains its importance. Each bowl of modern muesli rehabilitates the peasant porridge or gruel, and the antique and medieval discourse on diet, just as the turn-of-the-century life-reformers had done—Max Bircher-Benner's muesli, John F. Kellogg's corn flakes, and Werner Kollath's oat flakes (Wirz 1993).

Communities and communes which radically relive the old "good life", such as the oldest anthroposophist farm Marienhöhe east of Berlin, where forty people have farmed since 1927 without chemical fertilizers or pesticides, are symbols and beacons of hope for these new ways of life. In the final years of the German Democratic Republic and since the fall of the Wall in 1989, the people of Marienhöhe were, and continue to be, virtually overrun by enthusiastic visitors and followers. Although their anthroposophist beliefs doubtless give them something in common with religious fanatics and "fundamentalist sects", their radical rejection of numerous consumer goods and luxuries in favor of a simple life with communal meals also makes them social role-models.

Even in the city, however, communal cooking and eating are at the center of many collective living situations or "scenes" and, after the disappearance of the family dinner table, they have restored the forgotten meal as a communal activity. "Think globally, act [buy] locally" is no longer the view of only a marginal protest generation. People are well aware of the interactions between the individual and society. According to a survey by Emnid, 75% of all Germans are convinced that targeted purchasing practices can exercise substantial pressure on food manufacturers. In 1994, at least 65% of them said that they wanted to shop in such a way that they do not support companies that seriously damaged the environment, and 55%

said they did not want to support animal testing with their purchases ("Zitty" September 1994: 212-20). Two-thirds of Germans surveyed would prefer to buy organic produce if it were more affordable, and 80% opposed genetically manipulated foods.

Thus, vegetarianism is apparently the radical "symbol" of the new social movements, which have long since become a social fact and a source of hope not only for a "niche economy". In questions of animal rights and landscape conservation as well as the treatment of plants, many conservatives (at least in the realm of values) agree with the new alternative left, and this is true not only in Berlin. In England, 40% of the population have greatly reduced their meat consumption since 1994, and in the USA the organic food sector is booming, with 20% growth rates. In Germany, the meat processing industry reported a 20% drop in beef consumption in 1994. Over 10% of Germans, and a larger percentage of young people, report that they are vegetarians for ethical and ecological reasons.

In the tradition of the Pythagoreans, Brahmans, monastic ascetics and nineteenth-century life reformers, vegetarian food today continues to be associated with sun and light, "lightness", femininity and youth. Typically enough, the proponents of such a diet are often members of relatively privileged strata, such as the Brahmans in India, to whose mainly sedentary way of life not eating meat is appropriate. At the same time, abstinence from eating meat represents a symbolic identification with the hungry of the Third World, whose daily meals remain almost exclusively vegetarian even today. With their vegetarianism and their interest in animal rights, today's "youth without a future" have turned their attention to issues of everyday life. Now, at the end of the technological revolution, the question of our daily food is again central, as it once was in peasant subsistence culture. According to a study conducted by the University of Hohenheim, for most households that buy organic produce, such motives as "contributing to the protection of nature and the environment" and "supporting alternative farming and alternative forms of trade" are just as important as the "better taste of the products" and their "higher nutritive value" (Lünzer 1993; Kallenbach 1991).

The fact that this has caused many children of harmless alternative parents to become infuriating little vegetarian fundamentalists must apparently be considered nature's revenge. "Enlightened" ethical vegetarianism thus proves to be a worldwide response to a globalized economy of excess, a perilous growth with all its negative effects of corruption, decadence and war.The new dedication to enjoyment in growing strata of the population means that more and more people are eating away from home. According to newspaper accounts, in 1997 75% of Germans ate out once a week and, because their expectations of good food are rising, spent a good deal more money than previously. In Europe, too, both the well-heeled and young people are increasingly eating food prepared by new immigrants from the poor "South". Regular panics have broken out about this kind of self-alienation. It is the old fear of too many cooks spoiling the broth. Thus in the spring of 1995, following the old pattern of seeking scapegoats, Chinese restaurants were once again suspected of cooking with dog food. For the first time, Chinese people got together for a protest rally and their spokesman explained to journalists—probably with a smile, but not without a certain aggressive tone—that "only the stupid man eats meat; the wise man eats vegetables."

A fine pickle we've gotten ourselves into!

References

Allen, Ann Taylor (1991): Feminism and Motherhood in Germany 1800-1914, New Brunswick: Rutgers University Press.

Borgers, Dieter (1993): Cholesterin—Das Scheitern eines Dogmas. Die mangelnde Effizienz einer individualmedizinischen Präventionsstrategie, Wissenschaftszentrum Berlin: Edition Sigma.

Cremer, Hans-Dietrich (1980): Ernährung und geistige Entwicklung, in: Gießener Universitätsblätter, No. 1, pp. 51-69.

Duden, Barbara and Karin Hausen (1978): Gesellschaftliche Arbeit—geschlechtsspezifische Arbeitsteilung, in: Annette Kuhn and Gerhard Schneider (eds.): Frauen in der Geschichte, Düsseldorf: Schwann, pp. 11-33.

Ernährungsbericht 1988 (1988), ed. by Deutsche Gesellschaft für Ernährung e.V., Frankfurt a.M.: Deutsche Gesellschaft für Ernährung.

Ernst, Andrea, Kurt Langbein and Hans Weiss (1986): Gift-Grün—Chemie in der Landwirtschaft und die Folgen, Munich: dtv, updated ed. 1988.

Fèl, Edit and Tamas Hofer (1972): Bäuerliche Denkweise in Wirtschaft und Haushalt—Eine ethnographische Untersuchung über das ungarische Dorf Atany, Göttingen: Schwartz & Co.

Fleck, Ludwik (1935/1980): Die Entstehung einer wissenschaftlichen Tatsache, Frankfurt a.M.: Suhrkamp.

Fiddes, Nick (1993): Meat—A Natural Symbol, London und New York: Routledge.

Gamerith, Anni (1956): Lebendiges Ganzkorn. Neue Sicht zur Getreidefrage—gewonnen aus dem Urwissen bäuerlicher Überlieferung, Bad Goisern: Verlag Neues Leben.

Inglehart, Ronald (1977): The Silent Revolution, Princeton: Princeton University Press.

Kallenbach, Udo (1991): Vollwert-Ernährung und Öko-Landbau in der Bundesrepublik Deutschland, Bad Dürkheim: Stiftung Ökologie und Landbau.

Kapfelsberger, Eva and Udo Pollmer (1992): Iß und stirb—Chemie in unserer Nahrung, 2. Aufl. Köln: Kiepenheuer & Witsch.

Kleinspehn, Thomas (1987): Warum sind wir so unersättlich? Frankfurt a.M.: Suhrkamp.

Koch, Egmont R., Reinhard Klopfleisch and Armin Maiwald (1986): Die Gesundheit der Nation—Eine Bestandsaufnahme, Karten, Analysen, Empfehlungen, Cologne: Kiepenheuer and Witsch.

Köster-Lösche, Kari (1995): Rinderwahnsinn BSE: Die neue Gefahr aus dem Kochtopf, München: Ehrenwirth.

Krönig, Jürgen (1996): Tod im Topf, in: Die Zeit, 29.3.

Liehr, Heinrich (1996): Leber—Galle—Bauchspeicheldrüse, Stuttgart: Trias.

Lücke, Susanne (1985): Was essen wir wirklich?—Schein und Sein der modernen Lebensmittel, Frankfurt/Berlin/Vienna: Ullstein.

Lünzer, Immo (1993): Bio-Kost im Kommen, in: Jahrbuch Ökologie, Munich: C.H. Beck, pp. 228-237.

Maurizio, Adam (1927/1979): Die Geschichte der Planzennahrung Berlin: Paul Parey; Reprint Wiesbaden: Sändig.

Meyer-Renschhausen, Elisabeth (1991): The Porridge Debate—Grain, Nutrition and Forgotten Food Preparation Techniques, in: Food and Foodways—Exploration in the history and culture of human nourishment, Vol. 5, No. 1, pp. 95-120.

Meyer-Renschhausen, Elisabeth (1990): Die fürstlichen Mahlzeiten der Revolutionäre, in: Marieluise Christadler (ed.): Freiheit, Gleichheit, Weiblichkeit—Die europäischen Frauen und die Französische Revolution, Opladen: Budrich & Leske, pp. 127-140.

Meyer-Renschhausen, Elisabeth (1989): Weibliche Kultur und soziale Arbeit—Eine Geschichte der Frauenbewegung 1810-1927 am Beispiel Bremens, Köln/Wien: Böhlau.

Mintz, Sidney W. (1986): Sweetness and Power—The Place of Sugar in Modern History, 2nd ed. New York: Penguin.

Oikos—Von der Feuerstelle zur Mikrowelle. Haushalt und Wohnen im Wandel, Anabas-Verlag Gießen 1992.

Van Otterloo, A.H. (1993): Die Bewegung für Natürliche und Gesunde Nahrung als 'Petite Religion', Österreichische Zeitschrift, Vol. 18, No. 4, pp. 41-52.

Pestizid-Aktions-Netzwerk (1991): Zum Beispiel Pestizide Göttingen: Lamuv Verlag.

Randolph, Theron G. and Ralph W. Moss (1980): An Alternative Approach to Allergies, New York.

Ritzer, George (1993): The McDonaldisation of Society, Newbury Park, California: Pine Forge Press.

Schäfer, Herbert (1993): Tatort Lebensmittelmarkt, Vienna: Orac.

Schivelbusch, Wolfgang (1983): Das Paradies, der Geschmack und die Vernunft—Eine Geschichte der Genußmittel, Frankfurt/Berlin/Wien: Ullstein.

Sentker, Andreas (1996): Viren oder wildgewordene Proteine, in: Die Zeit, 29.3.

Sloterdijk, Peter (1990): Das Andere am Anderen—Zur philosophischen Situation der Alternativbewegungen, in: Dietmar Kamper and Christoph Wulf (eds.): Rückblick auf das Ende der Welt, Munich: Boer, pp. 94-125.

Spittler, Gerd (1987): Essen und Moral—Die Nahrung der Kel Ewey im Alltag und in einer Hungerkrise, in: Freiburger Universitätsblätter, Vol. 96, pp. 95-112.

Spittler, Gerd (1993): Lob des einfachen Mahles. Afrikanische und europäische Eßkultur im Vergleich, in: Alois Wierlacher et al. (eds.): Kulturthema Essen, Berlin: Akademie Verlag, 193-210.

Stern, 28.3.1996.

tageszeitung, 29.3.1996.

Tietze, Henry G. (1978): Das Essen—Eine Kulturgeschichte unserer Ernährung von den Anfängen bis heute, Hannover: Fackelträger.

Teuteberg, Hans-Jürgen (1990): Die Rolles des Fleischextraktes für die Ernährungswissenschaften und den Aufstieg der Suppenindustrie, in: Zeitschrift für Unternehmensgeschichte, Beiheft 70, hrsg. v. Hans Pohl und Wilhelm Treue, Stuttgart: Steiner.

The Times, 28.3.1996.

Umweltbundesamt (1997): Nachhaltiges Deutschland—Wege zu einer dauerhaften umweltgerechten Entwicklung, Berlin: Erich Schmidt.

Walletschek, Hartwig and Jochen Graw (1995): Öko-Lexikon, 5th ed. Munich: C.H. Beck.

Winkler, Ulrike (1996): Der Krieg—Das Fleisch—Der Tod. Die un-heimliche Bevor-mundung, unpublished master thesis, Institut für Erziehungswissenschaften, Leopold-Franzens-University Innsbruck.

Wirz, Albert (1993): Die Moral auf dem Teller, Zürich: Chronos.

Zitty, vol. 18, no. 19 (September 1994), pp. 212-20.

PART III

APPROACHES AND STRATEGIES TO OVERCOME HUNGER AND MALNUTRITION

16

Human Rights Requirement to Social and Economic Development:
The Case of the Right to Food and Nutrition Rights

Asbjørn Eide

1 The World Food Summit in Rome 1996: Reaffirmation and commitment

The heads of states and governments gathered in Rome at the World Food Summit at the invitation of the Food and Agriculture Organization of the United Nations and reaffirmed on November 13, 1996 the right of everyone to have access to safe and nutritious food, consistent with the right to adequate food and the fundamental right of everyone to be free from hunger. At no previous point in time has a declaration been made at that high level of authority on the importance of these rights.

There is ample evidence—and this is well documented in other parts of this book—that hunger continues to be widespread and that the right of everyone to adequate food is even more extensively violated. The heads of states and governments were fully aware of this gap between rights and reality. They declared that they considered it intolerable that more than 800 million people throughout the world, and particularly in developing countries, do not have enough food to meet their basic nutritional needs. They noted that while food supplies have increased substantially, constraints on access to food and continuing inadequacy of household and national incomes to purchase food, instability of supply and demand, as well as natural and man-made disasters, have prevented basic food needs from being fulfilled.

Since the realization of the right to food and at least the fundamental right to be free from hunger is something within our reach, what is required is to harness the necessary political will and to comply with obligations already undertaken under international human rights law. The leaders of the states assembled in Rome in 1996 pledged their political will and their common and national commitment to achieving food security for all and to an ongoing effort to eradicate hunger in all countries, with an immediate view to reducing the number of undernourished people to half their present level no later than 2015.

The commitment to an ongoing effort to eradicate hunger in all countries in the world requires immediate action. The target to reduce by half the number of undernourished people by the year 2015 gives a time span of less than two decades. It must be assumed that it was a commitment made in earnest. If that is the case, governments must immediately initiate steps which could systematically lead to the goal set – to reduce the number of undernourished persons from 800 million to 400 million. This would require, firstly, that those groups which presently have access to sufficient, safe and nutritious food will continue to have this access also in the future and that conditions will be created so that those groups which do not, will have such access in the future. The year 2015 is not far from now.

The heads of states and governments adopted the World Food Summit Plan of Action and pledged their actions and support to its full implementation. In it, they formally renewed their commitment to the right to adequate food and recommended—with a view to its realization—to better define the content of this right and to identify ways to implement it.

The Summit's Plan of Action, in its Commitment 7.4, stipulates as one of its objectives: "To clarify the content of the right to food and the fundamental right of everyone to be free from hunger, as stated in the International Covenant on Economic, Social and Cultural Rights and other relevant international and regional instruments, and to give particular attention to implementation and full and progressive realization of this right as a means of achieving food security for all."

In support of this objective, the Plan of Action invited "the UN High Commissioner for Human Rights, in consultation with the relevant treaty bodies, and in collaboration with relevant specialized agencies and programmes of the UN system and appropriate intergovernmental mechanisms, to better define the rights related to food in Article 11 of the Covenant and to propose ways to implement and realize these rights as a means of achieving the commitments and objectives of the World Food Summit, taking into account the possibility of formulating voluntary guidelines for food security for all."

The World Food Summit thus reflects a commitment by the international community through its highest representatives to take effective action in applying a right-to-food based approach to the immense food and nutrition problems of our time, and envisages a close co-operation between the High Commissioner and the United Nations human rights machinery with the food agencies and other relevant parts of the UN system. The UN Commission on Human Rights, reaffirming the right to adequate food in its resolution 1997/8, endorsed the Summit's request to the High Commissioner and encouraged the Committee on Economic, Social and Cultural Rights "to pay further attention in its activities to those rights recognized in Article 11 of the International Covenant on Economic, Social and Cultural Rights."

2 Evolution and scope of human rights

Throughout the evolutionary history of human rights, three aspects of human existence have sought to be safeguarded: human integrity, freedom and equality based on respect for the dignity of every human being. The way in which these issues have been addressed has matured over time, from initial, idealistic assertions of vague principles to the adoption of the comprehensive, international normative system now in existence. The debate emerged on the two sides of the Atlantic—particularly in Britain, France and the American colonies—during the 17th and 18th century, to be extended to a European-American concern in the 19th century and a global concern in the 20th century. The contemporary system of human rights is therefore the product of reflection and implementation over several centuries.[1]

Halfway into the present century, Marshall reviewed the development of attributes vital to effective 'citizenship' (Marshall 1959).[2] He distinguished three stages in this evolution, tracing the formative period of each of these types of rights to a different century. Civil rights had been the great achievement of the eighteenth century, laying the foundation of the notion of equality of all members of society before the law. Political rights were the principal achievement of the nineteenth century by allowing for increasingly broader participation in the exercise of sovereign power. Social rights were the contribution of the twentieth century, intended to make it possible for all members of society to enjoy satisfactory conditions of life.[3]

The contemporary international human rights system was born in 1948 when the United Nations General Assembly unanimously adopted the Universal Declaration of Human Rights (hereafter: UDHR) as "a common standard of achievement for all peoples and all nations, to the end that every individual and every organ of society, keeping this Declaration constantly in mind, shall strive by teaching and education to promote respect for these rights and freedoms and by progressive measures, national and international, to secure their universal and effective recognition and observance."[4]

The scope of the rights contained in the international human rights system included all the elements achieved during the evolution described by T.S. Marshall, and was affected by the emphasis given by the United States administration and the governments of other Western states prior to and during World War II who increasingly had recognized that economic and social rights had to be promoted as a parallel track to civil and political rights. Of special importance was the "Four Freedoms" address of U.S. President Roosevelt in January 1941, which included freedom from want as one of those rights,[5] the Atlantic Declaration of August 1941 jointly made by President Roosevelt and Prime Minister Churchill of Britain, and

---

1 Numerous contributions to the history of human rights could be mentioned here. A thorough study in the German language is found in Ermacora (1974). Highly interesting insights into the origin of the human rights discourse can also be found in Palley (1991).

2 The lectures were given in honour of the famous economist Alfred Marshall. R. Dahrendorf (1988) has dealt with the same issues in "The Modern Social Conflict: An Essay on the Politics of Liberty".

3 Marshall's neat description of three stages is somewhat simplified, particularly if we take into account developments in other parts of continental Europe. Some of the social rights, including the legislation in Bismarck's Germany in the 1880s, were aimed at improving the political legitimacy of relatively autocratic and authoritarian states in face of an increasingly radical labour movement. On this point, see further Flora and Alber (1981).

4 From the preamble of the Universal Declaration of Human Rights.

5 On the Roosevelt conception of freedom from want as a source of contemporary conceptions of human rights, see further in Eide et al. (1991).

the detailed preparations for a Bill of Human Rights carried out in the United States during World War II.

In the negotiations of the Universal Declaration of Human Rights in 1947-1948, the United States delegation played a major role, emphasizing that economic and social rights should be included as well as the civil rights which set out the fundamental freedoms, since—in the words of the US delegation—"a man in need is not a free man."[6] In his 1944 State of the Union address, Roosevelt had advocated the adoption of an "Economic Bill of Rights", saying that "we have come to the clear realization of the fact that true individual freedom cannot exist without economic security and independence. 'Necessitous men are not free men.' People who are hungry and out of job are the stuff of which dictatorships are made."[7]

When the UDHR was finally adopted in 1948, there was thus not much doubt that economic and social rights had to be included. The great contribution of this Declaration is, however, that it extended the human rights platform to embrace the whole field—civil, political, economic, social and cultural, and made the different rights interrelated and mutually reinforcing. It was widely recognized in Western societies that the political upheavals and the predominance of totalitarian regimes in the period between the two World Wars had been due to the widespread unemployment and poverty. As a result, there was a broad consensus in favour of securing economic and social rights for all. This was held necessary not only to ensure justice but also in order to preserve individual freedom and democracy. It was broadly agreed that even in periods of recession basic economic and social rights could and should be enjoyed by all.

These concerns are more relevant than ever in the present time, in view of widespread unemployment, poverty and growing disparities in income, not only in the Third World but also in Central and Eastern Europe and in the West. It is necessary, therefore, to increase the efficiency of international mechanisms in this field and possibly to develop new ones.

Internationally recognized human rights today are those included in the International Bill of Human Rights and those elaborated on in subsequent instruments adopted by the UN General Assembly. The International Bill includes the Universal Declaration (UDHR) and the two covenants prepared on the basis of that Declaration, the International Covenant on Civil and Political Rights (CCPR) and the International Covenant on Economic, Social and Cultural Rights (CESCR), both adopted in 1996.

3 The package of economic, social and cultural rights

Economic, social and cultural rights constitute three interrelated components of a more comprehensive package, with obvious links to civil and political rights. At the

6 Summary records of the Commission on Human Rights, UN doc. E\CN.4\SR 64.

7 For details on this statement by Roosevelt, see Alston (1990).

core of social rights is the right to an adequate standard of living (UDHR Article 25; CESCR Article 11; the International Convention on the Rights of the Child (hereafter called CRC) Article 27). The enjoyment of these rights requires, at a minimum, that everyone shall enjoy the necessary subsistence rights—adequate food and nutrition rights, clothing, housing and the necessary conditions of care. Closely related to this right is the right of families to assistance (CESCR Article 10; CRC Article 27). In order to enjoy these social rights, there is also a need to enjoy certain economic rights. These are the right to property (UDHR, Article 17), the right to work (UDHR Article 23; CESCR Article 6) and the right to social security (UDHR Articles 22 and 25; CESCR Article 9; CRC Article 26).

The economic rights have a dual function, most clearly demonstrated in regard to the right to property. On the one hand, this right serves as a basis for entitlements which can ensure an adequate standard of living, while on the other hand it is a basis of independence and therefore of freedom. The right to property, however, cannot be enjoyed on an equal basis by all and can therefore not stand alone as the only economic rights. It is supplemented by at least two other rights. The right to work is intended to ensure that everyone, also those without property can have an income ensuring an adequate standard of living. The right to social security supplements, and where necessary fully substitutes, insufficient income derived from property or from work—insufficient, that is, in regard to the enjoyment of an adequate standard of living.

4 The right to an adequate standard of living, including food, and to be free from hunger

According to Article 25(1) of the UDHR, "everyone has the right to a standard of living adequate for the health and well-being of himself and of his family." With the wording slightly changed, the term of the "right to an adequate standard of living" appears in Article 11 of the CESCR: "The States Parties to the present Covenant recognize the right of everyone to an adequate standard of living for himself and his family ..." Under Article 27 of the CRC, "States Parties recognize the right of every child to a standard of living adequate for the child's physical, mental, spiritual, moral and social development."

The right to an adequate standard of living sums up a large part of the concerns underlying all economic and social rights, which is to integrate everyone into a humane society. It is intimately linked to the foundation of the whole human rights system that everyone is born free and equal in dignity and rights and should act towards each other in a spirit of fraternity (UDHR art.1).

The rights to property, to work, and to social security mentioned above are all sources of subsistence or income which ideally should make it possible for everyone to enjoy an adequate standard of living. When nevertheless a specific right to an adequate standard of living has been included in the international system of human rights, it is to cover the loopholes and to address the most basic needs to which every human being is entitled.

The provision serves to address the rights of the most vulnerable members of society. In the developed countries, the large majority already enjoys an adequate standard and sometimes much more than that. In the developing countries, the numbers of those who are vulnerable are much larger, though it differs substantially in different countries. But there are, also in developing countries, significant parts of the population who have a standard of living which is far above what is required under the international human rights instruments.

The UN Committee on Economic, Social and Cultural Rights has noted that the most vulnerable groups are "landless peasants, marginalized peasants, rural workers, rural unemployed, urban unemployed, urban poor, migrant workers, indigenous peoples, children, elderly people, and other especially affected groups".[8] To this list could be added persons who are temporarily in very difficult positions, such as internally displaced persons, refugees, and persons in detention or in psychiatric institutions.

In Article 25 of the UDHR the term "adequate standard of living" means "adequate for the health and well-being of himself and of his family, including food, clothing, housing and medical care and necessary social services;" and in Article 11 of the CESCR it includes "adequate food, clothing and housing;" whereas the right of the child under CRC article 27 is to "a standard of living adequate for the child's physical, mental, spiritual, moral and social development."

Everyone shall be able, without shame and without unreasonable obstacles, to be a full participant in ordinary, everyday interaction with other people. This means, inter alia, that they shall be able to enjoy their basic needs under conditions of dignity. No one shall have to live under conditions where the only way to satisfy their needs is by degrading or depriving themselves of their basic freedoms, such as through begging, prostitution or bonded labour, nor depend on the grace of others.

4.1 Adequate food and freedom from hunger

The right to adequate food is included in article 11 para. 1 of the CESCR which states that "the States Parties to the present Covenant recognize the right of everyone to an adequate standard of living for himself and his family ..." In paragraph 2 of the same article, we find the following stipulations: "The State Parties to the present Covenant, recognizing the fundamental right of everyone to be free from hunger, shall take, individually and through international co-operation, the measures ... which are needed

(a) To improve methods of production, conservation and distribution of food by making full use of technological and scientific knowledge, by disseminating knowledge of the principles of nutrition and by developing or reforming agrar-

8 This list appears in the guidelines drawn up by the Committee for the periodic reporting by States Parties to the Covenant. See "Manual on Human Rights Reporting" (1996: 120).

ian systems in such a way as to achieve the most efficient development and utilization of natural resources;

(b) Taking into account the problems of both food-importing and food-exporting countries, to ensure an equitable distribution of world food supplies in relation to need."

The CRC, ratified by 191 states, recognizes food- and nutrition-related rights in the context of the "right of the child to the enjoyment of the highest attainable standard of health" (Article 24.1). In pursuing the full implementation of this right, "State Parties shall take appropriate measures: ...

(c) To combat disease and malnutrition ... through inter alia the application of readily available technology and through the provision of adequate nutritious foods and clean drinking water ...;

.....

(e) To ensure that all segments of society, in particular parents and children, are informed, have access to education and are supported in the use of basic knowledge of child health and nutrition, the advantages of breastfeeding, hygiene and environmental sanitation."

At the regional level, the right to adequate food is most clearly spelt out in the Additional Protocol (not yet in force) to the American Convention of Human Rights in the Area of Economic, Social and Cultural Rights (Article 12):

"1. Everyone has the right to adequate nutrition which guarantees the possibility of enjoying the highest level of physical, emotional and intellectual development;

2. In order to promote the exercise of this right and eradicate malnutrition, the States Parties undertake to improve methods of production, supply and distribution of food, and to this end, agree to promote greater international co-operation in support of the relevant national policies."

Adequate food can be broken down into several elements: adequacy of the food supply means that the types of foodstuffs commonly available (nationally, in local markets, and eventually at the household level) should be culturally acceptable (fit the prevailing food or dietary culture); furthermore, the overall supply should cover overall nutritional needs in terms of quantity (energy) and quality (provide all essential nutrients, including micronutrients such as vitamins and iodine), and, last but not least, be safe (free of toxic factors and contaminants) and of good food quality (for example, taste and texture).

Stability of the supply and access to food presupposes environmental sustainability, implying that there is a judicious public and community management of natural resources which have a bearing on the food supply, as well as economic and social sustainability in terms of conditions and mechanisms securing food access. Economic and social sustainability concern a just income distribution and effective markets, together with various public and informal support and safety nets. These supports could be public social security schemes, as well as numerous forms of community transactions, self-help and solidarity networks, the latter becoming particularly important when people need to cope with various crisis situations.

4.2 Adequate housing

Essential to a life in dignity is also the right to have adequate homes. This is important in itself, but also essential for the realization of the right to food. The household being the basic unit for the collaborative efforts to satisfy basic needs, there must be a house to hold. The right to housing is recognized in CESCR Art. 11.2 and in several other sources. Reality, however, is disturbing. The United Nations estimates that there are over 100 million persons homeless worldwide and over 1 billion inadequately housed. There is no indication that this number is decreasing.

The Committee on Economic, Social and Cultural Rights has observed that the right to housing should not be interpreted in a narrow or restrictive sense which equates it with, for example, the shelter provided by merely having a roof over one's head or views shelter exclusively as a commodity. Rather it should be seen as the right to live somewhere in security, peace and dignity. "...(T)he right to housing is integrally linked to other human rights and to the fundamental principles upon which the Covenant is premised".[9]

4.3 Adequate care

It is often overlooked that an adequate standard of living also requires adequate care, which is particularly important for children, the elderly, and for those who have immediate responsibility for small children. The concept of adequate care encompasses a number of extremely critical factors in the development of nutritional well-being among individuals, especially the most vulnerable groups in society: young children, especially poor young children, and mothers-to-be. Adequate care is pivotal also for other groups and individuals, such as the elderly and the disabled, and normally healthy individuals who are temporarily exposed to health hazards or other crises in their lives which may affect their ability to procure food, their food intake, and their nutritional status, and thus their health and productivity. Under international human rights law, these issues have found their clearest expression in Article 24(2) of the Convention on the Rights of the Child, which in part reads:

"States Parties shall ... take appropriate measures: ...

(b) To ensure the provision of necessary medical assistance and health care to all children with emphasis on the development of primary health care;

(c) To combat disease and malnutrition, including within the framework of primary health care, through, inter alia, the application of readily available technology and through the provision of adequate nutritious foods and clean drinking-water, taking into consideration the dangers and risks of environmental pollution;

(d) To ensure appropriate pre-natal and post-natal health care for mothers;

9 General Comment No. 4 (1991) para. 7, contained in Manual on Human Rights Reporting (1997: 126).

(e) To ensure that all segments of society, in particular parents and children, are informed, have access to education and are supported in the use of basic knowledge of child health and nutrition, the advantages of breast-feeding, hygiene and environmental sanitation and the prevention of accidents;

(f) To develop preventive health care, guidance for parents, and family planning education and services."

5 State obligations

5.1 General

The UDHR envisaged that everyone throughout the world should enjoy the rights contained therein. The rights would have to be absorbed into the legal, administrative and political culture of nations, firstly by their recognition and then by implementation in national law and administration through necessary political and social reforms. Global institutions had to be set up to monitor the implementation of human rights world-wide and to bring about the necessary co-operation in the fields of economic, social and cultural matters required to establish conditions for their full enjoyment world-wide. This effort has now gone on for half a century, and considerable progress has been achieved though much remains to be done, not the least in regard to economic and social rights.

The UDHR was initially an expression of ideal goals to be achieved. The process of transforming these ideals into "hard law" ("positivization" in legal language) at the international level started with the adoption of two covenants adopted in 1966, followed by numerous more specific conventions. While this created obligations for states under international law, the main task was to ensure that the rights were incorporated into national law and administrative practice. This transformation, whether into constitutions or into statutory law, can be fully achieved only when it goes hand in hand with the evolution of a human rights culture where individuals as well as politicians, administrators and security forces know and accept not only their own rights, but also their duties flowing from the rights of the other members of the community on a basis of equality.

Under international law, obligations to ensure the enjoyment of human rights are held primarily by the state. When a state seeks to implement these obligations in national law, it has a dual task: to respect the freedom of their subjects and yet to impose certain duties on every person subject to its jurisdiction. Duties to respect the right of other persons, and duties to contribute to the common welfare, make it possible for the state to assist and to fulfil (provide) in ways which enable everyone to enjoy their economic, social and cultural rights.

Under Article 2 of the Covenant on Economic, Social and Cultural Rights, States Parties have undertaken legally binding obligations to take steps, to the maximum of their available resources, to "achieve progressively" the full realization of the economic and social rights in that Covenant. The Committee on

Economic, Social and Cultural Rights has pointed out that while the concept of progressive realization constitutes a recognition of the fact that states will generally not be able to achieve a full realization of all economic, social and cultural rights in a short period of time, the phrase must be seen in the light of the overall objective, which is to establish clear obligations for States Parties to move as expeditiously as possible towards the realization of these rights. The more recent Convention on the Rights of the Child (CRC), which includes many economic and social rights and corresponding state obligations, does not contain the qualifying clause "progressive realization". Under the CRC, the obligations arise immediately, but their implementation is still qualified by the phrase "within their means".

A fundamental misunderstanding has negatively affected the implementation of economic and social rights. The misconception has been that such rights must be provided by the state. On that basis many oppose such rights, on the assumption that they are costly, undermine creativity, remove incentives and lead to an overgrown state apparatus. This view results from a very narrow understanding of the nature of these rights and particularly of the corresponding state obligations; consequently, and given their relevance to development policies, some words about their nature are required.

A realistic understanding of state obligations must take into account that, as stated in the Declaration on the Right to Development (Article 2),[10] the individual is the active subject, not the object, of economic and social development. Most human beings strive to take care of their own livelihood by use of own efforts and resources, individually or in association with others. Use of his or her own resources, however, requires that the person has resources that can be used—typically land or other capital, or labour, in both cases combined with application of the knowledge available to that person for optimal utilization of the resources she or he controls. The realization of many economic, social and cultural rights of an individual will in most cases take place within the context of a household as the smallest economic unit, as reflected in the language of the relevant human rights instruments.[11] This requires attention also to female/male division of labour and control over production and consumption, and to various forms of wider kinship arrangements which influence the concept and pratical operation of the concept of "family".

5.2 Four levels of obligations

Since state obligations must be seen in the light of the assumption that human beings, families, or wider groups seek to find their own solutions to their needs,

10 The Declaration on the Right to Development was adopted by the United Nations General Assembly by resolution 41/128 of 4 December 1986.

11 The CESCR Article 11 refers to "an adequate standard of living for himself and his family," and corresponding formulations are found in article 7 ("Remuneration which provides all workers, as a minimum, with ... a decent standard for themselves and their families"), and Article 10 describes the family as "the natural and fundamental unit of society".

states should, at the primary level, respect the resources owned by the individual, her or his freedom to find a job of preference, to make the optimal use of own knowledge and the freedom to take the necessary actions and use the necessary resources—alone or in association with others—to satisfy his or her own needs. Individual as well as collective or group rights are relevant here: resources belonging to a collective of persons, such as indigenous populations, must be respected in order for them to be able to satisfy their needs. Consequently, as part of the obligation to respect these resources the state should take steps to recognize and register the land rights of indigenous peoples and land tenure of smallholders whose title is uncertain. By doing so, the state will have assisted them in making use of their resources in greater safety in their pursuit to maintain an adequate standard of living.

The state cannot, however, passively leave it at that. Third parties are likely to interfere negatively with the possibilities that individuals or groups otherwise might have had to solve their own needs. At a secondary level, therefore, state obligation requires active protection against other, more assertive or aggressive subjects, more powerful economic interests, such as protection against fraud, against unethical behaviour in trade and contractual relations, against the marketing and dumping of hazardous or dangerous products. This protective function of the state is widely used and is the most important aspect of state obligations with regard to economic, social and cultural rights, similar to the role of the state as protector of civil and political rights.

Significant components of the obligation to protect are spelled out in existing law in most states. Legislation of this kind must be based on the specific requirements in the country concerned. This is one reason why the formulations of economic and social rights in international instruments are relatively vague—they should be given content by specific legislation within each country, taking into account the situation prevailing there. To take one example: legislation requiring that land can be owned only by the tiller of the land is essential where agriculture is the major basis of income for the majority of the population, but may be much less relevant in highly industrialized technological societies where only a small percentage of the population lives off the land. Protection against hazardous or undesirable elements in foodstuffs is an important obligation in ensuring a safe food supply as part of realizing the right to adequate food, and countries have established more or less effective surveillance and control mechanisms to ensure this.

At the tertiary level, the state has the obligation to facilitate opportunities by which the rights listed can be enjoyed. It takes many forms, some of which are spelled out in the relevant instruments. For example, with regard to the right to food, the state shall, under the CESCR (Article 11(2)), take steps to "improve measures of production, conservation and distribution of food by making full use of technical and scientific knowledge and by developing or reforming agrarian systems."

At the fourth and final level, the state has the obligation to fulfil the rights of everyone under economic, social and cultural rights. This fourth level of obligation is important as an emergency when conditions for survival are temporarily disrupted (severe draught or flood, armed conflict, or the collapse of economic activities within particular regions of the country.) As a more permanent feature, fourth level obligations increase in importance with increasing rates of urbanization and the decline of group or family responsibilities. Obligations towards elderly and disabled, which in traditional agricultural society were taken care of by the family, must increasingly be borne by the state and thus by the national society as a whole.

The obligation to fulfil could thus consist of the direct provisions of basic needs, such as food or resources which can be used for food (direct food aid, or social security) when no other possibility exists, such as, for example: (1) when unemployment sets in (such as under recession); (2) for the disadvantaged and the elderly; (3) during sudden situations of crisis or disaster; and (4) for those who are marginalized (for example, due to structural transformations in the economy and production).

6 International reporting and supervision mechanisms

When a state becomes a party to an international treaty, it is expected to review its domestic law and practice to ensure that it is in compliance with the obligations contained in the treaty. An essential component of contemporary international law of human rights is the practice of international monitoring and review of state compliance with universal norms of human rights.

The monitoring takes, at present, three forms:

- investigative reports, prepared for the United Nations Commission on Human Rights by special rapporteurs or working groups appointed by the Commission;
- individual complaint procedures by which nationals and other residents of a state can complain to international bodies for alleged violations of their human rights;
- reports prepared by states who have ratified international human rights conventions and who therefore, in legal language, are parties to the convention concerned. Such reports are submitted periodically to international expert bodies (treaty bodies) set up in conformity with the convention concerned.

In practice, the two first mechanisms have been applied only to civil and political rights, not to the economic, social and cultural rights. There is no inherent reason why this should continue to be so, and plans are under way to provide for a complaint procedure also for these rights, through the adoption of an optional protocol to the CESCR. This issue will here be left aside in order to concentrate on the reporting processes.

The international monitoring of the CESCR at present rests completely on a reporting procedure, established by Article 16 of that Covenant. Since 1987, the consideration of the reports has been entrusted to the Committee on Economic, Social and Cultural Rights, established by the United Nations Economic and Social

Council. State Parties are required to present comprehensive periodic reports every five years.[12]

Before submitting its initial report to the relevant treaty body, the State Party is expected to undertake a comprehensive review of national legislation, administrative rules and procedures and practices in order to ensure the fullest possible conformity with the provisions of the treaty. This, then, is the basis on which the reporting and the ensuing dialogue between the State Party and the Committee on Economic, Social and Cultural Rights should take place.

The Committee has adopted a set of guidelines for the content of the report.[13] Regarding the right to an adequate standard of living, States Parties to the CESCR are required to provide information about the current situation, in particular the vulnerable groups. They are called upon to provide a general overview of the extent to which the right to adequate food has been realized in the country. General statements do not satisfy; the state must present nutritional surveys and other monitoring arrangements. They are furthermore expected to provide detailed information (including statistical data broken down in terms of different geographical areas) on the extent to which hunger and/or malnutrition exists in the country, with particular attention to the situation of especially vulnerable or disadvantaged groups, including landless peasants, migrant workers, marginalized peasants, indigenous peoples, rural workers, children, rural unemployed, elderly people, urban unemployed and other urban poor, and other especially affected groups. Information should also indicate whether there is any significant difference in the situation of men and women within each of the above groups.

More importantly, based on this detailed and disaggregated information, states are requested to inform about the changes that have taken place over the past five years with respect to the situation of each of the above groups, and whether changes have been made in national policies, laws and practices, negatively affecting the access to adequate food by these groups or sectors or within the worse-off regions. Finally, the government is required to indicate the measures it considers necessary to guarantee access to adequate food for each of the vulnerable or disadvantaged groups and for the worse-off areas, and for the full implementation of the right to food for both men and women, with specification of measures taken and time-related goals set.

Following an oral hearing, the Committee on Economic, Social and Cultural Rights adopts its concluding observations in relation to a specific state report, expressing its positive appreciation where improvements have been made, and its issues of concern where implementation is proceeding too slowly or where there have been regressive lapses. In addition to the country-specific observations, the

12 The United Nations has published a comprehensive "Manual on Human Rights Reporting"(1997), in collaboration between the UN Office of the High Commissioner for Human Rights, the United Nations Institute for Training and Research and the United Nations Staff College Project.

13 The text of the guidelines for reporting under the Covenant are contained in Alston (1997).

Committee also uses the means of "general comments" and "general discussions" for reaching a better understanding of the contents of the treaty obligations.

The reporting process is taken more or less seriously by states. A conscientious preparation of state reports takes time and requires the use of human resources, but advances the awareness of shortcomings and the need for domestic policy-making to remedy these. International procedures and control mechanisms can never be considered as substitutes for national mechanisms and national measures. Preparation of the periodic report on the implementation of a treaty should be seen as an important document destined for a domestic as well as an international audience. Human rights treaties seek to promote and enhance not only a government's international accountability, but also its accountability to its own citizens. The preparation of the report thus provides an important occasion for consultation of the appropriate social, economic, cultural and other sectors of society.

Reports shall provide not only the legislative and administrative measures adopted and the situation as it exists in practice. A precondition for effective reporting is the existence of an adequate system for internal monitoring, within each state, of the situation with respect to each of the rights, on a regular basis. Many human rights problems can be resolved merely by amending the relevant legislation, by changing administrative practices, or by issuing appropriate instructions to the authority concerned. Others, however, are not susceptible of such rapid resolution and require the formulation of a long-term set of policies designed to ensure full and lasting compliance with treaty obligations. In such instances the reporting process can act as a catalyst to the formulation of carefully tailored policies designed to respond to the problems that have been identified.

A variety of states from different regions of the world have begun to experiment with different forms of consultation. Some have sought inputs from non-governmental groups on particular issues, others have requested such groups to submit comments on the draft reports, and still others have entrusted the preparation of the reports to a group, which includes representatives of the non-governmental sector.

Since states prepare successive periodic reports, the Committee on Economic, Social and Cultural Rights can assess the progress, if any, over a period of time. States should be encouraged, in their early reports, to set targets which they want to reach over a defined period of time; it will then be possible for the Committee and the state itself to determine whether the targets have been met. If they have not been met, a reassessment can be undertaken of the obstacles encountered and the means by which these are sought to be overcome.

The principal human rights treaties generally request States Parties to report not only on the progress that they have made, but also on any "factors and difficulties" that have affected the realization of the rights in question. In practice, states are reluctant to acknowledge the internal problems they face in seeking to advance the realization of these rights. They would be better served, however, by recognizing the difficulties. This would make it easier both for their own inhabitants to collaborate better in realizing the rights, and for the international monitoring body to address adequate recommendations.

Some states have ensured the widespread dissemination of their reports so that the public at large might comment, and thus contribute to an on-going national policy debate. This public scrutiny function can be further enhanced by ensuring easy access for the public at large to the United Nations summary records which document the examination of the state's report by the appropriate treaty body. There is reason to believe that there would be much to learn from the transparency of the international human rights machinery for agencies and institutions dealing with development issues. There, the principle of confidentiality often seems to reign beyond any logical reason.

7 International obligations?

At the World Food Summit, the heads of states and governments emphasized that food should not be used as an instrument for political and economic pressure, and reaffirmed the importance of international cooperation and solidarity as well as the necessity of refraining from unilateral measures not in accordance with the international law and the Charter of the United Nations and which endanger food security. This gives rise to reflections on the scope, if any, of international obligations related to the enjoyment of the right to food.

States are obliged to respect the freedom of other peoples to maintain their access to food. Deprivation of food as a weapon in international relations is unacceptable, though its relationship to sanctions adopted by the United Nations is unclear and controversial, as illustrated by the case of Iraq.

Do states also have obligations to protect peoples in other countries, by ensuring that persons, including enterprises, with residence/headquarter in their own country abstain from actions which cause deprivation of access to food in other countries? The World Food Summit, and Article 2 of CESCR, refers to the duty of international co-operation, the content of which is not very clearly spelled out. International co-operation can best be harnessed through the use of intergovernmental organizations and in some cases through the support to broadly representative international non-governmental organizations. The role of the intergovernmental organizations may be both to facilitate and to provide development and emergency aid, which should be tailored to the realization of the right to food and other human rights for all.

It should re recognized, however, that at the present stage in the evolution of international law, states generally do not accept that they are under international obligations to ensure the enjoyment of human rights, including the right to food, in countries other than their own. It is a highly debated issue, and the long-range trend can be expected to be towards a growing recognition of such obligations as a necessary corollary to the process of economic globalization presently taking place.

8 Concluding remarks

Economic and social rights form part of the human rights system as it has been formulated and consolidated since the adoption of the Universal Declaration in 1948. The right to an adequate standard of living for all, including food, is a core component of that system. Nevertheless, it remains a weak link, due to limited political will for its enforcement.

The Declaration and Program of Action adopted by the World Food Summit has significantly changed this situation, and the follow-up by the High Commissioner for Human Rights as well as by FAO and its Committee on Food Security, other food organizations, UNICEF, the Sub-Committee on Nutrition of the UN Administrative Coordinating Committee (ACC-SCN) and other bodies are likely to place the issue of the right to food more centrally on the international agenda. A firm commitment is now required to meet at least the target set by the World Food Summit, to reduce by half the number of those chronically malnourished. If it is achieved, it will be one of the quantitatively most substantial contributions which have been made to the realization of human rights worldwide.

References

Alston, Philip (1990): U.S. Ratification of the Covenant on Economic, Social and Cultural Rights: The Need for an Entirely New Strategy, in: American Journal of International Law, Vol. 84, p. 387.

Alston, Philip (1997): The International Covenant on Economic, Social and Cultural Rights, in: Manual on Human Rights Reporting, pp. 65-170.

Dahrendorf, Ralf (1988): The Modern Social Conflict: An Essay on the Politics of Liberty. London: Weidenfeld and Nicolson.

Eide, A., A. Oshaug and W.B. Eide (1991): Food Security and the Right to Food in International Law and Development, in: Transnational Law & Contemporary Problems (University of Iowa), Vol. 1, No. 2, pp. 415–467.

Ermacora, Felix (1974): Menschenrechte in der sich wandelnden Welt, Vol. 1, Wien: Verlag der Österreichischen Akademie der Wissenschaften.

Flora, Peter and Jens Alber (1981): Modernization, Democratization, and the Development of Welfare States in Western Europe, in: Peter Flora and Arnold J. Heidenheimer (eds.): The Development of Welfare States in Europe and America, New Brunswick: Transaction Books.

Manual on Human Rights Reporting (1997), published in collaboration between the UN Office of the High Commissioner for Human Rights, the United Nations Institute for Training and Research and the United Nations Staff College Project, Second Edition, New York and Geneva: UN sales number GV.E.97.0.16.

Marshall, T.S. (1959): Citizenship and Social Class and other Essays, Cambridge University Press.

Palley, Claire (1991): The United Kingdom and Human Rights, The Hamlyn Lectures, forty-second series, London: Stevens and Son.

17

Food Security: The Policy Dimension[1]

Frances Sandiford-Rossmiller and George E. Rossmiller

1 Governments and food security

Since the early 1980s, policy reforms initiated in many countries have been biased in favour of greater market orientation and a more open economy.[2] There has been a movement away from the concept of development, including agricultural development, as planned change by public agencies. Indeed, this period has seen a serious questioning of the very role of government—what it should and should not properly do in a market economy. In this context, it is clear that government has a vital role to play if a functioning free-market economy, rather than one that is merely a free-for-all, is to emerge in such a way that the sustained and sustainable economic growth on which long-term national food security depends can occur, and that its benefits are distributed equitably.

1.1 Role of government

What then is the role of government—what can a government do that no other body can? Put simply, governments need to govern. This has traditionally been taken to mean securing the borders and protecting the population from both external and internal threat, i.e., keeping the peace without which food security is threatened. It also means ensuring the establishment and enforcement of a legislative and judicial system that defines the rights and obligations of individuals and legal entities, regulates their activities in the public interest, and protects their agreed rights. A strong, fair and stable legislative framework is necessary to guide and regulate the individual players in the market, and ensure that they all play by the same set of rules through enforcement of the law so that market activity can contribute to food security for all. Only government can create the favourable and stable macro-economic and trade environment that can enable national food security to be realized. For countries in transition, be it from centrally-planned to market economies, or because of the implementation of structural adjustment policies, or simply as a part of the normal process of economic development, the role of government is especially difficult. Government needs to invest in the infrastructure

1 This chapter is based on the Special Chapter entitled "Food Security: Some Macroeconomic Dimensions" published in the 'State of Food and Agriculture, 1996', ©FAO, Rome, 1996. Permission by FAO to use this material is gratefully acknowledged.

2 The main pressures underlying these policy reforms are presented in (FAO 1995a).

for progress. Inherent in this must be the recognition that investment in the development of human resources (building human capital of both women and men) and action to alleviate poverty add to, rather than subtract from a country's growth potential, and is essential for ensuring food security for all sections of the community. This type of investment includes the provision of those services and infrastructure that have a large public good component and cannot therefore be provided adequately by the private sector, such as education, health, public utilities and roads. In addition, the exigencies of adjustment or development might in some cases require the government to provide temporarily some services that can in principle be provided by the private sector once the successful implementation of policy reform has allowed its capacities to develop sufficiently. In order to avoid stifling the development of the nascent private sector, any such activities, whether undertaken by governments or other agencies, need to be carefully planned and coordinated.

The achievement of food security on a sustainable basis therefore requires that governments take action on a number of different policy fronts. Trade and macroeconomic policies are needed that permit and foster overall economic growth and increase competitiveness in export markets; they should also correct past distortions that favour one sector of the economy to the detriment of others. Agricultural sector policies should be designed to promote sustained and sustainable sector growth in order to increase both domestic food supply and agricultural and food exports for which the country has a comparative advantage. Although economic growth is so important for addressing the underlying causes of food insecurity, "economies cannot be expected to grow quickly enough to eliminate the chronic food insecurity of some groups in the near future, even under the best of circumstances. Moreover, long-run economic growth is often slowed by widespread chronic food insecurity. People who lack energy are ill-equipped to take advantage of opportunities for increasing their productivity and output" (World Bank 1986). Further, gross inequalities of income distribution may prevent the resource-poor from participating in the growth process, and certain policy reforms may of themselves have substantial negative impacts on vulnerable groups in society. Special measures may be needed in the short and medium terms to deal with specific cases of food insecurity, and to ensure that essential food imports can be financed. Over the long run, some special measures will always be needed, although their nature may change.

It must be re-emphasized that the successful implementation of agricultural and food policies alone cannot achieve a national objective of food security. The elimination of absolute poverty, the root cause of food insecurity, requires action across the board to enable people to escape the cycle of poverty and malnutrition that traps successive generations. Yet the achievement of food security does not have to wait on the eradication of poverty. It is repeatedly stated by international agencies, donor governments, world summits, and just about everybody else involved in development that the resources and the means exist to eliminate food insecurity, the problem is "just" the lack of political will. If governments would only readjust their priorities accordingly, the problem could be solved—although discussion about the time-frame required is studiously avoided. "Success stories" tend to concentrate on the policies that a particular country has implemented without delving too deeply into the socio-political circumstances that enabled it to implement those policies. Rarely is it asked why the political will might be lacking.

"Political will is journalistic shorthand for the overcoming of the conflicting interests, ideological blinkers and structural constraints that usually make it impossible for governments to do what is technically feasible and clearly necessary to solve a serious problem. The term contributes to good journalism, but poor social science. Social scientists have to explain why political will is lacking and what might be done to produce it" (Barraclough 1991).

The findings of research on food systems by UNRISD (the United Nations Research Institute for Social Development) are unusual in that the question of political will is raised explicitly. They cast doubt on the political possibilities, rather than the strictly technical ones, of rapidly improving food access for the very poor. This applies to rich industrialized countries who have widely differing levels of social and economic deprivation as well as countries at other stages of development. Governments are, after all, dependent on the groups to whom they owe their support, and their room for manoeuvre is correspondingly restricted.

"If the problem is really systemic, as the UNRISD team believes, then it can be dealt with effectively only through both fundamental public policy and social change. The latter implies new power relationships among individuals, social classes, groups and nations. Social changes do not come about easily. Convincing political leaders that hunger and poverty are serious and solvable social problems does not bring about political will, although in some circumstances it might help. ... In alleviating hunger, politics matters. ... How are sufficient political pressures generated to force governments to adopt effective strategies leading to rapid diminution of poverty and hunger? Answers are unique for each time and place. Where social forces have emerged capable of bringing about such policies, however, there have been at least three broad and closely inter-related social processes at work" (Barraclough 1991).

1.2 Social and political processes

The three social processes referred to are identified as modernization processes—the social impact of economic growth and technical change; the rapidly increasing availability and dissemination of information, which contributes to social change by changing perceptions and ideologies; and popular participation—the mobilization and organization in a real sense of those previously excluded by lack of control over resources or influence over government. The interactions between political, social, economic and ecological systems and processes as they affect people's access to food—locally, nationally and internationally—are extremely complex and the problems admit of no easy solutions. It follows logically, and is observed over and over again, that there is rarely anything as simple as a technical solution to a complex problem. To take a simple example, assume crop yields can be increased by increasing fertilizer applications: whether fertilizer will in fact be applied depends on many other factors, e.g., are fertilizer imports regarded as being sufficiently important for the government to guarantee foreign exchange availability on a reliable basis? Can the distribution system get it to the right place at the right time? Do the farmgate prices for output justify its use? Can farmers obtain the resources to buy it in the first place? Are some farmers restricted in their access to fertilizer for political or other non-economic reasons?[3] Note that we are not talking here about the political will to establish state interventions or subsidies to encourage an otherwise uneconomical fertilizer use, but the political will to remove existing distortions or privileges.

There are many technical questions (covering a wide range of professional disciplines) concerning food insecurity that require technical answers. Should fertilizer be applied? Yes, in a given set of agro-ecological circumstances if yields are to be increased. Because the basic problems of food insecurity are not purely technical, however, the solutions are not purely technical either. So will fertilizer be applied? No, unless the political, social and economic configuration determines that it shall be. The rest of this chapter examines some of the economic questions of food security, and the policy implications for the governments concerned.

2 Rural and urban food security—growth with equity

In countries with a large agricultural sector, policies to achieve food security at the national level, and perhaps even more at the household level, must include policies for agriculture and the rural economy within which it operates. This is so self-evident that household food insecurity in the urban areas sometimes tends to be overlooked. In this section, therefore, we look at some of the relationships between the urban and the rural economies, and the macroeconomic policies that affect the two sectors differentially. In particular, income, employment, taxation and public expenditure policies are of great importance in ensuring accessibility to food supplies: understanding the economic linkages between the urban and rural areas throws a different light on the effects that those policies have on households in the respective areas.

2.1 Rural growth and urban bias

One major consequence of the economic policy bias against agriculture that has hindered its growth in so many developing countries has been the extremely high incidence of rural poverty and hence food insecurity. A second is a rate of urbanization that is faster than it would have been in the absence of such a policy bias. More than three-quarters of the poor in sub-Saharan Africa and south Asia live in

3 As an example, there have been cases where the control of input supplies has been through a government agency that has restricted, say, fertilizer supplies to those supporting a particular political party.

rural areas. Despite rapid urban growth of almost 6 percent per annum in sub-Saharan Africa since 1960, resulting in a population that is about one-third urbanized, the absolute size of the rural population continues to grow (Gleave 1992). Southeast and southern Asia have slightly lower levels of urbanization than sub-Saharan Africa, and also annual growth rates of the urban population of less than 4 percent. Although Latin America is much more highly urbanized (over 70 percent), a substantial proportion of the poor are rural. Achieving food security therefore requires policies to encourage the development of the rural economy. However, the magnitude of the numbers should not blind us to the fact that there is also a serious and growing problem of food insecurity within sections of many urban populations—and one that has become more serious given the exigencies of structural reform policies[4]—that governments need to address. It should also be said that between the definitional inconsistencies and the data deficiencies, there is insufficient information about the real incidence of urban versus rural poverty and food insecurity, and of the effects of progressive urbanization on urban food insecurity:

"An urban bias in much of government policies for food security coexists with a rural bias in much of the detailed food security research. It has long been recognized that developing country governments are more responsive to the urban poor than to the less vocal rural poor. Urban bias in food policies has been criticized by the research community and rightly, especially if transfers affecting food consumption were financed by the rural poor through the implicit and explicit taxation of agriculture" (Von Braun 1987).

The distinction between the urban[5] economy and the rural economy is not one conventionally made by economists, who tend to view the system as comprising the macroeconomy at the most aggregate level, and as a set of sectors—agriculture, extractive industry, manufacturing industry and services—at the first level of disaggregation. Yet analysis approached in this way implicitly assumes a strong and complete set of linkages between the different sectors, which is manifestly not the case in many developing countries. The urban-rural distinction is perhaps a more useful subdivision for analytical and policy purposes, and one that has meaning for countries at all stages of development: it is particularly relevant in the least-developed country context because the linkages between the urban and rural economies as a whole, especially through the labour and food markets, are often more important than those between the main economic sectors as traditionally defined. In other words, the lack of development of the non-agricultural sectors in the rural economy means that there are few "vertical linkages" within a sector such

4 See Demery and Squire (1996), who note that the evidence suggests that urban poverty appears to have increased significantly. They also emphasize the continuing data problem, despite the recent increase in the number of household surveys.

5 There is no standard definition of "urban" in terms of size of town. Further, definitions can include administrative and commercial importance, and non-agricultural activity criteria. Thus "urbanization" is characterized more by diversity of economic base with relatively low dependence on agriculture than by size in the developing country context. See Gleave (1992).

as manufacturing that cross the urban-rural divide and form cross-linkages with the agricultural sector; similarly, the urban services sector may have few such vertical linkages with service provision in rural areas: the connections are more between the urban economy in general and the agricultural sector through distribution, perhaps of imported goods.

The urban-rural distinction is also relevant to the countries in transition from centrally planned to market economies whose agricultural policy reforms have had a serious impact on the rural economy. The provision of many economic and social services in the rural areas, such as rural road maintenance, nursery schools and cultural and leisure facilities, was formerly the responsibility of the heavily subsidized collective and cooperative farms. The privatization of agricultural holdings has left a vacuum in terms of rural services provision. At the same time, the sharp reductions in agricultural subsidies are leading to contraction of the industry with associated rural unemployment and urban migration. Having said that, in some of the transition economies there is strong anecdotal evidence that some areas have seen quite a substantial migration of the unskilled unemployed from industry to agriculture.

2.2 Agriculture as a growth leader

In most developing countries, agriculture is still the motor of the rural economy, and, directly or indirectly, the main source of rural incomes. There has therefore been a tendency to stress the need for the development of agriculture *per se*. The argument runs as follows: in economies that are predominantly agricultural, capital scarcity limits the absorption capacity in the urban areas for labour migrating from agriculture. Thus growth of agriculture and related rural enterprises is the main vehicle by which employment and income can be increased on a widespread basis. Land-augmenting technological change is the key to higher agricultural productivity. Consumer food prices fall in consequence, and national income rises. The decline in food prices also has a multiplier effect on national income as urban wages need not rise as much as would be necessary without the fall in food prices. This results in additional employment and greater output for the whole economy. Agricultural growth has other multiplier effects. The increased agricultural production generates effective demand for goods and services produced by the domestic non-agricultural economy: as a result, relative prices (the terms of trade) shift in favour of the non-agricultural sectors, and resources—including labour and capital—are transferred from agricultural to non-agricultural uses. This stimulates growth in the non-agricultural sectors. The positive impact of agriculture-led development strategies where such are appropriate is well documented in empirical studies.[6]

But the issue is rather more complex. A sectoral development focus on agriculture, which is more pointed given the bias against agriculture in favour of other

6 A good summary is given in Vollrath (1994).

sectors, obscures the fact that agriculture as a sector operates predominantly in the context of the rural economy, a complex subset of the national economy that extends beyond any single sector. It also ignores the high and growing dependence of the rural poor on non-agricultural sources of income, such as craftwork, services, remittances and non-agricultural wages that can together equal—or even exceed—the agricultural income share (Von Braun 1989). This phenomenon is not confined to the landless rural poor, but includes also a large proportion of small-scale farmers who are net food purchasers. Tackling rural food insecurity clearly therefore requires the development of the rural economy as a whole, not just agriculture, and will therefore contribute to tackling urban food insecurity through increased food supplies at lower prices.

The other sectors of the rural economy are related to the agricultural sector by way of the backward and forward linkages, as well as through the multiplier effects on consumption and production. Von Braun (1989) notes that "a review of the farm/non-farm linkages in rural sub-Saharan Africa suggests that agricultural growth multipliers appear to be significant though somewhat lower than in some Asian countries". This implies that policy measures for sub-Saharan Africa in particular need to be geared towards developing the linkages in the first place, rather than just to increasing those that already exist, if agricultural development is to lead to broadly based growth of the rural economy, and if the agricultural sector is to be integrated into the national and international economies (see Section 4 below). At the same time, agricultural development itself requires the creation and continuing expansion of those linkages within the rural economy and with the national (urban) and international economies. This offers the prospect of increasing rural employment opportunities and incomes. For example, on the input supply side (the backward linkages), there will be a growing demand for capital goods, such as tools and agricultural machinery, as well as for the associated service inputs. The forward linkages include such factors as output marketing and food processing. Some of the consumption goods that will be increasingly demanded as agricultural—and indeed non-agricultural rural—incomes grow can also be produced in the rural areas.

2.3 But agriculture is not enough

Such a focus on the development of the rural economy, with agricultural development as its driving force, could have major benefits in the longer term for the urban economy. At the moment, the situation in the many developing countries that have not had broadly based development is rather difficult. The lack of growth in the rural economy has spurred rural-urban migration at a rate that has exceeded the capacity of the formal urban employment sector to absorb it. Food subsidies for urban consumers provided additional encouragement, especially perhaps in Latin American and some other countries where the bi-modal agrarian structure led to extreme rural poverty and destitution. In looking at sub-Saharan Africa, for example, Gleave (1992) argues that "present levels and rates of urbanization and the size of major cities in the subcontinent are not the result of economic development but a reflection of the lack of it. ... The problems include employment (and unemployment), housing, traffic congestion, electricity supply, water supply, sewerage and waste disposal." (This is in sharp contrast to the Asian newly industrialized countries (NICs) where urbanization increased in line with employment opportunities.) The demand-reducing policies that form part of many structural adjustment programmes[7] have exacerbated this already difficult situation, especially in the urban areas: cuts in public sector employment, reductions in food subsidies, the imposition of indirect taxes and falling real wages have a disproportionate negative effect on the urban poor with a concomitant rise in the incidence of urban food insecurity. The reduction in labour opportunities and real wages in the formal sector increases the labour supply in the informal sector, and puts a downward pressure on the returns to labour. This occurs despite the rise in the price of food as a wage good because labour in the informal sector is not organized so as to articulate an effective demand for higher wages. The linkages with the rural sector primarily through labour and food markets and remittances ensure that some of these negative effects will be transmitted to the rural economy.

The long-term, broadly based growth of the economy is a precondition for improving food security. This must necessarily involve the development of the rural economy as a whole, which requires agricultural sector growth, and greatly strengthened linkages within the rural economy and between the rural and the urban economy. But growth of itself, while necessary, is not sufficient. We need to look to growth with equity for all of the population, rural and urban, bearing in mind that, even if the absolute numbers of food insecure are greater in the rural areas, there are still many people in urban areas who are malnourished. And given the linkages between the urban and rural areas, poverty and food insecurity in either will have negative effects on the other.

In the longer term, growth with equity requires that the food-insecure poor acquire more control over resources so that the benefits of growth are shared more equitably, which will of itself lead to more growth. More immediately, there are policy measures that can be implemented to improve the food security position of the poorest (Stewart 1995), taking account of the need to protect the most vulnerable from the negative effects of structural adjustment programmes whilst allowing the long-term benefits for economy-wide growth from those programmes to be realized.

2.3.1 Taxation policies

Taxation policies critically affect the poor. Changes in the tax base that increase government revenues through the imposition of indirect rather than direct taxes generally affect the poor disproportionately. Direct taxes tend to be progressive

---

7 A theoretical and empirical analysis of the different components of structural adjustment programmes and their impact on poverty can be found in Stewart (1995).

whereas indirect taxes are regressive if they are imposed on goods and services that are purchased by the poor (food, public transport, fuel for cooking) or if the inputs into such goods and services are taxed; indirect taxes can be designed to be progressive if they are levied on luxury goods and services. Thus whereas reducing the disproportionate direct and indirect tax burden on the agricultural sector removes some of the anti-agricultural and anti-rural bias of earlier policies, its replacement by inappropriately designed taxes can lead to a more widespread anti-poor bias.

2.3.2 Public expenditure policies

Public expenditure policies are equally important. Cuts in public expenditure can be made so that spending on vital services such as primary education and primary healthcare in both urban and rural areas is maintained. It is easier of course if the economy is growing, even though this may still mean a temporary falling expenditure per capita. Negative growth poses more intractable difficulties, but priority can be given to those services most needed by the very poor. In practice, there is too often a bias in favour of the upper and middle income urban population, with expenditure on hospitals and secondary and tertiary education being accorded higher priority than the provision of free access by the very poor in both urban and rural areas to a more basic level of service that they otherwise cannot afford and that is essential for the development of their human capital (Demery and Squire 1996). Investment in infrastructure and budgetary allocations for infrastructure maintenance are needed for the achievement of development goals in the longer term: in particular, the neglect of maintenance invariably turns out to be a false economy.

Public expenditure choices also need to consider the provision of food subsidies, an important mechanism for transferring income to poor households where the majority of the income is devoted to food expenditures. Food subsidies have mostly benefitted urban consumers, and have in many cases been universal. Largely for budgetary reasons, the tendency has been to replace the universal subsidies with targeted subsidies, and much time and effort has gone into devising targeted schemes. That replacing universal with targeted subsidies has reduced costs is indisputable. However, the success of targeted subsidies in achieving full coverage of the target groups is far less obvious. Stewart (*op. cit.*) lists four main reasons for this: lack of information about the targeted schemes among the target groups; costs of acquiring entitlements to targeted schemes; qualifications for entitlement that exclude some of the poor as well as the non-poor; and social stigma. Although a narrow benefit-cost analysis of targeted interventions may well be positive, such an approach does not take into account the real costs of excluding some of those in need, which includes both short-term and long-term losses in labour productivity, and inter-generational effects arising from maternal malnutrition and reproductive efficiency. Another point is that although universal subsidies may in some cases benefit the richer groups more in absolute terms (much as agricultural price supports benefit larger farmers more in absolute terms), the benefits to poorer groups in terms of income effects because of the substantially higher proportion of income spent on food are greater. Further, if the coverage of food subsidy schemes, whether "universal" (in the sense that all buyers of, say, imported wheat and wheat products benefit from the subsidy) or targeted, does not extend to the rural areas as well as to the urban areas, the majority of the poor are in any event not going to benefit from the subsidy. The received wisdom has been that the rural poor, as food producers, will better receive their benefits in the form of higher agricultural prices. But as we have seen, a large proportion of the rural poor, be they semi-subsistence farmers or landless labourers, are net food purchasers in many developing countries, and so an increase in food prices will often tend to outweigh the income effects of higher farm-gate prices for agricultural produce. Thus the provision of food subsidies, and the form they take, are important determinants of food security directly and the ability through enhanced labour productivity and income effects to take advantage of opportunities to improve the food security position of the household.

2.3.3 Labour market policies

This brings us to the vital question of government policies and the labour market. The only resource that many poor people possess is their labour, and it is usually limited by being unskilled or at best semi-skilled; its productivity may be reduced by malnutrition, ill health, and the lack of affordable opportunities for education and training. Nevertheless, employment-based growth offers the most effective way of tackling poverty and food insecurity in both urban and rural areas (Demery and Squire 1996). This requires government policies that improve labour productivity; enable the poor to access labour opportunities;[8] remove or avoid anti-labour biases in the factor markets; and, in the sequencing of policy reforms, allow for the slower adjustment of labour markets relative to capital markets. The World Bank (1990) found that: "Many countries make imports of capital goods cheap (through low tariffs and over-valued exchange rates), offer tax breaks for investment in capital equipment, and subsidize credit—all of which tend to reduce the price of capital. Subsidized energy prices often exacerbate this bias and, furthermore, have adverse environmental consequences. In contrast, social security taxes, labor regulations, and high wages (especially in industries in which competition among producers is weak) all tend to raise the cost of labor in the formal sector. ... Labor-market policies ... are usually intended to raise welfare or reduce exploitation. But they actually work to raise the cost of labor in the formal sector and reduce labor demand. Studies from the 1970s and 1980s found that job security regulations reduced the long-term demand for labour by an estimated 18 percent in India and 25 percent in Zimbabwe. There is little poverty, in any case, in the formal sector.

---

8 "Where the poor are concentrated on the periphery of urban areas, as in many developing countries, the costs and availability of public transport become key factors in their ability to obtain employment" (World Bank 1994).

Yet by trying to improve the welfare of workers there, governments reduced formal sector employment, increased the supply of labor to the rural and urban informal sectors, and thus depressed labor incomes where most of the poor are found."

In most developing countries, and increasingly so under structural adjustment programmes, formal employment accounts for only a minor proportion of available labour. Recognizing the importance of the informal sector, agencies such as ILO and the World Bank are more and more advocating policies that will strengthen the informal sector by reducing or eliminating restrictions on its activities, even though this has certain negative features in the short to medium term.

"For developing countries, there is no alternative but to accumulate sufficient investments to generate a high rate of employment-intensive growth. Employment creation is a unique instrument for achieving such an objective since it is a vital input in the creation of wealth, and, at the same time, the most efficient mechanism for income distribution. Creating the conditions for a growth regime that maximizes employment and restrains unemployment and deprivation will require a coherent strategy for poverty reduction" (Von Braun 1995).

2.4 Putting it all together

Governments, sometimes in partnership with international agencies, have implemented a wide range of employment-creating programmes with a greater or lesser degree of success.[9] At their best, such programmes provide productive employment for the very poor—productive in the sense that the work undertaken creates useful social infrastructure such as roads, water supply and sanitary facilities, or addresses resource constraints such as land quality and irrigation. While government or international funding (in cash or in food wages) may provide the necessary resources, it is sometimes possible to involve the private sector in the actual implementation. As so often happens in countries at all stages of development, it is easier to build the infrastructure than to ensure its maintenance when the responsibility is transferred to another level of government without the provision of additional funding. Although most schemes seem to have been implemented in rural areas, there is no inherent reason why appropriate schemes cannot be designed for urban areas. The significance of the locality depends in large part on the physical and financial mobility of the labour force. Planning is important, for budgetary reasons and also for the institutional and technical support needed for success.

9 A good account of the types of programmes that have been attempted in different countries and regions, and the lessons that can be learnt is given in von Braun (1995).

3 Reliability: Dealing with short-term fluctuations and long-term trends

It is an accepted legal precept that hard cases make for bad law: one could with equal justice say that short-term crises make for bad policy. This chapter was written against the background of a perceived global grain crisis, which is of its nature short term while nevertheless having serious longer-term impacts on several low-income, food-deficit countries. In the understandable desire to react to an urgent situation, we must still keep our eyes on the long view.

The reliability component of food security concerns both availability and access, and is often confused with stability, although the question "stability of what and for whom" is rarely addressed explicitly. Weather and other acts of nature affect the stability of supply; abrupt changes in demand affect the stability of price; the interaction of macroeconomic and sectoral policies within and across countries can affect both.

3.1 Price impact of supply fluctuations

Supply-side fluctuations in cereal production have a disproportionate impact on prices because of the relatively small short-run price elasticity of demand for cereals in the aggregate. A major cause of supply instability is a weather-induced shock such as occurred in the early 1970s, when the 1973 cereal crop fell 3.5 percent below trend, and again in 1995 when the production fall was 3 percent below trend, the effects of which are still being played out. Adverse weather conditions in north America, northern Europe and major parts of the former Soviet Union, together with failure of the monsoon in south Asia, resulted in the 1973 cereals crop being 3.5 percent below trend. This, given that the US Government decided in the late 1960s to get out of the stocking business, together with a number of other factors that occurred simultaneously (e.g., the first oil price shock and its aftermath, which inter alia, increased the prices of many agricultural inputs, and the change in Soviet policy to import cereals during domestic shortage rather than slaughter livestock herds) caused a sharp and rapid escalation of prices in international cereal markets (see Figure 1).

A similar weather-induced phenomenon happened in 1995, with a drop in global production of 3 percent below trend. World grain prices rose sharply during 1995, with unusually low policy-induced stocks and problematic growing conditions in several producing areas. During January-June 1996, US wheat export prices were up about 30 percent from a year before, but importers of US grain were frequently facing price increases of 50 percent or more owing to the reduction or elimination of the export price subsidy. The US export price of maize, the leading coarse grain, rose by 46% over the same period, as reflected in prices paid by importers. Rice prices also rose markedly, despite significant stocks in India and China. The grain import costs faced by many importing countries increased even more because key exporters largely suspended export price subsidies. Exporter supplies were tight, and world grain stocks had dropped to the lowest level since the early 1970s, the stocks-to-use ratios for cereals stood at only 14 percent.

Figure 1: Wheat export prices 1970-1996 (constant 1990 and nominal US Dollars per metric ton)

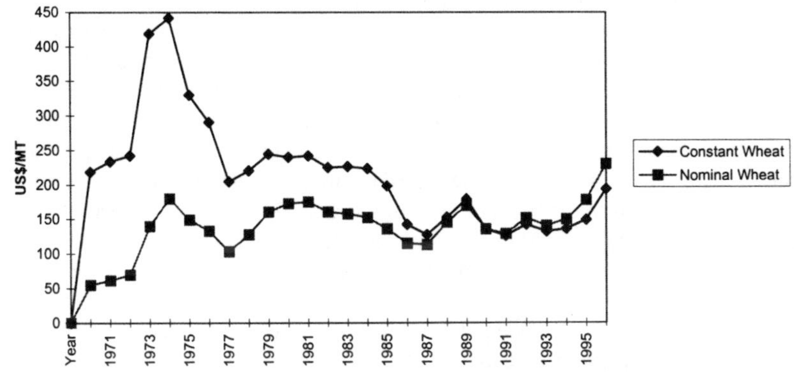

1996: Jan-Jun Average

Source: FAO, World Bank (Deflator).

Thus the grain market phenomenon is one of short-term fluctuations—sharp price rises and less sharp price falls (the price falls are naturally of less concern to the importing countries, although not to the exporting countries whose policies have been designed to mitigate the falls to a greater extent than the rises)—around a long-term decline in the trend of real world grain prices. The rate of decline appears to be slowing down, but there is as yet no real evidence that it has bottomed out. Even at its peak, the 1995/96 price spike reflected a lower real price than at any time since 1985, and has never exceeded about 40 percent of the real price in 1974 (see Figure 1). The commodity markets for the major tropical agricultural export crops also show great price variability around even more steeply declining long-term real prices.

The price impact of the weather-induced supply shocks of 1973 and 1995 on international markets was of longer duration in both instances than it would have been in an open-market, liberal trading environment because many countries, both exporters and importers, have policies that isolate the domestic market from the international market. This isolation means that price signals from the international market do not reach domestic producers or consumers, who therefore do not adjust to the international market conditions. In effect, longer-lived instability is exported to the international market by those countries. The adjustment that occurs takes place within the few countries that have relatively open agricultural economies, and tends to be large because the adjustment burden is not being shared by all.

As Johnson (1984) so cogently put it, "much of the price variability in international market prices is man-made—it is the consequence of policies followed by many governments. In short, national policies that stabilize domestic prices for consumers and producers do so at the cost of international price variability unless the domestic price stability is achieved by holding stocks of sufficient size to create what is in effect a perfectly elastic supply curve for the relevant food product. But countries other than Canada, India and the United States have not held stocks of such size; consequently almost all national programs of domestic price stability are achieved by varying imports and exports to make supply equal domestic demand at the predetermined and stable price. In this way, all the potential price effects of domestic demand and supply variations are imposed on the world market." Nevertheless, changes are occurring in the global environment within which international trade takes place; from the point of view of global and national food security, future strategies need to differ from those of the past. It is also clear that the food security policy responses to the short-term fluctuations and long-term trends need to be different.

Over the past four decades, the US has been the major inter-temporal (inter-seasonal) stock-holder of cereals, with the EU also maintaining significant grain reserves since the late 1970s when it became a net cereal exporter. Canada has at times carried much smaller grain reserves while neither Australia nor Argentina have had the storage capacity to do so. Food reserve stocks in India until very recently have been strictly domestic. The stocks held by both the US and the EU were the result of agricultural policies that supported the domestic price above market clearing levels, requiring the authorities to purchase and hold stocks until a pre-determined market price trigger allowed their release into the market. In addition, the various area set-aside schemes and the conservation reserve programmes that held land out of cereal production acted as a further complementary stock of grain, albeit in the form of idle land rather than physical quantities of grain. These so-called policy-induced stocks will be drastically reduced or eliminated as market and trade liberalization occurs. This means that the world will no longer be able to rely on such policy-induced stocks to cushion the price effects of a production shortfall.

3.2 Uncertainties in a more liberal trade environment

This raises two separate but related issues. The first is just what is likely to be the behaviour of the global cereals market in a more liberal trade and markets environment. Work is underway at FAO and elsewhere on analyzing this question, but unfortunately only preliminary results are available at the time of writing. Economic theory and an empirical understanding of markets, however, can lead to some informed qualitative speculation. Consider the case of a reduction in world production. Without the cushion of the policy-induced stocks to buffer the price rise in response to the production shortfall, the international price rise is likely to be sharper. But with more open economies and liberalized markets there will be greater international market price transmission to more producers and consumers in more countries. This should mean that a larger and quicker supply and demand adjustment will occur in response to the price change, with producers increasing output and consumers shifting consumption in favour of relatively cheaper foodstuffs. Thus future international market price spikes are likely to be more violent initially, but shorter lived. A sub-question is to what extent the private sector will take on the stock-holding function formerly borne by governments with policy-induced stocks. The private sector would not be expected to carry stocks of a similar magnitude, as such levels would most probably be unprofitable. Nevertheless, the private sector will hold stocks up to a profitable level, and to that extent those stocks would buffer and reduce the magnitude of market price spikes.

This discussion has focussed on upward price movements. An examination of Figure 1 shows that hitherto downward price movements have been much less sharp and deep, reflecting the policies of some of the main grain producing countries which have been designed to protect their farmers from severe price falls. To the extent that liberalization and policy reform remove or reduce the effects of such policies, the international market would see greater downward price variation than it has in the past. Thus in years of good harvests, price falls would be more pronounced, enabling importing countries to reap the benefits, and providing perhaps greater profit incentives for private sector stocking.

3.3 Need for stocking?

The second issue is that a number of countries may still feel the need to hold some level of food security reserve, as distinct from any working stocks held by private importers and traders. (Countries that do not will bear the full brunt of market instability.) These countries have basically two options. One is to hold a foreign currency fund for food security reserve purposes rather than holding a physical stock of the commodity. The main advantage of this option is that the country does not incur the significant costs of holding the actual commodity and of stock management, and can indeed earn interest on the hard currency account. However, the use of such a fund during periods of global supply shortfall will exacerbate the price spike. The tradeoff for the country involved is the additional import cost due to the price spike minus what has been earned on the foreign exchange account as compared with the cost of holding the commodity reserve until it is needed.

Whilst a foreign exchange food security fund has both fiscal and monetary implications (e.g., tax revenues or borrowings to establish the fund, a positive balance of payments item and earnings on the fund until it is needed), a physical commodity stock reserve has mainly fiscal implications if purchased locally, but also monetary if acquired through imports. Firstly there is the expense of establishing the stock reserve either through tax revenues or through borrowing. Then there are the maintenance costs associated with the reserve including stock administration, transport, storage, handling, rotation and so forth, which will need to be financed from the same sources. Finally, distribution and replenishment costs are incurred when the food security reserve is called upon in accordance with the pre-existing rules governing its use. Ideally, the stock would be replenished when prices are low and depleted when high: but, as we have seen, policy reforms that permit substantial price falls have yet to feed through to the international market. The government budget for establishment, operation and management of the physical commodity food security reserve has an opportunity cost over and above the monetary cost either by government or by the private sector. This opportunity cost may be great or small, depending on the alternative uses that might have been made of the funds. Given the shortage of both capital and recurrent budgetary funds in developing countries, the opportunity cost if properly calculated is likely to be very high.

4 Trade- and balance of payment-related economic policies

A country's trade-related economic policies influence food security indirectly through their effect on the growth of the economy as a whole and of particular economic sectors. They also have a more direct impact on food security and nutrition status by affecting such factors as rural and urban household incomes, the ability to import food to meet domestic shortfalls and demand for food items not produced locally, and the earning of foreign exchange to finance the varying share of food imports in total imports.

"The expansion of agricultural trade has helped provide greater quantity, wider variety and better quality food to increasing numbers of people at lower prices. Agricultural trade is also a generator of income and welfare for the millions of people who are directly or indirectly involved in it. At the national level, for many countries, it is a major source of the foreign exchange that is necessary to finance imports and development; while for many others, domestic food security is closely related to the country's capacity to finance food imports. ... Agricultural trade policy has long reflected the widely held belief that, because of its importance and vulnerability, the agricultural sector could not be exposed to the full rigours of international competition without incurring unacceptable political, social and economic consequences. This view has led to high and widespread protection of the sector" (FAO 1995b).

4.1 Protection or bias against agriculture?

It has been argued that the instability in commodity markets that has apparently resulted from agricultural border protection has in its turn led to further pressures for protection. Whether or not this is true, many developing countries have nevertheless implemented economic policies that have been biased against the production of tradable goods in general and exports in particular, as well as against agricultural products. Taxation of the agricultural sector has been high in several countries. A major research study by the World Bank[10] covering 18 countries over a 25-year period found that "the indirect tax on agriculture from industrial protection and macroeconomic policies was about 22 percent on average ... nearly three times the direct tax from agricultural pricing policies (about 8 percent). The total (direct plus indirect) was thus 30 percent" (Schiff and Valdés 1992). The overall effect has been an average income transfer out of agriculture of 46 percent of agricultural GDP, ranging from 2 percent for the countries that "protected" agriculture to 140 percent for the heaviest taxers. In such countries, investment in food production has therefore been sub-optimal, and agricultural growth has been stifled, as has economic growth as a whole. Trade-related economic policy reforms and the ongoing structural adjustment programmes should lead towards correction of the long-standing anti-agriculture bias, if the reforms are carried out with real commitment and consistency. "The adjustment in Africa displays several weaknesses. From the evidence of recent policy actions, African governments have yet to display a real commitment to policy reform. Macroeconomic imbalances continue to characterize many economies, even those ... that have been engaged in adjustment for more than a decade. Governments continue to interfere in markets" (Demery and Squire 1996).[11] The same authors stress the critical role of exchange rate policy in stimulating growth and reducing poverty through the correction of economic disequilibria.

The maintenance of over-valued exchange rates is of particular significance as they impose a tax on exports and subsidize imports. This tool has been used at high cost to stabilize and hold down domestic food prices for urban consumers at the expense of the domestic producers of import-competing and exportable agricultural products, often in the face of severe domestic inflation which has been poorly controlled or exacerbated by economic policy measures. In the long-run, therefore, the effects are damaging for food security as (i) structural changes in the tastes and preferences of urban consumers that do not take account of real international prices, as well as increasing urban incomes, exert pressure to maintain and increase food imports; (ii) the ability to pay for those imports has been reduced by depressing the expansion of agricultural and food exports which, for many low-income countries, are the main source of export earnings; (iii) the benefits of long-term falling real cereal prices have not been realizable in the face of high domestic inflation; and (iv) greater exchange rate overvaluation is related to lower GDP growth. Correcting over-valued exchange rates, which increases the domestic price of tradable food items, and controlling inflation, which slows down the rate of increase in domestic food prices and reduces the cost of stabilization measures, should therefore be put high on the policy reform agenda, and kept there. Rather than delay painful macro-

10 The results are published in five volumes under the overall heading of "The Political Economy of Agricultural Pricing Policy" (World Bank 1992). A summary of the major policy findings is given in Schiff and Valdés (1992).

11 The authors review evidence from six African countries using data from detailed household surveys.

economic adjustment, which needs to allow for balanced sectoral growth by removing the biases against agriculture, governments may be better advised to implement compensatory interventions targeted at the groups most vulnerable to rises in the prices of tradable foods.

As noted earlier, there appears to be a long-term shift in the terms of trade away from the traditional agricultural export crops in favour of food crops. Thus over time, a country's comparative advantage will change. Trade and macroeconomic policies, as well as sectoral pricing policies, need to permit the agricultural sector to respond to changes in comparative advantage patterns by reallocation of resources. However, in anticipation of these changes, governments need to invest in the long-term development of agriculture and the rural economy, as indicated earlier.

4.2 Importer's options

The implementation of appropriate trade and macroeconomic policies is critical for another important aspect of food security: the ability to finance the importation of food that is not produced domestically or is not produced in sufficient quantities, both in times of short-term price fluctuations and to meet the ongoing import, needs reliably. Whilst increasing food aid is often the alternative of choice in this type of situation, that solution does not appear to be feasible in the near future. The overall level of food aid has been declining recently. Higher prices can be expected to further reduce the quantity of food aid, as most aid allocations are planned and budgeted in value terms. It is to be hoped that the lower food aid availabilities result in tighter targeting to meet the needs of the most severely affected countries and regions.That leaves a significant number of other developing countries, which are generally in a marginal position with respect to financing grain import requirements, to search for alternative methods of finance in a period of higher prices.

The long-term issue concerns the ability of export earnings to keep pace with food import bills. The relatively rapid decline in real prices of agricultural export commodities has been exacerbated by increased supplies of such commodities by several low-income countries: if one small country increases its exports, it will not affect the world price. If a large number do, the effect will be to depress prices further and faster. Commodity agreements have had very little success in supporting world prices, and are unlikely to yield substantial benefits to the exporting countries in the aggregate. Schiff and Valdés (1992) suggest that for "the few export products where developing countries have market power, appropriate export taxes or quotas should be imposed." However, this might not prove easy to agree because the "appropriate" tax or quota in one country depends on the levels set by other countries exporting the same commodity. Further, the ability of exporting countries to do this will depend on the countervailing power by the importing countries or corporations.

There are a number of policy issues that governments can address to the end of financing food imports. For example, there are long-term measures that can be taken to increase a country's export earning capability over time, and also to increase domestic food production and reduce production, processing and marketing costs. To this end, government can implement non-distorting measures to increase the export earnings capability of the agricultural and food sector. This should not imply the promotion of export crops at the expense of food crops, nor the promotion of food exports at the expense of food security. The question is one of improving exportability, which must take account of international market demand, and is closely linked to improving domestic food availability, an important aspect of food security. The reason for this is that for the potential for exportability to be realizable by large numbers of farmers of different types exploiting different agro-ecological conditions, the internal domestic marketing system must be able to deliver inputs and outputs whenever and wherever they are needed to minimize production and marketing costs and meet market demand on competitive terms.

So policy measures to improve domestic and export marketing should address the needs for hard and soft infrastructure: an adequate agricultural and food research and extension base; improved processing, preservation and storage techniques and facilities; food standards for domestic and imported products, as well as quality control and grading to meet international requirements; information (production, domestic markets, nutrition, international markets); adding value in-country to the basic commodity, or producing high-value commodities such as fruit and flowers, including new product development; export promotion; export credit guarantees; and export insurance.

Where available and appropriate, governments could also take steps to make the maximum use of programmes such as the EU's STABEX scheme and Sectoral Import Programme,[12] and the increased availability of foreign exchange assistance (as opposed to balance of payments assistance) could be explored. There might also be possibilities for short-term assistance for financing commercial imports under the GATT/WTO Decision on Measures Concerning the Possible Negative Effects of the Reform Programme on Least-developed and Net Food Importing Countries, although the position is not yet clear.

4.3 Balance of payments support

The International Monetary Fund (IMF), as part of its statutory purposes, has funds and programmes under which it can make resources available to member countries in relation to certain balance of payments problems. These may include cases where members are facing difficulties resulting from a rise in international cereal prices. The IMF can provide financial assistance either under a special facility or by adjustments in regular Fund arrangements.

12 The purpose of the EU's Sectoral Import Programme is to provide foreign exchange for the purchase of certain high priority imports, e.g., fertilizer, agrochemicals, machinery and spare parts for agricultural processing, and fishing equipment. The equivalent amount in local currency must be forthcoming and the scheme is open to private sector agents as well as government agencies.

The Compensatory and Contingency Financing Facility (CCFF) is a special facility designed to help countries in the case of shortfalls in their export receipts or where there are excess cereal import costs. It is one of the financing tools provided to assist countries facing adverse external shocks in maintaining the momentum of their adjustment programmes. The conditions for use of the scheme are rather complex and contain several features that limit access by cereal-importing countries: the calculation of the excess costs of the cereal imports; constraints on total drawings; repurchases of drawings; conditionalities attached to drawings; and the integration of excess import costs and excess export earnings. The scheme was used to only a limited extent during the 1980s and early 1990s.

The current lack of use of the CCFF probably has two main causes. One is that in several country cases the prices of export commodities have also risen, reducing the balance of payments problem and also the eligibility of the member country to use the CCFF. This feature of the CCFF—the integration of excess costs of cereal imports with excesses in export earnings—has been criticized on a number of grounds, perhaps the most compelling being that of linking two components of the balance of payments where no real link in fact exists, as it would if a particular imported item was used to produce a specific export item. The food security argument for giving priority to financing cereal imports would arguably be better answered by decoupling the balance of payments support. However, empirical studies indicate that this would substantially increase the volume of drawings under the CCFF, putting the IMF's limited resources under severe strain.

The second reason for the low utilization of the CCFF is that most potential users have access to another IMF facility with more favourable terms, the Enhanced Structural Adjustment Facility (ESAF). Low-income member countries with excess cereal import costs who need balance of payments support have apparently preferred to apply for assistance under the ESAF for which the IMF has concessional loans. Recently the ESAF has been used for cases of excess import costs arising from the higher than usual cereal prices. ESAF financing is through concessional loans that carry an annual interest rate of 0.5 percent with repayments semi-annually beginning 5.5 years and ending 10 years after each disbursement. Recently, 81 low-income countries were eligible to use the ESAF. Of these, 27 had ESAF arrangements as of the end of February 1996, with a total amount approved of SDR 3.25 billion and undrawn balances of SDR 1.43 billion.

Financing under the programme can be obtained through inclusion of a contingency mechanism and/or through augmentation of access under an existing arrangement. Short-term balance of payments support is suitable for dealing with a short-term price fluctuation problem; it is quite unsustainable if the underlying problem is one of long-term adverse price trends unless, as in the ESAF case, the support is used to enable the process of adjustment to long-term changes to continue.

Economic Recovery Loans are generally designed to assist in restoring farmers' capacity to increase output following a happening such as a drought or other natural disaster that has seriously affected domestic food supplies. They are not likely to be appropriate for dealing with temporary price spikes in the world market, but could provide an indirect form of balance of payments assistance by reducing the medium-term demand for supplementary imports.

Apart from the limitations and restrictions of the balance of payments support programmes themselves, countries making use of such facilities face the problem of increasing their debt burdens. As the following section shows, some of the countries most in need of balance of payments support are likely to be low-income countries that are already severely indebted. Balance of payments support in such cases therefore raises important policy questions for both borrowers and lenders.

5 Debt reduction

The debt crisis of the 1980s, mostly in middle-income countries, was initially largely concerned with commercial debt and, as such, was perceived as posing a threat to the stability of the global financial system. The Brady Plan, amongst other initiatives, was a response to this crisis, which has now apparently receded. The 1990s have seen a different type of debt problem, which also has its roots in the 1980s—that of low-income countries mainly to developed-country governments and multilateral creditors. Much of this lending took place to help poor countries to cope with falling export commodity prices, rising world interest rates and escalating repayment schedules to commercial banks.

5.1 A picture of debt

Figure 2 shows the change in total external debt as a percentage of GDP by region since 1970. Of particular concern is the continuing sharp increase for sub-Saharan Africa, the region least able to sustain such a debt burden; the improving overall situation for Latin America and Asia masks the serious difficulties faced by a small number of countries.

In fact, thirty-two countries are classified by the World Bank as "severely indebted low-income countries" (SILICs), defined as having debt ratios for 1991-93 as either debt-service-to-GNP ratios of more than 80% or debt-service-to-export ratios of more than 220% (both measured as net present value). Twenty five of the SILICs are in sub-Saharan Africa, three in Latin America, three in Asia and one in the Near East.[13] Debt service repayments for sub-Saharan Africa were almost one-fifth of export earnings in 1995, up from 17.3 percent in 1994. Yet this understates the long-term and growing seriousness of the situation: in many countries, the stock of debt has been rising because actual repayments have been less than scheduled repayments; arrears have doubled since 1991 and now total three-quarters of annual export earnings. In 1994, for example, scheduled debt service payments for sub-Saharan Africa were over $US 20 billion, while actual repayments amounted to

13 The Financial Times of 20 May 1996 reports that there are now 40 heavily indebted countries, of which 33 are in sub-Saharan Africa.

$US 13 billion. The total debt stock of the SILICs was just under $US 210 billion in 1994, four times as much as in 1980. Further, whereas in 1980, the total debt as a proportion of national income was about one-third, in 1994 it was about 110 percent; the region's debt to total export proportion increased to 389 percent (and over 800 percent for three of the SILICs), compared with 150 percent for all developing countries. "The surge in interest arrears ($11bn since 1990) and capital repayment arrears ($23.5bn) highlights just how unsustainable the situation has become" (Financial Times 1996).

Figure 2: Total external debt as a percent of GDP (all regions)

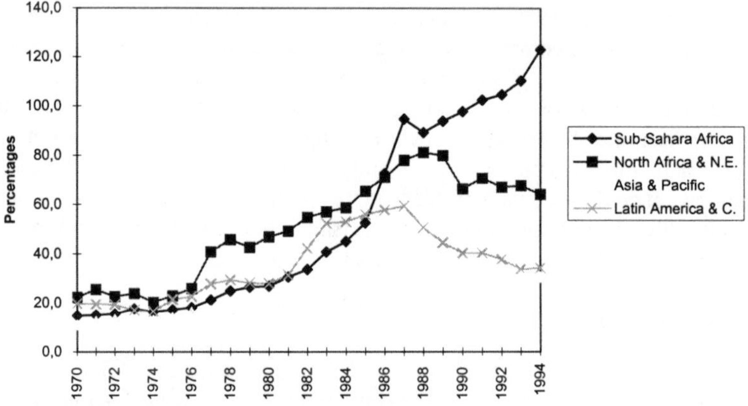

Source: World Bank, World Tables, various issues.

The Paris Club, the coordinating body for negotiating the rescheduling and restructuring of the credits of western governments, has taken a series of steps to reduce the outstanding debt of some of the poorest countries, but the conditions for reduction have severely limited the potential impact. However, one-quarter of the debt stock and one-half of the debt service payments for 1991-93 are accounted for by multilateral creditors.[14] The World Bank, together with its soft-loan affiliate the International Development Association (IDA), accounts for just over half of the multilateral total of debt stock, the IMF and the African Development Bank each accounting for 14 percent. Negotiations have started between the World Bank and the IMF to find ways of reducing the debt burden of the SILICs. The support of the G-7 governments will also be of vital importance for finding a solution to this problem. Whatever solution is reached should ensure that the qualifications for debt

14 The discrepancy between debt stock and debt service payments arises because the multilateral creditors are the first to be paid owing to the severe penalties incurred if a country falls into arrears with the IMF or the World Bank. For a detailed analysis of the issue, see Oxfam International (1996).

relief, including the definition of what constitutes an unsustainable debt burden, are not so tough that very few countries can ever hope to meet them.

5.2 Debt and food security

The debt burden has many negative implications for food security, not the least of which is the constrained ability to import food and nonfood items that could increase domestic food production. It is rather ironic that 14 of the SILICs have ESAF arrangements that could assist in supporting their balance of payments in the face of rising cereal prices—thereby increasing their longer-term debt burden. However, the problems caused by high levels of external debt go far beyond the balance of payments issue, and seem likely to have had a deleterious impact on long-term economic growth, including agricultural sector growth.

In the first place, the use of hard currency earnings for debt servicing has led to import compression: this has affected industry, as essential imported inputs have been cut, the effect being under-utilized industrial capacity; it has also affected agriculture through a reduction in the supply of agricultural inputs that cannot be produced domestically. The multiplier effects of slow-downs in sectoral growth rates, or even on occasion negative growth rates, must have been substantial. Among these should be numbered a thinner and perhaps narrower tax base, with all that that implies for government revenue collection. In addition, the ability to import capital goods for investment has been reduced. Then, there is the impact of external debt servicing obligations on domestic budgets if governments have to resort to domestic sources at high interest rates for financing public expenditure: this can of itself push up interest rates and "crowd out" investment.

Cuts in public expenditure or attempts at cost recovery often hit the poorest hardest, particularly those in rural areas, since it may be politically more feasible to cut rural health workers than city hospitals, for example, or village schoolteachers rather than university lecturers. This amounts to a disinvestment in human capital with very long-term repercussions. To put the problem into perspective, according to UNICEF, an additional $US 9 billion per annum would provide the resources necessary for sub-Saharan Africa to meet the main human welfare objectives agreed at the 1990 World Summit for Children, among which were universal access to safe drinking water and sanitation, and primary education (Oxfam International 1996). As noted above, the actual (as opposed to scheduled) debt repayments were $US 13 billion in 1994.

Further, the development of agriculture and domestic food supply is hindered by the lack of finance available for development purposes: a substantial amount of official development assistance (one estimate is about one-quarter (Oxfam International 1996)) is transferred to multilateral creditors for multilateral debt financing; this is in addition to the attempts by the World Bank and IMF to refinance debt through softer loans which has meant, for example, that in 1994, total IDA disbursements amounted to $US 2.9 billion, of which just under $US 2 billion was used to repay World Bank debt, and part of the rest was used to finance payments to the IMF! Not only is the quantity of the effective aid reduced, but also its quality as increasing amounts of aid money are diverted to balance of payments support rather than efforts to alleviate poverty. The ability to achieve food security is obviously compromised.

The existence of heavy external debt burdens has also tended to force the pace of structural adjustment programmes: the costs of adjustment are a rising function of the speed of adjustment (Killick 1993), and growth usually suffers more with shock-treatment adjustment. The corollary is that more gradual adjustment requires more external financial support to bridge the gap until the macroeconomy is balanced, and hence more debt.

Reducing the debt burden of the SILICs is not a panacea for the ills of poverty and food insecurity. But when the long-term impacts on the balance of payments and growth are considered, it is difficult to see a single positive factor that could have a potential effect of comparable magnitude, as long as the resources released are in fact used for the purposes intended. Any discussion of debt reduction invariably raises the perceived problem of moral hazard. In this context, it needs to be recognized that as well as borrowers, bilateral, multilateral and private sector lenders too have responsibilities, and to lend for the wrong reasons—perhaps because of political or institutional pressure on the lenders' side, perhaps to governments that lacked popular legitimacy and have since been removed, perhaps for projects that were not really appropriate for the country concerned, perhaps for consumption or for investments where the return flow could not cover debt service costs—argues for a more flexible approach to the whole question of indebtedness. There have been mistakes by all parties, and lessons to be learnt. If the over-riding concern is to assist the poorest countries to reduce poverty and achieve food security then it is this concern that should guide attitudes to and support the provision of resources for reduction of the debt stock, and not merely for partial subsidization of debt servicing. Perhaps the idea would be more acceptable to the creditors if any debt reduction were made conditional on an agreed proportion of the accrued benefits being used in approved ways to alleviate poverty and food insecurity in the long term.

6 In conclusion

This chapter has emphasized that economic growth alone—even growth with equity—cannot solve all of the problems of poverty, food insecurity and malnutrition. However, without equitable growth, it is difficult to see how there can be solutions. Whether policies for growth with equity will in fact be adopted depends on whether there is the political will. But governments everywhere are brought to power and kept in power by various coalitions of interests, and where those interests are very narrowly based because of a lack of control over resources, including political access, by large sections of society, it will always be difficult to take action that goes against those interests. Experience indicates that redistribution of resources is easier when the economy as a whole is growing. It is also the case that political support for measures that benefit the poor will be easier if the non-poor also benefit to some extent. Thus, for example, the replacement of universal food subsidies with targeted subsidies has in some instances led to a loss of political support for the programme. Governments have to make hard decisions about the realistic choices and compromises that lie within their power: policy advisors—even economists—can in the final analysis only advise about alternatives and possible outcomes.

"Visionaries have been preaching against human selfishness for millennia without spectacular success. ... Appealing to the longer-term self-interest of the powerful may occasionally be more effective than relying on their altruism. A healthy well-fed and well-educated labour force is essential for future profits and prosperity. Poverty and hunger breed crime, disease, riots, revolutions and war. Poor people make poor customers. Environmental destruction deprives future generations of their birthright. All these facts are well known. They have not been sufficient as yet, however, to produce the political determination to adopt effective strategies to eliminate poverty and hunger or protect the environment adequately even in rich countries, to say nothing of poor ones where economic and technical constraints are much tighter" (Barraclough 1991).

Whilst it seems necessary to stress the problems that lie ahead in achieving food security for all, we should nevertheless remember that, in many countries, the achievements to date have already been substantial. Economics may be popularly known as the dismal science, but sound economic policies that emphasize growth with equity have played their part in those success stories—and can continue to do so in the future.

References

Barraclough, S.L. (1991): An end to hunger? The social origins of food strategies. A report prepared for the United Nations Research Institute for Social Development and for the South Commission based on UNRISD research on food systems and society, Zed Books Ltd in association with UNRISD, London and Atlantic Highlands, New Jersey.

Demery, L. and L. Squire (1996): Macroeconomic Adjustment and Poverty in Africa: an Emerging Picture, in: The World Bank Research Observer, 11(1), pp. 39-59, February 1996, World Bank, Washington DC.

FAO (1995a): Policy Reform and the Consumer, in: The State of Food and Agriculture 1995, Rome.

FAO (1995b): Agricultural trade: entering a new era? In: The State of Food and Agriculture 1995, Rome.

Financial Times (1996): 20 May 1996.

Gleave, M.B. (Ed.) (1992): Tropical African Development, Longman Scientific and Technical: Harlow; John Wiley and Sons Inc., New York.

Johnson, D. Gale (1984): Alternative Approaches to International Food Reserves. Paper prepared for the FAO Symposium on World Food Security, Rome 3-7 September 1984, ESC: FS/SYMP/84/5.

Killick, T. (1993): The Adaptive Economy: Adjustment Policies in Small, Low-income Countries, EDI Development Studies, World Bank, Washington DC.

Oxfam International (1996): Multilateral Debt: the Human Costs, Oxfam International Position Paper, February 1996, London.

Schiff, M. and A. Valdés (1992): The Plundering of Agriculture in Developing Countries, World Bank, Washington DC.

Stewart, F. (1995): Adjustment and Poverty: Options and Choices, Routledge, London and New York.

Vollrath, T.L. (1994): The Role of Agriculture and its Prerequisites in Economic Development, Food Policy, 19(5), pp. 469-478.

Von Braun, J. (Ed.) (1995): Employment for Poverty Reduction and Food Security, IFPRI, Washington DC.

Von Braun, J. (1989): The Importance of Non-Agricultural Income Sources for the Rural Poor in Africa and Implications for Food and Nutrition Policy, Reprinted from PEW/Cornell Lecture Series on Food and Nutrition Policy, Reprint No. 189, IFPRI, Washington DC.

Von Braun, J. (1987): Food Security Policies for the Urban Poor, Reprinted from Andreas Kopp (Ed.) (1987): Scientific Positions to Meet the Challenge of Rural and Urban Poverty in Developing Countries (proceedings of a conference organized by the German Foundation for International Development and the Centre for Regional Development Research at the Justus-Liebig University Giessen, 22-26 June, 1987), Verlag Weltarchiv GMBH, Hamburg, Reprint No. 169, IFPRI, Washington DC.

World Bank (1994): World Development Report 1994, Oxford University Press for the World Bank.

World Bank (1992): The Political Economy of Agricultural Pricing Policy, Five Volumes, Johns Hopkins University Press, Baltimore and London.

World Bank (1990): World Development Report 1990, Oxford University Press for the World Bank.

World Bank (1986): Poverty and Hunger, A World Bank Study, Washington.

18

Effective Nutrition and Health Programmes

M. Anwar Hussain and William D. Clay

1 Introduction

Nutrition programmes in the broad sense could be defined as those ongoing activities that have nutrition improvement and maintenance of good nutrition as an explicit outcome. These programmes include a varied range of activities and take many forms depending on the type, nature, magnitude, causes, target groups, availability of resources, infrastructure, services and objective of the programme. The ultimate expectation from these programmes, however, is to create an environment in which all the population can meet its nutritional needs on a sustainable basis, particularly the vulnerable groups.

It is generally accepted that nutritional status is an outcome of many factors, and to be effective, nutrition programmes must address multiple causes. They must be food-based so as to ensure long-term and sustainable effects. Yet historically, most nutrition improvement programmes were primarily health based. This is unfortunate because health actions touch only the tip of the problem of malnutrition leaving the root causes, poverty, social deprivation and ignorance, unattended. Health actions also produce short-term, visible benefits which are, thus, more attractive to policymakers and donors. For the improvement of nutritional status nutrition improvement programmes must include both short- and long-term actions in a synergistic way.

2 Actions taken to improve nutritional status

Three types of actions are generally needed to maintain and improve the nutritional status of the population:

a) incorporation of nutrition objectives and actions into national, sectoral and integrated development plans and allocation of necessary human and financial resources so that these objectives may be achieved; a long term developmental approach to ameliorate social deprivation and poverty and to create a conducive environment to allow the nutrition programme to function smoothly;

b) specific nutrition improvement programmes directed at particular problems or groups; and

c) community-based actions with active participation and ownership by the community to improve the nutritional status.

It is commonly understood that the first group of activities are usually implemented at the policy and planning level of the governments and do not strictly fall into the category of nutrition programmes. However, these food and nutrition actions, as part of development programmes, are vital for creating a supportive environment which allows nutrition programmes at the community level to succeed in achieving their objectives more easily. They should also ensure that the benefits of development accrue to those most nutritionally at risk and that the outcome of the development programme is not in conflict with the food and nutrition possibilities of the people.

It should also be understood that at the programme level some specific actions have multiple outcomes while others are often needed to achieve a single nutrition outcome. For example, promotion of home gardening for the prevention of vitamin A deficiency, besides increasing the availability and consumption of vitamin A-rich foods, improves the overall quality of the diet and thus contributes to overall improvement of the nutritional status of the population. Yet simply producing and increasing the availability of fruits and vegetables is not enough; these acts must be combined with nutrition education to promote consumption and change dietary behaviour of the community. These actions are selectively reviewed in this chapter.

2.1 Incorporating nutrition objectives into development policies and programmes

The nutritional well-being of a population is an indicator of national development and as such reflects the combined performance of the social, economic, agriculture and health sectors. Nutrition is also an essential input for national development, with a healthy well-nourished population being the best foundation for promoting national economic growth. Development aims at providing all people with the social and economic environment necessary for them to lead an active and healthy life. To achieve this objective, development policies and programmes need to be directed towards improving human development, including nutritional well-being.

Factors influencing nutritional well-being fall under the responsibility of many sectors, and all of these factors must be addressed to achieve good nutritional results. A policy or programme which deals with one determinant of nutrition may be successful but might still not show any measurable improvement in nutrition or health if other negative factors have continued. Consequently, policymakers concerned with promoting and improving nutritional status must be aware of the potential effects that various development policies and programmes can have, either directly or indirectly, on the poor and the malnourished.

The effects of development policies on nutrition can be positive or negative. Maximising the positive nutritional impact of development, both at the national level and in different sectors, can significantly contribute to improve nutritional status. Economic development which increases incomes and national and community wealth makes it possible to improve the health and nutrition status of the population. Strategies of economic development which promote equity and enhance human capital are more likely to produce these beneficial outcomes. At the same time, to maximise impact from specific nutritional interventions, a favourable environment, both in terms of overall development policies and sectoral policies, is required.

To safeguard the nutritional well-being of the poor, it is essential that macro-economic policies do not discriminate against the food and agriculture sector or rural areas, where most of the poor often live. Unbalanced economic growth, employment and income distribution, compounded by structural adjustment programmes, as well as reduced government expenditure on social services, such as health or subsidised food distribution, may have indirect nutritional effects. Efforts must be made to ensure that the burden of adjustment does not fall disproportionately on the poor and nutritionally vulnerable.

A more direct effect would be the decrease in total or specific food consumption due to higher food prices resulting either from higher producer prices or removal of food subsidies. Cuts in government health services, especially primary health care, including immunisation and growth monitoring, and public sanitation, including both piped water and sewerage, have significant adverse impact on health and nutrition. Investment in infrastructure to promote effective market functioning, especially roads and transportation, and the communication of market information are likely to promote equitable access to economic incentives.

A growth-promoting external environment also has an essential role to play in improving the nutritional status of the poor. Policies in this domain encompass improving the international trade environment, alleviating the external debt problem and increasing the flow of external resources. At the national level, rapid population growth is a serious barrier to achieving a sustainable living standard. Consequently, the implications of population policies on nutrition are significant, particularly in food deficit countries where rapid population growth continues and where urbanisation is increasing—both often accompanied by a reduction in support to the agricultural sector and slow agricultural growth. Addressing population concerns is fundamental if sustainable improvements in nutrition are to be achieved.

Women's educational levels significantly affects fertility. Educated women are more likely to work in the paid labour force, and women who work outside the home have fewer children. Higher productivity of women, as measured by their income, is associated with delayed marriage and thus delayed child bearing and lower total fertility. Women's participation in the paid labour force is often associated with greater income control and increased influence on family's nutritional well-being.

Education provides better opportunities and better living conditions which can result in improved health and nutrition. The direct effects of education include improved dietary intakes and health status of children, participation in school feeding and school-based health programmes, and improved eating habits resulting from a better understanding of food and health. Maternal education and literacy, in particular, have a significant impact on children's survival, health and nutritional well-being. Indirectly, education and literacy affect development and income, which, in turn, contribute to improved nutrition. Education and training of people to address food and nutrition concerns at the community and regional level may have a great impact in those areas where such skills are lacking.

Environmental policies can also have a major role in influencing the nutritional status of the poor, especially those who live in environmentally fragile areas. Of particular relevance for nutrition objectives are policies that can promote sustainable development of agriculture, including forestry and fisheries. This should include the promotion of production and consumption of traditional foods from plants and animals. Policies should aim at creating an economic environment in which it is more profitable to manage and conserve natural resources than to destroy them. The most serious environmental problems that affect the attainment of nutrition objectives in developing countries are desertification and resource degradation of cultivated lands. Therefore, policy formulation should be based on a thorough understanding of why undesirable land use practices are employed. Policies should induce farmers, especially poor farmers on marginal lands, to adopt improved farming methods which are ecologically sound, socially acceptable and economically beneficial, and should provide sustainable livelihoods for the landless.

Intersectoral dialogue based on strong government commitment and political will is indispensable to encourage actions to improve nutrition that are realistic and complementary, recognising the benefits and trade-offs of the short- and long-term priorities within the various sectors. At local and regional levels some structure is needed to identify actions to be taken by various sectors that can improve nutrition and to foresee obstacles and better formulate operational objectives for such actions. Time is needed to achieve positive outcomes from development policies, particularly those aimed at behaviour change and hard-to-reach groups. Feasibility related to financial and resource costs and political costs, as well as institutional and human capacity will determine the appropriateness of various policy interventions.

Attention must be given to targeting the benefits of development preferentially to those most in need, for example landless labourers, the malnourished and other vulnerable groups. Development activities have different impacts on different population groups, and particular difficulties may arise for some groups when trying to incorporate nutritional objectives into development issues or policies. Individual participation and community involvement in developing programmes will ensure better focus and sustainability. Decision-makers need to be encouraged to incorporate nutrition considerations into development programmes and policies. This data should be presented convincingly by professionals in the food and nutrition sector, including health and education, to back up the recommendations made in light of the resources available and the recognition of the trade-offs of adopting alternative policies.

Recognising the long-term nature of development interventions is important as continuity is essential for their effectiveness. People and institutions will not change their behaviour in response to a change in policy if they have no confidence that the new situation will continue and last. The long-term feasibility and economic sustainability of a policy or programme must be realistically evaluated before deciding to implement it. One experience of a policy reversal on the part of government is enough to inhibit response to subsequent policy initiatives for a long time. The need for continuity in developing policy has implications for the international donor community as well, and the assurance of long-term support should be part of a government's decision to implement a programme or policy with outside funding.

The feasibility of a development strategy has much to do with its costs. These include financial and resource costs, the institutional and human capacity to carry it out, and the strategy's acceptability in political and social terms. As countries have different socio-political contexts and widely differing resource bases, actions and programmes which are quite reasonable in one setting may be inappropriate in another. Financial costs of an intervention are the most obvious, while the institutional and human resource costs receive far too little attention in the choice of development activities. The institutional base available to a country can greatly alter the feasibility of a programme. In a resource-rich environment, a variety of actions can be undertaken; where resources are scarce, identification of priorities need to be much more stringent.

2.2 Nutrition programmes addressed to specific problems

Specific strategies and actions to improve nutrition should be developed according to the particular needs, circumstances and available resources prevailing in each country. The International Conference on Nutrition (ICN), jointly convened by FAO and WHO in 1992, has identified priority areas for specific actions, including: improving household food security; protecting consumers through improved food quality and safety; caring for the socio-economically deprived and nutritionally vulnerable; preventing and managing infectious diseases; promoting appropriate diets and healthy lifestyles; preventing specific micronutrient deficiencies; and promotion of breast feeding. Most nutrition improvement programmes address these issues both directly or indirectly through their various activities.

2.2.1 Improving household food security

The recognition that household food security is integral to the process of social and economic development and is the basis for nutritional well-being was stressed by the International Conference of Nutrition in 1992 and strongly reinforced by the World Food Summit, which was held in Rome in November 1996. The Rome Declaration on World Food Security reaffirmed "the right of everyone to have access to safe and nutritious food, consistent with the right to adequate food and the fundamental right to be free from hunger." The objective of the World Food Summit Plan of Action is to ensure "food security at individual, household, national, regional and global levels." Commitment Two of the Plan of Action, in particular aims at "improving physical and economic access by all, at all times, to sufficient, nutritionally adequate and safe food and its effective utilisation."

A number of actions can be taken to improve household food security. These include:

Home gardening

Home gardening is a family food production system widely practised in developing and developed countries under myriad forms. A traditional tropical home garden typically includes a wide diversity of perennial and semi-perennial crops, trees, shrubs and condiments. Some gardens also include small animal rearing, particularly poultry and even fish raising. Home gardens make important contributions to household food and nutrition security, but their contribution to the overall food supply is generally overlooked in national and international consumption statistics. The dynamic role of home gardening in family nutrition and household food security must be more generally evaluated in the context of the whole farming system and in relation to other components that make up the household economy.

Typically the functions and output of home gardens complement the functions and output of field agriculture. Agriculture should provide the bulk of the energy needed by the household; the garden supplements other essential nutrients with minerals and vitamin-rich leafy vegetables and fruits, animal sources of protein and herbs and condiments. The continuance of this form of production, from time immemorial to the present, can be taken as proof of its intrinsic economic and nutritional merit. The importance of gardens is further affirmed by the fact that in times of emergency societies have had to return to the use of gardens to improve food security, as, for example, the Irish potato gardens during the Great Depression and household gardens in Europe during the Second World War (Niñez 1985: 3).

Home gardens contribute to food security in two fundamental ways. The first way is through the provision of a diversity of fresh foods that improve the quantity and quality of nutrients available to the family. Studies show that gardening households typically obtain more than 50% of their household supply of vegetables, fruits, plantains, and herbs from their gardens and in garden systems that include animal raising, their primary and often their only source of animal protein (Soleri et al. 1991; Marsh 1994, UNDP 1996). The Asian Vegetable Research and Development Centre (AVRDC) has provided evidence, after five years of experimental gardening in very small plots (16 sq. meters), that mixed vegetable gardens can provide a significant percentage of the recommended daily allowance of key nutrients for a family of five: protein (measurable amount); iron and calcium (20%), vitamin A (80%) and vitamin C (100%) (Marsh 1994).

Second, a large proportion of these gardeners sell surplus produce and animal products from their gardens. The income generated from garden sales, combined with the resultant savings in food and medical bills from home production vary seasonally. However, the average contribution makes up a significant proportion of the total household income, as for example, Bangladesh 25%, Cuba nearly 20% and Sumatra 18%. This income contributes to food security by increasing the family's ability to purchase food and meet other expenses that contribute directly to food security, for example, education, health and production inputs.

Credit to poor households

Promoting self-employment through private investment can be a useful policy instrument for strengthening food security. Credit programmes that have been found to be most successful for these purposes are those that combine small-scale credit with group motivation, technical advice and assistance. Credit programmes aimed at women have been particularly beneficial to food security. An example of a very successful income generation programme is operated by the Grameen Bank of Bangladesh which provides group credit with no collateral to poor women, allowing them to develop small enterprises and also providing them with a stock-holding in the bank. This scheme is being duplicated in many countries in the developing world with great success.

Increasing employment opportunities
i) Food for work

Labour-intensive public works, food for work and employment guarantee schemes often targeted at vulnerable groups, can be an effective instrument for improving food security.

The provision of employment obviates the necessity of either moving food to families or families to feeding centres, as work can be offered close to home, thus building up the assets of the community. Public work schemes may be preferential to women, who form a majority of the work force on such schemes, by raising their incomes and consequently improving their socio-economic status. Wage differentials between sexes should also be eliminated. These schemes can be most effectively used to combat seasonal food and employment shortage.

Food for work and employment guarantee schemes vary enormously in their scope and coverage. They also vary in their stated purpose: to provide employment, to provide income to the poor, to produce assets. Thus, they can provide short-term benefits—an increase in employment and income of poor households—and long-term benefits by increasing income earning capacity through productive asset generation.

Food for work programmes must be designed on the basis of local needs and priorities, and be compatible with the overall development framework of governments. It must be ensured that unemployed or underemployed labour is available and that there is a general scarcity of food or poor access to it.

Costs and effectiveness for food for work projects vary considerably depending on the type of project, degree of targeting and need, and the source, quantity and type of food given as payment. They are likely to be most cost-effective during seasonal food shortages.

Food for work projects are often self-targeting to the poor, providing wages below market rates. Food insecurity can be addressed by concentrating on disadvantaged regions where poverty is dominant. A major trade-off accrues between employing needy persons with low capabilities and maintaining a reasonable level of worker productivity. Participation that is limited to the destitute carries a social stigma. The size of food rations will determine both the numbers and the alternative occupations of those who enrol in the project.

ii) Income transfer schemes

Increasing the food consumption of poor household can be accomplished through direct feeding programmes, food stamps and food subsidies although they address somewhat different aspects of nutrition problems. The common element in both feeding and food-related transfers is that they transfer resources to target households, and thereby raise households' real income.

Feeding programmes

These programmes are generally implemented in two ways: direct, on-the-spot feeding of the beneficiaries and providing a take-away ration at regular intervals for home use. They generally cover vulnerable groups, such as pregnant and lactating mothers and children from six months to five years of age. School feeding programmes are also often included. Direct feeding involves provision of prepared food to target individuals, usually malnourished children at the feeding centres or schools, or full feeding of malnourished children at nutrition rehabilitation centres. On-site programmes call for a greater infrastructure and therefore cost more, but they ensure that beneficiaries actively consume the food: take-home programmes can cover wider areas and reach more beneficiaries, but leakage takes place through sharing with other family members and sometimes sale or exchange of all or part of the ration. Other problems include poor participation and sporadic attendance when the rations fails to provide a sufficiently strong incentive or when the distribution centres are too distant; difficulty of targeting programmes to the people who need them most and, at times, failure to respect the size of the ration. The cost of the programmes vary from country to country but are usually very high.

In general, supplementary feeding programmes are likely to be cost-effective if they are targeted to the most malnourished, to pregnant and nursing mothers, and to children from six months to three years of age; if the food supplement is large enough to provide incentive for regular participation; if the criteria are established for entry into, and exit from, the programmes on the basis of malnutrition and response to feeding; and especially if the programme is integrated with other inputs, such as health services, nutrition education and nutrition surveillance.

The efficacy and effectiveness of the feeding programmes have been studied by many scientific workers. These studies have shown that increasing dietary intake through supplementary feeding can have beneficial nutritional consequences in terms of growth, activity, cognitive development and compensation of energy lost during illness. These benefits were reported to be greater in poor socio-economic groups and have been found to persist even after fifteen years of participation in the programme. Evaluation of large-scale feeding programmes has shown mixed results. Beaton and Ghassemi (1982) found that the net increase in food intake by target recipients was 45 to 70% of the food distributed. The recipient response was higher when the supplementation was targeted to malnourished children. Leakages have also provided benefits to other members of the household. Cost to the family was the most important determinant of participation.

Food subsidies

Food subsidies are generally of two types: general and targeted. With general subsidies, the government pays a portion of the total production, storage and marketing costs, thus reducing the price of the subsidised food commodity below market level. All consumers are included. Targeting is mainly determined by marketing outlets. Such schemes tend to improve the real income and nutritional status of the urban rather than the rural poor, and indeed, the primary goal is a reduction in the urban cost of living and the prevention of urban unrest.

Food price subsidies influence nutritional status in three ways:

i) they increase the purchasing power of the recipient households;

ii) they reduce the price of food and thereby encourage households to buy more food, and;

iii) they may render certain foods cheaper relative to other foods, encouraging a change in diet composition. It has been reported that subsidies increase calorie consumption in households (Kennedy and Alderman 1985).

General subsidies are usually very costly but the cost will vary depending on the amount of food subsidised. In 1975, food subsidy costs accounted for 21% of Egypt's total budget expenditure; 19% of Korea's; 16% of Sri Lanka's; and 12% of Morocco's. They are difficult to implement on a small scale and administratively difficult to implement on a large scale in rural areas. Richer households usually end up receiving more per capita allocation than the poor for whom they are originally intended. For example in Egypt, the poorest quartile received only 29% of the total benefits. Market-wide subsidies are thus not generally regarded as a sustainable, cost-effective way of reducing chronic food scarcity among the poor. Politically, however, they are attractive and receive support. However, once they are in place, it is very difficult to dismantle them since political unrest and food riots, as happened, for example, in Egypt, Morocco and Algeria, could occur.

Targeted food subsidies

Targeting a programme to a specific population group almost always makes the programme most cost-effective but is often politically unpopular. Blanket targeting is generally preferred. An FAO study (1987) found that 53 of the 56 countries reviewed had general market-wide structures to benefit all sections of the population.

Subsidies may be targeted by community, household, season or commodity. Too narrow or refined targeting increases its administrative cost. Geographic targeting may be more effective in identifying those in need and be less burdensome administratively than using eligibility requirements based on household income, such as in the subsidy and food coupon programmes in Brazil and Colombia, respectively. Targeting by season to counteract seasonally variable food prices and shortages is a relatively unexplored approach to an efficient subsidy programme. Subsidies for weaning and other special foods for pregnant and lactating women are different options for reaching the most vulnerable. Chile's complementary feeding programme provided acidified milk to children in an attempt to reduce sharing this food with other household members. It was estimated that 80% of the calories from this food went to the target child (Harbert and Scandizzo 1982).

The cost of subsidy programmes can be substantially reduced by targeting, provided that supporting administrative and service infrastructure are available. There is always a trade-off between the degree of coverage that the population affected by malnutrition and inadequate diet receives and the cost of the programme. Narrow targeting criteria and vigorous enforcement reduce the errors of inclusion but increase the errors of exclusion. This means that narrow targeting improves cost-effectiveness and reduces cost but at the same time reduces the overall impact by including too few beneficiaries and excluding the needy.

Targeting by commodity may be another way of improving cost-effectiveness. The best foods to subsidise are those mainly consumed by the poorest group, e.g. coarse grains consumed by the poor. Excluding the non-needy reduces some leakage, but leakage also occurs when nutritionally needy households or individuals receive the subsidised food but use it for food already consumed, rather than as a net increment to food consumption.

2.2.2 Household food security during emergencies

In recent years, the number of people affected by natural and manmade emergencies has grown dramatically from approximately 4.4 million in the mid-1980s to more than 175 million in 1993 (FAO 1996). Most crises in the 1990s have been brought about by civil conflicts or war. Nothing is spared, lives are lost, property is destroyed and thousands of people are displaced. As a result of emergencies caused by conflicts and natural disasters, food security has deteriorated in all affected countries, particularly in the sub-Saharan region, resulting in widespread malnutrition affecting all population groups, specifically the disadvantaged and nutritionally vulnerable.

The provision of food, water, shelter, protection and medical care are essential lifesaving measures for refugees and internally displaced persons until the crisis is over and people either return to their homes or establish new ones. Temporary food distribution and supplementary foods for vulnerable groups and agricultural inputs are common humanitarian interventions to help people cope during an emergency situations.

There is an urgent need to initiate preventive and preparedness measures along with the designing of early warning and/or mitigation strategies to alleviate the potentially devastating impact of natural or socio-political events by establishing mechanisms and building capacities to respond rapidly and effectively to such circumstances. Such efforts can help to prevent natural disasters from turning into major emergencies. In countries prone to natural disasters, as, for example, Bangladesh, these strategies are part of development activities.

It has been widely recognised that emergency relief should be linked to rehabilitation, reconstruction and eventually to sustainable recovery. All three processes: relief, rehabilitation and development may also take place simultaneously, the exact combinations of activities, of course, depending on the situation in each country. By linking emergency assistance to development assistance, poverty and food insecurity can be reduced and the improvement in people's nutritional status can be sustained. Identifying and implementing appropriate rehabilitation interventions, which ensure that relief and development are properly linked, will require the involvement and commitment of recipient communities. The Rome Declaration on World Food Security and the World Food Summit Plan of Action, adopted in November 1996, have also underlined the need to link relief operations and development programmes (FAO 1996). Creating conditions in which households can meet their own basic needs and sustain their nutritional well-being is a fundamental aspect of interventions carried out during the different programmes of relief, rehabilitation and development.

In many emergencies, intervention strategies must include diverse sectors, such as agriculture, health, community development, education and planning, so as to create activities relating to both relief and development.

The conditions of infrastructure and availability of services will determine, to a large extent, the rehabilitation measures. Actions must be taken to rehabilitate services. Relief assistance must be targeted to the most needy and vulnerable groups. Nutrition surveillance measures can serve as an implementation tool in targeting since it not only identifies those individuals suffering from malnutrition, but can also provide relevant information about the effectiveness of the implementation. Poor families often lack assets to fall back on for survival. Agricultural interventions to improve household food security and nutrition, such as home gardening and crop diversification, should be designed for these vulnerable groups. A special focus on alleviating poverty and food insecurity can help speed and sustain their capacity to survive.

Whatever the intervention, timing is important to prevent loss of life and the waste of scarce resources. It is essential that disaster preparedness and mitigation measures be implemented at the onset of the emergency so that households may be able to safeguard their productive assets and protect food security. When mitigation measures are inadequate, households dispense their assets to survive.

Nutrition interventions should be designed on the basis of an assessment of the situation. Data on the levels of malnutrition, disease incidence, mortality rates, food habits, etc., should be collected and compared with the pre-emergency data. Household food security and nutritional status should be assisted. The needs for food aid and food for work should be linked with agricultural rehabilitation. Local capacity in these areas should be strengthened through proper training and above all, all relief and rehabilitation activities should be properly co-ordinated by a mechanism set up within the government and donor communities.

2.2.3 Protecting consumers through improved food quality and safety

A safe food supply of adequate quality is essential for proper nutrition; foods must have appropriate nutrient content and must be available in sufficient variety; they must not endanger consumer health through chemical and biological (i.e., bacterial, parasitic and viral) contamination; and they must be presented honestly. Food safety and quality start at the farm and continue throughout the processing and distribution chain to storage and final preparation by the consumer or food service industry. Good agricultural and manufacturing practices, including processing, distribution, and marketing are essential to ensure consumer protection. Any factor that leads to exposure to hazardous chemicals or biological agents, inadequate or excessive nutrient intakes, or impairs their optimal utilisation, contributes to malnutrition.

An effective food control system improves the nutritional status of the population, directly and indirectly. It operates through: (1) ensuring that nutrient composition of foods is retained during the food chain, i.e., production, storage, handling, processing, packaging, and preparation; (2) preventing and controlling biological and chemical contamination of foods; (3) promoting hygienic practices throughout the food industry by establishing appropriate codes and standards and training of food handling personnel; (4) reducing food losses caused by spoilage, contamination or improper storage or distribution; (5) promoting a safe and honestly presented food supply by requiring composition and nutrient information on food labels; and (6) protecting consumers against being offered foods that are injurious to health, are unfit for human consumption, or are nutritionally or economically debased. In addition to contributing to improvements in nutritional status, a food control system encourages the orderly development of a nation's food industries, creates greater outlets for farmers' produce, stimulates increased foreign exchange earnings through export of foods that comply with acceptable standards, and avoids losses that occur when sub-standard foods are traded. All these effects help to create jobs, increase incomes, and ultimately improve nutritional status as consumers' diets become more varied and nutritious.

Thus, strengthening food control systems and educating consumers about appropriate food handling practices are both essential to proper nutrition. Governments, the food industry, consumers and international agencies all have particularly important and interrelated roles to play.

Governments have a responsibility to ensure that a safe, nutritious, and varied food supply is available to enable their populations to choose a healthy diet. This requires, in addition to the food supply itself, comprehensive legislation, regulations and standards, together with an organization for effective inspection and compliance monitoring, including laboratory analyses. Publication of compliance and surveillance activities gives the public confidence in the safety of the food supply, as it also does to countries importing food. An effective food control system will in many cases be a prerequisite for food exports to some markets; it is therefore important in economic as well as public health terms.

Governments also have a role in educating consumers and advising the food industry about a variety of topics, including food handling practices, minimising food spoilage and avoiding contamination. Both industry and various groups of consumers should be made aware of food laws, regulations and standards. Governments also establish food and nutrition labelling regulations as well as guidelines for advertising to help consumers make better informed decisions.

Governments have further roles which include information gathering through general monitoring of the food supply for quality and safety, special surveys when problems are detected or suspected, and the gathering of epidemiological data on the nature and extent of food borne diseases. Governments should bolster their understanding of food quality and safety by conducting research in public health and in food technology. It is a special responsibility of governments to see that food quality and safety programmes are integrated into other government-sponsored, nutrition-related programmes, such as feeding programmes, nutrition education programmes, and other intervention programmes.

The role of industry in ensuring food quality and safety extends from agricultural production through food service. Good agricultural practices by primary producers include proper pre-harvest use of pesticides, fertilisers, veterinary drugs and post-harvest control of storage, chemical use, handling practices and transport. The food industry also has a role to play in developing alternative, cost-effective technologies for food safety. The industry must also play a role in consumer education.

Good manufacturing practices (GMPs) are an important part of a total quality control system. They include product design using ingredients meeting established standards, compliance with codes of hygienic practice and the use of suitable technologies and distribution systems that ensure that the product reaches the consumer in a satisfactory condition.

Consumers, individually or through organisations, can do much to discourage food adulteration and fraudulent practices. A major influence by consumers on food quality and safety can be achieved through the exercise of discrimination in the marketplace. Consumers and consumer groups can be invaluable in connection with consumer education about improved sanitation and safe food handling, better nutrition and improved general health. Community participation should be encouraged and used to the fullest extent.

International organisations have a role in assisting developing countries to establish or strengthen their national control systems and to develop suitable guidelines, educational and reference materials which can be adapted to local conditions in different countries. International organisations advise governments on food quality and safety, including the safe use of food additives and their permitted levels in various foods, and the recommended maximum levels of different contaminants in food. On a global basis, international organisations play an important role in the assessment of both the scope and magnitude of food contamination problems through the monitoring of selected contaminants in major food items, and occurrence of foodborne diseases.

In addition, international organisations have a unique role to play in developing standards and guidelines for food quality, safety and labelling, such as those standards developed by the Codex Alimentarius Commission (Codex), a subsidiary body of FAO and WHO. These international standards protect the health of consumers while ensuring fair trade practices. Food standards are important in the international and national trade of foods. Standards and codes of practice are an integral part of national and international food security systems, ensuring the quality and safety of food.

2.2.4 Promotion of healthy diets and lifestyles

Promoting better eating habits and positive health behaviour is one of the most challenging tasks in the overall effort to improve nutrition. Nutritional problems broadly fall into two categories: those due to insufficient intake relative to needs and infections, and those due to an excessive or unbalanced intake of food or particular dietary components. In both instances, improvement in nutritional well-being will depend on people having access to a variety of safe and affordable foods, understanding what constitutes an appropriate diet and knowing how to best meet their nutritional needs from available resources. This includes an understanding of the influence of different lifestyles on nutrition. Provision of correct nutrition information and an adequate level of nutrition education to the public on the nutritional value of foods, their quality and safety, methods of preparation, processing and preservation will allow for an informed choice of food for an adequate diet.

To encourage and promote overall health, official nutrition goals and dietary recommendations have been issued by government agencies in different countries and by various national and international panels of experts. Traditionally, recommended dietary allowances have focused on adequate and safe intakes to avoid deficiencies and to ensure that energy is adequate for the needs of nearly all adults, and for the growth, development and activity of children. More recently, however, dietary recommendations and guidelines reflect growing concern about diet-related, non-communicable diseases, and recommendations now frequently include recommendations for intake of those food components that are associated with risk of these diseases or are beneficial for their prevention. These food-based guidelines provide advice, appropriate for the populations concerned, on selecting a balanced diet that promotes health. Appropriate advice on food purchasing and preparation should be provided. The basic guidelines adopted in many developed countries are quite similar, and they include the following principles:

- eat a variety of foods;
- adjust energy intake to energy expenditure to maintain desirable body weight;
- avoid excessive fat intake and, especially, intake of saturated fat and cholesterol;
- increase intake of complex carbohydrates and dietary fibre;
- limit salt intake to a moderate level;
- limit alcohol intake; and
- keep physically active and fit.

In addition to qualitative dietary guidelines, quantitative nutrient goals have been proposed in some countries. The WHO Study Group (1990) has recommended population nutrient goals which provide upper and lower limits within which average intakes should fall for good health and nutrition. The group envisaged that the population nutrient goals would be useful as general planning tools to evaluate the adequacy of a given food supply and the effectiveness of social communication efforts. The recent Joint FAO/WHO Expert Consultation on the Preparation and Use of Food-based Dietary Guidelines, held in Cyprus in 1995, summarised that the underlying thinking of food-based dietary guidelines for use by the public are:

- Public health issues should determine the direction and relevance of dietary guidelines.
- Food-based dietary guidelines (FBDG) are developed in a specific sociocultural context, and need to reflect relevant social, economic, agricultural and environmental factors affecting food availability and eating patterns.
- Dietary guidelines need to reflect food patterns rather than numerical goals.
- Dietary guidelines need to be positive and encourage enjoyment of appropriate dietary intakes.
- A wide range of dietary patterns can be consistent with good health.

All recommendations to encourage and sustain appropriate diets and healthy lifestyles should be culturally acceptable and economically feasible. The quality of traditional foods should be emphasised, when appropriate. Promotion of dietary guidelines should be widely encouraged through government, health services, schools, feeding programmes, the mass media, food industry, advertising and by consumer and community groups.

The principal aim of information, education and communication in nutrition in developing countries is to give all levels of consumers adequate education, information and motivation to choose more nutritious diet. This would include improvement of family food resources and better utilisation of available foods for securing an appropriate diet. In developed countries, where the main problem is excessive consumption, nutrition education is directed towards promoting proper food selection and consumption. In both instances, education for better lifestyles, such as quitting smoking, taking physical exercise, improving general and personal levels of hygiene, should be included in the nutrition education programmes.

Reviews of nutrition education projects indicate that a well planned and executed nutrition education programme can change knowledge, attitude and other food habits and practices of the beneficiaries. Most successful behaviour change projects focus on a few, specific changes; more general communication programmes are less effective. The smaller the suggested change in existing practices, the better are their chances of being adopted by a specific audience. To avoid confusing and overwhelming the target group, successful programmes focus on improving or changing one or two dietary patterns.

Nutrition education programmes should be designed to include the entire public, with emphasis on all vulnerable sections of the society. This should include adequate coverage, and communication between social and professional groups and institutions. The aim should be to create a nutrition movement with the active participation of the public. It should involve urban and rural, rich and poor, youth and school children, and pregnant and lactating mothers. It should involve government and political institutions, people's organisations, and religious groups. To achieve impact in a nutrition education programme, specific messages, in addition to general nutrition education, need to be directed to each group.

Nutrition education and communication programmes should be developed in sequential steps. The first step should be an analysis of nutrition problems and identification of areas responsive to nutrition education. Nutrition education alone may not be appropriate when undesirable behaviour is the result of economic constraint. Actions will be needed to remove the constraints to facilitate behavioural change. The second step should be the definition of realistic goals and objectives of the programme with a specific timeframe for achieving them. This should be followed by elaboration of nutrition messages and production of education materials. These materials should then be field-tested in the target community to evaluate their sustainability and comprehension. Formulation of a communication strategy for dissemination of information follows, and finally, a decision is made on the criteria for measuring the programme's success.

Effective exposure of behaviour change messages requires the use of a mixture of communication channels, including mass media and interpersonal communication. Experience has shown that a multi-media approach in setting programme priorities, determining solutions and disseminating nutrition information is most effective in achieving healthy dietary practices in the public. For example, a trained health worker can allay a mothers' concerns about feeding vegetables to her six month old child. Radio can popularise selected foods and new dishes. Community-level discussions may help in the understanding of new food behaviour. The nature and complexity of the message and the intensity of the target population's exposure to mass media should determine the selection of communication channels.

Interpersonal or face-to-face communication should be emphasised when complex behaviour change is being promoted. Recent studies have documented that broadcast media (radio or television) are an extremely cost-effective way to reach large numbers of people. Although the cost of using these media is high, the number of people who change their behaviour as a result of exposure to new ideas on radio or television actually makes this option relatively inexpensive per person influenced. However, a long-term sequenced communication effort is necessary to achieve permanent change in food behaviour. Typically individuals will try out new food behaviour when attention is focused on a problem, but they will not persist with the desired behaviour unless the messages are repeated. Specialists in public health communication have noted the phenomenon of behaviour decay or reversion to original behaviour in the absence of periodic reinforcement of messages.

Nutrition education is best delivered as an integral component of other programmes of health and nutrition improvement. It can be an essential component of primary health care, agricultural extension, school feeding, women's welfare programmes, hospital services, nutrition rehabilitation and a variety of other social programmes aimed at the health and welfare of vulnerable groups. There are also free-standing nutrition education programmes.

A change in knowledge alone is not a sufficient measure of success for a nutrition education programme. The evaluation should measure the extent to which practices are modified, and, ideally, the effect of promoted practices on the nutritional status. Indicators of nutritional status should reflect expected changes in the target audience and should be selected based on available resources. For example, child weight gain, or the prevalence of child malnutrition before and after education could be appropriate indicators in a weaning food education project. Prevalence of eye damage (xerophthalmia) in children is appropriate for education focused increasing the consumption of vitamin A-rich foods.

2.2.5 Preventing specific micronutrient deficiencies

Four main strategies are used to overcome micronutrient deficiencies. These include dietary diversification, food fortification, supplementation and public health and other disease control measures. Each of these strategies is likely to play some role in most countries, but the appropriateness of each needs to be determined at country level. Successful programmes for prevention have to date been most notable for iodine deficiency disorders (IDD), and to a lesser extent, for vitamin A deficiency and anaemia. All three of these are currently receiving priority in public health programmes in developing as well as developed countries. Better planning and targeting of interventions could generally be possible following an assessment of the magnitude and severity of the problems. This assessment should identify the population groups and the geographical zones within each country that are affected by, or at risk from, each deficiency. The World Bank has estimated that investing in programmes to prevent micronutrient deficiencies is among the most cost-effective of all interventions to improve health.

The basic strategy for preventing micronutrient deficiencies centres on increasing the availability and consumption of micronutrient-rich foods. Food production, processing and preservation activities are part of this strategy. The main advantages of this, coupled with nutrition education, are its long-term sustainability and cost-effectiveness, its ability to improve overall human diet quality, and to correct multiple micronutrient deficiencies simultaneously, its toxicological safety and its contribution to people's self-reliance. In addition, diet diversification programmes are more sustainable at the family and community levels when food resources are locally available and have the advantage of providing other nutrients and dietary factors to improve absorption and utilization of micronutrients. These programmes also do not have to rely on a regular supply of pharmaceuticals, which often must be imported and purchased with scarce foreign currency, for effectiveness.

In rural areas, major food-based efforts will likely be in horticultural programmes. In urban settings, there is generally better overall food availability as well as potential for access to fortified food products. It is still beneficial to promote home gardens in periurban areas. Nutrition education activities strengthen and complement efforts to increase the consumption of micronutrient-rich food. Experience in a number of countries—India, Bangladesh, Ghana, Niger, and Vietnam—illustrates that home gardening combined with nutrition education have increased both the production and consumption of fruits and vegetables as well as improving the vitamin A intake of vulnerable groups. The cost-effectiveness has also been demonstrated by other projects. The marketing of vitamin A-rich food, conducted in northeast Thailand from 1988 to 1991, promoted the production and consumption of vitamin A-rich food at a cost of US$ .42 per capita. In Indonesia, the cost of increasing the consumption of green leafy vegetables was estimated at US$ .28 per mother/child. Obviously the cost will differ from project to project and from country to country and is likely to decrease substantially as the plans are implemented on a larger scale. Bangladesh undertook the largest initiative, which aimed at increasing both production and consumption and cost only US$ .13 per capita per year. When small animals are also included in the home garden, sources of other readily bioavailable micronutrients are increased, and absorption of some other nutrients are enhanced.

Food fortification is another successful method of reducing micronutrient deficiencies. Fortification of salt with iodine has proven, in many countries, to be the best solution for reducing IDD. As a result of salt fortification, iodine deficiency has already been eliminated in eighteen countries, one of the best records of success for addressing any micronutrient deficiency. Fortification of salt with iron has been successfully implemented in the control of anaemia, and fortification of sugar with vitamin A has obtained positive results in Latin America.

Many other vehicles have been identified as suitable carriers for micronutrients, including water for iodine, milk and margarine for vitamin A, monosodium glutamate for vitamin A and iron, and wheat and rice for iron. Although cost-effective, the main difficulties with food fortification activities are related to technical and distribution problems, the necessity of adequate legislation, and the need for an effective system for controlling the fortification process. Governments and the food industry need to work together to reduce costs and ensure product quality. Cost is, in fact, a great constraint as prices of fortified food products may increase and poor people may not be able to obtain them.

Micronutrient supplementation should, in general, be regarded as a short-term measure to be used only until more sustainable food-based approaches are implemented and become effective. Supplementation efforts have met with varying degrees of success. Distribution of vitamin A capsules can be effective in preventing eye damage and may be relatively inexpensive to distribute in countries with well-established health care systems. As a preventive method, however, this approach is not effective due to low coverage of capsule distribution as indicated by the results of some of the long ongoing programmes as, for example, in India. Iron tablets frequently are distributed to women through health centres and maternity clinics, but often with limited success due to problems of compliance. Iodine oil distribution campaigns in high at-risk areas which are difficult to reach by other methods, have been successfully attempted in various countries but often at a higher cost than if iodised salt were used. The disadvantages of these interventions, in addition to their unsustainability over the medium- and long-term, are the low percentage of population covered, the lack of capsules, tablets and injectable oils in the areas at risk, the monitoring of such programmes, the difficulty of reaching the populations most in need, the insufficient training of health workers and in the case of injectable iodine, the risk of HIV and hepatitis infections due to the use of non-sterilised syringes.

Public health measures provide necessary support for the above approaches. These include the prevention of infections through environmental health programmes, such as water quality, sanitation and food hygiene, and others such as immunisation, control of endemic diseases, mother and child health (MCH), essential drugs and all primary health care programmes.

Reaching these goals requires action at several levels, and co-operation among governments, non-governmental organisations, the private sector, international organisations and communities.

2.2.6 Preventing malnutrition and managing infectious diseases

Malnutrition-infection complex refers to a situation in which nutritional status influences the outcome of exposure to infection at the same time as infection contributes to a deterioration in nutritional status. Inadequate dietary intake leads to low nutritional reserves, which are manifested as weight loss or failure of growth in children. Depleted nutritional reserves are associated with a lowering of immunity.

Control of infectious diseases and dietary/nutrition interventions are of major importance in breaking the cycle of malnutrition and infection.

Both the traditional and modern health sector, through primary health care, have a role to play in controlling infectious disease. Immunisation, early recognition and intervention in growth faltering, breast-feeding promotion, emphasis on adequate dietary intake, especially during infancy, as well as family planning, are public health measures that contribute to preventing infections and malnutrition. Controlling infectious diseases also involves improving the health environment. These actions and their importance in improving nutrition are briefly described. They are usually implemented as an integral part of primary health care programmes but are equally important in community nutrition programmes.

i) Growth monitoring and promotion

"Growth monitoring and promotion of children is defined as an operational strategy for enabling the mother to visualise the growth or lack of it and to receive specific and relevant and practical guidance in ways that she and her family and community can act to ensure health and continued optimal growth of the child" (UNICEF 1997).

Growth is commonly measured through regular and serial weighing of the child and recording weight in a growth chart. Ideally growth monitoring should be a part of a nutrition monitoring, surveillance and improvement programme. It is not useful unless action is taken to correct growth faltering and advice is given to the mother to correct the situation and remedy the causes of growth faltering. It has been used for many purposes, for example to evaluate the usefulness of child nutrition intervention, to select beneficiaries for supplementation programmes, to estimate prevalence ratios of underweight children in nutritional surveillance, to determine the efficacy of treatment of sick children, and to trace children not attending or returning to the health centres for immunisation.

Growth monitoring has not served its purpose in many centres because of the lack of appreciation of the operators regarding the preventive nature of the monitoring. The mechanical way it is used by overloaded health workers as a record for immunisation and dates of vitamin A capsule distribution, etc., without establishing an effective dialogue with the mother to promote the nutritional status of the child, has defeated its purpose as opportunities provided by growth monitoring are lost. The main objective of growth monitoring can be attained through linking monitoring to the identification of at-risk children, individual counselling of mothers, and taking appropriate action to improve the situation.

ii) Promotion of breast-feeding and improved weaning practices

Experience in child care has proved that breast-feeding is best for the child. Breast milk passes directly from the producer to the consumer without any contamination and prevents diarrhoea and other childhood diseases through transfer of passive immunity from the mother. Continued breast-feeding during attacks of diarrhoea helps to maintain the nutrition of children. Exclusive breast-feeding is recommended for the first four to six months.

Lactational amenorrhea prolonged by active breast-feeding, resulting in increased birth intervals, allows the mother to breast-feed longer and allows time for the mother to take better care of the child.

Activities designed to promote breast-feeding should include measures to facilitate breast-feeding and removal of constraints, nutritional care of the mother, provision of proper antinatal and postnatal care and nutrition education.

Complementary feeding must be introduced to the child between four and six months of age. Care should be taken concerning the energy density, nutritional value and hygienic preparation of the complementary food. Contamination is reduced by the use of fermented foods. It is essential to promote frequent feeding with adequate energy density. It is also important to continue breast- and complementary feeding when the child is sick.

iii) Immunisation against common infectious diseases and prevention of diarrhoea

Childhood infectious diseases, including diarrhoea, are the most common precipitating factors of malnutrition in young children. It is very important to immunise all children according to a proper schedule.

Dietary management during illness seeks to modify the course and outcome of infection by the improvement of food intake during disease and recovery, particularly in young children. This includes: continuation of breast-feeding during infections; use of rehydration therapy in treatment of acute diarrhoea; maintenance of diet during persistent diarrhoea; administration of vitamin A in the management of measles, acute respiratory infections; and the administration of iron during the treatment of malaria and parasite control where intestinal parasite infestation is prevalent.

The prevention and control of malnutrition/infection requires substantial inputs from other sectors, in addition to health. Improvements relating to food safety, housing, water supply and sanitation are important steps towards preventing infection. Primary education has an important role to play by stressing rudimentary nutrition principles and health. At the same time, nutrition and health improvements are unlikely to be sustained if socio-economic status does not improve concurrently.

iv) Integrated nutrition programme

In most conventional nutrition improvement programmes, a number of actions already described are combined with the programme. Many large, well-publicised and successful nutrition programmes include nutrition education, health related services, supplementary feeding, growth monitoring, micronutrient supplementation and home gardens. An analysis of fifteen such projects by Gillespie and Mason (1991) showed that 93% had nutrition education, 73% had health-related services, 80% had supplementary feeding, 67% had growth monitoring, 27% had micronutrient supplement and 20% had home gardening. These programmes are the most publicised success stories of nutrition interventions, such as the Iringa Nutrition Project in Tanzania and the Tamil Nadu Nutrition Project in India. The basic point made by these success stories, however, is that multiple actions must be taken simultaneously in such a way that their effects are synergistic and long-term, establishing a certain momentum while also providing the necessary time for change.

3 Community-based actions for assessment of nutritional problems and actions for their amelioration

For the success and sustainability of nutrition improvement programmes at the community level, people's participation in the assessment of their own nutrition problems, in prioritising them, and in the design, implementation, monitoring and evaluation of them, is essential. People's participation creates ownership, a sense of belonging and self-reliance, and mobilises the community towards sustainable actions for improving its nutrition.

Formulation of participatory nutrition improvement programmes should be achieved in a systematic and sequential manner and in four distinct phases. First, the preparatory phase: this should include gathering and reviewing preliminary information; establishing/strengthening links with other local development institutions; selecting a community for action, and instituting food and nutrition dialogue with the community to stimulate interest in food and nutrition issues. This last step, community mobilisation, is crucial. Communities must be mobilised to take actions themselves to improve their own nutrition with minimum external assistance.

Second, the community must participate in the analysis of its own food and nutrition situation, identify its own nutrition problems and their main causes and constraints for improvement, identify vulnerable households and groups within them and prioritise their food and nutrition problems.

Third, goals must be set for each of the priority problems, activities should be identified to meet these goals, feasibility and cost-effectiveness of each activity must be discussed, the objectives and timeframe identified, the selection of activities agreed upon, community resources mobilised, local institutions contacted for technical support, and a proposal prepared should external support or funding be needed.

The fourth phase is project implementation, monitoring and evaluation. All project activities should be continuously monitored to assess their progress during implementation and, after a predetermined time phase, evaluated against set targets for achievements. To measure the success of each activity, an indicator must be agreed at the beginning of each activity and must be monitored through repeated time-bound measurements. The final progress or success should be gauged through measurement of progress against the baseline and matched against the initial objectives set out in the project

4 Elements for successful nutrition improvement programmes

The Fifth International Conference of the International Nutrition Planners Forum (1989) analysed major successful community nutrition programmes in a number of countries and concluded that the nutritional status of poor population groups in developing countries can be significantly improved through nutrition-oriented community development programmes if certain critical elements are built into the programmes from their inception. It also pointed out that nutrition projects and programmes cannot substitute for a country's and government's political commitment to sustainable and equitable economic growth and social development. A comprehensive strategy that either incorporates nutrition elements into development programmes or uses a community development approach in nutrition programmes was recommended. The Conference also suggested that institutional and individual commitment to community self-reliance in a broad development context is crucial to promoting nutritional improvement. Six crucial elements for programme success were identified:

a. Political commitment

Firm and consistent political commitment, reflected in concrete political actions and financing of nutrition programmes, is necessary. Political actions can be generated from the communities needing nutrition services through advocacy by the technical and scientific community and/or international organisations.

b. Community mobilisation and participation

Effective community mobilisation for active participation is essential for nutrition programmes to succeed. It is best achieved by involving the community in all phases of programme planning and implementation, including needs assessment, decision making and programme supervision, monitoring and evaluation. Decentralisation of power to the community facilitates organization and enables the community to identify its own needs, to search for solutions and to participate actively in the programme implementation.

c. Human resources development

Commitment to community work and strong leadership qualities should be the basic criteria for staff selection. These should also be sought in volunteer workers and staff paid by the community. Relatively large investments are needed for basic and frequent in-service training. This training should be skill-oriented, competence generating, comprehensive and multidisciplinary. Special attention should be paid to the training of trainers.

d. Targeting

Appropriate targeting improves the efficiency and cost effectiveness of nutrition improvement programmes by focusing resources on groups or individuals at highest risk and those most likely to benefit from the programmes. When malnutrition is widespread, geographic targeting may be adequate, but as the level of malnutrition decreases, it is necessary to use a combination of geographic, household, economic and individual criteria. In targeting the poorest regions or communities, development of a minimum service delivery infrastructure is often required.

e. Monitoring, evaluation and management information systems

A functional management information system for ongoing monitoring, evaluation and decision-making at the local and higher levels is an important element of programme success. A two-way, top-down and bottom-up flow of information and decision-making should be established, with regular collection of data, timely analysis and interpretation and immediate feedback. The information should be kept simple and contain a minimum set of data and indicators to be collected, analysed and used by the community, programme managers and policymakers for decision making. It should never exceed the data handling capacity of the programme or overload the community workers as data collectors.

f. Replicability and sustainability

Replicability is determined by the extent to which the programme elements, methodologies and implementation processes can be successfully applied in the same contextual situation. For nutrition programmes to make a difference in the long term, sustainability of positive outcome is crucial. Sustainability is enhanced by political commitment, active community participation, development of trained human resources and programme cost-effectiveness *vis-à-vis* resources available in the community. Sustainability should be built in from the planning stage when nutrition interventions are designed within the context and capacity of a country's local resources. Effective technology transfer or creation of cost-effective, locally developed technologies can increase a programme's sustainability.

5 Role of public and private entities in nutrition improvement programmes

Governments need to take a leading role in working toward solutions to nutrition problems. Their role should mainly involve sectoral activities, especially in the fields of agriculture, health, education and social welfare. Ministries could prepare a review of the nutritional impact of their policies, programmes and projects. They could incorporate nutritional considerations in project formulation and use nutritional indicators to assess the performance of the project. Intersectoral co-operation, especially between health and agriculture, is important in many areas, and there is considerable scope to increase this collaboration. Each country needs to evaluate its own experiences and processes of intersectoral co-operation and strengthen them as necessary in the light of their needs and resources.

Non-governmental organizations (NGOs) can play an important role in generating innovative action at the grassroots level. They should strive for full integration in the national system and address the issue of replication for wider impact. Consumer organisations can initiate a dialogue with the food industry and distribution network agents. Private enterprise has an especially important role to play in nutrition since most food and agricultural production is carried out by small-scale private farmers. Small-scale rural and other industries are also important, particularly in ensuring good food processing, food quality and safety and nutritious products. The contribution of industry to nutrition research is also important to benefit from the financial resources and expertise as well as to identify consumer and production problems requiring solutions.

Legislation regarding the quality and safety of food and its labelling, marketing and advertising is a government responsibility; however, implementation and monitoring are often in the hands of the private sector and consumers. Dialogue between all partners—namely, the government, consumers and private industry—is essential, and they must all co-operate if sustainable improvements are to be made.

The international community can provide support to national efforts through international organisations and bilateral agencies. Many UN agencies address food and nutrition problems directly or have an impact on nutrition through their general activities. Among these agencies, FAO, UNICEF, WHO and the World Bank have nutrition divisions or sub-divisions while many of the others have at least one full-time nutrition adviser. The concerned UN agencies participate in the United Nations Sub-Committee on Nutrition of the Administrative Committee on Co-ordination (ACC/SCN). The aggregate financial and technical contributions of bilateral organisations are substantial, and several of them have nutrition advisers.

International research support for nutrition is provided in the fields of both agriculture and health. The Consultative Group of International Agriculture Research (CGIAR) supports eighteen international centres worldwide, all of which have made important contributions to agricultural research development, sometimes with important nutritional implications. An active network of research institutions also exists to support nutrition in the health sector.

Successful implementation of nutrition programmes requires human resource development. At the national level, availability of a cadre of professionals who can guide national programme formulation, implementation, monitoring and evaluation are crucial for success. Their formal or in-service training should be problem-and-action-oriented. There is a need to strengthen national training institutions in all countries. An important concern is the development of capacities for nutritional analysis and action at the district level where, generally, no nutrition personnel are present. There is also a need to develop the capacities of community leaders to assess the nutritional situation and to design measures to improve it.

References

Berg, A. (1981): Malnourished People. A Policy Review Work Bank. Washington D.C.

FAO/WHO (1992): Nutrition and Development—a Global Assessment, International Conference on Nutrition.

FAO/WHO (1992): Major Issues for Nutrition Strategies, International Conference on Nutrition.

FAO (1987): The Fifth World Food Survey, FAO, Rome.

FAO (1996): Rome Declaration on World Food Security and World Food Summit Plan of Action, World Food Summit, 13-17 November 1996, Rome.

Harbert, L. and P. Scandizzo (1982): Food Distribution and Nutrition Intervention. The Case of Chile, Staff working paper No. 512, Washington D.C., World Bank.

Kennedy, E.T. and Alderman (1985): Comparative Analysis of Nutrition Effectiveness of Selected Interventions, ACC/SCN, State of the Art Project.

Marsh, Robin (1994): Production and Consumption Effects of the Introduction of Home Gardening on Target, Interaction and Control Groups: a Case Study from Bangladesh, presented at the International Symposium on System-oriented research, November 1994, Montpellier, France.

Niñez, Vera K. (ed.) (1985): Household Food Production: Comparative Perspectives, International Potato Centre, Lima.

Soleri, Daniela; David A. Cleveland and Timothy R. Frankenberger (1991): Gardens and Vitamin A. A Review of Recent Literature, prepared for vitamin A field support project (VITAL), Office of Nutrition, Bureau of Science and Technology, Washington D.C.

UNICEF (1997): Nutrition into the Nineties. Report of a Workshop on Nutrition Policy and Action, Naivasha, Kenya, 1 - 6 April 1997.

UNDP (1996): Urban Agriculture. Food. Jobs and Sustainable Cities, UNDP, N.Y.

United States Agency for International Development (USAID) (1989): Crucial Elements of Successful Community Nutrition Programmes. Report of the Fifth International Conference of the International Planners Forum, Seoul, Republic of Korea, 15-19 April 1989, Washington, D.C., U.S.A., USAID Bureau for Science and Technology, Office of Nutrition.

19

Famine Prevention During Armed Conflict: The Humanitarian Challenge

Marc J. Cohen[1]

1 Introduction

Violent civil conflicts have put 80 million people at risk of hunger, from shattered urban neighborhoods in Afghanistan to refugee camps in Zaire, as well as in former Soviet and Yugoslav republics. Hopes for a more peaceful and food secure world in the post-Cold War era have given way to a proliferation of "complex humanitarian emergencies." War and oppression have increasingly replaced natural disasters as the source of famines.

The lines between humanitarianism and politics, always somewhat blurry, have become increasingly difficult to discern. Timely delivery of relief supplies in situations of armed conflict may require military forces to distribute aid and protect civilian populations and aid workers. There is great potential for conflict between claims of national sovereignty on the one hand and the right to food and humanitarian assistance on the other.

The international community has yet to reinvent the global emergency response regime, created at the dawn of the Cold War, so that it can appropriately link relief, human rights protection, conflict management and development aid. At the same time, the system presently lacks adequate capacity, authority and resources. Once conflict ends, often enormous tasks of repatriation, reconstruction and reconciliation remain. Aid donors have provided far more resources for pursuing military conflicts than for repairing the resulting damage.

Because of budget constraints, donor countries are significantly reducing their overall aid programs. The spread of crises has channeled a higher share of what remains into emergency assistance. Yet the costs of responding to crises exceed the price of investing in prevention and mitigation.

2 The characteristics of complex humanitarian emergencies

Increasingly, violent conflicts occur within nation states, rather than between them. Of the 25 armed confrontations which led to 1,000 or more deaths in 1995, 23 were civil wars or other instances of internal strife (see Table 1). Up to 80 percent of the

1 This chapter is adapted from the Bread for the World Institute Report.

casualties are civilians, mainly women and children, often deliberately targeted by the warring parties(Karolien 1994; UNDP 1994; Watkins 1995: 43).

Table 1: Battlefields of 1995

Country	Circumstances
Afghanistan	Soviet intervention, civil war, 1979-
Algeria	Low-intensity insurgency, 1992-
Angola	Civil war, 1975-1997
Armenia-Azerbaijan	War over Nagorno-Karabakh, 1989-
Bosnia	Serbian and Croatian intervention, civil war, 1992-1995
Burma	Armed rebellions, 1985-
Burundi	Ethnic clashes, 1988-
Colombia	Armed rebellions, 1986-
Georgia	Separatist rebellions in Abkhazia and South Ossetia, 1992-
Guatemala	Civil war, 1966-1996
India	Separatist rebellions in Kashmir and Punjab, 1983-
Iraq	Unrest in Kurdish areas, 1991-
Kenya	Ethnic violence, 1991-
Liberia	Civil war, 1989-1996
Pakistan	Ethnic and religious violence, 1994-1995
Peru	Armed rebellions, 1980-
Philippines	Armed rebellions, 1972-
Russia	Separatist rebellion in Chechnya, 1994-1996
Rwanda	Civil war, genocide, 1992-1996
Sierra Leone	Civil war, 1991-1996
Somalia	Civil war, 1988-
Sri Lanka	Civil war, 1983-
Sudan	Civil war, 1984-
Tajikistan	Civil war, 1992-
Turkey	Kurdish rebellion, 1984-

Sources: Sivard 1996; United Nations Department of Humanitarian Affairs; press reports.

2.1 Definition of complex emergencies

According to Thomas G. Weiss and Cindy Collins, a complex emergency results from the combination of internal conflict, large-scale displacements of people, and fragile or failing economic, political and social institutions. "Other symptoms include noncombatant death, starvation or malnutrition; disease and mental illness; random and systematic violence against noncombatants; infrastructure collapse; widespread lawlessness and interrupted food production and trade" (Weiss and Collins 1996: 4).

2.2 The extent and roots of complex emergencies

The rise in civil strife has had an enormous human toll. Complex emergencies are behind the increase in the number of people who have crossed international borders as refugees from 2.4 million in 1974 to 14.5 million in 1996. In addition, over 3 million repatriated people remain in need of humanitarian assistance, and some 5 million live in "refugee-like circumstances," without official recognition of their status or entitlement to aid. An estimated 27 million "internally displaced" people have abandoned their homes without leaving their country of origin. Meanwhile, as many as 30 million more people are trapped within conflict zones, desperately poor and subject to the threat of malnutrition, starvation and death.[2] Table 2 indicates the populations (about 22 million people in all) in 23 countries dependent upon international humanitarian assistance for food, water, medicine, sanitation, medical care, seeds, farm equipment and assistance in mine clearing.

Civil strife stems from conflicts based on race, religion and ethnicity; competition over resources such as land, water and other assets and political power; or ideological disputes, e.g., religious fundamentalism vs. political, social and economic modernization. Hunger and poverty often cause or contribute to the flare-up of violence. Resource poor areas are especially prone to conflict, and conflict in turn is a cause of further environmental, social and economic stress. Hunger leads to mass refugee flight, which causes yet more environmental damage (Jacobsen 1994; Messer et al. forthcoming).

The Cold War contributed to civil strife in a number of countries, some of which are now at peace (e.g., El Salvador, Guatemala, Angola and Mozambique). Others such as Somalia are still coping with a legacy of conflict and arms. Superpower intervention suppressed factional and separatist conflicts in some other countries such as Yugoslavia. With the reduction in East-West tensions, these places became more, rather than less, dangerous, as power-hungry leaders exploited age-old tensions to gain political advantage.

---

2 Estimates of numbers of people affected by complex emergencies based on data from UNHCR and the U.S. Committee for refugees, as well as personal communications from Steven Hansch, Senior Program Officer, Refugee Policy Group, Washington, DC, USA, 18 December 1996 and 30 April 1997.

Table 2: Hunger in conflict and post-conflict countries, April 1996

Country	People in need of humanitarian assistance (millions)	Circumstances
Afghanistan	2.4	Civil War Internally displaced people, food shortages; of 2.7 million Afghan refugees in Pakistan and Iran, some 650,000 are at risk nutrionally
Angola	1.0	Post-Conflict internally displaced and war-affected people, demobilized troops
Bosnia	3.1	Post-Conflict Low income and elderly people continue to need assistance
Caucasus Region (Armenia, Azer-baijan, Georgia, Chechnya)	1.7	Post-Conflict Displaced people live in abject poverty in Armenia and Azerbaijan; difficult economic transition in Georgia; lasting political solutions to region's territorial disputes not yet achieved
Ethiopia	0.4	Post-Conflict Fragile reconstruction and reconciliation; widespread food insecurity; internally displaced people; Somali refugees
Great Lakes Region, Central Africa	Burundi: 0.6 Rwanda: 1.4 Tanzania: 0.3 Congo (Kinshasa): 0.6 Congo (Brazzaville): 0.7 Total: 3.6	Active Conflict Refugees, internally displaced people, food used as a weapon, military inter-vention, economic sanctions on Burundi
Iraq	2.1	Active Conflict International embargo, internal embar-goes, internally displaced people
Liberia/Sierra Leone Region	1.5	Active Conflict Internally displaced people in both coun-tries; fighting continues in Sierra Leone; 600,000 refugees in Côte d'Ivoire and Guinea
Somalia	1.2	Civil War Internally displaced people; no function-ing central government; drought and floods exacerbate security problems
Sri Lanka	0.5	Civil War War has disrupted normal economic activity in north
Sudan	2.8	Civil War Internally displaced people, food is weapon

Country	People in need of humanitarian assistance (millions)	Circumstances
Tajikistan	1.0	Post-Conflict Internally displaced and people affected by economic transition face serious undernutrition
Uganda	0.6	Civil War Internally displaced people; refugees from Sudan and Great Lakes region

Sources: Food and Agriculture Organization of the United Nations 1997; United Nations Administrative Committee on Coordination/Subcommittee on Nutrition 1997; United Nations Department of Humanitarian Affairs 1997; U.S. Mission to the United Nations 1997.

2.3 Conflict, hunger and disease

Hunger is a major feature of these crises. Warring factions loot and deliberately destroy crops, draw labor resources out of food production (through conscription, market disruption and displacement of farming communities) and use food as a weapon. In a study of 16 developing countries at war between 1970 and 1990, Frances Stewart, of Oxford University, found widespread food insecurity. In each case, per capita incomes declined and conflict heavily destroyed productive and social infrastructure. Food production per capita dropped in 14 of the countries. People had difficulty getting enough food because of reduced output, employment and earnings, and rising inflation. Landmines and destruction of infrastructure took farm land out of use (Stewart 1993).

People uprooted in complex emergencies frequently forfeit their meager assets, including land and tools. This makes return, recovery, long-term development and self-reliance—as well as productive activities in asylum countries—that much more expensive and difficult. In the Horn of Africa, for example, violent civil strife during the early 1990s raised mortality rates from malnutrition and disease more than 20-fold (U.S. Centers for Disease Control and Prevention 1993). In southern Sudan, a long-term conflict zone, 70 percent of all children were malnourished in 1993 and millions of people were at risk of malnutrition (Herwaldt et al. 1993).

All too often, conflict transforms food from the staff of life into a weapon of war. The problem is especially severe in southern Sudan, as John Prendergast (1994) has written: "Food becomes a powerful military instrument. Warring factions deny or disrupt access and distribution for relief; routinely divert food aid for their sustenance; use civilians as bait for internationally donated food; provide food aid to gain legitimacy; monetize, barter or otherwise manipulate food aid to obtain arms or fuel and differentially provide food aid to supporters at the expense of those most in need, who may be unsympathetic or of the wrong ethnicity, race or religion."

Complex emergencies frequently lead to serious micronutrient deficiencies ("hidden hunger"). Food aid rations may lack vitamins and minerals. Conflict blocks access to fresh food markets. Yet emergency relief efforts have not given high priority to fortification of food aid, providing supplements or encouraging the cultivation of household gardens.

Complex emergencies exacerbate—and are exacerbated by—disease epidemics. Efforts to control infectious diseases must contend with mass forced migration and regions rendered inaccessible by war and social breakdown. Health personnel migrate or are killed, and warring factions destroy clinics (World Health Organization 1995). Violent conflict limits access to clean water. The risks of communicable diseases and poor sanitation usually increase when uprooted people congregate in camps. The 80 million people who face food insecurity because of complex emergencies account for less than 10 percent of the world's 841 million chronically undernourished people. But known public health measures could readily avert most of the deaths from hunger and related diseases that occur in these crisis situations.

3 Crisis response[3]

Addressing complex emergencies requires multi-pronged approaches that combine food and health interventions with conflict mediation, negotiation with the warring parties for access to vulnerable populations, establishing safe havens, training in human rights reporting, tracking of dislocated populations and repatriation or resettlement efforts. Often, a multilateral peace keeping force must accompany humanitarian aid. All these need to be coordinated among regional governments, international organizations, and local and foreign nongovernmental organizations (NGOs). Crisis response, in turn, must be linked with prevention efforts and post-crisis development planning. The international community has yet to establish an effective global structure to manage all these tasks coherently.

3.1 Response to natural disasters: lessons and limits

The experience of the past 25 years in responding to natural disasters (drought, flood, earthquake) offers valuable lessons for dealing with complex humanitarian emergencies. But these lessons are insufficient for devising appropriate systems to respond to violent conflicts. Famines that result primarily from natural causes require quick and appropriate provision of food, water, shelter and medical aid, usually with the cooperation of the local government. As a result of their work in the famines in West Africa in the early 1970s and in East Africa in the mid-1980s, international relief agencies bolstered their early warning and response capacities.

3 This section is in part an effort to synthesize the pioneering work of the Humanitarianism and War Project at Brown University. See Minear et al. 1991; Minear and Weiss 1993; Minear and Weiss 1995a; Minear and Weiss 1995b; Scott et al. 1996.

In contrast, early warning systems to monitor social and political tensions that might escalate into violent conflict are in their infancy.

The enormous 1992 crop failure in East and Southern Africa did not cost millions of lives. Local communities, aid donors and African governments effectively coordinated their response. Similarly, in 1994, a timely aid response and effective use of local capacities prevented starvation following the poor Ethiopian harvest. When armed conflict threatens to create a famine, such a coordinated response is not always possible. One or more parties may not be open to outside assistance, and such emergencies are usually of uncertain duration, rather than only until the next harvest.

3.2 The changing humanitarian aid regime

The drama of crisis response includes an extremely large cast of characters. At present, coordination of the various players and their roles remains inadequate. The appropriate balance between humanitarian and political responses, especially, is the subject of much debate within the international community. Moreover, the current framework has yet to adequately address the important contradiction between state sovereignty and human rights that so often arises in complex emergencies.

Since the end of the Second World War, the United Nations system has had a key part in responding to crises, both natural and human-made. Specialized agencies such as the U.N. Children's Fund (UNICEF), the Office of the U.N. High Commissioner for Refugees (UNHCR), the World Food Programme (WFP) and the U.N. Centre for Human Rights have provided emergency aid and monitored the status of civilian populations. In 1992, the world body established a Department of Humanitarian Affairs (DHA) to coordinate humanitarian activities at the international level; in the field, the local office of the United Nations Development Programme (UNDP) usually has responsibility.

Peace keeping operations and conflict mediation efforts fall under the aegis of the U.N. Security Council, along with the Departments of Political Affairs and Peacekeeping Operations. In a number of cases, the United Nations has established field level bodies to integrate humanitarian and political aspects of crisis response, such as the U.N. Transition Authority in Cambodia and the U.N. Operation in Mozambique. But this happens only on a case-by-case basis.

DHA offers a framework within the U.N. system for institutionalizing a more integrated approach. Now, however, interagency and intergovernmental cooperation remain inefficient and insufficient. Inadequate funding and staff limit the capacity of relief agencies to respond to needs and to do so in a timely manner. The total annual budget for U.N. peacekeeping and humanitarian operations is currently less than that of the New York City Fire Department (Watkins 1995: 68).

Donor governments make substantial contributions to emergency response both as funders of the U.N. system and through direct activities. Among the key agencies are the Office of Foreign Disaster Assistance of the U.S. Agency for

International Development (USAID) and the European Community Humanitarian Office.

NGOs have long played a critical role in emergency aid. Because of their independence and commitment to humanitarian principle (many are motivated by religious principles), they are known for rapid response and willingness to work on the front-lines, often operating directly in rebel-controlled territory. Some NGOs insist on keeping their operations completely separate from those of governments and international organizations; others work in close partnership with official donor institutions. International and industrial country NGOs, such as CARE, Caritas Internationalis, the World Council of Churches, World Vision, Oxfam and Save the Children, have substantial emergency budgets comparable to those of the official agencies.

The International Committee of the Red Cross (ICRC) has a mandate under international law—the 1949 Geneva Conventions and 1977 Additional Protocols setting out the "rules of war"—to protect civilians in situations of international or civil war. The agency is funded primarily by governments but enjoys considerable independence, and maintains strict political neutrality. ICRC works closely with national Red Cross and Red Crescent Societies, which are major players in providing emergency assistance. These and other local NGOs and community based associations are critical and often under-recognized parts of the humanitarian aid regime. Government and rebel-controlled agencies in crisis countries also directly provide relief, as well as logistical support and access to vulnerable populations.

In recent years, NGOs have attempted to improve the coordination of their efforts through such bodies as the International Council of Voluntary Agencies and the Steering Committee for Humanitarian Response. In 1995, NGOs involved in disaster response adopted a Code of Conduct stressing the primacy of humanitarian principle, political neutrality and the need to draw on and foster local capacity. Significantly, the Code states, "In our information, publicity and advertising activities, we shall recognize disaster victims as dignified humans, not hopeless objects" (International Federation of Red Cross and Red Crescent Societies 1996: 147).

Finally, the news media are part and parcel of humanitarian response. Print and electronic media make the world aware of crises, focus attention on successes and failures of emergency response and shape public support (or lack of support) for humanitarian intervention, including the use of military forces.

During the Cold War, the United Nations generally deferred to the dictates of state sovereignty when humanitarian emergencies occurred or conflicts broke out. As an organization composed of national governments, it provided relief supplies or peacekeepers only if the affected national government requested them. Thus, when the Ethiopian government failed to acknowledge that it faced famine in 1973, no aid arrived and people starved. And national governments regularly ordered peacekeeping forces out, as in the Middle East in 1967.

At the other extreme, Cold War strategic calculations often influenced the shape of bilateral humanitarian aid efforts (or their absence) in such places as

Central America, Afghanistan, East Timor and Cambodia. Nevertheless, in the mid-1980s, the United States government (the largest provider of bilateral humanitarian assistance), under the pressure of public opinion, agreed to provide huge amounts of food aid to Marxist-ruled Ethiopia in order to forestall mass starvation. This principle that "a hungry child knows no politics" has continued to guide U.S. policy. The United States has provided emergency assistance to such longstanding "enemies" as Sudan and the Democratic People's Republic of Korea. Recently, though, senior U.S. officials have argued, "humanitarian aid must be linked more closely to our foreign policy" (Atwood and Rogers 1997).

In the 1990s, the international community has struggled to reshape crisis response to uphold humanitarian imperatives while at the same time addressing the political causes of the emergency. This is an ongoing process involving exceedingly thorny issues.

3.3 Problems in contemporary crisis response

Food and other relief supplies may be diverted to support warring factions—inadvertently, or as a necessary bribe for permission to reach people in need. Serious ethical questions face relief organizations, since providing assistance may further fuel the conflict and suffering, and postpone helping affected people achieve food self reliance or sustainable development. But failing to offer aid may lead to starvation.

People affected by civil strife have the right to protection and assistance. Their needs and opinions, whether expressed directly or through advocates, should be carefully weighed. Getting assistance to people affected by crisis depends on the willingness of warring nations and parties to adhere to humanitarian principles. During civil wars, reaching an affected population with relief supplies often becomes an international legal issue when governments assert national sovereignty. Sudan's government, for example, has tried to limit aid to its southern region based on such concerns. NGOs often work in rebel-controlled areas via neighboring countries.

In recent years, a consensus appears to be emerging that the international community may intervene to provide humanitarian assistance and defend human rights, regardless of the objections of the affected state. In April 1991, the Security Council authorized multilateral military intervention to protect the Iraqi Kurds, allowing unprecedented intervention in the internal affairs of a state. In January 1992, the council similarly authorized intervention in Somalia. The view seems to be that when state authority collapses, or the state denies its own citizens food, the international community must act. Yet the potential for casualties, which quickly became a reality in Somalia, has given the international community—and global public opinion—pause. Queasiness about the risks led to long delays before humanitarian-military intervention occurred in Bosnia and Rwanda, at a staggering human cost.

Even the most altruistic humanitarian intervention will be colored by the national, political and economic interests of the intervening country or countries. Hence, there is also a strong preference for international intervention, or at least multilateral action. Some emergencies are of such scale or immediacy that only a military force may be able to protect and assist people affected by crisis in a timely manner. In other situations, the intransigence of one or all warring parties, often coupled with the breakdown of government or deliberate policies of starving large populations, may make relief aid almost impossible without military protection.

Military intervention for humanitarian purposes raises both practical and ethical issues. Practical questions include the strength of national and international commitment and the conditions that accompany withdrawal of the forces. Many humanitarian emergencies cry out for diplomacy and mediation. Using the military to "force" delivery of assistance may complicate conciliation efforts. The main mission of any military force is not to provide relief, but to prevail. A military presence may also raise serious questions about the neutrality of humanitarian agencies that work with military forces. Military force for humanitarian assistance should always be authorized by the U.N. Security Council or another international body. To the extent possible, the force should be neutral with respect to the conflict at hand, multinational in make-up and utilized as part of a clear and comprehensive strategy of crisis response.

A final issue is the coherence of donor country policies. These often work at cross purposes and undercut humanitarian responses. For example, the five permanent members of the U.N. Security Council—the nations that the U.N. Charter designates as guarantors of world peace—account for more than 80 percent of the world's arms exports. As Oxfam has pointed out: "These weapons have wrought human destruction on a massive scale. From time to time they have also been used against U.N. troops, or on soldiers from the supplying country, as they were during the Gulf War and in Somalia. Apart from destroying human lives, arms exports have reinforced the underlying causes of conflict by diverting resources from development. Developing countries now account for 15 percent of world military spending, or $188 billion annually" (Watkins 1995: 59).

3.4 Uses and limitations of emergency food aid

In a number of recent emergencies, food aid has temporarily helped sustain the affected people. In Bosnia and Sri Lanka, food aid has allowed large populations to maintain relative food security in the midst of crisis. In some instances, food aid has played a role in creative efforts to promote livelihood security. In Somalia, WFP, CARE and other agencies were not able to deliver food aid directly to people most in need. Nevertheless, by selling food on the market, they were able to bring the price down for everyone and use the sales proceeds to pay for additional relief and rehabilitation activities (Sommer 1994). In carrying out such efforts, it is crucial to assure that falling prices do not harm local farmers. When possible, local or regional procurement of food aid supplies can help guard against such effects.

Another problem is male control of food aid. Women and their dependent children account for 75 percent to 80 percent of the world's refugee population. Yet when agencies consult refugees, they usually talk with men. The consequences of distributing food and supplies through male committees or male elders can be serious for women. Sometimes, the food is sold on the black market or diverted to the military. Sexual favors may be expected from single women and women heads of households in exchange for food. High malnutrition and death rates among refugee women have repeatedly been traced to distribution systems in which they have no say. In contrast, when refugee women have been given the lead role in food distribution, distribution is more equitable for the entire refugee community.

The future of global food aid is uncertain. The Uruguay Round trade agreement promises gradually to reduce industrial country agricultural surpluses and subsidized exports. This should reduce donors' temptation to use food aid for surplus disposal. In addition, the agreement pledges to maintain or increase levels of bona fide food aid, but in fact, donors have cut food aid budgets in the mid-1990s, as part of overall budget austerity. Rising commodity prices have meant substantial reductions in actual tonnage. Greater scarcity of food aid makes efforts to achieve sustainable food security all the more important in countries facing complex emergencies. In any event, food aid alone is not a long-term solution to either crisis or the uprooting of civilian populations.

4 Integrating relief and development

Relief efforts should not undercut, and will hopefully contribute to, sustainable development. In the rush to feed hungry people, it is important to monitor overall livelihood security. This refers to the ability of a household to meet all of its basic needs—food, water, sanitation, shelter, health care, education—without making tradeoffs (Frankenberger, no date). If emergency relief is not linked fairly quickly to long-term development efforts, it can lead to dependence for the affected communities. The transition to development includes rehabilitation of damaged physical and social infrastructure, restoration of human capital, reconstruction of institutions, and reinstatement of social and cultural ethics and values. Adoption of disaster preparedness plans provides local governments with resources and skills that can keep problems from turning into crises. Relief operations should, when possible, move to recovery activities, such as helping people restore assets and livelihoods, and food-for-work and other job creation projects that rebuild infrastructure, repair roads, plant trees, develop irrigation and conserve the soil.

In northern Ethiopia and in Eritrea, donors provided food aid through local NGOs. This helped build local capacity, and proved helpful for carrying out post-conflict rehabilitation. This is a two-way street: community development projects likewise create structures that can facilitate relief activities (Institute of Development Studies 1995). WFP's large refugee food aid program in northern Uganda represents a major effort to link relief and development. Over 300,000 Sudanese refugees in Uganda depend on food aid, most of which is produced and procured within Uganda. The Ugandan government has welcomed Sudanese refugees. When living in camps, they are permitted to grow food, build permanent structures and participate in local labor markets. In many asylum countries, however, there are numerous obstacles to self-reliance such as laws that deny refugees access to employment or land. In conditions of armed conflict, access to local markets is often difficult or impossible.

Humanitarian interventions should focus on maintaining communities and the activities of everyday life, if the security situation allows—even at some risk. It is essential to engage affected populations in designing and implementing relief and rehabilitation activities. Also, if people leave their homes for feeding camps, the process of rehabilitation and reconstruction becomes more difficult, especially if the conflict goes on a long time.

5 Reconstruction

Several countries are emerging from years of civil war as a result of peace agreements, often brokered by the United Nations or other outside mediators. While war and crisis draw international media and political attention, the world tends to lose interest in a country's struggle to reconstruct. U.S. aid to El Salvador, for example, which averaged $250 million annually in the 1980s, has fallen to $48 million as the country faces enormous reconstruction burdens. Post-crisis countries face physical reconstruction, social and political reconciliation and coping with the legacies of war. Environmental restoration and sustainable agriculture must sit high on the agenda. War-scourged economies are often extremely delicate. Uprooted people need help in returning and resettling, and ex-combatants have to find constructive civilian roles. Local people will, of course, do most of the rebuilding, but international aid for rehabilitation and development is often necessary.

5.1 Physical reconstruction

Warfare destroys physical and social infrastructure. Governments at war shift funds away from social services and infrastructure maintenance to help finance the fighting. Scarcity of funds can delay efforts to rebuild or repair the damage during and after the conflict.

5.2 Landmines

The removal of anti-personnel land mines and unexploded ordinance is often a crucial reconstruction task. Combatants most often sow mines in rural areas, and many of the countries most afflicted by mines depend predominantly on agriculture for income, employment and food security. Failure to carry out effective mine removal programs discourages and impedes refugees from returning home, leaves large areas of land inaccessible and seriously hinders reconstruction efforts (Renner

1994). The Red Cross has estimated that mines cause more than 800 deaths and 450 injuries every month. Civilians account for 80 percent of the deaths and maimings due to land mines. Estimates of the number of mines scattered in 62 countries range from 65 million to more than 120 million. In such countries as Afghanistan, Angola, Iraq, Kuwait, Mozambique, Bosnia, Somalia, Sudan and Ethiopia, there is one buried mine for every three to five people.

Land mines pose a major obstacle to Cambodia's reconstruction. Estimates of the number of mines range from 4 million to 7 million, covering more than 40 percent of the land once farmed in a country where agriculture employs over 75 percent of the workforce. Cambodia has the world's highest incidence of disabilities, with one of every 236 people affected. Each month, 300 to 700 amputations occur because of land mine injuries (United Nations 1992; Human Rights Watch and Physicians for Human Rights 1991).

In 1993, de-mining efforts removed roughly 80,000 mines worldwide, but combatants planted another 2.5 million mines. More than 250 million land mines have been produced over the past 25 years and at least another 100 million lie in stockpiles around the world (U.S. Senate Appropriations Committee, Subcommittee on Foreign Operations 1994; U.N. General Assembly 1994; Human Rights Watch/Arms Project and Physicians for Human Rights 1993; U.S. Department of State 1993).

Effective mine removal is dangerous, time consuming and very expensive. Unfortunately, it is not the trained personnel who eliminate most mines. Rather, unlucky civilians stumble across mines, accidentally detonating them at the cost of their lives or limbs. It takes roughly 100 times as long to detect, remove and disarm a mine as to plant it. The cost of clearance (including training, support and logistics) is $300 to $1,000 per mine, compared to production costs of less than $25. The United Nations has begun efforts to establish moratoria on production and sales of land mines.

5.3 Economic construction/reconstruction

Economic revitalization is another key to rebuilding a post-crisis country. Official reconstruction programs work best when they are flexible and support local initiatives to rebuild. Local and foreign NGOs, which generally work in partnership with local communities, can play an important supportive role.

Post-crisis economies are often weak, with few income earning opportunities to offer people returning home or those who never fled. In Mozambique, for example, with the achievement of peace, refugees and internally displaced people have eagerly gone back to their communities. UNHCR's efforts to repatriate 1.5 million Mozambicans represent the agency's largest operation ever in Africa. The number of people returning without official assistance is thought to be the largest such migration in history. Assuring economic opportunities for these people in a poor country is a huge undertaking.

5.4 Political reconciliation

Perhaps the most important and critical aspect of successful reconstruction involves the government, often newly formed, taking effective, inclusive and democratic steps to foster a sustainable rehabilitative environment. The opposing factions must bring armed conflict to an end. This involves the signing of a peace agreement and the demobilization of armies. Then, formerly hostile groups must find a way to share power. Frequently, this process takes the form of an election. The United Nations regularly steps in to help ensure that elections are fair and free. Once a new government takes office, the final stage involves the strengthening of democratic institutions to assure a lasting government, future periodic elections and respect for minority rights. If the country can achieve genuine political reconciliation, this greatly boosts the chances of successful reconstruction.

6 Prevention

It makes sense to develop the wisdom to anticipate, and strengthen the capacity to manage, those disputes most likely to erupt into violent conflict. The cause of contemporary hunger-producing crises is most often found in ethnic conflict. This problem affects industrial and developing countries alike. In Africa, for example, Rwanda and Burundi offer the most extreme, but not the only, examples. Ethnic conflict remains the major threat to the consolidation of a peaceful, democratic, post-apartheid system in South Africa.

Open strife is usually triggered deliberately by groups trying to enhance their own power or by politicians building their careers on ethnic hatred. In Rwanda and Burundi, Hutus and Tutsis do not periodically turn on each other with rocks and machetes without reason. As in 1994, they are incited by organized groups with political agendas.

6.1 Preventing and managing conflict

Steps can be taken to reduce the likelihood of conflict and to shorten the duration of ongoing crises. In the long run, the most important factor contributing to conflict prevention is sustainable development. It can help break the vicious circle of conflict and hunger by increasing available resources, offering peaceful avenues to resolve conflicts and giving communities greater capacity to withstand disruption without a serious humanitarian crisis. But sustainable development is a long-term process that will not stop ongoing violence or suddenly overcome long-standing conflicts. Some of the changes needed to bring about sustainable development in the long run can increase tension in the short run. The transition to more democratic government may lead many groups to feel threatened. Yugoslavia blew apart after multi-party elections were held in all its regions for the first time in half a century.

In the medium run, conflict prevention and management efforts should focus on helping countries and communities understand better the concerns of all groups involved, and agree on a set of rules of the game that can address those concerns. In cases of ethnic and religious conflict, the issue of the rights of the different groups is paramount. Usually, groups involved in ethnic conflict have legitimate demands and grievances, but they are unwilling to recognize the legitimate demands and grievances of others.

Measures that enable minorities to maintain their language and culture, as well as preserve a measure of autonomy in their local governments, can help avoid ethnic and religious conflict. Nigeria suffered a disastrous civil war in the late 1960s, triggered by the attempt of the Ibos to form their own state of Biafra. But Nigeria then established a redesigned federal system that maintained a degree of ethnic peace for 20 years. In South Africa, a combination of power-sharing at the center and regional decentralization opened the way to successful elections in April 1994, preventing the large-scale ethnic violence that appeared very likely only a few weeks earlier. In neither case was the problem entirely solved. Ethnic tensions remain and so does the potential for a new explosion. Nigeria appears to be moving in that direction now.

In the short run, measures such as those just described will probably not help much in defusing ongoing conflicts that have already become violent. U.N. interventions, with the deployment of large peacekeeping forces, is only one of many different ways to help resolve ongoing conflicts. U.N. interventions are costly, and the United States and other nations are now reluctant to fund them. U.N.-led military interventions also depend on difficult-to-achieve international consensus; they are hampered by narrowly defined, rigid rules and, often, continuing disagreement among the major powers. At the other end of the spectrum are modest interventions at the local levels by small organizations or even individuals.

In the Natal region of South Africa during the late 1980s and early 1990s, violence often flared between members of the African National Congress (ANC) and those of the rival Inkatha Freedom Party. Thousands of people were killed, mostly in night-time raids on the homes of sleeping families. Communities became deeply divided. Individuals were forced to take sides. One of the communities most deeply affected by this slaughter was the hill-top town of Mpumulanga. Yet in 1992, Mpumulanga became peaceful, despite continued slaughter in the region. No U.N. blue helmets occupied the town, no foreign countries sent in troops. The South African government did nothing different there than in the rest of the region. The secret was simple. Local leaders of Inkatha and the ANC decided that the villagers had suffered enough and that no one benefitted from the violence. They set out together to calm the community. They spoke to the young people in their respective organizations. They toured the trouble spots jointly, trying to defuse tensions, suggesting solutions and compromise. Mpumulanga settled down.

Interventions by regional organizations have been advocated recently as an alternative to U.N. action, particularly in the case of African countries. Regional bodies such as the Organization of African Unity do have an important role to play, but they cannot be expected to solve all problems on their own, providing the United Nations and the industrial countries with an excuse for doing nothing.

Regional organizations have severe limitations. They have even more difficulty than the United Nations raising money to pay for peacemaking interventions, so regional organizations depend on the often poorly equipped and disciplined armies of member countries. They bring to their peacemaking efforts a better understanding of the region and its people, but they can also become embroiled in the politics of the conflict more easily. Nigerian troops in Liberia are more likely to become part of the conflict they are attempting to solve than troops from Bangladesh, for example.

6.2 Role of NGOs

Many types of organizations and individuals can serve as mediators and help solve conflict. Southern NGOs are particularly well placed to work for conflict prevention and management in their own countries. Indeed, their role can be expected to become even more central in the future as their numbers and strength increase. Traditional institutions such as councils of elders are also reasserting their importance as instruments of conflict management in some countries. Most frequently, NGOs are able to work at the community level. This is very promising, particularly since a community may remain peaceful even if conflict continues in the rest of the country.

In southern Sudan, the Presbyterian Church (USA) helped settle a conflict over grazing rights and access to water between two communities. Because of the civil war that rages in the country, weapons are everywhere. This local conflict had become violent, costing 1,300 lives and destroying 75,000 cattle and large stores of grain. In July 1994, funding from the church made it possible to bring together representatives of all affected groups. The meeting continued for 45 days. All grievances were heard, and a compromise was reached on the basis of customary law and local mediation practices.

7 The crisis of aid

Underlying efforts to improve crisis prevention and response, as well as post-crisis reconstruction, is the question, "Who will foot the bill?" At present, aid donors are not operating along the "relief to development continuum" so much as dishing out ever-larger slices of a shrinking development aid pie for short-term emergency assistance (see Figure 1).

In 1995 (the last year for which complete data are available), official development assistance (ODA) from the member countries of the Development Assistance Committee (DAC) of the Organisation for Economic Co-operation and Development (OECD) declined 9.5% in real dollar terms to $58.9 billion, due primarily to budgetary restraint in donor countries (Michel 1997).[4] At the same

4 DAC members provided 98% of all ODA in 1995.

time, demand for emergency assistance has increased, mainly because of armed conflicts. Total emergency aid more than tripled (and more than doubled in real dollar terms) between 1987 and 1995, reaching $5.3 billion. This sum accounted for nearly 9% of DAC members' ODA in 1995 (and 11% in 1993-1994), compared to just 3.5% in 1987. These figures do not include associated costs, such as peacekeeping expenditures, which averaged $3 billion annually in the early 1990s, as these are not considered "aid" (U.S. Mission to the United Nations 1996; Randel and German 1996).

Figure 1: Emergency Assistance as a Share of Official Development Assistance, 1987-96

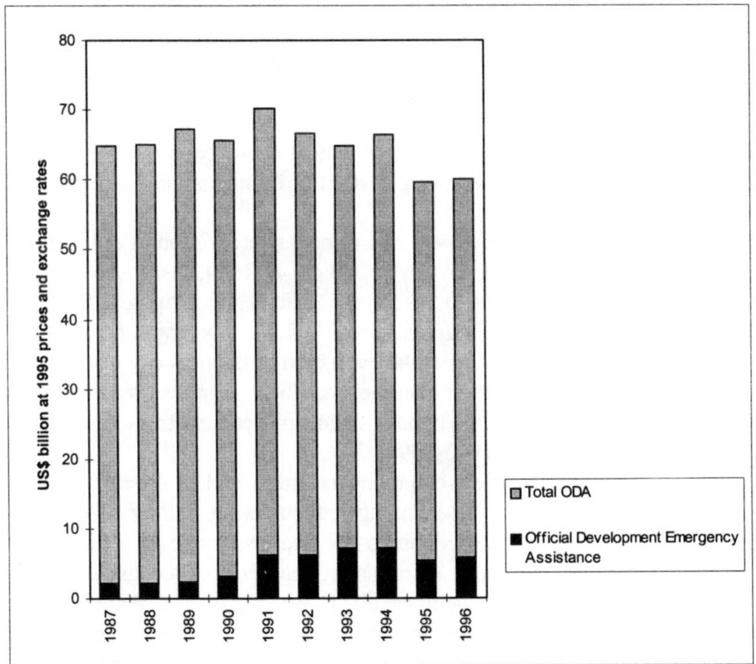

Sources: Development Cooperation Directorate, OECD; UNHCR; UNICEF; WFP.

Emergency operations budgets of agencies such as UNHCR, UNICEF and WFP have increased over the past decade, and emergency assistance now accounts for 50% of all U.N. aid. Development budgets for agencies such as the U.N. Development Programme (UNDP) have declined. WFP estimates that it devoted two-thirds of its shipments to emergency activities in 1995. A decade earlier, it devoted two-thirds of its tonnage to development purposes. Total food aid tonnage from all donors declined 25% in 1995. Emergency aid accounted for one-third of the total, about the same as in 1994.[5]

It is important to note that many relief activities have development or rehabilitation components built into them. This is particularly true of food-for-work projects. Forging such linkages in a creative manner becomes ever more important as funds decline and crises multiply.

The end of the Cold War deprived aid of its most powerful political motive. Aid to former communist states, which received $9 billion in 1995, has drained resources from poorer countries (Michel 1997: A96). DAC members provided 52% of their aid to developing countries classified as low-income by OECD in 1995, down from an average of 55% during the previous decade. Aid to sub-Saharan Africa, where most of the poorest countries are located, declined by 4 percent between 1992 and 1995, to $18.3 billion.

While trade and private investment flows from the industrial to the developing world are considerably larger than the volume of ODA, aid remains the most significant channel of external funds for the poorest countries. It is essential for physical and social infrastructure development in these countries. Significantly, OECD considers 16 of the 21 countries in need of humanitarian assistance identified in Table 2 to be low-income.

Emergency relief aside, however, only a modest proportion of aid contributes to sustainable development and poverty reduction. In 1994, just 0.6% of total aid funded basic education programs; 0.5% funded basic health activities. The share of aid from OECD donors going to agriculture fell from an average of almost 12% between 1987 and 1989 to 7.5% in 1994, even though the majority of poor people in the developing world get their income and food supplies from agricultural activities. Aid to agriculture in the poorest countries declined from nearly 16% of all aid in 1990-1991 to 11% in 1993-1994.

Globally, the squeeze on development resources and proliferation of emergency needs is likely to continue. Funding reductions are falling mainly on the programs which could help poor countries become less prone to conflict, human rights abuse and hunger. Ironically, many policy-makers now recognize that development assistance can help prevent crises. J. Brian Atwood, Administrator of USAID, argues, "Sustainable development that creates chains of enterprise, respects the environment, and enlarges the range of freedom and opportunity over generations should be pursued as the principal antidote to social disarray" (Atwood 1994).

The widespread assumption that citizens in donor countries have little interest in development contributes to politicians' willingness to cut aid. But surveys suggest that popular support for aid remains strong in Europe and Japan (Hewitt 1994). Even in the United States, where it is often asserted that foreign aid is wildly unpopular, recent surveys have shown strong levels of support for development assistance, especially if it goes "to the poor people who really need it."

---

5 <www.wfp.org>, December 1996.

Committed supporters of aid—anti-hunger and environmental advocates, nongovernmental relief and development organizations, concerned people in the academic and religious communities, ethnic organizations and businesses that directly benefit from aid programs—need to organize and mobilize existing but passive public good will into a coherent constituency. Otherwise, funding will continue to dwindle, while the world's crisis zones continue to require humanitarian relief.

8 Conclusion

Ethnic diversity can enrich human communities, from the local to global level. But differences are also a source of tension, subject to manipulation by leaders pursuing personal or ideological agendas. When tension escalates to open conflict, the more vulnerable members of society are the first to suffer hunger and privation. Food itself often becomes a weapon.

The international community can respond more effectively to the threat of food insecurity among the 80 million people affected by complex humanitarian emergencies. This will require mobilizing political energy and funds; learning from experience with recent crises, including natural disasters as well as human-generated emergencies; engaging affected communities in every aspect of crisis response; and complementing and coordinating relief with peacemaking, reconstruction and development.

Just as people create violent conflicts, they can resolve them. People can instead create a world where food and livelihoods are secure, where everyone is accorded their full measure of human dignity and where diversity of ethnicity, religion, color, gender and age enrich life together. It is a matter of collective choice.

References

Atwood, J. Brian (1994): Suddenly, Chaos, Washington Post, July 31.

Atwood, J. Brian and Leonard Rogers (1997): Rethinking Humanitarian Aid in the New Era, in: International Herald Tribune, March 12.

Food and Agriculture Organization of the United Nations (FAO) (1997): Foodcrops and Shortages, No. 5, November/December.

Frankenberger, Timothy R. (no date): Conceptual Issues Related to Food Security, Atlanta (mimeo).

Herwaldt, Barbara et al. (1993): Crisis in the Sudan: Where is the World?, in: The Lancet, No. 342, pp. 119-120.

Hewitt, Adrian, ed. (1994): Crisis or Transition in Foreign Aid, London.

Human Rights Watch and Physicians for Human Rights (1991): Landmines in Cambodia: The Cowards' War, New York.

Human Rights Watch/Arms Project and Physicians for Human Rights (1993): Landmines: A Deadly Legacy, New York.

Institute of Development Studies (1995): IDS Policy Briefing Issue 3, Sussex.

International Federation of Red Cross and Red Crescent Societies (1996): World Disasters Report 1996, Oxford.

Jacobsen, Karen (1994): The Impact of Refugees on the Environment: A Review of Evidence, Washington.

Karolien, Bais (1994): Development and Conflict, Amsterdam.

Messer, Ellen, Thomas Marchione and Marc J. Cohen (forthcoming): Food from Peace: 2020 Vision Discussion Paper, Washington.

Michel, James H. (1997): Development Cooperation: Efforts and Policies of the Members of the Development Assistance Committee, 1996 Report, Paris: Organisation for Economic Co-Operation and Development.

Minear, Larry et al. (1991): Humanitarianism Under Siege: A Critical Review of Operation Lifeline Sudan, Trenton, New Jersey and Washington.

Minear, Larry and Thomas G. Weiss (1993): Humanitarian Action in Times of War: A Handbook for Practitioners, Boulder.

Minear, Larry and Thomas G. Weiss (1995a): Humanitarian Politics, New York.

Minear, Larry and Thomas G. Weiss (1995b): Mercy Under Fire, Boulder.

Prendergast, John (1994): Sudanese Rebels at a Crossroads: Opportunities for Building Peace in a Shattered Land, Washington, Center of Concern.

Randel, Judith and Tony German, eds. (1996): The Reality of Aid 1996: An Independent Review of International Aid, London.

Renner, Michael (1994): Budgeting for Disarmament: The Costs of War and Peace, Worldwatch Paper No. 122.

Scott, Colin, Larry Minear and Thomas G. Weiss (1996): The News Media, Civil War and Humanitarian Action, Boulder.

Sivard, Ruth Leger (1996): World Military and Social Expenditures 1996, Washington, World Priorities.

Sommer, John G (1994): Hope Restored? Humanitarian Aid in Somalia 1990-1994, Washington.

Stewart, Frances (1993): War and Underdevelopment: Can Economic Analysis Help Reduce the Costs?, in: Centro Studi Luca D'Agliano-Queen Elizabeth House Development Studies Working Paper No. 56.

United Nations (1992): The Secretary-General's Consolidated Appeal for Cambodia's Immediate Needs and National Rehabilitation, New York.

United Nations Administrative Committee on Coordination/Subcommittee on Nutrition (1997): Report on the Nutrition Situation of Refugees and Displaced Populations, 22, 12 December.

United Nations Department of Humanitarian Affairs (1997): <www.reliefweb.int>, accessed 5 and 9 January.

United Nations Development Programme (UNDP) (1994): Human Development Report 1994, New York.

United Nations General Assembly (1994): Moratorium on the Export of Anti-personnel Land Mines, Report of the Secretary-General, New York.

U.S. Centers for Disease Control and Prevention (1993): Morbidity and Mortality, Weekly Supplement on Refugee and Famine-Affected Public Health Measures, Atlanta.

U.S. Department of State (1993): Hidden Killers: The Global Problem with Uncleared Landmines, Washington.

U.S. Mission to the United Nations (1996): Global Humanitarian Emergencies, 1996, New York (this is an unclassified version of a Central Intelligence Agency study).

U.S. Mission to the United Nations (1997): Global Humanitarian Emergencies (New York, April 1997 (public version of report prepared by U.S. Central Intelligence Agency).

U.S. Senate Appropriations Committee, Subcommittee on Foreign Operations (1994): Hearing on the Global Land Mine Crisis, Washington.

Watkins, Kevin (1995): The Oxfam Poverty Report, Oxford.

Weiss, Thomas G. and Collins, Cindy (1996): Humanitarian Challenges and Intervention: World Politics and the Dilemmas of Help, Boulder, Colorado, p. 4.

World Health Organization (1995): The World Health Report 1995, Geneva.

20

The Green Revolution, not Green Enough for Asia's Rice Bowl

Klaus J. Lampe

Rice is not only the principal staple food in Asia—90% of the world's rice is produced there. More important also, in view of the beneficiaries of new rice technologies, is the fact that 90% of that rice is grown on small family farms of mostly less than 3ha in size. Even today, no more than half the total harvest is marketed at all. The rest is eaten by those who farm the riceland. Nobody has yet calculated the labor force absorbed in the production of rice—a highly laborious and painstaking undertaking.

Up till now, the international rice market has been almost negligible. Less than 5% of the annual world harvest of about 580 million t are traded internationally. But an Asian diet without rice is almost unthinkable, even in areas where rice is not grown. In modern Japan, about a quarter of the total calorie intake per capita stems from rice. Bangladesh and Myanmar (Burma), with 74% and 77% total calorie intake per capita respectively, are the countries most dependent on rice for their national food supply.

10% of Asia's arable land—or 150 million ha—are planted with rice, compared to only 87 million ha 50 years ago. The quality of rice land, however, is highly diverse; only 50% of the total area planted with rice is irrigated and belongs to soils most suitable for this crop. Another 25% or 36 million ha belong to the rain fed lowland ecosystem that does not need to be irrigated or cannot be due to water shortage. Given good soil and water conditions, yields can equal those of irrigated land. The most disadvantaged rice-growing areas are those of the upland, deep-water and tidal wetland ecosystems. They cover roughly the remaining 25% of the total rice land and contribute about 6% or 30 million t., very little of the world's production. They supply local markets only, and the farmers belong to the most disadvantaged and poorest peasant community in Asia.

Those who would prefer to neglect these production systems altogether need to know that out of the 320 million poorest people living in the world's low potential rural areas, 265 million—more than 70%—are Asians. Most of those again are rice farmers who have not yet benefited from any green revolution. If those who still grow rice today suddenly were to move to the demand side of the urban poor, social unrest would doubtless become uncontrollable.

1 The new role of rice research

Never before in the history of modern agricultural science has any innovation been debated in a more controversial and emotional fashion than that which is commonly known today as the "green revolution." The reasons are multifold, complex, and perhaps often linked more to political objectives than to biological science. Forty years might be too short a period of time for a balanced review of the development; this even today sometimes produces unbalanced assessments of its successes and failures.

Development studies of the 1950s do not mention Africa but Asia as the continent of unmanageable food and poverty problems for future decades. Those who began to be concerned about the long-term future were not the various governments of the region or the economically rehabilitated post-World War II Western states. It was rather private organisations, like the Rockefeller Foundation and the Ford Foundation, who realized the magnitude of the challenges ahead and the need for fast and bold action. The dilemma Africa is faced with today was not foreseen at that time and those few who did sound the alarm were not heard. But that does not diminish the far-sightedness, the vision, and the preparedness of all those who advocated joint efforts in research and development, not only to prevent hunger tomorrow, but to combat existing hunger through food production where there is need. We need to be reminded that at the same time, be it with good or more selfish intentions, many groups in the West were still advocating"food aid" specifically in times of domestic surpluses. Only too often, such programs have been used to ease the problems of oversupply at home, promote export, or to gain the political support of the domestic farming community. It is true that food aid beyond emergency programs and carefully planned Food for Work projects is counter-productive with regard to domestic production efforts. This fact has been common knowledge for a long time now.

Those who in the late 1950s were thinking three decades ahead when they decided to establish, finance and manage what is still today the International Rice Research Institute (IRRI) had no information systems similar to those available today, no simulation models, no data bases projecting the future. What they knew was that, for example, in four countries alone—Bangladesh, India, Indonesia, and Pakistan— their populations increased between 1950 and 1960 by 110 million people, equaling the total population of South America in 1950! What they had, was the foresight that there was not much time left and that they had the possibility to act professionally. In less than a year a fact-finding mission came up with a proposal for a rice research center to be established in Asia. A little more than six years later, the first varieties of a new semi-dwarf plant type with the potential of a new yield plateau had been developed. That, in a nutshell, is how IRRI, the basis for the "green revolution" for the rice-eating world, was established.

Today, more than one third of the total daily world calorie supply per capita originates from a single commodity: rice. With hunger on the horizon not only in India but, for example, in South Korea, similar to the present situation in the North, research at IRRI was intensified by the two Foundations in the first joint program they both agreed to undertake. Simultaneously, governments in Asia, as well as multilateral and bilateral development programs, concentrated on the development of the rural infrastructure specifically through investments in irrigation, extension services and promotion of the agricultural input sector. Equity, gender consciousness, sustainability, and natural resource conservation were not yet marketed as buzzwords. But there are many examples that prove the environment consciousness and social sensitivity of many key players at all levels of decision making in the public and private sector. Fighting hunger and the fear of political unrest because of food shortages were, however, the driving political forces at the national level for investing in rural development infrastructure and agriculture. That still does not explain the speed and the enthusiasm with which new production technologies for a crop used by human kind for 10,000 years have now been accepted. No doubt, there has been government pressure, at least in two larger Asian countries, to get seed-agrochemical packages introduced through credit schemes quickly. But the continent-wide and, later on, global acceptance of new varieties had other reasons. There is an old farmer's saw seldom mentioned in lecture rooms: give us technology with more than 10% profitability gains and you do not need an extension service to get the message widely accepted. In its first breeding program, good luck was with the Institute. From a single crossing of Dee-Geo-Woo-Gen (DGWG), a dwarf rice variety from Taiwan, and Peta from Indonesia, a line was selected which led directly to what very soon became known as IR8, the first high-yielding variety of the new generation that triggered a seed exchange of hitherto unknown dimension.

The success story of rice growing during the last 30 years is strongly linked, if not limited, to the irrigated and favorable rain fed lowland ecosystems of the world. To a large extent, this is due to the favorable physical and agro-climatological conditions. The great similarity of the irrigated rice production systems and their potential for increased productivity was seen—and rightly so—40 years ago as the research location with the highest success potential. Breakthroughs in breeding, soil management or fertilization could be transferred quite simply without much adaptation not only elsewhere within Asia but to other continents as well. Research, therefore, was concentrated on a few selective locations and the major genetic and agronomic constraints. Yield increase, fertilizer response, resistance to lodging have been the major concerns. Breeding for tolerance or resistance against biotic and abiotic stresses has been high on the agenda for all breeders, even before international efforts in agricultural research started. There was, however, a parallel development of new and effective pesticides by the chemical industry following the pressure for reduced losses, i.e., higher yields. The early—in retrospect perhaps too early—release made possible by those responsible for the breeding, testing and releasing of the new high-yielding lines is difficult to validate today. Most of us with the knowledge available at that time would have decided in the same way. It was the starting point of a seed-fertilizer-pesticide technology we could today compare with the first introduction of the automobile 70 years ago, lacking proper brakes, lacking a clean exhaust system and without safety belts.

Because of diminishing rice stocks and the obvious new yield potential, the spread of modern varieties was ceaseless. Today in China, India and Japan, all irrigated rice land is planted with modern varieties. In Vietnam, Indonesia, the Philippines, Malaysia, and Sri Lanka which have a high rate of irrigation and a favorable rain fed lowland area, the adoption rate varies between 75% and 90%. Thailand, *the* high-quality rice exporter within the warm humid tropics, is an exception. The early-maturing modern varieties (MVs) still lack the high aroma of the traditional Thai rices, which fetch high prices at the world market, more than compensating lower yields. Breeding efforts during the last years to improve the flavour and aroma of new rices are quite promising. With the pressure on rice land, increasing land prices and improved quality standards, the spread of MVs in Thailand will only be a question of time.

2 Reasons for concern

The more than doubling of rice production during the 1970s and 1980s can be attributed by about 80% to increases in productivity. Only 20% of the total production increase was due to the expansion of rice land. In the years to come, investment in irrigation will be very low due to high costs, limited opportunities, and lack of funds. Production increases through expansion of riceland is, therefore, most unlikely. On the contrary, it can be expected that more fertile rice land will be lost to urban and industrial use than new land for rice production mobilized.

The unprecedented increases in production, notably between 1975 and 1985, have slowed down research and development efforts because of the false assumption that the problems have now been solved. Agriculture and rural development have been shifted to the back burner or removed from the priority list altogether. Development banks and donor institutions have closed their agricultural departments, withdrawn their experts and shifted to more tangible, short-term, low risk, high prestige projects. All that at a high long-term cost.

Now already, some traditionally high production systems are showing signs of stagnating yields and factor productivity. Over the last 20 years, new lines released by national systems as varieties have remarkably improved levels of resistance and tolerance against old and new pests and diseases. They have also helped to reduce the risk of crop losses, the costs of pest control and clearly contributed to environment protection by reducing the need for pesticide use. However, science was, up to only a few years ago, unable to improve the yield potential itself. What is true today for the irrigated system is, to a much larger extent, relevant for the less favorable systems. Because of their multi-faceted soil fertility and water availability constraints, investment in research for the less favorable rice areas has at all times been very low, with political interest limited. Given the financial constraints, the research community always was—and still is—inclined to allocate funds not in long term, risk-prone research for low production potential areas, but for those with the highest probability of large returns in research investment. The fact that such priority setting is favored by many donors limits the likelihood of change. If poverty alleviation, equity, and sustainability—key buzzwords of the 1990s—really are taken seriously, these ecosystems must receive much more attention by intensified long-term research with additional resource allocations. Close collaboration among existing national research institutions through already established research consortia would allow the use of methodologies and approaches that could take care of the specific regional and subregional constraints. The criticism that green revolution technology has still not reached the poorest rice farmers is correct. This is so, not because of lack of scientific commitment, but lack of secured long-term funding to tackle the very complex, locally specific, difficult production constraints that can only be overcome through intensified research only.

3 Growing Populations—Shrinking Resources

Short-term planning is a convenient excuse for avoiding confronting the problems of tomorrow.

Our soil and water base is not only limited. It is shrinking and we have to share it with a second wave of 5-6 billion people. This is an almost trivial, but in today's decision making, a fact generally ignored. In about 25 years, many of the larger developing countries will have less agricultural land per capita available than highly industrialized ones in the Western world today. Population growth, urbanization, infrastructure and the misuse of arable land leading to degradation are the reasons often described. The potential area for agricultural production in South- and South East Asia is estimated to be 297 million ha, out of which 274 million ha are already being utilized. The other 23 million ha might be usable for agriculture but only at a high cost and high ecological risk. But another even more difficult problem also remains unsolved: water. The irrigated production system of Asia with 80 million ha and yields between 3.0 to 9.0 t./ha per crop is today providing more than 75% of the world's total rice production. The concentration of rice research on this system was to a large extent based on the assumption of secure water availability. Today, agriculture is using 70% of the world's available sweet water supply. The water consumption by agriculture has increased tremendously over the last 50 years. In 1950, out of the 1,360 km^3 used globally, Asia's share was about 860 km^3. By 1990, the consumption in Asia had almost tripled to 2,500 km^3. For the year 2000, the demand is estimated to pass the 3,000 km^3 line equal to the global consumption of 1980.

The demand and consumption pattern for fertilizers is no less a matter for concern. This holds true especially for one very important and irreplaceable macro nutrient: phosphate. The present known world reserves, i.e., those deposits economically exploitable with the most modern technologies, are estimated to be less than 20,780 million tons, whereby total existing world resources of phosphate do not exceed 90,755 million tons. Given the present annual consumption of about 150 million t and no foreseeable major technological breakthrough, the year 2150 must be seen as the depletion date of the world's resources of phosphate, one of the most crucial plant nutrients. Nobody, therefore, can claim that our present food production systems are sustainable, not even for a couple of hundred years.

Reliable knowledge about population dynamics and what must be expected and accounted for has been available for several decades. Countless documentations about land and water availability and the shrinking of non-renewable resources are published annually. The figures are reliable enough to justify action; proposals for action have been available for a long time. Population development projections, published in 1988, calculated for 2025 a total world population of 8.6 billion. Exactly 10 years later, the world's population for 2020 has been estimated to be 8.0 billion. Does the difference of 600 million really justify the level of ignorance we manifestly display in view of what we now know:

- a fourfold increase of the world's population during the last 100 years;
- a population of South and South East Asia of 3.36 billion people in 2050 equaling the world's population of 1965;
- already 800 million people now undernourished;
- 500 million poor people—50% of the world's total—in South Asia alone?

Table 1: Population—Key development indicators (South and South East Asia) in millions

Country	Population			
	1950	1970	1990	2050
Bangladesh	45.6	67.4	115.8	265.8
India	370.0	555.0	850.1	1591.0
Pakistan	39.4	65.7	113.2	423.8
South Asia	472.3	713.8	1117.0	2373.6
Indonesia	83.4	122.7	191.3	359.7
Philippines	21.1	38.7	66.6	203.9
Vietnam	25.3	42.4	68.5	166.0
South East Asia	182.9	291.3	455.3	982.0
World	2,565	3,721	5,320	10,805

Source: Urban and Philip 1988.

What we need perhaps more urgently than 40 years ago are "basic needs" oriented policies, strategies and action programs toward long-term food security, based on self-sufficiency.

4 Where the green revolution was not green enough

South Asia's per capita food production index increased from 100 in 1961-1965 to 117, and that of East and South East Asia to 125 in less than 30 years. In sub-Saharan Africa, where the green revolution technology was not applicable, beginning only in recent years with maize and cassava, the food index decreased during the same period to 96. Before reviewing the failures of modern production technologies, the question must be asked: what would have happened in Asia without the production increases of the last 30 years?

Total rice production in Asia increased between 1968 and 1982 from 141 to 211 million t. Total cereal production increase, including maize and millets, was even higher, with more than 60%. More than 30% of these increases must be directly attributed to the genetic improvement of all major cereal crops. Asia's population at the same time grew from 1.9 to 2.7 billion people. Today, this figure is getting close to 3.5 billion. Would we be able to feed them with the technology of the 1950s? With the land races of the 1950s? With the fertilizer ratio of that time? The answer is clearly: "No". India alone would need 100 million ha more agricultural land to do so.

Unfortunately, the opposition from the most vocal and most critical circles vis-a-vis the green revolution is to a large extent rooted in personal animosities, professional egoism, emotions and a political agenda, intentionally ignoring scientific facts as well as economic and political realities. It is too often seen as inopportune to address these issues; therefore the noisy criticism is receiving undue public attention. One of the most violent and vocal opponents often cited is V. Shiva in her book entitled "The violence of the green revolution" in which she tries to review the post-war, post-independence development of agriculture specifically in the Punjab. Her study can be seen to be a masterpiece of reductionism. Almost all the problems of the Punjab and the rest of India, including crime rates, can be traced to the creation of IRRI, the Ford- and Rockefeller activities in agriculture in Asia, and to the private sector in general. In more than 250 pages, all efforts are made to prove that pre-World War II technologies of subsistence farmers were superior to those of modern agriculture. The social and financial cost and the impact of new cultivation systems, including high-yielding varieties, are seen as unjustifiably high, almost criminal. What is missing in the same publication is at least one single paragraph about the food needs of India, the population dynamics of the country from 320 million in 1950 to 900 million today and the urbanization trend. There is not one single mention of the implications of India's industrialization, the new division of labor, the need for increased labor productivity in agriculture in order to compete at least at a minimum level with other employment sectors. Subsistence farming is described as a highly desirable way of life. All those who have plowed behind a pair of oxen, harvested and threshed by hand, harvesting hardly enough to feed a family, will strongly disagree.

These groups of opponents of a modernized agriculture are not so much in disagreement with modern technologies and their use *per se*, but the linkage of modern agriculture to an open market-system. It is not so much a conflict over levels and different systems of production, but the political and economic systems influencing agricultural production and marketing. Unfortunately, this ideological confrontation and its emotional roots are seen as attractive battlegrounds by politically animated action groups oriented predominantly toward political change. Integrated Pest Management, Biological Diversity, Environment Protection, important as they are, are not always the primary objective, but are used as tools for fueling the controversy over modern, labor divided, market-oriented forms of agricultural production in the light of the need to supply urban populations. Such reductionism would still be tolerable as part of a very broad and diverse spectrum of opinions about what agriculture today and tomorrow should look like. Unfortunately, even defamation of individuals is part of the weaponry in this ideological warfare. Robert Chandler, the founding Director of IRRI, a pioneer in agricultural research management, and M.S. Swaminathan, who headed the Institute from 1982-1987, and Ralph Cummings, agricultural frontrunner in India's food struggle in the 60s and 70s are misused as targets. They have contributed beyond any doubt, more than all political action groups together, to the present level of food security in Asia. They have, with their leadership, changed lives in many parts of rural Asia. To try to tarnish their names with false allegations, by citing old professional animosities, must fail in the long run. Since the number of these opponents is very small, continually the same papers, persons and incidents are cited again and again. All these actors of the first green revolution generation have reached retirement age. Their personal conflicts, sometimes trivial, have been irrelevant to the process of agricultural research and development during the last decades. They could without exception be ignored were they not kept artificially alive by a new politically motivated generation of opponents in order to misguide well-intended laymen and women, even for fund-raising purposes.

The most fundamental conflicts with those opposing the green revolution efforts are rooted in ideological, even political, controversies. Hybrid rice in China seems not to be a controversial issue, since seed production is managed by a state monopoly. Modern varieties in a market-oriented society, however, are the source of a whole range of fundamental conflicts, from farmers' rights to biodiversity. It must be realized that many political action groups in Europe, North America and Asia are not only closely inter-linked and financially inter-dependent. They have a common agenda opposing the globalization of markets and the internationalization of the agrochemical, seed and food market sectors. Governments and international organizations are aware of this no longer hidden agenda. They try to find common ground through permanent dialogues. Those who really suffer from this conflict are the predominantly agrarian structured countries in Asia, Africa, and Latin America. The most affected, however, will be the rural poor.

5 The green revolution—not without a real downside

Every innovation that has changed the world so far is linked with more than one undesirable side effect. With the spread of electric energy, the number of fire outbreaks has increased. With the introduction of railway systems, motor cars and airplanes the number of traffic accidents have multiplied. The side effects of the first green revolution followed the same pattern, but they are by far less severe than the public is made to believe. But when preparing for new yield and production plateaus for the next green revolution the experiences of the past must be taken account of.

5.1 Agricultural science and biodiversity degradation

During the 10,000 years that rice has been cultivated by human kind, its biodiversity has increased multifold because of the influence of farmer breeders, and lately, through modern science. With the development and quick acceptance of modern varieties the number of locally bred—and adapted—varieties rapidly decreased. This holds true for almost all cultivated crops and domesticated animals worldwide, more so within the more productive ecosystems, but not limited to them. To avoid a total loss of this invaluable genetic material collection, documentation and proper storage in seed banks has become part of agricultural research on national and international levels. Today, more than 1,000 gene banks exist, but the estimated number of accessions safeguarded through seed banks is not very reliable.Too many of these storage centers, due to lack of funds, storage capacity and management shortcomings especially in the economically constrained countries, have to work under very limited conditions. The major food crops are taken care of, to a large extent, by International Agricultural Research Centers. IRRI is at present the custodian of a gene bank in which more than 80,000 accessions of rice, including many wild species, are safely stored in optimum conditions. One may argue, however, that all the evolutionary processes these varieties were confronted with in nature have been interrupted with the acceptance and spread of new varieties. The fact that a particular variety—in former times sown only on a very limited area—has been replaced by "universal" varieties used on 5, 10 and more million hectares is rightly giving cause for concern. If the resistance or tolerance of such a variety breaks down, severe economic losses critically influencing the life of small farmers and landless poor are inevitable. Farmers used to reduce their risk by using a larger number of different varieties adapted, for example, to distinct soil and water conditions. This is, even today, the case in rain fed lowland and upland ecosystems where modern varieties have not yet made much progress. The effect on local varieties will be, however, even more severe since the diversity of upland rices considerably outnumbers those of the irrigated systems. Only joint efforts in very intensive collecting, documentation, and multilocation storage can help to minimize the negative effects of the replacement of old varieties by new.

At the same time every kind of breeding effort is contributing to biodiversity at different levels. Today, a new variety is based on a very large and complex system of crossings, including land races, and, with the help of modern biological tools, even with wild species which would have made their way into a domesticated line only haphazardly over a time span of a couple of hundred years. Modern breeding permits a careful selection of individual traits and their incorporation into a new variety specially designed for a specific environment. Therefore, more and more resistance and tolerance potential accumulated in wild species or old local varieties find their way through conventional and unconventional methods into modern varieties. But population growth and efforts to improve living conditions especially of the landless poor have their price. The yield potential of the old varieties was sufficient to feed the populations of the 1930s and 1940s; but not those of today and the decades to come. The price tag appears very diverse. One is the need for new genotypes for all staples, which will ensure stable yields at a high plateau with a minimum of external input and the highest possible factor productivity in terms of labor, capital and land. Simultaneously, joint efforts are needed to minimize the inevitable side effects on the biodiversity of wild and domestic species and varieties respectively.

Table 2: Threatened plant species

Country	Higher Plant Species	Total Threatened
China	30,000	1,009
France	4,500	704
India	15,000	1,256
Indonesia	27,500	281
Japan	4,700	704
Malaysia	15,000	510
Philippines	8,000	371
USA	16,302	1,845

Source: World Bank 1997.

Protecting plants—and to a much larger extent animal species—is costly, labor- and knowledge-intensive. Given the pressure to provide the essentials, such as drinking water, employment, energy and transportation, it cannot be expected that countries under population pressure will be able to put the protection of plant species on a high priority list. It is a supra-national responsibility that requires first and foremost international action. At the same time Table 2 shows clearly that the possible loss of plant species is not automatically linked to population pressure or GNP.

5.2 The price of pesticides

Economically and ecologically, the price of pesticide use is very often seen to be unjustifiably high. The first generation of modern varieties, specifically rice, were lacking the level of resistance that local varieties had developed over many generations. Also entomological knowledge at the beginning of the green revolution was not sufficiently developed to understand the complexicity of, for example, the irrigated rice ecosystem with its interdependence of several hundred different species of insects, of which only a very small number are harmful to the rice plant. The immediate and, therefore, convincing effect of powerful pesticides has indeed slowed down the learning process that has led, through many stages, to integrated pest-plant-, and finally, production management. Overconfidence in technological solutions has added to the problem. The many efforts to establish dialogues among the different schools of thought were severely hampered through unjustified generalizations aimed towards the discrediting of a technological breakthrough that has prevented hunger and malnutrition on the Asian continent.The pesticide industry unfortunately has to share part responsibility for that development. Strategies and policies at a company headquarter level, though open, environmentally conscious and end-user responsive, did not take account of the aggressive methods of marketing where sales and turnover rates had clear priority over the real need for chemical pest control. Preventive spraying in rice, for example, is known to be harmful. During the first four weeks after planting, rice should not be treated at all. The harmful side effects to useful insects and other organisms in rice, and to farmers' health, have been studied over the years without the necessary immediate reaction on the part of the pesticide producing industry; a fact that has reduced the level of confidence in the agricultural input sector in general. The growth of mistrust—justified or not—from local consumer groups in industrialized countries has finally helped to intensify the search for "softer" solutions. Pesticides seen before as the fastest, easiest, safest, and most powerful weapons have become one of many tools within the integrated system. Now it seems necessary to ensure that the necessity, the value, and importance of agrochemicals are not becoming undervalidated. Much will depend upon the policies the private sector will develop to ensure safer use and pro-active information strategies for farmers as end-users of agricultural products.

Compared to the environmental risks and the health hazards, the cost of pesticides is almost neglectable. Notably in irrigated and favorable rain fed lowland rice, even for small farmers, the cost of pesticides is affordable. If used properly, they reduce risk and indirectly increase yield through reduction of losses. Generous subsidies and government promotion programs in combined packages, including seed fertilizers for pesticides had led to overuse and misuse. These policies have now become part of the past.

5.3 Modern varieties and small farmers risks

The rice bowls which are of primary importance to ensure urban supply—the irrigated systems—have always received most attention from governments—even before modern varieties for these ecosystems were developed. This was because of the high yield potential and the controlled risk levels in harvest losses. In some parts of Asia—especially those in the Pacific Rim affected by typhoons—all agricultural production systems are high risk prone. Under traditional production systems with local varieties and almost no external inputs the loss of 50% or more of the harvest is identical with starvation or hunger. And this is not only true for the rice farmer in Asia. Up to the last century, hunger drove rural populations from Europe to America. Without what is now called "modern agriculture", this situation would not have been changed.

The introduction of new rice production technologies, combined with traditional collaterally bound credit schemes, has increased the risk for small farmers considerably. Especially in typhoon or drought-prone areas and in combination with increased pest or disease potential, the loss of the larger part of a small farmer's crop could mean more than hunger. With no crop insurance in place and credit schemes and contracts which forced especially small farmers to bear all the risks, they lost not only their crops, but in the worst cases, their land as well. Such cases did happen, and their number is not negligible; but the fact that such an overwhelming percentage of irrigated rice-land today is sown with modern rices, speaks for itself. The risk-related experiences of the introduction phase of green revolution technologies are by now well known. Today, new credit systems with combined crop insurance, better varieties and production methods have helped to reduce risks for the rice farmer, in favorable ecosystems at least, to an acceptable level.

The marginal rice farmer, though, still needs new solutions. Problem soils, drought, submergence, heat or cold tolerance are challenges the research community must face with much higher priority and vigor. If not, the disparity between different rural areas may lead to another wave of migration—from the least to the less favorable, and from these to the favorable rural areas and, in the worst cases, directly to the centers of urban poverty. The latest economic crisis in the industrial sector in many parts of Asia has clearly demonstrated the economic, social and political vulnerability of urban agglomerations with a high rate of low paid or even unemployed populations. It has hopefully also re-opened the discussion about food security versus self-sufficiency.

All those who once advocated confidence in international food markets must surely by now agree that most, if not all, agrarian structured developing countries must invest foreign currency not predominantly in food imports but in labor-generating capital goods.

6 Food supply and poverty alleviation—different goals?

The architects of the first green revolution were agriculturists. They were definitely not involved in national politics. The underlying idea was geared to hunger alleviation through increased food production. This linear approach has led to a conflict similar to the one during the first phase of chemical pest management. In countries where the introduction of new production methods had been combined with structural reforms such as in Taiwan and Korea, the green revolution ignited a rural evolution. Peasants became agricultural entrepreneurs and the rural economies, like in Europe 100 years before, provided the financial and, later on, also the human base for an unparalleled industrial development. The tremendous production increases would not have been possible without a policy that provided a distinct degree of freedom on the village and farm levels. In other countries where reforms were delayed or did not take place at all, production increases were much smaller, but in almost all cases large enough to feed the fast growing population and avoid famine.

The most striking example in this respect is Vietnam. In 1985, its rice export was minimal. Only less than seven years later and three years after introducing a farmer-friendly land tenure system and a somewhat liberalized trade policy, Vietnam exported in 1995 about 2.0 million tons of rice on the international market, becoming the third largest exporter in the world. In China, a similar development is taking place now. At least in Asia it has become common knowledge that modern technologies introduced in agriculture must benefit farmers—small and large alike—to be successful; and they have to be embedded in a political and social framework that provides chances for growth within a rural setting. The first green revolution has provided benefits to the urban poor through staple food supply for annually diminishing prices. Those in the backward, less favorable uplands, however, who still depend on traditional resources and technologies, find themselves confronted with yields they cannot sell because of lower prices for goods bought on the local markets, served mostly by public marketing boards with the surplus from lowland farming.

Therefore, a clear distinction between the neglected farming communities in marginal areas of resource poor ecosystems and those within the more favorable environments is needed. The common belief that small farmers generally did not gain from the new technologies is incorrect. The overwhelming majority of rice farmers in Asia are "small farmers". However, the testing of new technologies and introducing them on the farm level has always been in the first place the job of those who are open to new approaches, capable of taking and accepting risks. New technologies were first introduced worldwide by progressive "pioneer farmers". Since green revolution technology is predominantly seed-based, the capital requirements for its introduction were much lower than, for example, the mechanization of western farm communities. The new genetic material allowed the efficient use of commercial fertilizer with a full investment returns after harvesting. At the same time, rice seed has been almost exclusively developed, multiplied and marketed through government controlled institutions.

The price of new seed had been for many years very low; so low that the private seed industry until very recently did not show any interest in the rice seed market in developing regions. It took farmers only one season to realize the potential of the new varieties, and the technology was adopted despite non-existant or at least weak extension systems. The increased yields lead quickly to an oversupply compared to previous years, and as a result, reduced prices which benefited the urban poor and the rural landless directly. The farmers, large and small alike, were compensated only through increased yields. The real losers were those who did not adopt or could not get access to the new technologies. For rice farmers in the less favorable and really disadvantaged regions, there has been no green revolution yet. On the contrary, the small surpluses gained with traditional varieties had and still have to be sold for lower prices. With growing families over the last 40 years, the net surplus in rice production has been continuously reduced, resulting in a further reduction of family incomes from rice. There is no doubt the upland farmers are still waiting for a breakthrough, and the deepwater rice producers are wherever possible shifting to dry season, irrigated rice farming using modern technologies.

7 The "greener revolution" will take place

Five billion Asians in the next century are not a horror scenario but the reality of tomorrow. Neither on the scientific nor on the political level has the existing awareness been transformed into actions that take account of the magnitude and complexity of that challenge. Our Western societies in several ways share a major responsibility for these shortcomings. A generation having grown up in affluence, spending less than 20 percent of their income on food, is hardly able to understand the pain of hunger, the struggle for survival in the hinterlands of rural Asia and the political risks linked to it. For them, spending an additional 10 percent on food, paying a premium for "fertilizer-pesticide-chemical-free" products, is easily tolerable. For some parts of Europe this could theoretically be an "ecological alternative", if all consumers were willing to pay the price for "living green." To promote those production systems, for example in India, where about 50% of the total population—more than 400 million—have to live below the US $1 a day international poverty line, this is unrealistic. To advocate such ideologies financed mostly through the private donations of misguided citizens demonstrates an almost frightening absence of realism.

The need for intensified production incorporating as many food crops as possible into a high-yielding system is indispensable. This has been achieved in many parts of the world and efforts need to be intensified in future, using all the lessons learned from the past. The fact that the term "sustainability" has been overused, even misused, does not permit anyone to ignore the fact that long term agricultural production at a level needed for 10 billion people has to be secured.

One of the major potential solutions, even if sometimes questioned, is an increased yield potential not only for the three major grain crops—wheat, rice and maize—but also for the most important root crops, such as potato, cassava and sweet potato. These increases must be achieved through higher yield plateaus, earlier maturing varieties, increasing the number of crops per year, higher levels of resistance to and tolerance of biotic and abiotic stresses which could lead to reduced losses, as well as reduced harvest and postharvest losses with improved technologies for harvesting, transport, storage and conservation.

The sources for traditional research have not yet been fully exploited and intensified efforts are needed, since the potential for success is high. In addition, agricultural research, following the example of medical research, is beginning to open new doors through the use of the biotechnological research introduced first in human medicine. In Asia, today biotechnology and specifically the modern tools of gene technology are widely seen as potential for additional yield increases.

No doubt, the development of the agroindustrial sector, the horizontal and vertical concentration process, and the speed with which the number of independent seed companies is diminishing and being absorbed by the agrochemical sector is disturbing. This process is still continuing and it may well be that major parts of the maize and wheat seed sector will be concentrated in less than five combined seed agrochemical companies within the coming two decades. The controversial discussion related to the use of gene technology for food production in Europe, which is discouraging small and medium sized companies from investing in agrobiotech research, has accelerated this concentration process. The striking success in weed control, combining herbicide resistant transgenic food crops with the respective herbicides, is evident. This technology will spread with even greater speed than modern varieties that were adopted in the 1970s. In less than 8 years the transgenic maize and soya production has been expanded from zero to more than 20 million ha. Once developed for cassava, the African farmer might finally profit from the new agricultural technologies he has been waiting for for four decades. The use of biotech in agriculture today can hardly be underestimated. The history of inventions is full of examples where their introduction and general use was delayed due to technical, economic or political influences. Fear, lack of public understanding and support have often slowed their acceptance. Now it seems that in some affluent countries the introduction of transgenic food crops will be postponed. Others like the Swiss, in a general plebiscite, gave a clear signal to modern plant and animal breeding and the use of biotechnology for the development of modern medical tools.

The new green revolution will in the next century move to new crops with new properties serving specifically the needs of the poor. The 250,000 children who still go blind every year because of vitamin A deficiency will not go blind, once the staples of the world have been enriched with 4 genes from an ornamental plant, enabling the production of the provitamin A needed to prevent early blindness. Preventive medicine, improving the quality of low-cost staple food for the poor is not a priority area in societies that struggle with agricultural surpluses.

Biotech and genetech are, in rich countries, predominantly accepted tools in human medicine, despite the high cost. The respective seed companies have unfortunately underestimated the need for a proactive information program preparing consumers for what they still see as new, unknown and, therefore, potentially dangerous food, which they could easily miss out on. This ignorance has damaged consumer confidence in several European countries and, even worse, has directly supported all those opposing the transnational private food industry and fortified their efforts towards prohibiting the production and sale of transgenic food products.

8 Who owns what or the dilemma of intellectual property rights?

For some, seed is a commercial ware just like anything else. For others, the larger section of the Asian rice-producing countries, rice seed is linked to a part of their history, culture, customs, beliefs and traditions. Monetary and non-monetary values are, in such circumstances, in conflict.

Much more than with any other invention, new varieties, such as the present high-yielding rice varieties, are based on preceding breeding trials. Before the commercialization of plant breeding, the exchange of seed was embedded in a network of rural traditions. The market value was of very minor importance. With high investments in breeding and pre-breeding research, plantbreeders' rights gained more and more importance, leading in 1961to the "Union for the Protection of New Varieties of Plants" (UPOV). Their regulation of the marketing and use of protected varieties has been strengthened during the last 15 years and culminated with the successful patenting of newly developed varieties. With the use of modern biotechnological tools and the introduction of alien genes in commercially important plant varieties, decisions related to property rights over organisms and their parts have become more urgent. In some countries, the protection of plants, including food crops, under patent laws as in the U.S., is an undebatable fact. In others patenting is not possible at all. Given the international trade agreements already in force, harmonization of plant breeders' rights in view of the fast growing seed industry is urgently needed. The Consultative Group on International Agricultural Research (CGIAR) could take on a clearing house function in a search to balance the rights of farmers, the private sector, consumers and the public interest. An initiative, a proactive intervention could help to overcome the present unhealthy situation where some patents are granted which are justly opposed, thus leading to uncertainties and conflicts between seed producers and consumers. But even without patent laws, the latest UPOV regulation stopping farmers from replanting protected varieties which they have already grown on their own fields, is in conflict with too many local traditions, rules and customs to be observed at all. Enforcing such regulations is equally unrealistic and damages the image of seed companies most of all.

9 Towards a new level of commitment to agricultural research and rural Asia

Given the task ahead, the total population and the research structure, Asia's role in this sector is by far too low. The absence of political awareness has many reasons, but change is urgent. The CGIAR is now financing six international research centers in Asia of which five are concentrating on major food crops for the continent. The total budget for all sixteen centers in 1998 came to a total of US $335 Mio., to which Asian governments, excluding Japan, contributed only US $9.0 Mio. or 2,7%.

The questions to be raised are at least fourfold:

1. Has enough awareness been generated at government levels about the need to provide the scientific and technical base for responsible and sufficient food production?

2. What has brought about the lack of interest in developing rural Asia and the political disinterest in promoting agriculture, despite some striking national success stories in at least the South East Asian region?

3. Why is agricultural research, despite the incomparable internal rates of return, almost completely ignored at political levels as one of the most promising agents for food security, self-sufficiency and rural growth?

4. For how long will western governments continue to take the responsibility for financing Asia's staple food research?

The next phase of a green revolution has to be part of a rural reconstruction process that involves all relevant disciplines of research and all sectors of society: public, private, local, national and international. The belief in an automatic trickle-down effect of new technology based benefits has deservedly faded. It has to be replaced by policies and strategies combining the search for new technological solutions for a generation which is conscious and environmentally responsible, and a scale of neutral food production geared to income generating employment. In real terms on a global level, more than 2 billion additional jobs worldwide, half of them in Asia, have to be created within the next 40 years. Science and technology, industrial production and marketing, though, are today concentrating on intensified labor productivity, leaving more and more people unemployed. Again, short-term profit maximization instead of real need-oriented political decisions can lead to another red revolution by a growing number of poor who have nothing to lose. The alternative we have to search for is a new green revolution providing the basis for food production, combined with the socio-economically balanced development of rural and urban habitats with living and working conditions which will ensure economic growth and social peace. Agricultural science has to play a crucial role in this process: to bridge the gap between disciplines, to establish a joint force willing and able to formulate the research goals and objectives for the next century, define the strategies to meet these goals and convincingly enlist public and political support.

Ivory tower protected, value-free research belongs to the past. Scientists in agriculture as in space research need public support to establish a financial base for every larger research undertaking. It is self-defeating to leave public awareness and resource allocation to those who share political responsibility. Agricultural science is responsible for the formulation of a new agricultural research agenda towards a greener revolution and has to win support independently, convincingly and publicly for a new setting of rural priorities. Such a program must help generate massive employment and increased food production, equity and efficiency, a more careful use of biological land and water energy and nutrient resources and also a new yield plateau balancing economic needs with ecological and social responsibilities.

There is no alternative to this, and it can be done.

References

Alexandratos, Nikos (1995): World Agriculture Towards 2010—an FAO Study, Rome.

Asian Development Bank (ADB) (1985): Agriculture in Asia. Bank Staff Working Paper, Manila, 1985.

Brown, Lester R. (1995): State of the World 1995, New York/London: World Watch Institute.

Chandler, Robert F. (1982): An Adventure in Applied Science—A History of the International Rice Research Institute, Los Banos, Philippines: IRRI.

Chandler, Robert F. (1979): Rice in the Tropics—A Guide to the Development of National Programs, Boulder, Colorado: Westview Press.

Crucible Group (1994): Peoples, Plants and Patents, IDRC Canada.

Dahl, J. (1992): Die Verwegenheit der Ahnungslosen, Stuttgart.

David, C.C. and K. Otsuka (1994): Modern Rice Technologies and Income Distribution in Asia. London and Manila.

Evenson, R.E.; R.W. Herdt and M. Hossain (1996): Rice Research in Asia—Progress and Priorities, CABI-IRRI.

Falcenmark, M. and C. Widstrand (1992): Population and Water Resources: A Delicate Balance. Population Bulletin, Vol. 47, No. 3.

International Rice Research Institute (IRRI) (1997): Rice Almanac. Second Edition, Los Banos, Philippines.

Islam, Nurul (1995): Population and Food in the Early Twenty First Century, Washington, D.C.: IFPRI.

Lampe, Klaus (1994): Perspectives for International Rice Research and its Role to Ensure Staple Food Supply in Asia Beyond 2000, Hokkaido Nat. Agric. Exp. Station. Pub. 50/1994.

Lampe, Klaus (1995): Rice Research—Food for 4 Billion People. Geojournal, Vol. 35, No. 3.

Meadows, Donella H., Dennis L. Meadows and Jorgen Randers (1992): Beyond the Limits, London.

Pingali, P.L., M. Hossain and R.V. Gerpacio (1997): Asian Rice Bowls, The Returning Crisis, CABI-IRRI.

Shiva, V. (1991): The Violence of the Green Revolution, London.

The World Bank (1997): World Development Indicators, Washington, D.C.

Urban, F. and R. Philip (1988): World Population by Country and Region 1950-1986 and Projections to 2050, Washington, D.C., USDA Staff Report, Ages 880308.

Vlek, P.G., R.F. Kuehne and M. Denich (1996): Nährstoffresourcen für die landwirtschaftliche Produktion in den Tropen. Symposium Berlin 1996. Humboldt-Universität (SPIA).

21

Technology Generation, Adaptation, Adoption and Impact: Towards a Framework for Understanding and Increasing Research Impact[1]

Uma Lele and Javier Ekboir[2]

1 Introduction

International agricultural research, technology generation, transfer, adoption and impact (IARTGTAI) constitute components of a system that has evolved from a relatively simple structure in the 1960s to a complex network in the late 1990s. Its functioning is of great international interest. Despite major successes on the food front, there are still 850 million people who earn less than a dollar a day and go to bed hungry. Many studies of research, adoption and/or impact in agriculture exist, but they tend to look at specific aspects of the scientific and technology processes, such as priority setting or research impact. The recent changes in the science and technology processes and the resulting present structure have not been analyzed sufficiently yet as organizational innovations intended to alleviate market failures with a view to achieve specific social objectives. The innovations form part of a larger global science and technology process consisting of multiple actors, each with a different set of interests. A broader evolutionary framework offers an opportunity for a clearer understanding of the relationship between sources of technical change in agriculture, and the spread of its adaptation and adoption by producers and agroindustries.

In this paper we look at IARTGTAI as a complex social process in which actors (donors, international research institutions, the ministries of finance and agriculture, researchers, research administrators of the National Agricultural Research Systems (NARSs), as well as producers, industries and users), each with different interests interact, whether by design or by default. These interactions result in a number of research and technological outcomes, which in turn offer further technological options (Figure 1). Several of these options are developed further by the same or different actors into new lines of research or finished products. Other

---

1 This paper builds on an earlier paper by Uma Lele, Shiva S. Makki, Javier Ekboir and Edward W. Bresnyan, Jr. "Accelerating Adoption of CGIAR-NARS Collaborative Technologies: Towards a Framework for Understanding and Increasing the CGIAR Impact", May 21, 1997, The World Bank, 1818 H street, NW, Washington, DC., 20433, unpublished. We appreciate Michel Petit's comments on an earlier draft.

2 The views expressed in this paper are those of the authors and do not necessarily represent the views of the World Bank or the University of California.

options are "abandoned" either permanently or temporarily.[3] The process is not linear. Rather it involves the passage of information over time in several directions. Feedback from other participants in the scientific and technology processes assists researchers and research managers to establish and revise their research agendas. The results of the scientific and technology processes in any single period of time are the consequences of past interactions among the different groups participating in them. Besides, non-technology factors influence the spread of technology in a fundamental way, including effectiveness with which each individual component of technology generation or transfer processes such as policies and institutions operate. Better understanding of the forces that condition the interactions among actors, and the consequent evolution of IARTGTAI can provide useful information for research policies, funding and priority setting in agricultural research and technology transfer.

Figure 1: International Agricultural Research and Technology Transfer System—Its multiple actors and stages

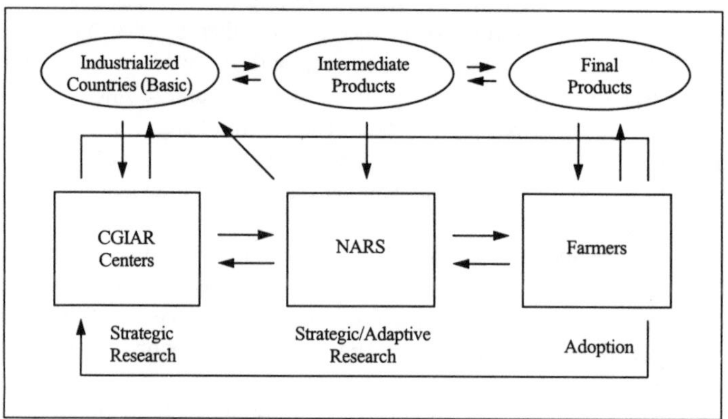

The actors in the Consultative Group for International Agricultural Research (CGIAR) system interact mainly through non market mechanisms, and each type responds to a different set of objectives and constraints. Major changes in the global economic and research systems are affecting the environment in which the CGIAR operates, leading to more active consultation with the private sector, the non-governmental organization (NGO) community, and the NARSs of developing countries. These changes dictate that IARTGTAI be viewed in an evolutionary and systemic perspective to understand the implications of these changes for future CGIAR research and technology transfer policies.

Several frameworks have been used to analyze the evolution of public sector research systems. Particularly in the case of the U.S. the competitive interest group

3 The structure of the DNA was identified in 1953; however, no applications for this discovery were found until the late 1980s.

model is said to offer the best explanation (Guttman 1978; Evenson and Rose-Ackerman 1985; Marcus 1987; Huffman and Evenson 1993; Khanna, Huffman and Sandler 1994). These types of "interest group" decision models have not been applied to the international agricultural research system of the CGIAR or to the research systems of developing countries which form an important part of the CGIAR system. Other authors have used the induced innovation model which suggests that allocation of resources to public sector research is influenced by relative prices (Hayami and Ruttan 1985). The validity of the assumptions underlying these "competitive" models needs to be assessed in the real world context in light of the recent developments in the field of institutional and organizational economics which have increasingly questioned the underlying assumptions of the competitive model.

A comprehensive analysis of the system also requires consideration of the technological possibilities available at each particular stage, the interactions among actors in evaluating these possibilities, including those whose interests are not expressed as direct contributors (such as funders or voters), and therefore actors who are not usually included in the analysis of technological development (trade associations), or the groups such as poor farmers or future generations. Demands of these groups for technology products and policies tend to be poorly articulated, yet they constitute important clients of public sector research. New approaches to the analysis of technical change (new institutional economics, evolutionary economics and ecological economics) provide a framework for the study of many of these interactions. The principal argument made in this paper is that IARTGTAI involves multiple actors and multiple feedback loops in several directions rather than a unitary "laboratory to farm approach" assumed in the traditional approaches to technological change. The outcomes depend fundamentally on the nature of interactions among these different actors and explain differences often observed in the spread of the same technology and its ultimate impact in similar agroecological areas, e.g., between the Indian and Pakistani Punjab on wheat or within India among different states on sorghum, or with regard to maize in sub-Sahara Africa.

Section 1 discusses the limitations of the current analytical approaches in understanding the relationship between processes and outcomes and offers an alternative framework. Section 2 explores the changing global environment for research and technology transfer. Section 3 discusses the changed climate affecting support for the CGIAR system.

2 An alternative framework to study IARTGTAI

Recent theoretical developments in economics (e.g., institutional economics, evolutionary economics, ecological economics) offer possibilities of a broad, dynamic, evolutionary approach and a new conceptual framework to reflect the role of different interest groups in the processes of technology generation and transfer and their ultimate impact (Coase 1972; North 1991; Nelson 1995; Lynn et al. 1996; Dosi 1997; Wright 1997).

The many interactions among different actors leading to processes and sub-processes cannot be sufficiently characterized with the use of a competitive model. The latter requires well-defined objectives, assumes that agents have full information to pursue those objectives, and choose the correct way to achieve them. It also assumes that there are no scale economies. Furthermore, the model typically focuses on outcomes, such as research investments, their efficiency or productivity, rather than on the processes, i.e., decision-making rules and sequences which individuals and organizations follow, and which in turn affect outcomes through their effect on processes.

A well known framework for analyzing research in agriculture, for instance, is the induced innovation theory (Hayami and Ruttan 1985). It posits that changes in relative prices, e.g., between agricultural and nonagricultural commodities, or among factors of production such as labor and capital, will induce investments in agricultural research. The theory implies the scientific and technology process as a linear sequence (from basic research to applied and adaptive research, transfer and, adoption), with one stage following the previous one in a smooth transition. Researchers and administrators respond to market signals to identify research needs (i.e., institutional signals and non monetary constraints are only relevant if they are reflected in relative prices). Given that technologies being adopted today may be a result of research initiated up to 30 years ago, it is not clear which market signals are appropriate (Dosi 1997). Finally, productivity increases can occur due to research which was not necessarily induced by demand; for instance, progress in basic research has stimulated strategic, applied and adaptive research in the fields of veterinary and human medicine, and plant and animal breeding, which would not have occurred otherwise.[4]

The induced innovation theory is also an explanation of outcomes after all "failed" alternatives were "discarded" over time. In that sense the approach confuses the outcome of a process with the process itself and does not inform us as to whether technology adoption and research impact would have been greater had certain other alternatives been selected. Understanding of the whole research and technology transfer process seems necessary to better understand which alternatives were rejected and why with what possible effects on the menu of technologies that emerged and spread. This requires a more comprehensive characterization of the research production function.

Other extensive sets of studies show very high rates of return to agricultural research, even after adjusting for certain biases in estimations. But they do not illuminate us on how research processes may affect returns. Besides, they do not inform us on the impact of research on institutions, human capital or the environ-

---

4 Some examples include genetics research on DNA, remote sensing research, geology research on soil formation and characteristics, mathematical and physics research in developing computers, space research leading to food production under zero gravity conditions.

ment. We propose the use of an evolutionary approach to the analysis of science and technology generation and transfer. The major building blocks of this approach are (Nelson 1995; Dosi 1997):

- The explanation of why something exists rests on how it became what it is; in other words, the evolution of processes (firms, markets, policies, etc.) matters and is path-dependent.
- Agents have limited information and understanding of the environment in which they live, and the paths the environment will take in the future; additional information cannot reduce the uncertainty about the future. Because of these limitations, agents are not assumed to maximize profits but to follow decision rules that are applied over an extended period of time.[5] Bounded rationality is the rule.
- Agents are always capable of discovering new technological and institutional opportunities, some of which will eventually be adopted. These changes, conditioned by the "external" process (markets, regulations, etc.), perform as selection mechanisms.
- Imperfect understanding, path dependence, and idiosyncratic learning routines imply persistent heterogeneity among agents, even if facing the same information and the same "objective" opportunities.
- Aggregate phenomena (market outcomes, adoption of new technologies, etc.) are the collective outcome of the individual actions and interactions characterized by bounded rationality.

This approach has been extensively used to analyze the evolution of specific industries (Burgelman 1996; Smith et al. 1992; Winter 1990), technology policies (Georghiou and Metcalfe 1993; Metcalfe 1994; Metcalfe 1995), and to develop new management tools at the firm level (Barnett and Burgelman 1996). The evolutionary approach has not yet been used to analyze the generation, transfer and adoption of agricultural technologies.

The new evolutionary framework has far-reaching consequences for the study of science and technology generation, its differential transfer and impact. First, the explicit recognition of the complexity and the dynamic nature of IARTGTAI means that its evolution cannot be measured by a single variable, but requires a number of indicators which may show opposite behaviors, e.g., a particular research may have failed in achieving high rates of return but may have contributed substantially to learning by doing or institutional development. A methodology for deriving implications from these contradictory results has to be developed. A more explicit exploration of what is measured, and whose values and indicators are used to measure impact (whether those of donors, scientists or farmers) would improve understanding of what determines which lines of research are pursued, why, and their potential

5 A relatively new body of literature analyzes decision processes in the presence of irreversibilities (Dixit and Pindyck 1994). In this case, agents are assumed to maximize over time a function that balances the expected benefits of a decision with the expected cost of making the wrong decision and having to reverse it. This process is observationally equivalent to bounded rationality; agents change actual policies sporadically.

impact, make better uses of the existing data sets often collected for other purposes, improve the choice of indicators and their measurement, while also helping to focus the priority setting process by providing more information to scientists and funders of research. A good example is the extent to which scientists in the past focused on yield growth alone while ignoring the many complex requirements of farmers dictated by labor availability, harvesting, processing, storage and marketing. These latter have consistently been shown to have affected the spread of technology and its impact. The other example is the possible difference in the objectives of donors and potential beneficiaries of new technologies. In the case of dairy development in India, two radically different viewpoints are found in the literature about the impact of commercialization and modernization in the dairy sector on women. Critics argue that these processes have generated hidden costs and increased the workload of women who provide most of the labor. They argue that modern dairying reduces women from 'doers and deciders' to 'doers only' (George 1991). Advocates on the other hand argue that the dairy development program in India known as Operation Flood provides an opportunity for women to improve their economic and social status (Somjee and Somjee 1989). The literature also draws attention to the social and cultural constraints which hinder active participation by women in modern dairying which technology development and transfer alone cannot address (Kumar 1997, World Bank Forthcoming).

Second, case studies conducted with this approach would collect and analyze a wider range of variables than that usually reported in the literature. In addition to the traditional agronomic and economic variables (e.g., yields, area planted or income), institutional and organizational indicators would be included (e.g., convergence between the goals of donors and the needs of users, information of communications systems, the state of universities and research institutions, or the development of intellectual property rights). Third, *a priori* models for organizing the information (such as the rational optimizing agent operating in a static environment) would be replaced by more flexible approaches that include the historical and social aspects of the process and enable reaching a more explicit convergence among the goals of the different actors so as to make the research priority setting and technology transfer process more efficient and impact greater or wider.

Lynn et al. (1996) propose the concept of innovation community to refer to the organizations directly and indirectly involved in the development and dissemination of new technologies. Within an innovation community, agents are categorized into groups with similar characteristics. Belonging to any particular group may be voluntary (as in the interest group theory), or the involuntary consequence of performing a particular function in the community (such as being a poor farmer). Groups interact in a complex web of social and economic relationships, having a specific set of competencies and performing a specialized role defined by a set of variables (e.g., size, economic and political power, degree of centralization or authority structures).

An important role in such a system is the coordination of activities, functions, roles, and contributions (Lynn et al. 1996). Coordination includes the passage of information (including funds and priorities of other agents), facilitating the interaction of agents within and between hierarchical structures, participation in negotiation processes, and definition of incentive structures.

Some agents organize themselves to gather and disseminate information through the community, information being any signal (e.g., market information, orders from authorities, funds) that helps other agents in their decision process. The extent to which information is converted to knowledge and communicated (e.g., within and between research institutions and extension agents), and how decisions are made can be critical to the performance of the system and central to understanding sources of growth (Stiglitz 1984). Yet this remains one of the least explored areas in empirical research on research and technology transfer. Communities that have better communication channels are more successful because technology generation and diffusion are network phenomena with substantial scale economies (Wright 1997). As technology becomes global, active participation in the international technological network becomes more profitable for countries with limited research capabilities. As Wright (1997) explains "... much of the benefit seems to derive, not from the generation of new, original technologies, but from maintaining the technical capacity to monitor, test, evaluate, and implement innovations originated elsewhere, selecting those that suit the local situation best."

The reverse side of this process is that unequal access to knowledge, or unequal capacity to convert information into useful knowledge, has become a major source of disparity. With the spread of new communication technologies, including increasing reliance on the internet, this source of disparity may likely increase. Countries with weak infrastructure and/or weak NARSs cannot take advantage of advanced technologies in part because they cannot screen new processes and products, and in part, because of lack of know-how and resources to protect or effectively deploy intellectual property. The economies of scale in technology scouting provides new opportunities for the CGIAR system because it has the potential to allow countries with relatively week NARSs to benefit from the new technologies, and to increase the efficiency of the technology network for all participants, from developed as well as developing countries.

The performance of the technological community is conditioned by the nature of its hierarchical structure. In developed countries the community has many communication channels among interest groups, while in developing countries communication channels have tended to be both more concentrated and often blocked. Indeed, in many developing countries access to information has been greatly constrained by the hierarchy in which scientists operate. Again, access to internet is changing that state of affairs in some respects, but may not do so in another, i.e., to the extent that access to computers themselves is determined by the hierarchical position of scientists rather than the extent to which they can make use of the information. Critics argue that in structures such as those, even in developed countries, powerful groups benefit and outcomes are short-term oriented, disregarding long-term environmental or equity considerations. But the recent changes in the content of public funded research toward natural resource management (NRM), food safety and biotechnology in developed countries reflect a change in the strength of competing interest groups (e.g. the increased power of consumer and environmental groups and scientists relative to that of agricultural producers and processors) suggesting that the evolution of the research community is not determined only by the dominant groups at any given point in time, but rather by the changing nature of those interactions among a multiplicity of actors and events. What implications does this way of looking at the system have for the CGIAR system given that the CG centers and the NARS are each not only at a different stage of development but are evolving at different rates in an international context which is currently very dynamic in several respects?

3 The changing environment for IARTGTAI

The CGIAR system currently involves annual commitments of around US$300 million, employs approximately 900 scientists and constitutes about 4 percent of the global agricultural research budget.[6] The circumstances in which the CGIAR system was created in the early 1970s have changed dramatically in many ways. The CGIAR was created to make up for an important market failure, i.e., adaptation of technologies generated in developed countries to address the problems of poverty and hunger in developing countries, and particularly the transfer of technologies to resource poor farmers, with whom the laboratories of the CGIAR centers often worked directly. Consistent with the way research was organized more generally at the time, the CGIAR was conceived as a unitary, relatively top-down system, in the sense of a lab to land approach. The recent changes in IARTGTAI present new challenges and opportunities for the CGIAR system. Among these changes are:

— The CGIAR's objectives, mandate, products and clients have all become more diversified. The most recent CGIAR mission calls for reducing poverty and ensuring food security through increased productivity, ensuring sustainability of natural resources, conserving biodiversity, and developing capacity of the NARSs. The number of CGIAR institutions has increased from four in 1971 to sixteen in 1997. Its clients now include NARSs, NGOs, farmers and their organizations and the private sector of both developed and developing countries. CGIAR's products now range from research methods and analytical tools, to training and institutional development, as well as being a role model in the type of multidisciplinary research conducted on crop and NRM technologies.

— Even though the number of donors has increased to over 50, the growth of financial support for the system has slowed while the composition of that support has changed. A smaller share of the contributions now comes from the US, and

6 In 1995, the donor community included 23 industrialized countries, 13 developing countries, 12 international and regional organizations, and 6 foundations. They contributed, respectively, 64 percent, 2 percent, 32 percent, and 2 percent to the CGIAR research funds (see Table 1).

increased shares from Europe and Japan. The share of the World Bank has increased to compensate for the US reductions (Table 1).

— The membership of developing countries has increased from 2 to 15, although the share of developing countries' contributions in the total is only 2 percent, explaining their expanding and yet still limited voice in the CGIAR system.

— Developing countries' NARSs have grown stronger in their research capacity (Bonte-Friedheim and Sheridan 1996). From monolithic publicly dominated organizational structures, NARSs are evolving into diversified systems with stronger participation of universities, NGOs, and the private sector (both local and international). However, the rate of change in various parameters is different among different countries.

— Regional organizations of the NARSs are becoming important players, increasing the possibility of exploitation of scale economies in applied research, which are weaker at the global level where the CGIAR centers operate. For example, development of more environmentally sensitive technologies is highly location specific research, with few scale economies. This calls for an increased "layering" approach in research and technology transfer including greater role for the regional and sub-regional research organizations.

— The desire for balanced budgets is making developed and developing countries alike to cut down on research expenditures and focus more sharply on priorities and research efficiency.

— The increasing strength of the international agricultural research system, which has entailed considerably stronger role for the applied and adaptive (and in some cases even strategic) research by the NARSs, now allows a two-way transference of technology between developed and developing countries. Whereas the early CGIAR varieties involved greater content of germplasm and technology from the north, Pardey et al. (1996) recently estimated the increased benefit of the CGIAR system to industrial countries: an investment of US$134 million (Centro Internacional de Majoramiento de Maiz y Trigo (CIMMYT) and International Rice Research Institute (IRRI)) in rice and wheat improvements led to a return of US$15 billion for the U.S. economy alone. The same applies to the benefits of stronger NARSs. A number of major NRM technologies, such as zero tillage and integrated pest management (IPM), come from farmer innovations in developing countries and have spread to developed countries. Additionally, NARSs scientists in developing countries are leading in developing hybrid rice, baby corn, long staple cotton and management of acid and sodic soils with potential benefits to developed countries.

— Intellectual property rights, liabilities, and government-industry relations are changing, leading to a rapid growth of private sector research, and their supply of agricultural technologies and inputs. Market-oriented trade policies have enhanced the role of trade and commerce, changing the setting in which issues of food security, poverty, equity, NRM, and environmental sustainability are discussed. Particularly challenging for the CGIAR is the increasing importance of intellectual property rights (IPR). If CGIAR centers do not patent their research, private

Table 1 CGIAR members, contributions, and international scientists, 1972-95

YEAR	Members of CGIAR[a]	Support to Agreed Research Agenda (Million $)[b,c]	Support to Non-Research Agenda (Million $)	World Bank Contributions (Million $)	Expenditure By Activity (Mil. $)[d]					Number of Scientists (IRS)[e]
					IP	PE	BD	PO	SN	
1972	16	20.7	3.1	1.3						
1973	18	25.0	3.5	2.8						
1974	20	34.5	4.5	2.4						
1975	22 (1)	47.5 (0.6)	6.0	3.2						
1976	25 (2)	62.9 (2.6)	8.0	6.5						
1977	27 (2)	77.2 (2.6)	9.5	7.9						
1978	27 (2)	85.0 (1.8)	10.7	8.7						
1979	27 (2)	99.5 (0.8)	16.2	10.2						
1980	30 (4)	119.6 (2.6)	18.7	12.0						
1981	32 (5)	130.9 (3.1)	20.2	14.6					20.3	
1982	32 (5)	143.8 (2.2)	26.9	16.3					21.8	
1983	34 (5)	164.7 (2.0)	23.7	19.0					25.8	
1984	36 (7)	173.2 (4.5)	29.9	24.3					26.2	775
1985	36 (7)	170.1 (2.4)	41.2	28.1					27.4	841
1986	38 (7)	192.2 (1.6)	43.4	28.4						835
1987	38 (7)	201.6 (1.3)	41.8	30.0						889
1988	39 (7)	211.5 (1.2)	50.6	30.0	79.77			4.07	37.97	925
1989	39 (7)	224.5 (1.0)	47.1	33.3	86.04			4.28	40.46	916
1990	39 (7)	234.9 (1.1)	51.3	34.3	87.01			4.19	42.84	912
1991	42 (9)	232.0 (1.8)	51.6	35.1	85.90			4.82	41.52	882
1992	45 (9)	247.3 (1.8)	71.4	37.6	127.4			25.5	56.1	973
1993	50 (10)	234.7 (2.3)	76.6	40.0	123.5	35.8	14.7	24.8	55.3	957
1994	54 (11)	268.1 (3.1)	57.1	50.0	124.3	40.1	22.6	26.0	51.7	888
1995	56 (15)	269.6 (5.0)	59.0	50.0	134.4	45.3	28.5	25.2	52.6	880

[a,b] Numbers in the parenthesis represent developing countries. [c] The actual budget of CGIAR is about 5% higher because of center-generated income which is not included in this table. [d] IP: increasing productivity; PE: protecting environment: BD; biodiversity; PO: policy; and SN: strengthening NARS. [e] IRS is Internationally recruited staff/scientists

Notes: The agenda funding consists of unrestricted and restricted contributions. Restricted funding is to the core agenda of CGIAR while unrestricted funding is used for other purposes within the research mandate. Non-agenda funding, on the other hand, is for research outside the CGIAR mandate (e.g. basic research). The break-up of expenditure according to research activities is available only for last three years. Since the classification has changed, systematic accounting of such expenditures is not possible.

Source: CGIAR Annual and Financial Reports (various issues)

researchers will do it, preventing the transference to NARSs and resource poor farmers; this means for research to be freely available, paradoxically, it may have to become private.

— An important question for the future is the extent to which the market will develop technologies suitable to the conditions of poor farmers. A related issue is that the traditional products and services of the CGIAR are likely to be under pressure from the growing importance of the private sector. Often these new commercial technologies, involving, for example, genetically engineered crops, entail different contractual arrangements with farmers, different technological trajectories, with substantial implications for patterns of competition, interindustry dynamics and market changes than those developed by the international agricultural research centers (IARCs). Importation of plant genetic material or acquisition of national seed companies by multinational corporations under the new liberalized investment regimes is, for instance, having a quicker, more dynamic impact on the sources of technology than the management of the resource system. However, these changes are more likely to benefit commercial crops and commercial producers rather than food crops produced by the small and marginal farmer which has been the focus of the CGIAR. Since present choices affect future growth performance and income distribution, and conditions the decisions that societies will have to make down the road, comparison of available technologies developed by the CGIAR, NARSs and the private sector is increasingly needed to anticipate future outcomes. For instance, the use of Monsanto's no till technologies may mean reliance on and availability of the chemical "Round-up." Other no till technologies may call for changes in the farming systems, each with different implications for the use of modern inputs, information sets, etc. As the current Anti-Trust debate on computer technologies in the U.S., and the related economic theoretical literature is revealing, power of individual industries could determine future choices in research, technologies and their impacts on the extent of intra-industry competition and impact of technologies.

— The agricultural research establishments in developed countries display at least five characteristics of diversification, leading to many different sources of research and technology for users which developing countries are likely to emulate, namely: (1) the share of private sector agricultural research, technology development and transfer increases relative to that of the public sector; (2) the share of public sector agricultural research in agricultural GDP increases, typically from less than 1% in developing countries to between 2% to 4% in Canada, U.S., Australia, and to up to 10 percent if private research is taken into account, meaning substantially greater investment in research, technology development and transfer relative to developing countries both in absolute and relative terms (Pardey and Alston 1995); (3) the role of universities increases vis-à-vis that of public sector research institutions; (4) the relative (not absolute) share of the public sector declines over time, with the public sector increasingly focusing on the "quintessential public goods research," i.e., research benefits of which are long-term, broadly derived and difficult to capture for the private sector; and (5) the role of the local and regional research and technology transfer systems increases in applied and adaptive activities relative to that of the federal/central government, with the latter playing a more strategic, catalytic role in stimulating research in the overall national research system (Lele 1996). It is interesting to view the international agricultural research system in this context.

4 The technology community of the CGIAR system

The main structures through which agents participate in the IARTGTAI community to which the CGIAR belongs are authorizing environment, operating capacity, and customers. Some groups participate in several of these structures; e.g., large NARSs contribute to the CGIAR budget and influence the priority setting process (authorizing environment), participate in joint research projects (operating capacity), and use technologies developed by CGIAR centers (customers) (Figure 2).

Figure 2: Adopting a Customer Orientation

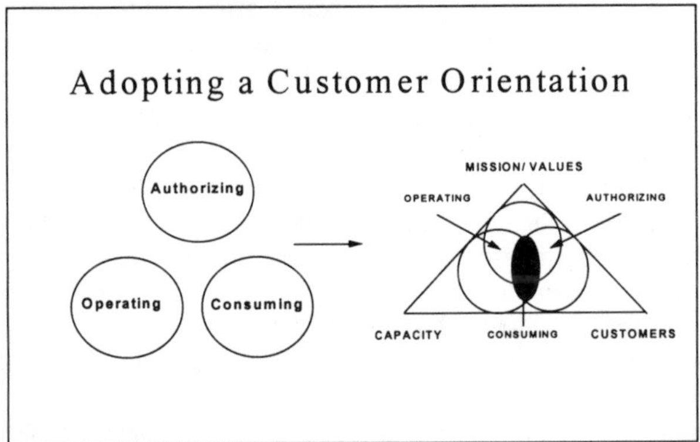

4.1 The CGIAR's authorizing environment

Those who fund and oversee the CGIAR system constitute the authorizing agents. This group has become more diversified since the creation of the system; also, individual agents have a more diverse set of objectives due to considerable pressure from their legislatures, universities, producer groups and (increasingly) the NGO community. They are demanding greater evidence of impact of the research they fund. The increasing diversity of the authorizing environment is the consequence of a new awareness both in developed and developing countries of the existence of inarticulated demands, such as technologies for poor farmers and NRM, and the increased capabilities of developing countries' NARSs.

The greater diversity of the funding community makes it more difficult for each donor to achieve its objectives. When specific donor objectives do not receive priority from the CGIAR's Technical Advisory Committee (TAC), the donors fund special projects. The proliferation of special projects reached a peak of US$59 million in 1995, or nearly 20 percent of the total budget (Table 1). The special projects became a parallel priority setting mechanism, in which the formal mandate of the CGIAR was partially overridden by funders. The problems created by conflicting mechanisms led the system's Chairman to suggest re-engineering the system, which involved (1) a matrix approach to research priority setting and its funding by donors; (2) increased consultation with donors, NARSs, NGOs and the private sector; and (3) focus on other agricultural research efforts including particularly the advanced countries' NARSs in the context of which the CGIAR system's mission is expected to be articulated and conducted.

The declining rate of growth of donor support has been a result of a number of factors, including reduced international food prices, the end of the cold war, the growing view of agriculture as the villain of the environment, the pervasive skepticism about the roles of the public sector and foreign aid, and budget constraints in industrial countries. Increased contributions from multilateral organizations, particularly the World Bank, have enabled maintenance of expenditures in real terms (Table 1).

The system's Chairman has also encouraged increased membership of developing countries, which more than doubled to 15 members since the early 90s. Although their financial contributions to the system were less than 2 percent of the total in 1995, developing countries make substantial in-kind contributions. A majority of the approximately 60,000 CGIAR germplasm accessions come from developing countries. Their NARSs now house two-thirds of the global agricultural scientific community, contributing to the production of the improved, more tropically derived germplasm issued by the CGIAR.

The poor in developing countries that the CGIAR aims to benefit have often had little voice in their countries' public decision making processes. Similarly, their governments have, in the past, had little voice in the governance of the CGIAR system. However, this state of affairs is changing rapidly. Democratization in developing countries and increased access to information has opened the way for greater participation of the institutions that represent the interests of the poor in developing countries as well as in the CGIAR system. Their economic growth and gains in human capital have also made their increased role in the CGIAR system imperative. These developments were reflected in the International Fund for Agricultural Development (IFAD)-led NARSs consultation process initiated in 1994, leading to the global consultation at the 1995 CGIAR meeting and the formation of a Global Agricultural Forum in 1996. Notwithstanding these gains, even large farmers in developing countries do not yet exercise sufficient political pressure to influence the research budgets of their countries. Furthermore, in spite of the recent reforms in the CGIAR system, developing countries continue to have a limited voice in the governance of the CGIAR system, in part reflecting their low financial contributions to the system.

Research expenditures in developing countries to date have come mostly through public finance. With structural reforms, several developing countries are trying to provide greater voice to the clients of research including farmers, agro-processors and exporters, diversifying sources of finance as well as research priority setting procedures. Farmer lobbies will have to finance a larger share of agricultural research in developing countries for budgetary reasons. Public sector rationalization and shortages in the operating budgets has meant that even the strong research systems such as those of China, Argentina and Brazil have to generate more revenues from the sale of products, services and research results. A positive aspect of this development is the need for research centers to connect with their customers. The negative result is that the earned resources from commercialization are not ploughed back into the research system, thus leading to a growing tendency to increase income earning activities, at the cost of research. Developed countries in the meantime are proceeding rapidly with patenting a large pool of new knowledge in the private sector which would be increasingly less accessible to developing countries. The extent to which developing countries continue to upgrade their physical, institutional and human capital to take advantage of the rapidly expanding scientific network will determine the extent to which they partake in the new scientific revolution. Even the more advanced developing countries have not yet caught on to the full implications of these changes for their research policies and strategies. It is in part a result of lack of sufficient information among the policy makers of developing countries regarding the nature of the scientific revolution and its implications for them. The problem for the poor low income countries is even more serious. Often, it is not simply one of information but of finances and political will.

One of the important tasks of the authorizing environment is the definition of research and transfer priorities. Priority setting and resource allocation within the CGIAR system takes place at two interrelated levels. At the system level, the TAC identifies priority areas (e.g. commodity research, NRM research, biodiversity) and provides the broad criteria or guidelines for resource allocation among the priority areas. TAC periodically revises priorities of the system to account for changing CGIAR mission, goals, and mandate, emerging trends in world agriculture, evolving scientific capacity in developing countries, and stakeholders' concerns (McCalla and Ryan 1992). For instance, the 1992 report of the TAC emphasized NRM research, based on ecoregions and land use systems, while the 1996 report focused on poverty alleviation, sustainable food security, and NRM while perhaps underemphasizing the ecoregional focus. Individual research centers then set priorities through their strategic and medium-term plans (Kelly et al. 1995; Walker 1996).

4.2 The CGIAR's operating capacity

The individual IARCs and the NARSs comprise the operating capacity of the CGIAR system. The greatest strength of the IARCs has been their humanitarian mission, a problem solving, interdisciplinary approach, access to global scientific knowledge, materials and institutions, and the convening power that the combination of these factors provides to the IARCs. The system has been an important catalyst for partnerships with the NARSs of both industrial and developing countries. Individual centers have been able to produce important products and services which the authorizing environment has been willing to underwrite by its funding. With the declining number of CGIAR scientists and the increased number of CGIAR centers the capacity of the CGIAR system to achieve impact is far more constrained now than previously, calling for wider partnerships with other research and technology transfer partners (Serageldin 1997).

The operating capacity of the IARCs represents an important socially concerned supply-side of technology generation. Publicly oriented scientists can contribute to decisions as to what technological responses are scientifically possible given resource constraints, their perception of the needs of their customers, and longer planning horizons.

The increasing strength of developing countries' NARSs both in absolute terms and relative to the CGIAR is creating a more diversified environment with increased opportunities to cater to local needs. Several NARSs in developing countries (e.g., Brazil, India, China) have gained strength in the last 30 years and are now conducting basic, applied and adaptive research. Producers associations are also conducting adaptive research in association with national research institutions or by themselves. Some of the strongest NARSs in developing countries are transferring technologies to weaker NARSs with similar agroecological conditions.

Some analysts argue that there is much scope for improvement in the division of labor among the CGIAR centers and the NARSs. For instance, it is estimated that nearly 40 percent of the total wheat varieties released in developing countries in the last three decades came from CIMMYT-NARSs collaborative research, 25 percent from indirect transfers and 10 percent from country-to-country spillovers (Maredia and Eicher 1995). For crops such as wheat, where international transferability of research is large, developing countries could allocate more resources at the margin to search for international research outputs so as to maximize spillins. This implies an increasingly important role for both regional research collaborations and NARSs in building sufficient capacity to capture spillins. Efficient access to the information network for weaker NARSs and the coordination of activities among NARSs becomes more difficult as the system's complexity increases due to increasing returns to investment in these areas. While the relative advantage of the CGIAR in direct research falls with the increased specificity of the problems tackled, its advantage as a coordinating organization and as a diffuser of information increases.

4.3 The CGIAR's customers

The consuming environment represents the demand side of the system. The producers and consumers of research all constitute distinct facets within this complex customer mix. They include NARSs, universities, NGOs, private sector researchers, as well as input suppliers, extension agents, processors, and producers (both in developed and developing countries). The choice of the term customer instead of the traditionally used term beneficiary has profound socioeconomic significance (Denning 1994). Beneficiary denotes a patron-client or a paternalistic relationship that the genesis of the CGIAR implied (Baum 1986; Lele and Coffman 1995), while customer implies an improved decision maker.

The customers' community has also become more diverse over time. The stronger NARSs in developing countries are demanding research inputs to be used in their own research programs while interacting more actively with developed countries' NARSs (e.g., the Global Research on the Environmental and Agricultural Nexus (GREAN) Initiative) and other developing countries' NARSs (e.g., Programa Cooperative para el Desarrollo Tecnologico Agropecuario del Cono Sur (PROCISUR)). Even though producers' associations and NGOs are also becoming active demanders of research products and transfer services, there are no formal channels through which latent demands can be represented, nor methodologies through which they can be identified. On the other hand, many smaller NARSs remain donor dependent and financially more hamstrung by their inability to effectively retain their researchers, even though their human capital base is stronger now than before.

The greater diversification of the customer community has allowed for a more active interaction with the authorizing environment and the operating capacity. The CGIAR system was created when the donor community realized the potential for large yield increases in developing countries; in other words, it was a top-down organization. Presently, different organizations negotiate directly or indirectly with the authorizing environment their demands for research in a more open political climate. In this way, users of technology that had previously been excluded from the decision process are now able to influence the allocation of resources.

5 The new roles for national and international innovation communities

The above discussion implies many diverse origins and paths of technology generation and adoption, some of which begin with the CGIAR system, move to the NARSs institutions, and finally, arrive to the producers. Others originate in developed countries' universities, multinational corporations or in the developing countries' NARSs, and move to the CGIAR. A customer-oriented process can ensure the feedback loops from the producer to the NARSs and the CGIAR system and information sharing throughout the system, including where necessary, input from the advanced countries' research.

Differences in the organization of research and transfer in different countries make it a challenge to forge effective linkages, not only between the CGIAR system and NARSs (including the private sector), but also among the NARSs of developing countries, between those of developed and developing countries, and farm households, producers and consumers. On the other hand, this diversity increases the potential for mutually beneficial interactions.

This paper analyzed the different interests represented in the decision making bodies (TAC, boards, etc.), and the ways in which these bodies gather information and support from both the users as well as the suppliers of technology, including technology transfer agents. A continuous and at some stages informal negotiating process takes place where priorities are negotiated among the interested parties based on mutual feedback. The extent to which the inarticulated demands of poor farmers, consumers, other users of natural resources, and future generations is represented in these decision bodies is an important issue still to be resolved.

At early stages of the system, the donors identified the latent demands of poor farmers in developing countries (which also happened to coincide with the self interest of developed countries engaged in the Cold War) and funded the system. Presently, the range of inarticulated demands is large and represents conflicting objectives, e.g., many traditional yield increasing technologies (traditionally in research) affect soil structure, and, consequently, future production (future generations' objectives); in other cases they do not have particular characteristics demanded by users (taste, processing or storage qualities demanded by the users of technologies).

To the extent that NARSs of developing countries intend to prioritize some of those demands, they will have to increase their contributions to the IARTGTAI system in order to influence the decision making process. Other demands (such as the right of future generations to use exhaustible natural resources) will probably continue to be represented by NGOs, both in developed and developing countries. Since the NGOs do not have resources to finance the research by themselves, they influence the system indirectly by pressing the donors. As all demands have to be negotiated in the process of setting objectives, some present donors will probably reduce their contributions (seeing that their interests are not being served as they hoped for) while others, including developing countries, will have to increase their support to have greater influence in the final decisions. Adequate support for the system in the future will depend on the ability of the authorizing environment to compromise on the individual objectives and on the capacity of the CGIAR system to convey its mission and specific research goals to the "right" donors. If the negotiation process is transparent, then the balance of power within decision making bodies becomes explicit, and remedial actions, if needed, can be taken.

Decisions about research priorities are made simultaneously at different levels, and these decisions are interconnected. For example, priorities in the CGIAR system are affected by decisions of donors, who need to promote the agenda and policies that maintain the support of their constituencies. But, in deciding their own policies, donors also interact with the CGIAR system and NARSs and receive feedback from the users in the process. In brief, the priority setting process entails formal and informal negotiating mechanisms where the different actors use their comparative advantages in articulating supply and demand for research, as well as in the conduct of the IARTGTAI functions.

An additional advantage of making the negotiation process more transparent is that the potential benefits are more readily perceived by the participants. Organizations or interest groups that are presently not participating in the process would find out that the potential benefits are large enough to justify the effort required to participate. Even though some of the present participants could lose interest in the CGIAR if the decision process becomes more participative, the likely outcome is that more customers will find it beneficial to participate, with the result that the scope of the system would be enlarged and international support would increase. The CGIAR's priority setting efforts have evolved considerably when viewed from this perspective, but are perhaps not yet fully informed by the views of the customers in the process whose lives the research process aims to impact.

6 Final remarks

This paper presented an alternative framework to analyze agricultural research, technology generation, transfer, adoption and impact based on a premise that understanding the process of research and technology transfer has significant implications for the extent, speed and the spread of impact. This framework is based on the premise that IARTGTAI is a complex process that evolves in a non linear iterative manner due to the interaction of a number of actors in several directions. Some of these are conditioned by the evolution of variables exogenous to the system. Particularly relevant for the understanding of this process is the study of the nature and the extent of the hierarchical structures and the channels that convey information and convert it into knowledge and decision-making through the system.

The evolutionary approach contrasts with other studies that have concentrated on the measurement of a few easily measurable and largely economic indicators of outcomes, e.g., productivity growth. They tell us little about the relationship between the processes and outcomes. In addition to advocating a wider scope for case studies of individual technologies, the evolutionary approach can use cross country and cross technology comparative studies to provide a better understanding of the interactions among factors that limit, or enhance the speed of technology development and transfer by better understanding the types of interactions outlined above.

The framework was used here to sketch the evolution of the IARTGTAI system to which the CGIAR belongs. The main features that characterized the process are:

— An increasingly diversified set of objectives. In addition to reducing poverty through the development of advanced technologies, the objectives now include ensuring sustainability of natural resources, conserving biodiversity, and developing capacity of the NARSs.

— Due to a larger number of actors participating in the authorizing environment, priority setting at the system level requires more complex negotiations, making it more difficult for each participant to objectively understand the factors that ideally should influence the research agenda so as to have maximum impact.

— Even though the number of researchers in the CGIAR centers has fallen, the operating capacity of the system as a whole has increased because NARSs in developing countries have become stronger. Also, regional organizations are becoming important instruments to capture economies of scale in research. However, with rapid advances in science, there is need to establish a different set of partnerships with industrial countries including with the private sector, universities etc., to work out a new set of comparative advantages.

The sketch presented here is still incomplete and needs further development. The aspect of the analysis which needs further exploration relates to the evolution of the hierarchical structure of the authorizing environment, and how the changing environment is likely to affect the division of labor among the institutions of advanced countries, the CGIAR centers, NARSs and other actors in research and technology transfer. Better understanding of these processes will help to improve research and technology transfer priority setting both at the level of individual NARSs as well as the CGIAR system as a whole and improve our understanding of the factors that determine impact. This is particularly relevant for understanding the impact of technologies, the benefits of which are indirect, take a long time to manifest themselves, require a change in traditional practices (e.g., NRM technologies or technologies addressing problems of resource poor farmers), and respond to other inarticulated demands for technology.

References

Barnett, W. and Burgelman, R. Summer (1996): Strategic Perspectives on Strategy, in: Strategic Management Journal, Vol. 17.

Baum, W.C. (1986): Partners Against Hunger: The Consultative Group for International Agriculture, The World Bank, Washington, DC.

Bonte-Friedheim, C. and Sheridan, K. (1996): The Globalization of Science: The Place of Agricultural Research, ISNAR.

Burgelman, R. Summer (1996): A Process Model of Strategic Business Exit: Implications for an Evolutionary Perspective on Strategy, in: Strategic Management Journal, Vol. 17.

Coase, R.H. (1972): Industrial Organization: A Proposal for Research, in: Victor R. Fuchs (ed.): Policy Issues and Research Opportunities in Industrial Organization, NBER General Series No. 96.

Denning (1994): Farmers as Customers: a Service Management Approach to Designing an Agricultural Research and Development Institution, IRRI Discussion Paper No. 3, Manila, Philippines.

Dixit, A. and Pindyck, R. (1994): Investment under Uncertainty, Princeton University Press, Princeton, NJ.

Dosi, G. (1997): Opportunities, Incentives and the Collective Patterns of Technological Change, in: The Economic Journal, 107, p. 1530-1547.

Evenson, R. E. and S. Rose-Ackerman (1985): The Political Economy of Agricultural Research and Extension, in: American Journal of Agricultural Economics, 67(1), p.1-14.

George, Shanti (1992): Generalization in Rural Development: 11 Villages in South Gujarat, India, in: Journal of International Development, Vol. 4, No. 4.

Georghiou, L.G. and Metcalfe, J.S. (1993): Evaluation of the Impact of European Community Research Programs upon Industrial Competitiveness, in: R&D Management, Vol. 23, No. 2.

Guttman, J. (1978): Interest Groups and the Demand for Agricultural Research, in: Journal of Political Economy, 86, p. 467-484.

Hayami, Y. and V. W. Ruttan (1985): Agricultural Development: An International Perspective, Johns Hopkins University Press, Baltimore, MD.

Huffman, W. E. and Evenson, R.E. (1993): Science for Agriculture: A Long-Term Perspective Iowa State University Press, Ames, IA.

Kelly, T.G., J.G. Ryan and B.K. Patel (1995): Applied Participatory Priority Setting in International Agricultural Research: Making Trade-offs Transparent and Explicit, in: Agricultural Systems, 49, p. 177-216.

Khanna, J., W.E. Huffman and T. Sandler (1994): Agricultural Research Expenditure in the United States: A Public Goods Perspective, in: The Review of Economics and Statistics, 76(2), p. 267-277.

Kumar, Nalini (1997): Operation Flood: Literature Review and Reconciliation, in: Occasional Publication 13, Institute of Rural Management Anand, Anand, India.

Lele, U. (1996): An International Comparison of Agricultural Research Policies, paper presented at a workshop on the Roles of Public and Private Sectors in Agricultural Research in Brasilia, Brazil.

Lele, U. and R. Coffman (1995): Global Research on the Environmental and Agricultural Nexus for the 21st Century: A Proposal for Collaborative Research Among U.S. Universities, CGIAR Centers, and Developing Country Institutions, Report of the Taskforce on Research Innovations for Productivity and Sustainability, University of Florida, Gainesville, FL.

Lewis, J. (1996): Indicators of Global Agricultural Research and Development Progress, Report on a workshop, September 27-29, 1995, University of Georgia, Athens, GA.

Lynn, L., N. Mohan Reddy and J.D. Aram (1996): Linking Technology and Institutions: the Innovation Community Framework, Research Policy, 25, p. 91-106.

Marcus, A.I. (1987): Constituents and Constituencies: An Overview of Public Agricultural Research Institutions in America, in: D.F. Hadwiger and W.P. Browne (eds.): Public Policy and Agricultural Technology: Adversity Despite Achievement, Macmillian Press, London, p. 15-26.

Maredia, M.K. and C.K. Eicher (1995): The Economics of Wheat Research in Developing Countries: The One Hundred Million Dollar Puzzle, in: World Development, 23, p. 401-412.

McCalla, A. and J. Ryan (1992): Setting Agricultural Research Priorities: Lessons from the CGIAR Study, in: American Journal of Agricultural Economics, 74, p. 1095-1100.

Metcalfe, J.S. (1995): Technology Systems and Technology Policy in an Evolutionary Framework, in: Cambridge Journal of Economics, Vol. 19(1).

Metcalfe, J.S. (1994): Evolutionary Economics and Technology Policy, in: The Journal of The Royal Economic Society, Vol. 104.

Moore, M.H. (1996): Creating Public Value: Strategic Management in Government, Harvard University Press, Cambridge, MA.

Nelson, R. (1995): Recent Evolutionary Theorizing About Economic Change, in: Journal of Economic Literature, Vol. 33.

North, D.C. (1991): Institutions, Institutional Change and Economic Performance, Cambridge University Press, New York, NY.

Pardey, P., J.M. Alston, J.E. Christian, and S. Fan (1996): Hidden Harvest: U.S. Benefits From International Research Aid, Food Policy Report, International Food Policy Research Institute, Washington, DC.

Pardey, P.G. and Alston, J.M. (1995): Revamping Agricultural R & D, A 2020 Vision for Food, Agriculture, and the Environment: a Brief, International Food Policy Research Institute, Washington, DC.

Petit, Michel (1985): Determinants of Agricultural Policies in the United States and the European Community, Research Report 51, International Food Policy Research Institute, Washington, DC.

Serageldin, I. (1997): CGIAR Chairman's Letter to Heads of Delegation on the 1997 Mid-Term CGIAR Meeting.

Smith, K., C. Grimm and M. Gannon (1992): Dynamics of Competitive Strategy, Sage, Newbury Park, CA.

Somjee, Geeta and A.H. Somjee (1989): Reaching out to the Poor: The Unfinished Rural Revolution, Macmillan, London.

Stiglitz, J.E. (1984): Information and Economic Analysis, in: The Economic Journal, 95, p. 21-41.

Walker, T. (1996): Background Information for Impact Analysis at the International Potato Center (CIP), Prepared for the CGIAR Impact Assessment and Evaluation Workshop at ISNAR, The Hague, The Netherlands.

Winter, S. (1990): Survival, Selection and Inheritance, in: Singh, J. (ed.): Evolutionary Theories of Organization, Organizational Evolution: New Directions, Newbury Park, CA.

World Bank (Forthcoming): The Impact of Dairying Development in India: The Bank's Contribution, Operations Evaluation Department, Washington, DC.

Wright, G. (1997): Towards a More Historical Approach to Technological Change, in: The Economic Journal, 107, p. 1560-1566.

22

The future role of bio-technology and genetic engineering

Gerhard Wenzel

1 Introduction

There is as much hope as there is scepticism concerning the future contribution of advanced biotechnology and genetic engineering, or as a more neutral synonym genomics, towards increased food supply in the next millennium. This section focusses on the expectations and uncertainties commending on the future, considerations which are always open ended. How open may become clear when looking back at the end of a century, and asking which predictions one would have made 100 years ago. At that time, the principles of classical plant breeding were just invented with the discovery of the Mendelian laws. Recombination, hybrid breeding or biotechnology were unknown words. This shows how vague any statement about the future role of biotechnology is at the beginning of the third millennium. To be at least a bit precise, the techniques encountered in biotechnology in connection to plant breeding are presented in figure 1. Other well known parts of biotechnology, often summarized as old biotechnology, like brewing beer or making bred will not be discussed here.

Figure 1: Overview of available biotechnological methods for plant breeding dealt with in this article

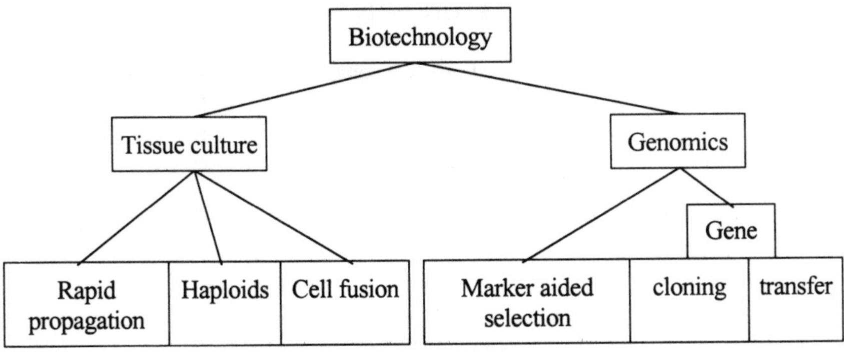

Table 1 summarizes the central present breeding aims, most of which are also relevant for third world countries. While the priority list in the industrialized world starts with quality and ends with yield, in developing countries this sequence is the opposite one. This shows a first future problem: Research in the northern hemisphere focusses on subjects like quality alterations while needs of the developing world like resistances to heat or drought stress are not of central interest. Since biotechnological research is extremely expensive compared with classical approaches, the concentration on objects of interest to industrialized countries has a priority now and in the future. Markham and Neuschwander (1997) worded it like this: "who pays the piper, calls the tune."

Table 1: Aims in modern breeding research according to the Third World's priorities
(topics where input from biotechnology is already a reality in existing cultivars are printed in bold)

1. Yield improvements	increase of photosynthetic activity	
	increase in nutrient uptake efficiency	
	facilitating hybrid systems	
	better adaptation to temperature	
	improved metabolic transport	
2. Production of resistances	against diseases	**viruses**
		bacteria
		fungi
	against pests	**insects**
	abiotic stress	shortage of water
		temperature
		salts
		gasses
	against herbicides	
3. Improvement of quality	of primary compounds	**starch/suggars**
		fats/oils
		protein
	of secondary metabolites	aromas
		drugs
	of new compounds	pharmaceuticals
		vaccines
4. Maintenance of biodiversity	in ecosystems	
	in variability of cultivars	
	in the genotypes	

2 General considerations

The production of the first cultivars being now in the market was mainly driven by available technical possibilities. Thus, it was easier in the beginning to transfer genes identified in viruses and bacteria than to identify and transfer genes from higher plants. As a consequence, the first varieties carry characters identified in bacteria and viruses. Now heavy research is going on in understanding the biochemical pathways of the higher plant to identify enzymes and to isolate the responsible genes. This allows a more efficient improvement of existing cultivars, less unpredictable influences and in consequence an easier acceptance of the new products.

Figure 2: The increasing number of transgenic plants and the corresponding additional transgenic characters

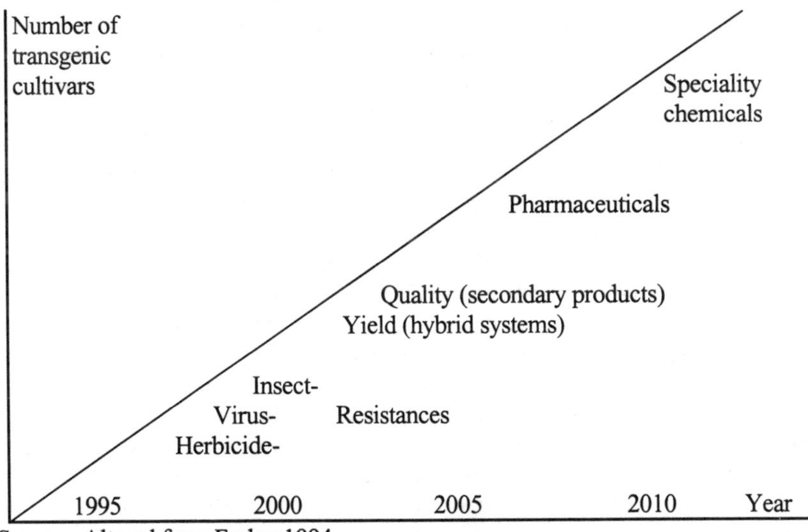

Source: Altered from Fraley 1994.

To guarantee the return of investments, all developments particularly in the field of genomics are patented as early and as broad as possible. The consequence is that presently the key technologies like DNA transfer by *Agrobacterium* (Horsch et al. 1987) and microbombardment (Sanford et al. 1987) or DNA multiplication with the polymerase chain reaction (PCR; Saiki et al. 1985) are not freely available. Looking from this angle at the phases of gene transfer (Figure 2), the first was the transfer of herbicide resistances—today, patented; then virus coat protein induced resistances followed by the use of *Bacillus thuringiensis* for the induction of insect resistance—today, patented. After the resistance phase work enlarged in the direction of hybrid systems causing heterosis—today, patented; and now the production of specific secondary products is taking over, and patents will come first. This situation will surely lead to increased research activities trying to develop alternative techniques in the molecular area to circumvent the existing policy.

3 Use of biotechnology for estimating changes of biodiversity

Since in the long run sustainability is the most crucial point, breeding and its influence on biodiversity shall be discussed first, although it is of last priority according to the list of Table 1. The more successful a newly bred cultivar expands, the less other cultivars can keep their areas. Moreover, leading cultivars are often closely related. A narrowing of the genetic basis is expected. Actually, uniformity is an essential prerequisite for registering a cultivar at seed boards. Coupled to uniformity is always the danger of rapid selection of new virulences in the pathogen population. Since in the Third World countries uniformity of cultivars is not progressed as far as in the industrialized world, it is often argued that specific programs have to be developed to maintain the variability with respect to increased sustainability. Biotechnology cannot contribute too much to preserve the ecosystems or a wide range of different varieties, but new biotechnological processes are expected to speed up the breeding process. Thus, replacement of old cultivars may become faster. To check whether the fear of an increased loss of biodiversity by this higher breeding speed is correct, Hatz (1997) compared the gene basis of more than 200 accessions of barley by the use of molecular markers.

Today, the analysis of DNA fragments generated by restriction enzymes (RFLPs) enables the correlation of specific fragment polymorphisms to phenotypes. DNA probes offer an uncoupling from environmental influences and thus a tremendous reproducibility (Beckmann and Soller 1983). Using 50 DANN probes in a wide range of different barley varieties, land races and lines reaching from wild varieties till cultivars, Hatz (1997) could demonstrate that although phenotypic variability is lost, the genotypic variability is not narrowed. Comparing the similarity of the DNA composition by measuring genetic distances, it became evident that newer and older types do not form any clear-cut genetic clusters. There exists a very normal distribution of the DNA differences over all genotypes. The fear that genetic variability is lost due to the selection process is not as large as anticipated. Furthermore, comparing such genetic distance patterns of parental varieties and new modern varieties originating from those, most of the genes in the younger ones can be traced back to the parental types but in addition, new genes show up. Presently it looks very probable that the recombination speeds up evolution and creates new variability. This means that the danger to loose biodiversity by breeding, and to loose it even faster by biotechnological approaches, is probably wrong.

Of course, there is a need to preserve the biodiversity of ecosystems and to do as much as possible to prevent the concentration of biotechnology on just a few major crops. National and international programs have to make sure that local plants and crops which are not of immediate interest to industrialized countries are not neglected. Perhaps there is not always the need to improve them with the most sophisticated gene-technological approaches, but it should be of general acceptance that at least classical and tissue culture procedures are adopted to as many species as possible. Here the system of the international agricultural research institutes has a central task.

4 Quality

One of the key issues for farmers engaged in food production today is the difficult concept of quality which is thought of as the sum total of physical characteristics embodied in the product. Shannon (1996) differentiates four categories of quality issues facing the producer and the customers with regard to an industrialized country: fitness for purpose, diet and health, safety and hygiene, and ethics and perceptions. At present the scientific community is not equipped to deal with the complicated situation of understanding the nutritional needs. From the point of view of developing countries the highest emphasis will certainly remain on the practicalities of production of quantity for quite a while although malnutrition is a crucial problem as well. Speaking about the future, one can predict that also in developing countries diet, health, and hygiene are of increasing importance, thus making breeding for quality a central goal worldwide.

Classical and biotechnological breeding techniques rely on the production and use of variability followed by the selection of the better plant type. Since classical breeding aiming at yield, resistances or quality follows the same procedures, it is normal to select always for several traits. A successful new variety is never better in only one trait but it is the successful combination of many. It should be stressed that even though there is a spectrum of new biotechnologies, the present breeding progress, documented by the annual licencing of better cultivars all over the world, is the result of classical breeding, and this will continue. Biotechnology is an addition to classical techniques only, and will never replace them. One example for success in improving the quality is the breakthrough of classical approaches in breeding of glucosinolate and erucic acid free rape seed (Röbbelen 1995). Both compounds restricted the use of rape seed for food and feed. Due to a rather simple genetic basis and a very efficient selection system working on single seeds, the breeding process was very fast.

Usually, selection is performed in the classical process at the whole plant level under field conditions. If clear markers or selection systems, likee.g. selection against toxic compounds, exist, the cell and tissue culture part of biotechnology might be helpful to achieve specific quality characteristics. Biotechnology allows to transfer this process into the test tube, uncoupling it from the natural environmental variability. Since the environment can modify the desired characters, the reliability increases by transferring the selection process into the greenhouse or to the petri dish. This gain in reproducibility is, however, counterbalanced by the increased artificiality. So it is necessary to have at least a final field test after any biotechnological selection. The increased artificiality is probably one reason why numerous lines or clones selected at the cell level did not express this character under field conditions (Wenzel and Foroughi 1993). For future considerations, in vitro selection is not a general way to go; there may be exceptions where this procedure pays, but not too much should be invested into this ambiguous approach.

The number of food plants which are modified by genetic engineering is increasing, and thus also the number of plants ready to enter the market or at least first field trials. This will surely start a discussion on the safety of such products. In Table 2 several possible modifications of plant quality are summarized.

Table 2: Some examples for the improvement of quality characteristics by gene transfer

New quality	Gene source	Example
Biodegradable plastics	Bacterium: *Alcaligenes eutrophus*	Potato
Altered sugars	Bacterium: *Klebsiella pneumonatus*	Potato
Improved protein	Chicken	Alfalfa
More lauric acid	*Umbellularia california*	Canola
More stearic acid	Rape seed	Canola
Altered starch composition	Yeast	Potato
Heat stable amylase	Barley	Barley

Source: Altered from Röbbelen 1995; Wobus 1995.

Strong emphasis has been placed on the main storage products, starch, oils, and proteins. A first result of gene transformation is the increase in the lauric acid content of rape seed, a nutritionally valuable short fatty acid, by the expression of a transferred gene from Umbellularia (Dale et al. 1993). For starch its composition out of amylose (long twisted chains) and amylopectine (branched chains) could be altered by gene technology. Presently, the first cultivar is on the market which produces only amylopectine (Koßmann et al. 1991). For the processing industries, this saves an expensive separation step. Modifications of the aminoacid composition of proteins of plants were an aim in plant breeding since long. Particularly in mutation breeding programs, lysin-rich cereals were of interest. The production of higher amounts of the essential amino acids in plants is surely a goal for future breeding programs.

For extensive agricultural systems the idea to vaccinate animals via feeding is realistic. It should not be too difficult to incorporate genes which will produce chemicals active as a vaccine directly in the plant. Such approaches might be of particular interest for countries with extensive animal farming.

5 Disease resistances

The incorporation of genes for resistances is the most effective, economical and prophylactic means of plant protection. Thus it is commonly agreed that a need exists all over the world for breeding plants with genetical resistances against diseases. Increase in genetical resistance is fast when the resistance is monogenic. For more complex resistances, oligo- or polygenic ones, the selection process needs rather large populations and several repetitions. In vegetatively propagated crops, like e.g. most trees, bananas or potatoes, any genotype can be made to a variety. In all other instances, homozygosity or at least homogeneity has to be achieved by selfing and selection. Biotechnology can help to achieve this goal more efficiently.

During the last 20 years, biotechnology backed the classical breeding system by cell culture and genomics (Figure 1). Rapid propagation has achieved a wide range of healthy plants, which yielded much more due to the absence of, e.g., virus diseases (Wenzel 1997). Such rapid propagation techniques usually can be economic only in vegetatively propagated crops. Many tropical fruits and most tuber crops are vegetatively propagated and thus can be improved by this technique (Rice et al. 1992). Since also numerous cash crops, like ornamentals, can be propagated with these in vitro techniques, it is this biotechnological tool which pays most at present. As it is a simple but labour intensive technique, it has very good economic chances in a number of developing countries, and surely will continue in the forthcoming decades.

Turning to the next process in biotechnology which creates new variability, namely gene transfer, the present situation is given in Table 3. For producing a new variety it would be ideal just to add one or a few missing traits to a superior cultivar. Although this can be achieved in principle by classical approaches, the big advantage is that with transfer procedures the existing optimized genotype is not destroyed by meiotic segregation during the necessary recombination processes. For gene transfer in principle the transfer procedures work, and thus today the crucial problems are no longer whether gene transfer will work but rather in which direction it can be directed and what the patent situation will allow.

Diversity at the resistance level is caused by corresponding differences in the DNA sequence. And thus DNA probes, already briefly mentioned in the section on biodiversity, can be used as markers for the identification of genes responsible for resistances (Graner et al. 1995). Most of these probes are still only detecting monogenic traits which are usually not very durable. Therefore an increasing interest exists to elaborate probes form oligo- or polygenic traits. A clear reproducible correlation between probes and polygenic, quantitative traits (QTLs) would result in a tremendous improvement of breeding programs (Backes et al. 1997).

Since in most cases the use of molecular markers demands the need to know the localization of the marker in the genome, genetic linkage maps are constructed (Graner et al. 1995). Presently, the most powerful application of such identified genes and molecular markers is opened up by marker aided selection (MAS). Such an identification of resistance genes needs, however, always the coupling with a difficile analysis of the genome of the corresponding pathogene. This is of particular importance when uniform monogenic traits are used. Coupled to uniformity is always the danger of the rapid selection of new virulences in the pathogen populations. The epidemiology of the corresponding pathogenes has to be monitored very carefully (Felsenstein 1995). Today, also for the description of the ecotypes of the pathogens DNA markers can be used. For example Saucke et al (1996) measured the genetic distances by the use of molecular markers for *Setospheria turcica*, causing the turcicum leaf disease of maize in Kenia, China, and Europe.

Table 3: Varieties with engineered genes, transgenic plants released to market with approval for sale

Year	Crop species	Variety	Area 1000 ha	Company	Altered trait	Country
1995	Corn			AgrEvo	Herbicide tolerance	Canada
1995	Corn	Maximizer		Novartis	Corn borer resistance	USA
1995	Corn	NatureGard		Mycogen	Corn borer resistance	USA
1996	Corn	Liberty Link		AgrEvo	Herbicide tolerance	USA
1996	Corn			DeKalb	Herbicide tolerance	USA
1996	Corn			PGS/AgrEvo	Male sterility	USA
1996	Corn	YieldGard		Monsanto	Corn borer resistance	USA
1996	Corn			NorthrupKing	Corn borer resistance	USA
1995	Cotton	Bollgard	500	Monsanto	Insect resistance	USA
1996	Cotton	Roundup Ready	6	Monsanto	Herbicide tolerance	USA
1995	Cotton	BXN Cotton		Calgene	Herbicide tolerance	USA
1996	Cotton			Dupont	Herbicide tolerance	USA
1994	Petunia				Flower colour	NL
1995	Potato	New Leaf		Monsanto	Beetle resistance	USA
1996	Potato		0.6		Starch quality	NL
1996	Potato			Monsanto	Insect resistance	USA
1995	Rape seed		40	AgrEvo	Herbicide tolerance	Canada
1995	Rape seed	Laurical		Calgene	Increased lauric acid	USA
1995	Rape seed			PGS/AgrEvo	Male sterility	UK
1995	Squash	Freedom II		Asgrow	Virus resistance	USA
1995	Soybean	Roundup Ready	250	Monsanto	Herbicide tolerance	USA
1996	Soybean				Protein quality	Canada
1994	Tomato	Flavr Savr	3	Calgene	Slower ripening	USA
1995	Tomato	Endless Summer		DANN Plant	Slower ripening	USA
1995	Tomato			Monsanto	Slower ripening	USA
1995	Tomato			Zeneca	Thicker skin	USA
1995	Tomato			Peto Seed	Different pectins	USA
1996	Tomato			Agritope	Slower ripening	USA

Source: Altered from James and Krattinger (1996).

6 Pest resistance

As can be seen from Table 3, the gene-technological incorporation of insect resistances by the use of *Bacillus thuringiensis* is widespread. With this bacterium, biological control was started already in 1928 (see Krieg 1986). The bacteria produce toxic proteins in their long-lasting forms. If an insect larva takes up such endotoxins, it is killed within a few days. The host spectrum and the action spectrum of the original *Bacillus thuringiensis israelensis (B.t.)* has been successfully modified. Since 1987 (Barton et al.1987) gene transfer of *B.t.* works and the present question is to find a strategy between too specific *B.t.* strains which do not help agriculture too much, and too general strains which may harm ecology. An additional concern is the fact, that the insects will develop resistances which will not only make the engineered plants susceptible but will also bring classical biocontrol into problems. Thus, a burning question for the future is by which strategy the genetechnological *B.t.* approach may be replaced.

In the meantime, engineered plants with insect resistance are of utmost importance for third world countries. To be able to use this system, arrangements about the patent situation have to be made. The example of the International Rice Research Institute (IRRI) which obtained free accession for the *B.t.* constructs of Novartis (Ciba) for the mandate countries of this international agricultural centre is certainly a recommendable way to go (Datta 1997). As soon as cultivars containing this construct come to non-mandate countries, the licences will go to Novartis. Such agreements are essential prerequisites to allow the spread of useful products of biotechnology to developing countries. It is hoped that other companies will follow a similar track. It is, however, doubtful whether this practice can be applied in general.

7 Abiotic stress resistance

In the area of environmental stress resistance the strategy is to influence physiological parameters or secondary products. Production of plants resistant to heat, frost or draught followed for quite a while mutation breeding procedures—actually with very limited success. In such mutants and naturally occurring stress resistant genotypes often very similar proteins were detected. These similarities give hope for a more general basis of the different stresses.

A very specific case is the herbicide resistance. Resistance to non-selective herbicides were the first practical results of engineered plants (e.g. Horsch et al. 1987). For this success several reasons may be quoted: The fact that the biochemical pathways of modern herbicides are known, allowing a straight-foreward strategy in developing resistances (tolerances). The fact that this tolerance was inherited by a single gene made it handable with the available transfer techniques. In the extensive agricultural systems of North America weeds are the dominant problem, and by the incorporation of a herbicide tolerance gene, the herbicide market is not lost for the companies. All this guarantees a good return on investment. For the more intensive cropping systems of the Third World and even Europe, herbicide resistance is not such a big gain. Nevertheless, weeds are a problem everywhere, and the search for additional alternatives, like allelopathy—not allowing weeds to grow next to the crop plant—are an interesting alternative. To understand and to find substances responsible for this known plant character and its transfer to crops would be a tremendous future gain.

Speaking about the future, some additional topics should be mentioned where biotechnology and particularly gene technology might contribute to the improvement of abiotic parameters. The physiological and genetical understanding of the control of day length as well as genes involved in the vernalization process are increasingly understood. Getting possibilities in hand to gear these processes, e.g. by increasing the efficiency of temperature dependent enzymes in countries with cold climates, and doing the opposite in countries with hot climates, will surely result in tremendous yield increases. A similar effect will be opened up by circumventing the day length dependence for many developmental processes of flowers or fruits.

8 Yield improvements

Yield is a polygenic trait. To select and produce cultivars combining several polygenic traits is the most difficult part of plant breeding. The strategy of hybrid production offers a way to combine at least complex characteristics from two parents. This is true for sexual hybrids as well as for somatic cell fusion products in vegetatively propagated crops like banana. Presently, no strategies exist, however, to transfer QTLs via gene technology. Reports exist about the transfer of at least two genes, one after the other (Brettschneider et al. 1997), but this is not yet sufficient for the transfer of complex characteristics.

The combination of complex characters became possible by somatic hybridization. Particularly in vegetatively propagated crops, cell fusion is the most efficient way to combine not only qualitatively inherited traits but also quantitative ones. This works already in potato, where besides virus resistances (Thach et al. 1993) also more complex traits as the non-monogenic resistance to Phytophthora could be combined in somatic hybrids (Möllers et al. 1994). In a somatic hybrid population even transgressions were found to both sides: less resistant as well as higher resistant to this fungus. Additionally, cell fusion was a successful procedure to rapidly incorporate cytoplasmic male sterility necessary for most hybrid systems. The first documentation was done in rape seed (Pelletier et al. 1988) and surely additional ones will follow.

The gene combination does not hold true only for the genes of the nuclear genome but also for the plasmon (Lössl et al. 1994). Plastids may belong to different groups, and thus different genome/plastome combinations can be selected after fusion. In the mitochondria, this effect is even higher since recombination and mixing of the mt-genomes take place. Some recombinations are better yielding than hybrids with the parental mitochondria. This possibility of the production of new cytoplasms is not restricted to vegetatively propagated plants; somatic hybridisation offers this approach in the future also for sexually propagated crops.

For a useful application of somatic hybridization, the haploid status is a prerequisite. Haploid cells exist as macro- or microspore, the egg cell or the young pollen grain. Both can be induced in vitro to form haploid plants. The microspore androgenesis has been improved so much that the necessary number of green haploid plants—usually 100 per donor genotype—can be produced in quite a number of crop plants (Foroughi-Wehr & Wenzel 1993). The genome of the haploids can be doubled by colchizine, or it doubles spontaneously resulting in doubled haploid (DH) lines. In a population of DH lines, the identification of specific traits is more secure as intermediate expressions resulting from heterozygosity are excluded. Thus, DHs of inbreeders allow a substantial shortening of the normal breeding process by omitting the time needed for achieving homozygosity. They further allow the efficient combination of qualitative traits by making the repeated recombinations during back crosses unnecessary (Wenzel et al. 1995). Since the technique is not too sophisticated, there are good chances to use it in developing countries. It might even be possible to produce such plants in those areas and reexport them for breeding purposes to Europe or North America.

For all hybrid systems, the asexual propagation of hybrid seeds via apomixis is of utmost interest. Its priority is, however, very different depending on economical considerations. In industrialized countries, hybrids are a secure protection against regrowing. In developing countries, the possibility for the seed production by the farmer is essential. As a consequence, in developing countries the potential of hybrids can only be fully exploited when an asexual propagation, e.g. via apomixis, becomes successful. Along this line the IRRI invests in its hybrid rice program also in the development of apomixis. Since apomictic grasses are known, there are chances for a transfer of this trait from e.g. Festuca to rice.

A further system for yield improvement will be the transfer of those genes responsible for the C3 or C4 carbohydrate cyclus. Particularly for the warmer climates of tropical and subtropical countries, such an alteration from the C3 to the C4 circle would pay with a striking yield increase. Of course also other improvements of the photosynthetic activity will help.

9 Increased mineral nutrient uptake

Plants always interact with soil ions and microorganisms. The central goals in breeding are: selection of low input varieties by improving the metabolic transport processes and optimizing the microflora of the soil including strategies for nitrogen fixation.

In cultivars, different sizes of the root system exist, allowing different efficiencies in the uptake of water and solved minerals. This uptake is partly an active one which is assumed to be under genetical control. Particularly for developing countries, a profile of low input plants, as given in Figure 3 number 3, would be advantageous. After an understanding of the responsible processes, it should become possible to influence this system positively by means of gene technology.

Figure 3: Different possibilities for nutrient uptake

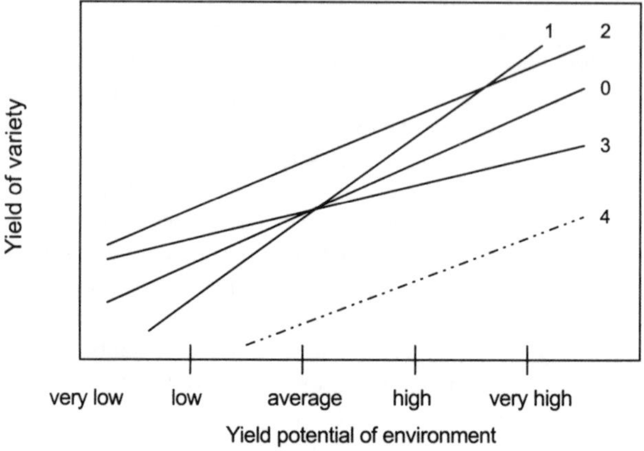

0=mean yield of all varieties; 1=high input variety; 2=all-purpose variety; 3=low input variety; 4=undesired type

Source: Spanakakis 1995.

A specific topic of low input is nitrogen fixation of the higher plant by symbiosis or directly. It is still a breeding goal to transfer the very efficient natural system, the symbiosis between *Leguminosae* and *Rhizobium* and several others like *Klebsiella*, *Azospirillum* and *Azotobacter* to other species. After a long period of frustration, new hope came up by making non-fixing plants to become a host for nitrogen fixing bacteria. Since fixing of nitrogen is a very crucial process in the whole agriculture, even strong failures were not discouraging, and research is now continuing with the help of biotechnology (for review see Ladha et al. 1992).

10 Conclusions

In summary we can say that the different biotechnological techniques have their advantages at different levels. The most striking challenges are summarized in table 4, they are, however, also the most difficult ones, and it will take some additional good ideas to make them applicable in breeding programs. Only by new ideas the natural evolution can be turned in an anthropocentric direction that helps man to survive.

Table 4: Central future challenges of biotechnology with special emphasis on developing countries

Aim	Classical approach				Biotechnological approach			
	Costs	Speed	Feasibility	Sustain-ability	Costs	Speed	Feasibility	Sustain-ability
Hybrids	++	+	++	++	+++	+++	++	++
C3 -> C4	?	+	+	?	+++	++	+	?
Day length	+	+	++	+++	+++	+++	+++	++
Allelopathy	+	+	+	?	+++	++	+++	+++
Temperature	++	+	++	+++	+++	+++	++	+++
Apomixis	+	+	+	++	+++	++	+++	++

To become a bit more realistic, Table 5 summarizes the different goals and techniques mentioned in this article. It demonstrates where advantages over the classical process are expected and to what extent. Such an evaluation is of particular importance when assuming that investments into biotechnology should be driven by demands and needs rather than by the available technology. We have to admit, however, that the coming up of technologies—the invention and discoveries—cannot be planned. Thus, biotechnology is one option which will help also in developing countries to improve crop protection and thus making yields more secure.

Table 5: Summary of biotechnological techniques and a subjective calculation of their expenses and advantages compared with the classical approach

Goal	Procedure					
	Classic	Rapid propagation	Somatic fusion	Haploids	Marker selection	Gene transfer
Quality	++	+++	++	++	+++	+++
Resistance						
- disease	+++	+++	++	++	+++	++
- pest	+	+-	+-	+-	+-	+++
- stress	++	+-	+-	+-	+-	+
- herbicide	+-	+-	+-	+-	+-	+++
Yield						
- temperature	-	-	-	-	+	++
- hybrids	+++	-	++	+-	+-	+
- C3-C4	-	-	-	-	-	+
- low input	+-	+-	+-	+-	+	+-

Before starting such biotechnological breeding activities, it should be checked, however, carefully whether they are cheaper, and/or faster, securer, more durable or not less sustainable than classical approaches. It would probably be a waste of time and money if they were used just because it is more fashionable. If used in the right manner, it is expected that the incorporation of biotechnology and particular of DNA technologies will be the most efficient way to combine economic and ecological aims.

Even the most intelligent approach may fail when regulations restrict this development; it will also fail, however, when light-minded strategies create problems which are difficult to overcome. Thus it is necessary that world-wide adopted regulations for the release of biotechnological modified plants are accepted. When making such regulations, one should keep in mind that classical breeding combines by chance two complete genomes in an unpredictable way while gene transfer works with identified DANN pieces. The reproduction of all thinkable ecological problems into biotechnological procedures is, however, not an intelligent way to go.

World-wide the ultimate success or failure of biotechnology in agriculture relies on the responsible cooperation of the scientific community and regulating authorities. To understand more and more how genetics and biology work, is the biggest challenge of the forthcoming years. It is, however, not only scientific interest by which this development is driven, it is also the need for more food and feed. By no doubt it is good luck that the new biotechnological techniques arose just when the number of breeding aims and the nutritional needs increased. The FAO conference in autumn 1996 stated clearly that there is a need to produce more food from less land. The acceptance of the processes will grow with its convincing results which by no doubt are on the verge to come.

References

Backes, G., G. Schwarz, G. Wenzel, A. Jahoor (1997): Comparison Between QTL Analysis on Powdery Mildew Resistance in Barley Based on Detached Primary Leaves and on Field Data, in: Plant Breeding (forthcoming).

Barton, K.A., H.R. Whiteley, N.-S. Yang (1987): Bacillus Thuringiensis Endotoxins Expressed in Transgenic Nicotiana Tabaccum Provides Resistance to Lepidoptera Insects, in: Plant Physiol., 85, pp. 1103-1109.

Beckmann, J.S., M. Soller (1983): Restriction Fragment Length Polymorphism in Genetic Improvement: Methodologies, Mapping and Costs, in: Theor. Appl. Genet., 67, pp. 35-43.

Brettschneider, R., D. Becker, H. Lörz (1997): Efficient Transformation of Scutellar Tissue of Immature Maize Embryos, in: Theor. Appl. Genet. (forthcoming).

Dale, P.J., J.A. Irwin, J.A. Schefler (1993): The Experimental and Commercial Release of Transgenic Crop Plants, in: Plant Breeding, 111, pp. 1-22.

Datta, S.K. (1997): Transgenic Rice in the Philippines, DSE Workshop Biotechnology for Crop Protection—Its Potential for Developing Countries (forthcoming).

Felsenstein, F.G. (1995): Ist die zyklische Nutzung von Resistenzgenen eine mögliche Strategie beim Aufbau dauerhafter Krankheitsresistenz im Getreide? In: Ber. Arbeitstg. Gumpenstein 46, pp. 177-180.

Foroughi-Wehr, B., G. Wenzel (1993): Andro- and Parthenogenesis, in: M.D. Hayward et al. (eds.): Plant Breeding—Principles and Prospects, London: Chapman & Hall, pp 261-277.

Fraley, R.T. (1994): The Contributions of Plant Biotechnology to Agriculture in the Coming Decades, in: A.F. Krattinger, A. Rosemarin (eds.): Biosafety for Sustainable Agriculture, Stockholm: ISAAA, pp. 3-28.

Graner, A., A. Kellermann, G. Wenzel (1995): Markergestützte Kombination von Resistenzen bei Gerste: Molekulare Kartierung verschiedener Pilzresistenzen, in: Ber. Arbeitstg. Gumpenstein 46, 189-192.

Hatz, B. (1997): Untersuchungen zur genetischen Diversität innerhalb Hordeum ssp. mit molekularen Markertechniken, PhD Thesis Technische Universität München.

Horsch, R., R. Fraley, S. Rogers, J. Fry, H. Klee, D. Shah, S. McCormick, J. Niedermeyer, N. Hoffmann (1987): Agrobacterium Mediated Transformation of Plants, in: C.E. Green et al. (eds.): Plant Tissue and Cell Culture, Liss, New York, pp. 317-329.

James, J., A.F. Krattinger (1996): Global Review of the Field Testing and Commercialization of Transgenic Plants, in: ISAAA Briefs 1-1996, pp. 1-31.

Krieg, A. (1986): Bacillus thuringiensis ein mikrobielles Insektizid, Acta Phytomedica 10.

Koßmann, J., R. Visser, B. Müller-Röber, L. Willmitzer, U. Sonnewald (1991): Cloning and Expression Analysis of a Potato cDNA that Encodes Branching Enzyme: Evidence for Co-expression of Starch Biosythetic Genes, in: Molec. Gen. Genet. 230, pp. 39-44.

Ladha, J.K., T. George, B. Bohlool (eds.) (1992): Biological Nitrogen Fixation for Sustainable Agriculture, Kluwer, Dordrecht.

Lössl, A., U. Frei, G. Wenzel (1994): Interaction Between Cytoplasmic Composition and Yield Parameters in Somatic Hybrids of S. Tuberosum L., in: Theor. Appl. Genet. 89, pp. 873-878.

Markham, R., P. Neuschwander (1997): Analysis of the Role of Biotechnology in Crop Protection in Developing Countries: a View from the International Agricultural Research Centres, DSE Workshop Biotechnology for Crop Protection—Its Potential for Developing Countries (forthcoming).

Möllers, C., U. Frei, G. Wenzel (1994): Field Evaluation of Tetraploid Somatic Potato Hybrids, in: Theor. Appl. Genet. 88, pp. 147-152.

Pelletier, G., C. Primard, M. Frerault, F. Vedel, P. Chetrit, M. Renard, R. Delourme (1988): Use of Protoplasts in Plant Breeding: Cytoplasmic Aspects, in: Plant Cell Tissue Cult. 12, pp. 173-180.

Rice, R.D., P.G. Alderson, J.F. Hall, A. Ranchhod (1992): Micropropagation: Principles and Commercial Practice, in: M.W. Fowler et al. (eds.): Plant Biotechnology, Oxford: Pergamon Press, pp.129-149.

Röbbelen, G. (1995): Beiträge der Biotechnologie zur Verbesserung von Qualitäts- und Leistungseigenschaften, in: von T. Schell, H. Mohr (eds): Biotechnologie—Gentechnik Eine Chance für neue Industrien, Heidelberg: Springer, pp. 201-214.

Saiki, R.K., S. Scharf, F. Faloona, K.B. Mullis, G.T. Horn, H.A. Erlich, N. Arnheim (1985): Enzymatic Amplification of ß-Globin Genome Sequences and Restriction Site analysis for Diagnosis of Sickle Cell Anemia, in: Science 230, pp. 1350-1354.

Sanford, J.C., T.M. Klein, E.D. Wolf, N. Allen (1987): Delivery of Substances into Cell and Tissue Using a Particle Bombardment Process, in: J. Part. Sci. Technol. 5, pp. 27-29.

Saucke, D., H.G. Welz, H.H. Geiger (1996): Genetische Diversität in kenianischen, chinesischen und mitteleuropäischen Feldpopulationen von Setospharia turcica, in: Mitt. a.d. Biol. Bundesanst. 321, p. 649.

Shannon, D.W.F. (1996): Food Quality—the Challenge to Agriculture, in: G.R. Fenwick et al. (eds.): Agri-Food Quality, Cambridge: Royal Society Chemistry, pp. 45-54.

Spanakakis, A. (1995): Stickstoffeffizienz bei Winterweizen: Neue Perspektiven in der Weizenproduktion? in: Bericht 17. Getreidetagung, Detmold: Granum Verlag, pp. 1-16.

Thach, N.Q., U. Frei, G. Wenzel (1993): Somatic Fusion for Combining Virus Resistance in Solanum Tuberosum L, in: Theor. Appl. Genet. 85, pp. 863-867.

Wenzel, G. (1997): Assessment of Resistance, in: H. Hartleb et al. (eds.): Resistance of Crop Plants Against Fungi, G. Fischer (forthcoming).

Wenzel, G., B. Foroughi-Wehr (1993): In Vitro Selection, in: M.D. Hayward et al. (eds.): Plant Breeding—Principles and Prospects, London: Chapman & Hall, pp. 353-370.

Wenzel, G., U. Frei, A. Jahoor, A. Graner, B. Foroughi-Wehr (1995): Haploids- An Integral Part of Applied and Basic Research, in: M. Terzi et al. (eds.): Current Issues in Plant Molecular and Cellular Biology, Kluwer, Dordrecht, pp. 127- 135.

Wobus, U. (1995): Stand und Nutzperspektiven der molekularen Pflanzengenetik, in: T. von Schell, H. Mohr (eds.): Biotechnologie—Gentechnik Eine Chance für neue Industrien, Heidelberg: Springer, pp. 163-180.

Glossary

Agrobacterium	Bacterium modified forms of which are used to transfer DNA into higher plants
Amylose	One of the two chemical compounds of starch; the sugar molecules form a twisted chain
Amylopectine	The other starch compound; the sugar chains form a net by cross links
Bacillus thuringiensis	A bacterium attacking larvae of insects and killing them by ejecting a toxic protein
Carbohydrate cyclus	Plants have two pathways for the production of sugar: either the C 3 or the C4 system which allows a better CO2 concentration in the plant and is—particularly at higher temperatures more efficient than the C3 way. A typical example is maize, which grows in a relatively short time with an enourmous speed due to its C4 photosynthetic pathway.
Genomics	Synonym to gene technology; generic term for gene transfer and gene/genome diagnosis including marker assisted selection

Haploids	Individuals with the simple genome in contrast to normal higher organisms containing one set of genetic information from each parent, resulting in diploids. The artificial doubling of a haploid genome results in homozygous diploids = doubled haploids (DHs)
Homozygosity	The genetic information of the two sets of genetic information is identical. In variety production of inbreeders like wheat or barley, homozygosity is a prerequisite to guarantee an identical offspring from the seeds sown
Lauric acid	A short valuable fatty acid with 12 C atomes
Markers	Visible (e.g. colours or hairs) or visualizable (DNA-polymorphisms) characteristics applied during selection
Marker aided selection (MAS)	Selection making use of (predominantly) DNA-markers = molecular markers identified normally by the use of DNA probes
Mitochondria	Cell organells responsible e.g. for the respiration. They contain circular DNA molecules
Plasmon	Non-nuclear genetic information of the cell. It consists of the DNA of plastids (Plastome) and the DNA of mitochondria (chondriome)
Polygenic trait	Character controlled by many genes—opposite: one gene = monogenic
Polymerase chain reaction	Procedure to artificially replicate DNA to such a quantity that it can be visualized without tricky staining or radiactive labeling
QTL	Quantitative trait locus, part(s) of the genome responsible for a polygenic trait
Restriction enzyme	Naturally occurring enzymes which cut the DNA molecule at specific sites
Somatic hybridization	Fusion of cells induced by chemicals or high voltage, resulting in somatic hybrids in which all characters of both parents are added
Stearic acid	A long fatty acid with 18 C atomes making fats solid.

23

Biotechnology in Third World Agriculture Some Socio-economic Considerations

Klaus M. Leisinger

1 Introduction: nature and limits of socio-economic impact analyses

Assessing the socio-economic impacts of agricultural biotechnologies in developing countries may "simply" be an academic task—the evaluation of the results, however, is subject to a great variety of interests and value judgements of a multitude of stakeholders. A review of the literature on the issue confirms this fact. Some authors consider agricultural biotechnologies to be amongst the most powerful and economically promising means,[1] while others perceive them as a threat[2] to development in Third World countries. Many critics of agri-biotechnology fear that it will lead to traditional farming becoming increasingly obsolete, that hunger and poverty will increase, and that technological and economic dependence of developing countries on industrialised countries will persist or even deepen.

These criticisms are not unique to biotechnology. They inevitably bring to mind comparisons with the debate on the Green Revolution of the fifties and sixties. In those times, mainstream development theory as well as dependency theory, although apparently at opposite ends of the ideological debate, postulated that underdevelopment was either the legacy of a traditional society to be overcome by modernisation or the negative consequence of "Western domination" over the Third World. In other words, the western model was either construed as the "problem" or the "solution" to the Third World predicament, and so was the Green Revolution. Today's debate about genetic engineering and agricultural biotechnologies is not any different, it seems like old vinegar in new bottles. Indeed, myths and clichés do die hard. Many seemingly new concepts are simple translations or relabellings of past Manichean categories—North/South, rich/poor, culprit/victim. It is still fashionable to deride the Green Revolution, although it has accomplished many great things:

- It saved some countries from bankruptcy over their food imports.
- It saved hundreds of millions of people from malnutrition and starvation.

1 See for example Jimmy Carter's appeal "Forestalling Famine with Biotechnology" in the Washington Post (Friday, July 11, 1997) and CGIAR 1992. See also the collection of working papers of the World Employment Programme Research of the International Labour Office in Geneva.

2 See for example Hobbelink 1991 and the publications of several nongovernmental organisations such as the Rural Advancement Foundation International (RAFI) in Ottawa (Canada).

- It brought millions of small farmers across the threshold from poverty to the rural middle class.
- It laid the basis for agricultural research systems in the South.

Ideologies only serve to further complicate the task of assessing the impacts of particular biotechnology applications or biotechnology-based products. After all, it is difficult enough to reach a consensus over the right assessment strategy. Not only do the various constituencies for impact analysis approach the issue from different perspectives, there is also a great diversity of possible levels of analysis. Thus, the point of view and methodological approach of a university-based sociologist are likely to differ widely from those of a regulatory official, an environmentalist, an economist or a representative of a biotechnological research institute. The levels of analysis reach from the broad impacts of biotechnological advances on patterns of international production and trade in the global economy, to in-depth analysis of the impacts of specific biotechnological applications or products on different development indicators at the national and regional levels.

Impact assessments are not ends in themselves. It is their objective to (i) identify ways in which positive effects of agricultural biotechnologies can be enhanced and negative effects minimised, and to (ii) integrate the impact assessment data into decision-making processes. There are three distinct levels of decision-making which affect agricultural biotechnology: individual scientific research projects, national policy and planning decisions, and decisions concerning international collaborative ventures. Again, in each case, the kind of analysis needed is different—from studies of consumer demand and "willingness to consume" regarding specific biotechnological applications or biotechnology-based products, to the evaluation of possible impacts of biotechnology on key national goals (e.g., growth, income distribution, employment), to the monitoring of technological trends and market characteristics in other countries.

Due to the complexity of the issues at hand and the diversity of possible approaches, any sweeping prediction of socio-economic impacts of agricultural biotechnology in developing countries must be regarded with great caution. Predictions will always involve simulations with key variables that are sometimes based on more or less subjective assumptions by the researchers—for example, on adoption rates of the new technology, the possible impact of changes in productivity on prices, demand and supply by crop, by region, and by type of holding, as well as the impacts of the prevailing policy environment. As in all exercises of this type, the results are critically dependent on the validity of the assumptions made about the exogenous environment, rates of changes in the individual variables, the interaction between the different variables, and the accuracy of the baseline data. Thus, the relevance of any impact analysis will be limited to a very particular biotechnological application or product in a very particular location at a particular time. *Ex-post* socio-economic impact assessments are similarly handicapped as *ex-ante* studies, since many questions cannot be answered because the impacts are yet to occur.

Sweeping statements on the impact of agricultural biotechnologies in developing countries are therefore highly questionable.

Nevertheless, this article ventures to evaluate the chances and risks associated with agricultural biotechnologies in developing countries, focusing on the socio-economic key variables to be used as impact assessment criteria:

- food security;
- employment and income;
- equity;
- environment, and
- economic growth.

By necessity very brief, this paper first roughly summarises the problems that poor developing countries are facing today with regard to these criteria and how they are caused and interrelated. This article can neither be comprehensive in the coverage of the manifold dimensions of socio-economic underdevelopment nor exhaustive in the treatment of the aspects it covers. More comprehensive treatments of the issues can be found in the list of references. What it tries to achieve, however, is to show that it is neither true nor helpful to make technology, especially agricultural biotechnology, accountable for the multiple causes of socio-economic underdevelopment—because socio-economic underdevelopment is prevailing especially there where technological development does not take place or only very slowly.

2 The socio-economic challenges in developing countries

2.1 Food security

The Food and Agriculture Organisation of the United Nations (FAO) defines "food security" as a state of affairs where all people always have access to safe and nutritious food to maintain a healthy and active life (FAO 1996: 5). Food security thus stands on three pillars:

- food availability or the sustainable production of food;
- economic access to available food;
- achievement of nutrition security—that is, adequate protein, energy, micronutrients, and minerals.

Food security can be measured at different levels, i.e., globally, nationally, at the household level and among individual household members. On a global level, food security for all requires that the supply of food be adequate to meet the total demand for food. While this is a necessary condition for the achievement of food security, it is by no means sufficient: currently, enough food is produced globally, but yet some 800 million people in the developing countries have inadequate access to food, fundamentally because they lack the ability to purchase enough, i.e., the means to exert effective demand. Anyway, global food availability cannot be taken for granted over the long term in view of continuing population growth, increasing land scarcity and mounting difficulties in achieving sustainable increases in food-crop yields. Already today it is foreseeable that even under the level best conditions, food insecurity will remain a nightmare for nearly 700 million people over the next 15 years. It will remain on the agenda of the most important development problems to be solved (see Table 1). Although the 1996 World Food Summit predicted good chances for further progress in the years to come, improvements cannot be expected in all countries, for all members of society, and without substantial investments in good governance efforts, environmental care and technological progress.

Table 1: Estimates and projections of the incidence of chronic undernutrition in developing countries

Region	Year	Total population	Number of undernourished people	
		Millions	% of Population	Millions
Sub-Saharan Africa	1969-71	268	36	103
	1990-92	500	43	215
	2010	874	30	264
Near East/ North Africa	1969-71	178	27	48
	1990-92	317	12	27
	2010	513	10	53
East Asia	1969-71	1,147	41	475
	1990-92	1,665	16	268
	2010	2,070	6	123
South Asia	1969-71	711	33	238
	1990-92	1,138	22	255
	2010	1,617	12	200
Latin America	1969-71	279	19	53
	1990-92	443	15	64
	2010	593	7	40
Total	1969-71	2,583	35	917
	1990-92	4,064	21	839
	2010	5,668	12	680

Source: World Food Summit Technical Background Documents, Vol. 1, p. 9, FAO, Rome 1996.

Within countries, the food-insecure poor comprise different sub-groups, differentiated by location, occupational patterns, asset ownership, race, ethnicity, age, and gender. Most of the poor and malnourished live in rural areas. They tend to be landless or unable to create a food-secure livelihood on the land available to them. In urban areas, household food security is primarily a problem due to low real wage rates (i.e., the rate relative to food prices) and low levels of employment. The prevalence of food deficiency and malnutrition tends to be lower in urban areas than in rural areas. However, urban food insecurity and malnutrition could become an increasingly important problem in the future as rates of urbanisation increase. For instance, by the year 2025, 57 per cent of Africa's population may be urban, as opposed to only 34 per cent in 1990. In South Asia, the figure may be 52 per cent. In Latin America, the urban population had already reached 72 per cent in 1990 (United Nations 1991).

Having adequate household access to food is necessary but not sufficient for ensuring that all household members consume an adequate diet; and consuming an adequate diet is necessary but not sufficient for maintaining a healthy nutritional status. At the household level, access to food can depend on factors such as the age and composition of family members, and the state of their health. In many countries, female-headed households with no adult males are especially likely to have insufficient food. Within households, pregnant and lactating women, whose need for calories is especially high, may consume less than they require to bear and sustain normal-weight, healthy babies. Infants and children (especially girls and children born lower in the birth order) are also less likely than other family members to receive sufficient food.

What factors contribute to food insecurity?

Poverty. Hunger is most prevalent in countries with low per capita incomes. Countries with low per capita incomes tend to have very low agricultural output. For most developing countries, increasing agricultural output for home consumption and export is essential to stimulating economic growth generally, and improving the diets of the poor and hungry. This is so because, despite trade, 90 per cent of the world's grain is consumed in the country where it is produced. Agricultural growth stimulates economic growth in non-agricultural activities, which results in increased employment and reduced poverty. Fostering rural and agricultural development especially among small-holders would make powerful contributions towards increasing household and national food security.

High rates of population growth. The world's most food-insecure countries are also generally those with the fastest growing populations. Countries with low per capita food supplies and with fast growing populations must pay special attention to raising agricultural output. Otherwise, demographic growth alone will increase the total number of hungry people. Rural development, particularly measures that raise the health and productivity of women, can lead to sharp reductions in birth rates, and an increase in well-being for women and children alike.

2.2 Employment and income

From the above, it becomes clear that food insecurity is the characteristic of some people not having enough food. It is not the characteristic of there not being enough food. While the latter can be a cause of the former, it is but one of many possible causes. In explaining hunger and famines, Sen focuses on the failure of entitlements to food acquired by production and trade activities, usually through a market mechanism (Sen 1981, Drèze & Sen 1993). Therefore, while production adequacy is of course important and efforts to increase it need to continue with vigour, it is only part of the picture: In the absence of sufficient purchasing power—or other exchange entitlements—people are unable to exert effective demand for food. Whether and how food security relates to supply in adequate quantity and quality is therefore a matter of empirical investigation.

The distribution of food insecurity is becoming more concentrated among the landless and the urban poor, and, in a regional sense, in Africa and South Asia. With increasingly limited land resources per capita in rural areas, the poor in many low-income countries lack resources. Rapid population growth is paralleled by increasing scarcity of land, which further limits the earnings of the rural poor from farming. Estimates suggest some 13 per cent of rural households in developing countries are landless, and almost 60 per cent have too little land to subsist (UNCHS 1986). Thus, the only resource that many poor people possess is their labour.

There is a large literature on the labour position of the poor and how this differs from the non-poor (e.g., Lipton 1988). Labour constraints tend disproportionately to affect poor people, although in many societies wealth and labour are not independent variables. Labour constraints arise from various factors, and the ways that these are affected by poverty, e.g.,

- poor health;
- lack of appropriate education and skills;
- poverty, because it constrains people's ability to increase their "human capital" via investments in health, education etc.;
- socially defined divisions of labour.

Over the last few years, it has been possible to reach an international consensus on the requirements for the elimination of poverty and on how poverty reduction contributes to other development objectives. This now widely shared view is most clearly expressed in the World Development Report for 1990 (World Bank 1990). The three central elements of this poverty alleviation agenda are:

- economic growth designed specifically to increase the assets and incomes of the poor, with a central focus on employment to promote the productive use of poor people's most abundant asset: labour;
- greater access to social services, especially better health and more education, so as to help poor people realise their potential and reduce their vulnerability; and
- well-targeted transfers and safety nets as an essential complement to the basic strategy.

2.3 Equity

To say that food security depends not merely on food supply but also on its distribution, i.e., on equitable social conditions, is essentially right. It is, however, not remarkably helpful: Countries that have seen negative (or stagnant) growth rates of agricultural production and GDP with a growing population have an ever-diminishing "cake" (and often one that was very small to start with) to share amongst an increasing number of people. Thus economic growth is necessary, and experience shows that it is easier (although never easy) to implement measures that increase equity, particularly if growth is broadly based to include the agricultural sector. Boosting agricultural production stimulates overall economic growth and development, particularly in those countries that have a high economic dependence on agriculture. In such countries, agricultural and rural development acts as an engine for sustainable economic development and poverty alleviation. Agricultural growth, however, requires the availability of new agricultural technologies.

Three aspects of new agricultural technologies influence its effects on equity: (1) the crop, (2) the environment in which the technology is effective, and (3) the factor bias of the technology. Thus, research work on staple foods that are consumed in large quantities by the poor, grown in disadvantaged environments, and produced with labour-using and land-saving technologies tend to promote equity (Barker et al. 1985). Appropriate technological innovations in agriculture reduce the unit costs of production and marketing and induce economic gains by stimulating agricultural growth, improving employment opportunities and expanding food supplies, all of which involve and benefit poor producers and consumers and help to reduce food insecurity. If new agricultural technologies are available, the expansion of agriculture is usually accompanied by increases in income and spending on goods and services, also in non-agricultural sectors. The beneficial effects of agricultural growth are thus spread beyond agriculture.

2.4 Environment

The environment and its natural resource base is one of many kinds of livelihood sources for poor people. Where there is a lack of alternative production factors, a healthy and productive environment is especially important in the livelihoods of the poor. However, based on data compiled by the World Bank, IFPRI and UNCHS, 60 per cent of the world's poorest people live in ecologically vulnerable areas, or so-called "poverty reserves", including rural areas of low agricultural potential, and squatter settlements within urban areas. This spatial distribution of the poorest differs from that of the non-poor (Leonard et al. 1989). Figure 1 shows the distribution of the poorest people across all developing countries by type of environment.

There are various apparent causes of the "poverty reserve" effect. Discriminatory policies and population growth within "poverty reserves" appear to be the most important. Poor people are poor not so much because they live in ecologically vulnerable areas, although environmental degradation may mean they get poorer; it is more often the case that they live in or move to ecologically vulnerable areas because they are poor (Leach and Mearns 1991). This finding makes Sen's entitlement theory even more significant with regard to poor people's access to environmental resources and their ability to make effective use of them. A wide range of factors structure environmental entitlements; among the central factors are:

- natural resource tenure arrangements,
- labour access and arrangements,
- social relations and interactions of kinship, power and status, etc., but also gender relations,

– capital endowments and access to credit.

Figure 1

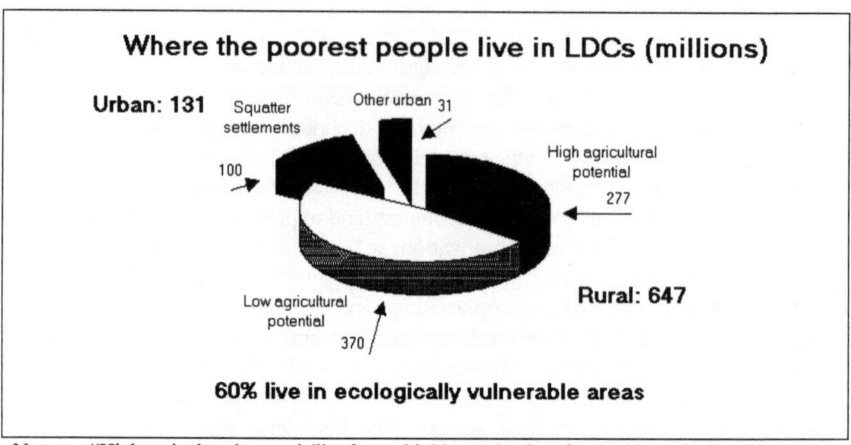

Notes: "High agricultural potential" refers to highly productive, favourable agricultural lands that are either irrigated or have reliable and adequate rainfall, as well as generally high or potentially high soil fertility. "Low agricultural potential" refers to marginal agricultural land, where inadequate or unreliable rainfall, adverse soil conditions, fertility and topography limit agricultural productivity and increase the risk of chronic land degradation.

Source: Leach and Mearns 1991.

The most critical factor, however, appears to be population growth. Of the poorest fifths of developing country households, between 55 and 80 per cent have eight or more members, whereas among all households at national level the proportion is only 15 to 30 per cent (Lipton 1985). These people are usually dependent for their survival upon the environmental resource base of soil, water, forests, fisheries and biota that make up their main stocks of economic capital. Regrettably, they often see scant alternative to exploiting their environmental resource base at a rate they recognise is surely unsustainable. They thereby undercut their principal means of livelihood, thus entrenching their poverty. In turn, poverty appears to reinforce their motivation to have large families (Keyfitz 1990). The problem of land shortages, accompanied by farmland fragmentation, is becoming widespread in many if not most developing countries. This drives many poor people to seek livelihoods in environments that are unsuitable for sustainable agriculture, thus aggravating the pace of land degradation.

The scientific understanding is there, the relevant technologies are available, the economic analyses are in place and the policy imperatives are established to tackle the vicious circle of poverty, population growth and environmental degradation. The urgency of the problem has been acknowledged and concerns have been expressed repeatedly at every conference dealing with these issues. What seems is left is mobilising the political will, improving governance and setting the right priorities.

2.5 Economic Growth

The world economy has grown by an average of 3.5 per cent per year during the last quarter century. However, the pattern of growth has been uneven among countries and within countries. A significant number of developing nations have achieved broad-based economic growth and thereby reduced poverty substantially, but many others have not. A quarter of the world's people remains on the margin of survival, struggling with malnutrition, poor housing, illness, and unemployment. Poverty on this scale is a global problem that makes other global problems worse.

The long-term, broadly based growth of the economy is a precondition for improving the situation. This must necessarily involve the development of the rural economy as a whole, which requires agricultural sector growth, and greatly strengthened linkages within the rural economy and between the rural and the urban economy. In the majority of the low-income countries, where the bulk of the population depends on agriculture, inadequate growth of demand reflects that of incomes of most of the population whose very incomes depend on the growth of agriculture itself.

Whether policies for growth with equity will in fact be adopted depends on whether there is the political will. However, since governments everywhere are brought to power and kept in power by various coalitions of interests, and since those interests are often very narrowly based, it will be difficult to take action that goes against those interests.

2.6 Conclusion

The above paragraphs briefly sketched some interdependent socio-economic factors which account for many of the problems the majority of people face in the low-income countries of the South. Contrary to a still very popular theory, they have neither been created by modern technology, nor will they be solved by modern technology, or better: they cannot be solved by technology alone. There are no technical solutions to social and political problems.

Since agriculture remains a key sector of the economies of most developing countries, nearly independent of their development level, its improvement is a critical factor for the economic development of these countries. However, the socio-economic environment in which this has to happen is characterised by high population pressure, a growing rural exodus, changes in food preferences associated in part with urbanisation, a rapid deterioration of natural resources as well as an unstable and often decaying socio-economic situation. The fast demographic growth in developing countries will push back the agricultural frontiers in many regions, and will increase the intersectoral competition for the use of resources that are progressively getting scarcer, such as water (e.g., drinking water, water for irrigation purposes). In such a context, agriculture in developing countries is confronted with three major challenges in decades to come:

- to increase the availability of nutritious food to an increasing population,
- to use natural ecosystems (including marginal lands) more efficiently and environmentally sustainable in food production, and
- to make a contribution to economic development.

It is not conceivable that this can happen without modern technologies, although more sustainable development policies and improvements in governance are needed first. Thirty years from now there may be 2.5 billion more people to feed in the world, and most of them will live in developing countries. Given that the food security problem is concentrated in these countries, it is proper to speak of it as being a problem of production, even if world markets fail to express it in the form of rising prices. The challenge is world-wide, and both technological and political in nature. The technological challenge is enormous, requiring the development of new, high productivity, environmentally sustainable technologies and production systems. It would therefore be cynical if biotechnology, which has enormous benefits to offer, would be prevented from realising its potential through discredit and mistrust in the minds of an ideologised public, thus leading to the curtailing or withdrawal of funds and leaving the whole of biological research in disarray. The fault of agricultural biotechnology does not lie in its existence, it lies in the fact that it mobilises so much political and ideological resistance against its rational application, especially in the context of countries where it is most needed. Thus, the prophecy that biotechnology will not have helped developing countries solve their most pressing problems, could in the end—ironically—fulfil itself.

3 Agriculture as a growth strategy

For many developing countries, especially those with low per capita income, agriculture is the most effective and frequently the only viable sector to generate economic growth. Very few countries have experienced rapid economic growth without agricultural growth preceding or accompanying it. In the last twenty years countries that experienced real declines in agriculture had the lowest economic growth rates. Agricultural growth stimulates economic growth in non-agricultural sectors, which, in turn, results in increased employment and reduced poverty. This further stimulates demand for agricultural goods, acting as a growth engine in the agricultural sector.

The limited availability of new land, however, means that agricultural intensification—increasing the productivity of land already under cultivation—is the key to alleviating poverty through an agricultural growth strategy. Current concerns that agricultural intensification may lead to degradation of natural resources, while valid, are somewhat misplaced. Lack of access to appropriate technology and modern inputs for agriculture is a much more serious cause of environmental degradation than excessive intensification. Rural poverty, exacerbated by increasing population densities and an inability to produce sufficient food due to inadequate agricultural intensification, is responsible for much of the forced exploitation and consequent degradation of environmentally fragile lands. It is also a major driving factor for the destruction of tropical forests and the consequent loss of biodiversity.

Thus, agricultural growth without technical improvement is possible for a limited time only through resource mining and area expansion (where excess land and labour exist). Such growth, however, neither raises incomes nor is it sustainable. It typically leads to resource degradation. In marginal areas, appropriate agricultural technology can go a long way towards stabilising food availability and facilitating food access for the poor. When agriculture expands into marginal areas or when resource mining occurs, primary and secondary environmental degradation effects may result. Thus, increases in agricultural output or productivity require sustained efforts to improve agricultural technologies and their rate of adoption and to avoid or reverse environmental degradation so that the output increases are not only sustained but sustainable. In other words, sufficient resources must be committed to investment in agriculture on an ongoing basis if the potential output increases at global, regional and country levels are to be realised.

3.1 The importance of biotechnology for agricultural development

3.1.1. The benefits

Agricultural biotechnology can be used to improve the resistance of plants to pests or to environmental stresses, or to increase the commercial value of agricultural products. Other uses for biotechnology include environmentally friendly industrial processes that may reduce the use of harsh or toxic chemicals. The spectrum of anticipated benefits from the application of recombinant genetics and biotechnology in agriculture ranges from diagnostic aids, for example in plant diseases, through to gene mapping, where the genetic characteristics of plants are visibly cartographed, thus enabling a more rapid identification of relevant genetic material for all kinds of plants used in agriculture or forestry.

Genetic engineering and biotechnology are expected to produce seed varieties that enable reliable high yields at the same or lower tillage costs through qualities such as resistance to or tolerance of plant diseases (fungi, bacteria, viruses) and animal pests (insects, mites, nematodes) as well as to stress factors such as climatic variation or aridity. Equally important objectives are the transfer of genes with nitrogen-fixing capacity onto grains, and the improvement of food quality by overcoming vitamin or mineral deficiencies (e.g. in rice). The realisation of these objectives will bring tremendous benefits—benefits that can easily be demonstrated using rice (the staple food for 2.4 billion people) and cassava (the staple food for 500 million people)[3] as examples:

3 All examples quoted from the work of Prof. Ingo Potrykus from the Swiss Federal Institute of Technology in Zürich (Institute of Plant Sciences, ETH Center LFW E.32.1., CH-8092 Zürich, Switzerland).

Rice

— Fungal diseases destroy 50 million metric tons of rice per year; varieties resistant to fungi could be developed through the genetic transfer of proteins with antifungal properties.

— Insects cause a 26 million tons loss of rice per year; the genetic transfer of proteins with insecticidal properties would mean an environmentally friendly insect control.

— Viral diseases devastate 10 million tons of rice per year; transgenes derived from the *Tungro virus* genome allow the plant to develop defence systems.

— Bacterial diseases cause comparable losses—transgenes with antibacterial properties are the basis for inbuilt resistance.

— Vitamin A deficiency is the cause of health problems for more than 100 million children—transgenes will provide provitamin A with the rice diet.

— Iron-deficiency in the diet is a health problem for more than one billion women and children—transgenes will supply sufficient iron in the diet.

Cassava

— The African Mosaic Virus causes immense damages in cassava; transgenes interfering with the life cycle of the virus could lead to virus-resistant varieties.

— Cassava contains toxic cyanogenic glycosides; the integration of transgenes could inhibit their synthesis.

— Cassava roots efficiently store starch but do not contain protein; the transfer of genes for storage proteins would substantially improve their nutritional quality.

— Cassava roots have a basic capacity for provitamin A synthesis, transfer of appropriate genes could lead to regulated accumulation.

A. The physical qualities of modern varieties as they affect the poor

Response to soil nutrients. Many critics claim that if poor farmers cannot afford fertiliser they gain nothing by planting modern varieties (MV) because without fertiliser these varieties yield less than do traditional varieties. MV are indeed designed to produce higher yields if provided with higher levels of soil nutrients, but they convert the nutrients into grain weight more efficiently under any circumstances. In addition, the denser crop cover of MV keeps down weeds. Thus, most MV outyield traditional varieties even if no fertiliser is applied.

Response to light. Direct breeding for greater photosynthetic efficiency was an important accomplishment of CIMMYT and IRRI and their partners in the sixties. The creation of MV with low sensitivity to day light was another. Because such varieties often permit double cropping and a more even food supply during the year, the poor gain most, since agricultural and non-agricultural employment rises and prices stay within a smaller fluctuation or even decrease.

Response to water. MV have been criticised for raising yields only with more water and for being more drought prone than traditional varieties. Actually, most modern varieties are bred to give better returns per unit of water, especially (but not only) where higher nitrogen inputs are used. This fact raises the payoff to farmers.

Fortunately, many MV mature more quickly than traditional varieties and are thereby more likely to escape moisture stress at the end of the growing season. Amongst other crops, barley, millets and sorghums are bred for short maturation times and strong root systems.

Resistance to diseases, pests and weeds. Many critics continue to claim that modern varieties are more susceptible to pests and diseases. Some early MV were indeed highly susceptible, but later varieties have had a significantly better resistance. For example, IR 20 rice lasted ten years before it became susceptible to a newly evolved pest; Sonalika wheat has lasted 20 years. Currently yield increases are sought mainly by raising robustness rather than by sacrificing robustness to greater yield.

B. The distribution of benefits

Over the past four decades, yield increases in the major foodgrains throughout the world have been substantial. Yield levels of maize, rice and wheat nearly doubled over the 1960 to 1994 period. These yield increases are attributable largely to improved varieties, irrigation, fertilisers, and a range of improved crop- and resource-management technologies. Much of this has been part of the Green Revolution. The Green Revolution has expanded farm and non-farm output, employment and wages, thus contributing to food security (Hazell and Ramasamy 1991; Barker et al. 1995). Higher productivity has also reduced the conversion of forests, grasslands and swamplands for cultivation of food crops, thus contributing to the preservation of biodiversity.

Development of short-duration varieties has contributed to higher food production and improved the returns to costly resources used by poor farmers, while crop- and resource-management technologies have improved environmental and resource sustainability. Cultivation of less-favourable lands made possible by new plant varieties (for example drought-tolerant crop varieties) has also contributed to higher food production (Plucknett 1993). Furthermore, it must not be forgotten that innovations in the chemical industry have allowed the price of fertilisers and other agrochemicals to come down in relative terms. Similarly, investments in irrigation infrastructure have helped irrigated agriculture. With cheaper inputs, production costs have come down, and production has been stimulated.

Rapid productivity gains have, in general, decreased food costs and improved food security, particularly for vulnerable sections of society. The urban poor have been important beneficiaries of this downward trend. While landowning households often benefit most from the direct income effects of agricultural growth, landless and small food-deficit farmers often benefit most from the indirect effects such as the generation of off-farm employment. Indirect employment effects that help the poorest households are further facilitated by infrastructural development.

Conventional seed-breeding programs will remain important also in the future. They, however, have a competitive disadvantage in that they have to proceed in small steps towards single targets and are thus time-consuming. If, in contrast, selection systems are developed for the test tube—through characterisation of genetic markers for certain properties, for example—then research can be carried out with a notably greater efficiency. For farmers both large and small this is of sizeable importance (Bunders 1990). The empirical evidence already compiled on the effects of genetic engineering and biotechnological interventions in the agriculture of developing countries allows for the conclusion that the positive impact could prove more far-reaching than that resulting from the application of present-day mechanical and chemical technologies (Bifani 1989; Komen and Persley 1993; IRRI 1992, 1993).

3.1.2 The risks

Despite the widely recognised favourable potential of genetic engineering and biotechnology, their acceptance in the industrial countries is very low. This is mainly due to the perception of the following social and ecological/biological risks:

- dangers to public health and the environment,
- aggravation of the prosperity gap between North and South,
- growing disparities in the distribution of income and wealth within poor societies, as well as
- loss of biological diversity.

The current debate on the "gene revolution" often suffers—like that centred on the Green Revolution—from a failure to distinguish risks inherent to technology from those transcending technology. It is, however, important to make such a differentiation, as only then it is possible to make a rational risk-benefit assessment and to identify ways in which positive effects of agricultural biotechnologies can be enhanced and negative effects minimised.

A. Risks inherent to technology

Risks inherent to technology may be defined as potential hazards that might occur during the research, development or implementation phase of a technology designed to improve an existing situation. The unexpected and harmful interaction of genetically engineered organisms with the environment is an example for this type of risks (biosafety).

(i) Biosafety issues

Since the early 1970s, recombinant DNA technology—the ability to transfer genetic material through biochemical means—has enabled scientists to genetically modify plants, animals and micro-organisms rapidly. Modern biotechnology can also introduce a greater diversity of genes into organisms, including genes from unrelated species, than traditional methods of breeding and selection. Organisms genetically modified in this way are referred to as "living modified organisms" derived from modern biotechnology. Although modern biotechnology has demonstrated its utility, there are concerns about the potential biosafety risks posed by living modified organisms. Many countries with biotechnology industries already have domestic legislation in place intended to ensure the safe transfer, handling, use and disposal of those organisms and their products (these precautionary practices are collectively known as biosafety, see Krattiger and Rosemarin 1994; Persley et al. 1993). However, there are no binding international agreements addressing situations where living modified organisms cross national borders.

There are categories of intended use of living modified organisms: contained use and field release. Living modified organisms intended for contained use are usually research material and are subject to well-defined risk management techniques involving laboratory containment. Living modified organisms developed for agricultural biotechnology are intended for field release. Field testing of living modified organisms is a new undertaking, and the interaction of living modified organisms with various ecosystems continues to generate questions about safety. Some of the concerns about field release of living modified organisms include: unintended changes in the competitiveness, virulence or other characteristics of the target species; the possibility of adverse impacts on non-target species and ecosystems; the potential for weediness in genetically modified crops; and the stability of inserted genes. There is a wealth of scientific literature on the deliberate release of living modified organisms into either new environments or into areas where it could prove particularly harmful. Until today, not one severe biosafety risk has materialised. Therefore, there is a broad consensus amongst scientists that many of the concerns about the release of living modified organisms is unwarranted (Gendel 1990: 341). This judgement supports the early principle of the US National Academy of Science that the safety assessment of a recombinant DNA-modified organism should be based on the nature of the organism and the environment into which it will be introduced, not on the method by which it was modified (Persley 1990: 67 ff.). As a social scientist, I am not competent to pass more than a lay-person's judgement on matters of biosafety. I therefore refer the readers to specialised literature.

(ii) Reduced use of biodiversity

The extent of biological impoverishment all over the globe has been a source of great concern for many years (Vogel 1994; Raven 1985: 8-14). More recently, in the context of genetic engineering and biotechnology, the term "biodiversity" has gained an even wider currency and has tended to become increasingly confusing. Therefore, a little more precision will be required:

The term "biodiversity" is commonly used to describe the number, variety and variability of living organisms. It has become a widespread practice to define biodiversity in terms of genes, species and ecosystems, corresponding to three fundamental and hierarchically related levels of biological organisation: genetic diversity, species diversity, and ecosystem diversity. These conceptual differences are not trivial: the losses in these diversity categories have quite different causes. Not all of them include technology directly or indirectly, and measures intended to maintain one facet of biodiversity will not necessarily maintain another. For example, a timber extraction programme that is designed to conserve biodiversity in the sense of site species richness may well reduce biodiversity measured as genetic variation within the tree species harvested. Clearly, the maintenance of different facets of biodiversity will require different strategies and resources, and will meet different human needs. Different goals have different implications for the elements and extent of biological diversity that must be maintained.

Losses in species diversity are caused by two broad types of human activity: directly by hunting and collection, and indirectly through habitat destruction and modification. Genetic diversity, as represented by genetic differences between discrete populations within wild species, is liable to reduction as a result of the same factors affecting species. The genetic diversity represented by populations of crop plants or livestock is liable to reduction as a result of mass production; the desired economies of scale demand high levels of uniformity. Virtually any form of sustained human activity results in some modification of the natural environment. This modification will affect the relative abundance of species and in extreme cases may lead to extinction. This may result from the habitat being made unsuitable for the species (e.g., clearing of forests[4]), or through the habitat becoming fragmented. A major, though at present largely unpredictable, change in natural environments is likely to occur within the next century as a result of large-scale changes in global climate and weather patterns. There is a high probability that these will cause increased extinction rates, although their exact effects are at present unknown. (Enquête Commission 1990).

Evidently a certain level of biological diversity is necessary to provide the material basis of human life: at one level to maintain the biosphere as a functioning system and, at another, to provide the basic materials for agriculture and other utilitarian needs. The most important direct use of other species is food. Although a relatively large number of plant species, perhaps a few thousand, have been used as food, and a greater number are believed to be edible, only a small percentage of these are nutritionally significant on a global level. It is clear that successful cultivation of agricultural crops on a large scale requires a number of other organisms (chiefly soil micro-organisms and, in a few cases, pollinators) but these probably amount to a statistically insignificant percentage of global biological diversity. But highly productive agricultural systems require the virtual absence of some elements of biological diversity (pest species) from given sites.

Loss of biodiversity as crop varieties and livestock breeds is of near zero significance for overall global diversity, but genetic erosion in these populations is of particular human concern in so far as it has implications for food supply and the sustainability of locally adapted agricultural practices. For domesticated populations the loss of wild relatives of crop or timber plants is of special concern for the same

---

4 The extinction of species has always been a concomitant of evolution but the speed and extent of this process have increased dramatically as a result of the destruction of forests, growing pollution, and other changes in the habitats of threatened species. For details see: Enquête Commission "Vorsorge zum Schutz der Erdatmosphäre" of the German Bundestag 1990: 495.

reason. These genetic resources may not only underlie the productivity of local agricultural systems but also, when incorporated in breeding programmes, provide the foundation of traits (disease resistance, nutritional value, hardiness, etc.) of global importance in intensive systems and which will assume even greater importance in the context of future climate change. Erosion of diversity in crop gene pools is difficult to demonstrate quantitatively, but tends to be indirectly assessed in terms of the increasing proportion of world cropland planted to high yielding, but genetically uniform, varieties. The availability of improved varieties in the field has direct consequences for the diversity of varieties used for food production: Farmers who gain access to varieties that produce higher yields because they are resistant or tolerant against plant diseases and animal pests as well as to stress factors such as poor soil quality will not continue to cultivate inferior varieties. If traditional varieties are not preferable in taste or attractive for cultural reasons, it will simply not be in the farmer's interest to continue to use them. Precisely because farmers find new varieties advantageous, the number of food crop varieties has diminished throughout the world over the last 100 years; farmers discontinue cultivating traditional varieties because modern varieties are more remunerative (see also Smale 1997).

To fight against genetic engineering and biotechnology because they make available superior varieties to the small farmer in developing countries would be the wrong way to join battle against the continuing loss of biodiversity. The availability of high yielding, resistant and tolerant varieties allowed for a substantial increase in hectare productivity: in 1991–93, India produced on average 196 million tons of grain a year, with an average yield of 1.98 tons per hectare. In 1961–63, the yield figure stood at 0.95 tons per hectare. If India would still be using the varieties of the sixties, 208 million hectares of arable land would be needed—116 million more hectares than were available in 1961–63. If the yield per hectare had not doubled, achieving the results recorded in 1991–93 would have required doubling the land under cultivation—a sheer impossibility without causing an ecological disaster by destroying the last remaining forests and converting them to cropland.

To slow down the continuing loss of biodiversity, the main battlefield must be the preservation of tropical forests, mangroves and other wetlands, rivers, lakes and coral reefs. The fact that—from a farmer's economic production point of view—inferior varieties are replaced by superior varieties does not at all have to result in an actual loss of biodiversity. Varieties that are under substitution pressure can be preserved through *in vivo* and *in vitro* strategies and hence be saved from extinction. If this is not done, a highly regrettable loss of biodiversity is likely to occur. As this would be the result of a lack of political will for appropriate conservation strategies, the loss of biodiversity associated with the introduction of improved varieties must be considered to be a technology-transcending risk. Improved governance and international support are necessary to limit this risk. Actually or potentially useful resources should not be lost simply because we do not know or appreciate them at present.

According to my value judgement, however, a risk-benefit analysis is necessary and not only an isolated focus on risks or benefits: in a society with limited resources, also biodiversity has to be evaluated in the light of the benefits it is likely to yield and the costs that are necessary to maintain it. This resource value or cost-benefit approach to conservation, however, may not satisfy those who strive to maintain all currently existing biological diversity. Such justification usually devolves onto two principles—ethics (see also Gendel 1990: 340 ff.) and aesthetics.

Ethics. For some cultures, ethical beliefs provide the strongest grounds for maintaining biological diversity. However, without recourse to an absolutist moral code, it is difficult to argue compellingly for an ethical imperative for the maintenance of all existing biological diversity. Whilst the killing of any living organism may be morally unacceptable to some people, there are problems in extending this argument to the conservation of biological diversity. It seems clear that not all species should be saved from extinction—the HI-virus, the tuberculosis bacteria are obvious examples for this argument. It may be understandable to object to the killing of an elephant on moral grounds, but is it any less moral to eat wheat, which is grown from genetically diverse seeds, than to eat potatoes, most of which are grown from genetically identical clones? Similarly, there are difficulties in demonstrating that one specific species has any greater right to existence as an entity than any one of the individuals of which it is comprised. The fact remains that ethics provides a powerful argument against the destruction of biological diversity. In practice, this argument is often contingent on other grounds, particularly the precautionary principle. For example, it may be considered immoral to destroy something that is now, or may be in the future, regarded as valuable to others. This is embodied in the "stewardship" argument. The principle of inter-generational responsibility underpins the ethical case for conservation in the developed world, although it may be of little practical relevance to a desperate farmer faced with the reality of survival in a developing country.

Aesthetics. Arguments for the maintenance of biological diversity for its aesthetic appeal are compelling but have limited force—especially under conditions of widespread poverty—, as they must be dependent on relative aesthetic judgements. Such judgements could presumably discard some organisms (those not visible to the human eye, for example) as not worthy of being maintained. They are also unlikely to hold sway in the face of counter arguments that certainly exist for the destruction of harmful organisms, such as malarial Plasmodium species. Further, because genetic diversity cannot be subject to aesthetic appreciation, aesthetic criteria can be applied only to species and ecosystem aspects of biodiversity.

Overall, while it is evident that neither ethical nor aesthetic arguments provide of themselves sufficient grounds for attempting to maintain all existing biological diversity, a more general and pragmatic approach recognises that different but equally valid arguments (resource values, precautionary values, ethics and aesthetics, and simple self-interest) apply in different cases, and between them provide enough reason for biodiversity conservation.

B. Risks transcending technology

Risks that transcend technology include the potentially harmful effects on the socio-political fabric and the economy of a society. The most critical fears in this regard are the following:

(i) Aggravation of the prosperity gap between North and South

What is usually discussed under this heading is an international trade issue of a very general nature, i.e. economic risks for some[5] developing countries due to a loss of export opportunities. With genetic engineering and biotechnology it will become possible to produce, in the laboratory or in temperate zones, agricultural products that have hitherto been grown exclusively in the tropics. This prospect gives rise to concerns that the resultant competitive edge could drive a number of tropical products off the market. The example commonly used to shed light on this issue is the production of vanilla aroma in the laboratory using biotechnology threatening the existence of several tens of thousands of vanilla-producing small farmers in poor African countries.

Similar but even more far-reaching consequences could materialise in connection with sugarcane. Countries like Cuba or Mauritius which depend on sugarcane for a significant share of their export earnings could find themselves extremely hard-pressed if the low-calorie protein sweetener thaumatin or similar substances would substitute sugarcane on a broad basis (Sasson 1988: 269-276; Jacobson et al. 1986: 96; Hobbelink 1989: 46; Walgate 1990: 161). The story of thaumatin is one that fits very much into the context discussed here. Some 10 years ago, Nigerian researchers at the University of Ife identified the sweetener thaumatin in the berries of *Thaumatococcus danielli*, which is common in the forests of that part of Nigeria. At that time, no industry was interested in using the fruit as a sweetener. With the advent of modern biotechnology, the gene for thaumatin, a protein weight-for-weight about 1,600 times sweeter than sugar, has been cloned and is now being used for the industrial production of sweeteners in the confectionery industry.

For food crops grown in developing countries this category of risks is of no importance.[6] Nevertheless the risk of aggravation of the prosperity gap between North and South must be addressed: From a holistic political perspective it cannot make sense to uncouple the North from the agricultural raw materials of the South, for this would plunge a large part of humanity into dire misery. It is incompatible with global sustainable development and a peaceful future for all the inhabitants of our planet, if life goes on getting better for a relatively small segment of the world's

5 It is not admissible to make generalizations for "developing countries" lumped together, as this impact differs very much between countries that are net agricultural exporters, for example, and those which must import much of their food (see Commandeur and Roozendaal 1993).

6 There are, however, other technology-trancending risks coming from the "North" such as inappropriate food aid and subsidized export of surplus grain to developing countries, having both a deflating effect on food prices and creating a taste for foreign foods. Both effects work to the economic disadvantage of food crop producers in the South.

already affluent population, while for billions of others their already low living standard stagnates or even shrivels.

From the perspective of economic rationality, however, it has to be expected that superior goods will conquer the market. Copper can serve as an example. Its price is determined by its electrical conductivity. Once electric current can be conducted more efficiently by glass or carbon fibre, or telephone calls are made in future by mobile phones, for instance, copper will in due course no longer be used for this purpose—with corresponding consequences for demand and thus price. The substitution will take place even though crumbling prices may lead, in countries like Zambia or Chile, to mass unemployment with all the human distress this involves.

The same market "logic" tells us to expect that if "lab vanilla" or "lab sugar" should prove cheaper or exhibit some other advantage—be healthier than the real thing, for example—over products previously imported from the South, then substitution will follow. Ultimately, this process cannot be forestalled, not even by sizeable government intervention—which is not desirable anyway. The solution to the product substitution problem must therefore lie in international endeavours to diversify the production structure in vulnerable countries and not in counter-market intervention.

In the context of the aggravation of the prosperity gap between North and South there is one further important issue that has to be examined: who shall compensate whom for the use of genetic material from developing countries and how much shall the compensation amount to? There is widespread fear that private enterprises and research institutes could gain control over plant genetic resources of the developing world free of charge, as it were, and use them for developing and producing superior varieties that would then be sold back to developing countries at high prices. Suppose a private seeds company would discover a property in an Ethiopian barley strain, make it resistant to certain plant diseases and genetically transfer this property to a wheat variety that would afterwards be commercialised in Ethiopia. Obviously, the farmers of Ethiopia, both male and female, have contributed something by selecting and preserving this variety over a long time. It is also obvious that without the research and development work of the seeds company the "something" would not have been turned to use outside Ethiopia or in food grains other than the native barley. So, both parties, the farmers of Ethiopia and the seeds company, have contributed to the new wheat variety, and therefore both have some kind of an intellectual property right and thus a right to compensation.

The basic question whether compensation is due has been clearly and positively answered by Article 19 of the Rio Convention on Biological Diversity (UNCED 1992) and the virtually unanimous consensus of the agencies engaged in development. Whereas the general political decision in favour of compensation has been taken, the technical details of how it should be handled in specific nations are still unclear. What especially needs unequivocal regulation is who should compensate whom for what, and how much this compensation should be. As a rough first approach, I would recommend that the issue be dealt with in terms of a licence agreement and the price left to the mechanism of supply and demand. Those who benefit should pay the license fee to those who over centuries through their hard agricultural work helped to preserve the varieties in question. The unimproved genetic wealth of the world's Vavilov centres should be considered as common heritage of humankind.[7]

As money resulting from a fair compensation arrangement should not land in the private pockets of a corrupt upper-class that, because its members are politically powerful, has ready access to the pot, I would further recommend that such funds are dealt with multilaterally and go into the CGIAR system. As the Consultative Group for International Agricultural Research already exists and does excellent work for the poor farmers of the world, one would not have to create a new institution. Instead, CGIAR or its subsidiary, the International Service for National Agricultural Research (ISNAR) could be requested to draft a proposal outlining how to deal with such compensation fees in a fair and constructive way.

(ii) Risks rooted in growing disparities in the distribution of income and wealth in poor societies

The use of genetically modified seeds adapted to the specific conditions of difficult biotopes can no doubt provide most desirable driving forces to national agricultural development as well as tremendous benefits to all farmers who use them. In a socially and politically deficient setting, it can hardly bring about improvements in the condition of those who are not able to use the new varieties. Where land ownership and tenancy systems, access to extension services, credit and marketing channels as well as to new technologies are governed by a socio-political power structure that favours only a small minority, technological progress cannot possibly be neutral in impact.

The answer to the question of who benefits and how much from the advent of new technologies and to what extent economic and social progress can be achieved virtually depends on the social and political configuration in place. Disease-resistant cassava, millet richer in protein or rice tolerant to stress can contribute to prosperity and thus enhanced food security only if the new varieties and other social advances come within the reach of the broad mass of the population, male and female. Whether this is possible and within what time depends on the political will to create the necessary national development framework. As poor farmers tend to be risk-minimising and not output-maximising, even under the best social circumstances, early adopters stand to gain earlier.

Today's review on the effects of the Green Revolution shows that in countries where small farmers were supported by agricultural extension services, where they had access to land, inputs and credit—in other words, where the agricultural development framework assisted the endeavours of the small farmers—they were able to

7 This does, however, not exclude that commercial enterprises which have an interest in the biological inventory of a specific biotope must pay a negotiated amount of money for the right of prospecting. See in this context the contract between Costa Rica's Conservation Program/National Biodiversity Institute (INBio) and Merck & Co., Ltd. in: Reid et al. 1993: 255.

benefit much more and earlier. Even where the Green Revolution made the "rich" richer because they could use the new technologies earlier, on better land, with better inputs and less expensive credits, the poor also benefited over time becoming less poor as agricultural modernisation proceeded. This may not be the best of all social results one could imagine, but in a world where more than 1.3 billion people live in absolute poverty such achievements should not go unappreciated.

Like the Green Revolution, genetically engineered crop varieties are a land-saving technology and, as such, can be of particular importance to those who have little or only marginal land. Whether the potential benefits become economic and social reality for the small farmers is not a question of the technology but of the social quality of the development policy. If land and tenure reforms are implemented, if there is support for the small farmers and other elements of a development-friendly environment, the benefits of a new technology can be scale-neutral. Where 90 per cent of the land belongs to three per cent of the population and where the agricultural extension and credit services are only available to the big landholders, the introduction of a new technology will deepen the gap between incomes. The economic and social impact of genetic engineering and biotechnology can only be as good as the socio-political soil in which the resulting new varieties are planted.

4 Conclusion: Ambivalence of technological progress

In assessing the impact of genetic engineering and biotechnology on food security, we must live with ambivalence: on the one hand, there are clear benefits from genetic engineering and biotechnology for food security. They have the potential to increase production and productivity, enhance the environment, and improve food safety and quality (Wambugu et al. 1995). These desirable contributions towards food security and the common good in general have to be set against a number of economic, social and ecological risks, most of which are of a technology-transcending nature, i.e. neither caused nor preventable by the technology as such. In this respect, progress with genetic engineering and biotechnology is no different from any other form of technological and societal progress, which, as the German theologian Helmut Gollwitzer (1985: 142) said, is "nothing other than the unremitting struggle to secure its positive aspects, learning to live with the dangers that come with it and surmounting the impairments it causes." Exactly what constitutes the "positive aspects", "dangers" and "impairments" in a given case is disputable. The value of a certain effect of technological progress is very much a function of individual value judgements. Solutions in the sense of a final decision on the ethical dilemma thus conjured up are not possible. Depending on how someone judges the worth of a good gained or lost through the march of technology, either the gain or the loss will have a heavier weight.

Technological innovation is no panacea—it is just one stone in a large and complex socio-economic mosaic. Whether the economic blessing becomes a social curse depends on the political and the broad social ramifications. A technology can only be as good as the social fabric permits. Only when poor small farmers have access to land, agricultural extension services, marketing opportunities, working equipment and fair terms of credit, can higher-yielding bring noteworthy advantages and more food to the masses of small farmers.

There is no way of evading the ambivalence that is intrinsic to every technical advance. But the existence of ambivalence and ethical dilemmas should not paralyse us. On the contrary, it must serve to clarify the course of action and expand our horizon of responsibility. Only action that is informed by an awareness of the ambivalence makes the socially meaningful deployment of top-class technology possible.

To secure positive economic and social development possibilities in the South and the North, what is needed are political and social national as well as international reforms (Serageldin 1994). At the same time, along with its utilitarian alignment it would be desirable that technological progress take on a socio-ethical orientation.[8] If genetic engineering and biotechnology were oriented to a greater extent on the needs of the poor in developing countries they could become indispensable to the whole development effort.

More publicly financed research North and South is summoned to make a bigger contribution to finding expedient solutions. The emphasis is on public research, because the fruits of public research can be passed on to small farmers at cost or, via government channels, even free of charge. This cannot be done with the results of research sponsored by private enterprise. For this reason public research must be strengthened. The Consultative Group on International Agricultural Research (CGIAR) with its focus on the needs of the developing countries could play a conspicuous role in such an effort. In a number of countries, agricultural biotechnology seminars are already under way to assess research priorities and turn them into feasible programs (Komen, Cohen and Ofir 1996; Komen, Cohen and Sing-Kong 1995; Brenner 1996).

More ought to be done in this respect. And there must be more and more intensive cooperation between the private and the public sector. The special knowledge and know-how and the different experience—and patented intellectual property as well—that are at the disposal of the private sector but are used only selectively for lucrative markets in the industrial countries could be passed on via donated transfers or very favourable licensing terms to public research institutes in developing countries. This can be done, as a concrete example shows: Novartis has made available a gene of *Bacillus thuringiensis* to IRRI, the International Rice Research Institute. Cooperation with the private sector and other "coalitions for food security" could be an important unconventional way to make progress faster and less expensive.

Sustainable food security will not be achievable without better governance and a new dimension of solidarity between the "rich" and the "poor" of this world—but also not without new technologies such as genetic engineering and biotechnology.

8 For an introduction see Qizilbash and the references.

References

Ambio (Journal of the Human Environment) (1992): Economics of Biodiversity Loss, Vol. XXI, No. 3, May.

Barker, R., R.W. Herdt and B. Rose (1985): The Rice Economy of Asia. Resources for the Future, Washington, D.C.

Bifani, P. (1989): New Biotechnologies for Rural Development, ILO (Technology and Employment Programm), Geneva.

Brenner, C. (1996): Integrating Biotechnology in Agriculture—Incentives, Constraints and Country Experiences, Paris.

Bunders, J.F.G. (1990): Biotechnology for small-scale farmers in developing countries—Analysis and assessment procedures, Amsterdam.

CGIAR (1992): Feeding the World—Protecting the Environment. UN Briefing Co-sponsored by the World Bank, UNDP and FAO, Washington, D.C.

Chen, Z. and H. Gu (1993): Plant Biotechnology in China, in: Science, Vol. 262.

Commandeur, P. and G. Roozendaal (1993): The Impact of Biotechnology on Developing Countries—Opportunities for Technology-Assessment Research and Development Cooperation. A Study Commissioned by the Büro für Technikfolgen-Abschätzung (TAB) in the German parliament, Bonn 1993, Chapter 3.

Coppenger, M. (1985): Bioethics—A Casebook, New Jersey.

Drèze, J. and A. Sen (1989): Hunger and Public Action, Oxford.

Edwards, R. (1996): Tomorrow's bitter harvest, in: Scientist, 17.8.1996, p.17 ff.

Ehrlich, P.R. (1988): The Loss of Biodiversity. Causes and Consequences, in: Wilson, E.O. (Publ.): Biodiversity, Washington, D.C.

Ehrlich, P.R. and A. Ehrlich (1992): The Value of Biodiversity, in: Ambio, Vol. 21, No. 3, pp. 219-226.

Enquête Commission "Vorsorge zum Schutz der Erdatmosphäre" of the German Bundestag (Eds.) (1990): Schutz der Tropenwälder. Eine internationale Schwerpunktaufgabe, Bonn.

FAO (1992): Nutrition and Development, a Global Assessment. Rome.

FAO (1995): World Agriculture: Towards 2010. N. Alexandratos, ed. Rome, FAO and, Chichester, UK, John Wiley. (Published also in French by Polytechnica, Paris, and in Spanish by Mundi-Prensa Libros, Madrid and Mexico.)

FAO (1996): The sixth world food survey, Rome.

FAO (1996): Food Security Assessment (Document WFS 96 / Tech/7), Rome.

Gendel, S.M. (1990): Biotechnology and Bioethics, in: S.M. Gendel, A.D. Kline, D.M. Warren, and F. Yates (Eds.): Agricultural Bioethics. Implications of Agricultural Biotechnology, Ames.

Gollwitzer, H. (1985): Krummes Holz—Aufrechter Gang: Zur Frage nach dem Sinn des Lebens, München.

Hazell, P.B.R. and C. Ramasamy (1991): The Green Revolution Considered, Baltimore.

Hobbelink, H. (1989): Bioindustrie gegen die Hungernden, Reinbek, p. 46 ff.

Hobbelink, H. (1991): Biotechnology and the Future of World Agriculture, London.

International Rice Research Institute (IRRI) (1992): Sharing Responsibilities: Irri 1991-1992, Los Baños.

International Rice Research Institute (IRRI) (1993): Rice Research in a Time of Change, Los Baños .

Jacobson, S., A. Jamison and H. Rothman (Eds.) (1986): The Biotechnological Challenge, Cambridge.

Keyfitz, N. (1990): Population Growth can Prevent the Development that Would Slow Population Growth, Laxenburg, Austria.

Komen, J. and G. Persley (1993): Agricultural Biotechnology in Developing Countries, ISNAR Research Report 2, The Hague.

Komen, J., J.I. Cohen and Z. Ofir (Eds.) (1996): Turning Priorities into Feasible Programs, The Hague.

Komen, J., J.I. Cohen and Sing-Kong Lee (Eds.) (1995): Turning Priorities into Feasible Programs, The Hague.

Krattiger, A.F. and A. Rosemarin (Eds.) (1994): Biosafety for Sustainable Agriculture, Stockholm.

Leach, M. and R. Mearns (1991): Poverty and the Environment in Developing Countries: An Overview Study, London.

Leonard, H.J. with M. Yudelman, J.D. Stryker, J.O. Browder, A.J. De Boer, T. Campbell and A. Jolly (1989): Environment and the Poor—Development Strategies for a Common Agenda, in: US-Third World Policy Perspectives, No. 11, Washington, D.C.

Lewis, W.A. (1953): Report on industrialization and the Gold Coast, Government Printing Office, Accra,Ghana.

Lipton, M. (1988): The Poor and the Poorest—Some Interim Findings, World Bank Discussion Papers No. 25, Washington, D.C.

Miflin, B.J. (1992): Plant Biotechnology—Aspects of its Application in Industry, in: Proceedings of the Royal Society of Edinburgh , Vol. 99b, Nr.3/4, pp. 153-163.

Miller, K.R. (1996): Balancing The Scales—Guidelines for Increasing Biodiversity's Chances Through Bioregional Management, Washington, D.C.

Myers, N. (1979): The Sinking Ark—A New Look at the Problem of Disappearing Species, New York.

Perrings, C., C. Folke and K.G. Müller (1992): The Ecology and Economics of Biodiversity Loss—The Research Agenda, in: Ambio, Vol. 21, No. 3, p. 205.

Persley, G.J. (1990): Beyond Mendel's Garden—Biotechnology in the Service of World Agriculture, Washington, D.C.

Persley, G.J., L.V. Giddings and C. Juma (1993): Biosafety—The Safe Application of Biotechnology in Agriculture and the Environment, ISNAR Research Report No.5, The Hague.

Plucknett, D.L. (1993): International Agricultural Research for the next century, in: Bioscience, Vol. 43, No. 7, pp. 432-440.

Qizilbash, M.: Ethical Development, in: World Development, Vol. 24, No. 7, pp. 1209-1221.

Raven, P.H. (1985): Disappearing Species—A Global Tragedy, in: The Futurist, Vol. 19, No. 5, pp. 8-14.

Reid, W.V. et al. (1993): Biodiversity Prospecting—Using Genetic Resources for Sustainable Development, Washington, D.C.

Report of the International Conference on Population and Development, Cairo, 5-13 September 1994.

Report of the United Nations Conference on Environment and Development, Rio de Janeiro, 3-14 June 1992, Vol. I, Resolutions Adopted by the Conference (United Nations publication, Sales No. E.93.I.8).

Sasson, A. (1988): Biotechnologies and Development, Paris.

Sen, A. (1981): Poverty and Famines: an Essay on Entitlement and Deprivation, Oxford.

Serageldin, I. (1994): Nurturing Development—Aid and Cooperation in Today's Changing World, Washington D.C.

Smale, M. (1997): The Green Revolution and Wheat Genetic Diversity: Some unfounded Assumptions, in: World Development, Vol. 25 (1997), No. 8, pp. 1257-1269.

The World Resources Institute, UNEP, UNDP and the World Bank (1996): World Resources—A Guide to the Global Environment 1996-97, New York.

UNCHS (1986): Global Report on Human Settlements, 1986, United Nations Centre for Human Settlements.

United Nations (1974): Assessment of World Food Situation, Present and Future, World Food Conference Document E/CONF. 65/3, New York, NY, USA, United Nations.

United Nations (1991): World Population Prospects 1990, Population Studies No. 120, New York, NY, USA, United Nations.

United Nations (1993): World Population Prospects: the 1992 Revision, New York, NY, USA, United Nations.

United Nations (1994): World population prospects: the 1994 revision. Annex, tables. New York, NY, USA, United Nations.

Vogel, J.H. (1994): Genes for Sale—Privatization as a Conservation Policy, New York.

Walgate, R. (1990): Miracle or Menace—Biotechnology and the Third World, London.

Walker, J.M. and E.B. Gingold (1992): Molecular Biology and Biotechnology, Cambridge.

Wambugu, F., E. Zandvoort and K.V. Raman (Eds.) (1995): Biotechnology and Risk Assessment in an African Perspective. Special Issue of the African Crop Science Journal on Biotechnology/Biosafety, Vol. 3.

World Bank (1988): Social Indicators of Development 1988, Baltimore.

World Bank (1990): Poverty: World Development Report, Oxford.

World Bank (1996): Global Economic Prospects and the Developing Countries, 1996, Washington, DC, World Bank.

World Commission on Environment and Development (1987): Our Common Future. Report of the World Commission on Environment and Development, Oxford.

24

Linking Grassroots Solutions to Global Policies: The Role of Southern NGOs in the Fight Against Hunger

Peter Uvin

The war against world hunger is fought on many battlefields by troops seeking to increase agricultural production, improve basic health care, increase people's incomes, improve the quality of the environment, change dietary practices, protect households against exceptional entitlement shortfalls, curb fertility rates, assure access to land, water, seeds, etc. It is often forgotten that it is poor households, rural and urban, that do most of this fight, on a daily basis—just as they are the casualties when the battles are lost. Third World governments, and bi- and multilateral development agencies sometimes assist households and communities in these battles, but their capacities, willingness, and resources are often limited.

Increasingly, people in the development community have come to realize that the answers to the problems of hunger, poverty, and environmental degradation must come—and are coming—primarily from the local communities themselves; they have consequently set out to develop mechanisms to tap into these local dynamics, strengthen and support them. In this respect, the veritable explosion of community-based, participatory, grassroots action in most of the Third World over the last two decades is very encouraging: everywhere one looks, people are organizing to fight erosion, increase production and incomes, create safety nets, supply credit and other inputs, improve their own and their children's health, etc.

This chapter seeks to present a brief overview of the potential of NGOs and GROs for contributing to the eradication of hunger and poverty. Part one will briefly present the extent and the origins of recent explosion in the NGO sector. Parts two to four will discuss the impact of these new organizations on hunger, distinguishing three roles they play that affect hunger: they work with and provide services to poor and hungry people worldwide, lobby for new policies by governments and international organizations to overcome hunger, and participate in the implementation of these policies. The article's focus is primarily on Third World NGOs and GROs, although it will sometimes also touch upon their First World NGO partners.

1 The multiplication of actors

Throughout the world, tens of thousands of NGOs now exist, and hundreds of thousands if not millions of grassroots organizations (GROs) have come into being. Estimates for international NGOs (operating in more than 3 countries) hover around 20,000, which represents a doubling in the last half-decade. National NGOs have grown faster still and number at least 50,000 in the Third World; they are multiplying quickly in the rich countries also. The number of GROs runs into the millions and is growing exponentially. All in all, there is now a vast and diverse array of peasant associations, neighborhood committees, people's movements, alternative trade organizations, community initiatives, urban action committees, support NGOs, producer cooperatives, women's associations, consumers' organizations, savings and loan associations, and NGO networks and federations, filling the ranks of what is often referred to as the "associative" or "third" sector (as distinct from the "first" or public and the "second" or private/corporate sector).

The causes of this trend are multiple. In the field of overcoming hunger and poverty, they relate first and foremost to "government failure," i.e., the fact that, for various reasons, governments throughout the world have been unable to provide goods and services in the quantity or the manner desired by people—or promised by governments themselves. In many countries, this government failure was accompanied by the early 1980s by massive public debts, often leading to profound financial crises and slowdowns in economic growth.

This has led to movements both against the state and against politics-as-usual. As to the latter, the growth in NGOs has coincided with a profound crisis in political party affiliation and voting behavior in Europe, the US, and South America. As to the former, the legitimacy of the state is questioned, and there is a widespread feeling that the public sector is an inefficient, ineffective, unjust, and costly mechanism for promoting social change.

This questioning of the legitimacy of the state took place at two distinct levels, and from two very different perspectives. At the international level, and foremost within the Bretton Woods institutions and some bilateral donor agencies (USAID, ODA), a longstanding conservative ideology of state disengagement, privatization, and unbridled free market competition (re-)gained dominance. This ideology favors the private sector: enterprises to produce wealth, and NGOs to redistribute it—whether in the U.S. and Western Europe, the former Soviet bloc, or the Third World. In the Third World, structural adjustment, mandated by the debt crisis, turned out to be a powerful tool for realizing this ideology. In the second half of the 1980s, country after country was forced to liberalize, dismantle state interventions (in agriculture and food, this primarily meant dismantling marketing boards and quotas, and cutting subsidies on inputs and consumption), and favor exports.

From the grassroots level, this disappointment with the state led to an explosion in self-help initiatives and agencies for social change. Many of these sought to substitute for the state, and propel local change while preserving their autonomy from the state. Others sought to combat what they considered inefficient or bad state policies. Still others had new goals of cultural or environmental preservation, human rights protection, etc. All were characterized, however, by a similiar attitude of going it alone, of promoting change outside of the state.

To a certain extent, this movement was parallelled by a third dynamic: a more or less longstanding, none-too-radical, rather managerial concern with participation and community mobilization among development practitioners. Evaluation after evaluation had shown that the development projects financed and managed by international and bilateral organizations and governments lacked sustainability, and that the prime cause for this was the failure to involve local communities and to ensure their participation. NGOs were seen as having comparative advantages in precisely these fields: flexibility, community trust, capacity to work with the poorest households, often in remote areas, and in-depth knowledge of local situations (Clark 1994: 5-6). Hence, increasing amounts of development aid have been channelled through Northern and Southern NGOs (and through them, to GROs), and their creation has been actively supported, even in projects that do not have "community development" as their prime goal.

All three of these factors interact in complex ways. The availability of international funding clearly provides opportunities for local professionals and grassroots leaders to expand beyond what could have been done by internal means alone; on the other hand, the preponderant role of foreign money poses the risk that the agendas and dynamics of these new organizations may be determined by foreign interests. The financial-economic crisis of most Third World governments and the withdrawal of the state provides institutional niches that people can seek to fill through the creation of new organizations; on the other hand, reduced and weakened states are not necessarily beneficial for NGOs and GROs or for development on the whole.

More generally, the surprising ideological alliance between grassroots empowerment groups—usually quite radical, anti-establishment or anti-status-quo—and neo-liberal, balanced budget/free market advocates, is quite unique, and it is unclear if it will last long. As to many Third World governments, their acceptance of NGOs is often reluctant, the result of international pressure and their own lack of resources or alternatives, rather than a real appreciation of the benefits of grassroots empowerment. For many governments and most donors, NGOs are now the preferred subcontractors, but that can imply roles for NGOs that may not be to their best interest or those of the communities they serve.

At the same time, and partly as a result of this explosion of new organizations, the older, existing actors have changed their roles. Extension agents from Ministries of Agriculture all over the world are adopting modes of operation that seek to create and support local initiatives, while peasant leaders emerge as credible partners in research and extension systems; traditional village authorities are asked to become co-managers of common property resource management systems, while NGO staff substitute for commercial banks in developing innovative financial services; government agencies are redefining their role as the creation of "enabling environments" rather than the execution of programs or the provision of economic services, while private companies are being established by NGOs now selling directly into foreign markets. Thus, old and new actors are redefining their roles and building often tentatively bridges with each other.

2 NGOs working with the poor and the hungry

The first way that these new non-governmental organizations impact on hunger is through their direct work with poor and hungry people. As said above, the enormous institutional diversity of NGOs, and the range of their fields of action, makes it hard to generalize. In other work, we have analyzed the records of 25 Third World NGOs and GROs that had been nominated for, or awarded, the Alan Shawn Feinstein World Hunger Award, an annual prize given at Brown University to organizations that have made "extraordinary efforts or contributions to the reduction of hunger in the world or its prevention in the future." These 25 organizations are considered by their peers to be especially meritorious in combating world hunger.

These organizations include both NGOs and GROs; they range from large, famous organizations such as BRAC (Bangladesh Rural Advancement Committee, the Third World's largest NGO, active in education, health, credit, rural development, etc.) and Sarvodaya Shramadana (a Buddhist inspired grassroots movement in Sri Lanka seeking economic and spiritual development) to much smaller and lesser known ones such as the Committee for the Fight to End Hunger (COLUFIFA, Senegal, a farmers' group active in various aspects of food production) and the Women's Organization of Independecia (WARMI, Peru, managing a series of soup-kitchens). Some of them are supported with tens of millions of dollars of external aid money, and increasingly resort to subcontracting for both the state and international organizations, while others have budgets in the tens of thousands of dollars, and volunteer effort is the key to their dynamics. It is interesting to see the type of activities these organizations—all supposedly successful in combatting hunger—are active in.

None of these NGOs remained limited to their original activity, and quite a few of them are active in a great many areas of human life. Most of them went through broad processes of diversification, reflecting the needs of their members or clients. An organization such as BRAC, for example, now manages dozens of programs in health, education, and economic activity, but even COLUFIFA is engaged in health, agriculture, food, and education.

In quite a few of these cases, the functional scaling up that took place was of a "horizontal integration" type, such as adding activities in forestry, environmental protection, education, or artisanal production to agriculture. Sarvodaya Shramadana has become active over the years in preschools, literacy, conservation, drug and alcohol rehabilitation, legal aid, micro-enterprise, relief and rehabilitation in war zones, and water supply. Similarly, Gram Vikas, an Indian NGO working with tribal people in Orissa, is active in the fields of social forestry, primary health care, adult education, legal aid, small enterprise credit, irrigation, fishery, bio-gas plants, and disaster relief. This is a typical process for many community-based organizations: as they scale up, they are drawn into all other aspects of life, eventually becoming integrated rural development (IRD) agencies, covering everything from basic human services to income generation. Note that the donor agencies have largely abandoned IRD projects, finding them too difficult to manage.

Other organizations followed paths of vertical integration. WARMI, for example, after a decade of managing soup kitchens, began developing an alternative food purchasing and distribution network; it also entered the health sector. BRAC added factories and outlets to its artisan training program. The most common case of vertical integration consists of the addition of savings and credit mechanisms to the original activities of the organizations. This seems to indicate the great lack of access to credit by the rural poor in the Third World—a fact now (overly) enthusiastically recognized by the development community.[1]

Twenty-one out of the 25 organizations studied primarily focused on economic activities. This reflects the fact that, for the majority of poor people, any investment of their time, energy and money depends foremost on the perceived capacity of that investment to generate additional income. Only later, when a higher and more stable productive base has been assured, were non-economic activities added: health, nutrition, education and training, etc.

Looking at hunger and the processes that lead to it, we observe that only four of the 25 organizations started out in areas directly designed to fight hunger: cereal banks, soup kitchens, improved food production methods, and vegetable gardening. Approximately half of them, though, had activities to increase food production. Two of them also invest in improved storage, again with the explicit goal of reducing hunger. Often, it is impossible to separate whether an action is designed to increase income or fight malnutrition. The introduction of vegetable gardening by COLUFIFA, for example, was justified both by improved nutrition and by income generation.

None of the organizations studied started in health, but most of them took on health-related activities. This is justified less by the goal of reducing hunger than by the fact that for most people, recurrent sickness and the absence of decent health care are among their main frustrations in life. If they feel they can change that, they are willing to invest their own resources. For the vast majority of these organizations, family planning or the provision of contraceptives is not an important field of action. To my knowledge, only BRAC and IIRR (International Institute of Rural Reconstruction, a Philippine-based research and training NGO) have some activities in that sector, as part of their health programs.

1 The recently created Consultative Group to Assist the Poorest (CGAP) under the leadership of the World Bank is basically a mechanism to directly finance Grameen Bank-type micro-credit schemes throughout the world: it is very popular in the development community.

3 The conceptual (r)evolution

The institutional change in the development community is paralleled by a shift in the definition of food security and the ways to overcome hunger from an almost exclusive focus on national/food production issues to a much broader attention to household/well-being ones. The capacity of NGOs and GROs to influence the policies of their own governments—often non-democratic ones—and international organizations—non-accountable to citizens—is of as much importance as their role in working directly in communities. It is the only way to modify the agendas of some of the world's major players, and ensure supportive policies from them.

Hunger for the first time moved high on the international agenda early in 1974, when, on the initiative of the U.S. and the Group of 77, the World Food Conference was organized in Rome. At the time, food security was defined as access by states to stable quantities of food. This state-centric definition was no accident: state representatives were the only participants at the Conference, and it was generally believed that the world had inadequate food to feed its population and that the situation was becoming worse. The global food production shortfall and the simultaneous Asian and African famines of the years 1972-74 were considered the first dramatic warning signs of this trend. Thus, the emphasis lay on the Green Revolution and agricultural technology, national and international food stocks, and food aid and trade.

Twenty years later, the FAO, in collaboration with the WHO, organized the International Conference on Nutrition. Among the participants at that conference, we find the UN Member States, joined by 150 or so NGOs; there were also a fair number of NGO members on official delegations. A much more complex and holistic approach to hunger became dominant, and food security was now defined in terms of household and individual access to adequate food, income, and health care. The 1996 Food Summit, a high-level worldwide conference, also involved hundreds of NGOs, whose opinions were solicited, before and during the conference, in dozens of regional conferences. Its scope of work was the broadest, dealing with the traditional aspects of research, education, population, fisheries, extension, and marketing, as well as new ones such as water, women, forests, the environment, urbanization, and climate change. Many of these issues owe their place on the international hunger agenda to NGO pressure, especially if we include a group neglected until now—scientific and research organizations—within the NGO category! And the recent arrival of micro-credit at the top of the development/hunger agenda is almost entirely due to NGO policy innovation, from the famous Grameen Bank in Bangladesh and American PVOs such as Trickle Down, Technoserve, or Accion, to thousands of small programs throughout the world.

Also of interest are two lesser known recent international conferences on hunger in which the central participants were not states and their representatives, but NGOs and GROs. The first one was the November 1993 World Bank Hunger Conference, held in Washington; the second one the November 1995 IFAD Conference on Overcoming Hunger and Poverty in Brussels. In both these conferences, the agendas were set by international organizations and NGO representatives together, and concrete follow-up mechanisms were developed in which NGOs are playing a key role.

Not surprisingly, at these conferences the emphasis lay on different issues, in particular popular participation and empowerment, defined not only in terms of access to decision-making but also in terms of access to productive resources, came to be the key concepts of both these conferences. The participation agenda is also a prime way for the NGOs to use international organizations to put pressure on their own governments to become more receptive to the voices of the grassroots—what Sikkink in another context has called the "boomerang effect."

At both conferences, structural adjustment was strongly condemned by the NGO sector. More generally, the world trading system, including the new GATT/WTO rules, or the policies of the Bretton Woods institutions are subject to profound and longstanding NGO criticism. Contrary to the environment and participation agendas, these criticisms have been almost entirely without effect, as they are crucially related to the political and ideological core of the global political economy.

Also of interest is the absence of the NGO sector in certain other areas related to hunger. One of the most important, and vocal, schools of thought links hunger causally to over-population. This vision of hunger, and the resulting actions in terms of family planning, is very widely accepted among the major development institutions in the North, and strongly promoted by a small set of very vocal American NGOs (and increasingly strongly counteracted by an equally small and vocal set of conservative, religious American GROs!). Third World NGOs, however, have been by and large absent from this field, both in their operational activities and in their advocacy work. At the International Conference on Population and Development in Cairo, 1995, Southern and Northern NGOs have managed to reframe family planning as a matter of women's rights and health care—a quite different vision of the usual "overpopulation" ones.

Another hunger-related field in which NGOs are conspicuously absent concerns agricultural research. It is clear that technological breakthroughs will be required to feed the world's growing population into the 21st century, while at the same time funding for agricultural research has been decreasing consistently for many years now. Moreover, most of the world's GROs and NGOs are active in the agricultural sector, occasionally collaborating with national or regional agricultural research institutions. Yet, the NGO community has not spoken out loud on this matter, and no major international coalitions have formed around it. The reasons for this may be a combination of the lack of technological sophistication of most NGOs, as well as a history of mutual indifference, if not antagonism, between them and the national and regional agricultural research institutions.

One last issue the development NGO community has not touched at all is the one of human rights. The separation between development NGOs and human rights NGOs remains almost total—a surprising and unfortunate situation, given that, for many GROs and NGOs, human dignity and people's rights constitute their raison d'être. In this respect, the NGO community seems to have adopted largely the same technical vision of development as the international aid community, characterized by an almost total blindness to human rights (Tomasevski 1989).

4 NGO participation in international policies to overcome hunger

NGOs and GROs have not only been able to infuse new voices into international policy discourses related to hunger, they also increasingly participate in the implementation and surveillance of the resulting policies.

NGOs have taken upon themselves an important function of surveillance. They collect and disseminate information so as to hold governments and international organizations accountable to the policies they commit themselves to. By far the most famous and successful field of surveillance by NGOs is the human rights one, which is usually limited, however, to the defense of a few basic civil rights. FIAN (the Food First Information Action Network) is a unique international NGO devoted to protecting the right to food. Combined with their lobbying capacity, NGO networks are now increasingly able to monitor policies at all levels that violate international standards, bring pressure to bear on governments and international organizations to change these policies, and at the same time lobby public opinion for more vigilance on these issues. Hence, it is hardly an overstatement when the Secretary-General of ICN states that "when we all go home, it will be the NGOs that will continue the pressure on governments."

In order to monitor effectively, NGOs need access mechanisms that allow their voices to be heard. While human rights NGOs are closely involved with (part of) the work of the UN Commission on Human Rights, the same does not hold in the field of development. The World Bank's Inspection Panel, created in 1994, can deal with complaints by private citizens and NGOs that the World Bank is violating its own procedures or that their interests are harmed by a proposed project. During its first two years of existence, five formal requests were received by the Inspection Panel. Two of these cases have received extensive follow-up: a hydro-electric project in Nepal was abandoned, while the fate of a natural resources management project in Brazil is still pending. Both these projects were far advanced in their preparation, and it is likely that without the Inspection Panel procedure, these projects would not have been halted. The World Bank is the only international organization with such a mechanism, however: in other cases, NGO monitoring is more ad-hoc and un-institutionalized.

However, it is in the field of project implementation that NGOs have become most active. Since a decade or so, all UN resolutions urge governments to integrate NGOs in the implementation of international programs. NGOs are now involved in the implementation of a large number of internationally financed projects. UNICEF, FAO, UNFPA, the UNHCR and even the UNDP, all accord NGOs sometimes major operational, sub-contracting roles in their projects. According to a recent brochure by the World Bank, "more than 40% of the total number of Bank projects approved in 1993 involved NGOs."

Of the sample of 25 organizations discussed above, approximately one-third is involved in sub-contracting for governments or international organizations. This can involve the implementation of (often sizable) project components, the conducting of training sessions for government and international organization staff, the execution of evaluation and identification mandates, the organization of conferences and workshops, specific consultancies, etc. Many analysts caution against sub-contracting to the state or to the aid system, arguing that it may tempt or force NGOs to "sell out" their principles for the sake of income—to become "co-opted." Yet, in the cases of our sample, extensive subcontracting seems rather to entail a recognition from external actors that the mode of functioning and expertise of these NGOs is sufficiently valuable to pay for. Hence, it seems that for the NGOs, this is a way both to expand their impact and to increase their degree of auto-financing.

On the other hand, the actual extent of participation is often kept very low, and NGOs can find themselves in the role of simple executants of externally designed programs, or mobilizers of local resources for externally defined goals. Indeed, much NGO participation in World Bank projects seems to be limited to using community workers for information, and in-kind or financial contributions by villagers. In its annual list of "World Bank-financed projects with potential for NGO involvement," the type of involvement sought is systematically "implementation", and rarely "design." And when the Bank mentions NGO participation in "input" rather than "implementation," it is in half of the cases only for small sub-projects within the confines of much larger ones.

5 Conclusion

During the last two decades, the institutional networks battling hunger and its causes have become much more varied and dense. In most countries, multitudes of different organizations now exist, many of whom were not there only 15 years ago; they engage in new relations of confrontation and collaboration with each other. The multiplicity, ambiguity, and redundancy of these organizations provides a source of diversity that renders generalizations—as well as on the ground coordination, for that matter—close to impossible. It is likely, however, that these same features increase pluralism, innovation, and representativity, at least to some extent.

These organizations manage thousands of projects and programs throughout the world. They have primarily economic goals, but most of them also eventually become active in the fields of health, education, and food security. What distinguishes them most from the other actors is their more participatory, small-scale, integrated way of working. Apart from some large and well analyzed cases, such as the Grameen Bank, BRAC, or the Aga Khan Rural Support Program in Pakistan (which has been evaluated three times by the World Bank), little is as yet known about their effectiveness and efficiency in overcoming hunger, making absolute or general judgments very dangerous (and typically reflective of ideology rather than analysis).

A major contribution of these organizations has been in the strategic/policy field. They have spearheaded new issue areas, such as environmental protection, micro-credit, and gender analysis. Among other results of their contributions, the dominant thinking about hunger has changed considerably: it has become more holistic, complex, and people-centered. However, the progress has been highly uneven and "consistently short of the transformations the NGOs seek": parts of the NGO agenda are remaining on the level of discourse rather than practice (participation, empowerment); other parts have been entirely devoid of follow-up (structural adjustment, fair trade), while on other issues (population, for example) still the NGO community itself is deeply divided. Finally, there are a set of blind spots in the NGO community that limit its impact further (research, human rights).

NGOs have fulfilled a third function, e.g., implementation and surveillance of government (and international organization) policies. The prime tension when fulfilling these functions is between the goals and modes of functioning of governments and international organizations on the one hand, and those of NGOs on the other. There is no evidence, however, allowing us to condemn all such action as cooptation, as is often done; rather, it reflects the fact that NGOs have become powerful, respected, and acceptable partners. There is, however, a price to pay for subcontracting: decision-making about the overall goals and priorities of organizations and projects tends to remain tightly controlled by the agencies NGOs subcontract for, and remain outside of their direct control. However, the increase in NGO resources, as well as the potential for upgrading the level of joint decision-making from contracting to partnership and true collaboration, may make it worthwhile.

References

Union of International Associations (1994): Yearbook of International Associations, Brussels.

Bebbington, A. and J. Farrington (1992): NGO-Government Interaction in Agricultural Technology Development, London: Earthscan.

Bebbington, A. and G. Thiele (1994): Non-Governmental Organizations and the State in Latin America. Rethinking Roles in Sustainable Agricultural Development, London: Routledge.

Carnegie Commission on Science (1993): Facing Towards Governments. Nongovernmental Organizations and Local Development, Discussion Paper 40, Washington D.C.: World Bank.

Clark, J. (1994): The Relationship between the State and the Voluntary Sector, electronic message, International Development and Global Education List, intdev-l&uriacc.bitnet.

Edwards, M. and D. Hulme (1996): Beyond the Magic Bullet? Lessons and Conclusions, in: M. Edwards and D. Hulme: Beyond the Magic Bullet. NGO Performance and Accountability in the Post-Cold War World, West Hartford, Kummarian Press, pp. 254-266.

Escobar, A. and S.E. Alvarez (1992): Introduction: Theory and Protest in Latin America Today, in: A. Escobar and S.E. Alvarez: The Making of Social Movements in Latin America. Identity, Strategy and Democracy, Boulder: Westview, pp. 1-17.

FAO/WHO (1992): Improving Household Food Quality, ICN Theme Paper No. 1, Rome.

Fisher, J. (1993): The Road from Rio: Sustainable Development and the Nongovernmental Movement in the Third World, Westport, Connecticut: Praeger.

Guthrie, R. (1994): Civic, civil or servile? Geneva, INTERPHIL (International Standing Conference on Philantropy):

James, E. (1990): Economic Theories of the Nonprofit Sector: A Comparative Perspective, in: H.K. Anheier and W. Seibel: The Third Sector: Comparative Studies of Nonprofit Organizations, Berlin, New York: Walter de Gruyter, pp. 21-29.

Monday Developments (1993a): PVOs Influencing Agenda for World Bank Conference on Reducing Global Hunger, in: Monday Developments, Sept. 13, p. 10.

Monday Developments (1993b): NGOs Seen as Key to Achieving Nutrition Conference Goals, in: Monday Developments, April 19, p. 21.

Monday Developments (1994): Southern NGOs to Join in Bank Hunger Conference Follow-Up, in: Monday Developments, Feb. 14, p. 7.

Nelson, P. (1995): The World Bank and Non-Governmental Organizations. The Limits of Apolitical Development, paper prepared for the ISA Meeting, Chicago, Febr. 1995.

Reutlinger, S. (1993): Addressing Hunger: An Historical Perspective of International Initiatives, background paper prepared for the World Bank Conference on Overcoming Global Hunger, Nov. 29-December 1, 1993, Washington D.C.

Salamon, L.M. and H.K. Anheier (1996): The Emerging Nonprofit Sector. An Overview, Manchester: Manchester University Press.

Sikkink, K. (1995): Nongovernmental Organizations and Transnational Issue Networks in International Politics, in: American Society of International Law Proceedings 1995, pp. 413-415.

Tomasevski, K. (1989): Development Aid and Human Rights, New York: St. Martin's Press.

UNDP (1994): World Development Report 1994, Oxford, Oxford University Press.

Uvin, P. (1994): The International Organization of Hunger, London: Kegan Paul.

Uvin, P. (1995): Fighting Hunger at the Grassroots: Paths to Scaling Up, in: World Development, 23 (6), June.

Uvin, P. (1997): Scaling Up, Scaling Down: the Role of NGOs in Overcoming Hunger, in: T. Marchione: Scaling Up, Scaling Down: Capacities for Overcoming Malnutrition in Developing Countries, Yverdon: Gordon & Breach.

World Bank (1991): List of World Bank-Financed Projects with Potential for NGO Involvement, Washington, International Economic Relations Division, Sept.

World Bank (1994): Working with NGOs, Washington D.C.: World Bank.

World Bank (1996): The Inspection Panel Report, Aug. 1, 1994 to July 31, 1996, Washington D.C.: IBRD/IDA.

25

Targeting Social Security Programs

Bernd Schubert

Social security is concerned with securing the sustainable access of households to all goods and services required to lead a healthy and active life. Food security concentrates on the access to food and nutrition. From the perspective of poor households there is not much difference between social security and food security. For very poor households, which have to allocate more than 75 % of their total expenditure on food, social security needs and food security needs are nearly identical. Social security programs, especially when targeting poor households, are to a large extent food security programs and vice versa.

The analysis of targeting approaches given in this contribution is based on the concept of social security as defined below. However, due to the reasons given above, the findings and conclusions given are in many ways also valid for the targeting of food security programs.

Policy makers and managers of social security programs have to make decisions which take into account the complexity and heterogenity of social security problems and social security systems. In order to do so they have to find answers to the following questions:

— How to define the target groups and objectives of social programs and activities?

— How to ensure that the needy and only the needy are effectively reached by social programs? In other words: What methods are available to achieve a high coverage of the target groups and to avoid at the same time, that the benefits leak to other persons which are not members of the target group.

— How can formal and informal social security be interlinked by using an appropriate targeting approach?

Without answering the first question, the second question does not make much sense. Without clearly defining which types of persons or households should be reached for what purpose and without having at least an approximate idea how many of such persons or households need to be reached, targeting cannot be done. And without an approach which facilitates that different social security organizations and systems interlink their activities, social security will remain a patchwork.

1 Defining the objectives and target groups of social security systems or social security programs

The following three tasks are internationally accepted as the purpose of social security systems:

— The most fundamental task of a social security system is to guarantee the physical survival of all members of a society by ensuring access to the most basic means of survival in terms of food and health.

— A somewhat more ambitious task is to ensure that all members of a society have access to those goods and services which are necessary to lead a healthy and active life.

— The most demanding task is to protect all members of a society against social and economic risks caused by events like unemployment, diseases, disabilities, old age or death of a bread winner. This protection should facilitate that the persons affected by such events can maintain a standard of living consistent with their social status.

Having these tasks in mind social policy makers have to analyse which groups in the society do already enjoy the three different levels of social security, and which do not. Based on this analysis and having their financial and institutional resources and potentials in mind, they have to define target groups and objectives for social policy interventions. Target groups are by definition homogeneous groups of persons or households which a policy or program wants to reach.

Defining target groups and objectives of social policy interventions means discriminating. Given scarce resources and limited budgets not all potential target groups and not all potential objectives of a social security system can be achieved at once. Priority setting with regard to target groups and objectives of social policy interventions is essential. It has to be done on national level for defining the social policy of a country. It also has to be done on all other levels and by all organizations which are involved in social programs and activities.

When defining target groups and objectives of social programs (on all levels) there is a temptation to use general terms like "the poor" or "the vulnerable." Such general terms tend to lead to the false conclusion that social insecurity can effectively be alleviated by one single approach like "making the poor productive" or "give the poor access to credit." A systematic analysis leads to the conclusion that in reality, social insecurity (like poverty) always has a variety of forms and a variety of causes. Social insecurity and poverty are heterogeneous phenomena. Therefore, social policies have to include a mixture of different programs and activities which together meet the heterogeneous needs of the different target groups.

The matrix given below is an analytical tool which can be used to divide the heterogeneous mass of "socially insecure" or "poor" into more homogeneous subgroups or potential target groups.[1] The matrix distinguishes by degree of poverty

1 In farming systems analysis this process is called: Identification of recommendation domains.

and by causes of poverty. Depending on the purpose of the analysis other dimensions of poverty have also to be included (like urban-rural or seasonal-permanent). However, in the context of this paper I would like to use the matrix in a simple form.

Figure 1: Poverty matrix

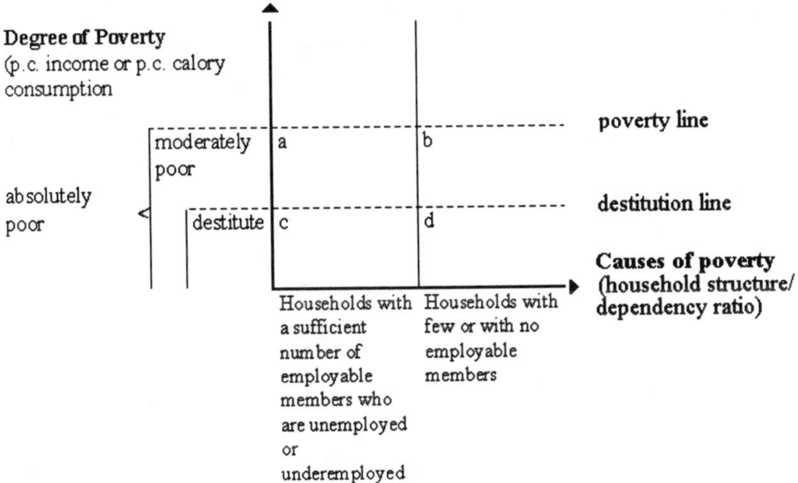

1.1 Degree of Poverty

With regard to the degree of poverty the matrix distinguishes between non-poor, moderately-poor and destitute households:

— The non-poor who have incomes in cash and/or in kind above the so-called poverty line.[2] In Mozambique,[3] the poverty line which permits a calory consumption of 2000 kcal per person per day is 15 US-Dollar per month.

— The absolutely poor who have incomes which are below the poverty line, but not so low that underconsumption endangers their health and survival. Some authors call this group the moderately poor. In Mozambique, this group are households which have incomes per head per month between 10-15 US-Dollar.

2 The poverty line defines a critical income threshold which is just sufficient to enable those basic needs to be satisfied which are essential for being able to "lead a healthy and active life." The emphasis is on meeting physiological energy requirements by using the cheapest available sources of energy.

3 The examples from Mozambique given in this paper are cited from Schubert (1994).

— The absolutely poor who live on incomes which reach less than 70% of the poverty line are called destitute. In Mozambique, destitute households live on incomes of less than 10 US-Dollar per person per month permitting an average calory consumption of less than 1400 kcal. In destitute households the underconsumption affects the ability to work and endangers the health and the survival of the more vulnerable household members (children, pregnant women and elderly).

The distinction between these three categories is important for priority setting. Human rights oriented organizations would, for example, tend to argue that the right for survival should have top priority and that scarce resources should be concentrated on ensuring the survival of the destitute. Other polical groups could argue that the most important objective of social policy is to lift as many households as possible over the poverty line. This objective would best be reached by concentrating on the moderately poor. Some organizations like the ILO seem to be mainly concerned with improving the social security of formal sector employees who are mostly not absolutely poor or destitute (ILO 1984: 3). They aim at protecting the non-poor from falling into absolute poverty or destitution.

1.2 Causes of poverty

With regard to the causes of poverty or social insecurity the matrix distinguishes between structural causes and conjunctural causes:

- Households which suffer from structural causes of poverty or destitution lack gainful employable labour. This has a quantitative and a qualitative aspect:
  a. The quantitative aspect is an unfavourable ratio (dependency ratio) between the number of household members who are in the working age (potential bread winners) and the total number of household members (mouths to feed).
  b. The qualitative aspect is related to structural constraints which the economically active members of a household in the working age face with regard to access to renumerative employment. One example of such structural constraints is their educational status. For instance, illiterate female adults are structurally excluded from formal-sector employment.
- Households affected by conjunctural causes of poverty or destitution have sufficient labour power to earn an income which is adequate to provide for basic needs. However, this productive capacity is unused or underused because one or more adult members of the household are unemployed or underemployed.

1.3 Poverty matrix

By combining the degree of poverty and causes of poverty we arrive at a poverty matrix. In its simple form this matrix distinguishes between four groups of poverty or social insecurity:

a. Households in a conjunctural situation of absolute poverty but not destitute. Of all the absolutely poor households these are in the most favourable situation.

Their most urgent need is productive employment for the unemployed or underemployed members of their households.

b. Households in a structural situation of absolute poverty but not destitute. These households cannot benefit from employment generating programmes because they have no unused or underused labour power. Most of these households will remain in the situation of being absolutely poor but not destitute as long as the household structure does not change.

c. Households in a conjunctural situation of destitution. These households are in urgent need of productive employment, like those in group (a). However, due to their destitute situation, their chances of achieving productive employment are small. Because of their acute malnutrition they have less physical strength, initiative and hope to search for employment. If they stay in this situation for a long period their health will deteriorate to an extent where even the employable adults will become unemployable. In other words, they face the danger of gliding into the group of structurally destitute. They need temporary social assistance (income transfers) to ensure their survival and their ability to work, and they need employment opportunities. Once they have found employment the social assistance can be terminated.

d. Households in a structural situation of destitution. Of all types of poverty this is the worst. Households in this group have no or extremely limited income-earning capacity and receive no or insufficient social transfers (e.g. pensions or donations from other households). Even if additional employment opportunities were available these households could not use them because they are scarce in labour power. To ensure their survival the households in this group need income transfers. These transfers are needed as long as their household structure (ratio between the number of employable adults and the total number of household members) does not change. In addition to income transfers, many households in this group need other social welfare interventions, such as access to health care.

The poverty matrix shows that different groups of poor and socially insecure households need different programs. It shows at the same time that specific programs like "small credit schemes" or "cash for work" are suitable for some poverty groups but are not suitable for others.

Elaborating a poverty matrix on the basis of whatever empirical data is available can facilitate decision making with regard to which target groups and objectives should get priority and which programs are suitable to reach these specific target groups and achieve the objectives.

This analysis can be done on national level, on provincial level, on district level and on communal level. It can serve to identify which poverty groups are reached by existing formal, informal or traditional social security activities, and which are not. It can serve as a tool for designing social security programs in a target group oriented manner. As a result of this target group oriented (versus program oriented) approach, a mix of programs can be designed which is tailored to the needs of the different poverty groups and which uses the scarce resources available for social policy in a rational way.

Example: Using the poverty matrix for designing a low cost social safety net for the cities of Mozambique

The analysis of household survey data indicates that in 1991 approximately 50% of the 400,000 urban households living in the 13 cities of Mozambique were absolutely poor. Using the poverty matrix approach the 200,000 absolutely poor households were disaggregated into four more homogeneous sub-groups:

Estimated number of absolutely poor households in Mozambican cities by degree of poverty and by main causes of poverty, 1991 (absolutely and in % of all urban households)

		Main causes of poverty		**Total**
		Conjunctural (unemployment; underemployment)	Structural (high dependency ratio)	
Degree of poverty	Absolutely poor, but not destitute	a) 30,000 (7.5%)	b) 50,000 (12.5%)	80,000 (20%)
	Destitute	c) 40,000 (10.0%)	d) 80,000 (20.0%)	120,000 (30%)
	Total	70,000	130,000	200,000

The next step was to investigate which of the four sub-groups were reached by which development or social security oriented programs. As a result of this analysis it became evident that most of the existing programs (e.g. credit schemes, small entrepreneur development, social insurance, food ration and price subsidies) benefited mainly the non-poor and the sub-group a) of the absolutely poor. The most neglected groups were c) and d).

Based on this analysis income generating programs and cash for work programs for group c) were designed (and partly implemented). Simultaneously a social assistance program called GAPVU was started. GAPVU's objective was to reach at least 60,000 destitute households, mainly concentrating on group d), with monthly cash transfers sufficient to increase their average daily calory consumption by 400 kcal per person. This has been implemented. Since 1994 GAPVU is reaching 70,000 households with monthly payments of approximately 2.5 US-Dollar per person which is sufficient to ensure the survival of destitute households.

Source: Schubert 1994.

The example given above shows that for priority setting, for defining target groups and objectives, and for planning social programs it is useful to disaggregate the heterogenous mass of poor households into more homogeneous groups. In many cases it is necessary to further disaggregate these groups. Group d) could e.g. be sub-divided into old persons, disabled persons, chronically deseased persons (all either living alone or being head of household with no other person in the working age living in the same household). In spite of limited resources (Mozambique is one of the poorest countries in the world) and in spite of the complexity of social problems and their roots, policy makers and managers can achieve significant improvements of social security by using an appropriate analytical approach for defining priorities, target groups, and objectives.

2 Dimensions which have to be taken into account for designing or evaluating targeting procedures

2.1 Horizontal and vertical targeting

The goal of horizontal targeting is to reach a high proportion of those households which belong to the defined target group. If in a certain region 10,000 households are in a destitute situation but less than 5,000 are reached by all existing formal and informal social activities then the effectivity of horizontal targeting is low.

The goal of vertical targeting is to concentrate the benefits of social programs on those who need them most. When the benefits of a certain program which aims at reaching destitute households are mainly captured by moderately poor households or by non-poor households then the effectivity of vertical targeting is low.

Many social sector organizations or programs have no information on how effective their horizontal and vertical targeting is. Only few have established goals with regard to how effective they want to be. Some do not even know the approximate size of their target groups. They are perfectly happy with reaching 500 households while their target group may consist of 50,000 households which all need to be reached. I sometimes wonder how the managers of such programs can sleep while people are suffering and dying because the horizontal targeting of these programs is so poor.

Other social sector organizations pretend that they are targeting the most vulnerable groups while their benefits go mainly to the high income groups. This is often the case with food price subsidy schemes. In Maputo for instance, 67% of the benefits of a Food Ration and Subsidy Scheme were captured by those 40% of the population which had the highest incomes whereas the 40% lowest income households received only 16% of the benefits (Schubert 1994: 166).

2.2 Targeting individuals, households, communities or other social units

The target groups of social programs can be individuals, households or other social units or organizations. The choice of the appropriate unit depends on the type of social problem that has to be solved, the means by which the problem should be solved and the socio-cultural frame conditions.

If, for example, child malnutrition is the problem to be solved, if the means to solve the problem is a balanced diet for the respective children, and if the frame conditions are such that the children are regularly attending health checks where their nutritional status is controlled, then it may be most appropriate to target individual children and to provide them with therapeutic nutritional interventions.

If extreme poverty of certain households like female-headed households with many children and no employable household members is the social problem and if the means to solve the problem are tansfers in cash or in kind, then the units of targeting will have to be households.

If the problem concerns a group of households (like no access to safe water) or a whole community (like no access to basic health care), then the units to be targeted will have to be bigger social units.

2.3 Costs of targeting

When choosing between different approaches to targeting which are described in chapters 3 and 4, the costs of targeting have to be taken into account. Here we have to distinguish between political, social and administrative costs of targeting.

The political costs of targeting have their root in the fact that disadvantaged and vulnerable groups are in many countries politically not well represented. This can lead to the situation that a social program which is rigidly targeted to the most disadvantaged groups and excludes the middle class loses political support. This is happening in Germany at the moment where unemployment benefits and social assistance are reduced while cuts in the rather luxurious social security provision for the working population meets strong resistance. The so-called welfare states in Western Europe are not characterized by spending a large amount of public funds on the poorest section of the population but by having very elaborate and costly social systems to protect their middle class. However, there are countries in Africa (like Mozambique) and in Asia (like Sri Lanka and a number of Indian States) which have succeeded in transforming untargeted transfer schemes into effectively targeted programs for the poorest. This indicates that the political costs of targeting (in terms of loosing political support) are different from country to country.

The social costs of targeting are the costs which the applicants have to pay in terms of loss of privacy, self-respect and dignity when going through the application and selection procedures. These costs depend partly on the typ of targeting approach used and partly on the attitudes of the officials who administer the targeting procedures. A good program management should ensure that applicants are treated as clients who have to be served, and not as beggars.

Another area of social and economic costs is the so-called "incentive distortion effect" which may occur as a reaction to certain forms of targeting (Sen 1994: 3). Such an effect can be caused if beneficiaries change their social and economic behavior in order to qualify for certain programs. If, for instance, malnutrition of a child is an eligibility criterion for welfare payments to a family, a desperate family could be tempted to keep a child in the status of malnutrition. There can also be positive effects: when the existence of an old person in a household is an eligibility criterion of a program (old age benefits), the behavior of other household members towards that old person may become very caring and supportive in order to ensure that the old person stays in the household and lives a long life. When designing a targeting system such behavioral changes have to be taken into account in order to minimize social and economic costs and to maximize social and economic benefits resulting from targeting.

The administrative costs of targeting are the expenditures required to implement all activities which have to be done by social sector organizations in order to ensure effective targeting. Depending on how the targeting is organized these expenditures can be considerable. In addition, bureaucratic procedures can cause delays which may reduce the value of the benefits for the beneficiaries.

There seems to be a correlation between the effectivity of targeting and the political, social, and administrative costs of targeting. Achieving 100% effective horizontal and vertical targeting would be extremely costly. Social programs should, therefore, try to achieve an optimal compromise between the effectivity and the costs of targeting. This optimum can be reached by systematic experimentation and can be different under different circumstances. Each social sector organization should, however, constantly assess its targeting approach by asking and answering one of the following questions:

— In case a program has reached a high effectivity of horizontal and vertical targeting: can the political, social, and administrative costs of targeting be reduced without reducing the effectivity of targeting?

— In case a program has already achieved low political, social, and administrative costs: can the effectivity of targeting be increased without increasing the costs?

In order to answer these questions each organization has to consider which of the following approaches to targeting or which combination of approaches is most suitable, taking the specific circumstances into account under which the respective organization is operating.

3 Conventional targeting approaches

This chapter will not deal with targeting of individuals who suffer from directly observable problems and who need direct sectoral interventions like therapeutic nutritional interventions for severely malnourished children or literacy campaigns for the illiterate or institutional care for helpless people like abandoned elderly people. It will also not deal with targeting groups of households or communities. It will concentrate on the most difficult targeting problem: the targeting of households which suffer from the complex problems of vulnerability, poverty, food shortages, and destitution.

3.1 Self-targeting

Self-targeting leaves the decision who should participate in and benefit from a social program to the individual households. Most social sector programs are self-targeted:

— Most food price subsidy schemes leave it to the individual household to decide if and how much of the subsidized commodities it wants to buy.

— Most free or subsidized health care services leave it to the household to decide who wants to use this service and who not.

— Most Food for Work and Cash for Work schemes are open to anyone who wants to participate (and is physically able to participate).

How effective and how costly this targeting approach is depends very much on the combination of target groups which should be reached, on the framework in which the approach is used and on the specific objectives of the respective program. This can be demonstrated using the three examples given above:

— Food price subsidies tend to be very poor with regard to vertical effectivity of targeting (reaching only the poor). They also fail to reach many of the poorest households (horizontal targeting) which have no cash to buy food, even if food prices are low. The effectivity of targeting can be improved by concentrating the subsidies on such food which is only consumed by the poor and by making this inferior food so cheap that also the poorest can afford it. Yellow maize seems to be such a type of inferior commodity in many parts of the world. However, where yellow maize has been used for self-targeted food subsidies a number of social and economic costs were observed: it was humiliating for the poor population to be forced to consume food which they considered as not fit for human consumption. Some not so poor households bought it and used it for feeding animals. Once parts of the population got used to yellow maize the countries became dependent on imports from North America. As a result of all these problems food price subsidy schemes have been terminated in many countries.

— With regard to basic health care self-targeting has been relatively successful and has contributed much to improving the health status of the poor. However, due to cuts in government budgets introduced as part of structural adjustment policies, user fees have been introduced in many countries which tend to exclude the poor. Some countries try to charge user fees from the non-poor and give free access to basic medical services for the poorest. This means they have given up self-targeting and use other targeting approaches.

— Self-targeting for Food for Work or Cash for Work employment schemes have a high effectivity of vertical targeting because only poor households who have no other alternatives join these schemes. But one has to realize that many of the poorest and destitute households cannot benefit from employment schemes because the household members are too old, too young, disabled, chronically diseased or for other reasons not able to do physical work. These schemes target such households successfully which are poor or destitute for conjunctural reasons but do not reach households which are poor or destitute for structural reasons.

3.2 Targeting by using eligibility criteria related to income

Income is an important means for meeting basic needs. If income is defined not only as cash income received from formal sector employment but as the total flow of products, services, and money which a household produces, earns, or receives as donations and which the household can use for meeting its basic needs, then income is an important criterion for poverty. At the same time it is difficult to verify the income of poor and destitute households. It involves high administrative costs, can easily be manipulated, and taking income as an eligible criterion can have negative incentive effects.

In order to avoid these problems different possibilities of using income-related proxy indicators have been used. Such proxy indicators use easily observable variables which are believed to correlate with low income. Such variables are for example:

- households which live in poor areas,
- characteristics of the housing situation like thatched roof, distance to source of drinking water, type of toilet, non-possession of any "luxury goods" like radios,
- incidence of malnutrition of children or of pregnant women in a household,
- number of meals consumed per day.

These criteria can be used in combination like: households living in a poverty area and having a severely malnourished child.

The problem with proxy indicators is that the correlation between these indicators and the level of income or poverty is not certain, that they can be manipulated and that they can be an incentive for negative behavioral changes like keeping a child in a status of malnutrition. An organization which is using proxy indicators should, therefore, carefully study if the resulting effectivity of targeting and the incentive effects are acceptable.

3.3 Targeting by structural criteria which determine the income earning capability of a household

Structural criteria of a household determine to a large extent its income-generating potential (in cash and kind). Types of households which are usually not able to survive without social transfers because of limited coping capabilities are:

— old people who are living alone or who are head of a household with no other able bodied persons in the working age living in the same household,

— severely handicapped or chronically diseased persons living alone or being head of a household with no other able bodied person in the working age living in the same household,

— female-headed households with three or more young children when the female head of household is illiterate (in an urban setting) or has limited access to land (in a rural setting) and has no other able bodied person in the working age living in the same household.

These are only examples. The specific criteria to be used to identify households with extremely low income-earning capabilities have to take local cultural and socio-economic frame conditions into account. The Grameen Bank for instance uses three screens of structural eligibility criteria: female gender, landlessness, and rural residence.

Once households with low income-earning capability have been identified a second screening can be used to verify if and to what extent these households already receive transfers from other private households (children, migrant workers), from organizations (pensions), or from their communities (religious groups). Households which have no or very limited income-earning capabilities and which are not receiving social transfers have a high probability of being extremely poor or destitute. However, in many regions the identification of transfers from other households is difficult and involves considerable administrative costs.

4 Using participatory and integrated approaches to targeting in order to link communities with formal and informal social security organizations

Participatory approaches aim at including all parties concerned into the process of analysing social problems, identifying solutions and in planning and implementing such solutions. Participation means sharing information, sharing power, and sharing responsibilities. Integration means that formal and informal organizations and community groups do not work in isolation but work together in order to attack the different roots of social problems and in order to make use of the different potentials of formal and informal systems in a coordinated way.

This type of approach has been used on a broad scale in the context of the Janasavija Program in Sri Lanka (Gunatilleke 1992: 136). It was based on a sequence of community level workshops which served to analyse the social problems of the respective community and to select a poverty alleviation committee. The technical details of this program for each household were planned and implemented jointly by the beneficiary households, committee members, and representatives of various local representatives of Government Departments and NGOs.

The advantages of a participatory and integrated approach are that it is decentralized, bottom-up, and holistic. Poor households are no longer considered as objects of social security activities but as subjects. Social security is not treated as a matter where each social security organization selects its beneficiaries and acts independently of other organizations and of the community but as a complex task which can only be solved if all actors plan and work together.

In my view, participatory and integrated targeting offers the possibility to link formal, informal, and traditional social security activities and to elaborate comprehensive social security systems on community level. A participatory approach may also lead to other improvements: Felt needs and specific cultural and socio-economic conditions of each community can be taken into account. Overlapping of programs can be avoided. Gaps in coverage can be closed. By applying the principle of subsidarity, the potentials of local groups and organizations can be strengthened for solving social security problems.

The participatory and integrated approach for the targeting and implementation of social programs in Africa is new. There have been some promising attempts to use Participatory Social Appraisal for evaluating and improving social security programs in Mozambique (Schubert 1995). There are also a number of positive experiences with using a participatory and integrated approach in community development (World Bank 1995). These experiences could be used to develop a similar approach for social security.

If participation is increasingly seen as one of the main approaches (and objectives) of development, why should it not also have a considerable potential for targeting and implementing integrated social security programs? It may be worthwhile to experiment with this approach. To elaborate in detail how this can be done is, however, already beyond the scope of this contribution.

References

Ahmad, E. et al. (1991): Social Security in Developing Countries, Oxford.

Alderman, H. et al. (1990): Maize Stamps and Market Liberalization in Mozambique: New Ideas for Urban Food Security, Cornell University, Washington.

Buvinic, M., Rao Gupta, G. (1992): The Costs and Benefits of Targeting Poor Woman-Headed Households and Woman-Maintained Families in Developing Countries, Seminar on Women in Extreme Poverty: Integration of Women's Concerns in National Development Planning, Vienna, 9-12 November.

Cornia, G.A. and Stewart, F. (1994): Two Errors of Targeting, in: van de Walle, D. et al. (eds.): Public Spending and the Poor, Washington.

Gosh, M. (1992): From Platitude to Practice: Targeting Social Security Programs in Latin America, World Bank, Washington.

Gunatilleke, G. (1992): Social Security in Sri Lanka: A Country Case Study, in: Getubig, I.P. et al. (eds.): Rethinking Social Security, Kuala Lumpur, pp. 136-166.

ILO (1984): Introduction to Social Security, Geneva.

Midgley, J. (1984): Social Assistance: An Alternative Form of Social Protection in Developing Countries, in: International Social Security Review, Vol. 84.

Schubert, B. (1994): Reaching the Unreached—Social Assistance as an Integrated Part of a Low-Cost Social Safety Net in Mozambique, in: Economics, Volume 49/50, Tübingen, pp. 159-176.

Schubert, B. et al. (1994): Facilitating the Introduction of a Participatory and Integrated Development Approach (PIDA) in Kilifi District, Kenya, Berlin.

Schubert, B. (1995): Participatory Social Appraisal of the GAPVU Cash Transfer Scheme, Maputo.

Sen, A. (1994): The Political Economy of Targeting, in: van de Walle, D. et al. (eds.): Public Spending and the Poor, Washington.

van de Walle, D. (1992): Whether to Target—and How, in: OUTREACH, No. 6, December 1992, World Bank, Washington.

van de Walle, D. (1994): Incidence and Targeting: An Overview of Implications for Research and Policy, in: van de Walle, D. et al. (Eds.): Public Spending and the Poor, Washington.

World Bank (1995): World Bank Participation Source Book, Washington.

26

The Role of Rural Financial Services for Improving Household Food Security—Concept, Evidence, and Policy Implications

Manfred Zeller and Manohar Sharma

1 Introduction

At first glance, many might be tempted to say that the poor in developing countries, earning incomes of less than a dollar per day, are neither creditworthy nor are able to save. That these common assumptions are unfounded has been shown by recent socioeconomic research. Yet, much of rural financial policy right until the end of the 1980s was based on these faulty premises, and frequently still is, leading to well-meant, but inefficient or outright detrimental policies for development of rural financial markets in Latin America, Africa and Asia. Past policy neglected to provide savings and insurance services, and much, if not all of the emphasis was put on giving loans. Credit was often limited to specific export crops while ignoring the demand for credit for other farm and non-farm enterprises as well as for smoothing consumption. The latter demand is being particularly important among poor households, as will be shown in this paper.

In policy practice, the concept of lending was and still often is being mixed up with that of providing relief or assistance. As soon as borrowers find out that loan default is not being penalized, or as soon as credit is perceived as government's or donor's assistance, or as efforts to gain political patronage, repayment rates drop to unsustainable lows. As a result, most, if not all so-called credit projects quickly degenerated into transitory income transfer programs with doubtful coverage of the poor, but with never-ending need for injecting public resources to keep rural state-driven, top-down banks and cooperatives from collapsing.

In recognition of these past failures[1], and in conjunction with the structural adjustment policies implemented since the last fifteen years, donor and government support for development banks and parastatal agricultural credit institutions substantially dwindled, leading to the current state in many developing countries which is characterized by the lack of any functioning rural financial institution operating on a substantial, if not a national scale. Credit for smallholder and tenant agriculture appears to have been especially hard hit, although the authors are unable to come up with hard numbers to confirm this assertion. The basic underlying constraints to

1 For a comprehensive critique of past credit policy, see Adams (1988), and Adams and von Pischke (1984).

financial market development are information asymmetry between market partners, political instability, weak governance and inadequate framework for bank supervision and legal enforcement of contracts, poor rural infrastructure, and high covariate risks, especially in agriculture-dependent rural economies. The result of all these factors are high information and transaction costs for the financial institution, the borrower and the saver alike. Because these transaction costs are so intrinsic to rural financial systems in many developing countries, the macroeconomic and financial sector policy reforms that have been implemented in many countries have proven to be only a necessary but not sufficient condition for developing sustainable rural financial markets in developing countries (Aryeetey 1997; Krahnen and Schmidt 1994; Zeller et al. 1997). The neo-classical view that liberalized markets—through changes in relative factor prices that then reflect the true scarcity of resources—trigger by themselves sufficient innovation and development in financial market institutions which serve more than just the affluent urban elite must be seriously questioned. Instead, public action complementary to market liberalization is needed to develop and eventually expand institutional innovations which can cut transaction costs in rural financial markets. Just as the public sector has a role to play in technological innovations, it is asked to provide an enabling environment and financial and technical support for developing institutional innovations that address market failures that result in inefficiency or that pose serious equity issues. Indeed, in the two decades, public action by donors, governments, nongovernmental organizations and community groups in the field of microfinance has generated successes, as demonstrated by the development of innovative rural financial institutions which are able to offer savings and credit services to many landless microentrepreneurs, tenants and smallholders in developing countries such as Bangladesh, Bolivia, Indonesia and Thailand. However, much of this recent institutional expansion took place in densely populated, high-potential areas of Asia, or in semi-urban areas and cities in Latin America. Innovative financial institutions also exist in Sub-Saharan Africa, but their scale is still very limited compared to those found in Asia or Latin America (Christen et al. 1994; Webster and Fidler 1996). The best-known microfinance institution in this region probably is K-Rep in Kenya. But this institution only served about 7,000 borrowers in 1994. An enormous public effort is therefore required to expand financial systems and to make them more sustainable, in particular in Sub-Saharan Africa.

This paper explores the role of financial services for improving household food security, and seeks to do so by presenting a conceptual household-level framework and supporting empirical evidence. The constraints to financial market development are highlighted, and the role of social capital or member-based financial institutions to mitigate these constraints is identified. The paper concludes with recommendations for future policy.

2 How can improved access to financial services enhance household food security: a conceptual framework[2]

2.1 Policy instruments for improving household food security: the role of rural finance

Food security, at the household level, is defined in its most basic form as access by all people at all times to the food needed for a healthy life. Access to the needed food is necessary, but, of course, not a sufficient condition for a healthy life; a number of other factors, such as the health and sanitation environment and household or public capacity to care for vulnerable members of the society, also come into play (von Braun et al. 1992).

The food-security concept addresses people's risks of not having access to needed food. These risks can be related to income and food production, for instance. Typically, these risks are higher the closer a household is, even in a "normal situation," to inadequate dietary intake. Food insecurity entails the short-term temporary shortfall of consumption of food below needed levels, also called "transitory food insecurity," and a situation of long-term chronic food shortage, often called "chronic food insecurity." An effective food-security policy aims to ensure that all households and their members have adequate dietary intake without excessive risks in attaining it.

There are many potential policy instruments for improving household food security. In general, packages combining a range of policy instruments are more effective in improving food security than ones that rely on few sector-specific, single policy instruments. Given the determinants of the household's food security, available policy instruments can be systematized into policies that (1) aim to increase the household's income; (2) stabilize and/or lower food prices; or (3) improve the households' access to intertemporal markets (Zeller et al. 1997).

The first two policy sets are geared towards increasing household's income and purchasing power—either in particular seasons or years or as part of long-term strategies. Key policy instruments for achieving long-term food security are the transfer of technology and investments in agriculture and rural infrastructure, combined with extension and credit programs. These measures must be part of any development strategy. Policies to directly address problems of income and purchasing power during specific periods are the stabilization of key commodity prices and targeted interventions, such as income transfers, food subsidies, or public works projects for the food insecure. The third policy set aims to improve the household's ability to adjust its consumption and investment between periods via access to savings, credit, and insurance markets.

In contrast to the other two policy sets, the immediate goal of the third set of policy is not to directly influence income in a particular period, but to enable households to make intertemporal adjustments of disposable income. Savings

2 This chapter heavily draws from Chapter 2 and 3 of Zeller et al. 1997.

reduce disposable income and, hence, consumption in the current period, but increase it for future periods. For food-insecure households, savings in the form of cash, food, and other assets are an important means of self-insurance against anticipated or unanticipated food insecurity in the future. Borrowing, on the other hand, increases current disposable income at the expense of available income in future periods. It enables investment into human and physical capital that may improve future income and consumption, or avoid shortfalls in current consumption. Acquiring insurance enables the household to transfer part of its risks to an insuring institution. The household pays an insurance premium that reduces disposable current income, but is able to lower the variance of consumption in future periods. Access to credit, not actual borrowing, can serve as an insurance substitute.

Policy instruments that directly aim to diversify and increase incomes are necessary, but not sufficient, for ensuring household food security. Many poor households face the risk of transitory food insecurity, even if, on average, over several years, their incomes are sufficient to provide a sustainable standard of living. Thus, there is a potential demand for savings, credit and insurance services which can more efficiently contribute to consumption smoothing. Sources of risk in rural households are manifold, and the time pattern, intensity, and food-security impact of income fluctuations are difficult to anticipate for household members and policy-makers alike. Government policies to influence and stabilize household incomes via direct income transfers and price stabilization often need considerable response times and may not be cost-effective in targeting specific groups among the food-insecure rural poor. In contrast, intertemporal markets for savings, credit, and insurance could potentially offer households quick and effective means of smoothing their disposable income and therefore consumption. With well-functioning institutional arrangements, the household's flexibility to alter disposable income via savings and disinvestment, credit, and insurance contracts is likely to be faster, more cost-effective, and more specifically adapted to the household's needs than ex-post income stabilization programs of governments.

2.2 Linking financial services with household food security: a conceptual framework

The concept of finance for food security involves exploring the potential effects of financial services on stabilizing consumption and reinforcing the household's wealth and income base. This concept is much broader than the one of credit for promoting particular income generation activities, which has often been adopted in the past for agricultural production credit, and, more recently, for off-farm microenterprises. Many credit programs and institutions narrowly focus on the enterprise or farm, without taking into consideration the socioeconomic context within which the household or individual members invest, produce, and consume.

The broadened role of rural finance for food security addresses credit and savings needs for agricultural production and off-farm enterprises, but also includes other demands for financial services, such as financing food consumption and health care, as well as providing households with more effective savings, credit and insurance services for smoothing consumption, holding precautionary savings, and diversifying the asset portfolio.

Based on a review of the theoretical literature, Zeller et al. (1997) distinguish three pathways through which access to financial services (or lack thereof) influences the food security of households and individual members. The systematization of these pathways sets the framework for identifying institutional arrangements that address the diverse demand for savings, credit, and insurance services by the poor, for evaluating them, and for comparing their costs and benefits with alternative policy measures aimed at improving food security (Figure 1):

- Pathway I: via income generation,
- Pathway II: via asset (dis-)investment strategies to smooth disposable income over time at sufficient food consumption levels, and
- Pathway III: via direct use of credit to finance immediate consumption needs.

In Figure 1, the process is depicted through the link of boxes. Each of the boxes indicates a component of the overall process of altering household's food security through improved access to credit, insurance, and savings options. Time subscripts are not shown, but the process is perceived as dynamic.

Pathway I: Improved income generation. The hypothesized effects of access to credit are twofold. First, additional capital can be temporarily used to enhance the level of the household's productive human and physical capital. This is the traditional argument for credit. Second, apart from this direct effect on factor income, access to credit and to savings services suitable for precautionary savings will increase the risk-bearing capacity of the household (Eswaran and Kotwal 1990). This will then favor more risky, profitable income-generating activities, and will partially substitute for traditional risk-coping measures, such as crop diversification and field fragmentation.

The allocation of credit to specific uses will be determined by the level of opportunity costs in the various consumption, production, and investment activities. In general, the opportunity costs of (capital-intensive) assets will be reduced relative to family labor. For example, instead of growing low-yielding local crop varieties with low input and, therefore, capital intensity, improved access to credit may lead to an increased use of improved seeds and to a higher crop output per unit of labor. This may, in turn, encourage labor-saving technologies, such as animal draft power in crop production and equipment for crop processing. Due to its positive effect on risk-bearing capacity, access to credit may also enhance the adoption of new, more risky technologies and enable the household to expand agricultural or nonagricultural production (Feder et al. 1985).

Access to credit and savings schemes may therefore alter the profitability and mix of agricultural, nonagricultural, and household activities through changing opportunity costs of family and hired labor, inputs and durables, and consumption items. The expected increase in income will contribute to the formation of human and physical capital, leading to potential second-round effects.

Figure 1: Access to financial services and its effects on household food security

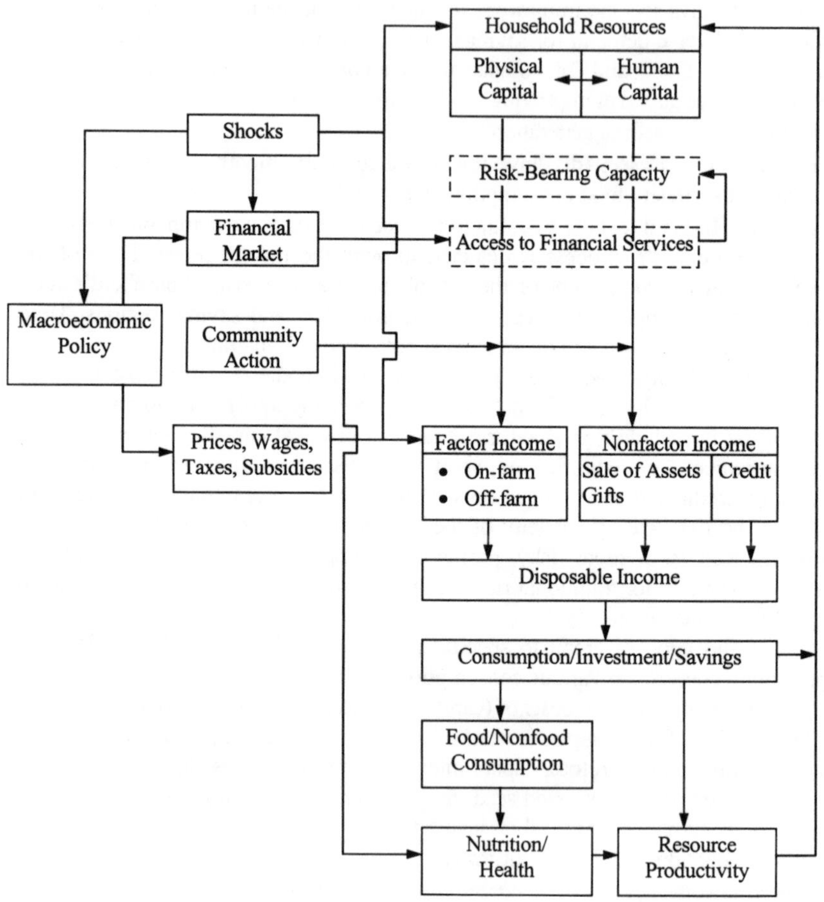

Pathway II: Decreasing costs for self-insurance through more cost-efficient assets and liabilities of households. Improved access to credit, insurance, and savings services may induce the following hypothesized changes in the household's composition of assets and liabilities:

– Decrease in holding of assets with lower risk-adjusted returns. Traditional forms of savings such as cash, jewelry, staple food, or livestock may be exposed to various risks (inflation, theft, loss, or disease). They are likely to be partially substituted if savings opportunities with higher risk-adjusted returns arise. This response, however, is conditioned by the quality of household's access to food and labor markets. For example, if food markets during the hungry season are fragile and food prices are expected to be highly volatile, households may continue to save in the form of food, even if formal savings options with high liquidity and low transaction costs are accessible. This example highlights the importance of financial products that are adopted to the local socioeconomic environment.

– Decrease in the level of assets held for precautionary savings.

– Increase of investments in and allocation of human and physical capital to current and future income generation, as discussed in Pathway I.

– Decrease in the level of credit obtained at high costs from informal sources.

– Decrease of emergency sales of productive assets at low prices. Thus, a depletion of productive assets (land, livestock, seeds) may be avoided.

In summary, improved access to credit and innovative savings and insurance schemes may alter the structure of assets and liabilities of households. The expected cost reduction for consumption stabilization may make more household income available for financing consumption, production inputs, or investments, and mobilize unproductively-held resources for economic growth.

Pathway III: "Consumption" credit. Households attempt to smooth their consumption by adjusting their disposable income. If factor income is insufficient because of shocks, various traditional consumption smoothing techniques are employed to generate non-factor income, such as that derived from the depletion of stocks, the sale of assets, the call for gifts from relatives and friends, and so forth. Factor and non-factor income constitute total disposable income for consumption and investment.

Non-factor income for stabilizing consumption in the current period can be alternatively generated by borrowing. Access to credit has hereby the potential of substituting for some higher-cost traditional savings, self-insurance, and community-level coinsurance strategies, as well as substituting for some of the higher-cost informal credit sources. Credit and savings services may be particularly demanded in environments of considerable interannual and seasonal income fluctuations.

Traditionally targeted production credit focuses exclusively on a reduced version of Pathway I by disbursing credit for "income-generating, productive" assets, such as fertilizer, seed, or machinery. To prevent the diversion of loans to other uses, loans are often disbursed in kind. However, when household priority needs for consumption, such as food, health, and education, which may be highly productive, and credit project perceptions do not coincide, in-kind disbursements will not succeed in restricting loan use, but simply increase its transaction costs for diverting loans to uses with higher economic returns. This practice can therefore reduce the net economic benefit of the financial transaction (von Braun et al. 1993).

It appears likely that rural financial policies will perform better in alleviating poverty and contributing to food security and economic growth when they address all of the above three pathways for food-insecure households and its members. The broader role for rural finance encompasses the three pathways shown in Figure 1, not just what is termed above as the direct effect of credit on income generation and the mobilization of savings for on-lending to more efficient users of capital. Recent theoretical models of precautionary savings and of credit constraints support the call for this broader agenda. When adopting it for the formulation of future rural financial policies, not only credit, but also savings and insurance services, will have to be emphasized much more. With respect to developing savings products for the rural poor, it follows that more emphasis ought to be placed on liquidity and low transaction costs than on attractive interest rates. Providing financial services to enhance food security comprises traditional "production" credit, be it for agricultural or off-farm enterprises. In addition, however, rural finance policy—if it aims at increasing its relevance for the food-insecure—should address the demand for credit, savings, and insurance services for consumption smoothing.

3 Recent evidence on impact of rural finance on household food security

The conceptual framework outlined above indicates that savings, credit and insurance services can play a potentially important role in increasing household income, food and non-food consumption, accumulation of physical and human capital, including improved nutritional and health status. In recent years, policy research has intensified its efforts to quantify the impacts of rural financial services. Much of the work focused on access to credit, and less on the impact of improved access to savings and insurance services. In the following, without trying to downplay the latter two services and without trying to be exhaustive for capturing the impact of the former, we will present some empirical evidence on the credit-food security linkage. Before doing so, we cite some evidence that highlights the problem of lack of access to credit by the rural poor in developing countries.

3.1 Lack of access to credit services

In most developing countries, rural financial services are sadly inadequate. In countries as diverse as Ghana, Madagascar, and Pakistan, access to credit and savings facilities is severely limited for small farmers, tenants, and entrepreneurs, particularly women. In these countries, of those who do not apply for a loan, up to 80 percent do so because they are deterred or discouraged by the strict collateral requirements and high transaction costs frequently involved in doing business with formal institutions, including time spent in travel and doing paperwork. Based on results from household surveys of IFPRI's multicountry research program on rural finance, the percentage shares of discouraged nonborrowers vary much by country, being the highest in Ghana, and the lowest in Madagascar (Table 1). When comparing all sample households with the lowest expenditure quartile, no systematic differences can be observed.

Table 1: Reason for not borrowing, by country

	Ghana	Madagascar	Pakistan
All households			
- Voluntary nonborrowers	20.9	55.9	36.8
- Discouraged nonborrowers	79.1	44.1	63.2
Poor households			
- Voluntary nonborrowers	10.6	59.1	54.9
-Discouraged nonborrowers	89.4	40.9	45.1

Source: Zeller et al. 1996. All nonborrowers in the household surveys were asked to state the reason why they did not apply for a loan. Those who did not apply because they did not want a loan for various reasons were categorized as voluntary nonborrowers. Those nonborrowers who were denied a loan after having applied, or those who did not apply for a loan because they perceived of having no chance of getting a loan were categorized as discouraged nonborrowers. The poorest households are defined as belonging to the lowest expenditure quartile.

While these figures describe the frequency of inadequate access to credit, it is incorrect to assume—as it is frequently done—that all households lack access to sufficient credit. In fact, Table 1 shows that the percentage share of voluntary nonborrowers among all nonborrowing households ranges from 21% in Ghana to 55% in Madagascar. In other words, between a fifth and a half of nonborrowers in these samples did not have a demand for credit. Most important reasons for not borrowing included to have enough equity capital or a lack of profitable investment opportunities that could carry the cost of the loan. The latter reason points out to the need for complementary public investments in rural infrastructure, markets, extension, and education which may have to precede rural financial market development in order to enhance the production possibilities of rural households and stimulate credit demand. It is by no means coincidental that credit programs and banking institutions are most frequently found in high-potential areas with relatively well developed infrastructure.

Nonetheless, households that borrow or would like to do so represent the majority in all IFPRI household samples from nine African and Asian countries. Some of these households are in such need of credit that they are willing to pay extremely high interest rates in the informal markets—sometimes higher than 100 percent per year. Table 2 shows average annual interest rates of all informal loans received by the sample households. When considering first the results for the full sample, the average interest rate for all loans ranges between 36 to 47%, with the exception of Pakistan where over 95% of loans do not carry any interest charge because of religious reasons. Moreover, in the other countries, the percentage of interest-free loans is also quite high, ranging from 26% in Cameroon to 83% in Madagascar. These interest-free loans are mostly given for a short duration by friends or relatives. Their overriding use is for consumption. These loans are therefore best to be considered as mutual insurance contracts where today's lender increases her stake in becoming an eligible borrower in the future if in need. The remainder of loans are provided by socially distant landlords, traders, and moneylenders, charging interest rates as high as 100 percent or more.

Table 2: Interest rates and loan duration of informal loans, by country

	Bangladesh	Cameroon	Nepal	Madagascar	Pakistan
All households					
- Average annual interest rate (%)	48	40	36	37	1.6
- Average duration of loan (days)	86	140		65	171
- Percentage of loans with no interest charge	60	26	28	83	96
Poor households					
- Average annual interest rate (%)	66	37	47	24	1.3
- Average loan duration (days)	71	140	...	48	210
- Percentage of loans with no interest charge	12	37	27	90	97

Source: Zeller et al. 1996.

A number of reasons account for this large divergence in interest rates. First, the amount of zero-interest credit available from friends and relatives is limited, and it can vary with idiosyncratic or covariate shocks that affect lenders and borrowers (see for example, Udry 1990). A bad harvest can for example reduce the total amount available for lending, while driving up the local demand for credit, and forcing disadvantaged households to borrow at very high interest rates. Moreover, most informal loans are short-term, and are meant to cover temporary shortfalls in consumption. Most of these consumption loans are between friends, neighbors and relatives, and carry no explicit interest rate. Second, the duration and the purpose of the loan also determine informal interest rates. The average duration of loans varies from 65 days in Madagascar to a high of 171 days in Pakistan. Loans of only 3 months are not long enough to finance a complete production cycle for most rural income-earning activities, except for poultry and vegetable production and certain types of non-farm enterprises. The majority of informal loans are therefore not suitable for financing seeds, fertilizer, and other working capital for farm production or for investment in durables, such as equipment. Several household surveys in Sub-

Saharan Africa found that consumption loans—when given among social networks—are usually cheaper than production loans (see Schrieder 1995; Shipton 1990; and Zeller et al. 1997).

Third, since informal loans are mostly not secured by collateral, sufficient knowledge of the lender about the creditworthiness of the borrower, and the lender's ability to sanction a defaulter, is required. Yet, this personalization of loan contracts implies that each village lender only deals with a finite number of creditworthy loan applicants. Vice versa, a borrower only knows a limited number of lenders. All of them have finite resources for lending, and therefore are able only to lend so much at a time. A borrower will first seek to exhaust all her low-cost credit sources, and gradually pay higher transaction-cost adjusted interest rates when contracting with the remaining number of lenders until she reaches her credit limit with all potential lenders. In view that credit demand and supply in rural areas moves with the agricultural production cycle, interest rates vary seasonally to a great extent. Forth, risks in loan default can systematically vary, and lenders may seek to cover some of this risk through higher interest rates. Compared to the full sample, the poor pay on average higher interest rates in Bangladesh and Nepal, but lower ones in Cameroon, Pakistan and Madagascar. It appears that the poor's self-help, reciprocal insurance systems in the two former Asian countries are either weaker or monopolistic village credit markets are more frequent.

In summary, considering the evidence on lack of access to credit and the high interest rates paid by some households, one can conclude that a considerable share of households have excess demand for credit that cannot be met by the informal and the formal sector.

3.2 Improving access to credit: Impact on household food security

Current or possible future binding credit constraints create opportunity costs. The optimal levels of consumption, saving, and income of a household that faces the possibility of a binding credit constraint are different from, and provide lower utility than the optimal levels in the absence of credit constraints (Feder et al. 1990). Following this argument, compared to households that do not face credit constraints in current or future periods, credit-constrained households will, ceteris paribus, hold more (precautionary) savings, and consume less and borrow less in the current period. Since precautionary savings are held to increase the flexibility of the household for cushioning shortfalls in disposable income in the short run, these savings will be held in liquid form. Credit-constrained households will therefore, ceteris paribus, not only hold more savings in absolute terms, but their share of liquid assets in total assets will be higher. Zeller et al. (1997) show that the poorest tercile of households in a rural sample from Madagascar had a higher share of liquid assets in their asset portfolio. However, higher liquidity of an asset usually comes at the expense of the asset's return. Thus, households that invest in liquid assets may end up investing less in more remunerative, but less liquid production durables such as agricultural equipment, as well as making less liquid investments in human capital.

Ceteris paribus such households, therefore, realize lower incomes in the short and long run than households with no borrowing constraints. Apart from this indirect effect of credit constraints inducing liquid, but low-yielding asset portfolios, credit constraints, also, have a direct negative effect on the available physical and human capital for income generation.

Rural financial institutions which enable the poor to access formal credit services can substantially reduce the occurrence of binding credit constraints. For Bangladesh and Malawi, Diagne et al. (1997) show that 35% and 61%, respectively, of members in credit programs faced a binding credit constraint in the informal or formal credit market. On the other hand, 84% and 92% of households, that never were members of group-based programs in Bangladesh and Malawi, respectively, experienced a binding credit constraint during a recall period of almost two years.

The evaluation of the impact of microfinance programs is not easy. Few recent in-depth studies have so far sought to address the methodological shortcomings of previous work in this area, and much more remains to be done. However, the few comprehensive studies available point out that improved access to financial services can yield significant improvements in income and food security of the poor. In the following, some of these research results are discussed, without trying to be comprehensive.

The manner in which improved credit access (that is, this relaxing of the binding credit constraint) affects different measures of household welfare is of ultimate interest for evaluation of public policy. A number of studies have attempted to examine this aspect. The study by Mark Pitt and Shahidur Khandker (1994) analyzed the welfare impact of the Grameen Bank and the Bangladesh Rural Advancement Committee (BRAC). They found positive and significant effects of credit program participation on outcome variables such as school enrollment, asset holdings of households, consumption, and nutritional status of children. Andrew Foster (1995) relates household participation in credit markets to smoothing fluctuations in the weights of pre-school children in Bangladesh. His findings show that growth patterns in landless households were influenced by credit market imperfections. Hanan Jacoby (1994) investigates the effect of borrowing constraints on the timing of human capital investments in Peru. Jacoby confirms the hypothesis that if parents are credit-constrained and child time has opportunity costs in the wage labor market, then the desire to smooth consumption will lead parents to withdraw children from school.

The results from IFPRI's own multicountry research program also point out to positive effects on income, technology adoption and food consumption. The methodologies for impact evaluation in IFPRI's country studies are described in Zeller et al. (1996). To account for selection bias, all IFPRI country studies use a two-stage econometric estimation procedure. The first stage measures the influence of factors that affect either access to or participation in the formal and informal credit market. The second stage then estimates the effects of predicted credit access or program participation on various outcome variables, as shown in Table 3.

In the table, effects are recorded as positive or negative only when statistical significance exceeded the 90 percent confidence interval. It is to be noted that the differences in data or estimation techniques across countries do not allow for a direct comparison of the absolute level of the impact. Nonetheless, the results show a uniform pattern that households can better adopt technology, increase incomes and improve their food security. The effects on calorie intake and nutritional status have been found to be more mixed, and mostly statistically not significant.

The effect of access to credit or of participation in a formal credit program on household income was found to be significant and positive in five out of six countries, except for Ghana where total household expenditures were used to proxy household income. Three country studies (Pakistan, Madagascar, and Malawi) specifically examined how improved access to credit affected use of modern inputs in agriculture. Each study concluded that improving credit access of rural households increases the use of productive inputs in agriculture, especially chemical fertilizers and improved seed. The results were also quite uniform with regard to effect of credit access on total food expenditures. For all five countries (Bangladesh, China, Malawi, Nepal, and Pakistan), a significant relationship was found. In three out of seven studies, the effect of credit access or participation in a credit program on calorie intake was found not to be significant. Substitution for higher quality foods with rising incomes may explain much of this weak effect on calorie intake. Finally, in all countries, except for a specific credit-cum-nutrition program in Ghana, no significant relationship between nutritional status of children and access to a credit program was found. Nutritional status of children is the result of a complex interaction between food intake, access to safe water and sanitation, nutritional knowledge of caretakers, and access to medical services; higher income (through access to financial services) is therefore only one of many determinants of good nutritional status.

It is apparent from these studies that far from having the effects of being one-shot transfers, repeated loans from such institutions have helped poor families make permanent positive changes in the quality of their lives. Of course, whether these apparent social benefits at the household level exceed the social costs of rural financial market policy (i.e., the opportunity costs of public subsidies), is an important research question (Zeller, Schrieder, von Braun, Heidhues 1997). Moreover, while rural finance definitely offers promise for enhancing food security, the lack of capital is only one factor from keeping poor rural households from improving their welfare. In rural areas of developing countries, illiteracy is high, basic social and market infrastructure is lacking, and many people are in poor health. When seed or irrigation water for the farmer, market access for the rural producer, or elementary bookkeeping skills for the would-be entrepreneur are absent, the returns to financial services will be low or sometimes even wasted. It is not a coincidence,

Table 3: Effects of credit on welfare: a summary of findings

Indicators of Welfare Outcomes	Observed Impact of Credit Programs							
	Bangladesh	Cameroon	China	Ghana	Madagascar	Malawi	Nepal	Pakistan
Household income level	(+)	(+)	(+)	(?)	(+)	(+)		
Technology adoption					(+)	(+)		(+)
Total food expenditure	(+)		(+)			(+)	(+)	(+)
Total calorie intake	(+)	(?)	(+)	(?) [a]	(+)	(+)	(?)	
Nutritional status of children	(?)	(?)		Mixed [b]	(?)	(?)		
Consumption variability	(-)						(-)	

[a] No significant effect on caloric intake was found, but note that 75 percent of the households already meet at least 80 percent of total caloric requirements.

[b] Regressions were run separately for each major type of credit program. One credit program showed positive effects on pre-schooler height-for-age. The results for two other programs were not significant.

Note: (+) or (-) indicates positive or negative impact statistically significant at the 10-percent level. (?) means that the effect was not statistically significant. Blank cells mean that the impact was not analyzed in that country.

Source: Zeller et al. 1996.

then, that in several countries the most successful rural financial institutions have operated in relatively well-endowed rural areas. In other cases, innovations have offered financial services in combination with other complementary services. For example, microfinance institutions such as the Bangladesh Rural Advancement Committee (BRAC) and the Grameen Bank combine credit services with basic literacy programs, training in enterprise management, and education in health and family planning. This bundling of services has, among other things, enabled these institutions to successfully serve the rural poor, and to achieve repayment rates in excess of 95 percent.

4 Institutional innovations and the role of policy

Ensuring a liberalized macroeconomic and financial sector environment is a necessary, but not a sufficient condition for the development of financial systems that reach and benefit the poor. The generation and transfer of technology which stimulate savings and credit demand is another necessary, but not sufficient condition. At the heart of the problem, i.e., in fulfilling the sufficient condition, lies the need for bringing transaction costs down—both for the financial institution and the clients who can only borrow or save little at a time.

In general, transaction costs can be brought down by improved infrastructure, such as roads, schools and communication infrastructure, by land titling to enable land to serve as collateral, or by improved institutions (Huppi and Feder 1990). While improved infrastructure and land titling may prove politically or economically feasible only in the very long run, institutional innovations could be brought about—in the medium run—through public action, i.e. through the concerted efforts of donors, governments, nongovernmental organizations and beneficiaries.

Reducing transaction costs is the central problem in improving outreach of financial systems to the rural poor. Much of these transaction costs arise from the need to acquire information about the market partner. For example, a lender must know about the reputation of the potential borrower, her wealth and current indebtedness, the expected returns of the project for which the loan is sought, and her ability and willingness to repay the loan. Furthermore, a lender would like to identify effective mechanisms for sanctioning defaulters so that loan repayment rate remains high. Obtaining such information proves prohibitively costly for microloans if a socially and geographically distant bank agent in the rural town is asked to gather this information. Traditional banking techniques, for example judging the loan application based on a written information, are either not feasible because of illiteracy or too costly. Yet, this information about the creditworthiness of a loan applicant is readily available in the community. Neighbors and other peers know about the character, previous credit history, ability to work, and ability and willingness to repay of their fellow neighbor. In other words, such information can be less costly obtained by networks or institutions that are based on social capital within the community. A solution to the transaction cost problem therefore lies in economizing on this locally available information through member- and community-based institutions.

While there are many different forms of institutional innovations in rural finance, a common characteristic of them is precisely to build on locally available information, and to exploit the cost advantage of informal monitoring and enforcement systems. In essence, what is being done, is that the bank asks peers to judge the creditworthiness of the loan applicant. In order to avoid strategic collusion of the peers against the banking institution, both the peers and the loan applicant are usually threatened by sanctions imposed by the bank if the loan contract is not fully fulfilled. For example, in credit groups under joint and mandatory liability, the peers and not the bank agent in the village decide on whether an individual is able to join a group and hence become eligible for a loan. In case of loan default of an individual, the entire group will lose access to future loans until all loans are repaid. Such a sanction is expected to encourage group members to carefully select fellow group members since a willingful defaulter will incur costs for themselves. In case of loan default beyond the control of the individual, fellow group members may even decide to bail out the defaulter, and to repay the loan (see for example Zeller 1996 and Wenner 1996). Like in credit groups, cooperatives and village banks also adhere to the principle of self-control, self-help and self-discipline for achieving greater individual and common benefit.

Hence, in innovative financial institutions, the functions of information acquisition, and monitoring and enforcement of financial contracts are to a large extent transferred from an individual bank agent to a group of people who share not only a common interest, i.e., gaining access to credit and savings services, but also possess information about themselves, including more cost-effective ways and means of sanctioning those who do not comply with the rules of their informal institution.

The major difference between traditional and innovative banking for the poor is therefore as follows: In traditional banking, the agent of a rural bank branch directly facilitates savings or loan contracts between the retail banking institution and the individual. Innovative approaches, on the other hand, are characterized by the existence of an institution that mediates between the bank and the individual, and that assumes many of the screening, monitoring and enforcement functions that are impossible or too costly to be executed by a bank agent. In other words, the bank transacts with these member- and community-based institutions, not with the individual borrower or saver as such. Compared to the traditional system, this can result in a considerable reduction of transaction costs for the bank, and also for the individual borrower or saver.

While the private banking sector should potentially derive benefits from investing in institutional formation at the community level to reduce transaction costs and increase market volume, so far, most institutional innovations in microfinance have been generated by nongovernmental organizations (NGOs) that do not have commercial profit as their principal objective. By taking fresh approaches, these new microfinance institutions have penetrated rural financial markets and serviced an underclass of borrowers in a way that was unimaginable some 20 years ago. In 1988, IFPRI published one of the most detailed studies then available of the innovations in group-based banking introduced by the Grameen Bank of Bangladesh, which has provided credit to 2.1 million women in 36,000 villages.

Yet, many microfinance institutions heavily depend on subsidies and technical assistance provided by governments and donors (Christen et al. 1995; Webster and Fidler 1996; Gurgand et al. 1994). Many of them are built on the principles of self-help, cost recovery and the objective of achieving financial sustainability—at least in the medium to long run. But in their infant stage, cooperatives, village banks or credit groups all depend on a minimal amount of external technical—and to some extent—also financial assistance. Technical assistance is for example needed for training members in reading and maintaining loan and savings records, in learning about and complying with rules of the savings and credit contracts offered, in setting up control committees, and in holding meetings. Financial assistance may be required to mobilize capital for on-lending—even if it is lent at market rates as banks often are unwilling to lend to such novice institutions without a past repayment record. Only later on, when the group or village bank has proven its creditworthiness over a series of NGO-assisted loan cycles is there hope that the local member-based institution can directly transact with a commercial bank. But this then often also requires changes in the banking law. In a nutshell, financial systems development for the poor incurs considerable investment cost that neither the clients nor the banks are willing or able to fully cover in the short-run. Moreover, in most cases, one does not know the successful prototype of a community-based institution which is best adapted to local conditions and that will be accepted by the local banking industry. This phase of institutional experimentation and development necessitates public action that precedes the take-up of the eventual few viable prototypes by the private sector.

In essence, much of the recent innovations in rural finance should be seen as the outcome of public action to develop new institutions that are able to reduce transaction costs and increase outreach to previously excluded clientele. It can be argued that the development of a new institution generates a public good, similar to the development of a new high-yielding crop variety that can be readily copied or used by those who did not contribute to the cost of its development. The rapid growth in credit groups within and outside of Bangladesh, in regions and countries as diverse as Malawi, the United States, Egypt, and China, which learn from and replicate Grameen Bank principles, is a vivid example for an institutional innovation serving as an international public good.

5 Conclusions

Improving the poor's access to rural financial markets can potentially contribute to the reduction of transitory and chronic food insecurity. Covariate risks and various imperfections in intertemporal markets, such as uncertainty, information asymmetry, moral hazard, and lack of suitable collateral impede the development of integrated rural financial markets. The resulting capital constraints limit the welfare of a large share of poor creditworthy households, and force them to choose less risky, but less rewarding, income generating, consumption, and investment activities. A broader role of rural finance for food security of the poor is called for. It encompasses credit, savings, and insurance services for improved consumption smoothing, thus addressing transitory food security, and for improved allocation of assets and income generation, thus alleviating chronic food insecurity.

If one accepts the theoretical arguments on credit market imperfections and the resulting reductions in household welfare and economic growth, the question follows: what is the role of the state in the development of rural financial markets?

As a necessary condition for developing financial markets, the state has to implement policies which ensure macroeconomic stability, a market-determined allocation mechanism for capital and a reliable and enforceable legal and regulatory framework. Additional policies which tend to address additional necessary conditions to be fulfilled are: (1) agricultural price, tax, and subsidy policies, including those affecting real interest rates which do not discriminate against tenant and smallholder agriculture and related off-farm enterprises, (2) investments in rural infrastructure for reducing information and transaction costs in real and financial markets, (3) investments in enabling environment for human capital formation, such as primary and secondary education as well as improvement in the health and sanitary environment, and, fourth, but not least, policies for promotion of institutional innovations in the rural financial sector for low-income people, including the provision of a regulatory framework for strengthening the legal status of member-based financial institutions.

Regarding the fourth necessary policy instrument, linkages between third-tier, member-based nonbank financial institutions and the banking sector appear especially promising for sustainably offering a broader array of financial services at low transaction costs.

In recent years, much of public resources was devoted to experiment with new institutional arrangements, such as various forms of savings and credit groups, village banks and savings and credit cooperatives. All these institutions seek to cut transaction costs by utilizing locally available information and contract monitoring and enforcement mechanisms. Moreover, collateral is no longer provided by physical capital, as it is in traditional lending, but by social capital of the borrower or a group of borrowers. In other words, friends, relatives and fellow group or cooperative members guarantee the fulfillment of the financial contract.

While it is fair to say that much of these experiments did not ultimately lead to the development of new institutions, several successes, in particular in Latin America and Asia, nonetheless exist. The few studies so far investigating the impact of these institutions on income generation, household food security and formation of physical and human capital show encouraging results.

It is not surprising though that failures in creating new institutions outnumber successes. After all, socioeconomic and agroecological conditions vary between countries and even within a country and among different target groups, so that institutions need to be developed in view of these local conditions. This requires time, money, political will and skill. What can we learn from this? First of all, that it is feasible to invent new institutions by building on existing social capital of the poor, and that such institutions can help to improve income generation and food security for the rural poor. Second, if we were to rely on market forces, institutional innovation may be slower, and may go into directions that are less equitable. History shows that important innovations, such as the group-based banks in this century and the savings and credit cooperatives in the last century, were not created out of market forces alone. It was the financial, human and social capital raised or formed by altruistic leaders, such as Friedrich Wilhelm Raiffeissen in Germany that brought about the cooperative movement which eventually led to the development and expansion of credit and savings cooperatives in the second half of the nineteenth century all over Western Europe. These cooperatives succeeded in integrating farmers that were previously excluded from the formal banking system.

And much of the recent innovations have not been generated by the private banking sector, but by national or international nongovernmental organizations which were supported by governments, donors and foundations in many developing countries. Group-based banks, such as the Grameen Bank, and village banks, such as those promoted by FINCA, as well as innovative rural banks, such as the Bank for Agriculture and Agricultural Credit in Thailand or the Bankya Rakyat in Indonesia, have much contributed to providing access to credit and savings services to millions of poor people, in particular women. Many, but not all of these institutions require subsidies, albeit frequently on a modest level.[3]

Designing, experimenting with, and building financial institutions for the poor require economic resources and adequate consideration of longer-term social returns. As policymakers seek to make rational policy choices, they must weigh the social costs of designing and building financial institutions for the poor against their social benefits. Well-directed support, including initial subsidies, to promising microfinance institutions are likely to have payoffs in both equity (services to the poor) and long-term efficiency (reduced cost of services). This is a point of view that those who argue for a complete removal of subsidies should not ignore.

References

Adams, D.W. (1988): The Conundrum of Successful Credit Projects in Floundering Rural Financial Markets, in: Economic Development and Cultural Change, Vol. 36, No. 2, pp. 355-367.

Adams, Dale W., and John V. Pischke (eds) (1984): Undermining Rural Development with Cheap Credit. Boulder, Colo., U.S.A.: Westview Press.

3 Yaron and McDonald (1997) show that the village banks or Unit Desas of the Bank Rakyat Indonesia have consistently made profits since 1987 while serving a rural low-income clientele of farmers and micro-enterpreneurs.

Aryeetey, E. (1997): Rural Finance in Africa: Institutional Developments and Access for the Poor. Proceedings of the Annual World Bank Conference on Development Economics 1996, The World Bank: Washington, D.C.

Von Braun, J., H. Bouis, S. Kumar, and R. Pandya-Lorch (1992): Improving Food Security of the Poor: Concept, Policy and Programs, Washington, D.C.: International Food Policy Research Institute.

Von Braun, J., S. Malik, and M. Zeller (1993): Credit Markets, Input Support Policies, and the Poor: Insights from Africa and Asia. Paper presented at the 1993 American Agricultural Economics Association Pre-Conference on Post-Green Revolution Agricultural Development Strategies in the Thirld World: What Next?, Orlando, Fla., U.S.A.

Christen, R.P., E. Rhyne, R.C. Vogel and C. McKean (1995): Maximizing the Outreach of Microenterprise Finance: An analysis of Successful Microfinance Programs, U.S. Agency for International Development, Program and Operations Assessment Report No. 10, Washington, D.C.: USAID.

Diagne, A., M. Zeller, and M. Sharma (1997): Empirical Measurements of Households' Access to Credit and Credit Constraints in Developing Countries: Evidence Using a New Methodology, International Food Policy Research Institute (IFPRI), Washington, D.C. Mimeo.

Eswaran, M., and A. Kotwal (1990): Implications of Credit Constraints for Risk Behavior in Less-Developed Countries, in: Oxford Economic Papers 42.

Feder, G., R.E. Just, and D. Zilberman (1985): Adoption of Agricultural Innovations in Developing Countries, in: Economic Development and Cultural Change, Vol. 22, No. 2, pp. 255-296.

Feder, G., L.J. Lau, J.Y. Lin, and X. Luo (1990): The Relationship Between Credit and Productivity in Chinese Agriculture: A Microeconomic Model of Disequilibrium, in: American Journal of Agricultural Economics, Vol. 72, No. 5, pp. 1151-1157.

Foster, A. (1995): Prices, Credit Markets, and Child Growth in Low-Income Areas, in: Economic Journal, 105 (430), pp. 551-570.

Gurgand, M., G. Pederson, and J. Yaron (1994): Outreach and Sustainability of Six Rural Financial Institutions in Sub-Saharan Africa, Discussion Paper No. 248, Washington, D.C.: The World Bank.

Huppi, M., and G. Feder (1990): The Role of Groups and Credit Cooperatives in Rural Lending, in: World Bank Research Observer, Vol. 4, No. 2, pp. 187-204.

Jacoby, H. (1994): Borrowing Constraints and Progress through School: Evidence from Peru, in: Review of Economics and Statistics, 76 (1), pp. 151-160.

Krahnen, J.P., and R.H. Schmidt (1994): Development Finance as Institution Building: A New Approach to Poverty-Oriented Banking, Boulder, Colo., U.S.A.: Westview Press.

Pitt, M.M., and S.R. Khandker (1994): Household and Intrahousehold Impacts of the Grameen Bank and Similar Targeted Credit Programs in Bangladesh, Brown University, Providence, R.I., and World Bank, Washington, D.C., Mimeo.

Schrieder, G. R. (1995): The Role of Rural Finance for Food Security of the Poor in Cameroon, Frankfurt. Germany: Peter Lang Verlag.

Shipton, P. (1990): How Gambians Save—And what their Strategies Imply for International Aid, Agricultural and Rural Development Department, Working Paper 395. Washington, D.C.: World Bank.

Udry, C. (1990): Credit Markets in Northern Nigeria: Credit as Insurance in a Rural Economy, in: World Bank Economic Review, Vol. 4, No. 4, pp. 251-269.

Webster, L., and P. Fidler (eds.) (1996): The Informal Sector and Microfinance Institutions in West Africa. A Regional and Sectoral study, Washington, D.C.: World Bank.

Wenner, M.W. (1995): Group Credit: A Means to Improve Information Transfer and Loan Repayment Performance, in: Journal of Development Studies, Vol. 32, No. 2, pp. 263-281.

Yaron, J, and B. McDonald (1997): Recent Developments in Rural Finance. Paper presented at the 23rd International Conference of Agricultural Economists, Sacramento, California, August 1997.

Zeller, M., S. Broca, M. Sharma, J. von Braun, A. Diagne, F. Heidhues, J. Zhong Yi, E. Payongayong, G. Schrieder, and Z. Ling (1996): Financial Services for the Rural Poor: A Multicountry Synthesis and Implications for Policy and Future Research, Final Report to German Agency for Technical Cooperation (GTZ), International Food Policy Research Institute (IFPRI), Washington, D.C. Mimeo.

Zeller, M., G. Schrieder, J. von Braun, and F. Heidhues (1997): Rural Finance for Food Security of the Poor: Implications for Research and Policy, Food Policy Review 4, International Food Policy Research Institute (IFPRI), Washington, D.C.

Zeller, M. (1996): Determinants of Repayment Performance in Credit Groups: The Role of Program Design, Intra-group Risk Pooling, and Social Cohesion in Madagascar. Food Consumption and Nutrition Division, Discussion Paper No. 13. International Food Policy Research Institute (IFPRI), Washington, D.C. (Revised version appears in Economic Development and Cultural Change, January 1998).

PART IV

THE INTERNATIONAL INSTITUTIONAL FRAMEWORK

27

Multilateral Development Co-operation for Improved Food Security and Nutrition

D. John Shaw[*]

1 The multilateral network: an overview

Food security, one of the most fundamental of human rights, has been the subject of countless international conventions, declarations, compacts and resolutions. According to one calculation, more than 120 have been addressed on various issues relating to the right to food since 1920 (Pinstrup-Andersen et al. 1995). A series of international conferences organized by UN bodies have been held on key issues—habitat, children, nutrition, environment, human rights, population, social development, women—that relate directly or indirectly to food security and nutrition between the World Food Conference of 1974 and the World Food Summit of 1996.

Over 30 UN bodies are directly or indirectly involved in food security and nutrition objectives (see Figure 1). They include the UN Secretariat and Departments in New York, the specialized agencies (such as FAO, ILO, UNESCO, UNIDO and WHO), the multilateral financial institutions (the IMF, World Bank and the regional banks for Africa, Asia and Latin America), the major funding programmes (IFAD, UNDP, UNFPA, UNICEF, WFP), trade-related organizations (UNCTAD), special UN entities (UNEP, UN Centre for Human Rights, UN Centre for Human Settlements (Habitat), UN Centre for Social Development and Humanitarian Affairs), five UN regional economic commissions, emergency and relief agencies (DHA, UNHCR, UNRWA), and research and training institutes (UNU, UNITAR, UNRISD, INSTRAW).

Between them, the UN bodies with an interest in food security and nutrition are responsible for a large annual aid flow to the food security and nutrition sectors of developing countries. This aid would be more effective if it was better co-ordinated. Data on aid flows for improving food security and nutrition are incomplete and difficult to calculate precisely owing to their cross-sectoral nature. With these limitations, it has been estimated that the annual average flow of resources from UN agencies and bilateral sources to nutrition and what are considered to be related sectors out of total Official Development Assistance (ODA) between 1987 and 1991 amounted to close to $10 billion or 17 per cent of total ODA (Table 1). About

---

[*] This chapter has benefited from many of the views of Professor Sir Hans Singer and Simon Maxwell of the Institute of Development Studies, University of Sussex, England and from the comments of the editors on an earlier draft. I alone am responsible for any errors and shortcomings.

Figure 1: United Nations Bodies with an interest in food security and nutrition

UN Body	Special Interest*	UN Body	Special Interest*
FAO	Agricultural production, rural development, employment, income generation, marketing, trade, food security, nutrition, food emergencies/early warning, agrarian reform, structural adjustment, environment	**UN Centre for Human Rights**	Food as a human right
		UN Centre for Human Settlements (Habitat)	Food security and viable and sustainable settlements
IAEA	Irradiation of food	**UN Centre for Social Development and Humanitarian Affairs**	Food policy in context of social development
IBRD/IDA	Macro policy, structural adjustment, programme and project lending for food security and nutrition improvement, management of consultative groups	**UNCTAD**	Food trade and agricultural subsidies
		UNCTC	Food production and trade of transnationals
IFAD	Agricultural production, rural development, agrarian reform, structural adjustment, employment, income generation, environment	**UNDHA**	Humanitarian operations
		UNDP	Technical cooperation and grant aid for programmes and projects for food security and nutrition, management of round-table process
ILO	Employment, income generation, training, social protection, entitlement programmes, structural adjustment, rural development	**UNEP**	Food production, food security, environment and sustainability
IMF	Macro policy, structural adjustment, financing of food imports	**UNESCO**	Formal and informal education on food and nutrition and related issues
INSTRAW	Women and food security		

Figure 1 continued:

UN Body	Special Interest*	UN Body	Special Interest*
UNFPA	Food security and population questions	**UNRWA**	Food security and nutrition for Palestinian refugees
UNHCR	Refugees and food security and nutrition issues	**UN Secretariat and Departments (New York)**	UN General Assembly and Security Council, general over-sight, political questions, macro policy, structural adjustment, population, environment, sustainability
UNICEF	Food security and nutrition programmes, mothers and children, structural adjustment		
UNIDO	Agro-industry, food processing	**UNU** (including **WIDER**)	Research and teaching on food security issues
UNITAR	Training programmes in food security, nutrition and related issues	**WFP**	Development and emergency food aid for food security and nutrition
UN Regional Commissions (5)	Food security and nutrition in regional policy and context	**WHO**	Health and nutrition programmes, food standards (with FAO)
UNRISD	Research on food security and related issues		

* The special interest indicated for each UN body is illustrative and not definitive. There are also 16 international centres of the Consultative Group on International Agricultural Research (CGIAR), including the International Food Policy Research Institute (IFPRI), related to the United Nations system. In addition, there are three regional banks and the World Trade Organization (WTO), whose special interests relate to food security, that have cooperative arrangements with the United Nations system.

Source: WFC 1990; Maxwell and Shaw 1995.

$4.8 billion came from the UN system or about 20 per cent of ODA channelled multilaterally, of which 60 per cent was provided by the World Bank. About half of ODA channelled through UN bodies other than the World Bank was provided for these purposes. Slightly more than $5 billion came from bilateral sources, or about 15 per cent of total bilateral ODA (ACC/SCN 1995).

About $2.4 billion was supplied in the form of food aid, which has increased in recent years mainly on account of the rapid increase in emergencies, especially those caused by civil wars. To quote a specific example, 50 million people received food aid from the World Food Programme alone in 1995 in a resource transfer of 2.8 million tons of food delivered at a cost of $1.2 billion, over half of which went to the victims of emergencies (WFP 1996).

Table 1: Estimated aid flows for nutrition and related sectors within total Official Development Assistance (ODA) (annual average 1987-1991 in US$ millions)

Category	World Bank	Other UN Bodies	Bilateral	Total ODA
Direct nutrition	87	41	16	144
Health	410	440	494	1345
Population	107	73	164	344
Water/Sanitation	755	102	1255	2111
Food care*	92	20	32	144
Child welfare	255	102	190	547
Women/Literacy	2	35	50	87
Community development	760	114	774	1648
Emergency/Rehabilitation (non-food)	385	143	537	1065
Food aid**	-	852	1543	2395
General resources***	17511	1974	29276	48761
Total	20364	3895	34331	58590

* Includes food safety, processing, quality control, storage, and reduction of post-harvest losses.
** For development and emergencies.
*** Other areas of development such as agriculture, education, industry, social, environment, general planning, etc.

Source: ACC/SCN 1995: Figure 1.

Total financial assistance (excluding food aid) for projects that have a direct impact on improving nutrition status in developing countries is estimated to have averaged $144 million a year during the five years 1987-91, representing 0.2 per cent of total ODA (Table 2). About 60 per cent of this assistance came from the World Bank, and 89 per cent from the UN system as a whole. On a per capita basis, these direct nutrition funds averaged 4 US cents per person a year for all developing countries. The regional distribution of these resources shows a wide range of per capita availabilities, up to 10 cents per person a year ($29 million) in South America, compared to 6 cents per person (total $31 million) a year in sub-Saharan Africa, and 4 cents per person (total $48 million) a year in South Asia. Related to the estimated numbers of malnourished children, South America received about $10 per malnourished child a year, sub-Saharan Africa about $1, and South Asia about 50 cents. Clearly, these external funds were unlikely to have had a major impact on the nutritional situation (ACC/SCN 1995: 15).

By contrast, by the late 1980s, world military expenditure had risen to about $1,000 billion a year, $800 billion in the industrial countries and $200 billion in developing countries. With an average of five per cent of the GNP of industrial countries, and rather more of Third World income, going to military expenditures, it is hardly surprising that so much of international life is affected (Sivard 1991).

Table 2: External funding for nutrition improvement projects by region (five year average 1987-1991)

	Five year average (US $ millions)	Per person (US cents)	Per malnourished child (US $)
Region			
Sub-Saharan Africa	30.7	6	1.15
Middle America and Caribbean	10.5	7	3.61
South America	28.9	10	10.31
South Asia	48.4	4	0.50
Near East and North Africa	2.8	1	0.57
South East Asia	12.6	3	0.61
China	0.7	*	0.03
Interregional	9.0	-	-
All developing countries	143.5	4	0.80
Source			
World Bank	87.1	2	0.48
Other UN Bodies	40.5	1	0.22
Bilateral	16.0	1	0.09

* Less than one US cent.
Figures rounded.

Source: ACC/SCN 1995: Table 7.

2 Multilateral aid: a balance sheet of performance

It is easy to be critical of multilateral development co-operation in the fields of food security and nutrition. Despite all the rhetoric, conventions, resolutions and resources, and the many UN agencies directly and indirectly involved, the number of people that remain exposed to food insecurity and malnutrition is a major impediment to economic and social development and peace, and a moral indictment of our civilization. However, some important gains have been made that should now be built upon. The balance sheet is not all negative.

2.1 Positive achievements

2.1.1 Understanding causes and providing solutions

United Nations bodies, individually and collectively, have contributed to major advances in understanding the causes of, and solutions to, food insecurity and malnutrition. Since the 1974 World Food Conference, with its emphasis on increasing food production and supply, and the creation of food stocks and emergency reserves, the concept of food security has "evolved, developed, multiplied and diversified", reflecting" the nature of the food problem as it is experienced by poor people themselves," and explicitly recognizing the complexity and diversity of the concept (Maxwell 1996: 155-156). To ensure food security, it is now realized that not only should there be increased food production, and stability of food supplies, but that poor people should have access to the food they need either by producing it themselves, through exchanges, by having the income to buy it, or through gifts and food aid programmes ("safety-nets") that provide them with food in difficult times (FAO 1982).

UN bodies have assisted in the implementation of thousands of development programmes and projects and emergency operations that relate to improving food security and nutrition. This practical experience has provided invaluable lessons in what to do, and what not to do. More should be done to synthesize this experience in each UN body, and to share this experience among the relevant agencies in the UN system, as well as in the international community generally. This would help improve programme and project design and performance, and provide an aid to advocacy and public information. The general public remains poorly informed about the importance of food security and nutrition, the successes (as well as the failures) of multilateral assistance, and the level of aid available.

The experience of UN agencies has shown the comparative advantages of different kinds of assistance programmes and projects. Ensuring employment is seen as a basic requirement for ensuring food security so that people can have the income needed for food purchases. "Today, understanding the labour market is as important for addressing the food security problems of the rural and urban poor in developing countries as understanding the food market" (von Braun 1995: 1). For the abjectly poor, who have only a single resource, their own labour, dependence on the labour market is crucial to their food security. At the same time, the potential and limitations of food subsidy programmes in developing countries (Pinstrup-Andersen 1988), and of supplementary feeding programmes for vulnerable groups, are now better understood.

The proper functioning of markets, liberalized world food trade, improvement of the inadequate infrastructure in many developing countries, which prevents food from reaching markets, and appropriate pricing policies to give incentive for increased food production without pricing the poor consumer out of the market, are also recognized as essential elements of a package of factors that are necessary for achieving food security (Pinstrup-Andersen 1994). On the other hand, the philosophy of "leave it to market forces" has been shown to be inadequate in attaining food security for all. A judicious balance of public and private sector involvement in the market place is necessary to ensure that the poorer segments of society are reached and benefited.

Conceptually, it is now appreciated that food insecurity can either be chronic or transitory (World Bank 1986). Chronic food insecurity involves a continuously inadequate diet caused by a persistent inability to acquire food by whatever means—production, purchase, sharing, foraging. Transitory food insecurity is a temporary decline in a household's access to enough food arising from instability of production, prices or household income. Policies and programmes for reducing chronic or transitory food insecurity differ. For the former, they may include increasing food supply (through production, imports or improved market integration), subsidizing consumer prices, and targeted income transfers. For the latter, they may involve stabilizing supplies and prices, and assisting vulnerable groups directly through aid programmes.

It is also recognized that food security and nutrition objectives should be made central and explicit outcomes of national development plans, not incidental or fortuitous benefits (UN 1989b). The complexity of these aims calls for multi-sectoral provisions and should not be left to the agriculture or health sectors alone. The costs and benefits of "food self-sufficiency" (producing all the food required) and "food self-reliance" (importing part of food needs from foreign exchange earnings) are now better understood. National and household food security are not necessarily the same: one can be achieved without reaching the other. There are no blanket or quick solutions, and each country has to draw up its own strategy according to its own circumstances.

Cost-effective programmes to improve food security should be tailored to the needs of the poor, and with their full participation (Oakley 1991; FAO 1990). The poor are not a homogeneous group. There are significant differences among them, and in the solutions to their problems. Their vulnerability to food insecurity changes over time, with increasing concentration on women and children, the landless, and the urban poor, in the resource- poor areas of Africa and South Asia (Crawshaw and Shaw 1995). Women are now identified as a key target group. Not only are they (and their children) often numerically and physically the worst affected by food insecurity but they played a pivotal role in the process of achieving and retaining household food security (Quisumbing et al. 1995).

It is increasingly being realized that there is a close, and growing, link between poverty, food insecurity and vulnerability to recurring emergencies. A concept of "human security" has been developed that combines two major components: freedom from fear and freedom from want (UNDP 1994: 24-25). If the food security of the most vulnerable people could be improved at the household and community levels through development projects that provided employment, income and assets, the continued need for emergency aid could be considerably reduced. Hence the need for a "relief-development continuum" through which development assistance would be provided to support national disaster mitigation and rehabilitation programmes and emergency aid would be used for development purposes, while addressing the immediate disaster needs.

A major focus should be on supporting labour-intensive works programmes that would provide simultaneously: (a) immediate employment and income, thereby alleviating poverty and strengthening capacity; and (b) construction and improvement of the infrastructure needed to increase agricultural production, stimulate rural development, and strengthen measures against future emergencies. Together with these labour-intensive programmes, targeted food, nutrition and health interventions could improve the well-being of the poor and help them withstand future food shortages. Much of this is built on the experience of countries in Asia, especially China and India (von Braun 1991; WFP 1992).

2.1.2 Advocacy

The UN bodies have played an important role in advocacy. The series of world conferences organized multilaterally through the UN system have been criticized for the costs they have involved at a time of scarce aid resources. They have been described as expensive talking-shops, with badly organized and inflated agenda, resulting in unrealistic programmes of action and inadequate commitment of additional resources, raising false hopes for progress. They have served, however, to galvanize world attention to key issues of global importance, provided forums for airing different views and opinions, and acted as instruments of advocacy and for co-ordinated action by the international community. At the same time, they have highlighted the global dimensions of the issues discussed, and established agreed goals and targets, as, for example, the specific targets developed by UNICEF and WHO, which were given prominent recognition at the 1990 World Summit for Children.

2.1.3 Technical co-ordination and standard-setting

There have been improvements in technical co-ordination and standard-setting in the food security and nutrition areas within the UN system. Standards are never as neutral as they appear, and the debates have been both technical and political as, for example, over the role of food industry interests, and the establishment of a code of conduct for the use of baby foods. Many technical and co-ordinating committees have played an important part in establishing standards, as in the case of setting a minimum ration scale for refugees.

2.1.4 Standardization and dissemination of data

UN bodies have made an important contribution to the standardization and dissemination of basic data on food, nutrition and other food security-related subjects. Good examples are: FAO's AGROSTAT system of agricultural statistics, and its

Global Information and Early Warning System on Food and Agriculture; UNDP's annual *Human Development Report* and its *Human Development Index*; UNICEF's annual publication on *The State of the World's Children*; UNHCR's yearly report on The *State of the World's Refugees*; WFP's international food aid data base (INTERFAIS); and the ACC/SCN's monitoring of the world nutrition situation. These, and other, data systems provide a regular overview of the dimensions of the problem, a measure of progress—or the lack of it, and a focus on critical points for action.

2.2 Shortcomings

Despite the important achievements indicated above, there is the more negative side to the balance sheet.

2.2.1 Problems of co-ordination

A major problem is that the record of co-ordination among UN bodies is at best chequered. Food security and nutrition are complex, multi-sectoral and multi-faceted subjects that do not lend themselves to neatly packaged solutions, and do not fall wholly within the mandate of any single UN agency or programme. They call essentially for policy and operational considerations that cross the boundaries of many aid bodies, and the organizational and administrative dividing lines within them. In addition, while there has been a growing tendency towards a common definition, and understanding, of the problems and their solution, important differences remain (Maxwell 1990; Maxwell 1996).

The UN system has grown up "like topsy". Each agency has its own mandate, constitution, governing body, funding arrangement and location. Given the multi-institutional structure and sectoralization of the UN system, extensive provisions have been made to try to ensure co-ordination among the system's institutions. At the political level, decision-making is co-ordinated by the UN General Assembly and Security Council in New York. At the inter-governmental level, the Economic and Social Council (ECOSOC) is charged with co-ordinating the economic and social work of the UN system. At the inter-secretariat level, the Administrative Committee on Co-ordination (ACC), consisting of the heads of the UN agencies and meeting under the presidency of the UN Secretary-General, was created to co-ordinate the activities of the UN bodies.

It was to provide a "co-ordinating mechanism ... for the successful co-ordination and follow-up of policies concerning food production, nutrition, food security, food trade and food aid, as well as related matters, by all the agencies of the United Nations system" that the UN World Food Council (WFC) was established at the ministerial level by the UN General Assembly in 1975, following a resolution of the 1974 World Food Conference (UN 1975: 18). In addition, to foster co-operation at the technical level, the ACC established a number of subcommittees and task forces, including a Subcommittee on Nutrition (ACC/SCN). At the country level,

UNDP was expected to play a co-ordinating role for the operational activities of the UN system. It was to serve as a central funding and programming agency, under the leadership of a UN resident co-ordinator, to ensure system-wide co-ordination in the country context. To facilitate policy dialogue and co-ordinate aid programmes among donors at the country level, the World Bank instituted the practice of chairing "consultative groups" in the early 1960s, and the UNDP initiated a process of "round table" discussions in the 1970s.

Despite these various arrangements, extensive reviews have found co-ordination within the UN system to be deficient. The UN agencies are still perceived to compete excessively and joint programming of their operational activities remain mostly inadequate (UN 1987; UN 1989a). Decisions are often taken without reference to decisions made on the same or similar subjects in other agencies and forums. It is hardly surprising, therefore, that co-ordination of both policy and action has been generally illusive. This has led to conflicting policy advice to developing countries, to lack of integration of aid resources—financial, technical and food, and to difficulties in linking relief and development assistance in a "continuum" of action.

While many UN agencies are engaged in some food-security and nutrition-related activities, few have focused sharply on hunger and poverty alleviation. There are important exceptions, including IFAD, UNICEF and WFP, which specifically concentrate their support on small farmers, the rural poor and nutritionally vulnerable groups, and the humanitarian aid agencies, DHA and UNHCR. UN agency priorities are generally widely set, reflecting different, and conflicting, interests within their governing bodies. The mandates of many UN agencies are directed at generally fostering economic development and human welfare. Some are specifically called upon to assist in raising nutritional levels, such as FAO, IFAD, UNICEF, WFP and WHO. Others address aspects relating to food security in terms of supply of, and access to, food as well as related macro-economic policies.

Often, hunger-alleviation and food security objectives are not well integrated into the overall activities of individual UN agencies, and there is need for more effective internal co-ordination within them, particularly the larger ones. With the dispersion of priorities, many UN bodies spread their limited resources thinly over a wide range of activities, generating large numbers of small-scale projects, endangering the quality of the agencies' work, and their impact on hunger and poverty reduction.

A major shortcoming has been the split between the Bretton Woods institutions (the IMF and the World Bank), both part of the UN system, and the other UN agencies. The IMF and World Bank policies and programmes of economic reform and structural adjustment have often resulted in a decrease in the real purchasing power of the poor and limited their ability to purchase food and other essential items (World Bank 1988). Adjustment programmes have also been found to have a negative effect on food security (FAO 1989) and have reduced basic nutrition, health and other social services for the poor, resulting in the plea for "adjustment with a human face" (Cornia et al. 1987).

In sum, there appears to have been an asymmetry between negative and positive effects. Negative effects of adjustment on the poor have often been certain and immediate, whereas positive effects have been uncertain and of long gestation (Shaw and Singer 1988). As a consequence, assistance provided by the non-Bretton Woods UN agencies has been undermined by the structural adjustment measures imposed on developing countries, and an increasing amount of assistance provided by them has gone to bailing out the poor from their negative effects.

Despite improvements, complexity and duplication in the UN system in the fields of food security and nutrition remain a cause of wonder. For example, there are five bodies (previously six) concerned with food aid, a resource which has an immediate appeal for addressing the problems of food insecurity and malnutrition. This applies to other areas. With so many UN agencies involved directly and indirectly, with different mandates and aid budgets, there is a real danger that because food security and nutrition issues are regarded as "everybody's business", they may become "nobody's business".

The demise of the UN World Food Council has provided sobering and instructive experience. At its final session in 1992, ministers agreed that "the Council has fallen short of achieving the political leadership and co-ordination role expected from its founders ... Food and hunger issues must remain at the centre of national and international development efforts ... There is therefore general agreement on the need for review of the role and functioning of the Council placed into the wider context of global food security management and the overall restructuring of the social and economic activities of the United Nations system" (UN 1992b).

There were many reasons for WFC's lack of success. The Council's membership consisted mainly of ministers of agriculture, who had neither mandate to cover the range of food security issues outside the agricultural sector, nor legally binding control over the activities of the UN agencies. The Council's role became a confused mixture of general advocacy and action plans. Its meetings, which took place once a year, were insufficiently focused on monitoring key action programmes, and were often too broad in scope. Insufficient attention was given to inter-sessional activities to keep the focus and maintain the momentum. Its Secretariat was too small. There was lack of co-operation—even resentment—from key UN agencies. And its location at FAO headquarters in Rome proved to be a major impediment, particularly as that organization saw itself as playing a major and co-ordinating role in UN policies and activities related to food security and nutrition. Yet the need for a central, undivided focus within the UN system on the elimination of hunger and malnutrition, and the achievement of food security for all, are as important now as they were when the decision was taken in 1975 to establish the World Food Council (WFC 1990).

2.2.2 Aid quality and operational performance

The quality of aid and operational performance of the UN agencies have been very uneven. The most effective appear to be those characterized generally by decentralized administrations, an action-oriented organizational structure, appropriate investment in research and analysis, and a commitment to advocacy. While agreement has been reached on overall objectives, and even targets, as at the international conferences mentioned above, it has been more difficult to reach consensus on how to tackle food security and nutritional problems. There has been a tendency to fudge difficult choices that might disadvantage certain interests, or to issue guidance only at the level of generalities. Furthermore, the UN system has been better at issuing general statements of intent than it has been at turning these into actionable statutes with some legal force. This can be seen, for example, in the area of food as a human right. So far, statements of the ideal in international conventions have yet to be turned into precise changes of policy and action at the country level. In addition, with some notable exceptions, such as the UN Conference on Environment and Development in 1992 and the GATT Uruguay Round of Multilateral Trade Negotiations that ended in 1994, the UN has generally not been successful in providing a forum for real international policy negotiations.

2.2.3 State sovereignty and international co-operation

There are a number of sensitive problems accounting for these lacunae. One is the extent to which the major powers are willing to cede their national interests in contending with global and regional problems through multilaterally co-ordinated international development co-operation. Greater co-ordination has been achieved in meeting large-scale emergencies than in providing development assistance. Another problem is the way in which the UN Charter and mandates of the UN agencies, crafted in different circumstances many years ago, may no longer be appropriate for tackling some of the major issues of today. Perhaps one of the starkest examples is the case of food security crises caused by civil war and state failures.

The principle of state sovereignty is enshrined in the UN Charter, although "this principle shall not prejudice the application of enforcement measures under Chapter VII of the Charter relating to 'Actions with respect to threats to the peace, breaches of the peace, and acts of aggression' " (UN 1945). Prior to the mid-1980s, the UN seldom intervened to provide relief in complex political emergencies without there being an agreed cease-fire in advance. By the end of the 1980s, however, an accepted form of intervention was to negotiate access to people in war zones through "corridors of peace" with the UN agencies concerned often devolving to NGOs the responsibility for delivering food and other relief supplies. This erosion of national sovereignty was further deepened during and after the Gulf War with the innovation of using military personnel to protect a UN- mandated relief operation, as in Angola, Bosnia, Iraq, Kurdistan, Rwanda and Somalia. Thus, humanitarian assistance has become closely integrated with the dynamics of violence. There are as yet no clearly established rules, guidelines or modalities, and there are no easy solutions. Much will depend on the nature of the conflict in each situation (Shaw 1996).

The new mood and challenge has practical consequences, calling for a review of aid agencies' mandates and activities that take them within the borders of sovereign states in food security and other fields. Few UN agencies have the mandate and experience of coping with emergencies as well as supporting development. The General Regulations of WFP, one of the UN bodies that provides both relief and development assistance, were amended in 1992 to allow it to supply humanitarian relief at the request of the UN Secretary-General instead of waiting for a request for such aid from a national government, which might never come. The World Bank has taken a higher profile in political liberalization. And there has been a lively debate about the scope for UN intervention in long-running political crises causing famine (Righter 1995; Parsons 1995; Gordon 1995).

2.2.4 Politico-bureaucratic problems

Politico-bureaucratic problems, both with and among UN agencies, are profound, leading to pressure for a major reform of the UN system. Leadership is seen as a vital concern, beginning at the top, if major progress is to be made in achieving the oft-pronounced aims of ending hunger and poverty. A lot has been said about the lack of "political will" among leaders in developing countries to achieve food security for all. Less is said about the lack of determination among leaders in the UN system to achieve that objective. This is perhaps hardly surprising given the way in which they are appointed.

The process of appointing the UN Secretary-General has been described as "a curiously haphazard affairs" (Urquhart and Childers 1990). Recommendations for an improved election process include: serious consideration by governments of the necessary qualifications for the post; a single seven-year term; cessation of the practice of individual campaigning; agreed rules concerning nominations and a timetable for elections; well- organized search for the best candidates worldwide; inclusion of women as candidates; high-level consideration of candidates by governments; and avoidance of an election or selection process that results in the appointment of the "lowest common denominator".

Concerning leadership of the UN specialized agencies and programmes, it is recommended that the process of appointment be "demystified", with far more imaginative and wider search procedures, single term appointments for a maximum of seven years, and major improvements in the selection process to ensure the highest standards and the most effective choices (Urquhart and Childers 1990). Leadership is, therefore, a special problem. It is perceived as being "self-perpetuating by whatever means, preoccupied with personal prestige and egocentric towards authority" (Abbott 1992). Executive heads have been described as "barons" who find it difficult to collaborate (Handy 1985).

Proposals have been made to "de-politicize" the UN specialized agencies, such as FAO, ILO, UNESCO, UNIDO and WHO, making them leading technical bodies in their respective fields. They would then have non-voting, decision-making procedures, or voting arrangements that avoided either domination by the major donors countries, or by consensus that would lead to stalemate between developing and developed countries, and a central financing of their activities to ensure co-ordinated programmes of action and avoid duplication (Williams 1987).

For the funding programmes (IFAD, UNDP, UNFPA, UNICEF and WFP), proposals have included their amalgamation into one consolidated fund, with a common location and common governing body, to maintain cohesion and common oversight, avoid duplication and waste, and reduce administrative and programme overhead costs (UN 1969; Urquhart and Childers 1994). Others have seen these proposals as retrogressive, and containing the hidden agenda of reducing aid resources, which would not only reduce the effectiveness of these programmes but also rob them of their particular comparative advantages in tackling specific aspects of emergency and development problems (Singer 1995b).

The structure of UN organizations is often ill-suited to tackling the multi-faceted nature of food security and nutrition problems, mirroring the difficulties experienced in governments in developing countries. A common feature is that aid agencies are vertically, rather than horizontally, organized. Growth in the number of special task forces, of cross-cutting inter-agency meetings, and of co-ordinating bodies in the UN system is taken as a sign of an organizational culture in crisis. This "patch and mend" approach is usually not sustainable, even when targets are agreed upon and a clear demarcation of agency responsibilities made. Responsibility for devising action plans to meet these targets is usually passed back to national governments, where the action plans to meet different sets of targets are unco-ordinated, overlap with each other, and replicate the organizational problems of the UN agencies.

2.2.5 Resource constraints

Finally, there remain the basic problems of providing the resources necessary to meet the challenge of providing food security for all, and of making the best use of the assistance that is provided, often confounded by the application by donors of conditionality on the aid they provide (Singer 1995a). Foreign aid is big business. Yet little is known by the general public, and even by some "professionals", about its intricacies. Much external assistance is given out of mutual self-interest. There are benefits for the aid giver as well as the aid receiver (Raffer and Singer 1996).

Increasing concern is being expressed about future multilateral development co-operation for a number of reasons. First, there is a general expectation that aid will decline in real terms. Second, an increasing proportion of that aid is going to address the symptoms, not the causes, of the development problems of developing countries, mainly in the form of emergency relief. Third, the trend seems to be for more aid to be provided bilaterally, rather than multilaterally through the UN system, in an unco-ordinated way, and directed mainly to serve donor political and commercial objectives. Fourth, of the aid that is supplied multilaterally, the major part is expected to be channelled through the Bretton Woods institutions (where the voting system favours the large donor countries), mainly for macro-economic adjustment and reform programmes, with the remainder going, in an unrelated way, to the rest of the UN agencies to look after what have been described as the "soft parts" of the development process relating to the development and protection of human resources. Fifth, assistance that is now going to the economies in transition of the former Yugoslavia and Soviet Union is at the expense of that going to the traditional developing countries. Sixth, increasing conditionality is being applied by donors in the provision of their aid. And, last, but by no means least, is the lack of clearly identified priorities, which must be tackled comprehensively in national development plans and programmes with the limited resources available, of which food security for all should be recognized as of the highest order.

Various ways are being examined for increasing aid resources, and for breaking the vicious circle of: inadequate and unassured resources, resulting in lack of capacity and impact on the problems of development; which, in turn, undermines political support; which further reduces the aid resources made available. A 20:20 global human development compact has been proposed by which governments in developing countries and donors would undertake to allocate 20 per cent of public spending and aid budgets respectively to human development priorities, including food security (UNDP 1994). Various forms of international taxation have been mooted that would give the UN system independent resources to enable it to tackle the problems for which it has responsibility, effectively and promptly, and perhaps in so doing elicit further support and contributions, thereby breaking the vicious circle (UNDP 1994: 70; Singer 1995b: 38).

Addressing emergencies and providing relief assistance is assuming greater urgency in aid agencies, attracting additional staff time and attention. The cost of peacekeeping has escalated at the expense of development assistance. The UN, in its first 48 years of existence, committed some $4 billion to peacekeeping operations. It spent that amount in 1993 alone. Meanwhile, the real value of development spending by UN agencies has remained stagnant, or even declined. Most agencies have had their staff levels frozen or reduced. This has inevitably resulted in decreased attention to development assistance to overcome chronic vulnerability to food insecurity as emergencies requiring immediate action have escalated. This shift in attention and resources is occurring despite much recent work that points to the complex interrelationships among the different causes of food insecurity and the need for more sophisticated approaches to overcoming it. Thus, at the very time when more is being understood about the causes of vulnerability to food insecurity, it appears likely that fewer resources, manpower and attention will be made available to help fight the problem (Crawshaw and Shaw 1995).

2.2.6 Aid conditionality

The policy statement of the aid ministers of the Development Assistance Committee (DAC) of the Organisation of Economic Co-operation and Development (OECD), which comprise the major donor countries, on development co-operation in the 1990s (OECD 1989) concluded that the vicious circle of underdevelopment can be broken only through integrating the objectives and requirements of: promoting sustainable economic growth; enabling broader participation of all people in the productive processes; a more equitable sharing of the economic benefits; ensuring environmental sustainability; and slowing population growth.

Subsequently, conditionality concerns have been added by donors to the provision of their assistance including democracy, human rights, good governance and accountability. But a principle of "contractuality," applied to both the donor and recipient of aid, rather than "conditionality" applied only to the latter, should be adopted. It is equally important for conditions to be applied to the donors of aid to ensure that their assistance is adequately and reliably provided, and on appropriate terms and conditions, as it is for the receivers of aid to use it effectively.

3 New opportunities

A bleak and dismal picture has been painted of multilateral development co-operation for improved food security and nutrition. Recent developments have, however, given rise to renewed optimism. The following are some examples.

3.1 A new general framework

A new general framework has been provided for the UN system by the global summit and development conferences of the 1990s. This framework has been encompassed in two interrelated initiatives taken by the UN Secretary-General, in response to UN General Assembly resolutions, *An Agenda for Peace* (Boutros-Ghali 1992) and *An Agenda for Development* (Boutros-Ghali 1995). Food security is a central requirement for both agendas: food insecurity is a major barrier.

An Agenda for Peace calls, inter alia, for preventive diplomacy (to avoid disputes escalating into conflicts, including early warning systems and fact-finding to provide timely and accurate information on impending crises), peacemaking and peace-keeping, and post-conflict peace-building operations. *An Agenda for Development* begins with the statement that "Development is the most important task facing humanity today. Yet ... we are in danger of losing sight of such an essential task. Beset by the growth of conflicts, and the necessity to maintain the peace in the tense post-cold war environment, we risk getting lost in the urgency of peace-keeping, at the expense of the longer term development effort." Development is recognized as a fundamental human right, and the most secure basis for peace. While there is want, no people can achieve lasting development.

3.2 Linking relief and development

The root causes of food insecurity, poverty and underdevelopment, are exacerbated by natural and man-made disasters. Yet, the division of external assistance into "development" and "emergency" compartments, each with its separate agenda, terms, legislation, financing and operating agencies, (even separate units within the same aid agency), has dichotomized what in the real experience of developing countries is not separated, the interrelationship between disasters and the development process. Attempts are now being made to remove the artificial dichotomy between relief and development assistance. A UN General Assembly resolution in 1991 (UN 1991) emphasized the inter-dependence between humanitarian assistance and development and the need for a "continuum of action" from early warning and prevention of, and preparedness for, disasters to the transition from relief to reconstruction, rehabilitation and development, not as a linear, but as a circular, process in which relief assistance supports and protects development and development mitigates the effects of disasters (Singer 1996a; Maxwell and Buchanan-Smith 1994).

In response to a call by the donor community to improve co-ordination among UN agencies in emergency situations, a Department of Humanitarian Affairs (DHA) was created at the UN in New York in April 1992 to provide leadership in the UN response to emergencies. It remains to be seen whether these arrangements will strengthen co-ordination in the UN system in times of emergencies significantly and permanently.

Experience has shown repeatedly that accurate, timely and commonly available information of impending disasters, coupled with sound and speedy response, are key factors in mitigating their effects. There are now good prospects for major improvements in early warning and tracking systems through the application of remote sensing and satellite imagery, linked to a worldwide computerized information superhighway. But such systems should have common, multilateral ownership that would have the confidence of all concerned, thereby helping to produce a common response. However, for the full benefits of these systems to be realized, they would need to be backed up by response systems on the ground with adequate resources in order to react quickly and effectively to the early warning signals. The returns from investment in these early warning and response systems would be considerable.

3.3 Country-level co-ordination

The centre-piece of the resolution is the formulation of a "country strategy note" (CSN) by governments in developing countries, which would be based on their priorities and plans. This would ensure effective integration of assistance provided by the UN system into the development process of developing countries, and facilitate assessment and evaluation of the impact and sustainability resulting from UN development assistance. While this provides an enabling framework for improved county-level co-ordination, it raises three conundrums. First, no reference is made to the assistance provided by the Bretton Woods institutions, which are treated as if they were not UN specialized agencies. They should be brought into the process of formulating CSNs, which could also act to ensure full consistency of the Policy Planning Framework documents which the IMF and the World Bank draw up as a basis for their assistance. Secondly, no reference is made to emergency assistance, although it is assumed that this will now be done in the context of the relief-development continuum. Thirdly, the need for co-ordination between assistance provided by the UN system and that supplied bilaterally and by NGOs should be addressed, although the CSN could provide an effective framework for bringing this about.

3.4 Trade and food security

The conclusion of the GATT Uruguay Round and the setting up of the WTO provide a major opportunity for improving world trade in food commodities as an essential contribution to achieving world food security. The outcomes of the Uruguay Round will be only one of a number of factors affecting world food production, trade and prices, but will they prove to be the swing factor? A major change has to be brought about by the Uruguay Round in the way food markets are viewed and in the rules under which countries must operate their national agricultural policies. This should prevent a return to old habits, ensure the emergence of improved opportunities, and provide a basis for the next episode of multilateral negotiations on agriculture under the auspices of the WTO (UNCTAD Secretariat 1994).

While the food-exporting developed countries are expected to gain substantially from the Uruguay Round, it is recognized that the least-developed and net food-importing developing countries may experience negative effects in terms of the availability of adequate supplies of basic foodstuffs from external sources on reasonable terms and conditions, including short-term difficulties in financing normal levels of commercial food imports (UNCTAD Secretariat 1994; Harrison et al. 1995). It has therefore been agreed to provide an adequate level of food aid to meet the needs of those countries and to give full consideration in the context of aid programmes to requests for the provision of technical and financial assistance to improve their agricultural productivity and infrastructure (GATT Secretariat 1994: 448; Shaw and Singer 1995; Konandreas/Greenfield 1996; Singer 1996b).

Much will depend on how effectively WTO will actually work. Questions have also been raised concerning its precise working relationships with the IMF and World Bank in a global compact linking macro-economic policies related to fiscal measures, development assistance and trade. Keynes's proposals at Bretton Woods in 1944 led to the establishment of the IMF and the World Bank but his "third pillar", an International Trade Organization (ITO), was not created. While the United Nations Conference on Trade and Development, held in Havana, Cuba in 1948, reached agreement on the structure and objectives of the ITO, the Havana Charter was never ratified by governments. Fifty years later, the WTO was set up but mainly as a mechanism to implement the agreements concluded under the GATT Uruguay Round, without the broad policy framework for international trade, and, in particular, without the function of commodity price stabilization that was foreseen for the ITO in the Havana Charter. As a result, the role and impact of WTO on incomes and employment in poor developing countries, particularly in sub-Saharan Africa, could be limited, or even negative.

In addition, restrictive business practices, which were included in the Havana Charter of the abortive ITO, are not included in the mandate of the WTO. Thus, there is no bar on multinational corporations exercising their power in international trade to increase international food prices even more than a reduction in supply brought about by the Uruguay Round. Restrictive business practices are to be dealt with separately in the UN system, mainly in UNCTAD, but given the lack of political and financial support, this may not be effective.

This suggests a definite need for a safety-net for the least-developed and net food-importing developing countries. Such a safety-net could either require financial assistance, which would involve the Bretton Woods institutions; or food aid, when it would involve WFP; or be trade-related, when it would involve discussion in WTO; or be related to global governance, when the UN in New York would be involved. In many cases, a mixture of all these solutions would probably be called into play. It is also imperative that WTO and UNCTAD work closely to evolve an integrated policy for international trade and development and undertake analytical work to assess the impact of the various agreements reached during the Uruguay Round, and recorded in the Final Act, on the poor developing countries.

3.5 Food aid and food security

While food aid alone is not the solution to solving the problem of food insecurity, it is a major resource for meeting transitory food insecurity, particularly during emergencies, and for supporting development programmes for achieving food security in the longer run (Shaw 1993; Shaw and Clay 1993). The Final Act of the GATT Uruguay Round and the creation of WTO have also provided an opportunity for establishing a new food aid regime within a liberalizing global economy (Shaw and Singer 1995). A large part of so-called "trade" does not take place as straight market transactions at free international prices. It is conducted through a labyrinth of various forms of bilateral agreements and export enhancement programmes that provide discounts from the "commercial" price (itself reduced by overhanging surpluses and domestic production subsidies) in many direct and indirect ways.

This "grey area" food aid, which is perhaps quadruple the level of statistically recorded food aid (12.9 million tons in 1994), is provided largely for donor short-run political and commercial (market protection and penetration) purposes and rarely benefits the poor and food insecure. If this hidden "food aid" is now forced out into the open, brought within the disciplines of food aid as defined in the Final Act, and focused on the needs of the poor and food insecure, a major step would be taken in dealing with the world hunger problem and, by extension, the eradication of poverty and food insecurity. A broader definition of what constitutes food aid is now required.

In the Final Act of the Uruguay Round, it has been agreed to establish appropriate mechanisms to ensure that the implementation of the results of the Uruguay Round on trade in agriculture does not adversely affect the availability of food aid at a level which is sufficient to continue to provide assistance in meeting the food needs of developing countries, especially the least-developed and net food-importing developing countries. To this end, signatories to the Final Act have agreed: (a) to review the level of food aid established periodically under the Food Aid Convention; (b) initiate negotiations in the appropriate forum to establish a level of food aid commitments sufficient to meet the legitimate needs of developing countries during the reform programme; and (c) adopt guidelines to ensure that an increasing proportion of basic foodstuffs is provided to least-developed and net food-importing developing countries in fully grants form and/or on appropriate concessional terms (GATT Secretariat 1994: 448-449).

Donors are required to ensure that the provision of international food aid should not be tied directly or indirectly to commercial export of agricultural products to recipient countries and that international food aid transactions are carried out in accordance with the FAO *Principles of Surplus Disposal and Consulting Obligations of Member Nations*, a code of conduct originally drawn up in 1954, to avoid harmful interference of food aid with normal patterns of food production and international trade (FAO 1992).

While the demand for food aid will increase as a result of the higher cost of commercial food imports resulting from the Uruguay Round, and for other reasons given above, the supply of food aid is now threatened by both a reduction of surpluses and by higher food prices, which will mean less volume of food aid for given budgetary allocations that are made in money terms. According to the Final Act, a balance between the two opposite forces will be found by maintaining food aid at an "adequate" level, presumably in volume terms to offset fluctuations in production and prices.

3.6 Sub-Saharan Africa

The special and acute problems of sub-Saharan Africa, and the need to give the region priority in the allocation of multilateral development co-operation, have long been recognized. Yet concern has been expressed over its increasing marginalization. Of the 47 least-developed countries in the world, 32 are in sub-Saharan Africa. And it is the only region in the world where poverty and food insecurity are expected to increase by the end of the century.

Faced with these acute problems, repeated calls have been made for "special programmes of assistance", a new "Green Revolution", or a "Marshall Plan", to provide assistance on the scale required, and in the most appropriate ways, to build capacities by investing in people and improving infrastructure, within sound macro-economic policies. The international community's generous response to meeting emergencies in Africa has been in marked contrast to that of providing development aid for the region, and co-ordination of the aid that has been provided has left much to be desired.

A new "United Nations System-wide Special Initiative on Africa" was launched in March 1996, described as "an unprecedented set of concrete and coordinated actions designed to maximize support for African development efforts" (UN 1996). This Special Initiative aims over a 10-year period to greatly expand basic education and health care, promote peace and better governance, and improve water and food security. Implementation of the Initiative will cost up to $25 billion. Most of this amount will come from a reordering of priorities in African national budgets and reallocations of existing levels of official development assistance (ODA). The World Bank has agreed to lead in the mobilization of over 85 per cent of this amount. Reallocation of existing resources will be required, as will better ways of managing aid. The Initiative therefore contains new measures to improve donor co-ordination and increase aid effectiveness. The food security component of the Initiative consists of three priority areas: land degradation and desertification control; soil quality improvement; and food security with special emphasis on women. Associated with this is the component of improving water management.

4 Conclusions

Two general conclusions can be drawn from this analysis if sustainable food security for all is to be achieved: the need for (i) a co-ordinated global overview and response; and (ii) co-ordinated national action (WFC 1990: 11).

4.1 Co-ordinated action in a multilateral framework

Food security and improved nutrition are issues of global dimensions. Their achievement will require cohesive global action: lack of achievement will have negative global consequences. Solution of the food security problem will lie not only in the food and agriculture sphere but in other economic and social sectors, and in the maintenance of peace and security. Overcoming food insecurity will require cohesive global political will and resources.

World food security is not a separate issue but is bound up with a series of impending and interlocking crises including food, population, employment, international migration, money and debt, energy, environment and human security—all with global dimensions, demanding global solutions. For this reason, various proposals have been made to strengthen the multilateral management of major global economic and social objectives, including food security, moving to the multilateral framework visualized at Bretton Woods in 1944 and San Francisco (where the United Nations was created) in 1945 (Singer 1995b).

The experience of the past 50 years suggests that a co-ordinating or supervisory authority for world food security cannot be located in a single agency with a limited sectoral mandate and membership. The fate of the World Food Council suggests that the solution does not lie in setting up a separate institution without executive authority and with a mandate that cuts across that of other bodies. A proposal was made at the World Food Conference in 1974, but not agreed, to establish a "World Food Security Council" (UN 1975: 37). Two closely related proposals have recently been made, which might overcome these problems. A UN "Economic Security Council" has been advocated as "a decision-making forum at the highest level to review threats to global human security and agree on required action" (UNDP 1994: 10-11; Haq 1995). The creation of a UN "Economic and Social Security Council" has also been proposed to "provide a structure to deal with issues of world economic governance and world action toward poverty and social needs in a systematic and politically realistic way" (Stewart/Daws 1998). In either case, achieving world food security would be one of the primary tasks. Whatever decisions are taken on UN reform, it is necessary to have a focal point on food security at the highest political level, which would ensure that this is advocated and managed as a central issue embedded in world and national action for economic and social development and peace, with cohesive and co-ordinated programmes of international development assistance.

4.2 National Action

At the same time, it is recognized that action to improve food security and nutrition must be focused at the level of individual developing countries where, first and foremost, it is the responsibility of national governments. Improved co-ordination is critically needed at the country level. Developing countries can most effectively contribute by formulating development strategies with clearly defined priorities, including the attainment of food security and improved nutrition for all and supporting policies and programmes, and by improving their own institutional and administrative capacities to foster co-ordinated management of national action and international support.

Multilateral assistance agencies, as well as bilateral agencies and NGOs, can effectively support developing countries' efforts by: (i) adjusting their own management and co-ordinating procedures to the needs of developing countries, including improvements in the internal co-ordination of action within the agencies themselves; and (ii) providing management support and training to improve the capacities of developing countries to plan and manage their national policies and programmes and external aid.

References

Abbott, J. (1992): Politics and Poverty: A Critique of the Food and Agriculture Organization of the United Nations, London: Routledge.

ACC/SCN (1995): Estimates of External Flows in relation to Nutrition. Doc. SCN 95, Resources, Geneva: Administrative Committee on Co-ordination/ Subcommittee on Nutrition.

Boutros-Ghali, B. (1992): An Agenda for Peace, New York: United Nations.

Boutros-Ghali, B. (1995): An Agenda for Development, New York: United Nations.

Braun, J. von (1991): A Policy Agenda for Famine Prevention in Africa. Food Policy Report, Washington, D.C.: International Food Policy Research Institute.

Braun, J. von, (ed.) (1995): Employment for Poverty Reduction and Food Security, Washington, D.C.: International Food Policy Research Institute.

Cornia, G., R. Jolly and F. Stewart (eds.) (1987): Adjustment with a Human Face—Protecting the Vulnerable and Promoting Growth. A Study by UNICEF, Oxford: Clarendon Press.

Crawshaw, B. and J. Shaw (1995): Changing vulnerability to food security and the international response: the experience of the World Food Programme, in: T.E. Downing (ed.), Climate Change and World Food Security, Berlin: Springer in cooperation with NATO Scientific Affairs Division, pp. 207-226.

FAO (1982): Director-General's Report on World Food Security: A Reappraisal of the Concepts and Approaches, Doc. CFS:83/4, Rome: FAO.

FAO (1989): Effects of Stabilization and Structural Adjustment Programmes on Food Security, Economic and Social Development Paper No. 89, Commodities and Trade Division, Rome: FAO.

FAO (1990): Participation in Practice. Lessons from the FAO's People's Participation Programme, Rome: FAO.

FAO (1992): Principles of Surplus Disposal and Consultative Obligations of Member Nations, Third Edition, Rome: FAO.

GATT Secretariat (1994): The Results of the Uruguay Round of Multilateral Trade Negotiations. The Legal Texts, Geneva: General Agreement on Tariffs and Trade.

Gordon, W. (1995): The United Nations at the Crossroads of Reform, New York: Praeger.

Handy, C. (1985): Understanding Organizations, Third Edition, London: Penguin.

Harrison, G., T. Rutherford and D. Tarr (1995): Quantifying the Outcomes of the Uruguay Round, in: Finance and Development, Washington, D.C.: IMF and World Bank.

Haq, M. ul (1995): An Economic Security Council, in: IDS Bulletin, Vol. 26, No. 4, pp. 20-27.

Konandreas, P. and J. Greenfield (eds.) (1996): Implications of the Uruguay Round for Developing Countries, Special Issue of Food Policy, Vol. 21, No. 4/5.

Maxwell, S. (1990): Food Security in Developing Countries: Issues and Options for the 1990s, in: IDS Bulletin, Vol. 21, No. 3, pp. 1-13.

Maxwell, S. (1996): Food security: a post-modern perspective, in: Food Policy, Vol. 21, No. 2, pp. 155-170.

Maxwell, S. and M. Buchanan-Smith (eds.) (1994): Linking Relief and Development, IDS Bulletin, Vol. 25, No. 4.

Maxwell, S. and J. Shaw (1996): Food, Food Security and UN Reform, in: IDS Bulletin, Vol. 26, No. 4, pp. 41-53.

Oakley, P. (1991): Projects with People: The Practice of Participation in Rural Development, Geneva: International Labour Office.

OECD (1989): Development Co-operation in the 1990s, Paris: Organisation for Economic Co-operation and Development.

Parsons, A. (1995): From Cold War to Hot Peace, London: Michael Joseph.

Pinstrup-Andersen, P. (ed.) (1988): Food Subsidies in Developing Countries: Costs, Benefits, and Policy Options, Baltimore, Maryland, U.S.A.: Johns Hopkins University Press for the International Food Policy Research Institute.

Pinstrup-Andersen, P. (ed.) (1993): The Political Economy of Food and Nutrition Policies, Baltimore, Maryland, U.S.A.: Johns Hopkins University Press.

Pinstrup-Andersen, P. (1994): World Food Trends and Future Food Security, Washington, D.C.: International Food Policy Research Institute.

Pinstrup-Andersen, P., Nygaard D. and A. Ratta (1995): The Right to Food: Widely Acknowledged and Poorly Protected, 2020 Brief 22, Washington, D.C.: International Food Policy Research Institute.

Quisumbing, A., L. Brown, H. Feldstein, L. Haddad and C. Pena (1995): Women: The Key to Food Security, Washington, D.C.: International Food Policy Research Institute.

Raffer, K. and H.W. Singer (1996): The Foreign Aid Business. Economic Assistance and Development Co-operation, Cheltenham, United Kingdom and Brookfield, United States: Edward Elgar.

Righter, R. (1995): Utopia Lost: The United Nations and World Order, New York: The Twentieth Century Fund Press.

Shaw, J. (1993): Poverty-Specific Policy Approaches, in: C. Easter (ed.), Strategies for Poverty Reduction, London: Commonwealth Secretariat, pp. 43-63.

Shaw, J. (1995): Future Directions for Development and Relief with Food Aid, in: J. von Braun (1995), pp. 252-274.

Shaw, J. (1996): The World Food Programme and Emergency Relief, Advanced Development Management Programme Series, No. 20, Tokyo: Sophia University.

Shaw, J. and Clay, E. (eds.) (1993): World Food Aid: Experiences of Recipients and Donors, Rome, London and Portsmouth, New Hampshire, U.S.A.: WFP in association with James Currey and Heinemann.

Shaw, J. and H.W. Singer (eds.) (1988): Food Policy, Food Aid and Economic Adjustment, Special Issue of Food Policy, Vol. 13, No. 1.

Shaw, J. and H.W. Singer (1995): A Future Food Aid Regime: Implications of the Final Act of the GATT Uruguay Round, IDS Discussion Paper No. 352. See different versions of this paper in: Food Policy, Vol. 21, No. 4, 1996, pp. 447-460, and in: H. O'Neil and J. Toye (eds.) (1998): A World Without Famine? New Approaches to Aid and Development, London: Macmillan for the UK Development Studies Association.

Singer, H.W. (1995a): Aid Conditionality, Advanced Development Management Programme Series, No. 13, Tokyo: Sophia University.

Singer, H.W. (1995b): Revitalizing the United Nations: Five Proposals, in: IDS Bulletin, Vol. 26, No. 4, pp. 35-40.

Singer, H.W. (1996a): Linking Relief and Development, Advanced Development Management Programme Series, No. 19, Tokyo: Sophia University.

Singer, H.W. (1996b): A Global View of Food Security, in: Food Security and Innovations: Successes and Lessons Learned, International Symposium, University of Hohenheim, Hohenheim, Germany: Eiselen-Foundation Ulm, pp. 5-14.

Sivard, R. (1991): World Military and Social Expenditure 1991, Washington, D.C.: World Priorities, Inc.

Stewart, F. and S. Daws (1998): An Economic and Social Security Council at the United Nations, in: D. Sapsford and J. Chen (eds.), Development Economics and Policy. Essays in Honour of H.W. Singer on his 85th Birthday, London: Macmillan.

UN (1945): Charter of the United Nations, New York: United Nations.

UN (1969): Study of the Capacity of the United Nations Development System, New York: United Nations.

UN (1975): Report of the World Food Conference, Rome 5-17 November 1974, Doc. E/CONF. 65/20, New York: United Nations.

UN (1987): Co-ordination in the United Nations and the United Nations System. Report of the Secretary-General, Doc. A/42/232, New York: United Nations.

UN (1989a): Operational Activities for Development, Doc. A/C.2/44/L.87, New York: United Nations.

UN (1989b): The Cairo Declaration, in: Conclusions and Recommendations of the World Food Council at its Fifteenth Ministerial Session, UN General Assembly Official Records, Forty-fourth Session, Supplement No. 19 (A/44/19), New York: United Nations, p. 5.

UN (1991): Strengthening of the Co-ordination of Humanitarian Emergency Assistance of the United Nation, United Nations General Assembly resolution 46/182, adopted 19 December 1991, New York: United Nations.

UN (1992a): Triennial Policy Review of the Operational Activities of the United Nations Development System, United Nations General Assembly resolution 47/199, adopted 22 December 1992, New York: United Nations.

UN (1992b): Report of the World Food Council on the Work of its Eighteenth Session, 23-26 June 1992, General Assembly Official Records, Forty-Seventh Session, Supplement No. 19 (A/47/19), New York: United Nations, p. 7.

UN (1996): The United Nations System-wide Special Initiative on Africa, New York: United Nations, 15 March.

UNCTAD Secretariat (1994): The Outcomes of the Uruguay Round: Supporting Papers to the Trade and Development Report, 1994, New York: United Nations, pp. 98-103.

UNDP (1994): Human Development Report 1994, New York: Oxford University Press for the United Nations Development Programme.

Urquhart, B. and E. Childers (1990): A World in Need of Leadership: Tomorrow's United Nations, Uppsala, Sweden: Dag Hammarskjold Foundation.

Urquhart, B. and E. Childers (1994): Renewing the United Nations System, New York: The Ford Foundation.

WFC (1990): Improving Co-ordination of National and International Action Towards A More Concentrated Attack on Hunger, Doc. WFC/1990/5, Rome: World Food Council.

WFP (1992): Disaster Mitigation and Rehabilitation in Africa, document CFA:34/P/7-B, Rome: World Food Programme.

WFP (1996): Annual Report of the Executive Director 1995: Ending the Inheritance of Hunger, Rome: World Food Programme.

Williams, D. (1987): The Specialized Agencies and the United Nations: The System in Crisis, London: Hurst & Co.

World Bank (1986): Poverty and Hunger. Issues and Options for Food Security in Developing Countries, Washington, D.C.: World Bank Policy Study.

World Bank (1988): Adjustment Lending. An Evaluation of Ten Years of Experience, Policy and Research Series No. 1, Country Economics Department, Washington, D.C.: World Bank.

28

Overcoming World Hunger: The CGIAR Prepares for the New Millennium

Ismail Serageldin

1 Introduction: Defining the challenge

Every second, three more human beings are added to the population of the planet, 200 every minute, 90 million each year. Nearly 95 percent are born in developing countries. The world's population is expected to exceed 8 billion by 2025, an increase of 2.5 billion in the next 30 years. Much, but not all, of the increase will occur in developing country cities, where urban populations will more than triple. Most analysts agree that, given moderate income growth, food needs in developing countries could nearly double. The challenge to world agriculture inherent in these projections is enormous. Nobel laureate Norman Borlaug calculates that "to meet projected food demands, by 2025 the average yield of all cereals must be 80 percent higher than the average yield in 1990" (Borlaug 1996). This increase will have to be achieved in increasingly complex circumstances (The World Bank 1997).

Future increases in food supplies must come primarily from increasing biological yields, rather than from area expansion and more irrigation, because land and water are becoming increasingly scarce (Feder and Keck 1994). Most new lands brought under cultivation are marginal and ecologically fragile, and cannot make up for the land being removed from cultivation each year because of urbanization and land degradation. The sources of water that can be developed cost-effectively for irrigation are nearly exhausted, and irrigation water will increasingly need to be reallocated for municipal and industrial use.

The challenge is worldwide, and both technological and political in nature. The technological aspect of the challenge is complex, requiring the development of new, high-productivity, environmentally sustainable production systems. The political task is to ensure that international and domestic policies, institutional frameworks, and public expenditure patterns are conducive to cost-effective and sustainable agricultural development (FAO 1996a).

The challenge of producing more—sustainably—to feed vastly more people is as formidable as it is inescapable. Helping to combat hunger, however, is not the only tasks of farmers and others engaged in agriculture. The challenge is much broader (Johnson 1997). Agriculture is the primary interface between people and the environment. Almost 70 percent of the land that is colonized by human beings is used to grow food and fiber. Seventy percent of the water globally is used for irrigation and agriculture: in developing countries between 80 and 90 percent of developed water supplies are used for agriculture and irrigation. Very few low-income countries have achieved rapid nonagricultural growth without corresponding rapid agricultural growth (IFPRI 1995). For these reasons sustainable agricultural growth is essential to economic growth in most developing countries. Such growth will not be achieved, however, without substantial investment in agricultural research; the source of new knowledge that fuels new technologies.

2 Delivering a response: the CGIAR

A major responsibility therefore falls on the Consultative Group on International Research (CGIAR), and the components of the CGIAR system, the only organization in the world that exists solely to mobilize the best in agricultural science on behalf of the world's poor and hungry. For more than a quarter of a century, the CGIAR has been committed to this goal (Baum 1986). Nine donor-members created the CGIAR in 1971. The CGIAR now consists of fifty-seven public and private sector members—countries, international and regional organizations, and foundations—supporting sixteen international agricultural research centers. The World Bank, the Food and Agricultural Organization of the United Nations (FAO), the United Nations Development Programme (UNDP), and the United Nations Environment Programme (UNEP) are cosponsors of the CGIAR.

The CGIAR system is a network that consists of the Consultative Group (the Chairman, Cosponsors, and other members), CGIAR committees (standing, advisory, impact evaluation, partnership, and *ad hoc*), international agricultural research centers and center committees, and a central service unit, the CGIAR Secretariat.

The mission of the CGIAR is to contribute, through research, to promoting sustainable agriculture for food security in the developing countries. Productivity research to help alleviate poverty, and natural resources management, are the twin pillars of CGIAR research on food crops, forestry, livestock, irrigation management, aquatic resources, and policy; and in its services to national agricultural research systems in developing countries.

The CGIAR is totally focused on agricultural research. The products of CGIAR-supported research are public goods, unconditionally available to poor farmers, national agricultural research systems, and other users. Coupled with this is a commitment to hold fast over the long term, recognizing that it can take up to 20 years to move a research result from laboratories to farmers' fields. Scientific excellence is the hallmark of the CGIAR system. The quality of work at international agricultural research centers supported by the CGIAR is maintained by the commitment to excellence of center scientists, by the strategic guidance of a Technical Advisory Committee, as well as by regular external reviews and impact assessments. Special awards for scientific excellence were inaugurated in 1996 to encourage young scientists and the research partners of CGIAR centers (CGIAR 1994-1997).

Another unique aspect of the CGIAR is that it does not exist, meaning that it does not have a juridical persona or legal standing. This most successful of all development cooperation efforts is really a "virtual" organization that exists solely by the goodwill of its members, and a shared commitment to a common goal. Some of the CGIAR centers are commodity specific, others have an interregional perspective, some have a policy focus, others have an institutional support focus. One is fully engaged in a range of activities connected with the conservation of biodiversity. All but three of the centers are located in developing countries—four in Africa, five in Asia, three in Latin America and one in the Middle East. All have active collaborative programs in the South.

Research supported by the CGIAR covers commodities that provide 75 percent of the food energy and a similar share of protein requirements in developing countries. The impact of CGIAR-supported research is widely recognized. Norman Borlaug, the originator of the high yielding varieties that lie at the heart of CGIAR endeavors, is a Nobel laureate. The CGIAR was awarded the King Baudouin International Development Prize. Six out of ten World Food Prize laureates are from the CGIAR. At the Mid-Term Meetings of the CGIAR held in Brasilia during May 1997, Maurice Strong said that "support for the CGIAR in the past 27 years has been the single most effective investment of nations and international institutions in official development assistance (ODA), with the greatest impact, bar none."

3 Renewal of the CGIAR

Despite these positive achievements which demonstrate the capacity of the CGIAR, a crisis of confidence afflicted the CGIAR early in the 1990s. The most visible aspect of this crisis was a decline in funding for the research agenda collectively formulated and defined by the CGIAR system. Several other issues needed urgent resolution as well, and these may be summarized as follows:

First, the CGIAR which was founded as a means of helping to create food abundance in famine-prone countries of the South, was required to deal with a new and complex set of research challenges, particularly in the area of natural resources management, including forests, fresh water, soils, coastal zones, and the sea. There was a need, too, to ensure—and ensure manifestly—that the needs of the poorest and the most neglected in society, including women, were encompassed in CGIAR endeavors.

Second, the research agenda had to be refocused, redefined and vigorously implemented at a time when the constituency supporting ODA in donor countries was shrinking or immobile, while demands for ODA were increasing, due mainly to changes in East Europe and Central Asia.

Third, the concept of agriculture as the cornerstone of development was receding from the center of public policy. The share of agriculture in total ODA dropped from some 20 percent in 1980 to around 14 percent in the 1990s.

Fourth, improvements in the effectiveness and efficiency of system management and governance, as well as in the system's instruments and processes for measurement and accountability were urgently needed.

Fifth, the CGIAR system had not adapted to the needs for greater partnership and interdependence with and among compatible institutions.

These issues were the focus of an eighteen-month program of renewal that began in May 1994 and was successfully completed by the end of 1995. The high-point of the program was a Ministerial-Level Meeting in Lucerne, Switzerland (February 9-10, 1995) at which participants adopted a Declaration and Action Program (CGIAR 1995) that serves the CGIAR as a road map to the future.

The renewal program clarified the vision of the CGIAR, refocused its research agenda, reformed its governance and operations, and secured renewed international support for its mission. Decision making has been streamlined, particularly in arrangements for reviewing and approving the research agenda. A matrix approach has been adopted to ensure transparency. Methods for assessing the impact of research are being embedded in the CGIAR system. Financial trends are positive. Funding for the research agenda has increased from an anticipated $215 million in 1994, the downturn year, to $320 million in 1997.

The renewed CGIAR confronts the challenges of promoting a people-centered sustainable development that helps feed the hungry, reduces poverty, and protects the environment in the context of a rapidly expanding global population that places increasing demands on the earth's fragile and finite natural resources. In pursuing these goals the CGIAR is not alone. It positions itself in the broader context of what is happening to address the problems globally. There are many actors and programs: the OECD, NARS, NGOs, the private sector, regional organizations, farmers groups and others, all have roles to play. Each of these actors can define problems and topics that lead to researchable programs. They are now part of a formally organized coalition of many different groups, the Global Forum for Agricultural Research (GFAR 1996).

The CGIAR is best known for the green revolution. And while the green revolution has been criticized, it has saved the hungry and destitute from starvation or death (FAO 1996b). But now we need to go beyond these achievements. We have to launch a "doubly green revolution," where genetically diverse new crop varieties are constantly being brought forward, where we minimize pesticide use through integrated pest management, and improve water use efficiency and nutrient management in terms of complex farming systems that are more efficient at the smallholder level. We need an even greater focus on environmental sustainability and the poverty impacts of the developments proposed, especially the benefits they bring to poor women farmers (SAREC 1994). These are the hallmarks of the new doubly green revolution that the CGIAR is pursuing, as it faces up to the challenges of our times (Conway 1997).

4 A framework for action

The challenge ahead is to sustainably intensify complex agricultural production systems while preventing damage to natural resources and biodiversity and improving the welfare of farmers. Doubling the yields of complex farming systems in an environmentally positive manner is an enormous challenge that is not going to be easy to meet. Can the world grapple with these new challenges? Yes, but only if we rise to the challenges by addressing a number of key issues, within a coherent framework for action.

Policies: On the policy front the most essential need is to remove the urban bias that discriminates against the rural world in general, and against agriculture in particular. Policymakers should make sure that fiscal, trade and, foreign exchange regimes, as well as taxing, pricing and subsidy policies do not discriminate against agriculture. Surely, urban and rural worlds both deserve to be treated fairly.

Institutions: Policies are translated into reality by effective institutions. For bringing about a transformation and renewal of the rural world many institutions, dealing with credit, titling, distribution, marketing, extension, research, infrastructure and social services must perform in an effective, enabling fashion. In many countries, rural infrastructure is key to get agriculture moving. Failure to build and strengthen the rural infrastructure neutralizes the impact of agricultural innovations. Effective user-associations, community-based groups, and vibrant local governments are badly needed. They should be complemented by decentralized public services, broader public-private partnerships and a functioning civil society. These are all part of the responsive institutional framework needed to meet the needs of the growing rural world, and must be nurtured. Communities with well-functioning local organizations are much better equipped to take charge of their own development.

Legal Structures: When farmers have security of tenure they invest in their land for long-term benefits, produce food more efficiently, use sustainable farming practices, conserve resources, and are less likely to be poor. With the shift toward a market orientation, the required changes can be explored. Also important are programs to strengthen land administration, generating many benefits, including improved efficiency of land markets, reduction in conflict over land, enhanced access to credit, and improved incentives to invest in agricultural production. Also critical are relevant research organizations, responsive, demand-driven extension systems, and institutions providing effective rural finance.

Financial Resources: Microfinance—providing loans and savings services to the world's poorest people—is an important and empowering tool in the fight against global poverty, particularly in rural areas. Studies from Bangladesh's Grameen Bank, and elsewhere, show that the very poor, especially women, repay their loans at the phenomenal rate of 98 percent. What is more important is that the benefits of such loans translate into improved conditions for the entire household, especially children. Very poor women can pull themselves out of poverty through successive loans of this type. Higher incomes for the poor result in increased investments in education, nutrition, and household welfare leading to an improvement in the overall quality of life. What are needed, therefore, are financial institutions that will in fact empower the poor, the weak, and the marginalized—especially women—to be creators of their own welfare, rather than the beneficiaries of aid.

It is heartening that the Microcredit Summit of 1997, a spontaneous peoples' movement is gathering momentum, and shows considerable promise of fulfilling the objective of reaching 100 million of the world's poorest families, especially women, with credit, self-employment, and other financial and business services by the year 2005.

5 Shifts in the agricultural research paradigm

Even with effective policies, responsive institutions and a proactive outreach program to provide the poor with access to financial services, agricultural renewal will not occur if the technology of agriculture does not change. It is here that the importance of agricultural research is highlighted. The challenges facing global agricultural science in the next century are arguably greater than at any previous time. And these challenges must be met in a political environment which is a dangerous mix of complacency, fiscal constraints, aid fatigue and fundamental disagreements about the magnitude of the problem and the appropriate paths to its solution (Strong 1996).

The closely intertwined problems of poverty, hunger, environmental distress, and population increase—problems held at bay by past achievements towards which the CGIAR made crucial contributions—continue to press on us, demanding resolution. Redoubled efforts to develop sustainable agriculture, particularly in the world's poor regions where agriculture is a major occupation, is vital to their solution. Confronting this challenge, the particular task of the CGIAR and its partners is to define and implement a research agenda for the next millennium that is innovative, appropriate, and effective. This task involves a double shift in the research paradigm.

The first of these shifts requires the integration of crop-specific research, which has been so successful in the past, into a broader, more holistic vision. This amounts to the contextualization of research. Research on crops would continue, but stronger attention needs to be given to ecoregional issues and sustainability. Thematically, it would focus on the livestock-forestry-aquaculture-farming continuum. On the socio-economic front, it would seek to increase the productivity and profitability of complex farming systems at the smallholder level. The second shift is to emphasize the genetic imperative. This second shift would enable the CGIAR to utilize the most cutting-edge work associated with genetic mapping, molecular markers and biotechnology to accelerate the breeding process and achieve the promise of all that science can do for the poor and the environment.

Biotechnology—one of many tools of agricultural research and development—could provide many advantages to institutions such as the CGIAR centers that pursue the mission of environmental protection, poverty reduction and food security centered on the small-holder farmer in the developing countries (MSSRF 1998). Although the first fruits of the new technology are already benefiting the commercial crops of the industrialized countries, there is no inherent reason why the tools of biotechnology could not be employed in pursuing the mission of environmentally and socially sustainable development (Kendall et al. 1997).

Looking to the next millennium, the CGIAR recognizes the importance of biotechnology in agriculture and natural resources management as one of a range of tools that can be used to increase productivity and address social and economic constraints to improving livelihoods for the poor in developing countries.

To further its mission of poverty reduction, food security and sustainable agricultural development while conserving the natural resource base, the CGIAR will:

— form strategic alliances and partnerships with both public and private sector institutions/organizations engaged in biotechnology, and

— develop need-based in-house biotechnology capability that will (a) address present and future needs of small scale farmers, and (b) contribute to relevant capacity building of NARS.

In all its operations the CGIAR is committed to complying with international and national biosafety requirements. The CGIAR recognizes that the issue of farmers' rights is important, and that such rights are easy to accept philosophically, but difficult to implement operationally. We all want to ensure that poor farmers are empowered to the maximum extent possible, and due recognition is given to their role in conservation and development of germplasm. The CGIAR has supported and will continue to promote this philosophy which is reflected in our ethical principles. These topics are being discussed in different fora such as the FAO Commission on Genetic Resources for Food and Agriculture, and the Convention on Biological Diversity.

The biotechnology revolution is here. Our task is to fashion a productive construct out of the diverse aspects—science, agriculture, law, farmers' rights, the working of civil society, and more—that together can ensure that this "revolution" has a positive and lasting impact on the lives of the poor and the hungry. It is our privilege not simply to help define a new paradigm but also to guarantee that it is effectively implemented.

6 Conclusion: Into the future

As we approach the new millennium, we know that the task of agricultural research is never done. However, in order to continue to be effective, the CGIAR has to meet many preconditions. We must:

- harmonize our research agenda with global concerns, initiatives, and actions;

- preserve the CGIAR system at all times as a true reflection of international realities;
- ensure that poverty reduction is the guiding impulse for all that we do;
- maintain the focus of the CGIAR system on increasing food productivity while protecting the environment;
- serve both as a provider and a catalyst so that the benefits of cutting-edge science, including biotechnology, reach the poor;
- improve institutional arrangements for strengthening partnerships with the civil society, the private sector, and all other "players";
- contribute our knowledge and resources toward resolving problems of a new world order for genetic resources;
- ensure that internal governance mechanisms promote effectiveness, transparency, and sustained financial support for research of an international, public goods nature.

The future beckons. We must move forward to meet it, especially for the sake of the poor farmers of developing countries. As an instrument of development cooperation, the CGIAR – built on a solid foundation of scientific excellence, and an outstanding track record of achievement – is ideally positioned to meet the challenge of achieving food security, conserving the environment, and promoting rural well-being in the new millennium. It deserves all-round support.

References

Baum, Warren, C. (1986): Partners Against Hunger, The World Bank, Washington DC, USA.

Borlaug, N. (1996): Feeding the World: The Challenge Ahead. Paper delivered at the Fourth World Bank Conference on Sustainable Development, Washington DC, USA.

Conway, Gordon (1997): The Doubly Green Revolution—Food for All in the Twenty-first Century, Penguin Books, London, UK.

Consultative Group on International Agricultural Research (CGIAR) (1994-1997): Annual Reports, Washington DC, USA.

Consultative Group on International Agricultural Research (CGIAR) (1995): Declaration and Action Program, Lucerne, Switzerland.

Feder, G. and A. Keck (1994): Increasing Competition for Land and Water Resources: A Global Perspective. Paper presented at Workshop on Social Science Methods in Agricultural Systems, Chiang Mai, Thailand.

Food and Agriculture Organization (FAO) (1996a): Declaration on World Food Security and World Food Summit Plan of Action, Rome, Italy.

Food and Agriculture Organization (FAO) (1996b): Role of Research in Global Food Security and Agricultural Development, Doc. WFS 96/TECH/12, Rome, Italy.

Global Forum on Agricultural Research (GFAR) (1998): Report and Work Program, CGIAR Mid-Term Meeting, Brasilia, Brazil.

Johnson, D. Gale (1997): Agriculture and the Wealth of Nations. In: Baldwin and Oaxaca (eds.): Papers and Proceedings of the One Hundredth and Ninth Annual Meeting, American Economic Association.

Kendall, Henry W. et al. (1997): Bioengineering of Crops, Report of the World Bank Panel on Transgenic Crops, The World Bank, Washington DC, USA.

International Food Policy Research Institute (IFPRI) (1995): Foreign Assistance to Agriculture: A Win-Win Proposition, Washington DC, USA.

Strong, Maurice (1996): Sir John Crawford Memorial Lecture, The World Bank, Washington DC, USA.

M. S. Swaminathan Research Foundation (MSSRF) (1998): Background Paper for Interdisciplinary Dialogue on Population, Science, and Food Security, Chennai, India.

Swedish Agency for Research Cooperation with Developing countries (SAREC) (1994): Sustainable Agriculture for a Food Secure World, Stockholm, Sweden.

The World Bank (1997): Rural Development, From Vision to Action, A Sector Strategy. The World Bank, Washington DC, USA.

29

The Current European Policy and Programmes on Food Security

Cesar Debén Alfonso and Pieter van Steekelenburg

1 Why reforms

Food security has been a central issue in the European Community development cooperation policy for almost 25 years. For a number of years, the issue pointed largely to food aid and to assistance for agricultural and rural development, support structures and policies, which corresponded quite well to the supply focus to food security adopted at the World Food Conference in 1974. The world food crisis of the early seventies demonstrated the vulnerability of food systems in many countries, especially in sub-Saharan Africa. Aid agencies including the EC responded to this crisis by increasing the share of project funding in favor of agriculture, and, within agriculture, there was a strong shift from export crops to food crops.

However, these increased financial efforts for agricultural and rural development did not improve the basic trend of the food situation. Gradually, attention was drawn to the wider economic environment of the agricultural sector, particularly to price policies, marketing, the provision of basic support services. It was concluded that more financing is not effective if the policy and institutional environment fails to provide the right incentives and services to agricultural producers, processors, traders.

This analysis and awareness led the EC in 1981 to launch a "Plan to combat hunger in the world", also known as the Pisani Plan. A central part of the plan consisted of support for the formulation and implementation of food strategies. The main characteristics of the food strategy approach were: to concentrate funding on the objective of food security (FS), to define and implement coherent policies to promote FS through a process of policy dialogue, to strengthen coordination among donors, and to better integrate different kinds of aid instruments. These characteristics subsequently became central features of the third Lomé Convention (December 1984).

The results of putting into practice this newly-conceived approach were varied: the concentration of funding was extended quite far; the process of policy dialogue was less effective than anticipated; coordination among donors on food-security related areas, and among ministries and parastatals with competencies in FS-related matters was facilitated and stimulated; integration of instruments concerned mainly project aid and food aid through counterpart funds resulting from food aid sales (projects should be, in principle, FS-related).

Under the fourth Lomé Convention, efforts were made for further improvements, such as the change in emphasis from food self-sufficiency to self-reliance, the complementarity of private and public sectors in FS matters, the importance of food processing, greater attention for direct measures for vulnerable groups, particularly so when revising general economic policies in a context of structural adjustment. Food policy dialogue faced severe limitations because various crucial policy measures can only be addressed within a wider context of structural adjustment.

In-depth evaluations of its food aid programmes in the early nineties, brought the European Commission to recognise that there was a need

— for greater flexibility in its food aid instruments;

— for a better balance between traditional operations, aimed simply at providing foodstuffs, and new operations aimed at supporting production and marketing and boosting the purchasing power of those most at risk;

— for food aid and food security operations to be integrated more effectively into a comprehensive development policy.

2 Objectives and main lines of the reform

Three key features of the new food aid management policy were pinpointed:

— the use of food aid as a basic element of development policy and of long-term food security policy in particular;

— an improved EC contribution to national development and food production of countries coping with food insecurity, particularly in the field of agricultural rehabilitation;

— enhancement of the ability of the poorest to obtain basic nutrition, instead of a focus on supplying food.

In the light of these orientations, the ways to supply food aid and the new special instruments to support food security have been rationalised within the overall policy framework to achieve a single intervention strategy which can be tailored to the individual situation of each country or region. This enables these interventions to be consistent with other EC policies and fit with other tools of EC development aid.

The starting point of the new approach is the wish to reduce or eliminate the negative effects of food aid, and reinforce its contribution as a tool for development. Therefore, the following orientations were taken:

— Food aid should no longer be provided on an *ad hoc* basis, but should be part and parcel of a national development strategy for agricultural development and household food security, in combination with other instruments of Community aid.

— Food aid will be purchased to a much larger extent on local markets or in neighbouring countries (in 1994 and 1995, more than 40% of food aid was purchased through so-called triangular operations), constituting a fundamental incentive to local production and regional trade and thus to food security.

— Food aid for free distribution should be limited to very vulnerable target groups under special conditions. Nevertheless, this does not affect the willingness to consider special food aid assistance in emergency situations, which is being provided in due coordination with the European Community Humanitarian Aid Organisation (ECHO). A recent case in point is North Korea.

— In cases where food aid is monetised (that is to say sold), the proceeds of the sale of food aid or agricultural inputs should be used primarily to support programmes addressing rural and agricultural development and trade in agricultural products.

— In post-emergency-situations, other products can be made available, such as agricultural inputs, small tools, in order to facilitate the transition from relief to development.

— A newly designed aid instrument is the foreign currency facility, whereby foreign currency is put at the disposal of private sector operators who can then import food and/or agricultural inputs. It is intended to support the participation of the private sector in the process of economic reform of low-income countries that have structural food deficits. Also financial aid can be made available for projects/programmes supporting food security. In 1997, the foreign currency facility was included in various country programmes.

Box 1: EC Food security support to Cape Verde

In "normal rain years", the country produces only 10% of its food needs, the remainder being provided as food aid and imports. Instead of continued food aid supply, a process was started in 1996/7 with the authorities and all donors involved, to reform the parts of the national policy which have a direct bearing on food security and income distribution. As a result, a 3-year support programme was agreed totaling 16 million ECU, in which EC food aid is largely replaced by financial aid to encourage economic growth and private sector involvement, among others through a financial facility in hard currency to facilitate commercial imports. The resulting counterpart funds are used to support institutional reforms and labour-intensive public works which will be more on a contractual basis, thus boosting capacity, rural incomes and infrastructure. Furthermore, the security stock will be built up, and changes are being introduced in targeting subsidies on bread, flour and other food items, in roles of State-owned companies and parastatals in the food sector (import, storage, distribution) in monitoring quality, prices and availability of food. In parallel, under the European Development Fund, multi-annual support is given to budgetary and macro-economic reform processes, in close coordination between most donors concerned.

As far as operators are concerned, it is envisaged that private operators, marketing co-operatives or associations, and NGOs will play a predominant role in the implementation of food aid and food security assistance, in conformity with current orientations in favour of an increasing use of the decentralised co-operation approach. They already do so under our current food security programmes: in 1997 a substantial part was implemented through NGOs and private operators.

Food aid and the specific instruments in support of food security constitute fundamental resources of EC policy to combat poverty. But they need to be adjusted to, and integrated into, an overall political framework and intervention strategy—and this strategy also has to be adapted to the specific realities of each recipient region or country. Moreover, such an approach has to be consistent with other Community policies and combined with the other instruments of development aid.

Similarly, in the field of conflict prevention, food aid and food security operations aim to avoid the social tensions which cause conflicts. They are often associated with other initiatives. Examples are efforts to increase the lowest incomes, the concentration on the most vulnerable categories such as children and women, the development of available resources, including agricultural ones, or job creation. In 1996, the Commission submitted a communication on this subject to the Council of Ministers for Development Co-operation of the European Union.

These various approaches today form part of an overall philosophy which is the basis for the co-operation policy that the Community follows with regard to a large number of developing countries, aiming at better coherence of objectives and of instruments.

In order to facilitate policy dialogue with the relevant authorities of recipient countries, seminars were held with representatives of ACP administrations. In 1997, three regional seminars were organised: for Latin America and the Caribbean, for Western Africa, and for Southern and Eastern Africa. While initially meant to explain objectives, scope, and mechanics of the new EC policy and programmes on food security and food aid, the seminars offer also an excellent opportunity for South-South information exchange and learning from experiences of neighbouring countries. It is planned to continue the series of seminars, especially for other regions (Central and Eastern Europe; Asia).

Another element aiming at continuous improvement of quality and relevance of food security support actions, is the preference to engage in multi-annual programmes for food security in a limited number of countries. To that end, in 1997 country strategy documents were prepared for the majority of this restricted group of priority countries, and discussed by the Committee on Food Security and Food Aid through which EU-Member States participate in managing the food security and food aid budget. The 1997 group consists of Bolivia, Haiti, Honduras, Nicaragua, Peru, Bangladesh, Yemen, Cap Verde, Ethiopia, Madagascar, Malawi, Mozambique, various members of the Commonwealth of Independent States (Azerbeidjan, Armenia, Georgia). Selection of priority countries is based on need (very low income/caput, structural deficiency in food production), experience (possibilities for a real policy dialogue and review), circumstances, budget volume, and Commission-internal capacity to handle adequately country programmes without spreading too thinly its human and financial resources.

In view of the continued importance of food aid and food security operations funded through NGOs and the need to facilitate procedures in that field, a major effort was undertaken to update and review the general conditions and standard contract to be used for that purpose. The final product will be formalised in 1998 (in 1997, 20 million ECU of NGO operations were funded on the basis of direct contracts between the European Commission and the NGO concerned).

Table 1: Figures on EC budget for food aid and food security programmes 1997

World regions	Planned (million ECU)	Committed (million ECU)	Committed/ Planned
ACP countries	256.3	248.0	97%
Near-East/North Africa	21.0	22.9	109%
Asia	69.2	102.0	147%
New Independent States	63.6	62.9	99%
Latin America	61.9	61.6	99%
Other	58.0	26.1	45%
Total	530.0	523.5	99%

3 Operational aspects

In order to have the envisaged impact of the revised policies, some measures were also taken on the operational side, in particular concerning technical assistance and support structures.

The number of small technical assistance teams in priority countries was increased, and its tasks somewhat revised. While originally meant to help channel food arrivals, purchases, storage and distribution, of late these teams increasingly assist in preparing and implementing sector-wide food security support programmes, and have a role to play in monitoring such programmes. The teams are often also useful in communication between the EC and national authorities on food security matters.

In order to further improve monitoring of policies and social and economic developments in priority countries, and to facilitate timely initiation and orientation of future actions, dialogue and coordination with other donors, a European Food Security Network (RESAL) of specialised consultants is being put in place. Each of the consultants selected will be involved in one country (when large, such as Bangladesh) or in a small group of countries (e.g. Sahel, or Nicaragua/Honduras). They are meant to support the programming and planning work of the Unit of the

European Commission in charge of food security and food aid. The consultants, based in Europe, will have a local economist in the country.

EC support to national FS programmes involves invariably an element of early warning and monitoring of food production, storage, price fluctuation, purchasing power of vulnerable groups and areas. This implies either the setting up of such a system, or to ensure an already existing one can operate adequately (e.g. in the Sahel the "Diaper" of the CILSS; in Southern Africa the Food Security Unit of the SADC).

Normally speaking, an early warning system operates in direct relation with an institutional provision that is in charge of government-held cereal stocks. Because modestly-sized and properly managed national cereal stocks continue to be quite important in the EC approach, in the first place as a buffer to flatten price fluctuations, and secondly for well targeted rapid distribution at subsidized prices, or free of charge, in case the need arises in certain parts (or certain vulnerable groups) of the country. However, the cereal market as such should be a private sector affair. A well-known case in point is the PRMC[1] in Mali, which operates since 1982 through sustained and coordinated support, by EC and other donors, to the government that includes, since 1996, operational costs of PRMC in its budget.

4 The reform process

In the early nineties, aware that ever increasing volumes of food aid will not provide a sustainable solution to hunger and food insecurity, various in-depth evaluations of EC food aid were commissioned, indicating the need for a major reform. In parallel, initiatives were taken to strengthen coordination between the European Commission and EC Member States in various areas related to structural adjustment programmes, including food security (the other were health care, poverty alleviation, and education). This lead to the Development Council's adoption of a resolution on food security in November 1994, underlining its wish to put the issue high on the policy agendas, setting out main lines while recalling previously adopted resolutions. Subsequent consultations with outside experts from EU Member States, meetings with academics, NGO and other representatives of civil society, and Commission-internal seminars, helped to lay the groundwork for the reform.

All of the year 1995 and the first half of 1996 were marked by hard work in the Working Party on Development Cooperation of the Council of the European Union, in the one of Food Aid, and later on also in the Working Party on Foreign Relations, between EC Member States representatives and the Commission on main lines and fine (legal) details of a new framework regulation, superseding five preceding regulations. Issues which attracted much interest during this process

1 PRMC: Programme de Restructuration du Marché Céréalier, comprising a stock of some 50.000 tons (OPAM), an early warning system, and a market information system.

were the flexibility to replace food aid shipment from overseas by local purchases or by financial aid, the hard-currency facility, the integration of food security support into other EC development cooperation programmes in a given country, the criteria for identifying priority countries and the harmonisation of food aid and food security policies throughout the European Union Member States. The issue of coherence between various policy fields, mentioned in Art. 130 of the Maastricht Treaty, and more specifically between the Common Agricultural Policy and Development Cooperation, was also considered.

The new regulation[2], approved by the Council of the EU in June 1996 and effective as from 4 July 1996, covers EC food aid and food security operations worldwide, except food aid for humanitarian purposes, and is also applicable in all EU Member States.

Box 2: EC food security support to Georgia

Based on the new FS policy, current assistance to the Newly Independent States takes the form of budget support, with utilisation of the counterpart funds to create a legal and regulatory framework that will be conducive to food security. In the case of Georgia, the initial assistance after independence was food aid in kind, in order to improve availability of food stuffs. In the present transitional phase, the multi-annual support programme for 1997-99 worth 42 million ECU, is focused on formulation and implementation of national food security policies and programmes. This includes a Monitoring system for cereal supply which is equipped with the financial resources to undertake purchases when shortages occur; the consolidation of the Agrarian Reform with privatisation of land titles, a land registry and land market; a reform of the cereal market and restructuring of state control of bread; and privatisation and reform of agro-food parastatals, in particular in the area of production inputs. Last but not least, there is support to improve the management of government budget and expenditures.

5 Future challenges

Aware that successful reforms of policies and programmes to reduce food insecurity of vulnerable countries and their inhabitant families, require shared analysis, joint commitment and effective operational coordination with all main parties involved, the European Commission puts substantial energy in strengthening donor coordination. Various initiatives were undertaken to that end:

---

2 Regulation (EC) No. 1292/96 of the Council of the European Union of 27 June 1996 concerning policies and magement of food aid and specific actions in support of food security.

— In April 1996, an international donor seminar was organised to look into worldwide long-term perspectives for food security, and the challenges posed to donors (the first "Brussels Forum on Food Security") by population growth, and resource depletion. One of its conclusions was that there is a need to prepare a Code of Conduct for Food Aid, as an additional mechanism to strengthen donor co-ordination, in view of the need to convert food aid into an effective development tool. In 1997, the issue was considered by the Council Working Group on Food Aid. In November 1997, the Development Council agreed to include work on such a Code of Conduct into the renegotiation of the Food Aid Convention during 1998. Preparations for that renegotiation have indeed started early 1998, including the idea to incorporate such a Code. It is too early to anticipate its outcome at the moment of drafting this text.

— A (third) International Food Aid Donor Forum, which is linked to the TransAtlantic Initiative, was organised in June 1997. This meeting also endorsed the initiative towards a Code of Conduct.

— The second "Brussels Forum on Food Security" in December 1997 looked into the subject of "Markets and Institutions for Food Security", considering (international) trade in foodstuffs in relation to national and local food security. In the aftermath of the Marrakech Agreement, the currently increased price volatility and market instability for food products because of lower government-held stocks, augurs ill for those low-income countries that depend substantially on imports. It was therefore concluded that greater coherence must be sought between trade and aid policies, and between agricultural policy reform and its effects on low-income food deficit countries and on market instability, including the question how to share out the cost of market instability and who will pay them.

The second conclusion was that agricultural market liberalisation needs to be completed by the establishment of international rules governing competition, similar to what already exists at national and at European level. This constitutes in fact a major issue which should be taken up at the beginning of a next international round of trade negotiations.

Donor coordination is also required to press for worldwide adoption of the principle that food aid should always be provided on a grant basis. Whereas all European food aid and food security support is systematically a one hundred percent grant, some other donors maintain that concessional sales of food aid should be included under the Food Aid Convention. Various researchers indicate that the volume of commercial food supplies with substantial grant elements in it, and of food aid supplies having commercial elements or strings attached to it, is probably more important than food aid on a full grant basis, and has therefore a decisive impact on food insecurity in vulnerable countries. It is questionable whether such mixed-character transactions should be listed at all under the FAC: the European position is that they should not. An intermediate solution of only listing under the FAC the grant element of food transactions involving the use of export credits, has not yet been considered seriously.

Nonetheless, at the same time it should be stressed that straightforward commercial transactions in food stuffs are valuable, and underline the world market's useful contribution to global food security, provided they take place between partners who can afford such transactions and that rules of fair competition are respected.

6 Emergency needs are not overlooked

The thrust of EC food aid and food security policy to strengthen the capacity of vulnerable countries to take up their responsibilities in this field, is in line with the views expressed at the World Food Summit (November 1996), that national governments have prime responsibility in ensuring food security for their country and its citizens. This is not to say that the European Commission will neglect short-term needs and emergency situations. Two cases in point can be mentioned: North Korea, and "El Niño".

Keeping in mind the disastrous effects of the last round of "El Niño" (1992/93) and in particular the resulting droughts in Southern Africa, the Commission considered it was necessary to anticipate and co-ordinate EU-responses and preventive operations for "El Niño". An interservice group, co-chaired by DG VIII and ECHO, with the support of DG I-B, was created to that end. A pre-programming exercise was made for the 1998 food security and food aid budget, in order to ensure that the Commission will be able to respond adequately to any additional requirements for (food) aid and food security support in 1998 as the result of the "El Niño" phenomenon.

In the case of North Korea (1997/98), the European Commission was the first to make available large quantities of emergency food aid in kind, from overseas. A package of more than 50 million ECU was put together to relieve urgent food needs of the population, which was largely implemented through WFP and NGOs.

Since emergency needs often stem from political instability, armed conflicts and massive movements of displaced persons and refugees, the EU response is generally threefold. In the first place to provide assistance, directly or through WFP and NGOs, to protracted refugee situations (e.g. Great Lakes area). Secondly, to assist in post-crises rehabilitation of productive infrastructure (e.g. Liberia). Third, to support conflict prevention efforts, as far as possible.

7 Concluding remarks

Food import needs of Africa alone are projected to increase to around 24 million tons in some 15 years from now, if present tendencies continue. We should furthermore recognise that the present favourable cycle of a series of years with generous rainfall conditions in what are traditionally drought-affected countries is bound to change sooner or later. It is therefore difficult to avoid the conclusion that the risk at stake is a sharply increased dependency on food aid of a substantial number of vulnerable countries which may be further marginalised in the world economy. On the other hand, it is doubtful that food aid supply in such massive quantities could be met in our post-Marrakech-situation with much-reduced government-held stocks all over the world that are only marginally replaced by additional stocks in the private sector. Apart from this, in view of current donor-fatigue, it is very doubtful that OECD countries would be willing to finance such massive food aid operations.

Most of us do agree that food aid from overseas can not provide the answer to such needs, nor should it because we do not want to go back to approaches perpetuating dependency. We believe that we should all adopt a longer time view in this field, without overlooking short-term needs, should support effective national FS policies and programmes in these countries, and seek coherence in approach.

Although we are quite conscious that everything can be improved upon, and that current EC policies on food security are no exception to that general rule, we firmly believe that the present line, as indicated above, is in all probability the way to eventually reduce the need to increase food aid shipments from overseas to what are now vulnerable countries. The main condition for success is, however, that all donors active in this field of food aid and food security, should adopt similar, or at least compatible, lines. Most EU Member States, and an increasing number of other OECD countries do already. We hope the last ones will follow soon.

30

Food Aid and Food Security—German Experience During Twenty Years of Cooperation

Friederike Bellin-Sesay, Günter Dresrüsse and Hans Pfeifer

1 Introduction

Access to food is a fundamental human right as it has been laid down in the UN Declaration of Human Rights (1948). Achieving food security for all is, therefore, an essential goal of the German Government's development policy and one of the major objectives of German development organisations. Policy approaches have changed over the years, reflecting many of the shifts in the international debate on food security. With growing experience in this field German development assistance was able to formulate comprehensive food security strategies and to develop a diverse set of specific instruments. This article explains the institutional background of German food security policy and illustrates how the existing approaches have been developed.

2 Developments in the German food aid and food security policy

In the aftermath of the Second World War the European Recovery Programme known as Marshall Plan was one of the largest food aid transfers in history. But sides have changed in the success story; Germany has shifted from one of the largest food aid recipients and become one of the largest donors for developing countries.

As in many donor countries German food aid in the beginning consisted of bulk supplies mainly in response to emergencies in developing countries; little consideration was given to directing its use to accountability. It was a common understanding that surplus disposal would be the key to food security for all. Countries with an agricultural overproduction granted free donations of food aid to overcome regional food shortages in poor states. At the beginning of the 1960s food security policies shifted from humanitarian objectives and surplus disposal towards assistance in economic development and agricultural production techniques.

The 1970s and 1980s brought again shifting views in the international discussion: the world food crisis of 1972/74 marked the transition from an era of abundant export supply of cheap food and excess productivity capacity to one of highly unstable food supply and prices. Policy-makers in these days were concerned with self-sufficiency measures and with price stabilisation. International efforts for establishing and maintaining adequate national, regional and international food stocks were promoted to stabilise food availability on various levels. Food security took the form of food insurance (Phillips and Taylor 1991).

The 1980s marked a turning point in the international debate: Food emergencies were no longer seen as shortfalls in food supply but as the result of loss of access of poor people to food (Sen 1981). It was also recognised that temporary and chronic malnutrition could be widespread within countries even when total food supplies at national level appeared satisfactory. At the same time, deteriorating satisfaction of basic needs became increasingly evident during structural adjustments. Food security discussions began to focus on household (and individual) level, stressing access, vulnerability and entitlement and called for multi-sectoral, but also multi-level nutrition planning (Maxwell and Frankenberger 1992; Maxwell 1996; Phillips and Taylor 1991).

Food first approaches in German development co-operation mirror international discussions and views of these decades. Food aid has widely evolved and diversified since the 1960s. Two comprehensive food security approaches emerged during the 1970s and 1980s: the "Integrated Food Security Programme" approach attempts to tackle food and nutrition insecurity at household level by combining entitlement protection with entitlement promotion. The second approach relates to the need to respond to food crises on national and subnational level and is called "Food Security Programme for Preparedness and Management of Food Crises" (BMZ 1997b).

The German Government responded to the diversification by creating a complex legal framework for different types of food aid and food security programmes. Over the years three special budget lines were created within the budget of the German Federal Ministry for Economic Cooperation and Development (BMZ), reserving funds for different types of food security programmes.

Most bi- and multilateral programmes concentrate on food supplies and on the accessibility of available foods; German programmes usually go beyond this and also emphasise the effective utilisation of available and accessible foods. This focus includes aspects of education, health, sanitation, personal hygiene, caring capacity, etc., leading to a broader approach towards food and nutrition security.[1] In the German debate on development policies, food and nutrition policy is considered to

1 Food security is defined as ensuring that all people at all times have access to enough food for an active and healthy life. Food and nutrition security is said to prevail if:

- all people at all times have access to sufficient as well as physiologically and culturally appropriate foodstuffs (food supply security);
- the people are healthy and therefore in a position to use and physiologically convert the foodstuffs available (food consumption security);
- health services are accessible to all people, thus enabling the effective treatment of all illnesses;
- the people responsible for food have both the knowledge and the time they need to prepare the available foodstuffs in an adequate form;
- fuel and water are available in sufficient quantities and quality to prepare meals (BMZ/GTZ 1997).

be a multi-sectoral task. The objective is to integrate and harmonise various sector policies towards the overall objective of achieving food and nutrition security (BMZ 1997b).

3 Objectives of Germany's food security and food aid policy

One of the main objectives of German development policy is "to assist developing economies secure their food requirements." The following more specific objectives are in accordance with the European Communities' rules and regulations on food aid and food security (EC 1996):

- promoting food security, especially amongst the poor population in developing economies;
- improving the nutritional situation in the recipient countries;
- improving the availability and access to food;
- contributing to a balanced economic and social development in the recipient countries;
- assisting recipient countries to improve their food production;
- reducing food aid dependency;
- contributing to development-oriented poverty-reduction schemes.

According to the ministerial policy paper on food security and food aid (BMZ 1997b), food security measures should be applied in low-income food-deficit countries (LIFDC). Exceptions to this criterion can be made in cases of emergency and severe food crisis. The German Government responds to the requests and demands of developing countries and international organisations. Appeals from the partner country usually include a proposal for a certain project or a specified region. The BMZ then sends an appraisal mission to map out the possible German contribution to a planned project.

The beneficiaries of German-funded food security programmes are acute or chronically malnourished people among the rural and urban population. Targeting is based on nutrition and indicators such as wasting, stunting and per-capita food supply.

Interventions are defined according to the nature of food insecurity and could thus focus on (inter-)national, regional or household level. Food security is therefore understood as a "multi-disciplinary, multi-sectoral and multi-level approach" (BMZ 1997b). The conditions and demands for food security and food aid projects differ widely. Thus, a set of tools and specific project types has been developed which take into account both the level of intervention as well as the aims of intervention. Table 1 shows the set of interventions reaching the target groups at different levels.

Table 1: Intervention levels and project types of food security measures

Objective	Operating Level	Project Type
Compensation of acute / temporary food deficits	Household / regional / national level	**Emergency Food Aid**
	National level	**Programme Aid**
Preparedness for temporary and acute food crises	National level	**Food Security Programmes for Preparedness & Management of Food Crises**
Sustainable and self-reliant food and nutrition security	Household / regional level	**Integrated Food Security Programmes**
Self-reliant food and nutrition security	National level	**Food Security Policy Advice (food security strategies)**

Source: BMZ 1997b.

These four approaches are the main instruments of the German Government's development policy in the field of food aid and food security. Projects can be implemented independently, but also as a preparatory supplementary measure within the framework of Financial or Technical Co-operation. However, whenever measures in the field of food security and food aid are implemented, the German sector concept stresses the importance and necessity of impact monitoring as an integrated part of the assistance for all stakeholders in the process. The improvement of nutritional status, but also other proxy indicators for poverty are seen as important criteria for the project progress. German policy is based on international agreements and an institutional and legal set-up that has developed over the years. In the following sections we illustrate how and why institutions, project types and budget allocations are interrelated. They form a coherent and flexible policy. The legal and institutional framework is described in section 4. The various project approaches (types) are described in sections 5 to 8 below.

4 The institutional and legal framework

At the beginning of German technical assistance food aid and food security programmes fell under the joint responsibility of the BMZ and the German Federal Ministry of Food, Agriculture and Forestry (BML). The latter was responsible for purchasing grains. The BMZ's task was to identify the beneficiaries. Since 1967, when Germany became one of the first signatory states to the Food Aid Convention (FAC), food aid programmes are the sole responsibility of the BMZ. It provides funds for bi- and multilateral programmes and develops policy guidelines which are compulsory for the implementing organisations. The BMZ is not directly involved in implementing projects but assures the standard of Germany's development projects through continuous evaluation and quality controls. German contributions to bilateral projects are usually implemented by the parastatal Deutsche

Gesellschaft für Technische Zusammenarbeit (GTZ) or NGOs such as German Agro Action, Caritas or the German Red Cross.

Germany's contributions to multilateral programmes are provided on the basis of the FAC and EC Regulation No. 1292/96:

The Food Aid Convention as part of the International Grains Agreement (1995). Under the FAC a total amount of 5.4 million mt of cereals are provided for food aid. The EU contributes 1.76 million mt, of which 193,000 mt are committed by the German Government.

EC Council Regulation No. 1292/96 on Food Aid Policy and Administration and on Specific Measures to Enhance Food Security (June 1996). This regulation resembles a European Food Aid Convention, which, in contrast to the International Grains Agreement, also includes non-cereal food products. It is important to note that the regulation aims at separating EU food aid from EU agricultural policies and at strengthening aspects of development cooperation. In addition, there is a lot of emphasis on the economic importance of purchasing the required food aid in neighbouring regions or countries rather than from the European market.

Germany's contributions to bilateral and multilateral food aid and food security programmes in developing countries are financed through special budget lines of the federal government's budget. For each programme type there is a special budget allocation:

Food aid, emergency and refugee programmes (Budget Allocation 686 25). Funds from this budget allocation are earmarked for the purchase of food products (mainly cereals and cereal products) mostly in bulk supply. The German contribution to the FAC (193,500 mt/p.a.) is also financed from this budget. Since 1995, programmes can also include rehabilitating infrastructure and social structures in emergency situations and strengthening self-help capacities.

Promotion of food security programmes in developing economies (Budget Allocation 686 08). Funds under this budget allocation are reserved for programmes aiming at sustainably improving the food security situation. To date, long-term food security measures (see Table 1) are financed through this budget line. Funding also covers project preparation and monitoring and evaluation of activities, reflecting a high flexibility in the application of these funds.

German contributions to the WFP (Budget Allocation 686 23). This budget allocation was established parallel to the foundation of the World Food Programme (WFP) in 1963. Funds from this budget allocation are reserved for German contributions to the WFP.

The following table provides an overview of the volume of Germany's contributions to bilateral and multilateral programmes in the field of food aid and food security.

Table 2: German food aid for developing economies (net payment in million DM)

	1989	1990	1991	1992	1993	1994	1995
Bilateral Contribution	193.5	204.5	154.4	244.6	161.1	192.3	180.0
Food Security Programmes	79.9	80.2	55.8	95.6	60.0	70.2	59.9
Food Security Programmes in connection with the Food Aid Convention	113.6	124.3	98.6	149.0	101.1	122.1	120.1
Multilateral Contribution	351.0	298.6	418.1	419.6	306.2	351.0	338.1
Food Aid through EU	308.3	253.6	373.1	370.6	241.2	286.0	293.1
Food Aid through WFP	42.7	45.0	45.0	49.0	65.0	65.0	45.0
Total	544.5	503.1	572.5	664.2	467.3	543.3	518.1
% of ODA	5.8	4.9	5.0	5.0	4.1	4.9	4.8

Source: BMZ 1996: 58-59, BMZ 1997a: 64.

Germany is one of the major donor countries operating world-wide. The broad involvement in food security issues is reflected in Germany's membership in the WFP, FAO, FAC, and the FAO's World Cereal Board and the Consultative Subcommittee on Surplus Disposal (CSSD). This involvement in the international food aid system is linked to Germany's contributions to the EU as well as to FAO/WFP's International Food Security Reserve. At this level the German Government is able to assert its influence on policies and programmes. Considering the volume of Germany's financial contributions to international programmes, the German Government has made relatively little use of its influence on policy matters over the last decades. The BMZ's policy focused primarily on implementing bilateral projects. Policies of international bodies and agencies also influenced implementing organisations' work.

Another important aim is to enhance cooperation at the level of regional institutions like the Comité Permanent Inter-Etats de Lutte contre la Sécheresse dans le Sahel (CILSS) or the Southern African Development Community (SADC). The idea is that these links will result in a harmonisation of policies and in an increased efficiency of food security programmes. The impact these programmes have on food security must, however, still be evaluated. The four main project types implemented by German development institutions (see Table 1) are described in the following sections.

5 Emergency food aid/programme aid

Food aid policy has undergone programmatic changes world-wide, shifting from a donor-driven to a demand-driven system. The idea of surplus disposal was initiated in the USA when it faced a tremendous grain surplus. For decades, surplus disposal implied that food aid derived exclusively from the European markets. It was the reduction of surpluses within the European Community (EC) that opened the way for food surplus purchases in developing countries. The German government, via the GTZ, was amongst the first to replace food aid shipments by local purchases or triangular business.

Already in 1987, a resolution was adopted by the German Parliament on "Food security in regions affected by hunger." This resolution urges the German Government to increase efforts to purchase food in surplus-producing developing countries. As a matter of fact, during 1994, procurements in developing countries amounted to 71.7% of the overall German cereal food aid (in MT of wheat equivalent) and 66.7% for non-cereal item (in monetary terms).

At the same time, other criteria have played an increasingly important role in food aid policies. Traditional food consumption habits, local production of food, market conditions, etc. were considered in political decision-making. Cereals, oil and sugar are the main products distributed as food aid. Fish is exclusively delivered by the WFP. Milk-powder has been abolished from the food rations since 1993 due to the frequently discussed risks of adverse effects on health. This demonstrates again how international discussions are reflected in implementing German development aid.

Food aid is granted in emergency situations, providing temporary relief for the population in a defined area (emergency food aid). Food aid can also be granted to substitute commercial food imports or as assistance for the purchase of food (programme aid) in Low-Income Food-Deficit Countries (LIFDC). Most of German food aid is provided in the form of emergency aid or as support supplies for food-for-work measures. In contrast, programme aid is decreasing and today only few countries (e.g. Cap Verde) receive regular donations.

Part of the food aid is delivered through multilateral food aid channels, being the German contribution to the World Food Programme (WFP). Under this programme, food aid is purchased and delivered by the GTZ, according to the quality and composition of foodstuffs agreed on by WFP/BMZ/BML.

The German policy recognises the importance of food aid, especially in emergencies where acute food deficits have to be overcome. In the area of food supply, German food aid policy takes a development-oriented approach (e.g. food-for-work schemes). Here, food aid is focused mainly at the household level. Programme aid plays a comparatively minor role in this context.

Emergency food aid/programme aid in Georgia

After the disintegration of the Soviet Union, Georgia faced tremendous food supply problems. The economy, based on the production and trade of tea, fruits, and citrus fruits, was confronted with severe shortages of cereals, flour and sugar which were previously exchanged with by the Soviet Union.

After the international aid appeal, the German government decided to supply wheat flour and sugar to Georgia in order to supplement the overall supply of basic foods for the Georgian population during the most difficult wintertime. The main share of the food supply was granted as aid (programme aid). Food donations were either sold to industrial bakeries or directly to the people through local markets. Part of the food aid was distributed free of charge directly to the most vulnerable groups, mainly to homes for children or elderly people.

Financed by the German Government the food was purchased in Turkey and shipped to Georgia (triangular business). Storage, transport and distribution of food aid falls under the responsibility of the Georgian Ministry of Trade and Transport as well as the Committee on Foreign Economic Relations. Distribution amongst the most vulnerable groups was coordinated by the German NGO Arbeiter Samariter Bund (ASB). The aid was directed at bridging the acute food shortage in Georgia. The timely and effective intervention contributed to balance temporary food deficits in Georgia and to stabilise the social situation in the country.

6 Food security programmes for preparedness and management of food crises

One of the lessons learnt from the emergency food aid operations during the severe Sahelian drought in 1973/74 was that food aid arrived too late. The lack of an early warning system, insufficient storage facilities in the recipient countries, poor transport facilities and an inefficient administration diminished the effectiveness of the food aid and thus worsened the effects of the drought.

As a consequence of this disaster, all Sahel countries established grain reserves or extended their existing capacities. Warehouses and transport facilities were financed by the international donor community. The facilities are usually managed by the national grain boards of the respective country. Buffer stocks were also built up to balance the seasonal price fluctuations on the local grain markets.

Buffer stocks have two functions: They are an instrument to control market prices within a country and to balance seasonal fluctuations in food availability. The grain board buys after a harvest when prices are low and sell in the period before harvest ("soudure") when prices are high. Buffer stocks of locally produced and of imported food are utilised to combat regional food insecurity. In cases of severe drought the warehouse capacities form the backbone of food aid operations.

The initial concept that profits from sales would cover the high storage costs proved to be unrealistic in almost all countries. Under the structural adjustment programmes (SAP) the rigid control of producer prices has been lifted, giving more incentives to small farmers and reducing the predominance of the parastatal grain marketing boards which were often criticised for their urban bias.

Buffer stocks, however, remain an absolutely crucial element of the national food security policy in countries affected by continued droughts, crop failures or other types of food deficits. The support of national systems for food security reserves remains, therefore, an integral part of the German Government's contribution to food security programmes of their partner countries.

These projects focus on strengthening management capacities in all governmental and non-governmental organisations concerned with the administration and controlling of food security reserves. Besides the support at management and policy level, these programmes also advise on practical issues like store keeping, stock protection, logistics, and administration (capacity building).

New instruments have been developed for the efficient administration of food security reserves. The GTZ developed a model to calculate the optimal size of a food reserve. Part of the funds programmed for buffer stocks is used as a food security fund which can be utilised for commercial imports in case of a disaster or drought. An early warning system combined with a market price information system help to reduce unnecessary and expensive buffer stocks. Such instruments help the grain boards to respond quickly and effectively to market changes and crisis situations. Linkage to a national disaster intervention plan assures the effective coordination of all relevant institutions in case of a severe drought.

Investing in preparedness and food security systems is considerably cheaper than any emergency food aid intervention or relief operation. In addition, one can say that the above-mentioned efforts played an important role during the 1985/86 crisis in the Sahel region. Compared to the effects of the crisis in 1973/74, this programme type contributed effectively to minimising the effects of this drought. The cost return of food security reserves is very obvious. Avoiding food imports of 10,000 t/year, for example, not only saves the government's budget for other important issues but at the same time prevents possible negative impacts, which are always being discussed in the context of food aid. Though the positive effect is obvious, high running costs of buffer stocks and preparedness systems remain a burden on the budgets of many developing economies.

Food security programme in Mali

After the 1973/74 drought in the Sahel region, it became evident that for many people in Mali food aid had arrived too late to save their lives. Thus, the German Government decided to support the national grain board, OPAM (Office des produits Agricoles du Mali), in its effort to built up a strategic grain reserve for the drought-affected country. Buffer stocks are kept which in cases of renewed emergencies can be utilised until commercial imports or food aid fill the gap between local production and demand.

The project supported OPAM in managing the food reserve and in technical matters (stock protection, grain marketing, market price information systems, etc.). In a first phase the infrastructure (warehouses) was set up and the reserve was strengthened either through food aid deliveries or through local purchases.

A legal framework has been developed to regulate the use of food security reserves. The Malian Government and the major donors agreed on terms for monitoring food availability and refilling grain reserves.

Considering the high costs of disaster prevention, the GTZ developed a system of instruments (grain reserves, early warning systems, food security funds, disaster preparedness plans) which made the system more efficient and cost-effective. With the technical facilities in place and with years of management experience in this field, OPAM is enabled to operate a complex food security system and to provide disaster preparedness. Funding for running costs, however, remains an ongoing problem in Mali as in many of the neighbouring states.

One major condition that made the whole system function was strong donor coordination to restructure the grain market in Mali and to coordinate food aid.

7 Integrated Food Security Programmes

Integrated Food Security Programmes (IFSP) have been the most frequent approach adopted by German development cooperation to combat food insecurity. These programmes target nutritional deficits at household level. They help improve the living conditions of groups suffering from acute and/or structural food insecurity.

IFSP have quite a long history. This approach was first developed in the context of emergency operations leading to large-scale food-for-work schemes. Between 1985 and 1991 poverty reduction became a more dominant aspect of food security measures to combat chronic food insecurity. Trends in current programmes, especially in complex emergencies in Africa, show that food security aspects regain the importance of the early years of IFSP. Integrated food security programmes as implemented today are an unique approach in the international aid system.

The following scenarios are typical starting points for IFSP:

— Severe food shortage caused by the effects of a natural disaster or a war. Such a crisis situation often surpasses the local self-help capacity and is normally characterised by the loss of productive resources even during rehabilitation and reconstruction.
— Chronic food insecurity, caused by structural inadequacies, mostly in extremely poor rural and urban areas.

IFSP are target-group oriented and focus on food-insecure people. The identification and preparation of projects starts with a baseline survey. On the basis of this data, experts can analyse to what extent food and nutrition insecurity is caused by availability of, access to or the physical use and physiological conversion of available foods. Following this analysis, target groups and project areas are identified. Such a survey also provides the necessary foundations for monitoring and evaluating project progress.

In order to reach the food-insecure poor, self-targeting approaches and participatory methods are employed. Participatory methods are also used to identify project activities together with the target groups.

IFSP pursue a twin-track strategy: on the one hand they aim at balancing transitory food deficits and, on the other hand, they serve to create productive and social investments for sustainable food security. The combination of interventions chosen - be it food- and/or cash-for-work, labour intensive employment schemes, training or extension services - will depend on the causes of the prevailing food insecurity. Focal points of IFSP range from food production, off-farm income, utilisation of food and health issues to disaster response or the rehabilitation of social and physical infrastructure.

Integrated food security programmes are as well an essential element of poverty alleviation which is one of the top priorities of the German Government's development policy. In addition, they contribute towards rehabilitating the environment, an important pillar of German development cooperation. Last but not least, these programmes follow gender-sensitive approaches at household level which is in line with German development policy.

There are three main fields of intervention for IFSP:

— improvement of physical resources (access to or better utilisation of existing resources),
— improvement of human potentials for development,
— strengthening of institutional capacities.

IFSP usually include measures that should either prevent emergencies or aim at improving post-emergency conditions. Hence, they are often seen as being a bridge between emergency aid and technical assistance.

Figure 1 shows the set of instruments employed in each phase. This implies decreasing inputs of food aid with increasing importance of extension programmes, training, institution building etc. Figure 1 also demonstrates how relief and development are linked and explains the transitory character of IFSP. IFSP can also be seen as a tool of technical assistance to reach the food-insecure poor and thus contribute to poverty reduction.

Figure 1: Instruments and phases of food security programmes

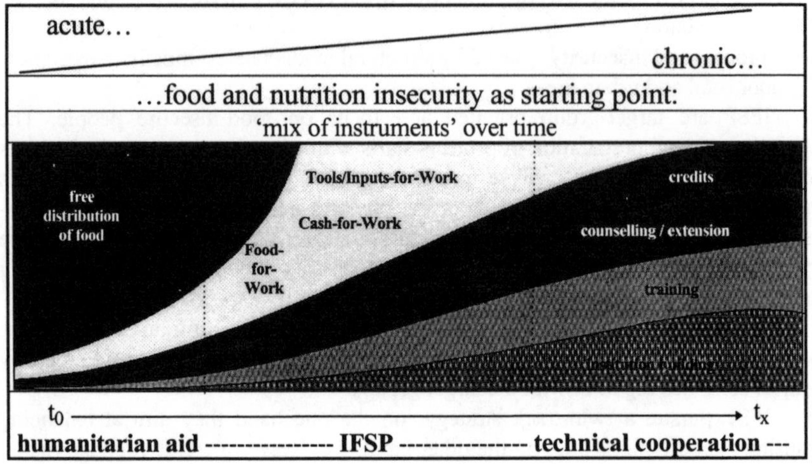

Source: BMZ/GTZ 1997.

This project type is one of the few which is able to show measurable improvements after a few years of implementation, using the nutritional status as an impact indicator. Presently, the nutritional status is also used as a poverty indicator, which again reflects that IFSP can be regarded as being poverty alleviation programmes.

The Integrated Food Security Programme Honduras

The overall goal of this project is to improve the nutritional status of approximately 3,000 families in three municipalities of the Department of Lempira, Western Honduras. The project started with an action-oriented start-up phase in 1990 and is currently in the second implementation phase.

According to a baseline survey, an average of 40 % of all children under five years are chronically undernourished in this area. Addressing the main causes of undernutrition, identified as insufficient food production on subsistence farms, inadequate food habits and high prevalence of certain diseases, the project activities are focused on agriculture, health, nutrition and infrastructure.

To improve food availability and access to food, agricultural activities concentrate on the promotion of sustainable agricultural methods and improved production of traditional varieties of food crops at household level. Health and nutrition activities aim at preventing nutrition-related diseases like diarrhoea and influenza, improving diets, breast feeding and child care. The extension methodology guarantees the integration of agricultural and nutrition-related activities, e.g. the selection of traditional food crops with high nutritional value.

In the infrastructure sector, the construction of drinking water supply systems reduces the work load especially of women, thereby creating more space for other economic activities or better child care. At the same time these measures help to reduce the prevalence of infections through contaminated drinking water.

Food-for-work programmes are mainly applied in road construction, reducing the temporary pre-harvest food deficit of affected households. This aid enables the families to avoid or reduce migration to the coffee plantations and therefore concentrate on their own agricultural production.

In order to achieve sustainability of food security related activities in the region, support is provided to relevant governmental institutions and local governments to improve their planning capacity and adapt their services to the specific needs of the food-insecure.

Project evaluations have shown the significant success of this approach. Participatory development of technical content and implementation by traditional institutions led to widespread application and diffusion of new technologies by the target group and resulted in improved living conditions.

New projects with similar approaches are currently being implemented in Honduras, Guatemala, Haiti, and Peru. Here, intensified institutional cooperation between local NGOs and the newly decentralised public administration forms a strategic element which aims at a broader impact.

8 Food Security Policy Advisory Services

Food Security Policy Advisory Services is a fairly new approach in the German development discussion. As yet, not much practical experience has been gained in this area. German development cooperation has neglected this very important area in the past, mainly as a result of historic developments, which started with food aid focusing emergency aid and relief programmes and moved step by step towards food and nutrition security.

The mode of intervention is to second advisors for policy and institutional advice, to elaborate inter-sector national food security strategies, following the sector guidelines. Policy advisory services also include effective planning and management of food aid and food reserves and support for elaborating food security programmes that aim at coping with the social and economic effects of structural adjustment. Donor coordination is another very important and frequently discussed task in this field.

One of the fundamental problems of this approach is that food and nutrition insecurity is a multi-sectoral approach. Policy advisory services must, therefore, be channelled through various line ministries. Food Security Policy must try to coordinate the policies of relevant sectors, such as agriculture, health, social affairs, education. Policy advisory services have been identified as one of the sectors which will receive increasing attention in development co-operation.

9 Conclusions

Food security programmes are an integral part of the German Government's development cooperation policy and constitute an important and independent programme within German development assistance. Over the last twenty years, a differentiated set of project types and programme approaches has been developed for appropriate interventions in the continuum from emergencies to technical cooperation. These projects impact at different levels ranging from household to national policy level. As the food-insecure are usually poor, food security programmes contribute significantly to poverty alleviation as the overall goal of food security.

However, in the 1990s the main feature of current food insecurity in the world is associated with the growing role of emergencies. German Development Cooperation reflects this situation. Assistance in the field of food security concentrates on post-war and post-disaster situations, giving regional priority to Africa. Food aid and food security programmes of the 1990s serve mainly to respond to increasing political demand from governments to link relief and development. This situation differs from that of the late 1980s where political priority in the field of food security was given to chronic malnutrition caused by structural poverty.

With regard to future challenges, the German Ministry for Economic Cooperation and Development (BMZ) has formulated new policy guidelines on food security and food aid (BMZ 1997b) which also underline the strong emphasis placed by the German government on education, environment, poverty alleviation and gender (four pillars of development cooperation). This policy paper provides guidelines for German implementing organisations and reflects the government's firm commitment to continue playing an important role in assisting partner countries to combat food insecurity. However, the successful implementation of these strategies will ultimately depend on the German Government's political willingness to secure sufficient funding for this sector in the future.

References

Bundesministerium für wirtschaftliche Zusammenarbeit und Entwicklung (BMZ) (1989): Sektorkonzept Nahrungsmittelhilfe und Ernährungssicherung, Bonn.

Bundesministerium für wirtschaftliche Zusammenarbeit und Entwicklung (BMZ) (1996): Journalisten-Handbuch, Bonn.

Bundesministerium für wirtschaftliche Zusammenarbeit und Entwicklung (BMZ) (1997a): Jounalisten-Handbuch, Bonn.

Bundesministerium für wirtschaftliche Zusammenarbeit und Entwicklung (BMZ) (1997b): Sektorkonzept. Ernährungssicherung und Nahrungsmittelhilfe als Instrument der Entwicklungszusammenarbeit, Bonn, Januar (English version to be published in 1997).

Bundesministerium für wirtschaftliche Zusammenarbeit und Entwicklung (BMZ)/Gesellschaft für Technische Zusammenarbeit mbH (GTZ) (1997): Integrierte Ernährungssicherungs-programme in der deutschen Entwicklungszusammenarbeit. Eine Orientierung für die Projektarbeit, Bonn, Januar (English version to be published in 1997).

EC (1996): Amtsblatt der Europäischen Gemeinschaften - Rechtsvorschriften. Ausgabe L 166, 39. Jahrg., 5. Juli 1996, Ausgabe in deutscher Sprache.

Maxwell, Simon and Timothy Frankenberger (1992): Household Food Security: Concepts, Indicators, Measurements. A technical review. UNICEF, IFAD.

Maxwell, Simon (1996): Food Security Post Modern Perspective, in: Food Policy, Vol. 21, No. 2, pp. 155.

Phillips, T. and D. Taylor (1991): Background Paper on Food Security: Draft Final, Centre of food security, University of Guelph, Ontario.

Sen (1981): Poverty and Famines. Clarendon Press, Oxford.

31

The Role of Northern NGOs in the Food Sector

Bernd V. Dreesmann

1 The food sector as a priority

The fight against hunger or, more positively expressed, the efforts to extend food security to all human beings, has always been a priority for the majority of non-governmental organizations (NGOs).

1.1 Names as an indicator

The names of some of the leading European NGOs provide a clear indication of the reasons for their creation and, in many cases, of the type of activities which guide them (OECD 1988: 18-28). OXFAM, the internationally renowned British NGO, was established in 1942 as "OXFAM Committee Against Famine". Soon afterwards it began to use its telegraphic address "Oxfam UK" as its "brand-name" and logo. In Germany in 1959, the Christian churches founded two aid agencies whose names, or part thereof, are indicative of the type of operations they carry out. The Diakonische Werk of the Evangelical Church in Germany called its development co-operation division "Brot für die Welt" and the German Catholic Episcopal Conference called its NGO "MISEREOR", adding "Action against hunger and illness" as a sub-name. At the same time, one of the most active and influential German secular development co-operation organizations uses the word "hunger" as part of its name: The Deutsche Welthungerhilfe.

The list of NGOs whose names contain food-related expressions can be easily extended. To mention a few:

- Action contre la faim, France
- Feed the Children International, Belgium
- Food for Life, USA
- Food for All, USA
- The Hunger Project, USA
- Freedom from Hunger Foundation, USA

The range of NGOs which support food-security programmes is not, however, restricted to the "name-bearers". Indeed, a vast majority of NGOs is active in this field.

1.2 Defining the food sector

The fact that definitions of the causes of hunger cover a broad spectrum of situations and events explains the wide outreach of the expression "food sector".

The US advocacy NGO "Bread for the World" listed the following causes of hunger in its 5th Annual Report on the State of World Hunger in 1995 (Bread for the World 1994: Table of Contents, p. iii):
- powerlessness and politics;
- poverty in a global economy;
- population, consumption and environment;
- racism and ethnocentrism;
- gender discrimination;
- vulnerability and age.

A similar approach was taken by the European Council of Ministers which, on June 27th, 1996, adopted a new regulation, that integrates European food aid policy into a comprehensive food security policy (European Commission 1996). Article 5 of Resolution 1292/96 contains a catalogue of measures which are regarded by the Council, i.e. the representatives of the 15 member states, and the Commission of the European Union, as an effective means to achieve a higher standard of food security.

Article 5 lists the following measures which will be implemented or funded by the EU Commission:
- the supply of seeds, tools and inputs essential to the production of food crops,
- rural credit support schemes targeted particularly at women,
- schemes to supply the population with drinking water,
- storage schemes at the appropriate level,
- operations concerning the marketing, transport, distribution or processing of agricultural and food products,
- measures in support of the private sector for commercial development at national, regional and international level,
- applied research and field training,
- projects to develop the production of food crops while respecting the environment,
- flanking, awareness, technical assistance and field training operations in particular for women and producers' organizations and agricultural workers,
- support measures for women and producers' organizations,
- projects to produce fertilizer from raw materials and basic materials found in the recipient countries,
- schemes to support local food aid structures, including training schemes on the ground.

Accepting that there is a wide range of causes for the existence of hunger and malnutrition, and taking into account the EU catalogue of measures to combat these problems and to achieve a higher degree of food security, then most programmes and projects of NGOs fall under the above-mentioned criteria.

This NGO-role of "food-fighters" applies not only to operational agencies which support field programmes, but also to those organisations that implement information, education and advocacy programmes. Since the International Conference on Nutrition in 1992, public campaign slogans and fund-raising appeals, such as "Freedom from Hunger" or "Food for All", have been replaced by the generally accepted definition: "Food security means access by all people at all times to the food needed for an active healthy life" (FAO/WHO 1992: v).

At the household level, food security refers to "the ability of the household to secure, either from its own production or through purchases, adequate food for meeting the dietary needs of its members".

2 Historical perspective

The strong involvement of NGOs in the food-sector can also be explained historically (Sen 1981). Famines have always been a great cause for concern and compassion. Indeed, in countries struck by famine, they are remembered by the people for generations. This applies to both the "Great Irish Famine" in 1845-51, and to the "Great Ethiopian Famine" in 1888-92, when one third of the population died. The same is true for the famine in Russia in 1921 or that in Bengal/India in 1943, which resulted in several million fatalities.

2.1 New NGOs

The advent of severe food shortages during and after the First and Second World Wars mobilized the European populace into undertaking relief actions. This led to the establishment of a number of NGOs, which today belong to the biggest and most active. Examples include the Caritas Agencies in several European countries and the "Fight the Famine Council", a predecessor of today's "The Save the Children Fund/UK". Relief and reconstruction programs led, in 1942, to the establishment of OXFAM/UK and the American NGOs Catholic Relief Services/CRS (1943) and CARE (1945).

2.1.1 The Freedom from Hunger Campaign

In 1959, following his own experience of severe food shortages and the power of civil society during the Indian fight for independence, B.R. Sen, the Director-General of FAO, proposed to the member-states of FAO the creation of a Freedom from Hunger Campaign/FFHC. This lead to the rise of a world-wide network of FFHC Committees.

In 1962 the German FFHC Committee came into existence as "Deutscher Ausschuss für den Kampf gegen den Hunger". It comprised representatives from the most influential groups in the country, such as political parties, the churches, the trade-unions, scientists, the media etc. The German Federal President, Heinrich Lübke, who, as Minister for Agriculture and Food of the Federal State North-Rhine Westfalia, was in charge of the extremely difficult food situation in the industrial Ruhr-area during the post-war period, volunteered as patron of the committee and became one of its most active supporters.

2.2 Focus on Africa

During the second half of the 1960s, the publicity surrounding the famine in Bihar/India and the civil war in Biafra/Nigeria caused huge public awareness and, consequently, fund-raising actions by NGOs all over the world ensued.

The Ethiopian famine in 1972-74, which led to the removal of Emperor Haile Selassie, has been called the “first fully media-covered food-crisis”. The horrific photos of starving children and the television reports of enormous camps full of “hunger-refugees," made the Horn of Africa synonymous with hunger, poverty and misery. A short time after the Ethiopian famine, the international community was mobilized once more by a drought in the Sahel-area. Governments, multilateral agencies and NGOs alike staged a huge aid campaign, which reinforced the impression of many people in Europe and North America, that Africa had become the “poorhouse of the world”.

In 1982-84, hunger and human misery was again uppermost in the public mind; or at least in the mind of those people who showed an avid interest in events in Africa, Asia and Latin America. The new rulers of Ethiopia admitted that there was another country-wide famine and an international relief-campaign was organized.

Following a few years of sufficient rains, Ethiopia, Eritrea and “the Somalias” were hit by another drought in 1991-92. This time the co-ordination of international aid operations to the area was especially difficult, since other parts of Eastern and Southern Africa were also suffering from a long period of dry weather. Even Zimbabwe, which in normal years was an exporter of cereals and an important source for the regional procurement of food aid, was forced to import food and simultaneously applied to the international community for food aid.

3 Institutional co-ordination

The significant involvement of NGOs in the food-sector has led to a high degree of institutional co-ordination between NGOs, both on the national and the international level. This is true not only for church agencies which have co-operated effectively for decades through special committees of Caritas Internationalis in Rome and the World Council of Churches, but also for the wide range of secular NGOs. The successful work of the FAO Freedom from Hunger Campaign/Action for Development has already been mentioned.

3.1 NGOs and international meetings

NGOs from all over the world also form coalitions, action groups, fora and "alternative platforms" which prepare their input into food-related international meetings such as the two World Food Congresses and the World Food Conference, not to mention events like the World Congress for Agrarian Reform, the International Conference on Nutrition and the World Food Summit. The fact that such NGO consortia attract a considerable amount of interest and attention by the media and, through them, by the public at large can, at times, frustrate the organizers of international meetings and cause significant tension between the different parties.

In this context it is interesting to note that the type of co-operation between international organizations such as FAO, WHO and UNCTAD and the NGO-activists has undergone noteworthy changes. While NGOs were regarded as equal partners and full participants during the World Food Congresses in Washington and The Hague, their critical comments throughout these meetings, and afterwards with regard to the insufficient results achieved, induced FAO to house NGOs some distance from the main meeting at its headquarters during the subsequent World Food Conference. An environment of co-operation and mutual respect returned during the preparation-phase and meeting of the recent World Food Summit, in 1996. In this instance NGOs were requested to contribute their experience and opinions and an NGO representative was invited to address the plenary session.

3.2 The European Union

Further examples of the operation of effective NGO-consortia, working together with respect to international food issues, exist on the level of the European Union. Ever since its creation in 1972, the NGDO/EU Liaison Committee in Brussels has been the main link between non-governmental development organizations and the Commission of the European Union. It has focused a lot of its attention and work on the food matters policy of European institutions, such as the European Parliament, the Council of Ministers and the EU Commission/EUC. When the Liaison Committee created five thematic working groups, one was designated to act as the "food sector watch" of the EUC. Throughout the following 15 years of its operation, the way in which the name of this working group changed continued to reflect the development and adaptations of EU policy in this area. The group was initially entitled "Food Aid Working Group"; this was followed by "Food Matters Working Group" and eventually "Food Security Working Group".

3.2.1 EuronAid

During the same period, European NGOs established another association entitled EuronAid, or European Association of NGOs for Food Aid and Emergency Aid, whose headquarters are located in The Hague.

The work of these two parallel structures was clearly demarcated during the first few years. That is to say, that whereas the working groups of the Liaison Committee concentrated their activities on political and programmatic questions and also had a leading role in lobbying the European institutions, EuronAid was in charge of facilitating the practical implications of food aid programmes of European NGOs that were funded by the EUC. However, the increasing amounts of EU food aid channeled through NGOs—which culminated in some 600,000 metric tonnes annually during the food crisis years in 1991-93—and the professional, low-cost services provided by EuronAid, shifted EuronAid's institutional influence from the discussion to the operational level.

EuronAid thereafter assisted European NGOs and the Food Aid Unit of the Directorate General "Development" of the EUC not only in logistical and procurement operations, but played an increasing role in food-aid programming, reporting and accounting. The Secretariat of EuronAid also developed support programmes in the form of training courses on funding procedures and regional NGO conferences based on central thematic issues. The growing importance of EuronAid led to a subsequent increase in its membership, although the association also serves non-member NGOs. At present, the majority of the most important and influential European NGOs are members of EuronAid.

3.2.2 The Joint Food Security Group

In 1997 the Liaison Committee and EuronAid joined forces once again by forming a Joint Food Security Group which consists of members delegated by the national NGO platforms or elected by the EuronAid General Assembly. The work of this group will have a number of consequences which will result in synergetic advantages:

- The divergence between policy planners and operational pragmatists has been overcome. There is, therefore, a united approach towards the food security and food aid policy of the EUC.
- The Joint Food Security Group will act as sole intermediary of the European NGO community *vis-à-vis* European institutions, especially the EUC. The slogan "unity creates strength" applies.

3.3 The USA

A situation similar to that found in Europe exists in the USA, in that some years ago the principal NGOs involved in food aid operations formed a project called Food Aid Management/FAM, located in Washington, D.C. Unlike EuronAid, FAM is not an operational agency, but an instrument used by NGOs, such as Catholic Relief Services/CRS, CARE, World Vision, Africare and others, to improve and harmonize programming, reporting and accounting procedures. This is of major importance for co-operation between American NGOs and USAID, which channels a large part of its food aid through NGOs. EuronAid and FAM have granted each other observer-status and have strengthened their co-operative ties as part of the New Transatlantic Partnership, developed with remarkable vigor between the EUC and USAID.

3.4 International organizations

Five other co-operation-schemes between NGOs and international organizations in the food sector deserve to be mentioned.

3.4.1 The World Food Programme

Since its foundation in 1961 the World Food Programme/WFP has developed a co-operative partnership with NGOs and at present has contacts with more than 1000 national and international NGOs. A regular operational and policy dialogue between the WFP and NGOs was set up in November 1995. One of the most important points on the agenda of the WFP/NGO Committee was the negotiation of "Memoranda of Understanding", clarifying the division of responsibilities between the partners. At field level co-operation is even stronger. In 1995, 92% of the WFP field offices reported that they had some form of relations with NGOs (The NGLS Handbook 1997: WFP/NGO relations, 255-259). The WFP is putting a growing share of its resources at the disposition of NGO programmes. For example, in 1996 German Agro Action, the Bonn-based NGO, received some 2.9 million DM from the WFP (German Agro Action 1996: 27).

3.4.2 The Food and Agricultural Organization/FAO

The Food and Agricultural Organization/FAO has, as already mentioned above, a history of co-operation with the NGO world since 1959. While co-operation weakened somewhat in the late 1970s and the 1980s, it recovered during the last decade and has been subsequently endorsed by a number of international conferences, including the International Conference on Nutrition in 1992 and the World Food Summit in 1996.

FAO/NGO co-operation falls into five broad areas: policy dialogue, information sharing and analysis, field programmes, promotion of partnerships, and resource mobilization. FAO's field programme includes components specifically targeted at capacity building for peoples' organizations/POs and NGOs. These activities aim at strengthening the ability of POs and NGOs to participate effectively in policy fora and to formulate and implement their own agricultural development strategies. Since 1996 a newly created Unit for Co-operation with the Private Sector and NGOs acts as the focal point for FAO's work with NGOs (The NGLS Handbook 1997: FAO/NGO relations, 22-25).

3.4.3 The International Fund for Agricultural Development/IFAD

Co-operation between the International Fund for Agricultural Development/IFAD and NGOs began in 1981 in the framework of a joint project with the Grameen Bank in Bangladesh. In the years that followed, IFAD concluded a limited number of co-operation agreements that led to the development of policy guidelines which stressed clearly the need to include NGOs from developing countries as active participants. IFAD also established an NGO consultative committee and created a special IFAD/NGO fund.

Another important step towards strengthening co-operation with NGOs was the IFAD Conference on Poverty and Hunger, which took place in Brussels in November 1995. The Conference adopted an action plan and NGOs are now actively involved in its implementation. The participation of NGOs in IFAD projects has also grown considerably. At present, approximately 150 NGOs participate in well over 100 IFAD projects (The NGLS Handbook 1997: IFAD/NGO relations, 34-39).

3.4.4 The World Bank

The World Bank has a long tradition and wide-ranging experience of operational collaboration with NGOs. In 1995, 41 percent of all projects approved by the World Bank were due to involve NGOs. Almost half of them supported the food sector, i.e., 29 percent were related to agricultural and rural programmes, whilst a further 19 percent fell into the category "population, health and nutrition" (The World Bank 1995: 22-24).

3.4.5 The Consultative Group for International Agricultural Research/ CGIAR

The most recent link between NGOs and an international body is the NGO Committee of the Consultative Group for International Agricultural Research/CGIAR. The committee was created in 1995 by CGIAR Chairman Ismail Serageldin, a Vice-President of the World Bank and as such, a reliable supporter of NGO-causes, such as the fight against poverty and the strengthening of micro-credit schemes. It is comprised of scientists and development specialists from both southern and northern NGOs.

As CGIAR stakeholder, the NGO Committee has developed and subsequently expressed its concern over the use of modern biotechnology in advancing research for sustainable food security in developing countries. Indeed, the NGO Committee went on record to voice its concern that the trend toward increased intellectual property protection in agriculture could endanger the range of collaborative research and therein reduce the free flow of knowledge on germplasm and technology. Furthermore, the NGO Committee is a strong advocate of greater biological safety and of the role of agro-ecology as a means to strengthen sustainable food security.

4 The interest of the donors

There are a number of reasons for the existence of a close co-operation between NGOs, public donors and international organizations. As regards public donors, the generally favourable image of NGOs is an attraction. Indeed, in a democratic society, the inclusion of the "civil sector" in government programmes and enabling "all relevant groups of society" to act as partners, are positive elements. Public opinion and voters get the impression that a consensus has been reached, in spite of the criticism of many NGOs at times, towards the policy and performance of governments .

4.1 The cost factor

For public donors, NGOs offer, in most cases, an extremely competitive cost-benefit relation. Although many NGOs have developed highly professional skills in preparing and implementing projects in the field, they regularly receive less overheads for their activities. This cost difference is especially noticeable in relation to the gaps in salary levels, for example, when a staff member of an NGO changes over to a consulting company or an international organization. Similar cost increases tend to occur when an NGO project is taken over and continued by the "non-NGO sector".

Recent examples which invite such a comparison are the "Local Food Security Units" and the "Food Security Advisors" of the EU Commission which form a global network of monitoring and control. Since it is very difficult to identify the exact costs involved, a glance at the material outfit of these units—staffing at the EU, salaries, size of offices and car—reveals that NGO representation in the respective countries are more than cost-competitive. The same is true for other international organizations, such as the WFP, FAO or the UNHCR, the local offices of bilateral donor programmes and consulting firms, all of which tend to be more expensive than NGOs. Small is not only beautiful, but also cost-competitive.

4.2 The grassroots connection

A third reason why public donors also co-operate with NGOs (in the food sector amongst others) is the close grassroots relations and the high flexibility of NGOs.

NGO activities are close to the grassroots and this leads NGOs to advocate and implement projects which aim at fulfilling the basic needs of the beneficiaries and which emphasize the fight against extreme poverty and its consequences. For NGOs the access to food is fundamental in order to cover the basic needs of the target population. It can be achieved in a number of ways, which include the funding of integrated, environmentally sustainable agricultural projects or the provision of food aid. NGOs are therefore a vital partner for public donors; both for programmes to improve agriculture and for the use of food aid in a broad variety of project types.

5 NGOs and food aid

It is therefore not surprising that big international food aid donors like USAID and the EUC have always channeled a significant part of their food aid allocation through NGOs. NGOs use food aid for emergency relief and social-humanitarian projects, as well as for development programmes, where food aid can be invested as food-for-work. Many NGOs continue to use food aid alongside their own resources. This approach increases the value of the food items, enabling them to be used for a wider variety of purposes than food aid alone. Examples are the construction of community kitchens, kindergartens, schools and homes for old people, as well as the provision of non-food inputs such as tools, machinery and other agricultural investment goods.

NGOs in America have developed a rather sophisticated system of monetising food aid, using the proceeds for the purchase of project-related non-food inputs and for covering their administrative overheads. For many years European NGOs have enjoyed a significant advantage, in that the EUC not only allocates food aid in kind to NGO food aid projects, but also funds the purchase of seeds and small tools. Monetisation activities by European NGOs are therefore less frequent than those of their American counterparts.

Another significant difference between NGO food aid projects funded by the EUC, as well as by some European governments, and USAID is the possibility for European NGOs to undertake local or triangular operations, where qualities and prices permit; that is to say that they are able to purchase the food items themselves, either in the recipient countries or in a third country.

5.1 NGO criticism

NGOs have traditionally cultivated an ambivalent role *vis-à-vis* food aid. There is a long list of critical publications which underline the detrimental consequences of food aid for agriculture, the food habits and self-help efforts of the recipients, just to mention a few negative aspects. Food aid has been condemned as a most dangerous outlet for the disastrous surplus effects of the Common Agricultural Policy of the European Union and the similarly bad farm policy of the US government.

There is no doubt that quite a number of these critical arguments are—or, at least, were—fully justified. This is, however, truer for American food aid, which is still tied politically to the "Farm Bill", than for the European Union where the ties between the Common Agricultural Policy and development policy were cut more than a decade ago. Hard-core critics refuse, however, to take notice of any improvements and continue to engage themselves in anti-food aid campaigns. The value of such criticism and negativity might increase, therein making the critics' arguments more acceptable, if they took account of the different types of food aid operations. There is a big difference between food aid as such and subsidised exports of agricultural products. For example, sending food aid to food-for-work programmes in drought-stricken Tigray is certainly not the same as dumping surplus meat into West African countries which already have their own flourishing cattle population. Another example might be the difference between food aid that is carefully targeted at an NGO-supported school-feeding programme in Haiti, a country which has to spend a considerable percentage of its extremely scarce foreign exchange reserves on commercial food imports, and bulk allocations made by national governments, the EUC or USAID, which are difficult to monitor.

5.2 The interest of NGOs

In spite of warnings and critical voices, which also emanate from within the NGO-community, food aid is nonetheless an important instrument for the successful implementation of NGO programmes. This is true not only in the case of emergency aid operations which alleviate human suffering following natural catastrophes or in the context of man-made disasters such as civil strife, ethnic disturbances or fully-fledged actions of war. NGOs also use large quantities of food aid for their social-humanitarian and development programmes.

5.2.1 The financial factor

Without a doubt, the intention to improve the access to food and the nutritional status of the poorest is the most important argument in favour of the use of food aid. However, its high value, especially if one includes transport costs, is a welcome source of income for NGOs: it helps to improve their balance sheets and has a positive effect on the percentage representing total overheads.

The 1996 balance sheet and profit and loss statement of German Agro Action can serve as an example of a development with which a number of NGOs has to contend. In their case, although all other major sources of income, such as fund-raising income and the cash contributions from public institutions like the German government and the EU Commission, showed an upward trend, a sharp reduction in the "contributions of food stuffs" led to an overall loss of income. At the same time, employment costs and some other expenses grew, therein increasing the percentage spent on overheads (German Agro Action 1996: 21-27).

5.2.2 The policy factor

Given the fact that the food sector plays a significant role in the activities of many NGOs, it is in the interest of NGOs to safeguard their position as one of the principal actors with regard to agricultural development and food security in the developing world. NGOs will undoubtedly endeavour to maintain and, if possible, strengthen their position as lobbyists and political activists, so that those areas which are deemed a priority for NGO programmes are not neglected. The food sector will also play a very significant role in the future, given its importance in all actions that try to fight absolute poverty and to put in place environmentally sustainable agricultural systems that are capable of eradicating hunger and of feeding the hungry.

6 Food aid in times of transition

The likelihood for such intentions to be realized is rather low. NGO reports in the "Reality of Aid, 1997" (Randal and German 1997: 243-257) and aid statistics for 1995/96 show a decline in aid given by DAC countries. The total amount of aid went down from US$58,800 million in 1995 to US$55,100 million in 1996. Since the four most important donors—Japan, USA, Germany and France—(accounting for 60 percent of total DAC aid) are in the process of cutting government expenditure for now and the near future, realistically there is little chance of a quick recovery in the amount dedicated to overseas aid.

6.1 Decreasing involvement of NGOs

Another prevailing trend is also affecting the food-sector programmes of the NGOs. The support for agriculture in developing countries declined in 1996 to 7.5 percent of the total DAC aid, in comparison with 1980, when 20 percent was devoted to the same purpose. Emergency and food aid sank to 8 percent. Food aid, taken as a separate aid instrument, has experienced such drastic reductions that even some of its most ardent critics have begun to warn against a continuation of this "implosion" of food aid.

Already in 1995, DEEP, a periodic review of FAO and NGO programmes, stated that: "Growing needs and decreasing availability call for a careful examination of the role of food aid" (DEEP 1995: 20-23). Since 1995, the trend towards decreasing the amount of money devoted to food aid has not only continued, but also the share of the NGOs has shrunk significantly. The amount allocated to NGOs out of the food security and food aid budget line of the EU Commission has been almost decimated. Whereas in normal years the level of allocations stood at approximately 150 million ECU, reaching 214 million ECU in 1994, the EU Commission reduced the amount for 1996 to 108 million ECU and for 1997 to a meagre 87 million ECU. The reasons given for such drastic decisions were the occurrence of two good harvests in most parts of developing countries and the "real absorption capacities of the NGOs".[1]

1 Quoted from an internal programming document of the EU Commission, 1997.

7 Future perspectives

The scenario of close and interwoven relations between NGOs, major donors and international organisations has undoubtedly been disturbed by the drastic decrease in food aid during recent years and, moreover, by the way in which NGOs now have a significantly reduced share of a much "smaller cake". If this trend continues to influence the political decision-making process, as well as the actual funding procedures, the role of NGOs in the food sector will be greatly reduced at the beginning of the next millennium.

References

Bread for the World (1994): Hunger 1995, Causes of Hunger—5th Annual Report on the State of World Hunger.

DEEP (1995): Development Education and Exchange Papers, How the international community can promote food security.

European Commission (1996): Official Journal of the European Communities No. L 166/5, July 5th (English).

FAO/WHO (1992): Major Issues for Nutrition Strategies, Rome.

German Agro Action (1996): Annual Report.

OECD (1988): Voluntary Aid for Development: The Role of Non-Governmental Organisations, Paris.

Randal, J. and T. German (eds.) (1997): Reality of Aid, EuroStep and ICVA.

Sen, Amartya (1981): Poverty and Famines, Oxford.

The NGLS Handbook (1997).

The World Bank (1995): Annual Report, Washington.

32

Towards a Global Policy Agenda: The World Food Summit in the Context of International Development Summitry in the 1990s

Uwe Kracht

1 Introduction

The 1990s have witnessed an extraordinary intensification of global summitry on development issues. The World Food Summit, held in Rome in November 1996, concluded a series of about a dozen summits and world conferences in just six years. The conference cycle started with the World Summit for Children, convened under United Nations auspices in New York in 1990, followed by the UN Conference on Environment and Development (UNCED), better known as the "Earth Summit", in Rio de Janeiro in 1992, and the International Conference on Nutrition (ICN) organized by FAO and WHO in Rome in the same year. Subsequent "megaconferences" included the World Conference on Human Rights (Vienna, 1993), the International Conference on Population and Development (Cairo, 1994), the Ministerial Conference on the Final Act of the GATT Uruguay Round (Marrakech, 1994), the World Summit for Social Development (Copenhagen, 1995), the Fourth World Conference on Women (Beijing, 1995), and the Second UN Conference on Human Settlements (HABITAT II, Istanbul 1996). One could add to this list the UN Global Conference on the Sustainable Development of Small Island Developing States (Barbados, 1994), the World Conference on Natural Disaster Reduction (Yokohama, 1994), the International Conference on Fisheries and Food Security (Kyoto, 1995), the Fourth Technical Conference on Plant Genetic Resources (Leipzig, 1996), as well as the Ninth United Nations Conference on Trade and Development (UNCTAD IX, Midrand/South Africa, 1996).

Many of these conferences have important historic predecessors. In the case of the "Earth Summit", this was the 1972 Stockholm Conference on the Human Environment, the first ever global conference on the environment. The World Food Summit's precursor was the landmark World Food Conference in Rome in 1974. There were three previous world conferences on women (Mexico City, 1975; Copenhagen, 1980; Nairobi, 1985) and two on population (Bucharest, 1974; Mexico City, 1984). The first human rights conference was held in Teheran in 1968, and HABITAT I took place in Vancouver in 1976.

What distinguishes the conferences of the 1990s from their predecessors is above all the much stronger emphasis on placing their specific agendas into a comprehensive economic and social development context, recognizing that effective action on "sectoral" problems requires an integrated, holistic development framework. Taken together, these conferences have shaped a coherent framework for the development agenda leading into the third millennium. A further distinguishing feature is a significant increase in the role and participation of civil society in the conferences and the action they propose, as a recognition of the trend of a diminishing role of governments in the era of globalization.

The conferences have not been universally well received. Looking back at a quarter of a century of world conferences on development, some people observe that such conferences come and go, but the problems they are meant to resolve remain. At the same time, they point to the costs of these international gatherings and suggest that the resources invested in them could more effectively be spent on addressing in practice the development issues that conference participants only talk about. According to the United Nations, the costs of most of the world conferences in the 1990s were in the range of US$ 1.8 to 3.4 million per conference, with the exception of the "Earth Summit" at a cost of US$ 10 million (United Nations 1997: 7). These costs may appear high in absolute terms, but they are certainly minute in relation to actual or required development financing, let alone non-development spending such as for military purposes. Yet, a quarter of a century of political consensus building is indeed a long time when compared to the progress achieved. While successive conferences undoubtedly have progressively built understanding and political consensus, achievements have been far below what is required and possible. Whether the summitry expenses in this decade were well spent will depend on whether the emerging global agenda for action is effectively implemented. And this means, above all, whether political consensus is translated into political determination to do what summit participants pledged their countries would do.

2 Common themes of the global development conferences of the 1990s

While each of the conferences had its specific focus, virtually all of them touched on an extensive list of cross-cutting themes, which assured a considerable degree of coherence in the decisions in the various fora. The following is an indicative set of such themes by broad categories:[1]

Group I: Enabling environment

(i) A stable macroeconomic policy framework conducive to development
(ii) External debt, finance for development, development co-operation
(iii) International trade and commodities
(iv) Science and technology

1 This listing is an adaptation from a presentation by the UN Secretary General to the Economic and Social Council in 1995 (United Nations 1995c: para. 58).

(v) Governance, democracy, human rights, accountability and transparency, participation, partnership with major groups and non-governmental organizations
(vi) Promoting social integration
(vii) Gender equality, equity and empowerment of women

Group II: Basic social services for all

Primary health care, nutrition, safe water and sanitation, education, population, shelter

Group III: Access to sustainable livelihoods

(i) Access to productive resources, employment and adequate incomes
(ii) Eradication of poverty, hunger and malnutrition
(iii) Sustainable food production and food security

Group IV: Environment and natural resources

The development paradigm which has clearly emerged from the consensus achieved at this decade's conferences is—in the words of the UN Secretary General—"that development is, above all, about human beings, that it should be sustainable to ensure intergenerational equity and that growth must be sustained over time to generate the resources necessary for broader development goals to be realized" (United Nations 1995b: para 55). These are fine words and, indeed, the express intentions of the summitry participants. However, policies and actions at national and global levels have yet largely to reflect acceptance of this paradigm. This is the challenge in the years and decades ahead.

Within this framework, combating poverty is one of the most pervasive goals in the entire conference cycle. It is a principal objective of the Social Summit, and figures prominently in Agenda 21, i.e. the "Earth Summit's" action plan, the conferences on population and women, HABITAT II and the World Food Summit. At the same time, it is the most elusive one in terms of action specificity and implementation.

Food and food security are prominent common concerns in most conferences. Agenda 21 emphasized the need to ensure food security at all levels, within the framework of sustainable development. The Action Plan of the International Conference on Nutrition dedicated an extensive chapter to the improvement of household food security. The Vienna Human Rights Conference emphasized the right to food of all people. The Cairo Population Conference underlined the linkage between population growth and food production and the need to respond globally to the ever-growing food needs of the world's population. The Social Summit in Copenhagen made the elimination of hunger and malnutrition and the provision of food security a central element of poverty eradication efforts. In Beijing, the Conference on Women reminded the world community that women provide over

55 percent of the world's food, in Africa over 80 percent. And HABITAT II drew attention to the role of cities in ensuring food distribution and drinking water supply. In a way, these conferences laid down a range of agenda items to be addressed with detailed action proposals and commitments by the World Food Summit.

3 The World Food Summit

The World Food Summit was to give *political* impetus to efforts concerning "all aspects of food security" and "the principal causes of hunger and malnutrition", *without creating "new financial mechanisms or institutions"* (emphasis added; FAO 1995, United Nations 1995b). The latter was a clear reference to the outcome of the 1974 World Food Conference, which created the International Fund for Agricultural Development (IFAD) as a financing institution, the World Food Council (WFC) as a political organ, and a number of other institutional arrangements. Generating political impetus without firm backing of financial commitment presents a general dilemma for the follow-up of all conferences. Although most of the financial resources for implementing the conference decisions will have to come from national sources, an indication of increased financial commitments from the traditional "donor" community in the form of increased flows of official development assistance (ODA) would have greatly stimulated that political impetus—certainly in the case of the World Food Summit, considering that ODA flows to food and agriculture have been declining over the years.

The Summit's political message is crystallized in the "Rome Declaration on World Food Security" (World Food Summit 1996). Detailed actions are put forward in the Summit's Plan of Action. Both were painstakingly negotiated in the framework of FAO's Committee on World Food Security (CFS) during a nine-month period prior to the Summit. For this purpose, the CFS had established an Inter-sessional Working Group (ISWG). When the CFS met in September 1996 for the finalization of the texts for the Summit (these were not to be reopened for negotiation at the Summit), it still had to address over 1000 items of bracketed, i.e. non-agreed, text. While there were no negotiations at the Summit itself, some countries registered reservations or interpretative declarations on contentious points, including population and human rights issues.

3.1 The Rome Declaration on World Food Security

The Declaration reaffirms "the right of everyone to have access to safe and nutritious food." But it also makes it clear that this right will not be realized for millions of people in the foreseeable future: Summit participants pledged their political will and their "common and national commitment to ... reducing the number of undernourished people to half their present level no later than 2015." This implies a tacit acceptance that in about 20 years from now over 400 million people will still be undernourished.

The Summit thus took a more sober and realistic stand than the 1974 World Food Conference, which set as its goal the eradication of hunger and malnutrition within a decade (United Nations 1974). It was also more cautious than the World Summit for Children (WSC), which set the goal of reducing severe and moderate malnutrition of children under five years of age by one-half within 10 years, i.e. by the year 2000 (United Nations 1990). The International Conference on Nutrition (ICN) had simply set as its goal to reduce substantially undernutrition, especially among children, women and the aged before the end of the decade (FAO/WHO 1992). Both the WSC and ICN set a number of additional quantified and time-framed goals for food security and nutrition.

The reduction by one-half of undernourished people is the only quantified goal pronounced by the World Food Summit. The remainder are general declarations of principles and intent. The Declaration underlines the importance of peace, democracy and a stable and enabling political, economic and social environment. It stresses the role of women and the importance of equality between men and women. It reiterates the demand that food should not be used as an instrument for political and economic pressure and identifies trade as a key element in achieving food security. The Declaration re-emphasizes that "the multifaceted character of food security necessitates concerted national action, and effective international efforts to supplement and reinforce national action," in support of which Summit participants made seven commitments:

- to ensure an enabling political, social and economic environment conducive to poverty eradication and sustainable food security for all;
- to implement policies aimed at eradicating poverty and improving physical and economic access by all, at all times, to adequate food and its effective utilization;
- to pursue participatory and sustainable food, agriculture, fisheries, forestry and rural development policies and practices in high and low potential areas, considering the multifunctional character of agriculture;
- to strive to ensure that food, agricultural trade and overall trade policies are conducive to fostering food security for all through a fair and market-oriented world trade system;
- to endeavour to prevent and be prepared for natural disasters and man-made emergencies and to meet transitory and emergency food requirements;
- to promote optimal allocation and use of public and private investments to foster human resources, sustainable food, agriculture, fisheries and forestry systems and rural development; and
- to implement, monitor and follow up the Plan of Action.

These seven commitments form the basis for the Plan of Action.

3.2 Plan of Action

Structured around the aforementioned seven commitments, the Plan of Action elaborates the political declaration by putting forward 27 objectives and 182 proposed actions. Taken together, these constitute a comprehensive agenda for action, covering about every area of direct or indirect relevance for global, regional, national and household food security. There are ample cross-references to relevant commitments and recommendations from other global conferences, thus ensuring that food security is placed into the broader socio-economic development framework as it has emerged from this decade's summitry. At the same time, the carefully negotiated and balanced text does not set priorities within the vast field of action nor does it launch any major new initiative which would galvanize international co-operation and finance around a specific area of activity—as did, for example, the 1974 World Food Conference and the 1992 "Earth Summit". Also, the lack of quantified and time-framed goals and targets, except for the single 2015 goal, and the absence of financial commitments by the international community for the implementation of the Summit outcome do not help to give the Declaration and the Plan of Action a strong sense of urgency.

Annex I summarizes the 27 objectives and highlights some of the broad lines of action proposed under each.

3.2.1 Enabling political, social and economic environment

As has become common in world development conferences, the World Food Summit's Action Plan lays out, at the outset, the broad conditions necessary for achieving food security and other development objectives.[2] The Plan's four objectives under this commitment address questions of conflict prevention and peaceful resolution, respect for human rights, "good governance" guided by transparency, accountability and equal participation of all people. They extol the virtues of stable economic conditions and sustainable development strategies, emphasize the importance of gender equality and the empowerment of women, and call for national solidarity especially in respect of vulnerable and disadvantaged people.

Broad lines of action to achieve these objectives include the strengthening of international mechanisms for conflict prevention and resolution; national measures to foster democratic processes, strengthen judicial systems for the protection of the rights of all people and advance land reform and the protection of property, water and user rights with a view to enhancing access to resources by the poor and women in particular. There are cross-references to relevant recommendations from the Cairo Population Conference, the Beijing Women's Conference and the Children's Summit.

2 The emphasis on aspects of an "enabling environment" was particularly pronounced at the Social Summit in Copenhagen, which devoted 10 pages of its 60-page Action Programme to this subject (United Nations 1995a).

3.2.2 Poverty eradication and access to adequate food

The four objectives in this area call for making poverty eradication and sustainable food security for all a priority, enabling food insecure households to meet their food and nutritional requirements, ensuring food safety, and promoting basic education and primary health care. The actions include many of those proposed at the Social Summit, specific aspects of the action plans adopted at the Cairo Conference and the ICN, as well as a series of measures in the context of food and nutrition safety nets and the provision of clean water and sanitation.

An innovative initiative among the proposed actions concerns the development of national food insecurity and vulnerability information and mapping systems, which have since become known under the acronym of FIVIMS.[3] These systems are to identify areas and populations affected by, or at risk of, hunger and malnutrition as well as elements contributing to food insecurity. Such information should facilitate the allocation of resources in support of food-insecure households, thus contributing to one of the objectives of the second commitment. Successful implementation of this initiative would also help reduce the "data gap", especially in Sub-Saharan Africa, discussed elsewhere in this book.[4]

3.2.3 Sustainable food and agriculture, fisheries, forestry and rural development

This third commitment can be considered the Summit's central commitment, with the most extensive list of activities of its action plan. Its five objectives and proposed actions build on Chapter 14 of the "Earth Summit's" Agenda 21, on "Promoting sustainable agriculture and rural development" (United Nations 1993) and subsequent conferences, which elaborated specific areas, such as the Kyoto Conference on fisheries and the Leipzig Conference on plant genetic resources. The objectives are aimed at sustainable, intensified and diversified food production through participatory means; at combating environmental threats to food security, including drought, desertification, pests, erosion of biological diversity, and degradation of land and aquatic resources; technology transfer; strengthened links between the public and private sectors in research and scientific co-operation; and at the advancement of integrated rural development.

The proposed lines of action run from the encouragement of appropriate technologies, the promotion of biodiversity, pest and disease prevention and control, natural resource rehabilitation and conservation, strengthened national and international research systems, national and international water management, and international climate forecast information to the social and economic revitalization of the rural sector, the organization of the rural population, rural market develop-

3 For an overview of objectives, management and utilization of such systems see FAO 1998a.

4 See the contribution by Theo Rauch in Chapter 5.

ment as well as measures already proposed at the 1979 World Conference on Agrarian Reform and Rural Development (see Annex I). The actions cover crop and livestock production, fisheries and forestry.

3.2.3.1 High and low potential food production areas

The third commitment makes explicit reference to "high and low potential" food production areas—an issue referred to again in the sixth commitment. This reference is the result of considerable debate in the preparatory negotiations prior to the Summit. Given the need for substantial food production increases, especially in Sub-Saharan Africa, there has been a tendency to focus attention on areas where such increases are most likely to be achieved. In the ISWG, IFAD and a number of countries pointed to the importance of food production in low potential areas, where a large part of the under- and malnourished people live, and called for more balanced strategies. The issue of a balanced approach to high and low potential areas goes, of course, beyond mere food production considerations. It raises the fundamental question of how food-security focused development can be realized in low potential areas.

3.2.3.2 The multifunctional character of agriculture

In this context, the pre-Summit negotiations also raised the issue of the "multifunctional character of agriculture," which has been integrated into the text of the third commitment. The group of countries emphasizing this concept, led by Switzerland and Japan and supported by African countries at FAO's 19th Regional Conference for Africa (FAO 1996), pointed to the manifold dimensions of agriculture in relation to food security such as food production, employment and income generation, as well as environmental protection, sustainable rural development and—in this context—conservation of traditional life styles, putting the human aspects of agriculture to the fore. The principle of the multifunctional aspects of agriculture had already been accepted at the "Earth Summit": Chapter 14 on "Sustainable agriculture and rural development" of Agenda 21 begins with the programme area of "Agricultural policy review ... in the light of the multifunctional aspect of agriculture, particularly with regard to food security and sustainable development" (United Nations 1993: 178-182). Also the GATT Uruguay Round basically recognized this principle.

This view met, of course, with strong opposition from the advocates of fully liberalized market economies such as the United States of America and Australia. These countries suspected in the multiple function concept a "backdoor" for reintroducing subsidies and trade distortions just banned in the Uruguay Round Agreement. In this spirit, Australia put on record that any suggestions that the concept of comparative advantage should not be applied to the agricultural sector need to be rejected. Both country groups admittedly had valuable arguments. In the end, concern for the human and other not purely economic aspects found their recognition through the inclusion of the multiple function concept in the third commitment.

3.2.4 Achieving food security for all through a fair and market-oriented world trade system

The three objectives under the fourth commitment re-emphasize the agreements reached in the Uruguay Round and in regional trade negotiations with regard to food, agricultural and overall trade and call for a continuation of the trade reform process. At the same time, they also emphasize the need for ensuring that essential food imports of all countries are met, considering world price and supply fluctuations and taking into account food consumption levels of vulnerable groups in developing countries.

With regard to the latter objective of developing country food imports with consideration for vulnerable group consumption, the proposed actions include an examination of WTO-compatible options to safeguard the ability of importing countries, especially low-income food-deficit countries (LIFDCs), to purchase adequate supplies of basic food stuffs from external sources on reasonable terms and conditions; and to implement WTO provisions concerning the possible negative effects of the reform programme on least developed and net-food-importing developing countries.

3.2.5 Disaster prevention and preparedness

The fifth commitment on disaster prevention and preparedness takes on particular significance in the light of recent dramatic increases in the number of victims of civil conflict, while the number of people affected by natural disasters fluctuates annually. The four objectives focus on enhanced efforts to prevent and resolve man-made emergencies and thus link up with the objectives of the first commitment on an enabling environment; on the establishment of prevention and preparedness strategies in LIFDCs; on improved emergency response mechanisms at international, regional, national and local levels; and on strengthened linkages between relief, rehabilitation and development programmes.

Among the broad lines of action is a reminder to establish the preparedness strategies and mechanisms already agreed upon at the ICN in 1992. There is also reference to the proposal of creating national volunteer corps or "White Helmets" in support of such strategies, as discussed in the UN General Assembly in 1994 and 1995. Other action proposals include the promotion of community-based and regional surveillance systems, national and regional vulnerability information and mapping systems (as already proposed under the second commitment) as well as climate forecast information, and measures for strengthening co-ordination and efficiency of international emergency assistance. Particularly noteworthy is the recommendation to pursue at local and national levels cost-effective strategic emergency food security reserve policies; an FAO-secretariat proposal for such policies at international level, as they were prominently discussed in the 1980s, was not accepted.

3.2.6 Optimal allocation and use of public and private resources

In the absence of a commitment to increased resource flows for food security and agriculture, the Summit shifted its emphasis towards more effective resource allocation and utilization. This is to be achieved through the creation of appropriate policy frameworks and conditions. However, the need for mobilizing—and optimally using—resources from all sources, including debt relief, in order to raise investments to required levels is recognized.

The proposed actions comprise well known calls for giving priority in resource allocations to human resource development, meeting the ODA target of 0.7% of GNP, reducing military expenditure and finding solutions to the external debt problems of developing countries, including the possibility of directing funds released by debt swaps towards the achievement of food security objectives. It is also proposed that public-private partnerships be encouraged to promote socially and environmentally responsible investment from domestic and foreign resources, and that the participation of local communities in investment be increased.

3.2.7 Implementation, monitoring and follow-up of the Plan of Action

Four of the five objectives under this commitment deal with issues common to the follow-up of any internationally agreed action plan: national implementation; subregional, regional and international co-operation; monitoring; and the sharing of responsibilities among individuals, households, governments and the international community. The remaining objective is peculiar in that it introduces a new set of (implementation-related) actions which could not be accommodated under the preceding commitments and action proposals, i.e. the human right to adequate food.

With regard to national implementation, countries are to review and revise their national development plans in the light of the Summit Action Plan and to complement national action plans already developed as follow-up to the ICN with food-security specific action as proposed by the Summit. They are to set up mechanisms for the establishment of priorities and the development, implementation and monitoring of action components and supporting management information systems, both for World Food Summit follow-up and that of other world conferences. Moreover, governments are to make every effort to safeguard food security goals and programmes in difficult times of economic transition, budget austerity and structural adjustment.

At the regional and international level, the action emphasis is on orienting development co-operation towards sustainable development, including agriculture for food security. International monitoring of the implementation of the Action Plan is to be realized, above all, through reporting mechanisms to be established by the CFS, which in turn will report to the UN Economic and Social Council (ECOSOC) overseeing the monitoring of all world conferences.

Concerning the shared responsibilities in achieving food security, the Summit emphasizes that individuals and households must be enabled to participate actively, on an individual and collective basis, that governments must provide the enabling environment, and that in an era of growing interdependence international co-operation and solidarity are indispensable.

3.2.7.1 The right to adequate food

The remaining of the five objectives under the seventh and last commitment deals with the right to adequate food as a human right and is the result of substantial debate during the pre-Summit negotiation process. The Summit's political declaration reaffirmed, as noted above, the "right of everyone to have access to safe and nutritious food," and then added "consistent with the right to adequate food and the fundamental right of everyone to be free from hunger." The added formulation is a reference to provisions in the Universal Declaration on Human Rights adopted by the United Nations in 1948 and the 1966 International Covenant on Economic, Social and Cultural Rights (ICESCR) to which some 180 States are Parties.[5] Among the few countries not Party to the ICESCR is the USA, which has persistently refused to accept the right to food as a human right, partly for fear that this may mean the State would be obliged to feed all inhabitants under its jurisdiction.

Still, the right to adequate food and to freedom from hunger continues to be cited as a fundamental human right. The 1974 World Food Conference, in its Universal Declaration on the Eradication of Hunger and Malnutrition, proclaimed that "every man, woman and child has the inalienable right to be free from hunger and malnutrition in order to develop their physical and mental faculties" (United Nations 1974)—a formulation which the USA appeared no longer willing to support in 1998. In the preparations for the World Food Summit, the Latin American countries took the lead in an initiative aimed at translating right-to-food rhetoric into operational meaning. The result is the fourth objective under the commitment under consideration, which calls for the clarification of the content of the right to adequate food and the fundamental right to be free from hunger, with a view to their operationalization.

In the corresponding action part, the UN Commissioner for Human Rights is requested to better define the right to adequate food and to propose ways to realize this right, including the possibility of formulating voluntary guidelines (such as a Code of Conduct) for its realization. The significance of this recommendation must be seen in the context of recent efforts in the UN system directed at applying human rights to development co-operation. This includes the emphasis in the UN Secretary General's reform programme that all UN funds, programmes and specialised agencies should be guided by the international human rights frame-

5 See also Asbjørn Eide's contribution in this book (Chapter 16).

work, and a recent directive by UNICEF that all its field activities be guided by the Convention of the Right of the Child (United Nations 1998b).[6]

Introducing a human rights dimension to food security and development has potentially profound implications for national and international development efforts. By introducing an ethical imperative—as strongly advocated at the 1995 Social Summit—accompanied by a juridical dimension, development co-operation at all levels within and between states becomes a question of responsibilities, duties and accountability as opposed to voluntary, non-accountable "basic needs" strategies (Kracht 1997). This would be consistent with the concept of "good governance" contained in the first commitment.

4 Progress in World Food Summit follow-up and monitoring

A first review of Summit follow-up by governments was undertaken by FAO's CFS, charged with monitoring the implementation of the Plan of Action, in June 1998. Out of the 186 countries which had participated in the Summit, 68 or just over one-third had presented national progress reports. In the absence of quantified and timeframed goals in the Action Plan and specific reporting targets and formats, these reports provided qualitative information on a vast array of activities difficult to summarize and to derive general conclusions from. However, one major conclusion points to "the predominance of continuing actions already in place at the time of Summit," although new actions undertaken or envisaged as a consequence of the Summit were also reported by a number of countries (FAO 1998b).

To advance policy review and development in support of Summit objectives, FAO took the initiative of drafting short strategy papers for national agricultural development towards 2010 for a large number of countries. These were reviewed by the governments concerned and further examined by panels of country-groups meeting in Rome. While the exercise helped sharpen priorities specific to individual countries and country groups, it did not replace the need for similar initiatives by the countries themselves. In fact, some countries observed in the CFS that such strategy briefs should be "country-driven ... under the ownership of the respective Governments" (FAO 1997b: para. 36).

With regard to supporting food insecurity and vulnerability information systems proposed under the second commitment (FIVIMS), follow-up until mid-1998 included (i) the establishment of an inter-agency mechanism, at the technical level, to oversee the development of FIVIMS internationally and ensure the necessary collaboration and co-ordination of all FIVIMS-related efforts; (ii) the designation of country focal points; (iii) the preparation of guidelines for the establishment of FIVIMS at the national level; and (iv) the preparation of case studies on the experience of 2-3 selected countries in food insecurity and vulnerability information and mapping (FAO 1998c). In addition to technical assistance to countries for

6 Idem.

the development and management of national FIVIMSs, follow-up envisaged for the near future includes implementation of a system of linked, commonly accessible international databases comprising global FIVIMS; and improvements in estimates of the number of undernourished people.

To ensure broad-based inter-agency collaboration in the Summit follow-up at agency and country levels, the UN Administrative Committee on Co-ordination (ACC), comprising the Heads of the specialized agencies under the chairmanship of the UN Secretary General, launched a Network on Rural Development and Food Security. Within its framework, UN Resident Co-ordinators are to organize thematic groups on rural development and food security at the country level, and "to ensure that all efforts are deployed to facilitate the coherent support of the UN system to national development efforts in the food and agricultural sector, and to implementing the WFS Plan of Action" (FAO 1997a: para. 4).

On the right to adequate food, a wide range of activities has been initiated or envisaged for the near future, including an expert panel on the content of this right held under the auspices of the High Commissioner for Human Rights in December 1997; discussions on this topic in the Committee on Economic, Social and Cultural Rights, the treaty body of the International Covenant (ICESCR),[7] which will also draft an interpretative commentary on the subject; the updating of a Special Rapporteur's report on the right to food for consideration by the human rights machinery; a detailed examination by the UN agencies in the ACC Sub-Committee on Nutrition in March 1998; and the drafting of a proposed voluntary Code of Conduct by a group of NGOs (FIAN/WANAHR/Jacques Maritain 1997), endorsed by over 800 NGOs.

4.1 Monitoring: World Food Summit and other world conferences of the 1990s

Beyond the current reporting arrangements, consisting of "three reporting streams (national governments, United Nations agency follow-up and inter-agency co-ordination, and other relevant institutions)" to the CFS (FAO 1998b: para. 1) and periodic reporting by FAO to the UN, there is still a great deal to be done to develop detailed monitoring methodology and procedures in order to achieve a meaningful monitoring system that would eventually function as a management information system in the sense of a true management tool. This is not just a challenge for the WFS follow-up, but concerns all of the world conferences. Most progress has probably been made in relation to the World Summit for Children and in certain areas of the "Earth Summit".

Most conferences of the 1990s developed their own monitoring system, supported by some inter-agency mechanism largely arranged through the ACC. But if the conferences of this decade are understood as constituting a common global development agenda, then much more is to be done to achieve a critical mass of a

7 Idem.

coherent global monitoring mechanism. The UN Secretary General has struggled hard with this issue, as his annual reports to ECOSOC and the General Assembly show. That this is a Herculean task becomes particularly evident from his 1998 report (United Nations 1998a) - and this report touches only the tip of the iceberg.

5 Conclusions

The World Food Summit concluded an unprecedentedly intense series of global development summitry in the 1990s. It closed the last missing gap in the development agenda leading into the third millennium. It took what might be considered a sober and realistic approach to the problems of hunger, food insecurity and malnutrition: while it was ambitious in the extent of ground covered, it was modest or vague in expectations of achievements. The Summit accepted that there would still be at least 400 million hungry people in some 20 years from now. It did not propose any major new initiative, which would rally the energies of the international community around a special effort to reduce the number of the hungry still further. Such an initiative would have meant greatly increased resources to be channelled to food and agriculture, rural development and to poverty eradication. Instead, the Summit focused on more effective allocation of available resources. However important this may be, it is simply not enough.

Yet, the Summit's outcome, seen in the context of the realities of the present economic "revolution" known as globalization, is maybe the best that could have been achieved. The global agenda emerging from the world conferences of the first six years of the 1990s taken together suggests that development is, above all, about human beings. However, policies and actions have yet to reflect this paradigm in practice. But the mere existence of this agenda, reconfirmed in about a dozen of world conferences, is a forceful reminder of the challenges ahead to bridge political intent and economic reality.

The seven commitments of the Summit—ranging from (i) an overall enabling policy environment, to (ii) special measures to ensure access to food, (iii) sustainable food and agricultural development, (iv) supporting world trade policies, (v) natural and man-made disaster prevention and resolution, (vi) efficient resource allocation and use, and (vii) an efficient, co-ordinated approach to implementation—constitute a plausible food security framework agenda for the early 21st century. The objectives and proposed actions put "meat on the bones" of that framework. There is clearly a need to set sharper priorities: at the international level, through cross-references to relevant priorities of other world conferences and possible linkages with already ongoing efforts; and at the national level, through a critical review of constraints and opportunities, taking into consideration existing action plans developed in the context of other relevant world conference commitments. In addition to more effective resource allocation and utilization, there is a need for more overall resources for combating hunger, food insecurity and malnutrition. Given the Summit's emphasis on "shared responsibilities", the international community should reconsider its position on external resource support.

The Summit's innovative initiative on the human right to adequate food, moving from conventional rhetorical declarations towards its operationalization, has potentially profound implications for future development activity, nationally and internationally. The human rights approach implies an ethical imperative, strongly advocated at the Social Summit, which together with a juridical dimension introduces a pattern of responsibilities, duties and accountability as opposed to voluntary, non-accountable "basic needs" approaches. Application of a right-to-food approach is no panacea for overcoming current obstacles to hunger- and poverty eradication, but it holds promise to make efforts in that direction more effective.

Annex 1: Summary of commitments, objectives and broad lines of action of the World Food Summit's Plan of Action

COMMITMENT	OBJECTIVE	BROAD LINES OF ACTION
1. Enabling political, social and economic environment	1.1 Peaceful conflict resolution and prevention, create respect for human rights, democracy, transparent and accountable governance, equal participation of all people	- international co-operation for peace - strengthen int'l mechanisms for conflict prevention/solution - develop democratic policy making, legislative, implementation processes, strengthen legal/judicial systems to protect the rights of all people
	1.2 Ensure stable economic conditions and implement strategies for equitable and sustainable development, including population and environment concerns	- promote nat'l and int'l policies for sustainable, equitable development - establish legal mechanisms for land reform, protect property, water, user rights - integrate population concerns into development strategies, consistent with Cairo Population Conference
	1.3 Ensure gender equality, empowerment of women	- implement Beijing Women Conference commitments
	1.4 Encourage nat'l solidarity and provide equal opportunities for all	- invest in human resource development, combat discrimination - special attention to needs of the child, consistent with Children's Summit
2. Poverty eradication, access to adequate food	2.1 Pursue poverty eradication and sustainable food security for all as a priority through policies aimed at employment, access to productive resources, maximization of incomes of the poor	- review and adopt corresponding policies, consistent with Copenhagen Social Summit commitments - promote access to land, genetic and other productive resources
	2.2 Enable food insecure households to meet their food/nutritional requirements	- develop nat'l food insecurity and vulnerability information/mapping - public works, social welfare/nutrition safety nets
	2.3 Ensure that food supplies are safe, physically and economically accessible and adequate to meet energy and nutrient requirements	- monitor food supply availability and adequacy - apply measures consistent with Agreement on the Application of Sanitary and Phytosanitary Measures - encourage use of traditional, underutilized food crops - promote improved food processing/storage/post-harvest technologies - support community based food/nutrition programmes - implement ICN micro-nutrient deficiency goals

	2.4 Promote access to basic education and primary health care	- promote access to primary health care, including reproductive health services consistent with Cairo Population Conference - promote access to clean water and sanitation - promote access to primary education, provide nutrition/health/sanitation education
3. Participatory and sustainable food, agriculture, fisheries, forestry, rural development policies/practices in high and low potential areas, and combat pests, droughts, desertification, considering the multi-functional character of agriculture	3.1 Pursue, through participatory means, sustainable, intensified and diversified food production	- implement policies and programmes to optimize production, especially of the main staple foods - encourage appropriate input technologies, farming techniques and other sustainable methods, such as organic farming, to assist farming operations to become profitable, with the goal of reducing environmental degradation - promote biological diversity in terrestrial marine ecosystems, notably through supporting the UN Convention on Biological Diversity, 1992 - promote more efficient and sustainable livestock production systems and acquaculture - ensure prevention and progressive control of plant and animal pests and diseases
	3.2 Combat environmental threats to food security, esp. drought and desertification, pests, erosion of biological diversity, degradation of land and aquatic natural resources, restore natural resource base, incl. water and watersheds	- monitor and promote rehabilitation and conservation of natural resources in food production areas, create incentives to reduce degradation - identify the potential and improve the use of national land and water resources, taking account of natural climatic variability and change - develop nat'l and int'l policies for water and watersheds and water management techniques - promote implementation of fisheries-related measures contained in various international agreements (e.g. UN Agreement on Straddling Fish Stocks and Highly Migratory Fish Stocks; FAO Code of Conduct for Responsible Fisheries; Agenda 21; Kyoto Declaration and Action Plan; UN Convention on the Law of the Sea) - promote the conservation and sustainable utilization of plant and animal genetic resources - reduce deforestation rate and increase forest coverage and implement related Agenda 21 provisions - promote implementation of Leipzig Action Plan; UN Convention to Combat Diversification, 1994; Convention on Biological Diversity, 1992; Montreal

		Protocol on ... Ozone Layer, 1987; UN Framework Convention on Climate Change, 1992 - prevent and control degradation and overexploitation of natural resources in poorly endowed, ecologically stressed areas
	3.3 Promote policies on transfer and use of technologies, skills development and training	- strengthen relevant education, training, skills development, ensuring equal gender opportunities
	3.4 Strengthen, in co-operation between the public and private sectors, research and scientific co-operation	- strengthen national and international research systems and co-operation - promote R&D leading to the use, at regional, nat'l and local levels, of appropriate technologies, incl. post-harvest and transformation techniques and locally adapted plant and animal breeding - promote research on int'l climate forecast information
	3.5 Formulate and implement integrated rural development strategies, in low and high potential areas, that promote rural employment, skill formation, infrastructure and services	- foster social and economic revitalization of the rural sector, with special attention to investment and employment and the promotion of political, economic and administrative decentralization - promote development of rural markets, reduce post-harvest losses and ensure safe storage, food processing and distribution facilities and transportation systems - further the social and economic organization of the rural population - promote the development of rural banking, credit and savings schemes, incl. Micro-credit for the poor - reinforce the follow-up to the 1979 World Conference on Agrarian Reform and Rural Development and implement relevant Agenda 21 provisions, esp. Chapter 14
4. Food, agricultural trade and overall trade policies conducive to food security for all through a fair and market-oriented world trade system	4.1 Meet the challenges of and utilize the opportunities arising from the international trade framework established in recent global and regional trade negotiations	- strengthen internal marketing systems to facilitate links within and between domestic, regional and world markets - implement Uruguay Round Agreement - ensure mutual supportiveness of trade and environment policies - WTO to address the relationship between WTO provisions and trade measures for environment purposes in conformity with Uruguay Round Agreement
	4.2 Meet essential food import needs in all countries, considering world price and supply fluctuations and taking especially into account	- examine WTO-compatible options and take any appropriate steps to safeguard the ability of importing countries, esp. LIFDCs, to purchase adequate supplies of basic food stuffs from external sources on reasonable terms and conditions

	food consumption levels of vulnerable groups in developing countries	- food exporting countries to act as reliable sources of supplies and give due consideration to the food security of importing countries, esp. LIFDCs - WTO members to fully implement the Decision on Measures Concerning the Possible Negative Effects of the Reform Programme on Least-Developed and Net Food-Importing Developing Countries
	4.3 Continue reform process in conformity with Uruguay Round Agreement	- promote the national and regional food security policies of developing countries, esp. in regard to their staple food supplies - support the continuation of the reform process and ensure that developing countries are well informed and equal partners in the process - int'l organizations to assist developing countries in preparing for multilateral trade negotiations
5. Prevention of and preparedness for natural disasters and man-made emergencies	5.1 Reduce demands for emergency food assistance through enhancing efforts to prevent and resolve man-made emergencies	- use int'l, regional and nat'l mechanisms to reduce situations which give rise to man-made emergencies - co-ordinate measures to combat terrorism and other activities contrary to human rights and human dignity
	5.2 Establish as quickly as possible prevention and preparedness strategies for LIFDCs and other countries and regions vulnerable to emergencies	- prepare/maintain for countries/regions concerned vulnerability information and mapping - establish, as quickly as possible, the preparedness strategies and mechanisms agreed upon at the ICN - support int'l efforts to develop and apply climate forecast information - promote community-based and regional surveillance systems
	5.3 Improve emergency response mechanisms at int'l, regional, nat'l and local levels	- strengthen co-ordination and efficiency of int'l emergency assistance - pursue at local and nat'l levels cost-effective strategic emergency food security reserve policies - consider the creation of nat'l volunteers corps, building upon "White Helmets", as defined by UN Resolutions 49/139B and 50/19
	5.4 Strengthen linkages between relief operations and development programmes	- keep under review the standards for the nutritional adequacy of food assistance to disaster-affected populations - ensure that emergency operations will foster the transition from relief, through recovery, to development - pursue well-planned post-emergency rehabilitation and development programmes

6. Optimal allocation and use of public and private investments to foster human resources, sustainable food, agri-cultural, fisheries and forestry systems and rural development, in high and low potential areas	6.1 Create the appropriate policy framework and necessary conditions	- give priority to human resource development and strengthen public institutions - encourage public-private partnerships in promoting socially and environmentally responsible investment from domestic and foreign resources, and increase participation of local communities in investment - strengthen co-operation at regional and int'l level to share the cost of investment in areas of common interest, such as appropriate technology generation and share experience and best practice
	6.2 Mobilize, and optimize the use of, technical and financial resources from all sources, incl. debt relief, in order to raise investments to the levels needed to contribute to food security	- strengthen efforts towards the fulfilment of the agreed ODA target of 0.7% of GNP - explore new ways of mobilizing public and private financial resources for food security, *inter alia* , through reduction of military expenditure and the arms trade - promote domestic, incl. rural, savings, access to credit, incl. micro-credit - intensify search for solutions to debt problems of developing countries, explore possibilities for directing the funds released by debt swaps towards the achievement of food security
7. Implementation, monitoring and follow-up of the Plan of Action	7.1 Adopt actions within each country's national framework to enhance food security and enable implementations of the commitments of the Action Plan	- review and revise nat'l plans in light of the Summit commitments - establish nat'l mechanisms to set priorities, develop, implement and monitor the components of action within designated time frames and provide necessary funding - encourage greater role for, and alliances with civil society - establish mechanisms to collect information on the nutritional status of all members of communities to monitor and improve their household food security - complement existing nat'l action plans, developed as follow-up to the ICN, with action on relevant aspects of food security, or develop such plans in accordance with the recommendations of the Summit and the ICN - plan and monitor in a co-ordinated manner the implementation of the relevant recommendations of all UN conferences aimed at eradicating poverty and improving food security and nutrition
	7.2 Improve sub-regional, regional and international co-operation and optimize the use of available resources to support nat'l efforts for the earliest possible achievement of sustainable world food security	- reinforce poverty eradication strategies and orient the development assistance policies of the int'l agencies of the UN system towards sustainable development, incl. agriculture for food security - improve information collection, analysis, dissemination and utilization - FAO and other int'l agencies to assist countries in reviewing and formulating

		nat'l action plans, facilitate a coherent UN system follow-up at the field level, through the resident co-ordinators - governments to make every effort that food security goals and programmes are safeguarded in difficult times of economic transition, budget austerity and structural adjustment
	7.3 Monitoring of the Action Plan	- establish, through CFS, timetable, procedures; reporting to CFS and monitoring through CFS, regular reports through CFS via FAO Council to ECOSOC - encourage effective participation of civil society in CFS monitoring
	7.4 Clarify the content of the right to adequate food and the fundamental right to be free from hunger, as stated in the International Covenant on Economic, Social and Cultural Rights and other relevant international and regional instruments, and to give particular attention to the implementation and progressive realization of this right as a means of achieving food security for all	- make every effort to implement the provisions of Article 11 of the Covenant - the Committee on Economic, Social and Cultural Rights to give particular attention to the Action Plan in the framework of its activities and monitoring of Article 11 - Relevant treaty bodies and UN specialized agencies to consider, within the framework of follow-up to UN conferences, including 1993 Vienna Human Rights Conference, how best to contribute to the realization to this right - UN Commissioner for Human Rights, in consultation with relevant bodies and agencies, to better define the rights related to food in Article 11 of the Covenant and to propose ways to realize these rights , including the possibility of formulating voluntary guidelines
	7.5 Share responsibilities in achieving food security for all so that the implementation of the Action Plan takes place at the lowest possible level at which its purpose could best be achieved	- individuals and households as key decision makers and actors regarding their food security must be enabled to participate actively - governments to provide enabling environment - regional and international co-operation

Source: World Food Summit (1996).

References

FAO (1998a): Guidelines for National Food Insecurity and Vulnerability Information and Mapping Systems (FIVIMS): Background and principles. 24th Session of the Committee on World Food Security, Rome.

FAO (1998b): Report on Progress in the Implementation of the World Food Summit Plan of Action, 24th Session of the Committee on World Food Security, 2-5 June 1998, Rome.

FAO (1998c): Report on the Development of Food Insecurity and Vulnerability Information and Mapping Systems (FIVIMS), 24th Session of the Committee on World Food Security, 2-5 June 1998, Rome.

FAO (1997a): The World Food Summit and its Follow-up; 29th Session of the FAO Conference, 7-18 November, 1997, Rome.

FAO (1997b): Report of the 23rd Session of the Committee on World Food Security, 14-18 April, 1997, Rome.

FAO (1996): Contribution of the 19th FAO Regional Conference for Africa to the Drafting of the World Food Summit Documents, Ouagadougou, Burkina Faso, 29 March 1996; WFS/ARC/REP, Rome.

FAO (1995): Conference Resolution 2/95 "World Food Summit", 28th FAO Conference, Rome.

FAO/WHO (1992): International Conference on Nutrition—World Declaration and Plan of Action for Nutrition, Rome.

FIAN/WANAHR/Jacques Maritain (1997): International Code of Conduct on the Human Right to Adequate Food. Food First Information and Action Network (FIAN International), World Alliance for Nutrition and Human Rights (WANAHR), Institut Jaques Maritain International, Heidelberg/Oslo/Rome.

Kracht, Uwe (1997): The Right to Adequate Food: Its Contents and Realization. An issues paper prepared for consideration by the UN Committee on Economic, Social and Cultural Rights at its "Day of General Discussion" on December 1, 1997.

United Nations (1998a): Integrated and Co-ordinated Implementation and Follow-up of Major UN Conferences and Summits. Report by the Secretary General, ECOSOC Substantive Session of 1998, 6-31 July 1998, New York.

United Nations (1998b): Administrative Committee on Co-ordination/Sub-Committee on Nutrition (ACC-SCN), Report on its 25th Session, Oslo, 27 March-4 April 1998, Geneva.

United Nations (1997): The World Conferences—Developing Priorities for the 21st Century, New York.

United Nations (1995a): Report of the World Summit for Social Development, A/CONF.166/9, New York.

United Nations (1995b): General Assembly Resolution 50/109 on the World Food Summit, New York.

United Nations (1995c): Co-ordinated Follow-up to Major International Conferences in the Economic, Social and Related Fields. Report of the Secretary General, E/1995/100, New York.

United Nations (1993): Report of the United Nations Conference on Environment and Development, Volume 1—Resolutions adopted by the Conference, New York.

United Nations (1990): World Summit for Children—Plan of Action for Implementing the World Declaration on the Survival, Protection and Development of Children in the 1990s, New York.

United Nations (1974): Report of the World Food Conference, E/CONF.65/20, New York.

World Food Summit (1996): Rome Declaration on World Food Security and World Food Summit Plan of Action, Rome.

PART V

CONCLUSIONS AND PERSPECTIVES

33

Food Security and Nutrition at the Threshold of the Third Millennium: Conclusions, Outlook and the Emerging Policy Agenda

Uwe Kracht and Manfred Schulz

1 Improving food security and nutrition: achievements and medium-term prospects

The record of addressing global hunger, malnutrition and food insecurity in their various manifestations over the past two decades is one of both qualified success and unjustifiable failure. On the positive side, one must acknowledge that the world is today feeding over 1.5 billion people more than some 20 years ago, and that on average food availability per person has increased by 15 percent. Food production growth has, in fact, outpaced population growth in all regions over the past two decades, except for Sub-Saharan Africa. The absolute number of undernourished people has decreased, albeit only slightly, and some regions and countries have achieved impressive success in increasing food production, improving its distribution and putting into place the necessary complementary measures to ensure access to food and meet the conditions for adequate nutrition for all people at all times.

Yet, there is no justification for over 800 million people to continue being chronically undernourished, for the increase in the numbers of people deprived of food due to wars, civil strife and the use of food as a weapon of political pressure, for the growing number of young children whose physical and mental development is impaired by protein-energy malnutrition, for the millions of malnutrition-related child deaths and for the effects of micronutrient deficiency disorders affecting some two billion people. While under- and malnutrition very much remain an Asian problem in terms of the numbers of people affected, their relative importance is rapidly shifting from Asia to Sub-Saharan Africa. At the same time, food insecurity is an emerging problem even in industrialized countries, both in the West and East, as unemployment increases, social safety nets erode and massive inter-country and intercontinental migration takes place, in the wake of profound economic and political changes, including the rapid globalization of the world economy.

The persistence of widespread hunger and malnutrition in a world of plentiful food supplies has over and again been condemned as morally unacceptable, by governments and civil society alike. There has been no scarcity of attempts of setting specific goals and targets for eliminating or reducing various kinds of food insecurity and malnutrition, from the 1974 World Food Conference's ambitious call for eliminating hunger and malnutrition within 10 years to the goals and targets in the United Nations International Development Decade for the 1990s, the 1990 World Summit for Children, the 1992 International Conference on Nutrition to the World Food Summit in 1996. Progress towards these targets has been lagging far behind of what was intended and what would appear perfectly feasible. As noted earlier (see Kracht, this volume, chapter 32), the World Food Summit—in the light of these experiences—was particularly cautious and committed itself only to the one, little ambitious target of reducing the number of undernourished people to half their present level no later than 2015. This implies acceptance by the Summit that in some 20 years hence over 400 million people would still not have enough to eat to lead a healthy, active life. Yet, achievement of even this modest target will require extraordinary efforts. As shown at the outset of this book (see Kracht, this volume, chapter 2, Table 1), a continuation of present trends, without policy change, would leave 680 million people undernourished in the year 2010.

In the medium term, food insecurity is not a problem of food production, but one of access to food. A recent study by the International Food Policy Research Institute, IFPRI (Pinstrup-Andersen et al. 1997), confirms earlier assessments in concluding that during the next quarter century the world will produce enough food to meet the demand of people who can afford to buy it. But the study reiterates that millions of people will not be able to afford the food they need, if "business as usual" continues.

2 Can the world feed its people in the long run?

Whether there will be a food production problem in the long run, given demographic developments and the finality of the Earth's resource base, has been an issue of ardent—and still inconclusive—debate at least since Malthus's times. The "confident experts", as von Blanckenburg calls those who trust in the capacity of our Planet (and the technological prowess of its inhabitants) to feed its growing population (see von Blanckenburg, this volume, chapter 4), point to the fact that all past Mathusian worries have not materialized, that technological progress has provided solutions to past food production problems and that there is no reason for believing that such progress would not continue. It is this latter point which is called into question by the "sceptics", offsprings of the neo-malthusianists, who doubt that more than double of the present world population could be fed in 2100. A prominent crusader among the neo-malthusianists has been Lester Brown, whose prolific writings on the subject have painted a bleak picture of food scarcity in the long run and have instilled a sense of urgency among at least some circles of the international community to devote greater attention to long-term prospects.[1]

There are no simple ways of predicting complex future situations and developments. Prominent among the many "great uncertainties" concerning the long-term food production potential are (i) the extent and effects of climatic change,

---

1 Among the more recent publications see Brown (1996).

notably the possible global warming resulting from the "green house effect"—the present intensified "El Niño" episodes may just be the precursor to more profound changes; (ii) the possible scarcity of fresh water, including the potential for political conflict and war over access to water resources and their repercussions for food security; (iii) mankind's ability to maintain soil fertility and avert soil erosion and desertification; and (iv) the contribution and risks of biotechnology and genetic engineering to future food production. There is also the issue of changing lifestyles resulting in shifts in food habits towards greater consumption of animal products and its impact on global food availability. A case in point are such changes in China, which are predicted to result in large demands on global cereal supplies. These are extremely pressing problems, and it is surprising and deplorable that the 1996 World Food Summit, while referring to them, did not manifest a greater sense of urgency for developing the understanding needed to deal with them. Without having a definitive answer to the question posed above, one may fairly confidently assert that current efforts are insufficient to guarantee a food-secure future for the generations to come.

3 An emerging agenda for action

Since the 1960s, there has undoubtedly been major progress in the scientific understanding of food security and nutrition problems, their causes and effective remedial action, and in related political consensus building. The 1974 World Food Conference was a landmark event with regard to the latter, and laid out the first major global agenda for food security and nutrition. In a way, the World Food Summit some 20 years later updated that agenda in accordance with developments in the intervening period. The contents of that agenda has become more complex—at the expense of clarity in its priorities, precision in its action proposals and forcefulness in conveying a sense of urgency for action, as much as the Summit's version is concerned.

As discussed in the preceding chapter, the seven Summit commitments can be considered a framework of a global agenda for food security. In a nutshell, these are:

1. an overall enabling policy environment,
2. special measures to ensure access to food,
3. sustainable food and agricultural development,
4. supporting world trade policies,
5. natural and man-made disaster prevention and resolution,
6. efficient resource allocation and use, and
7. an efficient, co-ordinated approach to implementation.

The Summit's 27 objectives and 182 proposed actions seek to give contents to that framework. However, these risk to remain a "global shopping list," unless they are translated into priorities and specific actions at regional and country levels. Yet, there are a number of overarching general concerns, many of which were raised in the preceding contributions.

3.1 The role of governments

The Summit's agenda is based on commitments which governments undertook to fulfil "in co-operation with civil society." Yet, the forces of market liberalization and economic globalization dictate a diminishing role of governments in managing their countries' economic and social affairs. How, then, are governments to assure the food security of future generations? IFPRI addresses this question in its "2020 Vision for Food, Agriculture, and the Environment" (IFPRI 1995).[2] At a time when it is fashionable to emphasize "less government," IFPRI calls for strengthening the capacity of developing-country governments to effectively perform their "appropriate functions"—a concept which is rapidly undergoing important changes. Such functions would include maintaining law and order, establishing and enforcing property rights, assuring private sector competition in markets, and a broad range of other measures falling into the category of ensuring an "enabling environment." Strengthening governments would include assisting them to improve accountability, transparency and continuity in policy making.

The quest for redefining the role of governments in liberalizing economies is a cross-cutting theme throughout the contributions presented in this book. For example, Sahn (this volume, chapter 6) points to the benefits to be obtained from government disengagement from liberalizing economies in the African context, but then presents a long list of "appropriate roles" for state engagement, ranging from ensuring macroeconomic stability to targeted food security interventions, investment in agricultural research and extension, regulatory functions related to address problems of decreasing soil fertility and related environment degradation, and the strengthening of analytical capacity and data and management information systems.

An underlying concern is the inadequacy of institutional capacity to support governments in efficiently exercising their roles. This applies generally to the implementation of the global agenda for food security, and not solely in Africa. Strengthening institutional capacity in support of "good governance" in the broadest sense of the term is part and parcel of that agenda.

3.2 Agricultural research and extension—and a new "green revolution" of a substantially different nature

Strong agricultural research and extension systems will be a *sine-qua-non* condition for the technological progress that must be achieved to meet the food needs of future generations, as the various contributions on this subject unanimously empha-

2 The 2020 Vision envisages, in the year 2020, "a world where every person has access to sufficient food to sustain a healthy and productive life, where malnutrition is absent, and where food originates from efficient, and low-cost food systems that are compatible with sustainable use of natural resources."

size (see Lampe, this volume, chapter 20; Lele and Ekboir, this volume, chapter 21; and Wenzel, this volume, chapter 22). As the World Food Summit stipulated, both high and low potential areas need to be considered. IFPRI's 2020 Vision points to the importance of focusing on sustainable productivity increases in areas with significant agricultural potential but with fragile soils, low or irregular rainfall, and widespread natural resource degradation and poverty. As emphasized by Leisinger, research and extension is a major responsibility of the public sector, i.e. governments and international institutions. Yet, there is also a need for greater interaction between the public sector, farmers and private sector companies. Leisinger's and Wenzel's contributions suggest that biotechnology and genetic engineering hold promise for productivity increases, improved food safety and quality, and environmental enhancement. However, at the same time they present a number of ecological, economic and social risks. Current judgement on the balance of opportunity and risk for the food security of future generations is still ambivalent, and much more needs to be done to advance scientific understanding in this regard.

There is no question about the need for a new "green revolution" to ensure future food security, as Lampe emphasizes. But the nature of such a "revolution" is to be substantially different from the original concept of the 1960s. A new "green revolution" will have to be guided by three strategic elements: productivity, sustainability and equity—the combination which did not apply to the first green revolution (Kracht 1993 and 1998). Specifically, it will have to have the following five directions:

- a focus on agro-ecological zones to achieve sustainable food security;
- a farming systems approach and livelihood research;
- an integration of "conventional" research with modern biotechnology;
- participatory research and extension; and
- improved links between research and policies.

3.3 International co-operation and financial resources for food security

The World Food Summit emphasized the "shared responsibility" for food security at national, regional and international levels. Throughout its Action Plan, it called for the co-operation between governments and civil society—an important acknowledgement of the participatory nature of development and a reflection of the changing role of governments. The concept of civil society is, for operational purposes, still an insufficiently defined term. It includes local community-based organizations (CBOs), national and international non-governmental organizations (NGOs), whose work is addressed in Dreesmann's contribution (this volume, chapter 31), and a host of other private sector institutions.

As far as international co-operation for food security and development is concerned, one must note the positive shift in "donor" policies from a food-aid mentality to a sustainable food-security orientation. At the same time, the contributions by Dresrüsse and Lele (see Bellin-Sesay, Dresrüsse, and Pfeifer, this volume, chapter 30; and Lele and Ekboir, this volume, chapter 21) point to the disappointing record of official development aid (ODA) flows and the declining share over the years of aid to the food and agricultural sector and agricultural research, in particular. More efficient resource allocation by developing country governments for food security purposes is important, but more international resources to support well defined priorities and action strategies are equally needed. One problem in this context is that food security, being a complex subject, is conflicting with the interests of other fields regarding funding—for example, policies directed towards influencing developments in population growth, employment, migration, energy supply, debt servicing, etc. (see Shaw, this volume, chapter 27). While acknowledging this, the World Food Summit was certainly not sufficiently emphatic about the need for increased ODA flows. When it comes to implementing the global food security agenda, "donor fatigue" is certainly out of place. And future—increased—resources should be preferentially allocated to low-income countries in Sub-Saharan Africa and South Asia where the potential for further deterioration of food security and degradation of natural resources is considerable (Pinstrup-Andersen and Pandya-Lorch 1997).

3.4 The ethical and human rights dimension

At the threshold of the third millennium, no development agenda would be complete and acceptable without an ethical dimension. For too long, development concerns have been considered to be the domain of economic reasoning, supplemented by secondary thoughts of charitable intentions. This was clearly recognized by world leaders participating in the 1995 Summit for Social Development, which like no other global event in recent years placed the ethical dimension at the centre of development (United Nations 1995). In its call for exploring the operational content of the right to food as a fundamental human right, the World Food Summit applied that recognition to the field of food security. That ethics and economics need to come together rather than being considered irreconcilable antagonists was also stressed in a recent address by a prominent world religious leader: in underlining the "advantages of a globalized economy", Pope John Paul II pointed at the same time to the need for "harmonizing the exigencies of the market with those of ethics and social justice" (John Paul II 1998).

That food security and nutrition can be cast into a human rights framework has been demonstrated by the ratification by virtually all states of the Convention of the Rights of the Child (United Nations 1989; see Eide, this volume, chapter 16) and in various national constitutions.[3] Undoubtedly, experience with its juridical and legal enforcement is still in its infancy. Much remains to be done to have development efforts in the third millennium be guided by ethical and human rights imperatives as much as economic reasoning. The UN Secretary General's reforms to this extent, as reported in the preceding chapter, are an encouraging step in this

---

3 See for instance the human rights provisions for food and nutrition in South Africa's constitution (Republic of South Africa 1996).

direction. Certainly, in the next millennium economic globalization must be matched by ethical globalization to eradicate hunger, malnutrition and poverty.

4 Outlook: The unknown dimension—and principal challenge ahead

The technical and socio-economic agenda to ensure food security for all has been mapped out. The resources for its implementation exist. There can therefore be no excuse for the widespread persistence of hunger and food insecurity in the medium term. One may state with some confidence that mankind's capacity to feed itself can be assured, provided that identified or suspected constraints are addressed in a systematic manner early on. One may fairly confidently forecast that mankind's capacity to feed itself can be assured, provided that suspected or identified constraints are systematically addressed early on; but a prime prerequisite is that some cohesive national and global political will for action exists.

There remains one unknown variable in the food security equation: how to galvanize the political determination, and in fact human resolve in general, to do what is known to have to be done. How to create the sense of priority needed to channel the required human, financial and material resources to the sustained eradication of hunger and malnutrition—at a time when in many parts of the world attention and energies are diverted to civil strife and war, to investment in the development of weapons of mass destruction, to arms race and arm trade. Who exercises the badly needed leadership in the fight against hunger? The United Nations, which are well placed to do so, have made honest efforts, but have fallen far short of making a major global impact (see Shaw, this volume, chapter 27). A few governments have been successful within their own geographical boundaries. In some countries, civil society organizations are beginning to make a difference in domestic policy formulation, in addition to helping at the grassroots level in a limited way. In some countries, civil society organizations are beginning to have some effect on domestic policy formulation, in addition to merely helping at the grassroots level in a limited way. However, it would be an illusion to assume that NGOs will be able to bring about coherent socio-economic development completely without support from the state. Anyhow, civil society organizations have also begun to influence decisions in international fora in areas impacting on food security, such as the environment, international trade and human rights. Recognition of the ethical dimension of development, the need for harmonizing economics, ethics and social justice, as implicit in the human rights concept, provides an imperative dimension to future efforts.

All of these are encouraging beginnings, but are not sufficient by themselves. More thought must be given to developing world leadership in the fight against hunger, food insecurity, malnutrition and poverty.

References

Brown, Lester R. (1996): Tough Choices. Facing the Challenge of Food Scarcity, New York/London.

IFPRI (1995): A 2020 Vision for Food, Agriculture, and the Environment: The Vision, Challenge, and Recommended Action, Washington, D.C.

John Paul II (1998): Address to the "Centesimus Annus-Pro Pontifice" Foundation, 9 May 1998, Vatican Information Service VIS 980511 (250), Vatican City.

Kracht, Uwe (1998): Does Africa Need a Green Revolution? Institutional and Policy Aspects of R&D for Food Security. Paper presented at the Toda Institute Symposium on Food Security and Governance, Durban, June 1998.

Kracht, Uwe (1993): Sustainable Agriculture and a New Green Revolution. International Symposium on Sustainable Agriculture and Rural Development (ISSARD '93), Beijing.

Pinstrup-Andersen, Per, Rajul Pandya-Lorch, Mark W. Rosegrant (1997): The World Food Situation: Recent Developments, Emerging Issues, and Long-Term Prospects, International Food Policy Research Institute (IFPRI), Washington, D.C.

Pinstrup-Andersen, Per, and Rajul Pandya-Lorch (1997): Food Security: A Global Perspective. IAAE Conference Paper, Sacramento, August 1997.

Republic of South Africa (1996): The Constitution of the Republic of South Africa, as adopted on 8 May 1996 and amended on 11 October 1996 by the Constitutional Assembly, Pretoria.

United Nations (1995): Report of the World Summit for Social Development. A/CONF.166/9, New York.

United Nations (1989): Convention on the Rights of the Child, New York.

APPENDIX

Abstracts

Part I Food Security and Nutritional Well-Being: Concepts, Trends and Issues

Joachim von Braun's contribution suggests that food security should be viewed from three different perspectives: food security as a basic human right, food insecurity as a symptom of broader poverty problems and finally food insecurity as a cause of poverty and underdevelopment. A comprehensive framework of causes of food insecurity and malnutrition including key linkages is presented; some principals for priority setting in food security policies are derived from his conceptual approach.

Uwe Kracht's article presents the actual global and regional situation on hunger and malnutrition. He also assesses achievements in the food sector that have been made over the last years. The record of addressing global hunger and malnutrition in its distinct manifestations (nature and man-made famines, large-scale undernutrition, child malnutrition, micronutrient malnutrition, overnutrition) over the last two decades is not one for the international community to be particularly proud of—nor is it one of total failure and despair. The world is feeding today 1.5 billion people more than some twenty years ago; the absolute number of undernourished people has increased, albeit slightly, and some countries and regions have achieved impressive success. Nevertheless, the absolute numbers of people affected by various forms of under- and malnutrition are morally unacceptable when compared with the given possibilities. The relative importance of undernutrition is rapidly shifting from Asia to Sub-Saharan Africa. In the eastern and western industrialized countries, greater policy attention is needed to growing problems of food insecurity and poverty within their own boundaries, especially as they move from planned to market economies or realign their economies to meet the challenges of economic globalization.

John Caldwell is a demographer; he analyses population growth, the single most important demand variable in the food sector. World population has more than doubled since 1950 and may quadruple by the time near stationary population is achieved perhaps a century from now when the global demographic transition is completed; actually we have only just entered the period of peak population increments. Because of differential population growth rates, the problem is more regional than a global one. In the early 1950s South Central Asia and Sub-Saharan Africa contributed 23 and 9 percent to annual population growth; that contribution is now 33 and 20 percent and by the late 2040s will be 30 and 44 percent or three quarters of all growth. The latest challenge will be presented by Sub-Saharan Africa where the non-farming market is small and where incomes are so low and slowly growing that there is little evidence that advanced scientific and capital-intense farming can be developed.

Peter von Blanckenburg analyses world food projections. The continued growth of the world population and increasing demand for food have raised new fears about world-wide food scarcities and hunger catastrophes in the future. It is, however, plausible that no really unsurmountable major emergency situation will occur within the next 15 to 25 years, although food security, especially for poor people in some regions of the world, will be seriously endangered. Timely mobilization of sufficient additional resources over longer periods will require enourmous efforts. Soil erosion, water shortages and various other environmental hazards stand in the way of assuring an increase in food production. It remains to be seen whether the measures already undertaken to raise agricultural productivity—more research and innovation, creating additional income by increasing employment and better controlling population growth—will be sufficient. Developmental strategists agree that the actions proposed are required immediately if catastrophes are to be averted.

Theo Rauch provides an unconventional view on food scarcity, especially with respect to Sub-Saharan Africa. He seriously questions the prevailing methodology of food security analysis and thinks that Africa is better off than it appears in the statistics. Macro-level figures on food production and consumption are not adequate indicators of people's food security situation. Nor can they say much about farmers' capability to feed a nation. Thus, by using a mix of macro- and micro-analysis, the author tries to identify major trends in food security in Africa and its determinants. Results show that the widespread perception that the African farmers are not able to feed the people is misleading. While starvation on the continent is predominantly a result of wars, the situation in regions not affected by wars is influenced by a complex range of factors which have altered since economic liberalization. While during the period of state-controlled systems and subsidized food imports from abroad farmers lacked incentives to intensify and to produce surplus to compensate for deficits elsewhere, the problem has since liberalization not been solved but only changed. The key issue nowadays is the affordability of food for those who depend periodically, or permanently, on purchasing food from the markets.

David Sahn's contribution also deals with Africa. We have focussed our attention to this continent since the food security perspective of this region is particularly bleak. The article explores the impact on food security and poverty of economic liberalization, with a particular focus on the agricultural sector and related food markets. The findings indicate prior to economic reform, state interference in the agricultural sector was ineffectual, and often resulted in heavy taxation of farmers. Likewise, poor consumers did not benefit from food subsidies and price controls. Consequently, economic liberalization has contributed to improved incentives for producers, stable and often lower prices for consumers, and overall improved growth and equity outcomes. While state disengagement has therefore been positive, the overall supply response in agriculture has been modest, reflecting the numerous structural constraints and institution failures. A new and active role for government is required in areas such as investing in agricultural research, improving information systems, the development of market infra-structure and investing in human resources.

Part II Empirical Studies: Cases and Multi-Country Experience

The social anthropologist *Gerd Spittler* presents a case-study, treating the most serious aspect of all in the food debate, famine and starvation. He has analysed a subsistence crisis on the Kel Ewey Tuareg in Niger/Africa, where he conducted research during a famine in 1984-85; his findings are incorporated in a theoretical discussion. There are several theories which explain people's behaviour during a famine. In the 1980s the disaster, or victim theory, was replaced by the theory of survival strategies. This research has considerably increased our knowledge of crisis behaviour, but the theory interprets the behaviour of people too mechanically. The crisis theory takes account of the fact that during a crisis people do not react automatically, but are seized by doubts and fears. In such periods they do not only try to survive, but also to maintain a dignified form of life. People communicate with each other in order to understand the crisis, to classify it historically, to come to an agreement about the moral order. Last but not least they try to communicate with each other in order to come to terms with the worst possible perspective during a crisis: that of death.

The article by *Friedhelm Steiffeler* is about urban agriculture which is becoming more and more important, especially in Sub-Saharan Africa, and above all in countries with a severe economic crisis like the former Zaire. The contribution distinguishes three forms of urban agriculture: household gardens, peri-urban agriculture and intra-urban agriculture. The latter is crucial for the survival of the urban poor. Whereas formerly urban authorities had a clearly negative attitude towards this form of urban agriculture, the present situation has become more differentiated, but often also more complex, and even confused. Social relations, especially the degree of cooperation, are important when practising urban agriculture.

Parto Teherani-Krönner looks through the veil in Iran. Here women have been ignored in the food security discussion for a long period of time. Women in Iran play a tremendous role in the economy, not only at the household level but on the national level too . They produce some of the most important goods except oil. If not statistically registered as such, it is mostly women and girls who make the world famous Persian carpets. This handicraft production makes up to 90% of the family income in regions lacking high agricultural production. In regions with intensive farming their share in rice and tea production is about 77%, according to detailed case studies in villages near the Caspian Sea. The article gives some inside information from field research conducted in recent years on gender policy in Iran and relates it to the food debate; food and meals are treated as materialized symbols of social networks.

Gabriele Zdunnek and *Peter Ay* begin their analysis of Nigeria with earlier findings by Ester Boserup on the importance of women in agricultural production and food security; she already had underlined an increasing gender-specific differentiation in the course of modernization processes. The multitude of empirical data collected since then, however, allow the reader to "revisit" Boserup's hypothesis on the perspectives of change and to examine reasons for the "gender blindness" of earlier studies leading to an underestimation of the perpetual work by women in agriculture. Results of two panel studies in south-western Nigeria show the complexity of factors influencing patterns and changes in the gender-specific division of labour, as well as in food security and agricultural production in general. Induced by the Nigerian oil boom economy, new opportunities for economic activities have emerged for men as well as for women since the middle of the 1970s and have often developed as parallel instead of competing options. In rural areas facilities for food production and processing were extended. Structural adjustment measures in the 1980s were intended to reduce the urban bias; in reality, though, they have seemed to contribute to a growing regional, social and gender-specific differentiation in rural areas and also in some ways to a reduction of cultivation and processing capacity, thus potentially affecting rural and urban food supplies.

Georg Elwert and his collaborators pose the question as to how far local knowledge systems could contribute to improvements in agricultural production, thus increasing food security. They analyse local knowledge systems in the rural economy of Benin/Africa based on their own field studies. In fields of high relevance these local knowledge systems prove to be most efficient and clearly outstrip the centrally planned, very expensive rural extension services which are meant to improve agricultural production based upon kowledge. The way peasants proceed is basically no different from the scientific approach, as the authors clearly show. Problems appear in those areas which are of low relevance, where oral communication does not offer opportunities to link scattered experience.

Bernhard Glaeser's article analyses the ecological requirements for increased food production; he draws his findings from a field study conducted in and around Madras/India. The natural environment and its exploitation by people are important factors for assessing the population carrying capacity and economic potential of a region. The changes to the natural system of a region are caused mainly by anthropogenic activities such as agriculture and energy use. This contribution views the environmental compatibility of land use in the relation between housing and home or kitchen gardening. Kitchen gardening is introduced as the "missing link", mediating between housing, energy management, and enviromentally compatible food production for an integrated social system on the household level. In conclusion, the house, or household, is conceived as a habitat organism organized around a kitchen garden and sometimes a bio-gas regime; it includes eco-farming methods and reforestation measures on a village scale.

In recent years food security analysis has been broadened; it incorporates now other aspects of well-being, above all health. *Detlef Schwefel* and his collaborators deal with food security related aspects in the Philippines. People's empowerment is part of the developing strategy of the Philippines. "Health in the hands of the people" is the battle cry of a Philippine movement towards self-help and self-help empowerment. The article presents the methodology and results of a discovery strategy to identify groups that take not only health, but also food and nutrition in their hands. It addresses risk and security assessments in the hands of the people; herbal medicine is a crucial option and nutrition security is a strategic issue. The paper explores the broader context: from income generating projects to food generating projects, from health to wealth, from food and nutrition towards a productive life-style. The authors conclude that food security and nutrition has to be seen in a broader perspective of a development strategy that is aimed at satisfying the basic needs of the population with a perspective of self-reliance and sustainability.

The contribution by *Hans Schoeneberger* discusses multidisciplinary measures to combat poverty and hunger in Bolivia. The UNICEF model identifies insufficient access to food, education, primary health care and basic sanitation, and finally to local decision making as underlying causes of malnutrition. As may be easily seen, this lack of access to basic human needs is coincident with the commonly used definition of poverty. In an Andean region of Bolivia, South America, where poverty is widespread among its mostly indigenous population, and malnutrition, child-mortality and illiteracy rates are high, it could be shown that the combination of multidisciplinary sustainable measures of rural development directed to increase food security, access to local health systems and nutrition education, combined with a process of structural political reforms which increased access of the poor to both, local decision making and financial resources, is a viable strategy to reduce poverty.

The contribution by *Elisabeth Meyer-Renschhausen* deals with changes in cooking and eating habits in industrialized countries, especially in Germany; she discusses the problems of luxury food consumption on the one hand, and the spread of a new lifestyle related to the use of organic produce on the other. With the advent of monocausal Cartesian thinking and the narrow market orientation of scientific economics, cooking, along with other household and subsistance activities, have largely disappeared from our realm of consciousness. Since the kitchen receded, the meal as a social act has also been disappearing. Leaving cooking to the commercial market is however not without its problems. Today, too much concentrated carbohydrate and meat is making us unhealthy and has led to an increase in diabetes and cancer. We are becoming increasingly "allergic" to the overuse of fertilizers, pesticides and food additives. Modern social movements, with vegetarianism taking the lead, have responded to this anomic development by turning anew to simple, mainly meatless meals, using "organic" produce. With their moral appeal to our consumer behaviour, they are restoring some of the lost significance of eating. With their new eating behaviour, which takes into account the ecological requirements and the social needs of the Third World, these movements are confronting the global market with a new cosmopolitanism.

Part III Approaches and Strategies to Overcome Hunger and Malnutrition.

Asbjorn Eide's article presents the normative framework of international human rights and the duty of states to cooperate for development, starting with the Charter of the United Nations and proceeding to examine the International Bill of Human Rights and the various international instruments (treaties and declarations) built upon it. By ratifying some of these instruments, a large majority of states have undertaken legally binding obligations to ensure freedom from hunger and to promote adequate standards of living including nutrition and care. The contribution notes that promotion of human rights and development have followed two separate trajectories, but efforts are now under way to bring them closer together, as manifested in particular by the Declaration on the Right to Development, adopted by the General Assembly of the United Nations in 1986. A major breakthrough in the recognition of economic and social rights occurred with their inclusion in the Declaration and Plan of Action adopted by the World Food Summit in 1996, especially in Commitment 7 and Objective 7.4. The article further points out that under international human rights law a comprehensive system of international reporting and monitoring by expert bodies has been developed. Full transparency has been achieved by ensuring that the state reports are made public and their examination by the international expert bodies are open to anyone interested.

Frances Sandiford-Rossmiller and *George E. Rossmiller* look at food security from a macro-policy point of view. Economic growth with equity is a necessary but insufficient condition to solve the problem of poverty, food insecurity and malnutrition. Governments of today have a diminished but essential role in creating the enabling macro-economic and trade environment to assure national food security. Agricultural sector policies must foster agricultural production that is sustainable and in line with a country's comparative advantage. But the eradication of poverty, the root cause of food insecurity, requires action across the full spectrum of economic and social policy. This requires the exercise of a degree of political will of which few governments have been capable.

The chapter by *M. Anwar Hussain* and *William D. Clay* analyses effective nutrition and health programmes. Nutrition programmes are broadly defined as those activities that have nutrition improvement and maintenance of good nutrition as an explicit outcome. These actions are divided into three groups and their rationale, outcome, coordination and limitations are briefly reviewed. These groups include: a) incorporation of nutrition objectives and actions into development plans and allocation of necessary human and financial resources for the realization of these objectives; b) specific nutrition improvement programmes directed at particular problems or groups; c) community-based actions with active participation and ownership by the community to improve the nutritional status. On the basis of these discussions and the experiences of other workers, elements of successful nutrition programmes were set out. The chapter concludes with a brief discussion of the role of public and private entities in the implementation of nutrition programmes.

Armed conflicts are a major cause of famine. The article by *Marc Cohen* deals with famine prevention in such armed conflicts. Violent civil conflicts have put 80 million people at risk of hunger. Conflict has replaced natural disaster as the main source of famine. Nations have a right to preserve their sovereignity, but their citizens have the right to food. This dilemma may require humanitarian intervention in armed conflicts, and military forces may be necessary to deliver aid and protect civilians. The current framework linking relief, conflict management and development aid lacks adequate capacity, authority and resources. Aid donors have provided far fewer resources for reconstruction than for pursuing military conflicts. Overall, industrial countries are slashing aid and devoting even larger shares of what remains to emergency assistance. Yet the costs of responding to crises exceed the price in investing in sustainable development, conflict prevention and mitigation.

The article by *Klaus Lampe* is about the Green Revolution. Population growth during this century created shortages in employment, income, and food supply of hitherto unknown dimensions. Science, ingenuity, flexibility, and willpower, starting in the early 1960s have developed a new plateau for growth and productivity in plant and animal production. The widespread hunger predicted for the 1970s would have become reality without a dynamic international and national effort in agriculture. In some countries, including Germany, the negative side-effects of this development are often highlighted. The truth is that more than two billion people today would now have insufficient access to food had it not been for a development called the "Green Revolution". However, we are today confronted with a challenge of even greater dimensions. To produce food for 10 billion people well before the year 2050—in a socially, economically and environmentally responsible manner—means doubling productivity.

Uma Lele's and *Javier Ekboir's* article is on the theory and practical experience with agricultural innovation diffusion. International agricultural research, technology generation, transfer adoption and impact are components of a system that has evolved from a relatively simple structure in the 1960s to a complex network in the late 1990s. Drawing on institutional economics the authors propose an evolutionary framework to analyze these changes as organizational innovations intended to alleviate perceived market failures. In the chosen framework the system is viewed as a complex social process in which different actors interact, where information about the objectives and actions of particular actors is conveyed to the other participants in the network. This framework is particularly relevant for the CGIAR because actors in this system interact mainly through non-market mechanisms, and each responds to a different set of objectives and constraints. A better understanding of the forces that shape the evolution of the system will allow improvement in the process of technology generation targeted to poor farmers, and improve their food and financial security.

Günter Wenzel analyses the future role of bio-technology and genetic engineering from a natural science point of view. There is as much hope as there is scepticism concerning the application of bio-technology to future plant breeding. The techniques concerned are: cell culture and genomics: the first involves rapid propagation, haploids and cell fusion, the second marker-aided selection, gene cloning and gene transfer. The possibilities of these new tools for biodiversity and breeding for product quality, as well as disease, pest and abiotic stress resistance, and also for yield improvements and nutrient intake are all summarized here. Finally, some judgements regarding costs, speed, feasibility and sustainability of the new methods—compared with the classical approaches—are given, particularly from the aspect of whether the procedures are also of help in developing countries.

Klaus Leisinger discusses the prospects of modern bio-technology in developing countries from a social scientist's point of view. Contrary to the mainstream of critical discussion, especially in Germany, he is an advocate of careful use of the new techniques. Agriculture in developing countries will be confronted with three major challenges in the decades to come:

- To increase the availability of nutritious food to an increasing population;
- To use natural eco-systems (including marginal lands) more efficiently and keep them enviromentally sustainable for food production; and
- To contribute to economic development.

It is inconceivable that this could happen without modern technologies, more sustainable development policies and improvements in governance. Ironically, the theory that a vicious circle of socio-economic underdevelopment has been created or aggravated by modern agricultural technologies is still very popular. The real tragedy, however, would be if bio-technology, which has enormous benefits to offer, were prevented from realizing its potential, if it were impossible for it to pursue its objectives rationally so long as it continues to face general mistrust; this would only lead to a curtailing or withdrawal of funds, leaving the whole of biological research in disarray. The article tries to show that it is neither true nor helpful to make technology, especially agricultural bio-technology, accountable for the multiple causes of socio-economic underdevelopment, because such underdevelopment is most pressing in those countries where technological development has occurred very slowly or not at all.

Peter Uvin discusses the role of NGOs in the fight against hunger. During the last decades, thousands of non-governmental organizations have come into being; they now play key roles in the eradication of hunger, confronting, collaborating with, or substituting for the traditional development actors: governments, international organizations, private enterprises, research institutions. The chapter presents an overview of this trend and an assessment of its potential for contributing to the eradication of hunger and poverty. Three roles of NGOs are distinguished: they provide services to the poor and hungry people, lobby for new policies by governments and international organizations to overcome hunger, and participate in the implementation of these policies.

Bernd Schubert suggests a better approach to targeting as prerequisite to reach groups badly in need of food. Targeting is done in order to achieve a high coverage of the target group while avoiding that the benefits of social security programs leak to persons which are not members of the target group. One of the preconditions for effective targeting are clear definitions of target groups and objectives of social security programs. To facilitate this a poverty matrix is introduced which analyses potential target groups with regard to degree of poverty and causes of poverty. The second part of the paper discusses conventional approaches to targeting like self-targeting, using eligibility criteria related to income and using structural criteria which determine the income earning capability of a household. The article concludes that in order to link communities with formal and informal social security organizations, participatory and integrated approaches to targeting should be explored.

The authors *Manfed Zeller* and *Manohar Sharma* explore the role that an improved access to credit, savings and insurance services can have in alleviating food insecurity and poverty. They draw their findings from research in several African and Asian countries. At first a conceptual framework is presented that distinguishes three pathways through which access to financial markets can improve household food security. The authors argue that all three pathways need to be considered when designing rural financial policies and programs for the poor. The paper further highlights recent empirical evidence from whom and for what the poor borrow, and how that is impacting their income generation, food and non-food consumption, nutrition and education. The paper concludes with a number of policy recommendations for financial market development that seek to more effectively address problems of transitory and chronic food insecurity. An important message of the article is that market liberalization is necessary, but not a sufficient condition for integrating the poor into financial markets. Institutional innovations, building on the social capital of the poor, are needed in order to cut transaction costs. Public action by the state, donors, non-governmental organizations, and community groups, have a pivotal role to play in generating much-needed institutional innovations.

Part IV The International Institutional Framework

John Shaw focuses in this chapter on the roles of multilateral development co-operation provided through the United Nations system. An overview of the multilateral network of 36 UN-agencies is given together with an estimate of the assistance they provide. A "balance sheet" of performance of the UN agencies is presented, identifying both positive achievements and shortcomings. An assessment is made of the adequacy of multilateral aid in quantitative and qualitative terms not only through direct food and nutrition interventions with financial, technical and food aid, but also in employment and trade, and investment in other, less direct, ways. The comparative advantages of different kinds of intervention programmes are evaluated, based on practical experience, and the critical issue of co-ordination of policy and actions is examined. The chapter ends with conclusions relating to the need for co-ordination at the global and developing country levels.

The contribution by *Ismail Serageldin* discusses the role of the Consultative Group on International Agricultural Research (CGIAR). As the dawn of a new millennium approaches, agricultural transformation will be essential to meet the global challenges of feeding the world's burgeoning population, conserving the environment, and reducing poverty, particularly in rural areas. This transformation will have to occur at the level of smallholder farmers so that their complex farming systems can be made more productive and efficient in the use of resources. The challenge is both technological (requiring the development of new, high-productivity environmentally sustainable production systems) and political (requiring policies that do not discriminate against rural areas in general, and agriculture in particular), and will have to be accomplished at a time when attention to agricultural development and rural well-being is diminishing. The Consultative Group on International Agricultural Research (CGIAR), created in 1971, is an informal association of 57 public and private sector members supporting 16 international agricultural research centers. The CGIAR's research products are international public goods, unconditionally available to poor farmers, national programs, and other users. As one of the most successful instruments of development cooperation, and based on a solid track record of scientific excellence and achievement, the CGIAR is ideally equipped to address some of the more compelling challenges facing humanity, both now and into the new millennium.

César Deben and *Pieter van Steekelenburg* from the European Commission present the main points of recent reforms to the European policy on food security in developing countries, where typical keywords are policy dialogue, integration of food aid into support for policy changes, flexibility, adaptability, triangular operations, monetisation, hard currency facility, food aid in kind as preferable in emergency situations, multi-annual approach, and so on. By presenting a few cases, the authors give the reader a picture of the effects of these reforms on the ground. Some views are also offered on future challenges to donor agencies, which need to improve their co-ordination at policy and operational levels in particular, but also to discover an appropriate balance between markets and institutions in order to protect the food security of vulnerable groups and countries.

The chapter by *Friederike Bellin-Sesay*, *Günther Dresrüsse* and *Hans Pfeifer* describes past and present trends in German food aid policy and elucidates developments leading to a comprehensive food and nutrition security policy. Having described the institutional and legal framework of the German aid system, the authors outline different types of programmes as defined in the sector policy paper of the German Federal Ministry for Economic Cooperation and Development (BMZ) on food security and food aid. The programme types include food aid, food security reserves, integrated food security programmes and food security policy advice. The commitment of the BMZ to promoting food security is a major focus of the authors' attention. At the same time, the authors stress the fact that the sustainable and successful implementation of these programmes depends on the political willingness of governments to secure sufficient future funding.

Bernd Dreesmann discusses the role of NGOs from an organizational aspect. The food sector has always been a priority for the majority of NGOs, who are a major channel for the employment of food-aid. Thus, fund-raising campaigns and large relief actions, followed by rehabilitation and development programmes targeted against hunger and malnutrition, play an important role with many NGOs. There are a number of efficient NGO networks which coordinate food activities among various NGOs. They are also partners of international organizations such as the FAO, the WFP, IFAD and the European Union in global co-operation programmes. However, there is a strong tendency for international donor countries to reduce the funding of food aid, as well as of agricultural development programmes. It is likely, therefore, that the role of NGOs in the food sector will be greatly reduced in the near future.

The last chapter written by *Uwe Kracht* analyzes the World Food Summit which was held in Rome in November 1996 and which concluded an unprecedentedly intense series of global development summits and conferences, which—taken together—mapped out the development agenda leading into the third millenium. The Summit did not propose major new initiatives which would have meant greatly increased resources to be channelled to food and agriculture. Instead, it accepted that hunger will be the scourge of millions of people for decades to come: even if its objectives can be met, there are likely to be at least 400 million hungry people in the world some 20 years from now. Against this background, one Summit initiative takes on particular importance: with its call for defining the operational meaning of the frequently invoked right to food, the Summit intended to move from the level of rhetorical declarations to applying an ethics-based human rights approach to development. Application of a right-to-food approach is no panacea for overcoming current obstacles to hunger- and poverty eradication, but it holds promise to make efforts in that direction more effective.

About the Authors

Peter von Blanckenburg

Peter von Blanckenburg is Professor Emeritus of the Humboldt-University of Berlin. From 1964-1986 he was Director of the Institute of Socio-Economics of Agricultural Development at the Technical University of Berlin. Between 1961 and 1993 he made numerous missions in developing countries in research, teaching and technical assistance, with long stays in Nigeria, Egypt, Sri Lanka and Zimbabwe. Main fields of scientific work are: agricultural policy in developing countries, instruments of rural development, world food economy. He has written about 150 publications including 8 books.

Prof. Dr. Peter von Blanckenburg
Lepsiusstr. 112 a
12165 Berlin – Germany

Joachim von Braun

Joachim von Braun is Professor and Director of the Centre for Development Research at the University of Bonn/Germany. Von Braun was Director of the Food Consumption and Nutrition Division of the International Food Policy Research Institute (IFPRI) Washington. Between 1993 and 1996 he held the Chair for World Food Issues at the University of Kiel/Germany. Von Braun serves on boards of publishers of several journals, is member of the Scientific Advisory Board of the German Ministry for Economic Cooperation and Development, and serves as President (elect) of the International Association of Agricultural Economists (IAAE).

Prof. Dr. Joachim von Braun
Centre for Development Research
Rheinische Friedrich-Wilhelms-Universität Bonn
Walter-Flex-Straße 3
53113 Bonn – Germany

John C. Caldwell

John Caldwell is an Australian demographer who was head of the Australian National University's Department of Demography for almost 20 years and is now Coordinator of the Health Transition Centre. Over the last 40 years, he and his wife, Pat Caldwell, have devoted much of their time to field work in developing countries, first in Thailand and Malaysia, and then in Sub-Saharan Africa (especially Nigeria, Ghana and Kenya) and South Asia (especially India, Bangladesh and Sri Lanka). He has published 20 books, of which the most influential has been "Theory of Fertility Decline", and over 150 chapters and journal articles. He has been the president of the demographers' learned association, the International Union for the Scientific Study of Population since 1994. He is Adjunct Professor of Harvard University's Department of Population Sciences and International Health.

Prof. Dr. John C. Caldwell
Health Transition Centre
National Centre for Epidemiology and Population Health
Australian National University
Canberra, ACT 0200 – Australia

Marc J. Cohen

Dr. Marc J. Cohen is Special Assistant to the Director General of the International Food Policy Research Institute (IFPRI) in Washington, D.C. From 1991 to February 1998, he served as editor of the annual report on the state of world hunger at Bread for the World Institute, a U.S.-based non-governmental organization. He received his Ph.D. in political science from the University of Wisconsin-Madison, and he has written extensively about hunger, human rights, conflict, food aid, and the relationships among development assistance, food security, and sustainable development.

Dr. Marc J. Cohen
International Food Policy Research Institute (IFPRI)
1200 17th Street, N.W.
Washington, D.C. 20036 – 3006 – U.S.A.

César Deben Alfonso and Pieter van Steekelenburg

César Deben is specialized in rural development and obtained a Ph.D. in Montpellier. Official at the "Centre International des Hautes Etudes Agronomiques Méditerranéennes" until 1996 when he joined the Directorate-General for Development of the European Commission. He is responsible for co-operation with West Africa, Head of the Evaluation Unit for programmes and policies in developing countries and currently Head of Food Security, Food Aid Unit.

Pieter van Steekelenburg who is an agro-socio-economist from Wageningen, served 6 years in Latin America for FAO and the Dutch Ministry of Development Cooperation. He then joined Foreign Affairs, moved on to the International Institute for Land Reclamation, worked extensively in Africa and Asia and joined the European Commission in 1991 where he is at present food security policies advisor.

Dr. César Deben Alfonso and Pieter van Steekelenburg
Food Security and Food Aid
Directorate-General VIII Development
European Commission
200, rue de la Loi
1049 Brussels – Belgium

Bernd D. Dreesmann

Bernd Dreesmann has occupied since 1991 the position of Secretary General of EuronAid, the European Association of NGOs for Food Aid and Emergency Aid in The Hague. Prior positions held: 1966/69 Legal Advisor to the Director General of the German Foundation for International Development in Berlin; 1969/91 Secretary General of Deutsche Welthungerhilfe in Bonn. Bernd Dreesmann has served on numerous NGO Committees, such as NGDO/EU Liaison Committee, the NGO World Bank Committee and the NGO/CGIAR Committee. He is trustee of the International Institute for Rural Reconstruction.

Dr. Bernd D. Dreesmann
EuronAid
Houtweg 60
P.O. Box 12
2501 CA The Hague – Netherlands

Günter Dresrüsse, Dr. Hans Pfeifer and Dr. Friederike Bellin-Sesay

Following ten years of field service with the FAO and the Deutsche Gesellschaft für Technische Zusammenarbeit (GTZ) GmbH (German Technical Cooperation), Mr. Günter Dresrüsse, an expert in business and economics, consolidated GTZ's Food Security Division. Following a period as head of the agricultural extension services department at FAO, he returned to GTZ, where he is currently responsible for the Planning and Development Department.

Dr. Hans Pfeifer also works in the Planning and Development Department at GTZ. Following 11 years of field service in Africa with different organizations he is now in charge of development-oriented emergency aid, food aid and food security in GTZ.

Dr. Friederike Bellin-Sesay is a nutritionist working with the GTZ food security, refugee and emergency aid department. During her former employment as assistant professor at Justus-Liebig-University in Giessen, she was mainly in charge of lectures and seminars in the field of nutrition in developing countries. She has gained practical experience mainly in Sub-Saharan Africa.

Günter Dresrüsse, Dr. Hans Pfeifer and Dr. Friederike Bellin-Sesay
Deutsche Gesellschaft für Technische Zusammenarbeit (GTZ)
Dag-Hammarskjöld-Weg 1-5
65760 Eschborn – Germany

Asbjørn Eide

Asbjørn Eide is Director of the Norwegian Institute of Human Rights, University of Oslo/Norway. He is a member of the United Nations Sub-Commission on the Prevention of Discrimination and Protection of Minorities. He is Co-Coordinator of the World Alliance for Nutrition and Human Rights (WANAHR).

Prof. Dr. Asbjørn Eide
Norwegian Institute of Human Rights
University of Oslo
Grensen 18
Oslo – Norway

Georg Elwert, Lazare Séhouéto and Albert Hoegner

Georg Elwert is a professor for social anthropology and sociology at the Freie Universität Berlin. Together with colleagues from sociology and history he organizes the graduate school on social comparison. His fieldwork regions are West Africa and Central Asia.

Dr. Lazare Séhouéto is director of the privately financed Institut Kilimandjaro in Cotonou/Bénin. He is trained as philosopher and sociologist and has done fieldwork in Bénin and other West African states.

Albert Hoegner is a graduate student of social anthropology and biology at the Freie Universität Berlin. He has a training as a musical instrument builder and as a bee-keeper (which is also his part-time occupation).

Prof. Dr. Georg Elwert, Dr. Lazare Séhouéto and Mr. Albert Hoegner
Institut für Ethnologie
Freie Universität Berlin
Drosselweg 1-3
14195 Berlin – Germany

Bernhard Glaeser

Bernhard Glaeser is trained in sociology and philosophy. He held the following positions: manager of a hosier mill (1971); assistant professor at the University of Heidelberg (Biology Department, 1972); senior researcher and project leader at the Social Science Research Center Berlin (WZB, 1976); professor of human ecology (chair) at Göteborg University, Sweden (1995). His research projects include topics like ecofarming in Tanzania, environmental policy in China, eco-housing in

India, sustainable coastal development in Sweden. He is a member of various international academic advisory boards.

Prof. Dr. Bernhard Glaeser
Avd för Humanekologi
Göteborgs Universiteit
Brogatan 4
41301 Göteborg – Sweden

M. Anwar Hussain and William D. Clay

M. Anwar Hussain is currently Senior Officer of Community Nutrition and Household Food Security in the Nutrition Programmes Service of the Food and Nutrition Division, FAO. He has held his post from 1985 to the present. Previously, he was senior lecturer and reader, Department of Human Nutrition, University of Ibadan, Nigeria (1976-1985). His prior experiences included: Associate Professor, Institute of Nutrition, University of Dhaka, Bangladesh: extensive work in community nutrition programmes, nutritional assessment and prevention of micronutrient malnutrition and maternal and child nutrition.

William D. Clay serves as the Chief of the Nutrition Programmes Service in the FAO Food and Nutrition Division. He joined the Organization in 1987, serving as the Senior Officer in the Planning, Assessment and Evaluation Service of the same Division. He was charged with the preparations and follow-up of the International Conference on Nutrition (ICN) in 1992. Prior to joining the FAO, Mr. Clay worked in Botswana as a Nutrition Planner for the Ministry of Health (1984-86), in Kenya as the Associate Director for Health and Water Development for the U.S.-Peace Corps (1979-82), in Sierra Leone directing the National Nutrition Survey (1978), and in Liberia where he worked as a nutritionist in the Preventive Medical Services Programme of the Ministry of Health, also teaching at the Tubman School of Medical Arts (1974-76).

Dr. M. Anwar Hussain and Dr. William D. Clay
Nutrition Programmes Services
Food and Nutrition Division
FAO
Viale delle Terme di Caracalla
00100 Rome – Italy

Uwe Kracht

Uwe Kracht is an agricultural economist and currently an independent consultant focusing on human-centered development, with emphasis on food, nutrition and poverty elimination. He is also Co-Coordinator of the World Alliance for Nutrition and Human Rights (WANAHR), a network of professionals and NGOs promoting the application of internationally agreed upon economic, social and cultural rights to development problems. He started his professional career as an international manager in the private sector, before joining the United Nations system. He contributed to the formulation of the food and nutrition objectives and policies of the United Nations' International Development Strategy for the 1990s adopted by the General Assembly in 1990 and he has extensively written on food and development issues.

Dr. Uwe Kracht
Viale delle Medaglie d'Oro 415
Interno 4
00136 Rome – Italy

Klaus Lampe

Klaus Lampe obtained his B.S. and M.S. in agriculture from the University of Bonn/Germany; from 1956-1959 he worked at his Ph.D. at the Federal Research Center for Agriculture (FAL) in Braunschweig/Germany. Until 1968 he served as a Project Manager at an Afghan-German Regional Development Program for the Paktia-Province in Afghanistan. Lateron he joined the German Technical Assistance Program (GTZ), where he was responsible till 1987 for the planning and implementation for Agriculture and later also for Forestry, Fisheries, Rural Development and Health. In 1987 he was elected to serve the International Rice Research Institute (IRRI) in Los Banos/Philippines as its 5th Director General, from where he retired in 1995. He received several awards, among others the Ordre du Commandeur du Mérite Agricole 1996 (France) and the Presidential Golden Heart Award 1995 (Philippines). He is an Honorary Professor at the University of Zeijang Province/China since 1989.

Dr. Klaus Lampe
Karl-Bieber-Höhe 29
60437 Frankfurt/Main – Germany

Klaus M. Leisinger

After studies in economics and social sciences and post-doctoral research in development sociology Klaus Leisinger became a Professor for Development Sociology at the University of Basel in 1990. As from July 1990 he is Executive Director and Delegate of the Board of Trustees of the Novartis Foundation for Sustainable Development. Additional affiliations: Member of the Swiss Federal Council's Advisory Committee for Cooperation in International Development; member of the European Academy of Science and Arts, member of the International Review Panel for the Consultative Group of International Agricultural Research (CGIAR).

Prof. Dr. Klaus M. Leisinger
Novartis Foundation for Sustainable Development
Basel II – Switzerland

Uma Lele and Javier M. Ekboir

Uma Lele is currently Advisor in the World Bank's Environmentally and Socially Sustainable Vice Presidency. From 1991 to 1995 she was Graduate Research Professor at the University of Florida in the Food and Resource Economics Department. She established the University's Office of International Studies. She was also the first Director of President Carter's Global Development Initiative which is established in Guyana in 1993 and 1994. Lele held various positions at the World Bank from 1971 to 1990 including Senior Economist, Division Chief of the Development Strategy Division, and Manager of Agricultural Policy in Africa. While at the University of Florida, Lele founded the GREAN (Global Research on Environmental and Agricultural Nexus) Initiative, a coalition of scientists from U.S. Universities, CGIAR centers and developing countries' agricultural research systems to foster long term collaborative research, teaching and technology transfer. Lele has authored, edited and co-edited 5 books and nearly 100 journal articles, working papers and book reviews. Lele's most recent honors include being elected Fellow of the Indian Academy of Agricultural Sciences and Distinguished Scientist of Asian Origin by the American Association of Agricultural Scientists of Indian Origin.

Javier M. Ekboir currently holds the position of Post Doctoral Researcher in the Department of Agricultural and Resource Economics at the University of California-Davis (UC Davis). He has worked as a consultant to international organizations, national and provincial governments, and private firms in the area of agricultural resource economics, livestock economics, trade, technical change and agricultural policy.

Dr. Uma Lele and Dr. Javier M. Ekboir
The World Bank
1818 H Street, N.W.
Washington, D.C. 29433 – U.S.A.

Elisabeth Meyer-Renschhausen

Elisabeth Meyer-Renschhausen has taken academic degrees in sociology and social sciences at the Free University of Berlin and at Bremen University. Since 1976 she has been teaching at different universities, namely in Berlin, Vienna, Innsbruck und Marburg. At present she is a university professor for women's studies in agricultural sciences at the Humboldt University Berlin. Her main fields of research are: social movements, gender studies, cultural anthropology, eating habits and women in rural development.

Dr. Elisabeth Meyer-Renschhausen
Institut für Soziologie
Freie Universität Berlin
Babelsberger Str. 14-16
10715 Berlin – Germany

Theo Rauch

Theo Rauch is an economist and geographer who has dealt with various aspects of rural development in "third world" countries in theory and practice. He was involved in project planning and evaluation in several countries like Zambia, Malawi, Tanzania, South Africa, Ethiopia and Nepal. His research focussed on the dynamics of regional rural development in the context of global markets, state power and peasant strategies. At present Theo Rauch is a development consultant.

Dr. Theo Rauch
Hektorstr. 2
10711 Berlin – Germany

George E. Rossmiller and Frances Sandiford-Rossmiller

Frances Sandiford-Rossmiller is an Agricultural Policy Consultant. She was formerly Reports Officer, Food and Agriculture Organization; Research Projects Officer, University of Manchester; and Chairman, Agricultural Economics Society.

George E. Rossmiller was most recently Chief, Comparative Agricultural Development Service, FAO. He formerly held positions as Director, National Center for Food and Agricultural Policy, Resources for the Future; Executive Director, International Policy Council for Agriculture, Food and Trade; Senior Official, Foreign Agricultural Service, US Department of Agriculture; and Professor of Agricultural Economics, Michigan State University.

Dr. Frances Sandiford-Rossmiller and Dr. George E. Rossmiller
The Conifers
Kennerleigh
Devon EX17 4 RS – United Kingdom

David E. Sahn

David E. Sahn is a Professor of Economics at Cornell University. He has written widely on issues concerning the effect of government policies on economic performance and living standards in Asia, Africa and the transition economies of Eastern Europe. Prior to joining Cornell University, David E. Sahn was a Research Fellow at the International Food Policy Research Institute. He received his Ph.D. from the Massachusetts Institute of Technology.

Professor Dr. David E. Sahn
Food and Nutrition Policy Program
Cornell University
3M28 Van Rensselaer Hall
Ithaca, N.Y. 14853-6301 – U.S.A.

Hans Schoeneberger

Hans Schoenberger is a German nutritionist who has been working for the last 20 years as a staff of the German Agency for Technical Cooperation (GTZ) in charge of planning, implementing and advising nutrition, health and rural development projects in different Latin American countries. At present, he is working as a Sectorial Coordinator for the German contribution to Rural Regional Development in Bolivia.

Dr. Hans Schoeneberger
Sectorial Coordinator for the German contribution to Rural Regional Development in Bolivia
Calle Magallanes No. 1530 y Av. Per.
Casilla 5647
Cochabamba – Bolivia

Bernd Schubert

Bernd Schubert is Director of the Center for Agricultural and Rural Development (CATAD) of the Humboldt University Berlin. He is involved in research and training in project management, organizational development and social security. The article on targeting has been produced on the basis of a series of consultancies under the Social Dimensions of Adjustment Program of the World Bank which focussed on social security in Mozambique.

Dr. Bernd Schubert
Center for Agricultural and Rural Development
Humboldt University of Berlin
Podbielskiallee 66
14195 Berlin – Germany

Manfred Schulz

Manfred Schulz is a sociologist and Professor at the Institute for Sociology at the Free University of Berlin/Germany. His regional interests go to Sub-Saharan Africa; he has done a number of studies on rural issues in West and East African countries.

Professor Dr. Manfred Schulz
Institut für Soziologie
Freie Universität Berlin
Babelsbergerstr. 14-16
10715 Berlin – Germany

Detlef Schwefel, Benjamin Ariel Marte and Noriko Kashiwagi

Detlef Schwefel serves as an advisor for health systems management in the Ministry of Health, Guatemala. Until recently he managed for 8 years health projects in the Philippines on behalf of the German Development Cooperation, GTZ. Before living in Asia he worked for many years in health system research in Germany and Europe. He holds a Ph.D. in sociology and also is professor at the Freie Universität Berlin.

Benjamin Ariel Marte is Program Manager in the Department of Health of the Philippines. He directs the health and management information program and the family health management program. Both programs started as Philippine-German Cooperation Projects. Dr. Marte is a medical doctor. His wide interests are encompassing informatics, management, herbal medicine, self-help organizations.

Noriko Kashiwagi is project assistant to the Health and Management Information System (HAMIS) of the Department of Health in the Philippines, a project that is supported by the German Development Cooperation GTZ. She holds a diploma in nutrition sciences from the University of Gießen, Germany.

Prof. Dr. Detlef Schwefel, Benjamin Ariel Marte and Noriko Kashiwagi
HAMIS at DOH
1003 Santa Cruz
Manila – Philippines

Ismail Serageldin

Ismail Serageldin, Ph.D., is Vice President for Special Programs at the World Bank, and since 1994, has been Chairman of the Consultative Group on International Agricultural Research (CGIAR). An ardent advocate of sustainable agriculture, he conceived and led the CGIAR's renewal program and argues that agricultural research is essential to addressing a number of pressing global issues such as hunger, environmental protection, equitable economic growth, and rural well-being.

Dr. Ismail Serageldin
Vice President
The World Bank
1818 H Street, N.W.
Washington, D.C. 20433 – U.S.A.

D. John Shaw

D. John Shaw was associated with the United Nations World Food Programme for over 30 years. He served as Economic Advisor and Chief of WFP's Policy Affairs Service. After studies in agricultural economics he was Senior Lecturer in Rural Economy at the University of Khartoum, Sudan. He was a founder member of the Institute of Development Studies at the University of Sussex, England; and Consultant to the World Bank and FAO. He has written extensively on development and food aid issues, and is on the Editorial Board of the journal "Food Policy". Among his current work, he is completing a history of the World Food Programme and he is writing a biography of Professor Sir Hans Singer.

Dr. D. John Shaw
112 Kenwood Drive
Beckenham
Kent BR3 2RB – United Kingdom

Gerd Spittler

Gerd Spittler holds the Chair of Anthropology at the University of Bayreuth/Germany; he was Professor of Sociology at the University of Freiburg/Germany. Gerd Spittler has done extensive fieldwork in Niger and Nigeria and particularly among the Tuareg nomads. His main interests go to the analysis of the relations between peasants and the state.

Prof. Dr. Gerd Spittler
Lehrstuhl Ethnologie
Universität Bayreuth

Geschwister-Scholl-Platz 3
95440 Bayreuth – Germany

Friedhelm Streiffeler

Friedhelm Streiffeler has a training in sociology and psychology. Between 1976 and 1979 he was Professor at the University of Kisangani/Zaire. Here he did research on rural-urban migration. From 1982-1985 he worked in an action-research project on urban agriculture financed by German Development Aid (GTZ). From 1987-1988 he did field research in the context of a research project on endogeneous conceptions of development in eastern Zaire. Since 1989 he is professor for rural sociology at the agricultural faculty of the Technical University of Berlin which was transferred in 1994 to the Humboldt University of Berlin. He has done further work on urban agriculture as expert for the FAO. He is member of the "International Network of Urban Agriculture".

Prof. Dr. Friedhelm Streiffeler
Institut für Agrarpolitik, Marktlehre und Agrarentwicklung
Landwirtschaftlich-Gärtnerische Fakultät
Humboldt Universität zu Berlin
Luisenstr. 53
10117 Berlin – Germany

Parto Teherani-Krönner

Parto Teherani-Krönner is an Iranian social scientist, living in Berlin. She is currently Lecturer in Women's Studies and Head of the Center for Women in Rural Development, Faculty of Agriculture and Horticulture at the Humboldt University of Berlin. Her fields of research are the socio-cultural dimensions of development and environmental problems in agriculture, women in rural and sustainable development, and the cultural ecology of nutrition. She has conducted a number of field studies in Iran and in Germany.

Dr. Parto Teherani-Krönner
Institut für Agrarpolitik, Marktlehre und Agrarentwicklung
Landwirtschaftlich-Gärtnerische Fakultät
Humboldt Universität zu Berlin
Podbielskialle 64
14195 Berlin – Germany

Peter Uvin

Peter Uvin is Associate Professor (Research) at the Watson Institute of International Studies at Brown University. He has published extensively on issues related to development, aid, food, NGOs, capacity-building, Burundi and Rwanda. He holds a Ph.D. in international relations from the Graduate School of International Studies in Geneva, Switzerland.

Dr. Peter Uvin
World Hunger Program
Brown University
Box 1831
Providence, RI 02912 – U.S.A.

Gerhard Wenzel

Gerhard Wenzel studied Botany, Genetics and Biochemistry at the University of Cologne. From 1971-1972 he worked at the Max-Planck-Institute (MPI) for Plant Breeding Research, Cologne and from 1972-1976 at the MPI for Plant Genetics, Ladenburg near Heidelberg; 1976-1981 MPI Cologne. From 1981-1996 he was director of the Institute for Resistance Genetics, Grünbach, of the Federal Centre for Breeding Research. Since 1993 he is Head of the Department for Agronomy and Plant Breeding, Technical University Munich, Freising-Weihenstephan. Main research topics are: combination of classical and biotechnical breeding strategies for improvements in disease resistances.

Prof. Dr. Gerhard Wenzel
Lehrstuhl für Pflanzenbau und Pflanzenzüchtung
Technische Universität München
85350 Freising-Weihenstephan – Germany

Gabriele Zdunnek and Peter Ay

Gabriele Zdunnek is a lecturer in the section development sociology at the Institute of Sociology at the Freie Universität Berlin. She has done empirical research particularly in Ghana and Nigeria. She has published on aspects of gender-specific differentiation, methods of empirical research, the informal sector and migration.

Peter Ay is a sociologist with strong links to agricultural economics and political science. He was involved in research and development programmes of universities and international research institutes, mainly in West Africa for two decades. His interests go to changes in local farming systems. At present he is working as a consultant for various development agencies.

Dr. Gabriele Zdunnek and Dr. Peter Ay
Institut für Soziologie
Freie Universität Berlin
Babelsberger Str. 14-16
10715 Berlin – Germany

Manfred Zeller and Manohar Sharma

Manfred Zeller is a research fellow at the International Food Policy Research Institute IFPRI in Washington. Before joining IFPRI he was an assistant professor at the Institute for Agricultural Policy, University of Bonn/Germany. His areas of specialization are rural finance, institutional economics, and food and agricultural policy. Mr. Zeller has worked as consultant on studies commissioned by the World Bank, the European Union, and the German Agency for Technical Cooperation GTZ.

Manohar Sharma is a research analyst at the International Food Policy Research Institute IFPRI. Agricultural economist by training, he works on issues related to food security and rural finance. He was formerly with the Agricultural Projects Services Centre in Kathmandu, Nepal.

Dr. Manfred Zeller and Mr. Manohar Sharma
International Food Policy Research Institute
2033 K Street, N.W.
Washington, D.C. 20006 – U.S.A.

Acronyms*

ACC	United Nations Administrative Committee on Coordination
ACP countries	countries in Africa, Caribbean and the Pacific who signed the Lomé Conventions for Development Cooperation with the European Community (involves at present 69 countries)
AVRDC	Asian Vegetable Research and Development Centre
BMI	Body mass index
BMR	Basal metabolism rate
BMZ	Bundesministerium für wirtschaftliche Zusammenarbeit und Entwicklung (Federal Ministry of Economic Cooperation and Development/ Germany)
BRAC	Bangladesh Rural Advancement Committee
CBO	Community-based organization
CCFF	Compensatory and Contingency Financing Facility
CCPR	International Covenant on Civil and Political Rights
CESCR	International Covenant on Economic, Social and Cultural Rights
CFA	Communauté financière africaine
CFS	Committee on World Food Security
CGAP	Consultative Group to Assist the Poorest
CGIAR	Consultative Group for International Agricultural Research
CILSS	Comité Permanent Inter-Etats de Lutte contre la Sécheresse dans le Sahel (Permanent Interstate Committee to fight Drought in the Sahel)
CIMMYT	Centro Internacional de Majoramiento de Maiz y Trigo
CRC	International Convention on the Rights of the Child
CSSD	Consultative Subcommittee on Surplus Disposal
DAC	Development Assistance Committee
DES	Daily energy supplies
DG IB	Directorate General IB of the European Commission: External Relations with Southern Mediterranean, Middle- and Near-East, Latin America, South and South-East Asia
DG VIII	Directorate General VIII of the European Commission: Bilateral and development cooperation relations with Africa, the Caribbean and the Pacific; Lomé Convention
DHA	United Nations Department of Humanitarian Affairs
Diaper	Diagnostic Permanent
EC	European Community

* The list of acronyms is selective; mainly internationally relevant organisations/activities are included.

ECHO	European Community Humanitarian Aid Organisation
ECOSOC	United Nations Economic and Social Council
ECU	European Currency Unit
EPM	Energy protein malnutrition
ESAF	Enhanced Structural Adjustment Facility
EU	European Union
EuronAid	European Association of NGOs for Food Aid and Emergency Aid
FAC	Food Aid Convention (London); Secretariate by the International Grains Council
FAO	Food and Agriculture Organization of the United Nations
FFHC	Freedom from Hunger Campaign
FIAN	Food First Information Action Network
FIVIMS	Food insecurity and vulnerability information and mapping system
GATT	General Agreement on Tariffs and Trade
GFAR	Global Forum for Agricultural Research
GLASOD	Global assessment of soil degradation
GREAN	Global Research on the Environmental and Agricultural Nexus
GRO	Grassroots organisation
GTZ	Deutsche Gesellschaft für technische Zusammenarbeit (German Agency for Technical Cooperation)
HAMIS	Health and Management Information System
IAEA	International Atomic Energy Agency
IARC	International Agricultural Research Center
IARTGTAI	International agricultural research, technology generation, transfer, adoption and impact
IBRD/IDA	International Bank for Reconstruction and Development
ICN	International Conference on Nutrition
ICRC	International Committee of the Red Cross
IDA	International Development Association
IDD	Iodine deficiency disorders
IFAD	International Fund for Agricultural Development
IFPRI	International Food Policy Research Institute/Washington
IFSP	Integrated Food Security Programme
IIRR	International Institute of Rural Reconstruction, Philippines
ILO	International Labour Organisation
IMF	International Monetary Fund

INSTRAW	International Research and Training Institute for the Advancement of Women
IPM	Integrated pest management
IPR	Intellectual property right
IRRI	International Rice Research Institute/Philippines
ISNAR	International Service for National Agricultural Research
ITO	International Trade Organization
LIFDC	Low-income food-deficit country
Lomé Conventions	Agreements between the European Community and (69) countries in Africa, Caribbean, and the Pacific, signed in the city of Lomé.Current Lomé IV Convention is 1990-1999, revised in 1995
NARS	National Agricultural Research System
NGO	Non-government organisation
NIC	Newly industrialized country
NNFTR	Iranian National Nutrition and Food Technology Research Institute
NRM	Natural resource management
ODA	Official development assistance
OECD	Organisation for Economic Cooperation and Development (Paris)
OPAM	Office des produits Agricoles du Mali
OXFAM	Oxford Committee for Famine Relief
PPP	Purchasing power parity
PRA	Participatory rural appraisal
PRMC	Programme de Restructuration du Marché Céréalier (in Mali)
RESAL	Réseau Européen de Sécurité Alimentaire (European Network forFood Security)
SADC	Southern African Development Community
SILIC	Severely indebted low-income country
STABEX	Stabilization System for Export Earnings
TAC	Technical Advisory Committee
TransAtlantic Initiative	Bilateral meetings USA-EU started by the Clinton Administration to look into specific areas of (development) cooperation
UDHR	Universal Declaration of Human Rights
UN ACC/SCN	United Nations Administrative Committee on Coordination—Sub-committee on Nutrition
UNCED	United Nations Conference on Environment and Development
UNCTAD	United Nations Conference on Trade and Development
UNCTC	United Nations Committee on Transnational Corporations
UNDHA	United Nations Department of Humanitarian Affairs

UNDP	United Nations Development Programme
UNEP	United Nations Environment Programme
Unesco	United Nations Educational, Scientific and Cultural Organization
UNFPA	United Nations Population Fund
UNHCR	United Nations High Commissioner for Refugees
UNICEF	United Nations Children's Fund
UNIDO	United Nations Industrial Development Organization
UNITAR	United Nations Institute for Training and Research
UNRISD	United Nations Research Institute for Social Development
UNRWA	United Nations Relief and Works Agency for Palestine Refugees in the Near East
USAID	U.S. Agency for International Development
VAD	Vitamin A deficiency
WANAHR	World Alliance for Nutrition and Human Rights/Rome
WFC	World Food Council
WFP	World Food Programme
WHO	World Health Organization
WID	Women in development
WIDER	World Institute for Development and Economic Research
WSC	World Summit for Children
WTO	World Trade Organization

Spektrum

Berliner Reihe zu Gesellschaft, Wirtschaft und Politik in Entwicklungsländern
herausgegeben von Prof. Dr. Georg Elwert, Prof. Dr. Volker Lühr, Prof. Dr. Ute Luig und Prof. Dr. Manfred Schulz (Freie Universität Berlin)

Manfred Schulz (Hrsg.)

Entwicklung: Theorie – Empirie – Strategie

Festschrift für Volker Lühr

Die Entwicklungssoziologie kennt eine analytische, eine empirische und eine normative Dimension. Die analytische Seite, d. h., theoretische Erklärungsmodelle von Unterentwicklung und Entwicklung sowie daraus abgeleitete Entwicklungsstrategien sind wegen ihrer geringen Tragfähigkeit ins Gerede geraten. Vielenorts wird in der Entwicklungssoziologie von einer Theoriekrise gesprochen. Die theoretische soziologische Entwicklungsdebatte bedarf u. E. neuer Ansätze: sie muß methodisch durch präzise historisch- empirische Einzelfallstudien sowie durch soziologisch begleitete Entwicklungsstrategien neu fundiert werden.
Der vorliegende Band ist im Kontext der aktuellen Entwicklungsdebatte angesiedelt. Im Abschnitt "Theorie" werden u.a. Überlegungen zum Verhältnis von Entwicklungssoziologie und allgemeiner Soziologie angestellt und auf neue, immer wichtiger werdende Wissenschaftsfelder, z.B. Umwelt und Entwicklung, eingegangen. Der Schwerpunkt der Aufsatzsammlung liegt indes eher auf den Bereichen Empirie/Methodik und neuerer Entwicklungsstrategie, u. a. der Transformationsdebatte.

Bd. 45, 1997, 248 S., 38,80 DM*, br., ISBN 3-8258-3245-7

Jörn Sommer

Die Herausforderung

Zum Weltmarktdiskurs der chilenischen Gewerkschaften jenseits ihrer Akteurfähigkeit

In der vorliegenden Studie wird die von der CEPAL proklamierte Komplementarität wirtschaftlicher Entwicklung und sozialer Gerechtigkeit hinterfragt. Ob beides kompatibel ist, hängt davon ab, ob verschiedene Akteure (Unternehmen, Gewerkschaften, Parteien, Militär) Strategien wählen, die eine qualitativ neue Phase der Weltmarktintegration einleiten. Am Beispiel des dynamischen Holzsektors Chiles wird gezeigt, wie Gewerkschaften ein Interesse hieran haben, doch nicht die Fähigkeit, entscheidend dazu beizutragen. Nur wenige können aufgrund innerer Gespaltenheit (multiple self) dies Ziel verfolgen, ohne die ihnen als Mitgliederorganisation eigene Probleme vernachlässigen zu müssen.

Bd. 46, 1997, 120 S., 38,80 DM*, br., ISBN 3-8258-3314-3

Gabriele Beckmann

Partizipation in der Entwicklungszusammenarbeit

Mode, Methode oder politische Vision?

Seit vielen Jahren wird in der entwicklungspolitischen Diskussion mehr Partizipation der Betroffenen gefordert. Trotzdem wird vielen Projekten der Entwicklungszusammenarbeit bis heute ein Mangel an partizipativem Vorgehen bescheinigt. Handelt es sich bei der selbstverpflichtenden Forderung nach mehr Partizipation also um bloße Rhetorik? Fehlt es am politischen Willen in den Organisationen der Entwicklungszusammenarbeit? Fehlen methodische Kenntnisse? Oder existieren andere Hindernisse, die eine Beteiligung der Betroffenen im Verlauf von Planung und Durchführung von Maßnahmen der Entwicklungszusammenarbeit erschweren?
Dieses Buch versucht u. a. Antworten auf diese Fragen zu geben. Eine Inhaltsanalyse von Dokumenten verschiedener entwicklungspolitischer Organisationen zeigt, daß der in der Entwicklungszusammenarbeit gebräuchliche Partizipationsbegriff mehrdeutig und problematisch ist.
Gelungene Partizipation ist an eine Vielzahl von Bedingungen geknüpft. Sie vollzieht sich im Spannungsfeld der konkreten Erwartungen und der Motivation der Betroffenen auf der einen Seite und dem Entwicklungsverständnis der in ihnen beschäftigten Experten auf der anderen Seite. Beckmann plädiert für eine realistischere Einschätzung von Partizipation in der Entwicklungszusammenarbeit. Sie muß in der Regel ausgehandelt werden und verläuft konflikthaft.

Bd. 47, 1997, 144 S., 34,80 DM*, br., ISBN 3-8258-3097-7

Omar Abdelgabar

Mechanised Farming and Nuba Peasants

An Example for Non-sustainable Development in the Sudan

This study examines the sustainability of mechanised farming in Habila as a form of agriculture and model of development. The study concludes that rainfed mechanised farming in Habila does not at all appear to be a sustainable type of development. This is reflected in that mechanised farming lacks aspects of compatibility between economic activity and local inhabitants. Mechanised farming lacks elements of fairness and equity in the relation between the Jallaba scheme holders and local inhabitants. It has intensifed destructive conflicts over resources between different production systems.
It has moreover encouraged the expansion and persistence of the civil war in the Sudan.

Bd. 48, 1997, 208 S., 38,80 DM*, br., ISBN 3-8258-3498-0

Thomas Bierschenk

Die Fulbe Nordbénins

Geschichte, soziale Organisation, Wirtschaftsweise. Mit einem Nachwort von Georg Elwert

Die Fulbe im Norden der Republik Benin (dem ehemaligen Dahomey) passen in keines der beiden Klischees, von denen die wissenschaftliche Literatur über Fulbe geprägt ist: Sie sind weder Aristokraten, Krieger, Sklavenhalter, Stadtbewohner, wie sie vor allem von Historikern und Orientalisten beschrieben werden; noch sind sie Hirtennomaden und Heiden, die für viele Ethnologen als der "reinste" Typ von Fulbe gelten. Die Fulbe in Nordbenin sind Rinderhalter, aber keine Nomaden: Sie sind vielmehr seßhaft und auch im Hackbau engagiert. Sie sind Moslems, aber keine "Aristokraten": In vorkolonialer Zeit waren sie als Spezialisten für Rinderhaltung mit einem relativ niedrigen soziopolitischen Status in das System von Berufs- und Statusgruppen des Borgou integriert, waren aber ihrerseits Sklavenhalter; heute sind sie dort eine ethnische Minderheit.
Bierschenks Studie, die sozialanthropologische und historische Ansätze verbindet, ist ein Beitrag zu den Diskussionen über Ethnizität und über die lokale Artikulation zentralstaatlicher Herrschaft und zur Wirtschaftsanthropologie des Agropastoralismus in Afrika.

Bd. 49, 1998, 288 S., 48,80 DM*, gb., ISBN 3-8258-2634-1

Manfred Schulz; Uwe Kracht (Eds.)

Food Security and Nutrition

The Global Perspective

The persistence of an unacceptably high level of hunger and malnutrition worldwide presents a serious challenge to the world on the threshold of the third millenium. Although enough food is produced to feed mankind, about 840 million people go hungry; among them are 185 million pre-school children that are severely underweight for their age. Since an additional 80 million people have to be fed each year, achieving food security is a central global challenge, if not the most important development issue.
The aim of the reader is to analyze actual problems in the field of food security and nutrition and to discuss present and future strategies to overcome hunger. Food security ist a complex subject. In order to master this complexity, we distinguish between four dimensions of analyses: Theoretical-analytical, empirical-descriptive, normative-political, institutional.
Contributors: Cesar Deben Alfonso, Peter Ay, Friederike Bellin-Sesay, Peter von Blankenburg, Joachim von Braun, John C. Caldwell, William D. Clay, Mark Cohen, Bernd V. Dreesmann, Günter Dresrüsse, Asbjorn Eide, Geog Elwert, Javier Ekboir, Bernhard Glaeser, Albert Hoegner, M. Anwar Hussain, Noriko Kashiwagi, Uwe Kracht, Klaus Lampe, Klaus M. Leisinger, Uma Lele, Benjamin Ariel Marte, Elisabeth Meyer-Renschhausen, Hans Pfeifer, Theo Rauch, George E. Rossmiller, Frances Sandiford-Rossmiller, David E. Sahn, Lazare Séhouéto, Detlef Schwefel, Hans Schoeneberger, Bernd Schubert, Manfred Schulz, Ismail Serageldin, Manohar Sharma, D. John Shaw, Gerd Spittler, Pieter van Steekelenburg, Friedhelm Streiffeler, Parto Teherani-Krönner Peter Uvin, Gerhard Wenzel, Gabriele Zdunnek Manfred Zeller.

Bd. 50, 1998, 608 S., 128,80 DM*, pb., ISBN 3-8258-3166-3

Evangelos Karagiannis

Zur Ethnizität der Pomaken Bulgariens

Bd. 51, 1998, 216 S., 48,80 DM*, br., ISBN 3-8258-3608-8

Thomas Hüsken; Olin Roenpage

Jenseits von Traditionalismus und Stagnation

Analyse einer beduinischen Ökonomie in der Westlichen Wüste Ägyptens

Die Fallstudie von Thomas Hüsken und Olin Roenpage über eine beduinische Ökonomie in der Westlichen Wüste Ägyptens ist eine faszinierende Lektüre und gleichzeitig eine ungemein anregende und unmittelbar praxisrelevante Erweiterung des analytischen Instrumentariums in der sozialwissenschaftlichen Auseinandersetzung mit vermeintlich traditionellen Ökonomien. Die Quintessenz der in ihrer empirischen Schärfe bestechenden Arbeit besteht in der Forderung nach einer theoretischen Neubewertung. Der tatsächliche Charakter einer beduinischen Ökonomie wird in seiner Vielschichtigkeit erkennbar. Die Vielfalt der Ordnungen, die flexible und strategisch geschickte Verschmelzung von Tradition und Moderne sind die Ingredienzien eines ökonomischen Erfolgsrezeptes, welches sich jenseits gängiger Stereotypen und Klischees über Niedergangstendenzen, Konflikte zwischen Tradition und Moderne, Subsistenz und Markt, Stamm und Staat bewegt.

Bd. 52, 1998, 256 S., 39,80 DM*, br., ISBN 3-8258-3762-9

Andreas König

"no saben ni hablar pobrecitos" – "sie können nicht mal sprechen, die Armen"

Formen des Sprechens und die Konstruktion der Identität in der Sierra von Huelva / Andalusien (Spanien)

Ethnologische Tätigkeit beruht in dreifacher Weise auf dem Dialog. Über den Dialog werden in der untersuchten Gesellschaft selbst Kultur und Bedeutung hergestellt und vermittelt: Gesellschaft wird in ihm ständig neu produziert. Das System von symbolischen Bedeutungen wird im Dialog der

Feldforschung vermittelt. Schließlich stellen Dialoge das zentrale empirische Material dar, auf dem die ethnographische Repräsentation der fremden Gesellschaft beruht.
Das Sprechen als grundlegendste soziale Tätigkeit des Menschen muß, wie alle Arten sozialen Handelns, kulturspezifische Eigenarten haben, die (vergleichend) zu untersuchen eine Hauptaufgabe der Ethnologie ist. Worin besteht aber überhaupt die kulturelle Prägung des Sprechens und in welchen spezifischen Formen kann sie gezeigt werden? Um die mündlichen Quellenmaterialien der Ethnologie auf ihre spezifischen Arten der Bedeutungskonstruktion hin zu untersuchen, muß eine eigene, genuin ethnologische Methodik entwickelt werden. Sprechwissenschaften wie die Kommunikationsethnographie, die Konversationsanalyse und Soziolinguistik haben wichtige Vorarbeiten erbracht, doch muß die Perspektivik ihrer Fragestellungen umgekehrt werden: Wenn das Sprechen eine kulturelle Form hat, was sagt diese dann über die Sprecher selbst und darüber aus, wie sie sich in Beziehung setzen? Um Verstehen zu erreichen, müssen die Sprecher verweisen: auf sich selbst, auf einander und auf ihre Gesellschaft. Besonders mit "leeren Zeichen" (z. B. Deiktika) leisten sie die Konstruktion personaler, lokaler und kollektiver Identität.
Anhand von Tondokumenten aus einer vergleichenden Feldforschung in zwei ländlichen Gemeinden im Bergland von Südspanien (Andalusien) bzw. Ostdeutschland (Thüringen) zeigt der Autor, welche Formen der Konstruktion von Identität die Sprecher verwenden und wie diese mit Blick auf die "sprechende Gesellschaft" lesbar sind.
Indem die Ethnologie den Dialog nicht allein als Vehikel kultureller Inhalte, sondern bereits selbst als eine kulturelle Tätigkeit nimmt, eröffnet sie sich einen neuen Zugang zur Frage nach der Konstruktion der kulturellen Bedeutung und gewinnt zum Status der reinen Beobachtungswissenschaft die Qualität der "Hörwissenschaft" hinzu.
Bd. 53, 1998, 488 S., 69,90 DM*, br.,
ISBN 3-8258-3877-3

Annerose Hammer
Aids und Tabu
Zur soziokulturellen Konstruktion von Aids bei den Luo in West Kenya
Bd. 54, 1998, 128 S., 34,80 DM*, br.,
ISBN 3-8258-3908-7

Anette Schade
Zwischen Armut und Statuswünschen
Fijianische Frauen als Haushaltsvorstände in der Hauptstadt des südpazifischen Inselstaates Fiji
Bd. 55, 1998, 208 S., 39,80 DM*, br.,
ISBN 3-8258-3916-8

Jochen Seebode
"Aduro kum aduro"
Ritual, Macht und Besessenheit in Asante (Südghana)
In den kosmologischen Vorstellungen der Asante-Gesellschaft Südghanas sind die spirituelle, unsichtbare und die materielle, sichtbare Sphäre untrennbar miteinander verwoben. In dieser Studie wird am Beispiel eines rituellen Experten die Diskrepanz zwischen idealtypischen, tradierten Vorgaben und konkreter Umsetzung in der sozialen Praxis verdeutlicht. Dabei wird besonderes Augenmerk auf individuelle Strategien bei den Aushandlungsprozessen um die Bedeutung von in den Ritualen getroffenen Aussagen gelegt. Die vorliegende Schrift bettet das Phänomen Besessenheit in das Alltagsleben ein, wertet historische Quellen aus und betont oftmals vernachlässigte emische Perspektiven der rituellen Praxis in Asante.
Bd. 56, 1998, 216 S., 39,80 DM*, br.,
ISBN 3-8258-3927-3

Clemens Beck; Stefanie Demmler
"From Resistance to Development"
Kontinuität und Wandel basisnaher Nichtregierungsorganisationen in Südafrika
Bd. 57, 1998, 184 S., 39,80 DM*, br.,
ISBN 3-8258-3987-7

Market, Culture and Society

edited by Helmut Buchholt, Hans-Dieter Evers, Rüdiger Korff, Gudrun Lachenmann, Günther Schlee, and Heiko Schrader

Helmut Buchholt; Erhard U. Heidt; Georg Stauth (Hrsg.)
Modernität zwischen Differenzierung und Globalisierung
Kulturelle, wirtschaftliche und politische Transformationsprozesse in der sich globalisierenden Moderne
Bd. 1, 1996, 256 S., 48,80 DM*, br., ISBN 3-8258-2782-8

Heiko Schrader
Changing Financial Landscapes in India and Indonesia
Sociological Aspects of Monetization and Market Integration
Heiko Schrader is an economist and sociologist. His present position is Reader in Economic Sociology and Social Anthropology at the Sociology of Development Research Centre, University of Bielefeld. He wrote his Ph.D. thesis and a book on traditional and contemporary trading patterns in the Nepal Himalayas and beyond. Furthermore, he edited a book, together with Hans-Dieter Evers,

* unverbindliche Preisempfehlung

on "The Moral Economy of Trade – Ethnicity and Developing Markets".
This book is the outcome of a five-year research project on the history of finance in India and Indonesia that he completed with his Habilitation at the Faculty of Sociology, University of Bielefeld. Presently the author is concerned with the study of business ethics in Southeast Asia.
Copublished with St. Martin's Press, New York
Bd. 2, 1997, 400 S., 48,80 DM*, br., ISBN 3-8258-2641-4

Han-pi Chang
Taiwan: Community of Fate and Cultural Globalization
Bd. 3, 1997, 296 S., 49,80 DM*, br., ISBN 3-8258-3559-6

Detlev Holloh
Microfinance in Indonesia
Between State, Market and Self-Organization
Bd. 4, 1998, 280 S., 48,80 DM*, br., ISBN 3-8258-3909-5

Günther Schlee (ed.)
Imagined Difference
Hatred and the construction of identity
The book addresses key concepts of modern anthropology like "difference" as "identity" in the light of ethnographic evidence from various local settings stretching from Morocco to Indonesia. As the antagonistic and destructive aspects of social identification are also discusses, the book is a contribution to conflict theory, it provides elements of orientation in a world marked by a proliferation of ethnic movements and of nationalisms which become more narrow and more aggressive.
Contributors: Artur Bogner; John Bousfield; Sovay Gerke; Georg Elwert; Hans-Dieter Evers; Mark Hobart; Jeremy Kemp; Mary Catherine Kenney; Rüdiger Korff; Thomas Rieger; Günther Schlee; Purnaka L. de Silva; Philip Quarles van Ufford; Bernhard Venema; Petra Weyland.
Bd. 5, 1999, 288 S., 49,80 DM*, br., ISBN 3-8258-3956-7

Politische Soziologie

hrsg. von Arno Klönne und Sven Papcke

Richard Albrecht
... fremd und doch vertraut
Skizzen zur politischen Kultur des Witzes gestern und heute
Bd. 2, 1989, 116 S., 19,80 DM*, br., ISBN 3-88660-502-7

Reinhard Löhmann
Der Stalinmythos
Studien zur Sozialgeschichte des Personenkultes in der Sowjetunion (1929–1935)
Bd. 3, 1990, 360 S., 29,80 DM*, gb., ISBN 3-88660-596-5

Franz Josef Brüseke
Chaos und Ordnung im Prozeß der Industrialisierung
Skizzen zu einer Theorie globaler Entwicklung
Bd. 5, 1992, 250 S., 29,80 DM*, br., ISBN 3-89473-205-9

H. C. F. Mansilla
Harmoniebedürfnis und Verewigung von Herrschaft
Elemente einer kritischen Theorie der Macht
Bd. 6, 1994, 300 S., 48,80 DM*, br., ISBN 3-89473-912-6

Paul Drechsel
Sozialstruktur und kommunikatives Handeln
Reflexionen über eine postmoderne Ethno-Soziologie
Bd. 7, 1994, 349 S., 68,80 DM*, gb., ISBN 3-89473-799-9

Werner Biermann
Die verratene Transformation
Ein soziologischer Essay über die neuen Machtverhältnisse in Rußland. Mit einem Vorwort von Arno Klönne
Vor nicht einmal 10 Jahren verabschiedete sich die UdSSR, nach den USA die zweite Weltmacht, von ihrem staatssozialistisch-imperialen Anspruch und wandte sich westlichen Politikidealen zu. Damit verband sich die Hoffnung auf eine weltweite Durchsetzung der "Zivilgesellschaft", und, bezogen auf die UdSSR, auf Wohlstandsökonomie und liberale, friedliche Zusammenarbeit der Nationen. Die Vormacht der "Zweiten Welt" schien sich auf den Weg in die "Erste Welt" gemacht zu haben – ökonomisch, politisch und ideologisch.
Heute, so stellt W. Biermann in diesem Band fest, hat der wirtschaftliche Umbau in Richtung auf einen staatsverschränkten, dennoch hemmungslosen Kapitalismus zwar die Erwartungen der früheren ökonomischen Elite an den Aufstieg in eine Bourgeoisie erfüllt, gleichzeitig jedoch die sozialen Spannungen in dramatischer Weise verschärft.
Welchen Verlauf die Transformationspolitik in Rußland nahm und welche sozio-ökonomischen und politischen Machtverhältnisse aus ihr hervorgingen, zeigt der Autor mit großer Präzision und Klarheit auf.
Bd. 8, 1996, 150 S., 38,80 DM*, br., ISBN 3-8258-2778-x

LIT Verlag Münster – Hamburg – London
Bestellungen über: Dieckstr. 73 48145 Münster Tel.: 0251 – 23 50 91 Fax: 0251 – 23 19 72
∗ unverbindliche Preisempfehlung